D1453071

 FRANCES POWER COBBE

Victorian Literature and Culture Series

*Jerome J. McGann and Herbert Tucker, Editors*

# FRANCES

# POWER COBBE

*Victorian Feminist, Journalist, Reformer*

SALLY MITCHELL

UNIVERSITY OF VIRGINIA PRESS   CHARLOTTESVILLE AND LONDON

University of Virginia Press
© 2004 by the Rector and Visitors of the University of Virginia
All rights reserved
Printed in the United States of America on acid-free paper

*First published 2004*

9 8 7 6 5 4 3 2 1


LIBRARY OF CONGRESS CATALOGING-IN-PUBLICATION DATA

Mitchell, Sally, 1937–
   Frances Power Cobbe : Victorian feminist, journalist, reformer / Sally
Mitchell.
       p.       cm. — (Victorian literature and culture series)
Includes bibliographical references and index.
   ISBN 0-8139-2271-2 (cloth : alk. paper)
   1. Cobbe, Frances Power, 1822–1904. 2. Authors, English—19th century—
Biography. 3. Great Britain—History—Victoria, 1837–1901—Biography.
4. Journalists—Great Britain—Biography. 5. Feminists—Great Britain—
Biography. 6. Reformers—Great Britain—Biography. I. Title. II. Series.
PR4461.C3Z78 2004
070.92—dc22

                                          2003022365

# Contents

# Illustrations

# Acknowledgments

First and foremost: to Frances Power Cobbe's great-great-great-nephews. This book in its present form could not have been written without their generous and friendly assistance. Hugh Cobbe provided access to family papers stored at Newbridge and granted permission to quote from letters and unpublished works by Frances Power Cobbe and from other materials to which he holds copyright. Alec Cobbe supplied further letters and papers, as well as showing me Frances Power Cobbe's albums and sketchbooks and sending copies of portraits and sketches, which are published with his permission.

Temple University supported the project with two study leaves and with research grants to buy microfilm of the *Echo* and subsidize additional illustrations. A National Endowment for the Humanities Fellowship in 2001–2 gave me time to complete a draft of the manuscript.

Librarians and archivists who helped in my search for letters written by Frances Power Cobbe and for other material include Pauline Adams (Somerville College), Richard Bond (Manchester Central Library), Susan Boone (Sophia Smith Collection, Smith College), Kath Boothman (Cheltenham Ladies' College), Susan C. Box (Augustus C. Long Health Sciences Library, Columbia University), Andy Breslin (American Anti-Vivisection Society), Bonnie Coles (Library of Congress), Julie Courtenay (Lady Margaret Hall), Rita Dockery (American Philosophical Society, Philadelphia), Bryan Dyson (Brynmor Jones Library, University of Hull), Margaret G. Foley (Mills Memorial Library, McMaster University), Joan Grattin (Milton S. Eisenhower Library, The Johns Hopkins University), John Hopson (British Library), Gwen Hough (Gwynedd County Archives), Jane Hudson (John Rylands University Library), Elen Wyn Hughes (University of Wales, Bangor), Keith Jones (Mable Smith Douglass Library, Rutgers University), Amalia G. Kakissis (British School at Athens), Caroline Kelly (Nottingham University Library), Susan Killoran (Harris Manchester College), Cornelia S. King (Free Library of Philadelphia), Bruce Laverty (Athenaeum of Philadelphia), Ceridwen Lloyd-Morgan (National Library of Wales), Kathleen Manwaring (Syracuse University Library), T. W. Mayberry (Somerset Archive and Record Service), Kathryn McCord (Royal Borough of Kensington and Chelsea Central Library), Alfred Mueller (Beinecke Library, Yale University), Kate Perry and Joan Bullock-Anderson (Girton College), Menna Phillips (National Library of Wales), Christopher Phipps (The London Library), Elaine S. Pike (Vassar College Library), Mark Pomeroy (Royal Academy of Arts), Angela Raspin (British Library of Political and Economic Science), Nancy S. Reinhardt (Miller Library, Colby College), Pearl Romans (Hartley Library, University of Southampton), Marion Rosenbaum and Judith Callard (Germantown Historical Society, Philadelphia), Deborah Harper Rouse (Special Collections, Florida State University), Callie Saliers (Huntington Library), Ellen M. Shea (Schlesinger Library, Radcliffe College), Margaret M. Sherry and AnnaLee Pauls (Princeton University Library), Robin Smith (National Library of Scotland), Linda Stanley (Historical Society of Pennsylvania), Vanessa Tyrell-Kenyon (*Spectator* Archives), Kathleen Whalen (Bryn Mawr College), Susan Woodburn (Barr Smith Library, University of Adelaide), and Roberta Zonghi (Boston Public Library). Additional help came from staff at the Bodleian Library, the British Library, the College of Physicians, Philadelphia, the Manchester Central Library, the National Army Museum Reading Room, the National Library of Ireland, the University of British Columbia Library, the University of Delaware Library, Dr. Williams's Library, London, and the Women's Library, London. As always, exemplary service was provided by Cathy Meaney, of the Interlibrary Loan Department of Temple University's Paley Library.

Permission to quote from materials in their possession was granted by Hugh Cobbe, Alec Cobbe, and the Trustees of the Cobbe Family Foundation; the University of Adelaide Library; the University Archives, University of British Columbia Library; the British Library; the British School at Athens; the Trustees of the Broadlands Archives, for passages from the diary of the seventh earl of Shaftesbury; Colby College Special Collections; Girton College; the Historical Society of Pennsylvania; Brynmor Jones Library, University of Hull; the Huntington Library; Special Collections, University of Illinois Library, for correspondence in the Bentley Archives; Archives Division, LSE Library; McMaster University Library; the National Library of Wales; Manchester Archives and Local Studies, Manchester Central Library; Manuscripts Division, Department of Rare Books and Special Collections, Princeton University Library; the Royal Academy of Arts; the Sophia Smith Collection, Smith College; the Principal and Fellows of Somerville College, Oxford, for letters from the Mary Somerville Family Papers on deposit in the Bodleian Library, as well as for material in the Somerville College Archives; Dr. Williams's Library, London; and the Women's Library, London.

Credit for illustrations is provided in the captions. If no individual, agency, or institution is listed, the illustration is taken from published material now in the public domain that is in my own possession. Photography and imaging were done by David Kerper Sr., of Kerper Studio in Wyndmoor, Pennsylvania. Margaret Godbey O'Brien helped read proof.

I am grateful for ten years' good fellowship on the VICTORIA Listserv (created by Patrick Leary) and to the following friends, colleagues, and e-mail correspondents who supplied information, clues, references, suggestions, and helpful questions: Nancy Fix Anderson, Nina Auerbach, Margaret Beetham, Valerie Bonham, Caroline Brick, Rachel Bright, David Budworth, Michaelyn Burnette, Barbara Caine, Julie Codell, Robert Colby, Vineta Colby, Ken Collins, Elizabeth Crawford, Eileen Curran, Sandra Donaldson, Adrian Dover, Maria Frawley, Richard Fulton, Barbara Gates, Peter Gran, Elizabeth Rose Gruner, John Hallock, Susan Hamilton, Linda Hughes, Fred Hunter, Anthea Jarvis, Ellen Jordan, Wendy Katz, Philip Kelley, Andrew King, Jack Kolb, Janet Larson, Mark Samuels Lasner, David Latané, Patrick Leary, Paul Lewis, Jeffrey M. Lipkes, Hugh MacDougall, Dorothy Mermin, Lisa Merrill, Cameron Moffett, Greg Murrie, Virginia K. Nalencz, Kate Newey, Barbara Onslow, Kathleen Peck, Deborah Pye, Denise Quirk, Patricia Rigg, Solveig Robinson, Gillian Rodger, Tracey Rosenberg, Janice Schroeder, Patrick Scott, Margaret Stetz, Gene Stratton, Beth Sutton-Ramspeck, Herbert Tucker, Rosemary VanArsdel, Martha Vicinus, Sue Wells, Stephen White, Joel Wiener, and Michael Wolff.

Special thanks go to Peadar Bates for helping me use the papers at Newbridge and also for his extraordinary work in the difficult job of examining and classifying them; to Richard and Valerie Foulkes for providing access to the commonplace book evidently kept by Mary Lloyd from 1849 to the mid-1850s and to Susan Hamilton for supplying information about its contents; to Joshua Schwieso (University of the West of England, Bristol) for sharing his research on the Agapemone; to Gerald J. Pollinger, of Laurence Pollinger Limited, London, for permission to consult the Lovelace-Byron Archive at the Bodleian Library; and to James A. Butler (LaSalle University, Philadelphia) for helping me with access to the drawing of Sarah Wister. I am also indebted to Clare Bates and Brigid Dunne for making my time at Newbridge House pleasant; to the man who told me where to find the key that would unlock the Donabate church; to Paul Hett, who showed me the remaining buildings at Hengwrt and shared local gossip; and, of course, to the readers and editors at the University of Virginia Press for supporting and improving the book. Finally, my thanks to Talia Schaffer and Andrea Broomfield for helpful reading and to Ruth Gayle for morning chat and good friendship; and my love to Molly and Dominic and Bridget and Skye.

 FRANCES POWER COBBE

# Introduction

Frances Power Cobbe (1822–1904) was celebrated in her time as a suffragist, essayist, journalist, theologian, and social reformer. By the last quarter of the nineteenth century she was the most important British woman writer of intellectual prose. Forceful, fearless, and effective, Cobbe worked to improve conditions for delinquent girls and for the sick poor, was the first person to formally propose that women be admitted to English universities, served for many long years on the Central Committee for Women's Suffrage, publicized marital violence, and founded two organizations to protect animals from medical experiments.

Her effect on people who met her was striking. One colleague wrote that Cobbe's "extraordinarily powerful personality . . . hypnotised all those who worked with her into complete obedience to her wishes." Elizabeth Cady Stanton described her as "one of the most remarkable and genial women" in England, "frank and cordial, and pronounced in all her views." Those who were less favorably inclined used terms such as *strong-minded* and *manly* or, in George Meredith's phrase, "a tone of the trousers." An obituary suggested that she had inherited from her father "a very strong will, a masterful and somewhat imperious disposition, and a somewhat impatient and fiery temper. Traces of the bitter and unforgiving spirit she had had to overcome in her youth remained in a considerable capacity for quick and lasting resentment."[1]

One lively description was provided by an American visitor to the home of Mentia (Clementia) and P. A. Taylor, which in the 1860s was a center of progressive activism. Presenting herself as an unsophisticated country girl, though already a published author in her thirties, Louisa May Alcott wrote that she was turning the pages of an illustrated book when

> the door suddenly flew open, and in rolled an immensely stout lady, with skirts kilted up, a cane in her hand, a fly-away green bonnet on her head, and a loud laugh issuing from her lips, as she cast herself upon a sofa, exclaiming breathlessly:
>
> "Me dear creature, if ye love me, a glass of sherry!"

The wine being ordered, I was called from my nook, and introduced to Miss Cobbe. I had imagined the author of Intuitive Morals to be a serious, severe lady, of the "Cornelia Blimber" school, and was much surprised to see this merry, witty, Falstaffian personage. For half an hour she entertained us with all manner of droll sayings, as full of sense as of humor, one minute talking earnestly and gravely on the suffrage question . . . the next criticising an amateur poem in a way that convulsed her hearers, and in the middle of it jumping up to admire a picture, or trot about the room, enthusiastically applauding some welcome bit of news about "our petition." Cheery, sensible, kindly, and keen she seemed; and when she went away, talking hard till out of the gate, and vanishing with a hearty laugh, it was as if a great sunbeam had left the room.[2]

The essays that made Frances Power Cobbe's reputation as an author are marked by impassioned earnestness, careful research, concrete details, and a biting edge that compelled public attention. She published well over one hundred articles in leading periodicals; produced some two hundred tracts for the antivivisection movement; wrote more than a thousand unsigned (and ungendered) second leaders on politics, public issues, and social causes for the London *Echo* between 1868 and 1875; and served as a *Daily News* correspondent in Rome and Florence. Bridging the worlds of popular and higher journalism, Cobbe was centrally located among the circle of London intellectuals who engaged the nineteenth century's significant debates. Like Thomas Carlyle, John Stuart Mill, and Matthew Arnold, Cobbe published in prestige journals as well as in popular monthly magazines. She was the only woman who wrote regularly for the *Theological Review,* the most progressive of the magazines published by Unitarians in the period during which faith was being transformed by scholarship, science, and textual studies. She was especially engrossed by the search for a new basis for ethics suited to an age of religious doubt and scientific advance.

Cobbe's most effective work supplied memorable phrases as well as provocative ideas. "Celibacy *v.* Marriage" (1862) and "What Shall We Do With Our Old Maids?" (1862) proposed that single women could be as happy as their married sisters. *The Red Flag in John Bull's Eyes* (1863) aroused support for the Union during the U.S. Civil War. "Criminals, Idiots, Women, and Minors" (1868) pointedly named those citizens who had few civil rights. Her 1878 campaign against domestic abuse, culminating in the article "Wife-Torture in England," secured passage of the act that let magistrates grant an immediate separation order to a woman whose husband had assaulted her. Antivivisection essays not only asked broad questions about health, medical care, and scientific values but also emphasized the moral damage done to physiologists and medical students who learned to ignore or even enjoy the pain caused by their experiments. American suffragists used *The Duties of Women* (1881) in persuading complacent middle-class women to take an interest in public life. In a journalistic London that was still primarily a male preserve, Cobbe established a reputation as a provocative writer whose essays were explicit, vigorous, witty, and memorable. Editors welcomed her work, knowing that it would arouse discussion, although even some activists thought her positions were too extreme. Individual essays, as well as books, were widely reviewed on both sides of the Atlantic.

The nearly four hundred admirers who signed a testimonial presented to Cobbe in celebration of her eightieth birthday in 1902 included Henry James, Florence Nightingale, Dr. Elizabeth Blackwell, Josephine Butler, W. T. Stead, Grover Cleveland, Julia Ward Howe, Thomas Wentworth Higginson, and Mark Twain. Within two decades after her death, however, Cobbe's name was almost forgotten. As the *Daily News* suggested in 1893, "It is the fate of social reformers worthy of the name to find their writings gradually becoming more or less obsolete." Reviewing a posthumous edition of *The Duties of Women* in 1906, the social theorist Helen Bosanquet was "reminded by this little book of lectures given nearly a quarter of a century ago of how great and silent a change has taken place in the position of women during that period. . . . The change is one which she herself had a large share in bringing about, but all the same it has the effect of making the book seem a little out of date." Theological writing praised for its "amazing courage" on first appearance had grown quaint or sentimental by the century's end.[3]

A more important reason for the lack of twentieth-century academic interest, however, may be that Cobbe was a woman writer who did not produce fiction. The American suffragist and temperance leader Frances E. Willard pointed out in 1897 that although "distinguished critical authorities have assigned her the rank of greatest among living English women . . . Miss Cobbe . . . has taken duty, not love, for her theme, and the essay, not the novel, as her literary vehicle." The analysis remains apt: nineteenth-century British women novelists and poets are valued for their imagination, emotion, and realistic depiction of female lives, but the women who published intellectual prose remain almost invisible. Although several Victorian sages, including John Ruskin (in *Fors Clavigera*) and Matthew Arnold (in "The Function of Criticism at the Present Time"), found Cobbe's ideas influential enough to ridicule, critics for much of the twentieth century remained deliberately uninterested. John Gross, for example, wrote in 1969 that although Cobbe's "Dreams as Illustrations of Involuntary Cerebration" was said to contain "some bold anticipations of psycho-analytic theory," he did not expect that he would ever read her work.[4]

Even feminist historians have only recently grown interested in Frances Power Cobbe. The high drama of the militant Women's Social and Political Union, founded at Emmeline Pankhurst's Manchester home six months before Cobbe died, has overshadowed the prior forty years of work. Among those who do consider the earlier campaign, Cobbe is generally included in the less interesting "conservative" faction, a move that is based on her political alliances and does not adequately describe her own activity. In many cases Cobbe worked within existing structures rather than founding new institutions; while some reformers devoted whole lives to one cause, she had dozens. She did establish two societies that still work to end the use of animals in research and testing, but the antivivisection campaign also damaged her reputation. She lost many feminist friends when she criticized physiological study at Girton and Somerville. Furthermore, the topical structure of Cobbe's autobiography gives the impression that she had withdrawn from women's causes by 1880 to devote herself to animal protection, although in fact the last article she published in a major periodical—when she was eighty years old—was revised from a suffrage speech she had given four months earlier.

Another difficulty in Cobbe's self-presentation involves social class. Some scholars are disturbed by her apparently elitist assumption of natural superiority. To an extent, however, her political success rested on her sense of entitlement. One of her cousins was married to a member of Parliament; another cousin was head of police for the Midlands; several more were high-ranking military men. Cobbe had longstanding connections with bishops and minor aristocrats. Gladstone invited her to breakfast. An 1886 letter to Millicent Garrett Fawcett mentions which titled ladies she could ask to help if a suffrage bill should reach the House of Lords. I am often struck by her ability to get country gentlemen and radical MPs, Tories and Liberals, evangelical Protestants, high church Anglicans, Roman Catholics, and an assortment of theists and Unitarians to sit on the same platform. This is of course now commonplace in social causes, but it was not easy in the nineteenth century. In March 1876 Cobbe urged the home secretary to introduce an antivivisection bill by organizing a delegation that included Lord Shaftesbury, Cardinal Manning, James Anthony Froude, and Leslie Stephen. Thomas Carlyle supported the cause but would not take part because he refused to be in the company of a detestable Roman Catholic like Manning.[5]

Over the last thirty years scholars interested in women's causes and in animal rights have begun to use Cobbe's activist essays, and some of her work is now found in classroom anthologies and specialist collections. For those who write about Cobbe, however, virtually the only source of biographical information has remained the autobiography she published in 1894. Like most such books, the *Life of Frances Power Cobbe* is vague in many details and reticent about important matters both public and private.[6] As a single woman whose "life-friend" (the term is her own) predeceased her, Cobbe had no survivor to gather her papers and preserve her reputation. In her will she left three hundred pounds to a literary executor, Blanche Atkinson, who was to bring out "a volume or volumes of remains from my unpublished M S S & Letters all of which are to be delivered to her," but aside from a slightly updated one-volume edition of Cobbe's *Life*, no such books appeared, nor have I located any significant collection of unpublished material, although the letters to Cobbe from eminent contemporaries (also left in Atkinson's hands) were purchased by the Huntington Library in 1949.

One of Cobbe's newspaper pieces might well make any biographer quail. She castigates the "bran-new style of biography" in which

> some person, chosen, not with an aptitude for biographical writing—for everybody somehow believes that he can do that sort of work, just as every one fancies that he can drive a gig, or steer a boat—is named, and the widow and the executors tie up all the papers, bills, pamphlets, diaries, and what not, and deposit them with the literary undertaker. He perhaps at odd moments finds out the dates of his hero's birth, schooling, and marriage; procures from an old friend a letter full of graphic reminiscences; asks the deceased's colleagues to send him a few testimonials of his talents and virtues. Here is the framework of a book; enough of letters to fill any vacuum are inserted; and the supreme result is launched into the world as a Life of So-and-So.[7]

Cobbe, by contrast, asks for inner life, evaluation, and judgment, for what she calls "the springs of action." She did not, however, make that task easy. Her own feelings stated in her own words are extremely rare, even in letters to close friends. Although it has been claimed that nineteenth-century women autobiographers generally negotiate their public discourse by and through representation of the private sphere,[8] Cobbe discloses very little about her intimate self. Her autobiography tells us a great deal about Ireland in the 1830s and 1840s, about what she saw and whom she knew in Bristol and Italy and London, and about the crusades and movements in which she had a part, but it is largely without what I would call personal content. She learned from her mother and the women of her mother's generation to keep social life comfortable by ignoring the flaws and errors of those around

her; in some cases she created cover stories that conceal her distress and disappointment beneath mildly humorous anecdotes. The *Life,* she claimed,
had a purpose: to show "how pleasant and interesting, and withal, I hope,
not altogether useless a life is open to a woman, though no man has ever desired to share it, nor has she seen the man she would have wished to ask her
to do so."[9] Yet though the book is vivid and often irresistibly quotable, it is
difficult to accept even as deliberately chosen self-representation because
many passages are only slightly revised from newspaper leaders or polemical essays written twenty or thirty years earlier. Periodical journalism is neither a transparent exposure of the writer's feelings nor a deliberate expression of the editor's (or publisher's) policy but something between the two;
it also depends on a personality negotiated for a specific public appearance.

In seeking to add depth and context to Frances Power Cobbe's public
and private history, I have been greatly aided not only by the new interest
in her work but also by other events of the past twenty years. The family
home at Newbridge, now in the care of the Fingal County Council, is open
to visitors, as are the two neighboring estates Malahide and Ardgillan, where
friends of the Cobbe family once lived. With the extremely helpful cooperation of Frances Power Cobbe's great-great-great-nephews, I have been able
to use significant materials still in private hands, including family letters and
account books, a diary kept by her father, Charles Cobbe, which runs from
the year after his daughter's birth until his own death thirty-four years later,
a manuscript account by Frances Power Cobbe of her journey to Egypt and
Palestine in 1858, and a number of her sketchbooks and photograph albums.

Cobbe also left a more extensive public record than has been appreciated. Following clues in her will, I located in the National Library of Wales
an uncataloged collection of scrapbooks and papers that contained more
than one thousand previously unidentified contributions to newspapers and
periodicals. Material in the London *Times* became much easier to discover
with the electronic version of *Palmer's Index.* The Fawcett Library (now the
Women's Library) and work by other feminist archivists have opened access
to records of the women's movement; the Internet has allowed many libraries
to describe their special collections online, and it helped me locate some five
hundred letters from Frances Power Cobbe in the papers of people to whom
she wrote.

Even letters, of course, are not transparent, no more than journalism: it
is necessary to consider when and to whom they were written and how the
author was framing herself for this appearance. Many additional letters that
once existed have not been found. "Please *don't* keep or return my letters but
*destroy* them," she wrote to a friend who fortunately disobeyed.[10] Elderly
people or their heirs often sent letters back to the person who had written

them; Cobbe had some of her own to quote when she wrote the *Life* but probably burned them afterwards. She may also have burned the journal or journals of her beloved friend Mary Lloyd. Blanche Atkinson's introduction to the posthumous edition of the *Life* quotes a letter Cobbe wrote in December 1900: "I have this last week broken open the lock of an old notebook of my Dear Mary's, kept about 1882–85. Among many things of deep interest to me are letters to and from various people and myself . . . which I used to show her, and she took the trouble to copy into this book, along with memoranda of our daily life."[11]

How many other journals or manuscripts or letters that might have revealed personal details and private friendships also went up in flames? Atkinson wrote that she had "an immense number of letters" to and from Mary Lloyd, as well as hundreds of Cobbe's letters to Atkinson. The latter were largely on antivivisection business, but some contained gossip, bits of reminiscence, and the casual chatter of an elderly woman who no longer had a companion with whom to share her passing thoughts. Other undiscovered materials include a lifetime's correspondence with Felicia Skene, who had been a friend since both were in their early twenties; frequent letters to Henry Cobbe, the brother closest to her in age; "nearly 50 years" of correspondence with Frank Newman, John Henry Newman's theist, suffragist, and vegetarian younger brother; a "whole volume" of letters from Mary Somerville; and "almost daily" letters to clergyman John Verschoyle, an antivivisection coworker, covering the last five years of her life.[12]

The biography of Frances Power Cobbe thus rests on a question that may have no answer: How did a daughter of the Anglo-Irish Ascendancy, raised on the estate of a father who was the major landowner in county Dublin, educated at an expensive Brighton finishing school with a curriculum of "French, Italian, German, the piano, the harp, singing, dancing, calisthenics, drawing, the use of the dumb-bells—with history, geography, and the use of the globes flung in as a slight ballast in odd corners of time, and science taught in nine lectures by an itinerant professor of omniscience," and governed by a mother described as a "refined, high-bred lady" and a father whose adult children, even into middle age, referred to him as "The Master," become a self-assured, sharp-tongued, socially aware feminist who staked out her own moral and intellectual positions, earned an adequate income, traveled alone both at home and abroad, lived for more than thirty years with another independent woman as her beloved friend, and was described in 1894 as "the oldest New Woman now living on this planet."[13]

Feminist biographies of prominent women, in the words of historian Barbara Caine, generally seek to discover "not just what they did, but . . . . how they felt about their private and familial life . . . [and] what it cost them to follow their own path."[14] Yet for me an important theoretical question arises: can we use twentieth-century psychologies to think about nineteenth-century lives? It is evident from Frances Power Cobbe's idealized account that she seldom spent time with her mother, but the same would be true for almost any upper-middle-class child of the period. Cobbe's autobiography suppresses a great many things, but some of the silences that seem to beg for deconstruction arise from Victorian standards of modesty, privacy, and personal reticence or from social conventions of the time (e.g., not to mention names, especially women's names, unless the person had a significant public reputation). Other discrepancies between Cobbe's account and external evidence are the kind of good stories that get enshrined in family lore. For example, she writes that she was born in Dublin at sunrise on 4 December 1822 and adds, "There had been a memorable storm during the night,"[15] while the *Dublin Almanac and General Register of Ireland for 1837* puts the "most tremendous storm recorded in our annals" a week later, on 12 December. Some omissions are very important: they denote secrets that were carefully kept and repressions that may be highly significant. Still others remain a mystery: why, for example, did Cobbe misrepresent by ten years the origin of her published concern for wife abuse?

Thus, my act of reconstruction is rather an act of constructing one version of Frances Power Cobbe's life, her family story, her relationships with brothers and cousins and friends, and her actions as an adult. The extent of new information available once I had discovered so much of her anonymous journalism and located so many letters (even aside from the material gleaned through family papers) presents a woman far too complex for easy interpretation. I therefore generally tell the events in chronological order and have depended on contexts and connections, rather than any psychological or theoretical mode of analysis, to suggest the experiences and influences that produced one of the most interesting and important women of the nineteenth century.

A note on names: One problem of biographers, especially biographers of women, is what to call the subject. During childhood she was surrounded by dozens of Cobbes, several of them, including her mother, also named Frances. In adulthood, close friends called her "Fanny," although she never signed letters that way and sharply criticized suffragists who put themselves "rather in the kittenish than the womanly category" by signing their names "Lulu" or "Vinnie."[16] Thus, until Frances Power Cobbe leaves home at the end of 1857 she is "Fan," a form sometimes found in family letters, and I also use first names for the rest of the Cobbes. Because the same names appear repeatedly in every generation, I designate relationships from Fan's standpoint to distinguish between, for example, "Uncle William," "brother Will," "cousin William Henry (Uncle Thomas's son)," and "cousin William Power (Uncle William's younger son)." After leaving Ireland she is "Cobbe." I also generally use surnames for private friends as well as for the public figures, male and female, in her adult world.

Geographical names also create a problem when writing about the nineteenth century. I use the English form customary during the period for places in Ireland, Wales, India, and the Middle East; the current designation is provided in parentheses on first usage and cross-referenced in the index.

A Child Well Born

*It is hardly to be measured, I think, how much of the best and tenderest family feelings amongst us are due to the old house, wherein all associations are centred, wherein each member of the race feels pride, where the pictures of our forefathers hang side by side on the walls, and their dust rests together in the vault hard by.*

FRANCES POWER COBBE, "A DAY AT THE DEAD SEA"

In the first sentence of her autobiography Frances Power Cobbe tells readers that she "enjoyed through life the advantage of being, in the true sense of the words, 'well born.'" A sound constitution and a relatively free outdoor childhood on a substantial estate twelve miles from Dublin gave her, in the words of a friend, "immense vitality and [a] ceaseless flow of animal spirits."[1] "Well born" also describes the generations that lay behind her: country squires, Oxford graduates, a regular infusion of aristocratic connections. An early-twentieth-century president of the American Social Science Association called her an exemplar of the "ruling class of England and Ireland during their remarkable career of conquest and government": "Strong qualities handed down from father to son, the instinct and the habit of command, courage invincible in the face of the most appalling odds, gracious manners clothing an inflexible purpose, keen wit, ready sympathy . . . a power of simple, strong affection . . . all these were as conspicuous in this youngest daughter of an Irish squire as in any statesman or admiral or great commander."[2]

The family genealogy put together by Fan's brother Tom claims to have "direct pedigrees from 1323," but for our purposes the story begins in the reign of George I, when increasing numbers of English-born administrators were appointed to high public office in Ireland. Among them was Fan's great-great-grandfather Charles Cobbe, the youngest son of an English landed family. Born in 1687 and educated at Trinity College, Oxford, he went to Ireland in 1717 as chaplain to his godfather, Charles Paulet, duke of Bolton, who had been appointed lord lieutenant. By the time Bolton left office in 1720, Cobbe was dean of Ardagh. Advancing quickly in the church hierar-

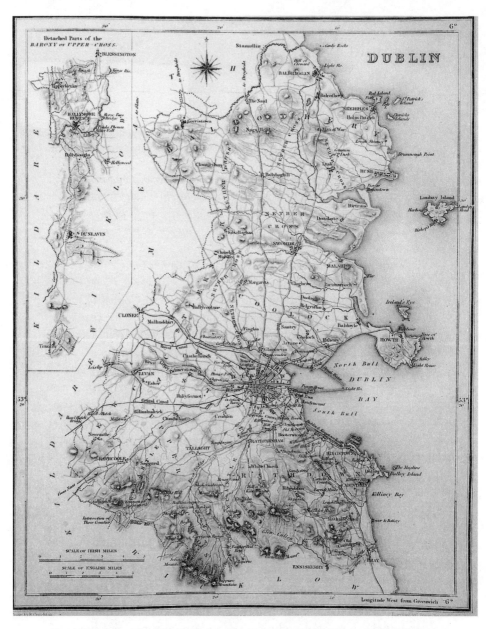

County Dublin. The Newbridge estate, just outside Donabate, is two English miles from the coast on a line with the southern portion of Lambay Island. (Samuel Lewis, *Atlas of Ireland*, 1837)

chy, he became archbishop of Dublin in 1743. Jonathan Swift was still dean of St. Patrick's at the time, although already near death and in a state of mental decay.

As his career prospered, Charles Cobbe started to buy land. On 19 June 1736 he paid £5,526 5s. 6d. for the properties Donabate, Lanistown, Haggardstown, and Newbridge and began building a house. "The Archbishop," wrote Frances Power Cobbe with more than a trace of ironic suspicion, "would seem to have well nursed the large revenues then pertaining to the See of Dublin." Ultimately he owned thirty-five thousand acres in four counties. By the 1920s another descendent's wife called him simply "the plundering archbishop." Nevertheless, family tradition asserted that although he "exerted himself strenuously in inculcating loyalty in Ireland" during the Pretender's Rebellion of 1745, he nevertheless strongly opposed a "severe penal measure against Roman Catholics" introduced in the Irish parliament later in the year.[3]

For eighteenth-century Anglo-Irish gentry, thoroughly outnumbered and many days' travel from England, social ties were necessarily very strong; relationships formed by friendship and marriage still influenced pragmatic affairs as well as the character of Cobbes in Fan's generation. In 1730 Archbishop Cobbe, then bishop of Dromore, married Dorothea Rawdon, a widow with two young sons. Her father, Richard Levinge, had served Ireland as solicitor general, speaker of the House of Commons, and lord chief justice of the court of common pleas. After she died in childbirth three years later the archbishop raised the Rawdon boys together with his own sons.[4] One of them became the father of Francis Rawdon, who was eventually the earl of Moira, governor general of Bengal, and a family connection of some importance.

Also related to the Cobbe family in multiple and complicated ways over the generations were Beresfords from both legitimate and illegitimate lines. In Fan's lifetime significant members of the Beresford clan included several members of Parliament, a field marshal, an admiral, and the Primate of Ireland. The Irish Beresfords, she wrote, were remarkable for their "tall stature, brilliantly fair complexion, well-cut features, and, lastly,—peculiarly large and powerful thumbs!" The latter trait "would now, no doubt, be generally recognised as an indication of strength of will." To claim the strength of will for her own, she added that her own thumbs "are so much out of proportion that I am obliged for their accommodation to wear gloves two sizes too large for my fingers."[5]

The archbishop's heir Thomas Cobbe (Fan's great-grandfather) was born in 1733, matriculated at Trinity College, Dublin, when he was sixteen, and earned his B.A. in 1753. His older brother, Charles, had died while taking a

European tour at age nineteen. Thomas stayed in Ireland and was married almost at once to Elizabeth Beresford, the eighth and youngest daughter of the first earl of Tyrone. Almost always referred to as "Lady Betty Cobbe," she was a dynamic and attractive woman about whom many legends circulate. Thomas Cobbe, who was "noted for his humourous and convivial temperament" (and known to his descendants in Fan's generation as "Old Tommie"), settled at Newbridge and began performing the duties of landowner well before the archbishop died.[6] In 1758 he held the largely ceremonial post of high sheriff for county Dublin, and from 1759 to 1768 and again from 1776 to 1783 he sat in the Irish House of Commons as a member for what his great-granddaughter called the "(exceedingly) 'rotten borough' of Swords."[7] He built a town house at 17 Palace Row (on the north side of Rutland Square, now Parnell Square) for the parliamentary season, served on the board of several philanthropic organizations (including a foundling hospital, a lunatic hospital, the Dublin public library, and a charitable loan society), and set out to make Newbridge into a showplace for personal and political entertaining.

Lady Betty's money helped add a forty-five-foot-long drawing room to the original square Georgian house. Much of the new furniture was Irish-made; Tommie and Lady Betty supported local trades instead of buying fashionable goods from France and England. The drawing room served as a gallery for the extraordinary collection of paintings Tommie assembled with the help of his parish clergyman. The vicar of Donabate and Portrane from shortly after 1722 until his death in 1784 was Matthew Pilkington, whose duties in a neighborhood with very few Protestant residents left him ample time for scholarship. In 1770 he published *The Gentleman's and Connoisseur's Dictionary of Painters,* the first book of its kind in English.[8]

Old Tommie's eldest son, Charles Cobbe (Fan's grandfather), was born in 1756. No records of his education have been located, but by 1783 he had taken his father's place as a member for Swords in the Irish House of Commons. He was, however, already deeply in debt by the time he turned eighteen, and according to Fan, his political service was mixed. Although he may have been one of the few members of the 1784 parliament who received no public office or pension in exchange for his vote, the only notices she found in the House journals referred "to certain charges made, and, I fear, proved against him, of 'bribery and corruption'!"[9]

In 1779 this Charles Cobbe married Anne Power Trench, a sister of the first earl of Clancarty. Anne originated the Newbridge "cabinet of curiosities," a family museum now filled with antiquities, weapons, carvings, beetles, shells, snakeskins, fossils, and other items sent home from nearly all corners of the British Empire. She too brought connections that would be useful to her grandchildren, although they were a drain on family resources

in the eighteenth century. They arrived "by coachloads, with trains of servants" and stayed "for months at a time."[10]

Like many other Anglo-Irish gentry of the period, Tommie and Lady
Betty lived too lavishly for their rents. In 1785 or 1786 they moved to Bath
and occupied number 9 in the Marlborough Buildings, a terrace located
just beyond the much more elegant Royal Crescent. Bath was by then a
place where, as Jane Austen wrote, a gentleman might "be important at
comparatively little expense."[11] Although aristocrats and royalty no longer
flocked to take the waters, a visitor's season lasted from September to May.
Entertaining could be done in public places instead of at home; there were
well-tended gardens, subscription libraries, and two assembly rooms with
space for card games and tea as well as concerts and balls. Fan suggested an
additional motive for her great-grandparents' relocation to Bath: that Lady
Betty, influenced by the Methodist countess of Huntingdon, "renounced
the vanities and pleasures of the world, and persuaded her husband to retire
with her and live quietly." "Quietly," however, does not seem quite accurate. A contemporary in Bath described Lady Betty as "a combination of
Calvinistic piety and aristocratic waggery. . . . a sort of head fuglewoman—
a busy, merry, witty lady, who thought the limitation of God's mercies to a
very select few the finest joke of the day."[12]

Tommie and Lady Betty had two daughters, who, as Fan's great-aunts,
brought still more useful connections into the family. Catherine married
Henry Pelham, a younger son of the earl of Chichester, and served briefly
as a bedchamber woman to Princess Caroline, wife of the Prince of Wales.
Although Henry Pelham died young, his widow and her two daughters
lived into Fan's adulthood. The other great-aunt, Elizabeth, married a naval
officer, Sir Henry Tuite. She too had a very long widowhood before dying
in 1850 at age eighty-five; she was among the relatives in Bath when Fan and
her brothers visited. Perhaps of more importance, Elizabeth Tuite was a
published author. Two of her books were written when Fan was in her teens.

Tommie's son Charles and his wife Anne produced five surviving sons
within ten years: the Charles Cobbe who became Fan's father was born in
1781, her uncle George in 1782, her uncle Henry in 1785, her uncle Thomas
in 1788, and her uncle William in 1790. Although Fan claimed that her
grandmother Anne sent each of her sons "out to be nursed at a cottage" at
Newbridge until they were three years old, feeling that her "motherly duties
were . . . amply fulfilled by occasionally stopping her carriage to see how
the children were getting on,"[13] some of the boys were born in Bath, and
Charles Cobbe left Parliament in 1790. Still heavily in debt, he and his wife
evidently preferred the pleasures of Bath to life on a country estate that was
still a half-day's carriage journey from Dublin. In January 1797, however, he

again became MP for Swords, although contrary to published accounts, he did not live long enough to see the Irish parliament through to its final act. An armed rising of Irish revolutionaries broke out on 23 May 1798. In its aftermath, Dublin's legislature was "induced to abolish itself" through the incentive of "a golden rain of titles and cash."[14] Fan claimed—and probably believed—that her grandfather Charles had been "almost the only one among the Members of the Irish Parliament who voted for the Union, and yet refused either a peerage or money," but this cannot be true, for he died in Bath on 9 July 1798, before the rebellion was brought to an end and two years before the Act of Union passed.[15]

Tommie, by then in his mid-sixties, did not return to live at Newbridge. Fan's grandmother Anne also remained in Bath at 22 Marlborough Buildings, just a few doors away from her father-in-law. Although absentee landlords have been justly criticized—by Frances Power Cobbe and many other Anglo-Irish writers as well as by the Catholic Irish—creating the "United Kingdom" destroyed one motive that had kept landowners (and the money their tenants paid as rent) in Ireland. Before the union Dublin had homes for 271 "temporal or spiritual Peers" and 300 members of the House of Commons, but by 1831 only half a dozen peers and 15 or 20 of the Irish members elected to London's parliament spent any part of the year in Dublin.[16] Until the very last years of his life, however, Tommie never became entirely an absentee but spent some time every year at Newbridge.

His grandson Charles (Fan's father) was not yet seventeen when his father died. There are some odd difficulties in interpreting the next ten years. The *Life of Frances Power Cobbe* reports that "his tastes were active rather than studious" and that "without much reflection or delay, he obtained a cornet's commission . . . and sailed for Madras."[17] These years when the eighteenth century turned into the nineteenth were war years. Not only was impoverished and overpopulated Ireland prime recruiting ground for Britain's soldiers but a disproportionate number of officers were country-bred Anglo-Irish gentlemen whose family estates supplied only a narrow income. Four of the five Cobbe brothers began military life about the time their father died. George entered the Royal Artillery as a cadet when he was barely fifteen and was commissioned eighteen months later, in October 1799. Thomas, who made a career as an officer in the East India Company's army, became a lieutenant a few days before his sixteenth birthday. William, the youngest, entered the Royal Navy as a midshipman at thirteen, two years before the battle of Trafalgar. Only Henry, born in 1785, was educated at Oxford and became a clergyman.

The eldest brother, Charles Cobbe, later to be Fan's father, joined the 19th Light Dragoons in India as a cornet on 24 January 1801, two and a half years after his father's death. In the days when commissions were purchased it took both money and influence to enter the cavalry. The 19th Light Dragoons had been created to serve in India and was for many years the only regiment of king's cavalry (as opposed to East India Company cavalry) on the subcontinent. George Tuite, a nephew of Charles's aunt Elizabeth's, became a lieutenant in the same regiment at the same time; the required influence may have been provided by Tuite's connections as well as by Beresford cousins. Charles Cobbe's purchase money was partly lent by his commander,[18] a man born in Dublin in 1769 as Arthur Wesley, later "Wellesley" and later yet the duke of Wellington. Wesley was elected to the Irish House of Commons in 1790 as MP for Trim. Although the elder Charles Cobbe was not then in Parliament, Trim was hardly thirty miles from his own constituency of Swords. By June 1796 Arthur Wellesley had become a colonel and sailed for India; two years later his brother was made governor general. At the time, the East India Company controlled most of Bengal and the south, Muslim rulers held the north and east, and the Mahrattas (or Marathas) held much of the central territory. Their internal conflicts gave the governor general and his brother an opening to enlarge the East India Company's domain.[19]

War against the Mahrattas began a little more than two years after Charles Cobbe and George Tuite got to India. The most significant battle was at Assaye on 23 September 1803. Long after his victories over Napoleon, Wellington still considered it the "'best thing' he ever did in the way of fighting." He also called it the bloodiest of all his battles. He had seven thousand men in the field, and the Mahrattas had at least six times that number; he had twenty-two cannon, and they had more than a hundred. At the most desperate moment for Wellington's outnumbered forces the tide was turned by a dramatic charge of the 19th Light Dragoons, among whose officers were Charles Cobbe and his friend George Tuite, which gave the infantry time to regroup. Operations continued for another three months, but Assaye virtually decided the war.[20]

The actions of those three months encompass all that can be discovered about Charles Cobbe's military service. In the autumn of 1805 his brother Thomas reached India and perhaps suggested that because of their grandfather's declining health Charles ought to be at home. Furthermore, Charles had contracted an "ague," probably malaria, which affected him intermittently for the rest of his life. The foolhardy (if heroic) charge of the 19th Dragoons haunted him. Decades later he marked the anniversary in his diary: "Tis 30 years this day since the battle of Assaye when I was engaged in a contest from which I could entertain no reasonable hope of escape."[21] The entry continues with a meditation on God's mercy in pointing out his follies and temptations. Whenever it actually took place, the conversion to evangelical seriousness that shaped the rest of his life may have originated on the battlefield.

Returning to England (possibly late in 1806, although the regiment sailed from India in October and disembarked on 18 April 1807), he found that Lady Betty Cobbe had died, but his grandfather Tommie and his mother, Anne, still lived in the Marlborough Buildings. As a man of twenty-five who had finished his youthful adventure, Charles Cobbe was ready for courtship. A story that Fan told in more than one version would have it that her father "carried on a pretty lively flirtation" with a second cousin, Louisa Beresford, but lost out to Thomas Hope, who "came into the little Bath world with the reputation of enormous wealth, great literary ability . . . supreme artistic taste, and almost abnormal ugliness." She then inserts her mother into the tale: "Going to call on Miss Beresford at this time my mother, then Miss Conway, found her reclining on a sky-blue silk sofa, appropriately reading the 'Pleasures of Hope.' Her marriage with Mr. Hope was, I believe, quite a happy one, though it was far from a love match; and after his death, her second marriage to her cousin, Field Marshall Lord Beresford, was entirely so." (The more public form of this narrative, in Cobbe's autobiography, omits the observation that Louisa Beresford's first marriage was "far from a love match.")[22]

Frances Conway, who was past thirty by the time Charles Cobbe came courting, lived at the west end of the Royal Crescent just a few steps away from Anne Cobbe's house. She must have been friendly with the family for many years, since Colonel Alexander Champion, with whose widow she lived, was godfather to one of Charles Cobbe's brothers. Frances Conway's early history is hard to piece together, partly because the version told in Fan's *Life* does not match some other records, but certainly she would have been interested in news from India. Her only brother, serving in the Madras Army as a lieutenant in the 6th Native Cavalry, had (like Charles Cobbe) fought in the battle of Argaum in November 1803; and her father, Thomas Conway, had sailed to India as a free merchant in 1766 and then spent ten years in the Bengal Army.[23] He married Sophia von Schramm, whose German father may have been an ambassador married to a Frenchwoman, Magdalen Rachel de la Brugére. Thomas and Sophia Conway settled at Morden Park in Surrey. Their daughter Frances was born on 18 March 1777, and their son Thomas in 1779.

Sophia Conway died in 1785, when her daughter Frances was eight years old. Frances then evidently came under the care of her father's widowed stepmother, also named Frances Conway, in Southampton. Her father, who according to his record at the National Army Museum was "a notorious gambler & had lost a fortune," returned to India and died there in 1794, the same year that her brother became an East India Company cadet. The older Frances Conway of Southampton died in 1792, leaving her step-grand-daughter with an inheritance but no close relatives in England. According to the account written by Fan many years after her mother's death, Mrs. Champion came to the rescue because Frances Conway's grandfather had helped her go out to India and marry Alexander Champion a generation earlier, when she was the orphan daughter of his parish clergyman.[24] By the time he retired to Bath, Champion was commander in chief of the East India Company's forces in Bengal and had, like many of the company's military and civil servants, become a wealthy man. Colonel Champion died in March 1793, at about the time his wife invited the friendless sixteen-year-old to share her house at Bath. No evidence suggests that Frances Conway had any other residence in the next fifteen years, although in January 1796 Mrs. Champion married Thomas Leman, who had been only eight years old at the time of her first wedding.

Yet there are difficulties with the stories about her parents' history that Fan told, sometimes with slight variations, in her autobiography, in the manuscript catalog of family paintings that she compiled in 1868, and as anonymous anecdotes in her journalism. The dates are slippery; some details simply cannot be made to fit. For example, the heartwarming story of her grandfather's kindness to the impoverished daughter of his parish clergyman in the account of Frances Conway's residence with Mrs. Champion is cast into doubt by other records describing Mrs. Champion as the heiress of a barrister.[25] Charles Cobbe's flirtation with Louisa Beresford is also problematic. Thomas Hope and Louisa Beresford were married on 16 April 1806, while the War Office *Army List* suggests that Lieutenant Cobbe did not leave India until later in the year.

These discrepancies force me to wonder why Frances Power Cobbe evidently had—or reported—so little accurate information about her parents' early years. Maybe incidents such as the Louisa Beresford flirtation were a kind of family joke, perhaps used by her mother to tease her father. (It would have been particularly entertaining by the time Fan wrote her autobiography, since Louisa Beresford and Thomas Hope became the parents of A. J. Beresford-Hope, the ultrareactionary MP for Cambridge University who could be counted on for an insulting speech whenever women's suffrage came up for debate.) Or perhaps her parents said very little about the past, leaving her to create plausible stories that codify the virtues she wanted to see in her forebears. Such a silence might reveal no more than a habit of reticence, the limited family contact in a household of substantial gentry, or a parental preference for educational and religious conversation instead of

trivialities about private life. Yet it is also possible that the entertaining anecdotes conceal awkward secrets and emotional tension. Nothing is known
about what Frances Conway did with her time in the fifteen years between
school and marriage. (Jane Austen, not quite eighteen months older than
Frances Conway, was miserable in Bath during four of those same years.)
Something more significant might well lie beneath the explanation that
young Charles Cobbe sought a cavalry commission—explicitly in India—
because "his tastes were active rather than studious" and the description of
him as a dashing young officer with fair hair tied back in a pigtail that reached
to his saddle.[26] If there were secrets, however, they remain well buried.

Frances Conway and Charles Cobbe were married in Bath on 13 March
1809. He was twenty-seven; she was five days short of her thirty-second birthday. Old Tommie, now in his mid-seventies, no longer made annual trips
to Ireland. By 1810 he had given up actively managing the estate; Charles
and his bride took up residence at Newbridge, although he did not actually
inherit the property until 1814, when his grandfather died. Thomas Cobbe's
will (proved 9 April 1814) left to Fan's father a great many debts and a heavily encumbered estate where most of the cottages were "miserable hovels" of
mud and thatch. Further difficulties surfaced in the form of unprofitable
leases, mismanaged property, and at least one promise that caused Charles
"infinite trouble & anxiety."[27]

Although the house had not been "deserted" for anything like the "nearly
thirty years" Fan said,[28] it too needed work. Her mother's money paid for
the new curtains and Regency furniture—most of it, once more, of Irish
manufacture—that are still in the Newbridge drawing room. Frances Conway had been well educated in accomplishments and social graces: she had
books of piano music carefully copied; the labels on the back of the paintings appear to be in her handwriting. Her school in Bloomsbury had provided "a great deal of careful training in what may be called the great Art of
Society; the art of properly paying and receiving visits, of saluting acquaintances in the street and drawing-room; and of writing letters of compliment."[29] While the house was being restored and the estate brought into
order she built new social networks. At about the same time that Charles
and Frances Cobbe took up residence at Newbridge, Edward Taylor and his
own new wife, Marianne Harriet St. Leger, came to live at Ardgillan, twenty
miles to the north. The two families visited frequently, and the men became
political allies.

Four sons were born to the Cobbes in their first ten years at Newbridge,
Fan's brothers Charles (on 17 August 1811), Thomas (8 December 1813),
William (6 March 1816), and Henry (11 November 1817). Fan's parents also
became partly responsible for some children of their own brothers, Thomas

Cobbe of the Bengal Army and Thomas Conway of the Madras Cavalry. British officers and civilians alike sent their children "home" from India at a very early age for the sake of health and character and schooling. Thomas Cobbe's eldest son, Henry Clermont, was born the same year as Fan's oldest brother; his second son, Charles Augustus, was the age of her youngest brother. Two daughters, Azélie and Florence, were for the time being in France under the supervision of Lady Granard, daughter of one of the stepsons the archbishop had raised with his own children. Thomas Conway and his wife had three daughters and a son during the same years that Fan's four brothers were born: Frances, Thomas, Isabella, and Anne. In February 1818 their mother, also an Anne Conway, brought the children to England herself. She found schools for the three oldest and left the youngest with the Cobbes at Newbridge.

In the decade before Fan was born, George III was formally declared insane and his son became prince regent, Jane Austen's major novels were published, Napoleon's defeat at Waterloo ended more than twenty years of war with the French, and postwar social unrest troubled industrializing England. Fan's father was high sheriff of county Dublin when the new king, George IV, visited Ireland in August 1821. Charles Cobbe met the king at Dunleary,[30] presented a formal address of allegiance, and escorted him to the boundary of the city, where, according to the letter of instructions, he was to break the wand he carried as high sheriff since the corporation of Dublin would be "inclined to resist any appearance of authority on your part within their bounds."[31] In preparation for this event, he had the Cobbe family arms confirmed by the Ulster king at arms.

The 1821 census recorded the residents of Newbridge as Charles, Frances, three sons (the eldest, who was almost ten, must have been away at school), their niece Anne Conway, three male servants, and eight female servants. The 1822 housekeeping expenses for food, candles, and supplies, not including clothing or wages, for family and servants came to £464 10s. 7d. Most of the meat and much of the other produce came from land Charles Cobbe farmed for himself, although the conscientious bookkeeping that helped restore the estate's prosperity charged the market value of homegrown food as a household expense. Purchases in January 1822 included only items such as lemons, saltpeter, and a bottle of fish sauce. A sheep was butchered for household and charitable use about once a week; pigs and chickens were also killed as needed.[32]

The comfort, plenty, and social position that made Fan aware of her fortunate background were well established by the time she was born, but the household's emotional temperature is almost impossible to judge. A few years later her father noted in his diary that he had heard at church "an admirable discourse on the dangers of prosperity God grant I may be the better for it . . . surrounded with more blessings, yet conscious of deserving fewer than others, will not more gratitude, more love, more zeal, more devotedness of those gifts to the author & giver of all be expected from me." What was the cost to his wife and family of the moral seriousness and watchfulness and zeal that followed his evangelical conversion? Fan wrote years later of such a man that "religion makes him take each event of his life (down often to the most trivial incident) as a specially designed reward or punishment." Although she admired her father's cavalryman's bearing and wrote several times about his share in the battle of Assaye, her pride was undercut by recognition of its underside: "At all times there was an aspect of strength and command about him, which his vigorous will and (truth compels me to add) his not seldom fiery temper, fully sustained."[33]

Her mother's feelings are even more difficult to imagine. There is an extraordinary essay in a notebook that once belonged to Frances Conway headed "Character of the Irish." Although not dated, it comes after a set of short compositions that seem be schoolwork. "The general Character of the inhabitants of Ireland," she begins, "is distinguished by the prevalence of Passion over Reason. Vainglorious, shewn in the conceit of genealogies & in infinite legendary tales of bravery, liberality & generosity—& what is frequent in savage nations, an excessive attachment to gambling." She then describes Ireland's two classes: descendants of the "Aborigines," who have "been the constant object of the tyranny and contempt" from the "Conquerors," who "are distinguished by romantic gallantry towards the fair sex & the Spirit of Chivalry, are remarkably negligent in their religious duties, cruelly oppressive to their tenantry & deficient in Charity to the poor. . . . The rich have all the intolerance of bigots, without any of their piety—The polished minority of the nation is one hundred years behind England in refinement & the rude majority of it is at least five."[34]

This passage suggests, among other things, that Fan may have come naturally by some of the acid in her own style. But did her mother write it as a schoolgirl? after she met Charles Cobbe and his family in Bath? or later, when she lived with her husband in Ireland? Letters from her brother seem to suggest that he disliked her marriage and thought the Irish gentry were barely civilized. But Thomas Conway writes in a virtually illegible hand and the rowdy schoolboyish language of a man who was on duty in India as a cavalry officer by the time he was sixteen; I cannot tell whether he was teasing or serious.

Charles Cobbe often marked the anniversary of their marriage in his diary: "Her happiness," he wrote on one occasion, " . . . would have been encreased by a union with one whose disposition had been more yielding or principle more compromising. . . ; neither can I help regretting how many opportunities I have lost of rendering her happy, but my temper is not good, I know & bewail it."[35] Given the critical self-examination that was a central motive for his diary, this expression too is capable of several interpretations.

Fan was born in Dublin, where her parents took a house to be near the doctor, on 4 December 1822. Her brothers were then eleven (Charles), just turning nine (Tom), six (Will), and five (Henry). Over the next few months her father got ready to close Newbridge and take the family to England, partly because the death of the Reverend Henry Cobbe, the only one of his brothers educated for the church instead of the military, had left him with greater responsibility for their brother Thomas's children but principally because he wanted English schooling for his sons. He remembered being so hungry at his own school that he had stolen food, and he also recalled seeing vice "practiced with impunity" there. Dublin was far from England until steam packets began service in the mid-1820s. A contemporary wrote about trips to school that took three days and nights in "stout cutters, with one narrow cabin" and food "reduced to salt junk and ship's biscuit."[36] Aside from the time and expense, Fan's brothers were too young to travel alone; a relative or servant had to accompany them on every journey.

Leaving Dublin with the younger children on 4 October 1823, Fan's mother went by way of Bristol, which meant an even longer trip by sea but only twelve miles overland to Bath. Will, Henry, Fan, and Fan's nurse stayed with their grandmother Anne Cobbe while their parents checked up on the other children in their various schools. The Conway cousins were in Hammersmith; Fan's brothers Charles and Tom, along with their cousin Henry Clermont, attended a preparatory school in East Sheen. One of their schoolmates was Alfred Gatty, later a clergyman and husband of the naturalist and children's writer Margaret Gatty. A biography by the Gattys' granddaughter describes the school, conducted by John Hearn Pinckney, D.D., as distinguished for scholarship and adds that "one of the occupants of Alfred's dormitory of eight boys was James Disraeli, a younger brother of Lord Beaconsfield."[37] The Cobbes stayed in Richmond, taking all of the children out of their schools for a long weekend, and then enjoyed London for some time before returning to Bath for Fan's first birthday on 4 December.

Meanwhile, Charles Cobbe arranged to have his brother Thomas's eldest girls, Azélie and Florence (then aged nine and eight), brought from Paris to attend school at Miss Ford's, close to their grandmother's house in Bath. After the Christmas holidays, Will and Henry and their cousin Charles Augustus went to board with Miss Morgan at Brislington, three miles from Bristol on the road toward Bath; and Henry Clermont was moved from Dr.

Fan's mother,
Frances Cobbe, née
Conway (1777–
1847). The miniature
by C. Linsell was
probably done be-
tween 1810 and 1825.
(Cobbe Papers, Alec
Cobbe Collection)

Pinckney's to a school near Bristol. His twelfth birthday, on 20 December 1823, was noted in Charles Cobbe's diary: "This is the birthday of nephew Henry Clermont, and as it had been determined he should henceforth be called by the family name I considered this the best occasion of acquainting him with the relationship in which he stood to us all. . . . He received the information & said less on the subject than I expected . . . but he is amiable & singularly sensible and I sincerely hope that nothing will . . . throw a shade on the prospect . . . of his doing well and fulfilling the wishes of his father—may all his birthdays be as happy as this."[38]

In 1810 Fan's uncle Thomas, then a lieutenant in the Bengal Army, had been united in a Muslim ceremony with a woman whose name is translated in the marriage contract as "Neeauze Baigum alias Nuzzur Baigum the Daughter of Azzeze Khaun."[39] The usual narrative about East India Company attitudes toward marriage or other relationships with native women is that it was commonplace during most of the eighteenth century but became forbidden, frowned on, or uncommon in the 1790s.[40] In 1791 the offspring of such unions were officially prohibited to hold "civil or military office with the company." Every time this narrative is introduced, however, there is immediately a list of exceptions. Indeed, when the East India Company absolutely prohibited intermarriage in 1835, the acting governor general (Baron Metcalfe) had three recognized sons by his Sikh mistress. One of them became a company cadet the next year and served as aide to a later governor general.[41]

Charles Cobbe did not view his brother's children as legitimate. Many years later Fan wrote a leader in the *Echo* arguing for changes in the marriage law in which she asked why "marriages of Englishmen with foreign women according to Mahometan or other rites" were not recognized.[42] Until Henry's twelfth birthday, Charles Cobbe used Clermont as a surname for the children under his care. The diary thus raises major issues about secrecy, distance, and the meaning of family. Had he really been looking after Henry Clermont and Charles Augustus, who were the same age as two of his own sons and went to the same schools, without telling them that he was their uncle? Did they never ask questions, or was Charles Cobbe deluding himself in believing the announcement was news to a twelve-year-old? On 20 February 1824, writing about the girls as well, he confessed to his diary, "I trust in God I shall fulfill the wishes of their father . . . yet I cannot feel that all is right."[43]

Another question involving family relationships and emotional distance is the difficulty in arriving at any understanding of Fan's mother. The saintliness and unreality of her portrait in the *Life of Frances Power Cobbe* were immediately evident; the reviewer in the *Nation,* for example, wrote that Cobbe's father "was a man of stern theology and violent temper, and his daughter's utmost consideration does not make him attractive; while her mother . . . moves through the earlier chapters of the book as a gracious, even exquisite, apparition." Elsewhere Fan wrote that her mother's picture "gives us as little idea of the sweetness and beauty of her countenance as words can do of her character!" Yet she wrote that her mother "regretted my birth, thinking that she could not live to see me grow to womanhood."[44]

Frances Conway Cobbe's personality seems to have been carefully constructed. Her school had given extensive training in decorum, with careful attention to "every movement of the body in entering and quitting a room, in taking a seat and rising from it." A friend of Fan's remembered her as "that lovely gracious lady with her almost angelic countenance and her perfect dignity of manner."[45] Information on the handwritten cards in the National Army Museum, however, suggests that Frances Conway was the daughter, granddaughter, and sister of men who lost money, got into debt, and left the country. The number of deaths and abandonments before she was sixteen seems unusual, even for the period. Since her mother was German and the maternal grandmother who lived with them until she was eight was French, it is not clear what language she spoke as a child. One of the books in Fan's library was *A Winter in Bath,* a silly romance about Adriana, age seventeen, whose uninterested wealthy parents go separately to France and then her grandmother dies, whereupon she lives alone in her grandmother's manor, and so forth. Published about 1808, the book probably belonged to Fan's mother. Perhaps the author was a friend, or perhaps she enjoyed the scenes of Bath as she knew it, or possibly Frances Conway found personal resonance in the story of death, disgrace, abandonment, and lovelessness.

Fan realized at an early age that her mother was unlike other mothers and felt vaguely guilty. She wrote that her mother was "in her forty-seventh year" when she was born (she was actually forty-five) and that since the youngest of her four sons was already five years old, "a girl was by no means welcome."[46] Nevertheless, Frances Cobbe made an adequate recovery from Fan's birth; during the following months she often traveled the twelve miles from Newbridge into Dublin for social events. What Fan almost certainly never knew is that in May of 1824, when she was almost eighteen months old, her mother suffered a miscarriage. She was bedridden throughout the summer and had only a few spells of good health for the remainder of her life, though she lived to be seventy. It seems that her illness was at least partly depression, or that depression became a consequence of her illness. Six months after the miscarriage Charles Cobbe wrote that she "has not recovered, and being low has served rather to increase my own lowness; I thought she made no exertion of mind and I reproached her perhaps too severely, but I was sorry for it afterwards."[47] Although a child of Fan's age and class would have been almost entirely in the care of a nurse under any circumstances, she could well have blamed herself in some dimly recognized fashion for her mother's condition. Even a child of eighteen months might pick up stray words that made her associate "baby" with her mother's illness, and she was then "baby." From her earliest conscious memory of her mother there was frequent illness and depression.

In 1825 Fan's father leased a country house near Melksham, fourteen miles east of Bath. Two-year-old Fan was sometimes taken to her grandmother's for a week or two. The only other trace Fan has left in family records during the period is the expenditure of £2 15s. to purchase a rocking horse. When school holidays arrived in June 1826 the whole family returned to Ireland. Fan was three and a half when Newbridge became home. The oldest boys could henceforth travel by themselves, especially since steam packets had dramatically shortened the passage from Dublin to Liverpool or Bristol. Charles Cobbe plunged into estate business and local politics, voted for his friend George Hamilton (who was trying to be elected to Parliament for county Dublin), and sought for a more satisfactory parish clergyman in Donabate. And before long his daughter crossed a boundary into the New-bridge childhood she remembered.

# 2 Childhood, Girlhood, School
## 1827–1838

*Miss Cobbe shows a temperament not merely poetical, but romantic, such as makes one say, "Had she been a* boy *what a harum-skarum being that boy would have been!"*

F. W. NEWMAN, "CAPACITIES OF WOMEN"

Fan turned five years old on 4 December 1827, a birthday she remembered as the boundary between infancy and childhood. She was taken into her mother's "darkened bedroom" and given an emerald ring, a set of bracelets, and a Bible and prayer book, and thereafter she went to church on Sundays and ate dinner with the family. Her old nurse, Mary Malone, retired to a cottage on the grounds; Fan's care was given over to Martha Jones, a servant who had worked for Charles and Frances Cobbe since their arrival at Newbridge. One cannot help wondering if it was from Irish servants that Fan learned the outgoing warmth and garrulous friendliness that so many acquaintances noted. Mary Malone had treated temper tantrums by locking Fan out of the nursery and threatening her with bogeys, but although Martha Jones, then in her mid-thirties, was responsible enough to escort Conway children to their London school, the girls playfully called her not "Martha" but "Joney."

Newbridge gave Fan a freedom that was impossible for middle-class town children. The house, sitting within its walled demesne, was surrounded by 360 acres of lawn, garden, pasture, woodland, and home farm. It is a brisk twenty-minute walk from the house to the gate closest to the village of Donabate. Most rooms used by the children were on the floor above the grand drawing room. Fan's nursery was, she said, "so distant from the regions inhabited by my parents that I was at full liberty to make any amount of noise." Enormous kitchens, along with a housekeeper's room and servants' hall, where children were sometimes welcome, were located beneath the formal rooms. Outdoors, in addition to the stable yard, with its "enchanting spectacle of dogs, cats, horses, grooms, gardeners, and milkmaids," was the ruin of a Norman peel tower. Roofless and floorless by Fan's childhood, Lanistown castle had "a large vaulted chamber, with huge yawning chimney," a secret stair, and a recess where flagstones could be raised so that defenders (or imaginative children) could "drop anything they might please . . . on the head of an intruder."[1]

The parish church is located directly outside one entrance to Newbridge. Since most villagers were Roman Catholic, the Cobbe family made up a large share of its congregation. The gallery, which had a fireplace, a window with a ventilating fan, and comfortable cushions, served as their family pew. Fan's father heartily disliked the clergyman, who abused the liturgy by "vulgar bad reading" and "slovenly indifference." For children the problems were somewhat different: "The Dublin confusion of the letter *a* for the letter *e*" turned "grace" into "grease," and the clergyman's "rendering of the list of nations converted at Pentecost was so astounding that his junior auditors, whose risible muscles were not under the best control, shunned the hearing of it with terror."[2]

Besides the children from India who came during holidays, two other families of cousins were nearby. Uncle George commanded the artillery that defended Dublin harbor and lived in the "Pigeon House," a fort built midway along the sea wall, which then extended more than three miles into the bay. His oldest son, Charles Henry, was already an officer in the East India Company's army by the time Fan was born, but the others—son Thomas Monck and daughters Frances, Anna, and Linda—remained in Ireland. Uncle William's children were all just younger than Fan: Charles (b. 1823), Jane (1825), William (1826), Flora (1827), and Elizabeth (1831). There were also adult visitors. When Fan was six her father's aunt Pelham and two unmarried daughters, then in their thirties, spent the winter at Newbridge. One of the daughters, Catherine Pelham, may have been a source of family legends; a hand-copied volume still in existence has versions of the "Beresford Ghost" and the "Advice of Lady Tyrone" for which "Miss Pelham's MS" is identified as the source.

In theory Fan had early lessons from her mother, although Martha Jones did most of the teaching. Her mother's influence was largely exercised through weakness and distance. "How different people's minds were in those days!" Fan once wrote to a friend, "and how refreshingly little they ever said or thought of their own feelings!" Yet she also understood the force of that restraint, describing the "mysterious potency of volition" exercised by "one who is physically weak and delicate." "To hundreds of us," she wrote elsewhere, "large donations from just and well-meaning but unaffectionate fathers have failed to waken the smallest throb of genuine gratefulness; while some mere trifle given by a loving mother . . . has filled our eyes with tears."[3]

In addition to learning her letters and numbers and reading from Sarah Trimmer's *History of the Robins* (1786), which promoted kindness to animals,

Newbridge House from the side, showing the long drawing room *(right)* that Thomas Cobbe (1733–1814), Fan's great-grandfather, added to the original house built by his father, Archbishop Charles Cobbe. The engraving, from a sketch done by Frances Power Cobbe, was published in her autobiography.

Anna Barbauld's *Lessons for Children* (1778), and the poetry of Jane Taylor (author of "Twinkle, Twinkle Little Star"), Fan may have been subjected to Priscilla Wakefield's *Mental Improvement; or, the Beauties and Wonders of Nature and Art in a Series of Instructive Conversations* (1799), which was in the library at Newbridge. In this book a Mr. and Mrs. Harcourt converse with their children on subjects that include whaling, hats, fossils, the Deluge, sugarcane, shipbuilding, the Crusades, chocolate, and porcelain. One passage may have some bearing on Fan's subsequent antislavery activities: Sophia Harcourt asks, "Why do the Kings of the African states suffer their subjects to be so cruelly treated?" Mr. Harcourt explains that Europeans have corrupted the rulers, fomented wars, and bribed Africans with rum. Sophia should not believe the gentleman who told her Negroes were stupid and hardly superior to brutes, he adds; although they have no education, "there is no reason to suppose that they differ from us in any thing but colour."[4]

Fan was no fonder of hard work than many small children. On one occasion, seeing her peacock sitting "with nothing earthly ever to do but to sun himself and eat nice brown bread," she "burst into a storm of weeping, and sobbed 'I wish I were a peacock! I wish I were a peacock!'" This story, like so many she recounted, emphasizes her naughtiness and rebellion and her passionate temper. Perhaps these incidents were vividly remembered because of their powerful emotions, or perhaps she selected them to foreshadow the strong-minded woman she would become. One year on Christmas Day Fan's father noted that all of his children were around him, healthy and happy, "children who fear to offend me because they love me."[5] He conducted morning prayers for the family and servants every day. Sunday was strictly kept: no secular amusements were allowed, and only religious books could be read.

Although Fan's autobiography reports that her "dear mother . . . was never once able in all her life to take a walk with me,"[6] Frances Cobbe's health during the late 1820s was better than her daughter remembered. In the spring of 1828 both parents went to the levee at Dublin Castle on 10 March, the drawing room on 13 March, and a ball the following day. As Anglo-Irish society came under new pressure the Dublin social season helped hold it together. Agrarian disturbances were growing more common. Charles Cobbe received a threatening letter and fumed in his diary that "had letters deterred me from doing what I think right, I might have quitted the country long ago." His efforts as a magistrate "procured the conviction of a ring leader of a mob who assembled to the number of 200 to compel a high rate of wages." On 7 April 1829 his diary recorded the end of Anglo-Irish political monopoly: "The Packet has this day brought the fatal news that the bill

Fan's father, Charles Cobbe (1781–1857). The chalk portrait by Alexander Blaikely is dated 1844. (Cobbe Papers, Alec Cobbe Collection)

to enable the roman Catholic to sit in parliament has passed the Lords by a large majority; the die therefore is Cast, and we must submit to whatever befalls us. . . . my fears are great that the sitting in Parliament is their least object & the struggle merely a preliminary one; we shall next have our religion to contend for, then our property. My fears may be groundless, but they predominate over every other feeling."[7]

Charles Cobbe was also in conflict with his strong-willed mother about educating his brother Thomas's children. In 1827, against his own inclination, he enrolled fifteen-year-old Henry Clermont in the Royal Military Academy at Sandhurst. Although the boy's mixed race barred him from an East India Company commission, the Royal Army had no such barrier. In the same autumn, Fan's brother Charles entered Charterhouse (then still in London, near Smithfield). Three of her four brothers ultimately attended Charterhouse, Charles from October 1827 to December 1830, Tom from September 1828 to May 1832, and Henry from June 1829 to June 1835. All were in Chapman's House. William Makepeace Thackeray—born, like Charles, in 1811—was also a Charterhouse pupil, though by 1827 he was a day boy living with a family nearby, and there is no proof that he knew the Cobbe brothers.

In 1829, when Fan had just turned seven, she and her parents spent part of the winter in Bath. They took a house in St. James's Square, immediately north of the Royal Crescent, very near to Grandmother Anne's residence in the Marlborough Buildings. Whether or not she realized it, conflicts between her father and her grandmother continued to seethe. Charles Cobbe recorded "a most painful discussion" with his mother: "I do not think it right or prudent that the natural children of my brother should be made prominent characters . . . and I have said what as their guardian I feel was my duty to say, but it gives offence." In particular, he continued, "I dare not . . . shew my children that I encourage illegitimacy, and attach no distinction to children born in wedlock or otherwise."[8]

Before they left England in the spring of 1830 Fan had her first trip to London; she was taken to the British Museum and to the view of Calcutta then displayed at the Regent's Park Diorama. By April they were back at Newbridge. There Fan had her first governess, Miss Kinnear. She was called a "nursery governess" and was probably quite young. After lessons finished at noon Fan was free to play outdoors or read whatever was in the house. "Paradise and the Peri," from Dublin-born Thomas Moore's long Orientalist poem *Lalla Rookh,* roused her desire to visit the Middle East. The practice of leaving Fan to herself in the afternoons was suggested by Maria and Richard Edgeworth's *Practical Education,* which proposed that "the pains of idleness stimulate children to industry."[9] The Edgeworths also suggested giving children a garden and a set of carpenter tools—Fan had both—and described a method she used in her late teens of drawing charts to organize facts.

At the time of Fan's eighth birthday, in December 1830, her father's diary shows constant activity: seeing to tenants, doing church business, attending quarter sessions, serving on the board of Kilmainham Prison (where he was trying to institute the new solitary system), having guests to shoot, engaging in local politics. Whether he was at home or away, he insisted on a rigid schedule: bells for prayers and meals, and dinner served promptly at six. Although in theory Fan ate with the adults, it is not clear how often either parent was actually present for meals. In early December she was the only child at home. At mid-month the boys started arriving for the holidays. On the fifteenth her brothers Charles, Henry, and Tom came from Charterhouse. Charles was nineteen and had already matriculated at Oxford, but no rooms were yet available in the college; Tom and Henry were seventeen and thirteen. Four days later three more boys came: brother Will, who was fourteen and prepping for Sandhurst at a school near Cheltenham, and two cousins. Henry Clermont turned nineteen the day after he got to Newbridge; he had done well enough on his Sandhurst exams to be commissioned without purchase. His brother Charles Augustus was thirteen and attended the same school as Will.

After a month of holidays, Tom and Henry returned to Charterhouse. Brother Charles stayed home; his father was looking for a tutor, but the first one he interviewed "was too young & too fond of billiards." Cousin Henry Clermont and the two younger boys were also still there. On 24 January there was a large crowd for dinner, and the next morning the hunt assembled at Newbridge. The older boys rode to the hounds; Will and Charles Augustus may have followed. Charles Cobbe was grumpy about both hunt and hounds: "I wish they were in the bottom of the sea," he wrote.[10] Whether or not the younger boys included Fan in their adventures, the excitement at Newbridge must have been delightful for a girl of eight. The boys were supposed to leave for school on 1 February, but the night before brought the biggest snow anyone could remember.

In mid-February 1831 cousin Henry Clermont was commissioned as an ensign in the 86th Foot and visited their grandmother in Bath before joining his regiment. Brother Charles went up to Oxford in April; a friend at Exeter College was his old companion from the school at East Sheen, Alfred Gatty. Some of the Conway cousins were also just leaving childhood. Tom Conway, eighteen, had spent two years at Haileybury, where boys prepared for the East India Company civil service. He sailed for Madras on 9 August. His sister Isabella, who had been at a London finishing school, also went out to India. Tom Conway was at Newbridge for much of the summer, as was another sister, Anne. The house was crowded for two months with all four of Fan's brothers, two Conway teenagers, and all five children of Fan's uncle William Power Cobbe. A half-pay naval officer, Uncle William died suddenly of "brain disease" on 8 April. His oldest son—yet another Charles Cobbe, usually called "little Charlie"—was less than a year younger than Fan. Her autobiography calls him her favorite cousin; the two of them together struck sparks that often led to mischief.

The Dublin zoo opened during 1831. Did anyone take Fan and some cousins to see the animals? She was not interested in "girlish" play. Her only comment about the beautiful old dollhouse at Newbridge was that some rooms were big enough for a child to climb into. When, in the 1890s the journalist Frances H. Low asked a number of famous women to write about their favorite doll, Fan had no memory to supply; she "loved the woods and living things better." Anne Conway wrote a nice duty letter to her aunt when she returned to school after the summer: "Pray thank Fanny for her letter which I shall answer soon. I am sorry she has not had much good luck at fishing. . . . I am glad my sampler has proved to be of use to her it was quite an agreeable surprise to hear she had *at last* taken to work." "Work," of course means needlework, and "at last" is underlined for emphasis. Brother Will wrote to Fan, "I hope you feed the Shelldrakes sometimes. I suppose you can ride a little by this time though not quite able to leap a ditch or paling."[11]

Reviewers of the *Life of Frances Power Cobbe* almost all mentioned Fan's solitary childhood; her self-sufficiency as a child and the remoteness of Newbridge were seen as shaping the independent woman. Yet if inventing her own occupations made her an adult not much damaged by conventional expectations, the delightfully social woman must have been partly created by the full house at holidays. "Often a party of twenty or more sat down every day . . . in the dining-room," she recalled. Children played blindman's buff, prisoner's base, and hunt the hare "through the halls below stairs, and the long corridors and rooms above." As they grew older, there were charades, dancing, pranks, comic verses, and forged love letters. Uncle George was musical, and his daughter Linda published a song that was popular in the 1830s. Cousin Charlie, writing from India many years later, nostalgically remembered acting plays "in the dining room at Newbridge."[12]

The composition and dynamics of such a family may explain what is recorded in Charles Cobbe's diary and retained in the papers. His sense of obligation was enormous, most crucially in finding an occupation for the boys. They were not given much choice. In 1829 he told his son Tom, then fifteen, "of my having designed him for the church, wherein I had the best prospects of providing for him."[13] When Tom resisted, after changing his mind several times, there was a flurry of other efforts: Uncle George helped look for a commercial post; Charles Cobbe called on a Beresford relative about getting Tom a cavalry commission, and when that failed, he wrote, with great reluctance, to the duke of Wellington. The boxes at Newbridge are crammed with replies to such letters. Would the family solicitor give a job to George's son if he were sent more business from the estate? Who could secure cadetships for Uncle Thomas's younger boys or take William Henry to Australia? Charles Cobbe knew what was best for the children. He believed it was wrong to tell "a boy the *profession* he is destined to prematurely; particularly if it be one of the *learned* ones; for they always set their minds against it." When Tom declined the church, it could only be that he was "impatient of school discipline & wants to be released even at the cost of his future prospects." Since most of her brothers did not do well in their first profession—a fact never disclosed by Fan—it is easy to suspect the flaws in such paternal control. Yet society also narrowly limited the acceptable occupations for men of their rank, especially in Ireland, where, according to a contemporary, the "classes are to the last degree exclusive."[14]

The diary kept by Fan's father began soon after she was born and continued up to his death in 1857. And in those thirty-four years there are exactly twenty-five mentions of Fan, most of them no longer than "Went to Bath from whence I brought my daughter."[15] Yet it may be that he wrote in such detail not only about his sons and nephews but also about his nieces because of his responsibility for their future. While he regretted the girls' "worldly" education and the attention devoted to their appearance, he understood its purpose. Neither Colonel Conway nor Colonel Thomas A. Cobbe had the means to leave a competence for that many daughters: they must marry. Fan may well have been fortunate to escape her father's conscientious attention.

As she grew alert to the wider world and her place in it, Fan must have noticed the different options provided to boys and to girls. The parliamentary reform of 1832 altered the property qualifications, so that about 14 percent of adult males in the United Kingdom could vote. Charles Cobbe saw "no reason to complain" since the bill would produce a respectable class of new voters.[16] As Fan's brothers reached twenty-one, he put enough property in their names that each could register as a fifty-pound freeholder. In July 1832 the other major landowner in the parish, George Evans of Portrane, who lived two miles from Newbridge, decided to stand for Parliament. His opinions were entirely unacceptable to his more conservative neighbor: Evans had threatened to vote for repeal of the Union "if justice be not speedily done to Ireland."[17] When Charles Cobbe refused to support him, the social relations between the two families came to an end.

The cholera that had spread from Bengal across Europe and appeared in England in the autumn of 1831 reached Dublin in the summer of 1832. For Fan's father the "Visitation" provoked a struggle between evangelical conscience, sharp intelligence, and social responsibility. Although he felt that the epidemic had been called into being by "our sins (national and personal)," he met with other landowners to ask that a board of health be established. The animosity of medical men toward one another, he wrote, "precludes their being of use to the sick." As the government in London prepared to abolish slavery in the British Empire, extra troops, including cousin Henry Clermont's regiment, were sent to the West Indies in case of disorder. In Ireland, resistance to using taxes to support a Protestant established church led to "agrarian crime . . . raging on a gigantic scale."[18]

The children at Newbridge in the summer of 1832, when Fan was nine, may themselves have been a rowdy crew. If schoolmistresses can be trusted, both Anne and Harriet Conway were active and self-willed. Harriet, the youngest Conway daughter, was ten and newly come to England. Miss Sawkins had nothing good to report: "There is much of evil in her character, which occasionally bursts forth with uncontrolled fury. The climate or the training in India may possibly have much influence in producing this effect. . . . She came full of bad passions & wicked ways." Fan took possession of an unused garret and the key to lock its door. She and Harriet tried, or pretended, to see the family ghosts. And influenced by the Irish troubles then stirring, they played "rebellion," stocking the garret with "bows and arrows, and old court-swords" and procuring whatever food they could lay hands on in case of siege. The cousins chased each other through the woods, jumped in the hay, and rowed on the pond. As an adult Fan vehemently criticized parents who forbade "dreadfully unlady-like" games. She also insisted that every adult, male or female, should know how to swim and that in warm months healthy people "ought to be like Newfoundland dogs, ready to get into any clean water they see."[19] She was allowed to ride her pony to the shore two miles from Newbridge, where the coastline was riddled with small caves among the rocks that provided enough shelter to change clothes.

Winter meant lessons. Miss Kinnear was followed by a second nursery governess, Miss Daly, and then by a "real" governess. Miss Worral, who came when Fan was eleven, was paid £3 13s. a month, which was toward the high end of the middle range for a resident governess. Whatever her skills, the description in Life reeks with dislike. Fan was still free in the afternoons, however, to read whatever she could find. The Newbridge library contained standard books for educational use—a Latin dictionary, texts on algebra, logic, and geography, an atlas, the works of Shakespeare, and so forth. More recent volumes that might have appealed to a young person included the poetry of George Crabbe, Mary Russell Mitford's *Our Village, Don Quixote,* and works by Walter Scott. The list is taken from a record in Fan's handwriting headed "Catalogue of Books left in the Library, Septr 1852." Very few were novels, but perhaps novels were not "in the library" but elsewhere, as personal possessions. When Fan as an old woman donated her books to the local reading room, the collection included a good deal of fiction by women writers that she could have read as a girl: Jane Austen, Maria Edgeworth, Anne Radcliffe, Elizabeth Inchbald, Susan Ferrier.[20]

Like many other intelligent and curious children accustomed to regular Bible reading, Fan in her early adolescence suddenly began to ask simple logical questions. A scene involving her father's Sunday evening reading about the loaves and the fishes was still vivid in her mind's eye when she was an old woman. Frank Turner believes that the visual details are more revealing than her thoughts: that she experienced a disruption "of family worship, social hierarchy, and her father's dominant religious role."[21] Turner's commentary, like Fan's own telling, may well be shaped by afterknowledge of her theological writing and social activism, as well as of the course of nineteenth-century religious thought. Fan began to question Scripture's literal truth at about the time Charles Lyell's *Elements of Geology* showed that the earth was far too old for biblical chronologies. For Fan the reaction soon set in, and like many adolescents, she pursued rigorous private rituals to perfect her faith. When adults at Newbridge discussed Alexander Keith's *The Signs of the Times: As Denoted by the Fulfilment of Historical Predictions: Traced down from the Babylonish Captivity to the Present Time,* she anxiously followed the news to find out whether the end-time was at hand.[22]

Anne and Harriet Conway were at Newbridge again during the summer of 1833. However much Fan welcomed the playmates—she and Harriet had begun to exchange letters—their presence troubled her parents. The bank Colonel Conway used had failed, and their schoolmistress refused to take them back until she was paid.[23] Putting Harriet in a much cheaper Dublin boarding school, Fan's mother paid four hundred pounds to send Anne back to India. By the time she went to spend two weeks in Bath the following May, Fan must have been considering the difference between plans for brothers or male cousins and those for girls. Even little Charlie, then ten, showed off his masculine privilege by writing in Greek at the end of his letters to her. Charles and Tom were both at Oxford, although Charles should have finished; he did not pass his degree examination in April 1834. Tom failed at his first public examination in June, and Will had managed to spend four years at Sandhurst while passing only one of the six examinations required to be commissioned without purchase. Tom was consumed by his interest in music, but it did not occur to a landed gentleman that his son might be trained as a composer any more than he noticed that his daughter's music lessons were wasted on someone who, as her piano teacher said, would never master the keyboard even if she practiced six hours a day until she was sixty.[24]

Fan observed other things about women. The "refinement" of their appetites, for example, was exposed when Flora Long and her sisters visited Newbridge. To Fan's "awe and admiration," they "never ate anything, except perhaps the wing of a chicken, or a spoonful of jelly, and a little wine and water." Some of the children "laid a trap for these ethereal beings" and caught them "surreptitiously in the luncheon-room—one was eating cheese, another carving a round of beef, and the third . . . had applied a huge silver tankard of beer straight to her delicate lips!"[25] Fan's own bedroom had a "large iron staple" from which her great-aunts had dangled to have their stays laced. One of these great-aunts, Elizabeth Tuite, was nearly seventy when Fan visited Bath in 1834. As a young lady she had been a notable horsewoman; even in old age she drove herself around Bath behind a four-horse team. A nephew described her as the "most gentlemanly old lady" he had ever known. On her death in 1850 she was buried, at her request, not with the husband who had died forty-five years earlier, but in the vault of her dear friend Mrs. Lysaght. A more distant relative of that generation was, Fan remembered, "much 'got up' in the George IV style" and "used to play with me good-naturedly . . . and call me his 'little wife.'"[26]

Fan's grandmother was putting her affairs in order. Perhaps she told her eleven-year-old granddaughter the family story that was still in Fan's mind seventy years later, when a telegram asking a trusted physician to sever her arteries so that she could not be buried alive was found beside her bed at her death. According to the story, Grandmother Anne's own mother, Frances Power, had fallen into "a state of apparent death" and would have been buried had not a friend insisted on postponing the funeral until the body showed some sign of decay. "I could never ascertain how long this comatose state lasted before she recovered," wrote Fan, "but she *did* recover, so thoroughly that . . . she became the mother of twenty-two children."[27]

Except, perhaps, for that of the gentlemanly great-aunt Tuite, the conversation of Fan's relatives in Bath was as discreet as their appetites were (in public) genteel. She described the model imposed by "those female voices of the last generation": "Nobody is going to say anything disagreeable to anybody! Everybody's small feelings and prejudices will be remembered. Kind things will be seen to be dropped gently, calling for no reply." Yet she also learned at a young age that "English adults generally live at a considerable distance" from those they love best because "we allow ourselves to say critical or frank things to relatives that we would never express to others." After almost every Christmas holiday from 1830 on, her father took to his room with gout, and he came to despise Bath: "Bath—Black, dull & disagreeable as usual, how many occurrences have taken place to render it painful to me."[28]

Thus, as she entered her teens Fan saw boys unable to satisfy her father's expectations and girls trained in subordination. She noticed that her grandmother Anne, an excellent whist player, "made a small, but appreciable, addition to her income out of her 'card purse,'" while other widows and single women with smaller incomes worried constantly about money yet had no conception of taking up any work. Fan's brother Charles passed his degree examination in the autumn of 1834 and came home to "enter on the duties of life" by preparing to succeed his father as landowner.[29] Brother Will went to work in a Dublin bank. A more revealing problem arose in finding a place for cousin Charles Augustus, who was then seventeen. The family papers I have seen contain only one explicit allusion to the race of the ten children born to Uncle Thomas and the begum Nuzzeer. In his diary for 26 December 1834, Charles Cobbe recorded that he had written to Charles Augustus "in reply to his letter wherein he wishes to go to Addiscombe; such a course could not do for him, his colour precludes it."

The published regulations for Addiscombe, the East India Company's equivalent to Sandhurst, specified only age, health, education, good character, and baptism in the Church of England,[30] but Charles Cobbe knew (though his nephew did not) that the company would not commission Eurasian men. After further exploration, Charles Augustus was apprenticed as a civil engineer. The arrangement was made through Uncle George, whose son Charles Henry—home on medical leave from India, where he had buried a wife and child—was engaged to marry Anne Gravatt. Anne's brother William Gravatt had worked under I. K. Brunel and was a fellow of the Royal Society, proof that his kind of engineering was a learned profession rather than a mechanical trade.

In March 1835 Fan's brothers Charles and Tom set off together for a trip to the Continent—yet one more thing young men could do at twenty-three and twenty-one that would have been impossible for their sister. Charles was gone only a few weeks before returning as escort for his cousin Laura, the fourteen-year-old daughter of Uncle Thomas, who had so far been educated in Paris. Tom, however, went on to Bonn and Geneva with an Oxford friend, Edward Marjoribanks. He stayed several months longer than his father had expected, and when he returned home there was yet another discouraging conversation—or argument—about his future. In November brother Henry failed to gain entrance to Balliol but did matriculate at Oriel. James Anthony Froude entered Oriel a week later, a fact that would be very important to Fan in the 1860s.

In mid-February 1835, not long after she turned twelve, Fan acquired a more advanced governess. Miss Montreau earned five guineas a month. Fan described her, with typical undercutting irony, as "a person of considerable force of character, and in many respects an admirable teacher."[31] With her Fan studied Plutarch and Gibbon, learned a system of chronology, followed lessons with an atlas, and was encouraged to ask questions about geography and economics. On her own she read about astronomy and eagerly watched for the reappearance of Halley's comet. Miss Montreau also worked on Fan's French and gave her some instruction in music theory. In addition, a guinea a week was being spent on dancing lessons.

Grandmother Anne Cobbe died at the end of 1835. When Fan's father returned from Bath after the funeral he brought cousins Azélie and Florence. Florence was almost twenty-one, and Azélie was about a year older. They had not been sent to their parents after leaving school because Uncle Thomas planned to retire. His career in India had received a major boost in 1813, when Francis Rawdon-Hastings, earl of Moira in the Irish peerage and subsequently marquess of Hastings, became governor general. His father was son of the archbishop's wife by her first marriage and thus was half-brother to "Old Tommie." Arriving in India, the new governor general had called on his young relative to act as aide-de-camp. In the next few years Fan's uncle Thomas had been promoted to captain and become secretary to the East India Company's military board. A solution to the difficulty that might have been presented by his marriage to a woman of Kashmir is suggested by a sentence in the governor general's diary. Until his wife "gave a private hint that colour never would be noticed," he wrote, "half caste ladies . . . were not admitted to Government House."[32] Perhaps the "hint" was given so as not to exclude family relations.

Before leaving India, Hastings had appointed Thomas as resident for the native state of Udaipur. Although he is not named, he must have been the resident described in an 1848 *History of British India* who "became virtually the Prime Minister," put down the "lawless tribes" ravaging the countryside, liquidated the ruler's debt, and restored the province to prosperity.[33] Since Udaipur was a Muslim state, Uncle Thomas's Muslim wife may have had something to do with his success in managing its rulers. Thomas's final posting was in Berhampore (now Baharampur), just over one hundred miles north of Calcutta. In 1836, after thirty years in India, he sailed for home accompanied by the begum and their two youngest daughters. Fan's father rented a house in Bath and gathered the other children to meet their parents. When the ship docked at Southampton on 2 August, they learned that Thomas had died of a stroke six days from home.

Two weeks later Charles Cobbe wrote that his brother's widow would soon return to India, "which cannot be regretted by any of *us* whatever it may be by his children; it was an unfortunate connexion in every sense of the word." He recorded no reason for the begum's change in plans. She may have recognized the grudging welcome and evident prejudice, and she may have been uncomfortable with the strange culture and people, the food and climate and way of life, as well as her position of helpless dependence. I do not know whether she even spoke English; her husband had been praised by other officers for his "knowledge of the native languages." In India she had been a woman of substance with property and friends. Thomas, well aware of British mores, had recorded a tribute in his will: "I owe it to her unceasing affection & good conduct to make this solemn declaration of the love and regard I bear her I have never for a minute regretted our union except in as much as the future fate of our children has created anxiety."[34]

Unmentioned in Charles Cobbe's version of the story is a fact revealed in a few surviving letters from Azélie. "When we parted," she wrote to him on 29 August 1836, "I thought it was with the conviction that we should in some months follow my mother to India, and now it appears that such a thought as a *serious* intention never really entered into your consideration." She understood that she ought to stay in England until the youngest girls— Sophia, usually called Sophy (age seven) and Eliza (five)—were ready for boarding school. She knew that Henry Clermont, who was briefly home from the West Indies, was the legal guardian of Laura (age sixteen) and could prevent her from leaving England. But she could not understand why, when "duty, feelings and our own happiness all lead us to follow our remaining Parent to India," she and Florence, "*being of age*" (her emphasis) could not judge for themselves.[35]

Fan, in the meantime, was being outfitted with a great many new clothes. Sending her to school was, her father wrote, "a necessity . . . much to be regretted . . . but her welfare required it."[36] Presumably that meant turning the tomboy into a young lady, getting an adolescent out of the house, and providing her with social connections. She and her mother left Dublin on 21 October 1836 together with brother Charles, who was twenty-five and acted as "courier." This journey was significantly more expensive than Fan's subsequent trips to school; her mother's health called for a more leisurely pace with overnight stops. Mother and daughter were closed up together for one day at sea and three in a coach across England to Brighton, but we cannot know if there was any substantive conversation or, as I suspect, only a long spell of perfectly correct public behavior.

Later, when campaigning to improve women's education, Fan wrote several accounts, some more serious than others, of her schooling. "The education of women," she asserted in the 1880s, "was probably at its lowest ebb about half a century ago." Or more humorously, when pleading for women's admission to London University, "In our own youth we acquired, in a certain shadowy way peculiar to the boarding-schools of that remote period, three or four languages and three or four instruments, the use of the globes and of the dumb-bells, Moral Philosophy and Poonah-painting."[37]

There were more than a hundred ladies' schools in Brighton at the time. Fan's, one of the more expensive, was at 32 Brunswick Terrace, in an elegant development facing the sea at the westernmost end of the esplanade. By 1831 the district was lit by gas; important politicians, diplomats, and distinguished foreigners wintered in Brunswick Terrace. The school's proprietors were Miss Runciman and Miss Roberts. "A better system than theirs," Fan later wrote, "could scarcely have been devised had it been designed to attain the maximum of cost and labour and the minimum of solid results." The basic fee for board, lodging, and "English subjects" was £120 or £130 per year, but "extras" tripled the expense, bringing the total charge for her two years' schooling to almost £750.[38] Although no prospectus for Fan's school has been located, an announcement by Miss Sawkins, who "finished" the Conway cousins, shows the relative value of girls' various studies. The basic fee covered instruction in history, chronology, geography, "the use of the Globes," and English literature. Extras at Miss Sawkins's school included piano and singing (each at twenty guineas a year), drawing, dancing, and Italian at twelve or fourteen guineas each, French at eight guineas, and "writing & arithmetic" at six guineas for the two.[39]

Fan's school had about twenty-five pupils ranging in age from nine to nineteen; all were "daughters of men of some standing, mostly country-gentlemen, members of Parliament and offshoots of the peerage." Although she claimed that the school was never rife with the malice and snobbery found in the novel G. H. Lewes based on it, Fan did not dispute the book's other details. While dressing in the morning, girls memorized a verse of Scripture; after prayers each one repeated the verse they had all just learned. Then they began to "march, heads up, chests expanded, toes out." Breakfast was next, followed by a half-hour's free time and then lessons. In addition to the din of competing recitations in the schoolroom, there were "five pianos—and five unhappy girls are always practicing on them." At noon they walked along the esplanade while reciting verbs in French, Italian, or German. At half past two they dressed for dinner "in full evening attire of silk or muslin, with gloves and kid slippers." The English subjects consisted of a history lesson one week and geography the next, both performed by memorizing assigned pages to recite back to the mistress.[40]

Fan hated everything about the school—hated the formal walks on the esplanade that took the place of romping and swimming at Newbridge, hated the fussy, constraining clothes, hated giving up the room of her own (and the attic with a key) for a shared bedroom and a noisy schoolroom. If she had any close friends at school or if she ever encountered a schoolmate in adult society, no evidence survives. When her father visited Brighton six months later, in April 1837, her joy "was too much for her spirits and it was long before she seemed to persuade herself of the reality." He, on the other hand, was disappointed: "School has as yet made little effect upon her."[41]

Fan's brothers and cousins continued to move erratically toward adulthood. Will, by then almost twenty-one, was not happy—or not satisfactory—at the Dublin bank. Since their cousin Charles Augustus had given up his engineering apprenticeship to escort his mother back to India, William Gravatt agreed to take Will on trial. Gravatt was then working up plans for the rail line between Bristol and Exeter, and surveying was the one subject Will had mastered at Sandhurst. Cousin Charlie entered Sandhurst at thirteen. Because he was a naval officer's orphan, his fee was reduced; if he did well, the value of his commission would be greater than the cost of his education. Brother Tom came to see his father in April, "nervous and looking thin" about his futile—or self-defeating—search for employment. After failing his degree examination at Oxford a year earlier, Tom had made inquiries about a diplomatic post; now he suddenly wanted to join the cavalry. The choice seems almost designed to ensure the failure of his father's efforts with Lord George Beresford and the duke of Wellington. Tom was still consumed by a "hopeless project . . . injurious to himself & painful to me," wrote his father,[42] though whether that was his wish to study music in Germany or another plan that he did carry out in due course is not clear. Fan was back at school amid the pounding pianos and gabbling verbs. Her newly adult cousins Florence and Azélie made a happy Maytime visit to brother Henry in Oxford. Finally, after seeing to the Christies' auction of goods his brother had shipped from India, Charles Cobbe fetched his daughter from Brighton and took her home for the holidays. Her joy at escaping from school after seven long months was "boundless."[43]

During that summer, on 24 June, a young woman named Victoria, just turned eighteen and less than four years older than Fan, became queen of England. With fast new steam packets, London newspapers reached Dublin only one day late. Cousin William Henry, a son of Uncle Thomas's who was one year older than Fan, was at Newbridge; I cannot tell whether he was willing to play the outdoor games she had shared with Harriet Conway and cousin Charlie in earlier years. Perhaps it was during this summer that Fan added paper, pens, and ink to a table in her attic and labored over long narrative poems in more or less iambic tetrameter couplets. All of her brothers were home in August. There must have been political talk when their father refused to be nominated as MP for county Dublin. Brother Will escorted Fan back to Brighton at the end of August. Everyone knew she was miserable at school. "She kept up her spirits very well untill [*sic*] she saw Miss Roberts," Will reported, "when as you may suppose she burst out crying."[44]

In January 1838 brother Tom finally settled on a profession and entered the Inner Temple to study for the bar. The same month, when Fan was fifteen, a string of family marriages began. Cousin Florence, a daughter of Uncle Thomas and the begum, married John Ensor of Rollesby Hall in England. She was twenty-two; he was sixty-four and had six grown children by his first wife. "There are objections enough that I can see," wrote Charles Cobbe, but they arose from "years rather than any thing else, and it is not for me to throw . . . difficulties in the way of one who so much stands in need of a protector."[45]

On 23 June, when Charles Augustus was back in Ireland after taking his mother to Calcutta, Archbishop Whately held a confirmation service in Malahide. The account in Fan's autobiography describes a comic disaster to her grown-up hairdo; her father's diary reports that those confirmed were "my daughter Fanny, my niece Harriet Conway & my 2 nephews Chas A and Will H. . . . I had hoped it would have been a day of calm & quiet reflection to them . . . [but] my nephew Chas . . . received the first notice of his getting a Commission in the Ceylon Rifle Regiment, and I cannot persuade myself that his thoughts travelled far from that subject for the rest of the day."[46]

The Ceylon Rifles was not an Indian Army regiment but a queen's regiment in which the officers were British but the rank and file were Malaysian men recruited in Singapore and Java. During the same summer, Henry Clermont exchanged into the 2nd West India Regiment, which had its home station in Jamaica. This was another regular army regiment raised specifically for tropical service. After realizing that the death rate among European troops in the West Indies could average more than 15 percent a year, the army created regiments of African soldiers. Until 1808 recruiting officers had first pick from incoming slave ships. By the 1830s most of the African troops had been born in the West Indies, though there was also a recruiting depot in Sierra Leone. For more than a hundred years these West India regiments—black soldiers, British officers—saw regular service in both Africa and the Caribbean.[47]

Fan's autobiographical account of walking back to her pew with locks "hanging down in disorder" after the archbishop had laid his hands in benediction upon her head, not merely her hair,[48] is the sort of vivid passage that often seems to stand in for events or feelings left undescribed. On the day the church affirmed that the four cousins had, in the words of the Book of

Common Prayer, "come to the years of discretion," Charles Augustus was just back from seeing Indian life with almost adult eyes. The mother Harriet had not seen for eight years was dead, and she had a new (unmet) stepmother in India, where her three sisters were now all married to officers. William Henry was the most rebellious and perhaps the most ambitious of Uncle Thomas's sons. The day might have encouraged Fan to think about marking out a future, about differences between peoples and societies, about questions of race, nationality, and empire.

Charles Augustus's commission in the Ceylon Rifles raises questions about why Henry Clermont had exchanged into the 2nd West India Regiment. Perhaps it was because he would be promoted more quickly in a regiment always stationed in unhealthy places, or perhaps it was because a man of twenty-six who found himself heading a family of nine younger brothers and sisters welcomed obligations that would keep him almost continually on the other side of an ocean. (In addition, there was by this time a natural son born to a woman in Portsmouth.) But it is also possible that he and Charles Augustus had both perceived that officers in more desirable regiments were prejudiced against men of mixed blood even if the Royal Army did not bar them from service.

Harriet Conway, Laura, Sophy, and Eliza Cobbe, their brothers Charles Augustus, William Henry, and Francis ("Frank"), and perhaps cousin Charlie as well, in addition to Fan's brothers Charles and Will, were all at Newbridge in the summer of 1838. It may have been the last summer when there was a big happy crowd of young people in residence. On 23 August word arrived that Fan's brother Tom and his first cousin Azélie had been married at Rollesby; the clergyman was one of Florence's stepsons, who had been up at Oxford with Tom. Tom was twenty-five, and Azélie was a year younger. He was still reading law; she had written to Charles Cobbe rather impatiently in July asking when she might find out what her income would be after her father's estate was settled. The prospect of this marriage had smoldered for some time. Their emotional entanglement had begun at their grandmother's deathbed in December 1835. Azélie might have been trying to evade the trouble when she begged to go to India. An incoherent letter from Tom to his father written during the conflict contained phrases such as "within a few days perhaps of appearing before Him who knows my heart" and "the last request *I* can make," which sound disturbingly like a suicide threat.[49]

Charles Cobbe was profoundly opposed to this marriage; he was deeply troubled when it took place, and time would prove him right. If she had been in any way a typical adolescent, Fan might have noticed the emotional signals passing between her brother and her cousin and found a runaway marriage (in defiance of her father) both romantic and thrilling, but nothing suggests whether it altered her perception of the male cousins close to her own age. It was, at any rate, almost the conclusion of her time at Miss Runciman's. When she arrived home for Christmas on 22 December 1838, she had turned sixteen and would not return to school.

*It is in the nature of things disgraceful and abominable that marriage should be made the aim of a woman's life.*

FRANCES POWER COBBE, "WHAT SHALL WE DO WITH OUR OLD MAIDS?"

Happily freed from the noise and drudgery of school, Fan was convinced she knew everything. Her brother Will complained about her "*Pride*," saying that she had "a very high opinion of her own talents & a very low opinion of every one's else."[1] She also had a great deal of time on her hands. Her father stayed in his own room for several weeks after Christmas, and her mother's health grew steadily worse. Her brother Charles took on more of the estate business. Cousins Frank and William Henry were at Newbridge during January. They were fifteen and seventeen, just younger and just older than Fan. For a month or more the three teenagers and the young man of twenty-seven were pretty much on their own, with neither parent regularly at meals, and Fan must have been forming opinions, or at least making adolescent judgments, about men and their ways.

When spring came Newbridge was closed for three months while the family rented a house at 29 Rutland Square (now Parnell Square) in Dublin. Substantial town houses surrounded a lying-in hospital and the Rotunda, a circular building "finished and decorated in a style of great elegance" where balls and concerts raised money for charity. The square was laid out in gardens and walks. Military bands played in the evening; "transparencies" produced by colored lights showed "Florence with the Arno, Vesuvius and Etna, also 'Venice' with the gondolas on the water all about the bridge." Another young Anglo-Irish woman in Dublin at the time saw Charles Keane and Ellen Tree at the Theatre Royal.[2] I do not know whether Fan's evangelical father allowed such entertainments; I am certain he would not have gone—he hated crowds and stuffy rooms—but she might have seen afternoon performances with her cousin William Henry, who was at school in Dublin, or with family friends whose names have not survived.

Fan was not officially "out," although her brother Will clearly had sus-

picions: "You seem to be going to flare up to no small account giving parties once a week, there must be something in the Wind or it would not pay
at no price '*Trot her out*' How nimbly she picks her steps How well she
bends her knee (I forget the rest of the Quotation) ask Chas."[3] But it was
her brother Charles who was courting: he and Louisa Brooke were married
on 21 May. It was an eminently suitable match. He was almost twenty-eight,
and she was twenty-one. Her father, George Frederick Brooke, was a landowner with a late Georgian house in Castleknock, four miles northeast
of Dublin. Louisa, like Charles, had political and aristocratic connections;
two uncles were baronets, another was Rear Admiral Percy Grace, and her
grandfather, like Charles's, had been a member of the Irish parliament.

   In June the family were back at Newbridge, and Charles Cobbe helped
negotiate two more marriage settlements, for children of Uncle George.
George's daughter Linda made an appropriate marriage to the landowner
Thomas Thompson on 2 August 1839, but the other union was more dubi-
ous. Although Thomas Monck Cobbe had some infirmity that kept him
from finding steady work, he married Sophia Tandy on 18 August. Meanwhile, Fan's brother Tom came "unexpectedly and indiscreetly"[4] to Newbridge at the end of June and left three days later. We can only imagine what
difficulties there were in the house of Azélie and Tom and what an alert girl
of sixteen might have perceived about his situation and about the three
weddings in her first months after leaving school. Her cousins Laura Cobbe
and Harriet Conway were both at Newbridge. Three girls on the verge of
adulthood (they were sixteen, seventeen, and eighteen) with marriage all
around them must have been thinking about their own futures. At the end
of August, Azélie gave birth to a son who died soon afterwards.

   There were frequent visits back and forth between Newbridge and Ardgillan. At the end of July the Taylors gave a large party to welcome Charles
and Louisa. The elder Charles Cobbe resigned as guardian for the poor and
from several other offices; his son became a magistrate and then did a year's
term as high sheriff of county Dublin. Fan's autobiography says that she had
a conversion experience that summer, though it also says that she was entirely
alone with her own thoughts, which cannot have been true. Filled with "deep
remorse for the failures of my school-life and for many present faults
(amongst others a very bitter and unforgiving temper)," she made religion
the focus of her life. If I were writing a novel, I would tell a somewhat different story: that during the summer of weddings and girl talk she became
aware of sexuality and then escaped from the "great and terrible perturba-
tions" in her inner life by "endless Bible readings."[5]

   She also learned from her father's example about responsibility beyond
the call of duty. Ever since taking possession of his estate almost twenty years

earlier, Charles Cobbe had been rebuilding and improving properties as money became available. In the vicinity of Newbridge the "miserable hovels" were gone; a visitor saw cottages that were "not cabins, but comfortable homes" and cottagers "burning coal instead of turf!"[6] He also owned property some thirty miles to the south, on the borderland of counties Dublin and Wicklow: rough country with inadequate roads, the scattered remnants of medieval open fields and, early in the century, the last Irish speakers in county Dublin. Charles Cobbe tried to rationalize the holdings into more consolidated farms, but even so, most were under ten acres in size and some only one or two acres. In the autumn of 1839 a London art dealer offered him £1,500 for two paintings from the drawing room. "I shall see them go with regret," he wrote in his diary, but "I can not reconcile it to my mind to leave so much value on Walls . . . when such a sum if laid out on [the] mountain property in comfortable houses for the poor tenants, with comfortable beds, instead of the wet wad of straw which so many now sleep on, would present a better picture to the Christian eye."[7]

He contracted with a builder for houses "built in a permanent and workmanlike manner of lime and stone" thirty-two feet long and sixteen feet six inches broad, with slate roofs, a fireplace and double chimney in the wall between the two rooms, and a window in each room. Fan helped by drawing plans and elevations based on the models in Arthur Creagh Taylor's *Designs for Labourers' Cottages . . . Suited to Irish Estates*. All in all, some £5,470 was spent on building and repairs in the mountains. There was no financial benefit to Charles Cobbe: most of the tenants paid less than £10 a year to rent their land, and nothing was added for the new houses.[8]

In 1840, when Fan was seventeen, she entered the final stage of her training for a career as a landowner's wife. School at Brighton was meant to develop her personal and social attractions; putting her in charge of the housekeeping at Newbridge not only unburdened her ailing mother but also served as a professional apprenticeship. Martha Jones, who had given Fan her early lessons in reading and arithmetic, now taught her the management skills needed to supervise a big house and its staff. The housekeeping budget in 1840 was more than £600. Fan did inventories, paid the wages, and learned to review the books and check the figures. She visited the housekeeper's room every day to plan meals for both family and servants. She supervised the training of new servants, which meant learning what a young girl from a cottage on the estate already knew and how to teach her the standards and manners required by gentry, as well as keeping notes so she could give "accurate and truthful recommendations" for servants who left. In addition, she had to discover how to give instruction and sometimes correction to older and more experienced servants, some of whom remembered her as a bothersome child in the years when she and her cousins had used the downstairs corridors as a playground. Fan's new authority induced some family teasing; a letter from her brother Will to his father has a postscript directed to "Miss Fanny, Housekeeper" saying that he is returning the jam pots "with grateful thanks for the *loan* of their contents" (probably a hint that he would like them back refilled). And though she did not take up the career for which this apprenticeship prepared her, the experience paid off in later years when she described the mismanagement of public institutions. She especially noticed how easily men were fooled by unscrupulous housekeepers because they failed to appreciate costs or understand budgets.[9]

A nearly adult Fan must also have been more aware of family problems. Her cousin Harriet Conway was at Newbridge until 30 May 1840, when Charles Cobbe took her to England and put her into the charge of the woman who would chaperone her to India. William Henry had been sent to Scotland to learn about sheep farming with the aim of going to Australia or New Zealand, but complaints were made about his "total absence of principle moral or religious."[10] And there were letters about a Mr. W. Fenton, who had proposed to cousin Laura. Since she was still underage, and since her father's will specified that any daughter who married before twenty-one without her guardian's permission would forfeit her inheritance, Charles Cobbe investigated and said no even though he thought it would be "well those poor children should all have protectors, as soon as possible." I have no evidence that he sought Laura's opinion. Fan and her cousins already knew "that no gentlewoman could possibly earn money. . . . The one natural ambition of her life was supposed to be a 'suitable' marriage; the phrase always referring to *settlements,* rather than *sentiments*."[11]

The diary kept by Marianne Taylor at Ardgillan during this period often has entries such as "3 Cobbes 6 Woods to tea."[12] The "3 Cobbes" were probably Fan, her brother Charles, and his wife Louisa. Visiting with neighbors eased girls into adult social life before they were formally out. Louisa found Newbridge dull; Fan's brother Will called her "worldly."[13] She, Marianne Taylor, and Harriet St. Leger, who often lived with her sister at Ardgillan, could provide Fan with wider interests and good-natured conversation. Marianne Taylor's diary includes an entry for 6 November 1840 that reads, "d[ined] Newbridge," which meant a full-scale dinner party for "Miss Fanny Housekeeper."

Nevertheless, those are only spots of time in a long stretch of days when Fan's actual duties took up no more than an hour or two. She would later describe the "unbroken monotony" of a young lady's life in a country home: "Her walks to her village school, or to visit her cottage friends in their sicknesses and disasters; her rides and drives along the familiar roads which she has ridden and driven over five hundred times already; the rare arrival of a new book, or of some old friend (more often her parent's contemporary than her own) make up the sum of her excitements, or even expectations of excitement, perhaps, through all those years when youth is most eager for novelty, and the outer world seems such an enchanted place."[14]

Still in the grip of her "conversion," Fan pored over the Bible and, as she had about the loaves and the fishes, once more began to ask questions. Some would grow serious, but others suggest a spark of naughtiness. The earliest letter to Frances Power Cobbe in the files at the Huntington Library—saved for a lifetime, preserved with the materials she assembled when writing her autobiography, mounted in the volumes meant to form an heirloom—is one that, according to a note in her handwriting, had been "dictated by Dr Pusey in answer to a hoaxing letter sent him by F.P.C. (then aged 18) in the character of a Mr. Jones who desired to enter the 'priesthood' but had qualms of conscience in consequence of a broken nose & St. Vitus's Dance." The reply begins, "My dear sir, The Mosaic law is certainly not binding upon us at present," and continues, "There may be a good deal of disfigurement without anything that would make it at all difficult to regard a person as one would wish to do the Minister of God."[15]

The letter Pusey was answering interests me because Fan dared to write it—signing a man's name—to the regius professor of Hebrew and canon of Christ Church, who was a central figure in the Oxford Movement; she sent it; and she preserved the answer for more than fifty years. Although she may have inquired about "a broken nose & St. Vitus's dance," the hoax was probably more significant; she may well have already wanted to know why the "disfigurement" of gender was an absolute bar to a person with a calling to be a "Minister of God."

By early 1841 Fan wanted something to occupy her mind. Gardening, sketching, and practicing the harp were not enough, and her social life was much less busy than it would have been had Charles and Louisa taken up residence at Newbridge. Remembering the advice in Maria and Richard Edgeworth's *Practical Education,* she worked up elaborate genealogical and chronological charts of the Egyptian dynasties and the modern dynasties. She would later use the dynastic tables with feminist intent, noting the "extraordinary fact" that "whereas the proportion out of the 2,760 kings and emperors who could be called 'illustrious' or even 'eminent' might be variously estimated at from 5 to 10 per cent, the proportion of illustrious Queens among the handful of female sovereigns amounted to something very like 50 per cent." At the time she had no real object for her study. She read her way through a great many standard works—Spenser's *Faerie Queen,* Milton, Dante's *Divine Comedy* (in Italian), translations of the *Iliad* and the *Odyssey.*

Using a biographical dictionary, she constructed a table of the principal Greek philosophers, with "their lives, ethics, cosmogonies and special doctrines" arranged in separate columns. What began perhaps as a means of filling time (an evangelical conscience did not permit idleness) turned into the "desire of knowledge" as an end in itself. "I should never like to represent the study of truth as merely or chiefly undertaken for the sake of fitting ourselves to teach and help others," she wrote, celebrating the "pure joy of it for its own sake."[16]

In the summer of 1841 Fan got to see electoral politics firsthand. The Whig government called an election and based its platform on repeal of the Corn Laws. Landowners vehemently opposed repeal, since the tax on imported grain supported prices for domestic farmers, who then earned enough profit to pay the rent asked by their landlords. Charles Cobbe chaired the election committee for county Dublin, canvassed for George Hamilton, and seconded the nomination for Thomas Edward Taylor of Ardgillan, who was the son of his "old & valued friend" and the same age as Fan's brother Charles. The polling took place amid bribery and violence; when Fan's father went to vote in county Louth, where he also held land, he "entered the town . . . with a guard of dragoons, and quitted it with an escort of Police, amidst a storm of stones and screams of abuse."[17] Conservatives carried the election with a plurality of seventy-six seats; both of the Cobbes' friends were successful. Edward Taylor would serve for many years as a Conservative whip and be instrumental in passing the second Reform Bill. George Alexander Hamilton, a cousin of Edward Taylor's father's, represented the University of Dublin until 1859. Whatever Fan thought about the issues, she saw pragmatic politics close up and realized that members of Parliament were men very like her brother and her father.

If she had been a conventional young lady, the first month of 1842 would have been a significant milestone in her life. On 26 January her father wrote in his diary, "Levee at the Castle, the first I have been at this ten years," and on the following day he recorded, "Drawing Room at the Castle with my daughter Fanny; for her sake I have again gone out at night to an heated atmosphere, & to me ungenial society; but her poor mothers health renders it imperative on me to take her out, & I fear will more than once do so again."[18] The levee and the drawing room mark Fan's official "coming out" as an adult, introducing her to the queen's representative who served as head of state for Ireland (in 1842 it would have been the lord lieutenant, earl de Grey) and opening a social season of balls and parties that exhibited marriageable young ladies to men of appropriate status. The gown for her presentation cost £17 5s. 10d., about the same as a comfortable trip from Dublin to London, or three times the monthly earnings of her best-paid governess.

A typical Dublin season lasted six weeks, culminating with a state ball at Dublin Castle on Saint Patrick's Day. Fan's recollection fifty years later was that her uncle George, who then commanded a brigade of horse artillery, took her to parties and supplied a series of young officers whose "really marvellous silliness and dulness made conversation wearisome in the extreme."[19] Some of her old companions were also available. Little Charlie, who had left Sandhurst with barely satisfactory qualifications, had nevertheless been commissioned and was barracked in Ireland; cousin Frank was at Trinity College, Dublin; even her brother Henry, who was ordained as a deacon on 27 February, did not take up his duties as curate in Kilmore until the end of March.

It is not possible to know what Fan's reaction to the whole game of romance and the marriage market might have been at the time. Much later, but not in her autobiography, she claimed that a "wise and loving woman, wife of a very worthy man, but a thorough disciple of the despotic school" (could this have been her mother?) had given her "two apophthegms as a general guide to the life we were then about to enter: 'Remember this, my dear: Woman proposes, but Man opposes.' 'Married women appear happy; single ones are so.'" I have only one other small clue about Fan's social life: One of her notebooks, mostly filled with quotations from books she was reading, contains an upside-down page with a half-legible pencil note in a different handwriting: "I have often noticed that clever women are the dullest & most disagreeable companions."[20] Was this a cousin's prank? a confirmation of young officers' empty heads? or was it possibly evidence of a painful experience?

Or perhaps she was completely untouched by heterosexual romance. The picture of herself at age twenty that she supplied to the *Strand* in 1893 had been artfully posed by someone who had demanded upwardly lifted eyes and a soulful expression and got a chubby face with the look of a suspicious bloodhound. It was not that she disliked men; as an adult she counted several men as close friends and companionable colleagues. But as she would say many years later, "Nothing is easier than to coax them to pet us like children, nothing more difficult than to persuade them to treat us like responsible human beings." As a young woman she noticed something else: "Several of my married acquaintances were liable to a peculiar sort of headache. They were obliged, owing to these distressing attacks, to remain very frequently in bed at breakfast-time, and later in the day to lie on the sofa with darkened blinds. . . . A singular immunity from the seizures seemed to be enjoyed . . . when their husbands happened to be in a different part of the country. By degrees, putting my little observations together, I came in my own mind to call these the 'Bad-Husband Headaches.'"[21]

Fan's room at Newbridge. Her sketch seems to focus on the large table with its sturdy desk and comfortable chair. (Cobbe Papers, Alec Cobbe Collection)

Frances Power Cobbe at age twenty, published in the *Strand* magazine series "Portraits of Celebrities at Different Times of their Lives" on 6 July 1893.

There is no evidence that Fan ever felt emotional attraction to any man, certainly nothing like the strong feelings aroused by several women in her life. A phrase she wrote about John Stuart Mill sticks in my mind: "Mill's death is a terrible loss to all women—& personally a grief to me. He was one of the two or three men in the world towards whom I ever felt one could love & honour them thoroughly as if they were good women."[22] Though it may not have been meant in the sense we read it today, her assumption that women could be loved in a way that men, generally, could not aptly describes her emotional expression as an adult. In the 1860s she would cheerfully enumerate the changes that had taken place in the twenty years since her own coming out: "A woman's lot is a freer, happier thing by far than it was when life's lottery offered her but the one prize of a congenial marriage, and all the rest of her chances were miserable blanks of unhappy wedlock or dreary maidenhood, pinned up in narrowest circles of conventionality."[23]

Returning home after she was officially adult, Fan began to take on the charitable work she called "the healthiest and best form of all female philanthropy."[24] After George Evans died in 1842, she was free to become friends with his widow, whose house at Portrane was two miles away. Sophia Evans, an aunt of Charles Parnell's, sponsored an excellent girls' school and helped her young neighbor learn the public duties appropriate to women from the landowning class. Fan subscribed to the *Church of England Magazine,* the *Penny Magazine,* and the *Saturday Magazine* (published by the Society for Promoting Christian Knowledge) for the village school she visited twice a week. Primarily supported by Charles Cobbe, the Donabate school was attended by Catholic as well as Protestant children. Most of their parents worked on the estate; an application made at Newbridge allowed children to attend free of charge.[25] Fan could easily have known every family in the immediate vicinity. The charitable needs of Donabate were probably not great. At the 1851 census it had a total of seventy-six houses, only four of which were of the "lowest class."

Child welfare occupied public attention during the 1840s. Elizabeth Barrett's poem "The Cry of the Children" was published in 1844, the year Parliament limited the workday for women and for all persons under eighteen to twelve hours. In the periodicals taken at Newbridge Fan could have read "Infant Labour" by Anthony Ashley Cooper (later to be her close associate the earl of Shaftesbury), as well as articles on public health, politics, and Irish issues. *Blackwood's* in September 1843 reviewed *Woman's Rights and Duties Considered with Relation to Their Influence on Society and on Her Own Condition,* by "A Woman," which argued that although women had some rights, men defined the limits of women's political and moral universe.[26]

I find no evidence that either parent pressured Fan to marry. Charles

Cobbe's diary makes no comment on her matrimonial prospects or their absence. The continued difficulties of some of the boys suggest her good fortune in having so little of his conscientious direction. Brother Will still worked with Gravatt on the railway between Bristol and Exeter but no longer liked engineering. Cousin William Henry proved intractable. On coming of age he left England at once, using his inheritance to become part owner of a merchant ship. His brother Frank wanted to join him, but Charles Cobbe, who was still Frank's guardian, refused permission. Frank ran away for a time. A letter he wrote on 7 March 1843 is full of self-justification but also shows the cost of Charles Cobbe's refusal to let boys know too soon about their future. "I suppose by my being in College that I am intended for either the law or medical profession," Frank began, and then he explained that it took only three weeks of study to get "the best marks in the Hall" on his thrice-yearly examinations, from which it might be inferred that he had a great deal of time left over for getting into trouble. Knowing his profession would let him pass his "idle hours" reading appropriate books.[27] Cousin Charlie was constantly in debt. Cousin Alick (Uncle Thomas's youngest son, Alexander Hugh), who had remained in India with his parents until he was eight, entered Sandhurst two years after Charlie. While Charlie accumulated reports that called him "idle and troublesome," Alick did so well on the public examination of May 1843 that he was not only commissioned very quickly into a choice regiment but also awarded a "Certificate of Special Approbation" for proficiency in the "higher branches of Mathematical Science."[28]

Fan's brother Tom was called to the bar on 29 January 1841 and had chambers in London, but whether he actually practiced as a barrister is not clear. From 1842 to 1846 he composed music and worked on an annotated edition of Shakespeare's plays with didactic critical prefaces. In later years he wrote a historical novel and a series of tales from the Basque and also published a work of history; that is, he undertook many ambitious projects, but perhaps because he lacked adequate training, he had no real success with any of them. In the prefaces he was writing as Fan reached adulthood, Mary Jean Gross finds that he admired "women characters in proportion as they are decorously fragile and helpless."[29]

During 1843 medical expenses for Fan's mother continued to grow. Fan spent a great deal of time out-of-doors. In the summer, according to her *Life*, she ceased to believe in Christianity. It was the culmination of four years' mental struggle that had begun with her "conversion" in 1839. Obsessive study of the Bible had alternated with rational doubt about miracles and with reading Gibbon. In her evangelical household, to be a Christian was to "believe implicitly in the verbal inspiration of every word in the Bible."

By age twenty Fan was an agnostic: she disbelieved in "human immortality" and "supernatural revelation" but "neither denied or affirmed" the existence of God. Profoundly miserable, she nevertheless took comfort in the beauty of nature and asked herself, in much the same evangelical spirit that organized her father's life, "Can I not . . . conquer my faults, and live up to my own idea of what is right and good?"[30]

She dared not share her disbelief with anyone available to her. Living in "complete spiritual solitude," she "did not know that there was another human soul in England (though of course there were already many) who had found that it was possible to walk in the star light, when the lamps were gone out—to worship outside the church walls as well as within them!"[31] The sense that she was unique provided a "morbid vanity" in her personal struggle and secret resolve. Her agnosticism was partly fueled by rebellion against her father's patriarchal authority, a way of silently resisting his will as well as society's rules for women, though ultimately she honored his faith by rebelling. "By far the most important result of the Individualism of the Evangelical system," she would later write, "has been the recognition of the spiritual equality of women."[32]

Despite Fan's proud independence, religious turmoil was already widespread. One year earlier, in 1842, another not-yet-famous daughter, then known as Mary Ann Evans, refused to go to church with her father. German higher criticism had for more than a generation pointed out discrepancies in biblical records, questioned the dating of texts and described the Bible as "the work of a myriad of authors, all writing at different times and with different standpoints."[33] To counter its threat, Edward Bouverie Pusey studied at German universities in the 1820s. Pusey, John Keble, and John Henry Newman published the first of their *Tracts for the Times* in 1833. Reviving doctrines such as apostolic succession, Newman built a case for Anglo-Catholicism in the Church of England as a middle way between Protestantism and Romanism.

It seems impossible that Fan knew nothing of these questions. Her brother Henry was at Oriel, which was Newman's college, from 1835 to 1840. In 1842 some members of the family were greatly relieved to hear that Henry had "given up the Oxford Tracts."[34] And while the Tractarians revived the forms and doctrines that led Newman into Roman Catholicism in 1845, militant evangelical literalism pursued additional text-based prophecies, such as the ones in *The Signs of the Times,* which had been discussed at Newbridge in 1832. Of this, too, Fan had an example very close to home.

Brother Will was initially enthusiastic about his work with Gravatt but found it hard to make friends. In mid-1838, a year into his apprenticeship, he asked Henry for books on religion and worried about what engineers would do when the railroads had all been made. A letter to his mother on 2 December 1839 marked "private" is a sort of biblical rebus with passages such as the following: "If it pleased him yet to spare you a little 38:13 Psalms, that you would not only be able to say like him 119:71,67,57 Psalms but after like him 51:13 Psalms."[35] During the next year Will grew ever more instructive toward his mother and criticized others in the family. In the summer of 1841 his work took him to Bridgwater, thirty-five miles southwest of Bristol, where he came into contact with Henry James Prince.

Son of a man whose fortune came from plantations in Jamaica, Prince had initially trained as an apothecary but had experienced several religious conversions, eventually becoming a Church of England clergyman. As curate in Charlinch, near Bridgwater, he began a series of charismatic revival meetings in October 1841. A sermon to schoolchildren was so powerful that most of them were "overcome by their feelings of distress . . . sobbing in the severest agony."[36] By May 1842 the bishop had revoked Prince's license, and he had begun to hold independent services in barns and out-of-doors. In addition to a doctrine initially based on "self denial" and "renunciation of self . . . a way of crucifixion of the flesh, and of dying to the world," Prince used a vocabulary drawn from geometry and physics, which might have appealed to an engineer. Diagrams of circles and lines showed the forces that bind souls to God: "They are all *without the circumference* of a sphere of which *He* is the center. . . . They likewise retard their progress towards God; for their straight line 2G must be shorter than the three straight lines 2K, KS, SG; because the shortest distance between any bodies, 2 and G must be the straight line 2G, which unites them."[37]

In 1843 Henry James Prince declared that he was the Holy Ghost. (This was the year that Fan was twenty and ceased to believe in Christianity, and it was also the year that her brother Henry was ordained a priest in the Church of Ireland.) Will, still working for the rail line but lodging at Charlinch rectory, explored ways to be ordained without attending college. By the end of the year he was preaching illegally, without a license. The *Somerset County Gazette* reported that a "fanatical Irishman, named Cob . . . has been haranguing audiences in the streets of this town, on the coming of Christ to judge the world, and declaring the end of all sublunary things is shortly to take place." Will used his engineering skills and much of his own money to build a church at a crossroads about halfway between Charlinch and Spaxton. At the end of August the *Somerset County Gazette* described the "'rant and bellowing' of the faithful" and reported that "cries of 'Behold He Cometh!', repeated at least one hundred times, could be heard half a mile away." A few months later, in January 1846, Prince announced that "Jesus had left the Mercy Seat, that the Door of Mercy was shut that therefore sinners could no longer be saved . . . but that it gladdened his . . . heart to think that all before him were safely shut up in the Kingdom of Heaven whilst others were left to the outer darkness." No longer searching the streets for converts, Prince and his followers withdrew behind the walls of a compound known as the Agapemone or the Abode of Love, where they lived communally until the end of the century and beyond.[38]

For a year or more before the Princites withdrew from the world, the family at Newbridge was deeply concerned about Will's activities. His brother Henry was sent to offer religious counsel, and his brother Tom sought legal advice. The *Times* of 15 July 1845 published an account of Will's marriage to Clara Nottidge of Brighton. In the same ceremony two of her sisters had married other "followers of a certain fanatic, who . . . predicts that the end of the world is at hand." All three sisters were heiresses, with eighteen thousand pounds between them. When brother Tom offered help in arranging a settlement to protect Clara's money, Will's answer was inevitable: "I have made no settlement & as Christ is coming so soon there will be no need whatever of my making one."[39]

During the autumn of 1846 there was a vast amount of correspondence about the Agapemonite sect. Tom wrote to clergymen in Bridgwater seeking information and talked to a Nottidge sister who was not involved. Cousin Tom Conway, home on leave after fifteen years in India, went to see Will and found him "cold and distant": Will had said that "the Bible was of no use now" and "his family were nothing to him." Will's father and brothers consulted with a commissioner in lunacy about having him declared insane. By the middle of 1847 communication between Will and his family had virtually ceased. Though "my brother at Sandhurst" is mentioned once in the *Life of Frances Power Cobbe,* Will's name never appears.[40]

I have leaped ahead of chronology to shape this narrative because in considering Fan's religious apostasy and her sense of its monstrosity it is important to realize that she was aware of turmoil elsewhere in the family. While she traveled a path of rational individualism that led eventually to open-minded universalism, her brother Will passed from biblical literalism through irrational enthusiasm to a state of communal unity attained by *"submission to their minister* . . . the messenger of the Lord of hosts."[41]

Fan, keeping her thoughts to herself, quietly read accounts by others who were searching for moral standards that did not depend on revealed religion, including *The Life of the Rev. Joseph Blanco White* (1845) and James Martineau's *Endeavours after the Christian Life* (1843). Her exploration of comparative religion revived her interest in the Middle East. Alexander Kinglake's *Eothen* was a successful new book in 1844, and Elliot Warburton, whose *Crescent and the Cross* was serialized in the *Dublin University Maga-*

*zine* from October 1843 through February 1844, paid a visit to her brother Charles at Newbridge.

At twenty-one Fan had a young adult's allowance of one hundred pounds a year. (Charles, who was doing much of the landowner's work, had £550; the other brothers had £200 apiece, the amount their father meant to secure in his will as a supplement to their professional earnings. It was also, eventually, the amount willed to Fan, though she had not entered the "profession" for which she was trained.) Physical independence and some degree of private mental and social life were very much simplified when the Dublin-Drogheda railway opened in 1844. There were six trains a day in each direction; Dublin was only twenty minutes from the Donabate station, and the first-class fare from Dublin to Donabate was 1s. 6d.[42] In the other direction, Edward Taylor allowed the tracks to be built across his demesne provided trains would stop by request at Ardgillan. Thus Fan could easily visit Harriet St. Leger. Although she was thirty years older than Fan, St. Leger was a noted bluestocking with an interest in metaphysics, as well as a handsome woman who dressed, like the Ladies of Llangollen, in a masculine style and shared her life with an intimate friend, Dorothy Wilson. Across the estuary at Malahide, which was far closer by rail than by road, the Talbot family had a number of young people, including one who during the 1870s became a member of the antivivisection society Fan established and a leader of the Irish Society for Women's Suffrage.

The railway made it simple to get a daily newspaper and visit Dublin bookshops. Fast trains from Liverpool brought London within one day's travel. Fan and her father made the trip together in March 1844. When they came back three weeks later, cousin Laura, now twenty-four, was with them. Laura was more cosmopolitan than Fan; since coming of age she had generally lived with one or the other of her married sisters. Florence Ensor, who by now had two young daughters, spent most of the year in Paris; Azélie and Tom had a house at 12 Queen Anne Street in London. Two of Laura's brothers spent August at Newbridge. Charles Augustus was on sick leave after six years in Ceylon, and Henry Clermont had been promoted to lieutenant colonel in May. At thirty-two, he was one of the youngest men then holding the rank, senior even to some officers who had been commissioned before he was born. The 2nd West India Regiment was ending a tour in Africa, and Henry Clermont took a six-month leave before rejoining them in Barbados. Fan must have already been acquiring the detailed knowledge of military issues found in her leaders for the *Echo*, especially during the Franco-Prussian War. Sadly, they also learned, a great many months after it had occurred, of the first death in their generation: cousin William Henry, who had been confirmed on the same day as Fan, Harriet, and Charles

Augustus, died on board ship near Indonesia at age twenty-two on 10 November 1843.

After the summer ended and the cousins left, Fan returned to her self-imposed studies. A few surviving pages from her notebook have formulas for finding the volume of a cone and similar problems. Like many people with minds more logical than mathematical, she "took an immense fancy" to geometry; she enjoyed working out the proofs and valued the training in reasoned demonstration. Her poem "The Joy of Youth," dated "Newbridge 1845," enthusiastically records the study and outdoor exercise of the following summer with phrases such as "My mind is free, my limbs are clad with strength which few may know." She also met the only woman friend her own age (other than cousins) known to date from her youth. Although denying any personal reference, she would later describe a father "not intentionally unkind or cruel, only selfish and systematically despotic," who "checks the warm friendships [his daughter] would have formed with other women, because he 'disapproves of female friendship'" and because he "has had enough of society long ago."[43]

The new acquaintance was Felicia Skene, whose family had moved to Greece in 1838. When they came back in 1845, Felicia visited a sister whose husband was then renting Glenasmoil, a shooting lodge in the Dublin mountains that belonged to Charles Cobbe. The two young women, almost exactly the same age, were introduced: "She attracted me exceedingly as a very powerful personality; strong and earnest in no ordinary degree, and very different from the young women of such society as existed then in Ireland." Skene had even published a book, *The Isles of Greece and Other Poems* (1843). Fan admired her looks, her singing voice, her manners, and in particular her intelligent conversation. They argued about theology—Skene was "quite orthodox in her views, with a slight tinge of Ritualism"—and tested each other's senses of humor. For a time Fan hoped that Skene would "form nearer ties with my family," which suggests the possibility of a romance with Fan's clergyman brother Henry or perhaps the hope of one illuminated by Fan's own fond admiration of a very attractive and sympathetic friend.[44]

The final act of Fan's introduction to adult society took place in October 1845, when her father took her around Ireland to meet relatives. A long letter to her sister-in-law Louisa is the first piece of her correspondence known to have survived, and its vivid descriptions and occasional witticisms show the style of her mature essays already forming. At Moydrum, the home of Richard Handcock, baron Castlemaine, who was married to a niece of Fan's grandmother Anne, Fan "endured a short boring . . . with the description of which I trust to draw tears (of laughter) from yr eyes." At Garbally, where the earl of Clancarty was another relative of Grandmother Anne, they arrived in time for the October cattle fair. "Lady C. is excessively good natured & makes a capital hostess—I may well say so for she put me the second night into one of the best rooms (so many blankets!) & crammed her uncle Mr Wynn of Hazlewood into the dressing room." Many of the guests—there were more than thirty for dinner on most days—were much older than Fan. Lord Devon, a high steward of Oxford University and a governor of Charterhouse, "gave me a long discourse on latin classics which seem his favourite pursuit." Lord Downshire "is a most witty pleasant person. ditto indeed old Ld Leitrim who told me numberless droll stories but whose ugliness is remarkable." They stayed at Garbally "nearly a week & I must say I never enjoyed society in the same way before. I liked everybody & if I had been Duchess of Draggletail nobody could have been more civil to me." At Parsonstown Castle (Birr) they saw the new telescope constructed by the third earl of Rosse, which was to remain the world's largest for seventy years. His wife amused Fan after dinner by telling her that the earl "was so terribly matter of fact she could not make him understand Punch."[45]

Fan's high spirits and joy in the company reflect the quality English visitors noted in Anglo-Irish gentry: "frank and cordial, tempered by playful good-humour and a keen relish for conversation . . . distinguished by the cheerfulness that borders upon mirth and the harmony produced by a universal aptness for enjoyments."[46] Fan's father had made similar visits with her brothers; looking after their future meant introducing them to the important people who had some family connection. For Fan it might have been part of "trotting her out," to use Will's phrase, though in the long run, she made better political use of these contacts than her brothers did. She tapped them to sign petitions and put them on the executive committee of her antivivisection society. Some names from that trip show up forty years later in the list of titled women she sent when Millicent Garrett Fawcett was looking for people to contact if a suffrage bill reached the House of Lords.

Just as it marks the beginning of Fan's adulthood, the autumn of 1845 was also a turning point in Irish history. The first public announcement was made in mid-September. When harvest began at month's end many potatoes appeared sound, but they rotted later, in storage. As they made their way back to Newbridge, Charles Cobbe noted in his diary a "part failure in the Potatoe crop arising from a disease we think unknown and not well understood."[47]

# 4    The Family Heretic
## 1845–1857

*The common disposition of children is to share in a very marked manner the emotional religious constitutions of their parents. . . . [But there is a] strong tendency of the different members of such religious families to adopt different creeds and types of piety from one another . . . the sympathy which ought to have united them in closer bonds than other households is too often converted into a source of dissensions.*

FRANCES POWER COBBE, "HEREDITARY PIETY"

When famine struck in 1845–46, the northeast part of county Dublin was relatively fortunate. Its primary crop was grain, not potatoes, and most of the land in Donabate parish belonged to responsible landlords. The village of Ballisk, however, was just over a mile from Newbridge on the estate of an absentee owner and near a common where squatters had put up one-room mud huts. Most of the squatters were laborers earning seven or eight shillings a week. Since the potato blight also affected England and the Continent, alternate foods became enormously expensive. One of Fan's notebooks has a page of careful calculations noting the price of wheat meal, oats, and Indian meal and working out how much a family would need. The result was that "if a man have a wife & 3 children to support his weekly wages at the present average fall short by 2 [shillings] of bare *food* exclusive of lodging clothes or fuel."[1]

Charles Cobbe's diary is full of references to relief-committee meetings, and Fan did what she could with food and stimulants for those dying of fever or cholera in the undrained squatters' village. But the description of Ballisk in her autobiography is tainted by its origin, since it is largely reprinted from an article she wrote for a popular magazine twenty years later. Entitled "The Fenians of Ballybogmucky," the article was designed to discredit the rising Irish nationalism of the 1860s by demonstrating—comically, as the substitution of "Ballybogmucky" for "Ballisk" reveals—the disorganization, incompetence, and shortsightedness of the native Irish when left to their own devices. Its most vivid details have political or religious targets that make unpleasant reading if taken as a picture actually remembered from the famine years.

In response to the misery around her, as well as to the unhappiness that followed her loss of faith, Fan grew increasingly absorbed by serious theological study. She could, she wrote in her autobiography, "go when I pleased and read in Archbishop Marsh's old library in Dublin." Narcissus Marsh's library, on the precincts of St. Patrick's Cathedral, contained twenty-five thousand volumes and was, according to *The New Picture of Dublin*, "generally open . . . from eleven till three, but its remoteness from the respectable part of the city, causes it to be little frequented."[2] Still, central Dublin was only twenty minutes from Donabate by rail, and Fan could afford a cab (or "car" in local terminology) to cross the river. Officially, only "gentlemen and graduates" could use the library, but presumably some arrangement was made for the great-great-granddaughter of the archbishop who was next but one after Narcissus Marsh.

Fan's notebooks for 1846 and 1847 are filled with quoted passages, biblical verses, and readings in history, linguistics, and theology, many of them followed by logical queries: "Joshua 11/21 . . . Incredible that the leader of a nomad tribe should have made law on the sale of houses." Eventually the notes were organized with an alphabetical index: "Aesthetics of Bible . . . Apocalypse . . . Aristotle . . . Asses."[3] Marian Evans's translation of David Friedrich Strauss's *Life of Jesus, Critically Examined*, a book Fan owned, was published in 1846. She may also have used her spending money to buy Robert Chambers's *Vestiges of the Natural History of Creation* (1844). Most importantly, she bought the first British edition of Theodore Parker's *Discourse of Matters Pertaining to Religion* (1846) as soon as she saw it mentioned in the *Athenaeum*.

Theodore Parker, the leading preacher and social reformer among Boston transcendentalists, taught "that God is absolutely, infinitely, eternally good . . . not good only to angels, Jews, and Christians . . . not good only in Time . . . but good to all, good for ever." And furthermore—especially important to a young woman struggling with patriarchy in many forms—"In God, the 'Parent of Good, Almighty,' we have both parents in One."[4] He addressed his prayers to "father and mother of the world." To whatever extent Fan had already come on her own to Parker's chief conclusions, his book helped her conceive of God's law as "written on our nature, revealed in various ways through Instinct, Reason, Conscience."[5] His New England transcendentalism was especially attractive to someone who sought escape from the claustrophobia of family prayers in her father's house and had come to feel religion most when she was out-of-doors.

Fan's life was far less lonely than would appear from her autobiography.

On 20 February 1846, for example, she left on a trip to England with her brother Henry. She was twenty-three; it was, I believe, the first time she had gone traveling as an adult without her father. In London they probably stayed with Tom and Azélie at 12 Queen Anne Street, north of Oxford Street, and they may have brought cousin Sophy back with them, for she spent much of 1846 at Newbridge. For this trip, as for Sophy's long visit and much else in Fan's private life, no record remains. A more troubling concealment in the *Life of Frances Power Cobbe* is that she evades major troubles through small comic narratives. Too honest to ignore the flaws of her favorite playmate but unwilling to expose him to serious criticism, she devised a brief valedictory for her cousin Charlie as "a very popular officer" who "died sadly while still young, at the Cape" and followed it with an amusing story about a nameless young officer at Malta who, according to a guest at Newbridge, "gives charming picnics" that he could hardly afford. He said, the visitor reported, "that he has an old uncle somewhere who—Good Lord! I am afraid I have put my foot in it."[6] Charlie had barely scraped through Sandhurst and usually was at the bottom of his regiment's promotion list. Fan's father rescued him repeatedly—from an order by a regimental court of enquiry, from the threats of a Dublin tradesman, by clearing his obligations at Longford barracks in 1843 so he could ship out. On 5 May 1845 Charlie wrote in desperation from Malta, afraid he would be court-martialed and cashiered.

Theodore Parker (1810–1860). Cobbe used this lithograph, signed "Saulini, Rome, 1859," as the frontispiece to *Discourse on Religion,* the first volume in her edition of Parker's collected works. (By permission of The Huntington Library, San Marino, California)

Charles Cobbe cleared his debts one last time, at a cost of £450 with a bond against his inheritance, and instructed him to write no more letters. Removed from his regiment in the army's post-Crimea reduction in force, Charlie was in fact forty-eight years old and an inspector of roads at Queenstown (now in Eastern Cape province, South Africa) when he died, "sadly while still young." Not quite willing to let her favorite playmate disappear without trace, Fan nevertheless elided the evidence of his failure to outgrow the thoughtless recklessness that had made him such an admirable companion for a bold and rebellious girl.

Later in 1846, affairs at the Agapemone made a stir, as did Will's part in them. Louisa Nottidge, Will's sister-in-law, was kidnapped by her relatives and committed to a lunatic asylum so that she could not give her money to Henry Prince. Will went to London in an unsuccessful attempt to free her. Tom got in touch with the Nottidge family, looking for evidence to bring a case against the Agapemone for misusing members' funds.[7] He heard rumors that both Will and Prince had "put off" their wives because the women were pregnant, presumably by other men since marriages among the enlightened were "spiritual only." The information was so horrifying that Tom and his brother Charles were not willing to tell their father.[8]

These stressful private concerns moved in counterpoint to Ireland's massive public disaster. The potato blight struck much harder in the second year: failure of the crop was immediate, devastating, and almost total. Like many others who remembered the summer of 1846, Fan described the night it came. Driving to a seven-o'clock dinner with Mrs. Evans at Portrane, they passed a field of potatoes, "and through the open windows of the carriage came the sweet smell of the potato-blossom. . . . 'What a fine field! How sweet the blossom is!' we remarked." But when they returned a few hours later the leaves and blossoms were a mass of rotting vegetation. Around Dublin early August brought torrential rains and floods. Food ran short even in the vicinity of Newbridge; on 8 October 1846 Charles Cobbe wrote to the lord lieutenant about "the necessity of calling the Relief Committee into operation." Brother Charles was "thoroughly occupied" with his duties as a magistrate—theft rose dramatically as people became desperate for money to buy food—and his work on other committees.[9]

The winter of 1846–47 was the "most severe in living memory." Cold and a population weakened by hunger led to epidemics of typhus and dysentery; misery was everywhere. Fan read not only biblical criticism but also Bacon, Rousseau, and Gibbon, and she copied into her notebook passages from Seneca and others on endurance, submission, and bearing pain. The new Irish Poor Law required landowners to fund the relief efforts, but tenants who spent their entire income on food could not pay their rents.

The more generous a landlord was in forgiving arrears and organizing relief, the more likely he was to go bankrupt. Although Charles Cobbe was never in that danger, his accounts show a number of loans to tenants, and the cumulative arrears in unpaid or underpaid rents had reached more than nine hundred pounds by the end of 1850. He had the same number of tenants, even very small tenants, in 1850 as in 1840; unlike the notorious landlord of stereotype, he made no evictions.[10]

Meanwhile, brother Tom had sent a plea for help. On 25 January 1847 Charles Cobbe wrote that he could not go to London, nor could he send Fan; aside from their duties at home, he would be hard pressed just then to pay for the trip. Barely six weeks later he gave Fan twenty pounds for her "expenses to London."[11] She arrived in the midst of a major crisis, one perhaps precipitated by her approaching visit. On 13 March Azélie left her husband's house and, it eventually became known, eloped to Paris with William Talmadge, who had been a fellow student of Tom's at both Oxford and the Inner Temple. Cousin Tom Conway, who was still on leave from the Madras civil service, spoke to the police about tracing Azélie, closed up Tom's house, arranged for someone to buy the books and goodwill of his legal practice, and asked Charles Cobbe about the instructions Tom had given: "I should be unwilling to act solely in accordance with his views, influenced, as they must be with the present excited state of his feelings. He says 'When you hear of her go *immediately* with the Police, & show her the enclosed writing. . . . If she will quit him I'll give up every thing possible for her.'" "I would gladly go to her," continued Conway, "but I could not undertake to say anything that might compromise Tom, in the event of legal proceedings being hereafter considered desirable."[12]

Ultimately there was a divorce. First there was an ecclesiastical suit, heard in Consistory Court on Wednesday, 14 June 1848; then a civil action against Talmadge for criminal conversation (the suit was not contested, and Talmadge paid five hundred pounds in damages); and finally a private member's bill in the House of Lords, reported in the *Times* on 24 April 1850. According to the evidence, Talmadge had often visited Azélie in the daytime while Tom was at his chambers. Then in June 1846 Tom's father had taken his son on a tour of Germany. While they were gone, "Mrs. Cobbe had frequently herself let Mr. Talmadge into the house . . . at unseasonable hours in the night, but also herself let him out at an early hour on the following morning." A servant testified that "before my master went to Germany he slept with my mistress, and so he did for the first two or three nights after his return; but after that, upon the ground that she was very much indisposed, they slept in separate rooms." (While everyone at Newbridge worried about Azélie's health, Tom surely must have known something even if he denied conscious knowledge.) Also, "the day that my mistress went away she had given her orders for the dinner as usual. She went out, but she never returned."[13]

This event, mentioned only in one, deliberately concealing phrase in the *Life of Frances Power Cobbe,* opens major new questions about Fan's analysis of relations between women and men. Given the rarity of divorce in the nineteenth century, it is astonishing that there were two in her family. The marriage of her cousin Thomas Monck Cobbe, Uncle George's son, was one of that first string of weddings when Fan was sixteen. Hardly more than a year later his wife was with another man, and he had secured an ecclesiastical separation. In both cases public evidence shows the woman at fault, thus making divorce possible. Yet there may well have been more to the story. What, for example, did Tom mean by writing that he would "give up every thing possible for her"? Certainly his preoccupation with music and Shakespeare suggests his disinterest in the profession he had reluctantly chosen. And did Azélie still resent not having been allowed to go back to India? She must have known she was never welcome as a daughter-in-law. Read in the light of subsequent events, fragmentary hints tell a circumstantial tale of friction and unhappiness: Tom's "indiscreet" trip to Dublin in 1839, the lack of any subsequent pregnancy after their newborn's death, the many references to her "low spirits," his own nervous instability. Azélie's anger may be revealed by the timing of her transgression in the summer of 1846, when Charles Cobbe took Tom to Ghent, Brussels, Cologne, Frankfurt, Aix le Chappelle, and Paris, while Azélie remained at home, and William Talmadge spent at least one night in her bedroom. One other suggestive fact: Azélie was not cut off by her brothers and sisters. She and William Talmadge married on 27 June 1850, almost as soon as the divorce was final; and although they lived in Paris, she was in the house of her sister Laura on the day of the 1871 census.

With all the distress both private and public, it seems remarkable that Fan's best-known poem is entitled "Thanksgiving" and dated "Newbridge May 1847." Perhaps it was partly a psychological ploy to give thanks in the face of evil. Sometimes entitled "A Litany of Thanksgiving" or "A Thanksgiving Hymn," it appeared throughout the century in Unitarian and non-denominational hymnals. The first stanza is as follows:

> For life, for health I bless Thee,
>     For hearing and for sight,
> For food, for clothing and abode,
> For the rest of the dreamy night
>         I bless Thee, O my God!

Although the epidemics were at their height during June, Anglo-Irish life went on much as usual. The actress Fanny Kemble appeared at Dublin's Theatre Royal and spent a few days with Harriet St. Leger at Ardgillan. St. Leger took her to lunch at Newbridge, where Kemble, who thought the room was full of people invited to gape at her, behaved with bare civility. After learning that they were all relatives, she vowed to make amends. In later years she would be Fan's friend and long-term correspondent. At the time, Kemble had just left her slave-owning husband, Pierce Butler, and would soon return to the United States for divorce proceedings. Marianne Taylor's diary for June 1847 records a trip to Newbridge by rail and notes, "Mrs Th," which means that she must have heard about Azélie's elopement. Tom was probably home for the summer, as were the three younger daughters of Uncle Thomas. Several of Uncle George's children lived in Ireland, Alick's regiment was still in Britain, and some of the Conway daughters had returned from India or had children who visited Newbridge. On 17 August, at Donabate church, cousin Laura was married to John Locke, probably introduced through Tom's legal connections. Laura was twenty-five; Locke was a substantial barrister of forty-two who in another decade would be elected to Parliament.

Throughout the year Fan's mother had been increasingly ill, enduring "sleepless nights" and "days of pain and grief," and her medical expenses had exceeded one hundred pounds. She died on 26 October 1847 "with her weeping husband and sons beside her bed and with her head resting on my breast," according to the *Life of Frances Power Cobbe*. She was "the only one who really loved me." Fan's anguish was compounded by her rejection of Christianity: "I could not see my way to any belief that she still lived, & the agony not only of my personal grief & loss but of the thought that that one most beautiful spirit was *extinguished* was never to be forgotten." The poem she wrote the next month expresses her sense of total absence: "Mother, O Mother! can it be / The grave holds all that once was thee, / And *thou* art but a memory." In the poem Fan calls herself "the light of thy dimmed eyes, / Whom others saw, but to despise."[14] Whether being despised by "others" was poetic overstatement or actual belief, it is difficult not to suspect that Fan's immoderate adoration grew from her mother's invisibility, which let her at least imagine a love she did not find anywhere else.

After another winter occupied with scholarship, charitable work, and housekeeping, Fan gathered her courage and wrote to Theodore Parker in Boston. His generous reply of 5 May 1848 reported his "great delight" in her letter. Perhaps her willingness to challenge him encouraged their intellectual friendship: "You ask me," his letter said, "if Jesus believed in eternal punishments, &c., or why I call myself a Christian if he did." He sent an autographed copy of his *Sermon of Immortal Life,* which explains his own opinion about hell, though it does not specifically answer her query about Jesus: "The notion of eternal misery . . . deserves all the . . . mockery which it ever met with."[15]

By the time Fan first wrote to Parker, in the spring of 1848, Ireland was seething with tension. On 15 March the nationalist Smith O'Brien urged a Dublin crowd to get military training. On 10 April, the day of the last great Chartist demonstration in London, he spoke in the Commons during debate on a new treason-felony bill. The old statute, requiring that treason be shown in overt acts and punished by beheading and quartering, had fallen into abeyance when the penalty became unacceptable. The new law, passed in late April, modernized the punishment but let the government act against those who promoted treason "by open and advanced speaking."[16] On 15 May Smith O'Brien was tried in Dublin for his speech of 15 March, but the jury could not agree on a verdict, and he was discharged.

In direct response to the new law another nationalist, John Martin, established a newspaper with the deliberately provocative name *The Irish Felon.* The first issue was published on 24 June. Meanwhile, Charles Cobbe had posted the following message in the villages of his neighborhood: "Whereas, several wicked and evil-minded persons are visiting the different parishes in this county, exciting the minds of the inhabitants, and calling upon them to form clubs, and to procure arms, with a view of accomplishing their own selfish and wicked designs. . . . I hereby caution all those who value their own lives and liberties, and all those who have anything to lose, to refrain from the formation of political clubs." The *Irish Felon* printed Charles Cobbe's message and a response that contained a barely concealed threat: "Benevolent Cobbe, Paris was deluged with blood because of the 'deep interest' which sweet-souled officials like yourself took in the affairs of all those who had 'something to lose,' while they forgot the very existence of those poor devils who had *nothing* to lose."[17]

On 22 July Parliament suspended habeas corpus in Ireland; the next day Smith O'Brien announced his intention to do battle. On 25 July Charles Cobbe wrote that "all the inhabitants of this district are looking to me to take . . . measures for their security" and made plans to enroll the gentry and farmers as special constables "in case of need."[18] By that time, however, the threat was virtually extinct. The only clash between armed people and armed police was at Ballingarry on 29 July, an incident quickly trivialized by the English press as "the insurrection in a cabbage garden." There were no casualties on either side. Whatever she actually experienced at the time, Fan's only account of the aborted rebellion originates in the entirely suspect (and largely comic) reporting of "The Fenians of Ballybogmucky."

Cousin Sophy returned to Newbridge for the autumn of 1848. She would turn twenty on the day before Fan's twenty-sixth birthday and was someone Fan could talk with about comparative religion. Toward the end of the year Fan let her father know that she was no longer a believing Christian. The passage describing this incident is quoted in virtually every account of her life or thought: "When my poor father learned the full extent of my 'infidelity,' it was a terrible blow to him. . . . He could not trust himself to speak to me, but though I was in his house, he wrote to tell me I had better go away. My second brother, a barrister, had a year before given up his house in Queen Anne Street under a terrible affliction, and had gone, brokenhearted, to live on a farm which he hired in the wilds of Donegal. There I went as my father desired and remained for nearly a year."[19]

Her father's diary, however, mentions nothing about religious questions involving Fan, although it has vast agonies over Will, soul-searching when Tom decided not to enter the church, and concern about Henry's flirtation with Puseyism. If I had to guess from the evidence in family sources, I would say that she was probably sent to Donegal to keep Tom from despair; his "nervous difficulties" and "mental distress" had been mentioned repeatedly since his mid-teens. On the day he left for Donegal, his father had wondered, "Shall I see him again? I sometimes think not."[20] Perhaps Fan's father never really heard what she said about her religion, or perhaps he thought men's doubts were important and women's were not, but it also seems possible that her own fear and guilt led her to project onto an unspeaking father the response she thought he must have had. In recalling her own stricken conscience at the enormity of disbelief, defiance of an earthly father stands in for the vastly greater risk of defying God.

Tom had leased a place on the river Inver, six miles from Donegal and a mile from the sea. He probably got the farmland on very moderate terms. Donegal was not as badly hurt as other counties on the west coast, but it was hard for landowners to find tenants with money to pay their rent. Fan described the residence, named Bonny Glen, as "a small house . . . bright enough, but somewhat dilapidated and oddly contrasting with the pretty London furniture imported by its occupants." It seemed a long way from civilization. By 1848 news reached Dublin by telegraph and twice-daily London mails. Donegal still had no rail service. A few years later Fan could joke: "If it should happen to any parent . . . to possess a son troubled with a strong desire to emigrate to Upper Canada or New Zealand, we should recommend, as the best possible remedy, that the youth should be induced to make a short and easy trial of how he really likes solitude by spending six months or so in the county of Donegal." At the time it must have been less amusing. Even had Tom been in the mood for society, there was "hardly a resident gentleman." A servant had to make a twelve-mile round trip to fetch mail, newspapers were virtually unavailable, Dublin's libraries were far out of reach, and "ink, books, and paper" could not "be procured short of a pilgrimage."[21]

Fan had no duties; even distributing charity was difficult when most of the poor were Irish speakers. Tom disliked her religious opinions and had no patience for discussing theology. Her notebooks for 1849 do, however, have quotations in Greek and Latin, so she must have persuaded him to give her some instruction in classical languages. Given the passages in the *Life of Frances Power Cobbe* suggesting that Tom engaged her feelings in ways that Charles and Henry did not, many other topics may have come out into the open. Fan's sense of the simultaneous necessity and difficulty of silence emerges in journalism two decades later, when she wrote of the hidden troubles in seemingly happy homes and the misery of entire families when divorce turns their secrets into public knowledge. More importantly, in writing about "justifiable publicity" and the morals of private life she asked, "What is to be done when the exculpation of one is the blame of another?"[22]

At the end of June 1849 brother Will's name showed up in the *Times*'s reports of a sensational trial. Early in 1848 Louisa Nottidge had escaped from the lunatic asylum, and Will had tried to help her get back to the Agapemone. They were intercepted at Farringdon Road station, but once Will learned where she had been, he asked the commissioner in lunacy to investigate. On 23 June 1849 the relatives accused of confining Louisa Nottidge against her will were put on trial in London. The heat was intense, the courtroom was crowded, and the testimony of Will and others aroused gusts of laughter. According to Lewis Price, the husband of another Nottidge sister resident at the Agapemone: "We have horses and carriages, and we live in style. . . . We abjure prayer altogether . . . we are glorifying God when we eat and drink. . . . All of us play at 'hockey' females as well as males."[23]

The trial ended with a verdict for Louisa Nottidge, although the jury awarded damages of only fifty pounds. The case was ultimately, however, extremely significant, since the presiding judge, Lord Chief Baron Frederick Pollock, instructed the jury that a person is "to be considered of 'non-sane mind' who is 'dangerous to himself, or to herself, and others.' Beyond these limits we must not travel." He further told the jury, according to the London *Times,* that he "very much doubted whether in this case, if the plaintiff had been a man, or living under the protection of a husband, the defendants would have dared to have taken the step they had." Pollock's second statement had important resonance for activist women, and his first infuriated the nascent psychiatric profession because the standard of "danger to self or others" put enormous restraint on doctors.[24]

During the trial another resident of the Agapemone explained that members did not pray because "it is the spirit of truth—the spirit within that God looks to. . . . God says we shall be joyful and happy, and why not?"[25] Despite their utter difference in practices, the sentiment is curiously similar to the theology Fan was developing. With a great deal of free time and the notes she brought along, she spent the months in Donegal producing a neatly copied, 405-page manuscript whose title page reads, "An Essay on TRUE Religion Being a reply to the question Why are you a DEIST? By Frances Power Cobbe 1849." The materials she used, which are bound in a separate volume, comprise about 350 pages of quotations with page numbers and careful documentation.[26] The project is very like a fairly competent Ph.D. dissertation, with summaries and evaluations of the sources arranged in a careful, if sometimes mechanical, outline. The language is clear, as if she were writing for an intelligent young person; she defines terms such as *demonstration* (in the mathematical sense) and *proof* (in logic) and uses examples from ordinary life to illustrate philosophical concepts. "I am a Deist," she affirms, "because it appears to me that Deism may be demonstrated to be true & that all other religions may be shewn to be false." *Deism,* she explains, means "the worship of one only God who reveals himself entirely in Nature & Conscience but never supernaturally or miraculously." Jesus, then, was the son of God, and the Bible an inspired text, "in no other sense than that all good men are the sons of God and all 'good gifts' come down from the 'Father of Lights.'"[27] The "Essay on True Religion" is a work of philosophy, not a spiritual autobiography; the struggle and turmoil have been surmounted and repressed.

By early 1850 Fan was back at Newbridge keeping house. She and her father had reached an accommodation of sorts. Religion was not discussed, she did not attend family prayers, and she spent Sunday in the "solitude of the woods and fields" instead of going to church.[28] Fifteen years later, when a group of London women formed a discussion society, the first question they took up was, "What is the basis and what are the limits of parental authority?" Frances Power Cobbe's response showed her prolonged deliberation. "The young child," she asserted, "owes its parent an obedience absolutely limitless. The adult son or daughter owes no obedience at all, but an amount of *service* which may assume the proportions of the most complete and life-long sacrifice." Her argument was balanced and gender-free; both sons and daughters must attend a parent in case of sickness, care for a parent who is old and feeble, and provide "pecuniary aid" if needed, but "if a parent ask his son or daughter to renounce a profession, to withhold a book, to abstain from a marriage—*not* on any ground connected with the parent's welfare but as a matter of arbitrary will, the son or daughter in such a case is always free (and *may* be, morally bound) to resist such demand."[29]

At home during the 1850s Fan felt "in a sort of moral Coventry, under a vague atmosphere of disapprobation wherein all I said was listened to cautiously as likely to conceal some poisonous heresy." Enduring, perhaps even learning to relish, the freedom of independent thought, she clung to high ground. "The solemn charge of moral freedom," she told the Kensington Society in 1865, "must be relinquished to no human master." An adult child "is bound to disobey" any commands of a parent that "clash with the decisions" of the child's own conscience.[30]

In her first spring back at Newbridge the account of her brother Tom's divorce appeared in the London *Times*. The costs, all told, amounted to almost a thousand pounds.[31] Although all of Fan's brothers were in their thirties, she had no nephews or nieces; Charles and Louisa remained childless even after ten years of marriage. Charles took an increasingly large role in managing the estate; in 1852 he replaced his father as deputy lieutenant of county Dublin. Some time during this period Fan and her brothers Tom and Henry decided to undertake a full, elaborate genealogy of the Cobbe family. Beginning with family stories and epitaphs copied in Bath and Winchester, they moved into published and then manuscript sources. They wrote "in the most audacious manner to everybody from provosts to parish clerks." Fan even had the sacristan at Dublin's Christ Church take her into the crypt so that she could read the brass plates on piled-up coffins. Reporting on work in progress to her cousin Alick in India, Fan mentioned a Saxon chief Cobba in the sixth century, a "Leuricus Cobbe . . . who held lands in Suffolk before the Conquest," and a direct ancestor, Richard Cobbe, who "to my infinite rejoicing proves to have been a good Republican" and "sat in the Cromwellian Parlt of 1650."[32] Ultimately she created a splendid illuminated volume with the armorial bearings of some twenty associated families for presentation as a gift to her father.[33] The genealogy was a useful exercise in research and a project to share with brothers who did not want to hear about her religious scholarship; and eventually her knowledge of the archbishops and ambassadors and men who signed the death warrant of Charles I must have helped supply the confidence (or audacity) to seek private meetings with eminent men whose policies she would then attack in her unsigned newspaper columns.

In the spring of 1851 gossip about the Agapemone reached a wide public through the *Illustrated London News*. Though the facts came from the 1849 court case, and brother Will was not mentioned by name, the article's knowing tone made painful reading. It reported that the "Family" had gained its wealth by making converts from "ladies of a certain age, who possess property, and have no objection to become wives." Members "have converted the chapel into a banqueting-house, and substitute feasting and enjoyment for privation and prayer."[34] At about the same time, brother Henry was involved in some difficulty that remains maddeningly opaque even though Fan was enlisted as intermediary between Henry and their father. "My dearest Father," she wrote from Donegal, where she was again staying with Tom, "you do not know how much I have felt for you in all this horrible business." A letter from Henry in the same month reads: "My dear Father, I made known your urgent wishes & have received an assurance that all shall be at an end. My letters are returned & all communication has ceased. . . . I can only now express my deep sorrow at having caused you so much pain . . . I give up what I still believe would have been to my happiness to your wishes & judgment."[35]

But what was the "all" that had ended? The return of letters suggests a love affair, though the fact that Henry had consulted his unmarried sister about the "horrible business" makes one pause, and his concession was thoroughly grudging ("what I still believe would have been to my happiness"). It would seem that Fan was not the only child of Newbridge who must have been existing in a "moral Coventry."

In the aftermath of this incident, Charles Cobbe offered Henry and Fan a gift of fifty pounds to go to London for the Great Exhibition. By 1851 the trip took little more than twelve hours: steamships crossed from Kingstown to Holyhead in less than four hours (compared with two or three days by sail when Fan was an infant), and there was a fast train from Holyhead to Euston station. Although it was not Fan's first trip to London without her father (she and Henry had gone in 1846), this one strikes me as possibly an occasion, if there ever was one, when relatives in her generation might have had adult conversations about things that could not have been said before. Fan was twenty-eight and had finished her manuscript "Essay on True Religion"; Henry had just experienced his disgrace (whatever it was); and Henry James Prince, the leader of the Agapemone, attracted notice yet again by his own visit to the Great Exhibition, "driving through Hyde Park in an open carriage recently purchased from the Queen Mother. . . . preceded by bareheaded outriders who proclaimed, 'He who cometh in the name of the Lord.'"[36] Henry and Fan stayed with their cousin Laura and her husband, John Locke. Cousin Florence was in England for the summer; her elderly husband had died, and she lived in France, where she must have seen Azélie. Cousin Charles Henry, Uncle George's eldest son, had retired from the Bengal Army and was also in London. His youngest daughter, Lucie Cobbe, who many years later would be Fan's protégée as a journalist, was then an infant.

Fan left no account of the exhibition. Its map shows that the displays from Italy, Greece, Egypt, and Turkey were just east of the fountain at the building's central crossing. Material from India—Laura and Florence may have had some memories of the subcontinent, where their mother still lived—occupied more than a thousand square feet on both sides of the central aisle to the west of the crossing. Fan and Henry spent some time on the genealogy; on 2 June they were both admitted to the British Museum Library, using John Locke's address. The round reading room had not yet opened; people examining books or manuscripts used a separate entrance in Montague Place. It would be interesting to know whether she read "The Enfranchisement of Women," later known to be by Harriet Taylor Mill, in the July issue of the *Westminster Review.* (Two years later her notebooks show that she regularly consulted the *Westminster Review.*) Also during the exhibition summer, in a foretaste of the growing celebration of empire that was to mark the century's final third, a medal was struck commemorating the battle of Assaye and "presented to the few officers and men then surviving."[37] Charles Cobbe received his at Newbridge on 23 July.

During the winters Fan continued to study theology. Research on religious history (and perhaps the Crystal Palace displays) revived her desire to see the East. She took notes from Harriet Martineau's 1848 account of her trip to Egypt and Palestine, *Eastern Life Present and Past,* and from John Lewis Burckhardt's *Travels in Syria and the Holy Land* (1822). She also thought about contemporary political ethics. A series of jottings headed "the morals of the Bible" includes observations that Mormons defended polygamy and slaveholders in the southern United States justified slavery on grounds they found in Scripture.[38] Fan, like some who had been her playmates, moved toward a new stage of life. In May 1852 her cousin Eliza, the youngest of Uncle Thomas's children, came of age. Parliament dissolved on 1 July, and during the election that followed John Locke unsuccessfully contested for Hastings. Fan made calls at Ardgillan, cataloged the books at Newbridge, and wrote poetry. A visit from Sophy made her "the happiest of the happy"; she felt she could "wish for nothing in life more than to have her always with me if it were possible she could be happy in so dull an existence."[39] In November her brother Tom thought he was likely to marry Lady Forbes, but nothing came of it.

The following winter, Fan, who turned thirty on 4 December 1852, suffered a severe attack of bronchitis and began looking for a faith more sustaining than her "Deism." Her friend Felicia Skene recommended Immanuel Kant's *Metaphysic of Ethics.*[40] With its help she began transforming her "Essay on True Religion" into the work that would be published in 1855 as *An Essay on Intuitive Morals. Part I. Theory of Morals.* (I refer to it henceforth as *Intuitive Morals,* the title most often used by contemporaries.)[41] At an early stage in the process, she added a further section to the despairing poem composed after her mother's death. In place of her anguish because "The grave holds all that once was thee," she proclaimed "Yon lonely grave can hold not thee; / Thou livest—blessed, pure, and free" and affirmed that people who love one another on earth will be reunited in an afterlife.[42]

During these years when Fan was buying new books and using Dublin's circulating library, as well as reading old treatises from the Narcissus Marsh collection, feminist ideas gained public currency. *A Brief Summary, in Plain Language, of the Most Important Laws Concerning Women,* by Barbara Leigh Smith (later Bodichon), was published in 1854. Fan copied out several passages from Anna Jameson's *Commonplace Book,* also published in 1854. "I have a great admiration for power," wrote Jameson, "a great terror of weakness—especially in my own sex." She argued wittily for a single moral standard and a single standard of behavior by editing Wordsworth's "The Happy Warrior" to substitute *woman* for *warrior.* Jameson observed that the idea that a woman's chastity belonged to her man, not to herself, "is a remnant of Oriental barbarism. . . . This idea of property in the woman survives still . . . and is one cause of the ill treatment of wives."[43]

Less than two years after the illusory news about Lady Forbes, Fan's brother Tom announced that he had been accepted by Janet Finlay Grahame, who would be called "Jessie" within the family. Charles Cobbe was (perhaps naturally) cautious. "I know so little of the lady, & know not whether to be glad or otherwise, but from all I hear, she is very amiable," he wrote on 28 June 1854, and in August he added, "I have seen her and she appears every way unobjectionable . . . she will bring an encrease to his income and is a good economist (very necessary for *him*)." Jessie, whose father was Thomas Grahame, of Stretton-en-le-field in Derbyshire, was twenty-seven and Tom was forty. Her younger sister Helen had been married three years previously to John James Nugent, of Clonlost, whose grandmother was a sister of Tom and Fan's grandmother Anne Cobbe's. John James Nugent was about Tom's age; once the families were brought closer together, Fan became very fond of his wife, Helen Nugent. The marriage was performed by brother Henry, either because of family feeling or because Jessie's parish clergyman was among those who would refuse to marry a divorced person.

The next marriage in the family reveals, as Tom's first marriage had done, that Charles Cobbe's habit of control fostered concealment and secret defiance by his sons as well as his daughter. On 20 October 1855 he "returned from the mountains, but only to hear from my son Henry that he had been married for more than a year, without my knowledge . . . or consent and to a person whose station in life must ever make her unfit to be a companion for the members of my family. Thus are my fond hopes & expectations for him blighted and my heart nearly broken with grief & sorrow."[44]

"More than a year" was a protective evasion on Henry's part. It is not possible to discover whether this marriage was a sequel to the events of 1851 and "all" had not, after all, been "at an end," or whether, on the other hand, the first experience had taught Henry not to consult his father about plans important to his own happiness. When he broke the news of his marriage, he may also have communicated that he had a six-month-old daughter, Mabel, born on 4 April 1855, but he certainly did not disclose that his marriage to Sarah Jane Taggart had taken place only eleven weeks before Mabel's birth.[45] Charles Cobbe was away from Newbridge during the first three months of the year; Henry and Sarah used the opportunity to establish residence in Dublin and be married by banns at St. Mary's Church, with the parish clerk as one witness and Margaret Taggart, presumably a relative of Sarah's, as the other.

During the first months of 1855, when Henry was quietly married in Dublin, Fan and her father lodged at 15 Connaught Square, just north of Hyde Park. She had a completed manuscript (which Harriet St. Leger had read) and an introduction from her Dublin bookseller to William Longman, whose firm published work by James Martineau and other advanced religious philosophers. Once Longman accepted her book, the publishing process was astonishingly quick. She got first proofs a sheet at a time and took them to the British Museum, where she made corrections, verified quotations, and inserted further evidence. The book was printed, bound, and in the hands of readers less than five months after she first walked into Longman's office. On 5 June 1855 Theodore Parker sent thanks for the copy he received in Boston "a few weeks ago." Parker admired the plan, the execution, and the details: "It is a noble work," he wrote, adding that "your learning also surprises me."[46]

*Intuitive Morals* was published anonymously so as not to annoy her father, Fan asserts, but probably also because William Longman knew there would be no market for a book of philosophy and theology by an unknown woman who, by the very fact of her sex, could have no professional credentials for the task. Women were writing about religion, but usually in some other guise, such as art criticism (Anna Jameson's 1852 *Legends of the Madonna*), conduct manuals, or instructions for educating girls. At virtually the same time that Fan started to rework her manuscript, Florence Nightingale was composing *Suggestions for Thought to the Searchers after Truth Among the Artizans of England,* but Nightingale, who, like Fan, was thirty years old when she began, undertook only a private printing, which allowed her to send copies to six readers.

Fan's goal in *Intuitive Morals* was to develop a system of morals that was neither too shallow for "thinking men" nor too abstruse to be widely understood and that required no religious commandments or divine inspiration but rested wholly on "certain necessary truths possessed intuitively by the Human Mind." The book was received more enthusiastically in North America, particularly among Unitarians and transcendentalists, than in England, but even reviewers who disapproved of the premise respected the writer's intellect. Except for a few Bostonians who knew the secret, it was generally treated as the work of a well-educated, if unconventional, clergyman. A friend of Theodore Parker's, noting that the author was "an Irish lady" (though he did not reveal her name), reported that he would "find it hard to name the English scholar of the other sex" who might have written the book. The final section of *Intuitive Morals* introduced gender issues that were not in the "Essay on True Religion." The "absurd difference" between "male and female Codes of Honor," she wrote, makes lying a disgrace for men and trivial in women, while the "cowardice which would bring ignominy to the Man" is "*taught* to the woman as the proper ornament of her sex."[47]

Fan was composing the passage on courage and cowardice during the Crimean War. In 1852 her cousin Henry Clermont, then forty years old, served temporarily as lieutenant governor of St. Lucia and hoped to get a permanent governorship in Tobago, near Trinidad. The war, however, intervened. In April 1854 he was put in command of the 4th Regiment, known as the King's Own, one of the oldest infantry line regiments, and set sail for Turkey. After taking part in almost all of the early battles, Colonel Cobbe was on the extreme left flank in the June 1855 attack on the Redan, perhaps the most costly high-level Crimean blunder. Essential to the Russian defense of Sebastapol, the Redan was an external battery with canon whose covering fire kept allied troops from reaching the city walls. In addition to its big guns, the Redan was crowded with ranks of infantry, elbow to elbow. The British high command had neglected to supply platforms or ladders for leaving the trenches, so soldiers—many of them, by this point in the war, young and almost untrained—tumbled awkwardly over the top in great confusion, while officers "rushed along the troubled mass of troops, endeavouring to get them into order." In the words of the magisterial history by J. W. Fortescue, "Altogether the assault of the 18th of June was a disastrous miscarriage."[48]

Colonel H. C. Cobbe, who was on the first casualty list as "severely wounded,"[49] died on 6 August. His sisters Sophy and Eliza, along with Laura and John Locke, came to Newbridge on 21 August and stayed for nearly a month. They were there when the allies entered Sebastapol on 11 Septem-

ber, essentially bringing the war to an end, and also for the baptism of Helen
Louisa, Tom and Jessie's eldest child. So far as Fan knew, Helen was her first
niece; although Henry was a baptismal sponsor, he had not yet revealed that
he had a wife and daughter of his own. In December 1855 the family gathered again to dedicate a memorial to Henry Clermont Cobbe on the wall
of their parish church: "His remains are buried on Cathcart's Hill on the
shore of the Crimea, which witnessed his unwearied fortitude and chival-
rous valour. . . . His memory lives in the house of his fathers, of which he
was the honour, and wherein he was beloved as a dear son and brother."

As Fan continued work on the second part of *Intuitive Morals* she paid
more attention to women's active lives. Until the Crimea, she wrote later,
"the adoption by ladies (not members of Romanist or Greek orders) of any
philanthropic tasks of a public kind had been altogether exceptional. . . .
A new and noble lesson for all their sex did they bring back from that holy
Eastern pilgrimage—that Woman's Crusade. . . . the thought that it is woman's province to do good, to devote herself (when no home duty or special
gift call her elsewhere) to relieve the miseries of mankind."[50]

In January 1856, a few weeks after the memorial to Henry Clermont was
put up on the church wall, a letter arrived from 135 Grove Street, Camden
Town, London, addressed "To the Owner of Newbridge House": "If I am
taking a liberty in writing to you I pray you pardon it I am the unfortunate
Son of your late Nephew Colonel Cobbe of the 4th In losing him I have lost
my only friend able to assist my advancement in life." And so forth. Written on mourning stationery in a neat, clerkly hand and signed "H. C. Willet," the letter went on to ask for money; Willet, who had been apprenticed
as a hairdresser, wanted to buy his own shop.[51] Charles Cobbe wrote at once
to Charles Augustus. The brother formerly in the Ceylon Rifles, Charles
Augustus had left the army and would, as soon as the 1856 County and Borough Police Act passed, become chief constable for the West Riding of Yorkshire. He confirmed that Willet had been born in the mid-1830s to a woman
who afterwards married a silversmith and moved to Edinburgh "with the
understanding that Henry should take care of the lad." Whether or not Fan
was told this fact about the cousin she continued to remember tenderly in
journalistic allusions to the graves on Cathcart's hill, the incident was one
more piece of evidence about the cost of authoritarian parenting. According to Willet, Henry Clermont had told him to "always do that which is
right and honest and fear nothing, had it not been for the fear of offending
my Uncle I should have done justice to your Mother and be a much happier man now."[52]

In February 1856 Fan's brother Henry resigned his post as parish clergyman. There may have been social stress caused by his wife and child or some

discontent with what Fan called the "false position" of Protestant clergy in Ireland, but the putative reason was ill health. Three of Fan's four brothers (Henry, Tom, Will) were apt to be ill when they considered departing from the path laid out by their father. In their childhood, she wrote, "Fathers believed themselves to possess almost boundless rights over their children . . . and the children usually felt that if they resisted any parental command it was on their peril."[53] Over the next few years Henry spent time at English spas and then in Switzerland, where his two younger daughters were born. He apparently lived on money provided by his father, though he might also have been taking pupils or doing locum service for other clergymen.

Fan's years at Newbridge were ending; already by 1856 it was evident that her father's life was drawing to a close. As her own achievements would make clear, she was a great deal like the man her autobiography so ambivalently admires and condemns. Her sense of solitude arose as much from her father's wide-ranging obligations and her mother's withdrawal as from any real isolation. A breadth of experience and knowledge came into the house not only through books but also through brothers, cousins, and friends: India, the West Indies, Africa; the law, the church, the military; money, sexuality, marital stress, and women who made happy lives with one another; familiar conversation with laborers and poor widows and very young working girls. Like her father, she would prove to be ethical, intransigent, stubborn, self-righteous, and endlessly hardworking.

Cousin Eliza visited Newbridge in 1857 and helped read proof for the second volume of *Intuitive Morals,* generally known by the short title *Religious Duty.* By 9 April the final sheets had gone off to London. During the summer Francis W. ("Frank") Newman, the younger brother of John Henry Newman, sent a copy to the Unitarian clergyman James Martineau with a letter suggesting that he knew its author was a woman. "This book has been to me most delightful and profitable," he wrote. "Such a revelation of a pure, tender, ardent spirit is itself an inexpressible stimulus, and has given me quite a flood of joy and sympathy."[54] Both Newman and Martineau became, and remained, loyal lifelong friends of Frances Power Cobbe.

As Charles Cobbe slipped toward death Fan pondered the next stage of her life, examined the possibilities for work and residence available to a single woman who chose not to remain under a relative's protection, and planned the trip she would take once her duty to her father ended. Lodgings in some quiet spot had no appeal. By this time Sophy and Eliza, as well as Uncle William's three daughters, were in Jersey; Fan would later write sadly about the life of women brought up in luxury who found in middle age that they could afford only "two sordid rooms and the solitary dinner of a lodging-house."[55] She knew from her reading that some middle-class women no longer feared the notoriety of public work. The January 1857 *Westminster Review* published "The Capabilities and Disabilities of Women," in which Caroline Cornwallis argued for women's economic independence. A February essay in the *North British Review,* J. W. Kaye's "The Employment of Women," reached the same conclusion. Both articles were cast as reviews of *The Communion of Labour* (1856), by Anna Jameson, whose work Fan admired. In April 1857 cousin Laura's husband, John Locke, was elected to Parliament as the Liberal member for Southwark, a seat he held for more than twenty years. In the last months of the year Fan began to form a plan for quasi-independent work and service. *Religious Duty* shows that she had read Mary Carpenter's *Reformatory Schools* (1855). At the 1857 annual meeting of the National Association for the Promotion of Social Science (NAPSS) Carpenter made two presentations, and Louisa Twining's paper took "the first public notice" of workhouse visiting as a sphere for women's interest.[56]

Charles Cobbe died at age seventy-five on 11 November 1857. All his children except Will were present. Fan's letter to Harriet St. Leger three days later is a conventional combination of sadness and consolation, though a small taste of self-justification creeps in: "I grieve that I was not more to him, that I did not better win his love and do more to deserve it," but "per-

Francis William Newman (1805–1897), rationalist, classicist, and intellectual polymath. Known to his friends as "Frank," he supported a great many reformist causes, including vegetarianism and women's suffrage. (I. Giberne Sieveking, *Memoirs and Letters of Francis W. Newman,* 1909)

haps he knows now that with all my heart I did feel the deepest tenderness for his sufferings and respect for his great virtues."[57] That is, maybe he appreciated her now that he was dead. His will charged the estate with annual payments of £200 apiece for Tom and Fan and £150 for Henry. (There was nothing for brother Will, who had effectively been removed from the family.) The net annual value of the landed property inherited by Fan's eldest brother, Charles, was just over £3,500, but the duties of landlord were a full-time job, and one that Charles had conscientiously done, by this time, for half his life. Of course Henry and Tom had been educated for professions, but neither was then working at his profession any more than Fan had taken up the one for which she was trained. Despite the evident resentment over the size of her inheritance expressed in her autobiography and elsewhere, Fan's father did not treat her any less well than he treated his younger sons. In addition, he left her an envelope with an extra one hundred pounds, a token perhaps suggesting that he sanctioned the plan he knew she had been forming.

Charles Cobbe was buried on 16 November in the parish churchyard; his will specified that "instead of any funereal pomp, a number of the oldest of [his] labourers were given new suits of their ordinary clothing to wear when carrying his coffin to the grave." A week later, Tom's wife Jessie wrote a letter of introduction to her cousin in Athens, banking arrangements were being made, and Fan cut off her hair so that she could travel in hot countries without a maid. By 4 December she was in London applying for a passport.[58] After spending a final night with Harriet St. Leger and her friend Dorothy Wilson on the coast at St. Leonards—looking out at the dark sea and the dark sky and the unknown future—she left for the Continent and found a new life.

⤳ *For viewing human nature . . . commend me to a long journey by a*
*woman of middle age, of no beauty, and travelling as cheaply as possible, alone.*
FRANCES POWER COBBE, *Life of Frances Power Cobbe*

By the time Frances Power Cobbe set out on her eleven-month trip through
Europe, Egypt, and the eastern Mediterranean, foreign travel, even in the
Middle East, was not quite the great adventure it had been fifty years before.
Half a dozen popular accounts besides Harriet Martineau's *Eastern Life Pres-
ent and Past* and William Makepeace Thackeray's *Notes of a Journey from
Cornhill to Grand Cairo* (by "Mr. M. A. Titmarsh") were written during the
1840s, and Murray's first *Handbook for Travellers in Egypt* came out in 1847.
The routes grew standard: Anthony Trollope stayed at the same Jerusalem
hotel as Cobbe in March 1858, and a few months later George Grove visited
the same spots she had seen.

Independent travel, however, especially by a woman on her own, was
not yet customary. Thackeray had gone on a tour arranged by the Peninsu-
lar and Oriental Company. Martineau had accompanied the Liverpool philanthropist Richard Yates and his wife Anne (later an important supporter
of Cobbe's antivivisection work); Florence Nightingale had traveled in the
winter of 1849–50 with Charles and Selina Bracebridge. Both Martineau and
Nightingale, that is, traveled in parties headed by a wealthy man; the Bracebridge group went up the Nile on a private vessel, and Nightingale was
escorted whenever she left her room. Even as late as 1882 the feminist *Englishwoman's Review* recommended that a woman should, at the very least,
take a maid: "If two ladies are travelling together the expense may well be
saved . . . but, if a lady is alone she cannot comfortably dispense with one.
. . . In many places the principal amusement is walking in beautiful scenery,
and for ladies who are tolerably strong nothing is more delightful, but one
cannot, in fact ought not, to take long rambles in very lonely districts quite
alone. . . . The solitary woman at an hotel is thrown on the companionship
of others, whether it happens to be congenial or not."[1]

Cobbe traveled entirely by herself, and although she sometimes shared excursions with others, she freely walked alone in both cities and "lonely districts." The *Saturday Review,* habitually hostile to independent women, was surprisingly gentle to the book that grew out of her trip. "Acting up to her theory of the equality of the sexes," wrote the reviewer, she "set off on a long pilgrimage unprotected and alone; and although dreadful things were prophesied . . . yet she got safely through, and saw and did all she wished." Her trip was a "long formed resolution," and she was determined to go at once; she needed to declare her independence so that she would not be absorbed into a life at Newbridge as maiden sister. But her income would not allow a maid or a packaged tour, and Sophy and Eliza were too hampered by their own, narrower finances to join her.[2] Her boldness was also a consequence of her life during the past few years. She had grown used to quietly going her own way without consulting anyone. Her intellectual interests and her decision not to marry made her less accustomed to thinking of herself as a woman. She turned thirty-five on the day her passport was issued. And finally, she had not only her share of typical British arrogance but also the firm assurance of her class position: she was used to moving freely in a community where her father was the major landowner and both father and brother were magistrates. It barely occurred to her that she ought to be anxious about setting off on her own.

Before leaving Britain she had bought a collapsible bath (on Louisa's recommendation), a railway rug, and a waterproof cloak and strong boots for walking. Messers. Hoare, of 37 Fleet Street, London bankers who advertised in Dublin directories, provided a list of correspondents in major cities to cash drafts. She hid a diamond ring of her mother's on a cord around her neck to sell in an emergency, bought guidebooks, asked friends and relatives for letters of introduction, and set off for Rome on the usual winter route: by rail through Paris to Nice and then by steamer to Civita Vecchia, which was eight hours from Rome by coach. The journey would have taken three days and nights if she did not stop at hotels along the way. Although winter dark had already fallen when she reached Rome, she began as she intended to continue, walking alone "through the colonnade of St. Peter's" for her first look at "the grandeur and beauty of the scene" while the coach went ahead with her luggage.[3]

*Murray's Handbook of Rome* recommended the Hotel de l'Europe in the Piazza de Spagna because it had "bachelor's rooms" as well as more luxurious accommodations and also a good table d'hôte. Cobbe got a cheap single room "on the top of the house." And alone at the Hotel de l'Europe in December, the unknown aging daughter keeping house for her father on a country estate outside Dublin was transformed into an independent woman and internationally acclaimed author. On 26 December she wrote to her sister-in-law Louisa about Christmas at St. Peter's, where she "saw the Pope's full state carried in on his throne like a gorgeous Guy Fawkes & perform-ing High Mass with endless Cardinals & bishops assisting . . . the whole scene impressed me as a . . . *pantomime* of worship rather than anything else—The Pope *kneeling* in *state* (!) seems utterly absurd." She had not planned to go but was asked to join some Americans staying in the hotel who saw her name and "came to ask me was I Miss Cobbe who had writ-ten the book they had read in America." These Americans—Eliza Apthorp, her husband, Robert Apthorp, and her sister, Sarah Henshaw Hunt—were close friends of Theodore Parker's. Imagining that moment makes my skin prickle: alone in a hotel at Christmas and suddenly recognized by strangers as author of a book they admired. "It is very curious & pleasant to me to find how those who only heard of me through my book are so glad to be friends with me," she wrote in that letter home.[4]

During her first week in Rome she went dutifully to monuments and museums, guidebook in hand, copying inscriptions, making notes on sculp-ture and paintings, setting down quotations in English, Latin, and Greek, and making rough sketches to fix details in her memory. Yet by 26 Decem-ber she had already met "Miss Hosmer the young sculptress . . . a very remarkable girl. I have seen a good deal of her in her studio here & am inter-ested in her not a little." Harriet Hosmer, who had been in Rome since 1852, was by this time twenty-eight years old. Her *Beatrice Cenci* had won high praise at the previous May's Royal Academy exhibition in London. Na-thaniel Hawthorne a few months later described her as "a small, brisk, wide-awake figure, of queer and funny aspect, yet not ungraceful . . . frank, sim-ple, straightforward, and downright." The introduction to Hosmer, no doubt supplied by Harriet St. Leger, whose friend Fanny Kemble had urged Hosmer to study in Rome, gave Cobbe entry into a circle of American and British expatriate women. The Italian sun permitted social freedoms not possible at home; new friends were made in public places, with English-speaking travelers, in hotel dining rooms, by mentioning the names of friends of friends of friends. "I am very glad to make some acquaintance-ship with pleasant people," Cobbe wrote to Louisa; "it cheers me more than the sight-seeing."[5]

Cobbe presented her letters of introduction to some of Louisa's Anglo-Irish acquaintances but spent very little time with them; new friendships were much more significant. Robert William Mackay, author of what she called "that awfully learned book," *The Progress of the Intellect, as Exempli-fied in the Religious Development of the Greeks and Hebrews,* invited her to join his family in a leisurely journey to Naples. She wrote to Harriet St. Leger that she was "really cheerful now" and "beginning altogether to look at the future differently." She was especially happy to discover that people enjoyed her for herself, even without the social advantages of her position in Ireland. "I don't think I deceive myself," she wrote, "in imagining that people easily like me, and get interested in my ideas."[6]

From Naples she went by steamer to Messina, in Sicily, and then to Malta, where she connected with a ship scheduled to reach Alexandria three days later. On what should have been its last night at sea a "tremendous gale" forced the ship almost a hundred miles off course. The seas were so high that Cobbe spent one day and two nights on a mattress on the floor to keep from being tossed about. "Presently," she reported, "in the middle of the night, an American lady, with whom I had only exchanged a few courteous words, came tottering into the little den, and sank down on the same mattress opposite me. . . . when that night was over, and we set foot at last upon the shores of Egypt, that brave good woman and I were no longer strangers, but friends, and as friends we lived together for many days." The ship reached Alexandria on a Tuesday, three days late, and was "boarded by hordes of half-naked porters and gorgeously-attired dragomans" clamoring to carry luggage and offer rooms. "Every figure is a picture, new in face, new in dress, new, above all, in bearing and character. . . . the strings of camels, whose large burdens fill the narrow streets from side to side; the innumerable donkeys . . . mosques of red and white stone, quaint and beautiful; shops all open, with all the goods displayed to the street, and the shopman seated cross-legged, playing with his child or his cat."[7]

Various difficulties detained her in Alexandria. None of the four post offices had the letters she expected; Hoare's draft was nowhere to be found. The transfer agents said her trunk would have to go on to Bombay with the luggage of the other British passengers, but "after an hour's pitched battle with the demented Arab-chattering guards and porters" her American friend managed to retrieve it. Then Cobbe found she could not afford Shepheard's, the favorite hotel for British tourists in Cairo; nevertheless, her letter to her brother Charles was resolutely cheerful: "I shall get on quite well, there is no fear—There are dozens of travelers all looking to make up parties & I could at once join some & with people who were on the packet only that they are rather middle class & I like the Symonds (the Americans) infinitely better."[8] The Symonds knew of a pension with a Piedmontese proprietor on the far side of the Nile, in the town called Old Cairo. Italian seems to have been the most useful European language, and the fact that "accomplished" women were taught modern languages, while their brothers spent years at Greek and Latin, gave them a pleasant opportunity "to assist our countrymen out of the multitudinous dilemmas to which their ignorance consigned them."[9]

From the pension, Cobbe made her way daily, sometimes on foot and sometimes riding a donkey, "to the city on one side, or into the desert on the other." One of Florence Nightingale's letters supplies an amusing account of donkey transport: "The donkey is very small, and you are very large . . . and you sit upon his tail; and as he holds his head very high, you look like a balance to his head. After mounting, a feat which is effected by curling your right leg round your saddle bow (the saddles are men's), you set off full gallop, running over everything in your way." Mr. and Mrs. Symonds were wintering in Egypt for Mr. Symonds's health, so they could not often share Cobbe's excursions. Her trip to see the Sphinx and the three pyramids of Ghizeh (Giza) was probably foolhardy. First the donkey boy led her out on a "sort of peninsula of mud," where two or three Arabs suddenly appeared to carry her across a stream and demand payment. When they finally got to the pyramids—a mid-nineteenth-century photograph shows them lonely and desolate amid drifting sand—a party of English-speaking tourists was just leaving. No one else wanted to go inside the great pyramid, so she asked the guard at its door to provide her with guides. Anthony Trollope would write, in "An Unprotected Female at the Pyramids," that the "entrance into the Pyramids is a terrible task, which should be undertaken by no lady. Those who perform it have to creep down, and then to be dragged up, through infinite dirt, foul smells, and bad air; and when they have done it, they see nothing."[10]

When they got to Cheops's burial vault the guides demanded more money. "Horror seized me," wrote Cobbe. "They had nothing to do but merely to go out and leave me there in the solitude and darkness, and I should go mad from terror." Drawing herself together, she "spoke out, angrily and peremptorily—'I'll have no more of this. *You* fellow there, take the light, and go out. *You* give me your hand. Come along, all of you.'" And it worked: "The slave habit of mind doubtless resumed its usual sway with them the moment that one of the free race asserted a claim of command. Any way, it was a simple fact that five Arabs yielded to a single Anglo-Saxon woman, who was herself quite as much surprised as they could be at the phenomenon." Though modern readers are made uncomfortable by her racist and imperialist assumptions, the habit of authority arising from her social position and her experience as the daughter of a man who expected unquestioning obedience gave her resources that balanced the disadvantage of gender. As Harriet Martineau had written, the inside of the pyramid "is a dreadful place in which to be seized with a panic: and no woman should go who cannot trust herself to put down panic by reason."[11]

Cairo's religious variety entranced the student of theology. One mosque she visited had "2 columns 10 inches apart thro which only true believers can pass." "Mrs. Simmons did so readily," but she herself, she wrote, joking about her size as well as her lack of faith, did not. Islam impressed her not only because of "its doctrine of the absolute unity and sovereignty of God" but also by the "profound reverence for spiritual things which strikes so forcibly the traveller who passes from the churches of southern Christendom, with their gabbling priests and distraught worshippers, to the stillness of the mosques of the East, and the solemn prayers of their prostrate crowds." Two Coptic churches seemed to retain a primitive Christianity that would still appeal to low church worshippers.[12] At Heliopolis, the original site of the Cleopatra's Needles, now located on the Thames embankment and in New York's Central Park, "it was curious to sit in the garden under the Obelisk" and think that Moses had once prayed there. She visited a "Latin convent of French and German nuns" and looked at the three institutions they ran. Her nondenominational theism controlled her response to non-European religions: "when we first pass beyond the bounds of Christendom, and see men worshipping God according to a wholly different faith" we are able to "feel the real brotherhood which underlies our variances . . . because form and name have changed, and nothing remains but the substance of religion—the simple relations of creature and Creator."[13]

Although she had to give up her wish to see "the ruins of Thebes and Memphis, Karnak and Philae," because she was "too poor by far" to hire a boat for the trip upriver, she wrote to Louisa without regrets: "I am very glad I came here. It has taught me more than any books could do—& all my life I am sure I shall rejoice to have done it." She had enjoyed the homely as well as the historical, collecting seeds that might grow in Ireland and a "gilt ear of Apis" for the museum at Newbridge. "One day spent in roaming aimlessly through the bazaars, and the gardens, and the mosques of Hassan and the Gama Tayloon, does more to reveal to us what Eastern life means . . . than could be gained by years of study."[14] The people of Cairo, she told Louisa, were "varied, four or five quite distinct types—One Turkish, one the Egyptian of the sculptures *really* to the life—one Negro—one Greek—The Jews do not resemble the English Jews, I cannot distinguish them from the mongrel Levantines." Or, more poetically, in a mode fit for publication, "crowds of men and women, some clad in magnificent robes, some with their broad chests and bronze limbs nearly bare; but all, without exception, possessing the unfailing birthright of Eastern races—grace, and ease, and dignity."[15]

After a month in Egypt Cobbe found "two very nice English ladies," Miss Giles and Mrs. Sieder, who were going on to Jerusalem. The party also included "a good natured young Irishman—a couple whose names I dont know—& two horrid old women from Louisiana a Mrs Thomas & a Mrs something like Killjoy! The Giles & I intend to leave them as soon as we get to Jerusalem for we know they will go on comparing the Jordan (as they do the Nile) to that eternal plague the Mississippi & tell us that the Mount of Olives 'they calculate is nothing to the Alleghenies.'"[16]

The trip from Alexandria to Jaffa took two days on a French steamer. Conditions in Palestine were primitive: Passengers disembarked into small boats because the harbor had no landing stage. There were no roads for wheeled vehicles, "merely mule-tracks between important places," and Jerusalem was thirty-five miles inland. The indispensable requisite for such a trip, Cobbe wrote, was the "power of riding on horseback. Any lady whose strength is unequal to such exercise, should not think of the journey." But although she had been warned of extreme danger—that some "English who tried to settle there have been murdered between Jaffa & Ramla"[17]—the risk had been exaggerated, as had some of the other difficulties. A ladies' saddle was easily hired. "I had given up riding, since the distant days of my girlhood," she wrote; "but finding myself once more on a good horse was like youth again. [The horses] gallop readily whenever galloping is practicable . . . pick their way down precipices; stumble about, but never fall." A Christian merchant at Lydda provided refreshment "in proper Eastern style; seated on carpets & cushions," and the convent in Ramla, where they spent the night, was enchanting: "The little wicket in the centre of the great gate; the jolly picturesque Franciscans; the court set apart for women; the hasty dismissal of such of us as ventured to put our profane noses into more sacred premises."[18]

The next day was more grueling. They were awakened at three and in their saddles "at halfpast 4 by moonlight." The "high-road to Jerusalem" was little more than a footpath: "I have since ridden over still worse passes in Lebanon & have also gained such confidence in the horses of the country as to lose the little nervousness which one feels at first," she wrote. "But that day was really terrible to us all." As evening fell they were still surrounded by barren hills. Cobbe "suggested writing to Dr. Strauss [the author of *Leben Jesu*] to inform him that Jerusalem itself was a myth & that we had proved it," when at last the city lay before them: "The talk and laughter at once died away. We sat motionless, to gaze at the City of Christ."[19] They went gratefully to their rooms at Christian Hauser's Mediterranean Hotel, where Cobbe slept for fourteen hours.

"It was a strange feeling to waken in Jerusalem," she wrote. "The quaint room in which I had slept opened out on a large deep pool: *that* was the Pool of Hezekiah!"[20] Yet although she was often moved by scenes that sprang alive after half a lifetime's Bible reading, she retained a certain distance: "It seems to me as if Christians must be, and in fact are, overwhelmed

Jerusalem as sketched by Frances Power Cobbe from the roof of Christian
Hauser's Mediterranean Hotel in 1858. (Cobbe Papers, Alec Cobbe Collection)

and confounded to find themselves in the scene of such events. To me it is
all pleasure." To cousin Eliza, who shared at least some of her religious opinions, she could report going alone "into the little spot hardly six foot square
where lies the plain marble altar-tomb said to be that of Christ. It was nearly
dark—a solemn place to any body's feeling—Never more than here have I
felt *how* monstrous is the creed which speaks of a Dying God!"[21]

In Jerusalem as in Cairo, the people were as interesting as the "sights."
Cobbe laughed with Anthony Trollope at the ridiculous blur of sacred and
silly in mealtime conversations at the Mediterranean Hotel; he provides an
example in *The Bertrams*: "Mrs Rose, we are going to have a picnic on Monday in the Valley of Jehoshaphat; will you and your young ladies join us? We
shall send the hampers to the tomb of Zachariah." (Trollope also disliked,
as she did, the English rudeness in holy places of other faiths.) Sketches and
pressed leaves in the manuscript of "A Lady's Ride" and in her notebook
commemorate visits to the "wall of Solomon's Temple called the Jew's Weeping Place," the Damascus Gate, the Mount of Olives, and Gethsemane. As
she looked at scenes first seen in Calmet's *Great Dictionary of the Holy Bible*—
one of the few books allowed on Sundays at Newbridge—she bid a last farewell to her childhood religion. "Gethsemane," she wrote, seems "the holiest spot on all the earth—far more so than Bethlehem, more so than Calvary
itself. . . . The story of the Agony is one that belongs to the life, not of Christ
alone . . . all deep and true lives have a Gethsemane—a time when a man

must decide to do the right, even when all hope of happiness . . . seems sacrificed thereby."[22]

After a week in Jerusalem Cobbe set off with a group of English and American travelers on a tour to "Hebron, Bethlehem, Marsaba, the Dead Sea, Jordan, and so back to Jerusalem by Jericho, the Mountains of the Temptation, and Bethany." It was "necessary to hire a regular Dragoman," who supplied horses, tents, meals, guards, and servants at a cost of about sixteen shillings a day for each person. "We shall have 3 nights in tents," she wrote to her cousin Eliza. "I am rather afraid of such awful roughing & fatigue but it is worth the trial."[23] And once again, she grew enormously as she discovered she could do it.

They started out by riding five miles to Bethlehem. At the Church of the Nativity everything was "covered up with red & yellow damask & crammed with the everlasting chandlery & jewellery, wherewith all the priests in Palestine make it a task to conceal & travesty their sacred places." Beyond Bethlehem they had "the unchanging lunch of all dragomen—hard-boiled eggs, cold roast fowl, a mysterious pot labelled 'Auzalozy Jam'—what is Auzalozy? I never could find anyone to tell me." The first night was spent in tents at Hebron, twenty miles from Jerusalem. Cobbe believed it to be "not only one of the oldest, but certainly one of the least-changed of all the towns in the world. Riding slowly thro' it in single file, making our salaams to the smiling & courteous people—we saw nothing to give us an idea that European civilization had begun to affect, even ever so lightly, the condition of things."[24] In thus dehistoricizing the East (a trait common among British tourists at the time) Cobbe gained support for her thesis of progressive religious evolution leading eventually to universal theism.

On the second day, they rode into the Judean hills, seeing very little evidence of human habitation. "I must doubt," she wrote, "how more than a 10th part of Judea can ever be brought into cultivation." They stopped near the monastery of Mar Saba (or San Saba), where the men were "courteously received and comfortably lodged within the noble walls," while the women had to sleep in a tent pitched in a nearby ravine. It was "not a nice place to sleep at—that is to say, for people with prejudices on the subject of centipedes. . . . it is quite impossible in a tent to exercise anything else but hospitality towards any visitors who may choose to 'drop in.'" They lay down with "terrible misgivings" but, even with the sound of jackals and hyenas in the night, slept "the sleep of people who have been eleven hours in the saddle."[25]

Despite the centipedes and her own love of comfort, after two or three nights Cobbe found the nomadic life "beyond all others attractive and fascinating" and "wished it could go on for months. . . . We learn there at last—what so many of us forget after childhood—that simply to exist in health is a blessing and a joy;—to breathe the morning air, awakened from the sound slumbers of real fatigue—to eat rough food with keen appetite— to mount the willing, spirited Syrian horse, and start for the long day's travel with the sun mounting into the cloudless sky of Palestine."[26] The next day, three or four hours of "hard riding & mane-holding" brought them to the Dead Sea, where Cobbe bathed but found the stones so sharp she could not go out "deep enough for a swim to prove its celebrated buoyancy." Another four hours brought them to the banks of the Jordan, where she gratefully washed off the stinging Dead Sea salt. That night, tenting among the ruins of Jericho, they found "a huge camp of pilgrims," some of whom "danced long and merrily in the starlight."[27]

Something on the trip, however, unsettled Cobbe far more than the punishing climate and the exotic local customs. When they got back to Jerusalem, she moved on at once without her companions, "*ostensibly* for the heat really because one of the ladies conduct did not seem to me satisfactory." To cousin Eliza she wrote more frankly that "Miss Alice Giles aged 50 made love to Mr Rowe in a manner unpleasant to see!"[28] The different accounts Cobbe wrote for various readers help us perceive the personal traits she developed, or revealed, on this trip. By the time she left Jerusalem she was prepared to travel quite alone, though she had remained pleasant and amusing under difficult circumstances and with companions she disliked, such as the flirtatious Miss Giles (recommended initially because she had been staying with the English chaplain in Cairo), and the two women from Louisiana, who were unbearable not only because of their endless talk about the Mississippi but also because of their rudeness to servants, which Cobbe came to believe was typical of Americans from slave-owning states.

She even grew contemptuous of other travelers' timidity. Her last dinner in Jerusalem "was somewhat troubled by the presence of a gentleman who had just ridden up from Jaffa." He said that "the great Arab chief Aboo Goosh was in the field with fifteen hundred followers, scouring the district and seeking to attack another robber chief." The "good, hearty English sportsman" who passed along this information "could not venture to come up to Jerusalem with a less guard than a khawass and five well-armed men." What was a lone woman to do? "I made up my mind," Cobbe wrote, "to arguments nearly connected with my purse, that a khawass and five guards were superfluous luxuries, and that *kismet* (destiny) must take care of me, with the help of Abengo and the muleteer."[29]

Of course it was perfectly safe, probably because Abengo paid protection money to the bandits, and after one more overnight stop at the convent in Ramla, Cobbe was back at Jaffa waiting for the next boat to Beirut (called alternately "Beyrout" and "Beyrouth" in her accounts) and walking along the shore to see the "low black rocks, on which Andromeda was chained when Perseus came to deliver her." At Beirut she could not find any other tourists heading for Baalbec. "I was obliged," she wrote, "to decide either to go by myself or to give up for ever the hopes of seeing the ruins which I had so longed to behold. On one side there was solitude, some larger expense; but on the other there was Baalbec & the grand Lebanon; to be enjoyed all the more, perhaps, alone."[30] Less than a month earlier she had dreaded roughing it; and three months before that she would hardly have imagined going off without any other woman for several days on horseback in the mountains. The British consul recommended a trustworthy drago-man named Hassan, she bought a used sidesaddle for twenty shillings, and they set off on the three-day ride to Baalbec.

On the first night she was awakened by "the arrival of a caravan with mules tumbling over the tent-pegs, and a general hubbub and chattering of Arabic. It was not very pleasant, but courage had come in my long wan-derings."[31] In the mountains "the snows were still heavy and the rains of the preceding days had turned [some passes] into quagmires. . . . In one place the horses were obliged to scramble without their riders, up a regular cata-ract, which was pouring down thro' a gorge in the mountains." That night they camped in a Maronite village she calls Zackly (Zahlah), a small collec-tion of mud houses "wonderfully like an Irish cabin, with the rough door & closed-up window & population of fowls, cats, dogs, & above all lovely rosy children." The Maronite women and girls were very curious about an English woman traveler:

> Having finished my dinner, giving bits of sugar to the children & bones to
> the big dog, who thenceforth became my ally . . . I retired into private life,
> closing the tent-door. Not, however, from "public gaze" could I retire. Rows
> of bright eyes continued to watch me thro' the slits in the canvas. . . . How
> did I comb & brush my hair? & what were the under-garments of "Angliss?"
> The thirst for useful knowledge for a long time overcame all other consid-
> erations, till a vast deal of kissing had been performed on my hands &
> cheeks; & finally, with many a soft word & bright smile, the pretty crea-
> tures departed.[32]

This is the only close encounter with Eastern women that Cobbe describes, although other women travelers of the period tend to concentrate on domes-tic scenes.

The next day, after another six hours in a cold rain, Hassan called out, at least in Cobbe's poetic rendering, "Signora, ecco Baalbec!" Thirty-five miles north of Damascus, Baalbec was originally sacred to the worship of

Baal as sun god and later known to the Greeks as Heliopolis. Its ruined temples may be the most imposing in the Roman world. Hassan refused to pitch Cobbe's tent among the ruins as she asked; he believed they had been built by "djinns" and were still inhabited by them. So she stayed at a lodging in the village: "Hardly had I time to dismount & walk in, when a mat was thrown on the divan & then a soft cotton mattress & a pile of cushions; while a hot pan of charcoal was brought from the adjoining house & placed beside me. The luxury I felt in resting my stiffened & frozen limbs thus comfortably, made me draw an unfavorable comparison between chairs & divans & fireplaces which take an hour to begin to smoke & charcoal-pans, which are carried about ready-lighted."[33]

Baalbec is richly described in "The City of the Sun," published in June 1861 as the first of the twenty-eight essays by Cobbe in *Fraser's Magazine*, but the initial impressions recorded in "A Lady's Ride" supply much more information about the goddess she admired. One of the temples had many examples of "a female half-length figure. It is in various attitudes, & apparently with various attributes. . . . Is this Astarte? If so, how comes this Temple to be called that of Jupiter. I have never read any discussion of the subject; but it seems we ought to have very sure grounds for calling it the temple of any male god, when figures of a goddess are the only ones visible in it." For most of three days she spent her time alone in the ruins drawing careful sketches. "Underneath Baalbec in all directions," she wrote to Louisa, "run subterranean tunnels also of gigantic masonry. I cannot understand their use. The roofs contain the same . . . relief figure of a goddess which appears under the portico of the temple."[34]

Despite an unpleasant attack of chills and fever, she decided to press on to Damascus, another two days' ride. As they climbed the Anti-Lebanon Mountains, however, the cold grew worse; the muleteer who was carrying their tents and baggage took a wrong turn; and a party of Arabs heading in the other direction told them the pass was still buried in snow. They turned back, spent one more night in Baalbec, and then made the three-day return trip to Beirut. After more than six days on horseback, Cobbe told Louisa, she was very glad to have seen Baalbec, "though the exertion was very great & the hardships I went thro' rather trying."[35]

Her voyage on to Athens was also "full of miseries." She had barely enough cash for a second-class steamer with no stewardess and no other woman passenger, though she wrote to Harriet St. Leger with typical good cheer: "Behold me seated *à la Turque* close to a party of Moslem gentlemen who alternately smoke and say their prayers all day long." After stopping at Cyprus, Rhodes, Smyrna, and other island ports, they reached Athens at sunrise on Monday, 5 April. There she "found 11 letters including one from

Baalbec. In this sketch by Cobbe the six immense columns are a fragment of the temple of Jupiter she describes in "A Lady's Ride Thro' Palestine." (Cobbe Papers, Alec Cobbe Collection)

Hoare" and went at once to collect fifty pounds from the bank. Eating a breakfast of bread and honey, she feasted also on the review her cousin Eliza had sent from the March *Eclectic Review;* it treated both volumes of her *Intuitive Morals* together with F. W. Newman's *Theism* and called the authors "two accomplished, sincere, and earnest men."[36]

Later in the day, after she had sent her sister-in-law Jessie's letter of introduction, George Finlay came to the hotel and offered his services. Not only was she back in civilization but she was introduced to people with valuable intellectual credentials. Finlay, described in the *Times* obituary published on 2 February 1875 as "probably the last survivor of that small band of enthusiasts who went out to Greece to join Lord Byron and the philhellenes," had settled in Athens and written a massive history of the Greeks. "All I ever expected of beauty is far more than fulfilled," she wrote to Eliza. "I ramble all day sometimes alone sometimes with Jessie's cousin Mr. Finley . . . it is a delight to me & I flatter myself pleasant to him to converse as we do about all old Greek history & the philosophy of evidence &c."[37] She spoke with him about Byron, pressed flowers from the Academe and the Acropolis, and sat up over a late dinner for the first time in months.

Next came a short stay in Constantinople (now Istanbul, the former Byzantium), which was "rather a disappointment"; still, she drew a careful sketch of the Scutari Hospital, where Florence Nightingale had worked only

four years earlier. She asked whether any "foreigners were going to obtain
the needful firmaun for visiting the Mosque" of Saint Sophia so she could
go along by paying a share of the expenses, but she located only some Americans who refused to let her join them. She had a sweet revenge later, in
Florence, since she had already mentioned her disappointment to the
Brownings and other literary people before the Americans arrived hoping
for invitations to enter their circle.[38]

After Constantinople she planned a trip to the Grotto of Adelsberg, in
Hungary. With a choice between the "rough and gloomy Black Sea, leading
(where I knew I ought to go) to the yet unvisited regions of the North, and
the sweet and smiling Bosphorus luring me to the already traversed Ægean,"
she found that the "stoic example did not exercize sufficient force." An extremely pleasant contrast to the second-class journey from Beirut to Athens,
the "good, nay splendid ship *Neptune*" had a congenial group of English-
speaking passengers, including the marquis of Headfort, a nephew of Cobbe's
old neighbor Edward Taylor of Ardgillan. The five-day trip took them past
the cliffs of Ithaca and "the Peak of Leucadia—'Sappho's Leap,'" a sight she
would describe in the feminist *Victoria Magazine:*

> There—down that sheer precipice of eight hundred feet (so tradition tells)
> fell the woman, whose name floats to us even now, like a perfume of orange-
> flowers wafted along the whole stream of History. Was that wild tale of
> genius and passion indeed a true one? Or was it but a dream, and this its
> fitting close . . . we shall never know. Sleep, Sappho! Ideal for all time of
> woman's passion and woman's despair. Sleep beneath thy rock in the depths
> of the unfathomable sea. May another ideal of woman's life and woman's
> hope, arise from the heart of the world ere long, and point to a far different
> doom!

Although literary women were already rejecting as pure fabrication the myth
of Sappho's fatal passion for the beautiful boatman Phaon, not until later in
the century did she become an emblem of love between women.[39]

They sailed on, enjoying pleasant conversation on deck in the brighten-
ing evenings of late spring, past the southernmost point of mainland
Greece. At Corfu, still under British administration, Cobbe spent a day visiting a second cousin she had met long ago at Newbridge. She left the ship
at Trieste, then in the Austrian empire, to make her way by train to the
famous underground caverns at Adelsburg (now Postojna), in southwestern
Slovenia, forty miles from Trieste, a labyrinth of colors, rivers, forms, sta-
lactites, vast aisles, and halls, "all a great, dim, uneasy dream." Once more
she had been drawn to a site that frightened her: "For the solemn gloom
which weighs down the heart and makes the breath come thick, surely there

are no places in the world like the mysterious dark vaults under Baalbec, the Catacombs, the interior of the Pyramids."[40] Returning to Trieste and then to Venice, she was lucky enough to find a pleasant and cheap ride to Florence in a coach that was returning empty.

Cobbe had a sheaf of introductions to expatriates in Florence, including the Brownings, who were pleasant although somewhat less than enthusiastic about Cobbe, and Anthony Trollope's brother Thomas Augustus. (His first wife, Theodosia, according to the *Dictionary of National Biography*, created at the Villino Trollope "one of the best known salons in Italy.") Cobbe also had a supply of good stories about roughing it in the Middle East to make her welcome among the British community. She may have shared quarters with Isa Blagden. "More remarkable," according to one obituary, "for the warmth of attachment she inspired in men and women of acknowledged genius than for the fame of her own intellectual gifts," Blagden was Elizabeth Barrett Browning's intimate friend. She published five novels, wrote for *Cornhill, Fraser's, All the Year Round, Once a Week,* and the *Athenaeum,* and lived economically in Florence by sharing rent with friends, taking care of convalescents, and serving as a companion for young women visiting the Continent. The qualities that made for instant attraction between Blagden and Cobbe may be glimpsed in Alfred Austin's preface to the 1873 edition of Blagden's *Poems,* which stresses her "beautiful Pagan side." She was "remarkably fond of society," always had a house full of dogs she had rescued, was habitually cheerful, and "delighted in bright textures and vivid colours for female adornment."[41] A persistent rumor that she was "the daughter of an unwed English father and Indian mother" seems to be based on no contemporary evidence other than Henry James's reference to her in *William Wetmore Story and His Friends* as having "the hint of East-Indian blood,"[42] but if it were true, it would simply have reminded Cobbe of cousins she liked.

Since early in her trip Cobbe had been making plans to meet people in Switzerland during the summer. After leaving Florence by way of Milan and over the Saint Gothard pass to Lucerne, she got together at various places with Mr. and Mrs. Symonds (the American couple who were friends in Cairo), her cousins Eliza and Sophy, her brother Tom, and, at Montreaux, her cousin Frank and his young wife. She had not seen Frank, who was the cousin closest to her in age, since he had left for India thirteen years earlier. Married in 1855, when he was thirty-two, to Alice, the daughter of Major General Charles Edward Faber of the Madras Engineers, Frank had become eligible for a year's leave soon after the Indian rising of 1857 ended. Frank would perhaps have brought news of his brother Alick, who had been awarded a medal for service in the recapture of Delhi on 23 September 1857, and of their mother, who still lived in Calcutta's most fashionable square. At Lausanne, on Lake Geneva between Montreaux and Geneva, her brother Charles gave her a Spitz she named Hajjin (the Arabic word for "pilgrim"); when he left he took the puppy back to Newbridge for later collection. At summer's end she joined Mr. and Mrs. Apthorp (Theodore Parker's friends) to travel down the Rhine through the German states to Antwerp and then back to London.

Cobbe had learned a great many things in eleven months on her own. When she had left Newbridge a sense of exile from her familiar world had struggled with a rather desperate declaration of independence. She was already intellectually self-sufficient; indeed, her work would have been improved by access to people trained in philosophy and theology. Liberated from her family role and her secure provincial world, she encountered people who knew more than she did about history, art, and society; many of them were engaged by her intelligent interest and her talent for remaining cheerful in difficult circumstances. She certainly had unpleasant experiences, probably more than she ever committed to paper; she was saddled with awkward companions, had to abandon plans because of expense, sometimes found herself alone with inadequate linguistic resources in frightening situations. But she learned to skip meals in order to save money, to make friends with strangers, to move through the world without the visible backing of family and class. She regained her health and spirits, learned to ride horseback again, and grew confident about handling money. (At home, her allowance had always been paid into her hands; when her father died, she said, she knew nothing about the simplest business matters—"how credits are open at corresponding bankers; how, even, *to draw a cheque!*")[43] She grew visibly stronger. On 8 March she had been afraid of "roughing & fatigue"; in mid-March she had gone with only a Turkish guide on a much longer trip into more isolated country; and by the first of April she had taken a second-class ticket on a steamer with no other women on board.

One hardship of returning to civilized life, at least in the accounts she wrote at the time, was having to wear proper clothing and take part in formal society. After dining with the Finlays in Athens she wrote to her cousin Eliza: "I have been rising at 5—riding or walking *all* day—dining at sunset & getting to bed *instantly*—for months back. . . . I have got a bottle of Samos wine here & I never fill my wineglass as you may be sure without saying 'Fill high the bowl with Samian wine' but I regret to state that if it 'made Anacreon's song divine' [as in Byron's "Isles of Greece"] it only gives *me* what Florence calls 'a cheap pain in the stomach.'"[44] She claimed she could "hardly sleep in a room with closed windows." Even more unpleasant was the return to city clothing. In her manuscript of advice to intending travelers, she reminded women that "every parcel must be packed on a mule every morning." The essentials included very strong boots, a broad-brimmed straw hat, and two cloth skirts short enough that they would not "continually get wet in passing thro' torrents."[45] For the remainder of her life Cobbe was impatient with fashionable clothing, especially ladies' garments that did not permit free movement.

Travel also opened her path into writing as a profession. Elizabeth Eastlake had written in "Lady Travellers" (which had been printed in one of the periodicals taken at Newbridge) that publication was acceptable for a lady when it was "merely the editorship of her own journal, undertaken for the amusement of her children . . . or the building of a school. . . . she can hardly be said to stand committed as an authoress." But from the moment Cobbe began writing up her own account, she hoped it would be "an amusing circulating library book."[46] Although they were not initially published in that form, her travel essays gave her entry into the profitable and intellectually reputable venue of *Fraser's Magazine*. And finally, the friendships made in Rome and Florence introduced her into networks of independent and activist women that showed how she might find both significant work and a rewarding personal life outside the family sphere for which she had been raised and educated.

*Descending from the Alps into Italy is always like passing from winter into summer. Be the season of the year what it may, we never fail to feel the same sense of coming into sunshine . . . we have left behind the atmosphere of black frosts, moral and physical, and may expand ourselves happily in a much milder medium.*

FRANCES POWER COBBE, *Italics*

During the final months of her trip Cobbe was, as she wrote, "looking out to see what use I could make of my life." She wanted to work, although not necessarily to earn money, and she wanted a respectable living arrangement that would give her some independence. She talked with Isa Blagden about nursing or hospital administration, much to the dismay of Elizabeth Barrett Browning, who told Blagden that she "might as well try to fly as do work in a hospital . . . be sure that there is good to be done in Florence even, and better truths to be taught to men and women and children than any reached by Miss Cobbe." Then on her way through London, Cobbe met what Theodore Parker called the "delightful company" of social activists that included Clementia ("Mentia") Taylor, who, with her husband, the Unitarian MP Peter Alfred Taylor, was at the center of many progressive causes. (The Apthorps had good transatlantic connections with radical Unitarians.) Through this group, by way of Harriet St. Leger, or perhaps through some old family connection, Cobbe was put into contact with Lady Noel Byron, who used the substantial income inherited from her father for charitable and educational projects, especially those initiated by her friend Mary Carpenter.[1]

Engrossed since the mid-1830s by the state of neglected and delinquent children, Mary Carpenter had established a successful ragged school (she preferred the term *free school*) at St. James's Back in Bristol and a reformatory school at Kingswood. She still managed both when she opened the first girls' reformatory school in England in a Tudor building known as Red Lodge in 1854. Although by 1857 she was already past fifty, Carpenter's mother had only just died. Lady Byron bought a house on the corner of Lodge Street and Lower Park Row, with side windows looking into the Red

Lodge garden, where Carpenter could live. The biography written by Carpenter's nephew says that she wanted "some one close at hand with whom to interchange sympathy and reciprocate affection" and sought "a friend who might be willing to share her simple way of living for the sake of studying the principles and methods of her work." With the help of Lady Byron, Frances Power Cobbe arranged to pay thirty shillings a week (somewhat less than half of her income from her father's will) for board and lodging and to be given "abundant occupation" in Carpenter's many projects.[2]

The arrangement had several attractions. Carpenter was an unusually well-educated woman who had been taught alongside male classmates, including James Martineau, at the school kept by her father, Lant Carpenter. Cobbe believed she would be "a very religious woman" yet "so completely outside the pale of orthodoxy that I should be sure to find with her the sympathy I had never yet been privileged to enjoy." Some of the drawbacks that later emerged should perhaps also have been evident. Carpenter probably did not want a companion. "I cannot tell you how thankful I am for . . . the sense of freedom which I now have," she wrote to a friend the summer before Cobbe joined her; she felt as if she were just "emerging from childhood." Cobbe, in her mid-thirties, had no experience in steady and demanding employment. The winter before she came had been especially burdensome at Red Lodge. The girls were unschooled, psychologically damaged, and often deformed by prenatal malnutrition and childhood disease; some had already served sentences in adult prisons. In 1857–58 an unusually unruly group began to steal from teachers, break up furniture and crockery, scream out the windows, and escape over the wall. Carpenter had to call the police for help. By November 1858 a new headmistress, who demanded and was given "the right to corporal punishment," had restored order, but the school's newly repressive atmosphere made Carpenter very unhappy.[3]

Furthermore, in September 1858 Carpenter had "adopted" a five-year-old girl. She was not only silly about Rosanna but also inexperienced in looking after young children: "Just think of me with a little girl of *my own!* about five years old. Ready made to hand, and nicely trained, without the trouble of marrying. . . . I feel already a *mère de famille,* and am quite happy in buying little hats and socks and a little bed to stand in my own room, out of my own money."[4]

After making the arrangement with Carpenter, Cobbe spent most of November at Newbridge. Her thank-you note to George Finlay, dated 8 November, reported that "Jessie's two darlings are growing up beautifully. She herself is well & promises us another ere long which we hope will be our little heir."[5] (Charles and Louisa remained childless, and Jessie's "two darlings" were both girls.) Tom, like his sister, had anonymously published a book. *The Noble Traytour: A Chronicle,* by "Thomas of Swarraton, Armiger," was a historical tale of love and religion in pseudo-Elizabethan typography and language. A review from the Dublin *Evening Post* for 11 November 1857 is pasted in Cobbe's scrapbook with "Thos Cobbe" at the top and "FPC" at the bottom, both in her handwriting. After a paragraph of summary and description, she had written: "The faults of the work are, however, hardly less obvious than its merits are great. The tale does not advance with sufficient regularity, and the plot is sometimes obscure. . . . To the dialogues we object even more decidedly than to the occasional lagging progress of the plot." Whether or not she told her brother who wrote the *Evening Post* review—it was published on the day their father died—the book had a full-scale notice in the *Dublin University Magazine* for May 1858. Itself a clever and facetious performance, the essay finds that "Thomas of Swarraton" must be an Irishman who is a proficient commentator on Shakespeare. The anonymous reviewer is not identified in any source I have located. Could it have been Tom himself?[6]

Late in November Cobbe left Newbridge for Bristol. "I like Miss Carpenter *very* much," she wrote soon after arriving. "I have seen her but little as yet, but I feel confident I shall have much happiness in her intercourse." Yet despite her desire to put the best face on everything, especially when writing to Harriet St. Leger, "I have seen her but little as yet" was ominous. By the end of two weeks Cobbe realized that "Miss Carpenter is fearfully overworked. . . . I never sit for a moment with her. . . . She does the work of three people on the food of half a one."[7] Carpenter was effectively the sole manager of the Red Lodge (reformatory) School, although a matron and teacher lived in the building; she paid weekly visits to another reformatory at Kingswood, a four-mile walk each way; and she taught almost daily at St. James's Back, where the ragged school had classes for both day and evening students. Cobbe soon found the work overwhelming and the comforts nonexistent. A notebook she began in Bristol on 3 December 1858 opens with meditations on religion and a few quotations in Greek, but the scholarly notes soon vanished. Already by the end of January Cobbe's friend Frank Newman worried about the grinding schedule and urged her to spend one day a week away from Bristol.[8]

Despite the crush of work, Carpenter found it almost impossible to delegate. Cobbe wondered if she was of any use. She had quickly seen the difference between giving an occasional lesson to a small group of children whose parents worked on her father's estate and coping with fifty or sixty "wild street-boys" in the ragged school. Although Red Lodge had been built as a suburban gentleman's residence in the sixteenth century, Bristol's industrial boom had left it crowded into the city's heart. Carpenter and Cobbe

Bristol social activist
Mary Carpenter (1807–
1877), engraved from a
photograph. (J. Estlin
Carpenter, *The Life and
Work of Mary Carpenter*,
1879)

lived in a tall, narrow house with a steep flight of steps leading directly up from the street, a basement dining room, and uncomfortable horsehair furniture. Even getting to St. James's Back meant walking half a mile through a neighborhood where policemen seldom ventured except in groups. At nine or ten o'clock on a winter night "half the gas lamps were extinguished, and groups of miserable drunken men and women were to be found shouting, screaming, and fighting."[9]

After three exhausting months Cobbe went to London for two weeks with Laura and John Locke. The letters Carpenter sent while she was away tell one side of a story of emotional tension, resistance, and misunderstanding. "You know me as little as any one," wrote Carpenter on 17 March 1859, "if you think that I shd love you one bit better for being a teetotaler [or] a delinquent." Cobbe had hoped for intellectual conversation about religion; Carpenter wanted help from someone dedicated to her work. Possibly both were looking for a mother substitute; though Carpenter was fifteen years older, her own mother's death was recent. "Be sure I am more grateful for your love than for any external help you can give me," Carpenter wrote. And then at once she contradicted herself: "You do not know me; I do not know myself. . . . So please to let it alone. I only desire to do the work given me by the loving Father." She was completely uninterested in anything else. "The other night we both came home late from our various schools," Cobbe wrote to a friend, and after prayers she had begun to talk about the "far-away summer mornings" at Newbridge. Carpenter "listened, as I fondly imagined, and smiled, though rather absently, and then suddenly said, 'I don't think those boys in the Industrial School will ever attend to Mr. Higginbotham if he doesn't take care.' . . . I could hardly answer her, so awful was the return from my beautiful dream to the ugly school and dirty boys."[10]

Though Carpenter's house provided no ordinary social life, it did receive visits from other earnest reformers. Mary Charlotte Mair Senior (later M. C. M. Simpson), daughter of Nassau William Senior, who had written the report on which the 1834 Poor Law was founded, spent two days at Red Lodge House, "where we were waited on by two obliging little thieves." Louisa Twining came with the latest news about London workhouses. Sarah Parker Remond stayed for a few days. A free person of color who had come to England early in 1859, she was, according to Elizabeth Crawford, "the first woman to address mass mixed audiences with lectures that covered both anti-slavery and women's rights." And Samuel May, an American Unitarian clergyman and early abolitionist who was also an uncle of Louisa May Alcott, came with a letter of introduction from Theodore Parker. Years later, Cobbe used his name to authorize her conversion to women's suffrage. He had asked her, she would say, "*why* I should not seek for political representation as the direct and natural means of aiding every reform I had at heart." Whether it was Sam May's "upbraiding" or her own observation of Mary Carpenter's constant appeals to members of Parliament and local authorities, Cobbe was evidently convinced, several years before the British suffrage movement began, that women needed the vote not on ideological grounds of "equality" but for the practical results they might achieve through direct influence on legislators and legislation.[11]

Among Cobbe's unmet hopes about life with Mary Carpenter, the worst was a lack of religious sympathy. Expecting Unitarians to be people of Theodore Parker's persuasion, she was distressed by Carpenter's "stiff and prickly orthodoxy" and her constant references to Christ. She tried to explain her discomfort, but Carpenter was "wounded by my remarks, however tenderly urged; and we never quite stood on the same ground" afterwards. Furthermore, she discovered, Carpenter "was an ingrained Stoic, to whom all the minor comforts of life are simply indifferent."[12] Meals, largely of salt beef and ham, were rushed through quickly. Seeing Hajjin one day "luxuriating on the rug before a good fire," Carpenter "turned solemnly away, observing, in a tone of deep moral disapprobation, 'Self-indulgent dog!'"[13] Trying hard to keep the peace, Cobbe sent Hajjin to some friends who had

Hajjin. This photo-
graph appeared in
Cobbe's *The Confes-
sions of a Lost Dog*
(1867). (Courtesy of
the Rare Book
Department, The
Free Library of
Philadelphia)

a garden; when that did not work, and summer came, she took the dog back
to Newbridge.

The summer trip to Newbridge, which lasted almost three months, was
advised by Cobbe's doctor. (He was, incidentally, John Addington Symonds,
the Bristol physician and long-term suffragist whose son and namesake
became well known as a writer.) Her trouble may have been emotional or
stress-induced as much as physical; her very erratic presence in Bristol reveals
how much she disliked teaching. Theodore Parker, writing on 5 July 1859,
wondered if she had "found the right niche" in a ragged school. Carpenter's
letters during the summer were again filled with contradiction. Cobbe considered some unknown plan involving a "college," perhaps a projected institution for women or working people in Bristol. (Theodore Parker mentioned "Mrs. Reid's scheme,"[14] probably referring to Elisabeth Jesser Reid,

founder of Bedford College, ardent abolitionist, and friend of Anna Jameson and Harriet Martineau.) "Leave me quite out of account," wrote Carpenter on 25 June, and then, two sentences later, "You might make R.L.H. your headquarters perhaps & go there at times? Yet that *mixture* would hardly do." After a summer of Newbridge comfort, seeing family and friends and swimming with Hajjin (who disliked the water very much), Cobbe realized that she wanted to plan her own time and make her own decisions. She would remain at Red Lodge House but take up a different pursuit. "I am glad that you are looking forward with pleasure to *working* at the poor Workhouse girls," Carpenter wrote on 12 August; "I should have attacked the subject many years ago."[15]

Six months of labor under Carpenter's direction had, however, broadened Cobbe's mental outlook. Visiting the children's homes—an essential part of Carpenter's program for successful free schools—she saw families disabled through no fault of their own and "rooms where whole families sleep together . . . rooms swarming with vermin—odious with intolerable stench." The marvel was, she wrote, "not that disease and wickedness result from such conditions of life as are here to be found, but that children ever grow up under them, and arrive at manhood and womanhood with some modicum of health and strength, some residue of modesty and uprightness. The notion that they can attain to natural vigour, or preserve complete purity, is the delusion of novelists and poets. 'Marian Erles' as often grow up with Marian Erle's training as orange trees spring on northern moorlands."[16]

Her experience with the ragged school gave Cobbe information that she would use effectively in describing the problems of board schools and truancy regulations after the 1870 Education Act. She understood that the "mother or sister who brings the child is herself a sad 'thing of shreds and patches'" whose lack of money and skills made exhortations about family reading and a good breakfast futile; education of the poor could not succeed unless schools took children as they were and provided everything they needed, including baths, food, medical examinations, eyeglasses, warm clothes, pencils, and caring adult eyes and ears. She explained these things in *Echo* leaders and in support for women school-board candidates in the 1870s. "These children are *ours,*" she wrote, quoting Mary Carpenter; "they will become the people of our land. It is not their fault that they exist in this state of degradation. . . . For our own sakes as well as theirs we ought to . . . prevent their growing up thus uncared for."[17]

The National Association for the Promotion of Social Science met in Bradford in October 1859. Whether Cobbe attended the meeting is not certain, but she certainly heard about it; Mary Carpenter read two papers.

Founded two years earlier to discuss social policy, the NAPSS welcomed women. Not only could they give papers and take part in discussions but they were also, as Ray Strachey revealingly remarks, "allowed to eat, and not merely to look on, at the public dinners."[18] And the association had significant political weight. Its first general committee included eighteen peers, at least twenty-eight members of the House of Commons, and many other well-known men, such as John Stuart Mill, John Ruskin, Charles Kingsley, Matthew Davenport Hill, and Frederic Denison Maurice. Cobbe's participation in subsequent meetings made her known to men in high places. The annual conferences also gave women who worked in provincial towns a chance to network, exchange ideas, make alliances—and socialize.

During the 1859 NAPSS conference, the Workhouse Visiting Society held its first annual meeting. Louisa Twining took Cobbe with her to see several London workhouses, as well as a hospital for incurables in Putney.[19] Twining had struggled long and hard to get permission for women with no official connection to enter workhouses for any purpose whatever. Under the 1834 Poor Law, the workhouse was intended not only to provide food and lodging for those who had no other means of support but also to enforce conditions so punitive that people would fall back on public assistance only as a very last resort. Visitors who came to offer some cheer even to the most helpless inmates—orphaned children, people with no one to care for them in a terminal illness, frail elderly women—were looked on with suspicion.

Of course, in a sense the workhouse bureaucrats were right; few public officials willingly submit to outside inspection. Workhouse visitors immediately documented mismanagement and made a nuisance of themselves getting regulations changed. Cobbe would explain in "Workhouse Sketches" that the Poor Law should have three aims: (1) to "repress pauperism," (2) to educate orphans and "fit them to earn their bread honestly," and (3) to provide for the sick, disabled, aged, helpless, and suffering "a shelter which should partake of none of the *penal* elements which belong to the treatment of the idle and vicious pauper." And as she showed through vivid examples, it failed at all three. For able-bodied men and women there were punitive conditions but no assistance toward self-support. Orphan children were undernourished, unloved, and given little vocational training. And workhouse infirmaries were badly constructed, badly managed, devoid even of proper arrangements for cleanliness, attended by the only medical men who would do the work—that is, either rank beginners or those who had failed at private practice—and nursed by "male or female paupers who are placed in such office without having had the smallest preparatory instruction or experience" and paid with "allowances of beer or gin." Like Louisa Twining,

Cobbe enlisted the assumption that women were naturally good at caring for infants, children, and the elderly to justify female supervision in workhouse management. Guardians of the poor were simply unsuited: "there never yet lived a man whom the matron of an institution could not perfectly deceive respecting every department of her work."[20] If this was a class-based argument—the matron was, after all, a working woman—Cobbe recognized that she was both badly paid and without any influence over the budget; male taxpayers, who elected the guardians, wanted most of all to keep taxes down. And even in the workhouse, Cobbe came to believe, men looked after their own: "wherever there was a choice between large and fairly good wards and others with some terrible defect . . . the *good* wards were given to the sick men, and the defective ones to the sick women!"[21]

Cobbe collaborated on workhouse projects with Margaret Elliot, whose father was Gilbert Elliot, dean of Bristol cathedral. Six years younger than Cobbe, Maggie Elliot took an intellectual as well as a practical interest in social reform. At Christmas 1863 Nina, countess of Minto, described a conversation between her husband and her cousin: "Maggie and William have descended from speculative to practical questions. Political economy is her hobby. . . . He always reasons in *circles, bird like,* soaring ever higher and higher. . . . She sits cat-like below, watching him, never for a moment losing sight of some tough, well-gripped fact." Conversations in that style were meat and drink to Cobbe. Through the Elliots, furthermore, she made other significant connections, including their relative John Russell, who was twice prime minister, and the redoubtable Lady Stanley of Alderley, who was described during the early 1860s as "joint whip" with her husband in the House of Lords.[22]

In addition to visiting St. Peter's workhouse, Cobbe helped Maggie Elliot and her sister Emma run a Sunday-afternoon class for young domestic servants. It gave girls with no family a place to go on their afternoon off instead of walking about the streets and access to helpful adults if they had problems with their employers. This class and similar projects in other towns ultimately gave rise to the Metropolitan Association for Befriending Young Servants, which was established in 1875 with Margaret Elliot on the governing committee.[23]

Across the Atlantic, in October 1859 John Brown and his companions marched on Harper's Ferry to seize weapons from the federal arsenal and give them to enslaved Africans for use in an armed rising. Theodore Parker, who was in Europe in the last stages of tuberculosis, had raised money for the raid. After Brown was executed, Carpenter and Cobbe collected aid for his widow and sent it to the American antislavery activist Lydia Maria Child. By the end of November, however, Cobbe was again ill. Dr. Symonds insisted that she needed better food and regular meals. Another series of fraught and contradictory letters reveals yet more tension. On 28 November Carpenter assured Cobbe that "I have never been hurt by any thing you may have said, because I *knew* you mean nothing unkind," but she continued, "I feel increasingly that I can never be a companion to any one." Three days later she was urging, "even *pressing*," Cobbe to return to Red Lodge House: "You can be *'your own mistress'* . . . & can take your meals at whatever time you like." Rosanna, the child Carpenter had adopted, was part of the problem. "I do not feel that it would be right to send her away," wrote Carpenter, "& am trying to bring her under more control. Still I will do all I can to keep her from annoying you."[24] After several more, increasingly emotional exchanges Cobbe decided to spend the winter in Italy and to take lodgings elsewhere when she returned to Bristol.

With access to only one side of the correspondence, it is not possible to tease out all the strands of stress and discontent between the two women. Health provided an acceptable reason for Cobbe to abandon a plan she had energetically defended to family and friends only twelve months earlier. I suspect that she found living with Carpenter simply too much like the last years with her father at Newbridge, with little social life, no emotional interchange, and no significant conversation. As she wrote to Harriet St. Leger, "It is rather an awful thing to live with a person whose standard is so exalted, and who never seems to comprehend, with all her pity for actual *vice,* the lax moral half-and-half state wherein most of us habitually muddle."[25] In Italy she had glimpsed other possibilities for single women, and "illness" let her return for another look.

Italy was in the throes of change during 1860. In 1859 the peninsula contained six independent states plus two provinces of the Austrian Empire (Lombardy and Venetia). By the spring of 1861 almost all of the territory had become a single country under King Victor Emanuel. When Cobbe arrived in February 1860, Florence was ruled by Leopold II of Hapsburg-Lorraine, grand duke of Tuscany. On 16 April she saw Victor Emanuel make his triumphal entry into the city: "The beautiful streets flamed with red, white, and green! . . . the free people and their own free soldiers, all one and in perfect unity and order, lined the way and filled the scaffoldings and balconies and roofs! . . . at last, when the cannon sounded, and we knew the king had reached the gates, there was a great hush, and then . . . there burst from the people's heart one low, deep cry of welcome, unlike anything my ears ever heard before."[26]

Cobbe lived with Isa Blagden in the Villa Brichieri, atop the hill of Bellosguardo. Henry James later called it "a picturesque, a vast & vaulted old villa" overlooking "the loveliest view on earth." Cobbe wrote that she and Blagden were both "poor, but in those days poverty in Florence permitted us to rent 14 well-furnished rooms" and "engage an open carriage with a pair of horses to do our shopping and pay our visits."27 For all that, including wages and food for two servants, they spent twenty pounds a month. Cobbe's share of ten pounds was less than twice what she had paid for salt beef in a narrow house on a dreary street in Bristol.

Cobbe and Blagden filled the large, handsome drawing room with guests at least once a week. Kate Field, later a successful journalist but then a very young American traveling with her mother, wrote about meeting "Hattie Hosmer, Emma Crow and young [Ned] Cushman, the great Charlotte's nephew; and we all laughed immoderately at nothing, as people always do whenever Hattie Hosmer is present." Field developed something like a crush on Cobbe and asked Cobbe to write something for her. The American publisher James Fields and his wife Annie (no relation to Kate Field) also visited. But although George Eliot was then in Florence staying with Thomas and Theodosia Trollope, Cobbe did not accept an invitation to meet her because, she explained in a private letter many years later, she had "a very strong old fashioned prejudice in favour of lawful matrimony & against such unions as hers. . . . What infinite pity it was that her real genius allied itself in such base fashion!"28

On 26 April, and on many subsequent days, Cobbe walked down the hill to visit Mary Somerville. Born in 1780 and therefore very nearly the same age as Cobbe's mother, Somerville had been known since the mid-1820s as the era's outstanding woman of science. Cobbe described her as "a slender woman of middle height . . . always dressed in some rich silk, dark brown or black, with soft lace and cap. . . . She drew every one nearer to her; and to younger women, whom she treated with motherly kindness, it was often impossible to forbear from passing an arm of protecting tenderness round the form which seemed so fragile, or caressing the aged hand which lay so readily in their own."29 Unlike Mary Carpenter, who had been fifty-two to her own thirty-six—not young or flexible-minded enough to be a "contemporary" but in no way motherly—Somerville became the perfect mother of Cobbe's dreams, with the voice and manners of her own mother's generation but with wide-ranging intellectual and social interests, a love of serious conversation, and a mind that could be worshipped.

As spring lengthened, invalids who had spent the winter in Rome made their way toward the more salutary air of Florence. Among them was Theodore Parker, traveling slowly and very close to death. On 28 April Cobbe saw him for the first time, "lying in bed his back to the light. . . . He took my hand tenderly . . . I kissed his hand and I daresay he felt a tear on it." Her notebooks thereafter record daily visits. By 6 May he was generally doz-

Mary Somerville
(1780–1872). Even in
her eighties, she still
wrote on scientific
topics. (*Personal Rec-
ollections of Mary
Somerville,* by
Martha Somerville,
1874)

ing, and he died four days later. "I saw him about three hours before he
died," she wrote to Frank Newman, "lying calmly, while life was ebbing away
unconsciously to himself. He left written directions for his funeral, limiting
to five persons the attending him to the grave, of whom I am one."[30] Harriet Beecher Stowe reached Florence just too late to see her countryman
before he died. On 19 May Cobbe wrote that Stowe "drank tea with Isa &
me on the terrace. She is much younger than I supposed . . . face not so
plain—full of intelligence yet not handsome—has a habit of not looking at
you."[31]

In addition to visiting and entertaining, Cobbe went to look for useful
ideas in Italian institutions. A letter about the Monte Domine Workhouse
appeared in Louisa Twining's *Journal of the Workhouse Visiting Society* for
July 1860. Concluding with the printed signature "C," this appears to be the
first essay Cobbe published. Soon after Cobbe had left Florence, Elizabeth
Barrett Browning wrote to her sister-in-law that Cobbe was "so perfectly
without Continental prejudices, that she didn't pretend to much interest
even in our Italian movement, having her heart in England and with the
poor."[32]

By the end of June Cobbe was settled in the Bristol suburb of Clifton.

She had two pleasant rooms facing the fine open spaces of Durdham Down in a lodging house kept by a widow named Catherine Stone, who was close to her own age and did not object to Hajjin. In the six months since Cobbe had left England there had been significant developments in what would soon be recognized as a women's movement: Maria Rye opened a law-copying office staffed by women at 12 Portugal Street in London; Emily Faithfull began the Victoria Press; Elizabeth Garrett entered on her private study of medicine; Isa Craig was appointed secretary to the NAPSS, which men such as Henry Fawcett and John Stuart Mill thought "a great thing" for women. In addition, *Essays and Reviews,* in which Benjamin Jowett and other liberal churchmen discussed recent biblical criticism, was published on 21 March. During that summer, when roses were in bloom, a flirtation or courtship or whatever it was between Jowett and Maggie Elliot began at a gathering in the garden of Brasenose College.[33]

Tom and Jessie had taken a house in Devizes, some thirty miles east of Bristol. (The child born in April 1859 was, to everyone's relief, a son.) In August Cobbe went to visit them and met Mary Somerville's great-nephew William Fairfax. They talked about genealogy, and Cobbe wrote to Somerville of her excitement on realizing they could not "be further than *6th* cousins!!" The letter then outlines a plan she and Maggie Elliot were drawing up for improving the treatment of incurable patients and describes Jowett's contribution to *Essays and Reviews* as "such a rational doctrine of the Interpretation of Scripture" that she found "wonderful little difference between him & ourselves."[34] Whether or not Somerville really agreed or was interested, Cobbe felt free to write openly about both charitable and religious matters that were close to her heart.

Back in Clifton, Cobbe used her research skills to assemble statistics about deaths from cancer and tubercular diseases. Freed from Mary Carpenter's sixteen-hour workday, she also enjoyed an adult social life. On 25 September she spent a "pleasant evening at Canon Guthrie's." Jowett visited Bristol several times—to see Maggie?—and came to tea with Cobbe. He encouraged her to write on social questions and to make her books more interesting by "throwing more feeling into them and adapting them more to what other people are thinking and feeling." "The great labour of writing," he advised, "is adapting what you say to others."[35]

Cobbe's first paper for the NAPSS was "Destitute Incurables," written jointly with Elliot for the Glasgow meeting of 24–29 September 1860. The core of their proposal was that since nothing could be gained by imposing a punitive workhouse regime on patients with incurable or terminal illnesses, guardians should put them in a separate ward and allow private charity to supply helpful comforts and better food. The published article that grew from their paper—the first Cobbe signed with her full name—demonstrates her political intelligence: she outlined a practical plan that could be put into operation at no cost to taxpayers, and she added heartrending accounts of the suffering endured by blameless elderly women.[36] She also understood the need for a wider public-relations campaign, since only people already interested in reform would be likely to read an essay published by the NAPSS. Helped by acquaintances who could influence editors, she managed to have eighty-four articles and letters about the misery of workhouse sick wards printed in fifty-four newspapers. Then she had the essay reprinted in a pamphlet that offered help from the Workhouse Visiting Society in carrying out the scheme and sent it to all 666 Poor Law unions in the country. Some fifteen workhouses ultimately adopted the plan.[37]

Cobbe happily spent Christmas 1860 with the family of her friends Rosamond (usually "Rose") and Florence Hill. Florence had joined her in workhouse visiting; Rose taught arithmetic and housework at the St. James's Back Ragged School. Their father, Matthew Davenport Hill, helped found the NAPSS and had been recorder of Birmingham, a post that gave him jurisdiction over the city's courts. Always looking for useful information, Cobbe asked him about "questions of evidence." He told her of a case that had been tried three times: with every trial the witnesses had grown more certain and remembered more details. Although Hill had endorsed female suffrage during an election campaign in 1844 and helped Barbara Leigh Smith draft her *Brief Summary in Plain Language,* like many busy Victorian men, he was in the habit of calling on his daughters for unpaid secretarial services. He once wrote to Mary Carpenter making fun of a women's convention in the United States. Carpenter received the letter with an extra paragraph:

> P.S. (by the Amanuensis).—Many thanks for the Women's Rights Report, which, notwithstanding I have been constrained to write so sarcastically of above, I heartily rejoice in. Could a more convincing proof of our "enslaved condition" be afforded than in my being made an instrument for ridiculing the struggles of our sex for liberty by one of our "tyrants?"
>
> Florence Hill

On the other hand, serving as their father's assistant provided both Rose and Florence with a valuable apprenticeship that would become enormously useful to women's causes over the next half-century.[38]

Early the next year, Cobbe broke into the field of intellectual journalism. Her wide network of contacts was one key to her rapid success. Mentioning the name of Elisabeth Reid, founder of Bedford College, she submitted an article to David Masson, who edited *Macmillan's Magazine.* It

was the first of the shilling monthly magazines that, around 1860, gained
wide circulation among a fairly well educated public by combining the political and religious essays found in substantial quarterly journals that sold
for half a crown with serialized fiction, poetry, travel sketches, and other
more popular material. While *Cornhill,* the second of the breed, made its
reputation with excellent fiction—its first editor was William Makepeace
Thackeray—*Macmillan's* became known for quality essays and nonpartisan
political analysis.

On 18 February 1861 Masson wrote an unusually complimentary letter
to an unknown author: "I have read your paper. Having an almost count-
less number of MSS. in hand, I greatly feared I might, though very reluctantly, be compelled to return it, but the reading of it has so convinced me
of the great importance of arousing interest in the subject, and the paper
itself is so touching, that I think I ought, with whatever difficulty, to find a
place for it."[39] He got it into the very next possible number, April 1861, where
it appeared as "Workhouse Sketches." Cobbe was paid fourteen pounds, the
first money she ever earned.[40]

Masson's letter asked her to make "a little abbreviation here & there,"
pointed out where it could be done, and gave sound editorial advice: "The
more compact it can be made in relation to the information conveyed, the
greater will be the effect."[41] He also asked if she would object to having her
name published. Anonymity, still common in mid-Victorian journals, has
often been seen as an advantage for women, both because of the prejudice
against "personal publicity" and because women with no professional qualifications could thus borrow the journal's authority to give weight to their
work; although Masson said that publishing names was "our usual practice,"
less than 80 percent of the material even in *Macmillan's* was signed. But
Cobbe already realized the importance of making her name known to editors and to the readers she hoped to influence.[42] The April 1861 issue with
Cobbe's "Workhouse Sketches" had installments of *Tom Brown at Oxford*
and Henry Kingsley's *Ravenshoe,* Dinah Mulock's incisive critique of *The
Mill on the Floss,* and an essay by J. M. Ludlow. Other writers favored by
*Macmillan's* during the period included F. D. Maurice, Henry Fawcett, Julia
Wedgwood, Augusta Webster, Caroline Norton, Harriet Martineau, Henry
Sidgwick, and John Duke Coleridge; both Masson and Macmillan admired
smart women. All in all, it was sterling company for a writer just beginning
to be heard on social subjects.

There is no evidence to show whether Cobbe had made serious efforts
to have "A Lady's Ride Thro' Palestine" published as a book, but when the
light short stories Anthony Trollope crafted from his trip were printed by
inexpensive magazines in October 1860 and January 1861, she may have

been inspired to look for her own periodical outlets.[43] By a piece of good fortune, the prominent historian James Anthony Froude, who had been a friend of Cobbe's brother Henry at Oriel twenty-five years earlier, officially became editor of *Fraser's Magazine* with the issue for January 1861. She sent him an essay on Baalbec slightly revised from the version in "A Lady's Ride," and he wrote a short, hasty, and very welcome note on 28 March: "Your article shall be inserted at the earliest moment that I can command."[44]

Thus in the space of less than six weeks Cobbe had articles accepted by two widely circulated monthly magazines. With the growing literacy and falling paper prices of midcentury, "higher journalism," as it came to be called, was becoming a reputable profession. "The young graduate . . . with a political frame of mind who towards 1860 found himself transported from Oxford in pursuit of a literary calling," wrote John Morley, who subsequently became editor of the *Fortnightly Review* and then of the *Pall Mall Gazette,* a member of Parliament, and eventually Viscount Morley of Blackburn, "had little choice but journalism."[45] For a woman, young or not, the attraction was even greater: journalism offered both public influence and the chance to earn a living wage. Frequent contributors to *Fraser's* in the early 1860s included John Stuart Mill, F. W. Newman, Matthew Arnold, and John Ruskin. Cobbe published twenty-eight articles in the magazine in the years 1861 to 1870. And while signed essays were the exception rather than the rule in *Fraser's,* Cobbe generally made sure that her name appeared.

While learning how to use her pen as an instrument of social reform Cobbe also published anonymously when need be. For example, in April 1861, the month war broke out in the United States, she anticipated "widespread desolation" from failure of the cotton trade and strongly recommended equalizing poor rates so the burden would not be insurmountable in the worst districts. The analysis no doubt came from her memory of the famine years in Ireland, when it proved impossible to provide adequate relief out of local taxes, and the essay appeared in the *Ecclesiastic and Theologian,* a Church of England monthly magazine, where the signature of a known "heretic" would have done no good.[46]

The NAPSS policy of meeting in a different city every year so as to draw on local experiences and encourage local activism took its conference to Dublin in August 1861. Charles Cobbe, who served as a governor of Kilmainham prison, was among the influential local men elected to the society's executive for the year. He gave a dinner at Newbridge for delegates interested in prison reform, including Matthew Davenport Hill, and invited his old friend Alfred Gatty to stay. With 1,671 people in Dublin to attend the conference, a familiar complaint was already heard: too many papers (theoretically limited to twenty minutes each) and too little discussion time.

James Anthony Froude (1808–1894), historian, editor of *Fraser's Magazine* from 1861 to 1874, and biographer of Thomas Carlyle. (Mary Evans Picture Library, London)

There were exhibits, concurrent meetings of groups such as the Workhouse Visiting Society, and inspection trips to local institutions—Louisa Twining saw a prison, a reformatory, and at least two workhouses—but there was also the great pleasure of conferences, a chance to visit with friends. In addition to sociable meals with other women, Cobbe and Twining spent a day walking in the Wicklow mountains and touring Powerscourt.[47]

Women were especially prominent in Dublin. Mary Carpenter, a mainstay of the organization, eventually read more papers than any other participant. Sarah Remond delivered a paper entitled "American Slavery and its Influence on Great Britain." The organization's Social Economy Department took up specific questions on women's employment. The list of women Cobbe saw in Dublin in 1861 is virtually a roll call of early feminist activism. Jessie Boucherett, like Cobbe the daughter of landed gentry, though she had a more substantial income, founded the Society for Promoting the Employment of Women and subsequently edited the *Englishwoman's Review of Social and Industrial Questions.* Emily Faithfull, whose printing press had secured the contract for printing both the NAPSS *Transactions* and the *English Woman's Journal,* gave a paper entitled "Female Compositors." Cobbe's Bristol friend Florence Hill spoke, and so did Maria Rye. Florence Nightingale did not attend, but the paper she sent attracted a packed house. Bessie Rayner Parkes, who was then, with Matilda Hays, editing the *English Wom-*

*an's Journal,* read her own paper and those of three other women in a single afternoon session.

Cobbe herself spoke twice. "The Preventive Branch of the Bristol Female Mission" reported on the free registration office opened by her friend Sarah Stephen to help girls between twelve and eighteen find employment and make sure they had safe working conditions. The second paper pursued her own interest in medical reform. "Destitute Incurables," presented at Glasgow the previous year, had taken up the easiest case. "The Sick in Work-houses," which she presented in Dublin, argued that all patients in work-house infirmaries, not only the dying, needed and deserved the same treatment that other sick people received in hospitals or at home.[48]

A growing proportion of women read their own papers. "Crowds came," said one report, "as if to witness a phenomenon transcending the limits of ordinary nature."[49] Although they lacked the public-speaking experience of the clergymen, barristers, and members of Parliament who were prominent in the organization, women like Cobbe had learned through teaching in schools or Sunday classes how to use vivid examples, make themselves heard, and keep the attention of squirming boys. But many people, not all of them male, disliked the innovation. Margaret Gatty, for instance, wrote to her daughters: "You are aware that *the ladies* form a very prominent feature of these Social Science meetings, and we have a friend among them whom I hope to hear. But, do what I will, it gives me a creepy-crawly sensation, to imagine a woman facing a court full of gentlemen and ladies, and giving them the benefit of her opinions! The opinions may be very good, and it may be very desirable for the gentlemen to know them; but—, yes! there is certainly a but." Even after hearing Cobbe's paper, Gatty remained unhappy. "No! I am not converted, though I was interested by what was said, and liked the lady who spoke. But to hear a woman hold forth in public, except when she is acting, and so not supposed to be herself, is like listening to bells rung backwards."[50]

Perhaps because there were so many of them, or because their papers were particularly good, women figured strongly in accounts of the conference. J. Beavington Atkinson's article in *Blackwood's Edinburgh Magazine* for October 1861 gives a fair sample of the patronizing yet acid tone often employed. "The sociability of science," he wrote, would have been "but dreary and desolate, had not woman come to charm the labours of the day." After devoting several columns of sentiment to the good old days when "man's business was in the bustle of the world," while "women's sphere was within the shelter and retreat of the tranquil home," and paying silly compliments to the "beauteous girls, apparently devoted to science, who, we would hope, had not yet met with their precise 'vocation,'" Atkinson admitted that papers by women were "written with praiseworthy care, and brought zeal, tempered by knowledge, to the elucidation of subjects of pressing practical importance" but objected that "open public controversy with ladies" would be "among all rightminded men, simply impossible." His final point must have especially delighted Cobbe for what it revealed about the man—she had met Atkinson, who was then lecturing on art in Bristol—and about male "protection" of women. He proclaimed: "Whenever, in fact, woman's vital interests came into debate—in marriage, divorce, and kindred topics—we confess ourselves to have been so ungallant as to have wished that the ladies, chiefly for their own sakes, had been out of hearing."

Atkinson's essay provoked Cobbe to compose "Social Science Congresses, and Women's Part in Them." David Masson wrote on 6 November delightedly accepting it for *Macmillan's:* "The whole portion respecting women's part in the congress and their work as substantially fair as it is skillful; & the retort on the masculine jestes most witty. Let me thank you sincerely for such a paper: it will, I believe, make 'a sensation.'"[51] He used it as the lead article for December 1861. Perhaps to add intellectual weight, as well as to build name recognition, it was credited to "Frances Power Cobbe, Author of 'An Essay on Intuitive Morals,' 'Workhouse Sketches,' etc." So far as I know, this was the first time in England that she publicly claimed authorship of her previously anonymous theological works.

Whatever women do, Cobbe wrote in "Social Science Congresses," they are harried by "little worrying terriers, with ears erect and outstretched tails . . . 'Bow, wow, wow! Don't go here—don't go there—don't separate yourselves—don't run together.'" Though she used palatable arguments about gender differences—"We want her [woman's] sense of the law of love to complete man's sense of the law of justice. . . . We want her genius for detail, her tenderness for age and suffering, her comprehension of the wants of childhood to complete man's gigantic charities and nobly planned hospitals and orphanages"—and made other rhetorical gestures to conventional ideas of women's role, she had much more fun poking holes in Atkinson's inflated chivalry:

> Ladies must not meddle with this school. Ladies must not interfere with that hospital. Ladies ought not to give evidence before committees of Parliament. Ladies cannot be admitted into workhouses. Ladies ought not to make a stir about the grievances they discover. . . . They must (we are driven to conclude) nurse the sick without going into hospitals, and look after children without meddling in schools and see evils but never publish them and write (if they *must* write) papers about babies and girls, and then get some man to read the same . . . while they sit by, dumb and diffident.

Thus at the end of the year that she broke into professional journalism, Cobbe produced the first published example of her expert feminist wit, developed both from the exhilaration of women's role at the 1861 Dublin conference and from the splendid opening handed to her by J. Beavington Atkinson and *Blackwood's Edinburgh Magazine.*

Meanwhile, after nursing Elizabeth Barrett Browning in her final illness, Isa Blagden had decided to "endeavour to live in England." She joined Cobbe in Clifton, where Benjamin Jowett met her one day at tea—"an amiable lady who has written a novel and is the owner of a little white puppy wearing a scarlet coat."[52] On 10 October Cobbe's brother Tom's youngest child was born in Clifton, where Jessie was lodging to be near her physician. On 1 November, still in Clifton, the boy was baptized as Hervic—the names of Tom's two sons (the elder was Leuric) were, they sometimes felt, an unfortunate consequence of their father's interest in early English history.

By this point Cobbe saw that she could do the best service, not in practical social work, but through analysis, argument, and persuasion. As soon as she finished the essay for *Macmillan's Magazine,* she mailed out a penny-pamphlet version of *Friendless Girls, and How to Help Them: Being an Account of the Preventive Mission at Bristol* to a long list of newspapers. Her scrapbook has a double-page spread of reviews and brief notices praising the scheme and quoting the essay, clippings from the *Daily News,* the *Illustrated London News,* the *Scotsman,* the *Examiner, John Bull,* the *Bristol Times,* the *British Standard,* and the *Daily Post.* The effort to spread information about practical reforms had an additional function, which she surely understood: it gave her widespread publicity as a responsible and interesting writer. The *Liverpool Mercury* for 13 November summarized "The Sick in Workhouses"; a *Daily Telegraph* second leader for 9 January 1862 quoted a great deal of *The Workhouse as an Hospital* and praised the remedies proposed by "Miss Frances Power Cobbe"; and a review in the *Daily News* for 21 January stated that "whatever subject Miss Cobbe discusses, no matter how dreary that subject may be, the fire of her earnest spirit lights it up, and shines on those who read." This was stirring praise and may have done her good, but it was not entirely disinterested. By the time it appeared, Cobbe was in Rome acting as a foreign correspondent for the *Daily News.*[53]

Isa Blagden had not remained long in Clifton. When she decided to return to Florence, Cobbe made plans to winter in Rome. Bessie Rayner Parkes booked Cobbe to write for the *English Woman's Journal.* "I like Miss Cobbe *exceedingly,*" she wrote, "but I don't agree with her as she very well knows." Although Parkes was the daughter of a Unitarian radical and had been described in 1850 as a startling young woman—"She will not wear corsets, she won't embroider, she reads every heretic book she can get hold of, talks of following a profession, and has been known to go to an evening party without gloves"[54]—she converted to Roman Catholicism in the early 1860s and would have profoundly disliked Cobbe's religious ideas.

When Cobbe arrived on 18 December 1861 Rome was in turmoil. Although the unified kingdom of Italy had been proclaimed on 17 March with Victor Emmanuel as monarch, Rome remained separate, ruled by the pope and defended by French troops. The *Daily News,* like most papers at the time, did not pay expenses for correspondents but did agree that a writer would submit material on a regular schedule and be paid at a specified rate. The anonymous articles pasted in scrapbooks held by the National Library of Wales include a series with Cobbe's note: "All written during my visit to Rome 1861–62. Recd for them £20-odd." The circulation of the *Daily News* was then around five thousand, which was relatively small for a serious newspaper, but it had a following among reformers, and its advertisement in the *Newspaper Press Directory* especially promoted its "Foreign Correspondence." Cobbe's contact might have been made through Maggie Elliot, whose father, Gilbert Elliot, helped secure press support for John Russell, or it may have been through the NAPSS or by way of London feminists; the paper was edited from 1858 to 1869 by Thomas Walker, who had contributed articles to *Eliza Cook's Journal.*

The first of Cobbe's reports from Rome with the byline "From Our Own Correspondent" was dated 19 December and printed on 27 December 1861. At that date she had published only three articles in journals that actually paid contributors, two on workhouses and social science in *Macmillan's* and one travel sketch in *Fraser's.* With the *Daily News* she discovered how to practice journalism as a profession, even as a man's profession. At this juncture in history, she wrote, "Rome is inhabited apparently by French soldiers, English ladies, a good many priests, and a small sprinkling of Italian laymen, exclusive of beggars. Seriously, the military and ecclesiastical elements have thrown into shade all civil life. Soldiers, French and Papal, parade about from morning till night."[55] She quickly learned how to generate the material for real political journalism and developed the language that made her work so vivid. Most of her reports are about politics or scandals or translations of "mysterious documents" circulated by unknown hands. There are eyewitness accounts of demonstrations, reports of rumors that the government was buying up lead to make bullets, and secondhand stories about arrests and troop movements.

Her other principal topic in 1862 was art, especially sculpture. Massive works in marble, including Harriet Hosmer's *Zenobia,* were being packed up for shipment to London for the summer's International Exhibition. Many in the art world did not want to believe that a woman had produced such an impressive and affecting work. An *Art Journal* obituary for a (male) English sculptor referred to "Zenobia, said to be by Miss Hosmer—but really executed by an Italian workman in Rome." (J. Beavington Atkinson wrote anxiously to Cobbe in fear that the slur might be attributed to him.)[56] Cobbe's unsigned article "The Fine Arts" described the process for readers of the *Daily News:* the sculptor makes a small clay "sketch," workmen build an iron armature and lay the clay roughly into form, the sculptor shapes the clay into an exact full-size model, and then stonecutters hew the marble with careful measurements into an identical copy of the sculptor's clay original. Without mentioning her friend's name, Cobbe as an anonymous journalist asserts that all great sculptors, including "Michael Angelo," worked in this fashion. Do people who say that the true artist is the stonecutter rather than the sculptor also think, she asks, that an architect is responsible for a building only if he has "with his own hands and trowel, laid the bricks and carved the columns?"[57]

Like most journalists of the period, Cobbe learned how to sell her material in several markets. "Sculptors at Rome and the Great Exhibition," signed "F.P.C." and printed in the issue for 1 February 1862, was her first identifiable piece in the *Spectator,* where she continued to publish until the 1890s. Political unrest during the pre-Lenten carnival season made five reports for the *Daily News,*[58] an article published in the *Inquirer* for 22 February with the signature "F.P.C.," one entitled "Why Romans Detest the Papacy. From an Occasional Correspondent" in the *Spectator* for 12 April, and "The Eternal City (in a temporary phase)" in *Fraser's* for May. While writing about Italian politics, Cobbe, perhaps because of what she had learned in the Bristol workhouse did not ignore rape and prostitution, an aspect of women's lives "of which I cannot speak, and yet which cannot be passed over in silence." That "the present Pope is himself a man of unimpeachable morals is a subject of almost boastful surprise," she wrote, "and that *many* of his cardinals, or 30,000 priests and monks, follow his good example, no one seems to believe for a moment."[59]

With her return to Rome, Cobbe fell happily into the circle of independent expatriate women that had so attracted her on her first visit. In early 1859 Charlotte Cushman, the American actress famous for her performances as Romeo, had rented handsome quarters at 38 Via Gregoriana, near the Spanish steps. After keeping company in England with Eliza Cook, Cushman had lived in Rome with the English writer Matilda Hays, a founding editor of the *English Woman's Journal.* Elizabeth Barrett Browning wrote, "I understand that she [Cushman] & Miss Hayes [*sic*] have made vows of celibacy & of eternal attachment to each other—they live together, dress alike . . . it is a female marriage."[60]

Florence Hill had once warned a young visitor that the "party of ladies" including Cushman and Hays "brought great discredit on the plans of young ladies being independent of chaperones, by the very extraordinary manner in which they conducted themselves."[61] Buried in the warning was a feature of expatriate life that Hill took as given: even young women expected to be free from chaperones when they were away from their own family and community. Whatever Hill knew or suspected that made her mention two women generally described in masculine terms can only be inferred; at any rate, Cobbe at thirty-nine was no longer young, and despite her friendship with Florence Hill, she was not put off. (Perhaps Hill knew better than to give her such a warning.) Cushman shared her new quarters with the American sculptor Emma Stebbins, then working on *Angel of the Waters,* the eight-foot bronze sculpture that tops the Bethesda Fountain in New York's Central Park, and had an apartment and workroom upstairs for Harriet Hosmer.

Contemporaries almost invariably described Hosmer as "boyish." To Elizabeth Ellet, writing in *Women Artists of All Ages and Countries* (1859), she was "a compact little figure, five feet two in height, in cap and blouse, whose short, sunny brown curls, broad brow, frank and resolute expression of countenance, give one at the first glance the impression of a handsome boy." Barbara Bodichon in a private letter called her a "most tomboyish little woman" who "smokes and wears a coat like a man."[62] With *Zenobia* already packed up for the 1862 exhibition, Hosmer was working on the *Fountain of the Siren,* commissioned by Marian Alford. (Known for supporting women artisans, Alford later established a school of art needlework at South Kensington and was on the original committee for the college that developed into Girton.) Cobbe spent enough time in Hosmer's studio to do service as a model: she wrote beneath a photograph of Hosmer's *Siren* that the "arms & hands" were "copied from F.P.C."[63]

After her life in Bristol, Cobbe reveled in the evidence that women could be cheerful, independent professionals without enduring stoic discomfort or constricted social lives. She saw young women "admirably working their way: some as writers, some as artists of one kind or another, bright, happy, free, and respected by all," and she wrote enthusiastically of the "happy way women club together in Italy." More than thirty years later she still remembered informal meals "including an awful refection menacing sudden death, called 'Woffles,' eaten with molasses. . . . There was a brightness, freedom and joyousness among these gifted Americans, which was quite delightful to me."[64] She called them all "young," which perhaps made their freedom and gaiety more acceptable, but by 1862 Hosmer was thirty-two, Cushman was forty-six, and Stebbins was fifty. They were energetic and vibrant women

Harriet Hosmer's *Fountain of the Siren* (1861). A photograph of the uppermost figure appears in an album of Cobbe's; a note in Cobbe's handwriting reads, "arms and hands copied from F.P.C." (Harriet Hosmer, *Harriet Hosmer: Letters and Memories,* ed. Cornelia Carr, 1912)

whose personalities suited her own. Hosmer had an "inexhaustible flow of wit, drollery, and genial joyous humour," and Cushman had a repertoire of comic Irish songs for entertaining her guests.[65] All were committed abolitionists. Cushman would tour the United States in the summer of 1863 to raise money for the Sanitary Commission, an organization originally proposed by women, which supplied nurses, ambulances, and emergency aid of all sorts to Union soldiers and their families. None of them subscribed to feminine conventionalities in clothing. Cushman often wore a plain skirt with a jacket that was fitted like a woman's but cut like a man's, with lapels open over a white shirt and black tie. Hosmer wrote to a friend when she began the full-size clay for *Zenobia,* "To-morrow I mount a Zouave costume, not intending to break my neck on the scaffolding, by remaining in petticoats." Cobbe herself was vastly amused by the crinoline fad; a letter from Bristol reported that "our boy thieves" steal sticks "to run into [women's] skirts," which would have made them rise at the other side, exposing the victim's underwear. She had continued to wear loose-fitting jackets with skirts short enough to walk comfortably. In 1864 a friend said to her, "My dear, it is not a question whether you dress ill or well—you don't *dress* at all!"[66]

Maggie Elliot was also in Rome. Benjamin Jowett wrote to her there in February 1862 in March Cobbe produced a four-line poem that sounds as if it might have been meant for a birthday:

To Margaret Elliot
My Margaret; What Fairy chose
Her god-child's name with so much art—
The simplest, purest flower that grows—
*The flower with the golden heart?*[67]

But whatever one might wish to read into this verse, a far more significant relationship began that winter: "One day when I had been lunching at her house, Miss Cushman asked whether I would drive with her in her brougham to call on a friend of Mrs. Somerville, who had particularly desired that she and I should meet,—a Welsh lady, Miss Lloyd, of Hengwrt? I was, of course, very willing indeed to meet a friend of Mrs. Somerville. We happily found Miss Lloyd, busy in her sculptor's studio over a model of her Arab horse, and, on hearing that I was anxious to ride, she kindly offered to mount me if I would join her in rides on the Campagna."[68] (It is interesting that Cobbe's account of their meeting invokes as proxy matchmaker the respectable elderly widow Mary Somerville rather than the boyish Harriet Hosmer, who was not only on the scene but also a good friend. Lloyd, like Hosmer, did some work in John Gibson's studio. The carriage ride is also curious, since Lloyd lived at 13 Via Gregoriana, and the Cushman-Hosmer residence was at number 38 on the same street.)

Mary Lloyd was thin, intense, dark, almost four years older than Cobbe, and, like her, independent. She was in Rome without any family member or chaperone and worked at sculpture. Lloyd too ignored many conventions, dressed in plain but distinctive clothing, and must have been smart about business, since her father made her executor of his will even though he had both sons and sons-in-law who could have acted. She had money enough to keep her own horses in Rome and offered Cobbe a chance to recapture the pleasure of her childhood and her liberating trip to the Middle East. "If you make any stay in Rome," Cobbe wrote to a friend during the last week of her life, "do take a long drive in the Campagna, where the air does one's very soul good. . . . Mary and I made our friendship riding together alone all over it, so it is sacred ground to me."[69]

On her way back to England at the end of April Cobbe visited Rosa Bonheur in her studio near Fontainebleau. Mary Lloyd provided the introduction; she, like Bonheur, made animals the primary subject of her art. And

Bonheur, with her practical trousers and her woman companion, served women of the mid-nineteenth century as a sort of touchstone. Whatever the specific signals were, and whatever the dimensions of recognition they identified, visiting Rosa Bonheur was one of the means by which they made known their bonds. Cobbe's essay "Celibacy *v.* Marriage," written and sent to Froude before she left for Rome, reveals that thoughts of discovering a life companion were in her mind. "The 'old maid' of 1861," she wrote, "is an exceedingly cheery personage, running about untrammelled by husband or children," and she is "far more independently happy" than a single man because she can "make true and tender friendships, such as not one man's heart in a hundred can imagine." She need not "contemplate a solitary age" since she can almost certainly "find a *woman* ready to share it." In Bonheur's studio Cobbe remarked that she envied friends who worked together and that she herself lived alone, to which Bonheur replied, "Je vous plains alors!" (I pity you, then!).[70] Cobbe reported this exchange in a letter to Mary Lloyd. It may have served as a safe way to begin asking a question.

When Cobbe returned to England in May she was technically still doing social work in Bristol, but she had crossed over a border that shifted her angle of vision. Her speech at the NAPSS meeting that year was not on charity but on her first unambiguously feminist proposal: women should be admitted to university examinations. The *Saturday Review* was scathing,[71] but the *Times* for 11 June called it the "most interesting paper of the day."

Held in London, the 1862 NAPSS meeting attracted a great deal of attention. On Monday, 9 June, the association was given an unprecedented opportunity to assemble at Westminster. The House of Commons was "crammed to suffocation, the green benches being filled with an enthusiastic multitude from floor to ceiling," and the "Treasury Bench was entirely occupied by a group of very determined-looking social science ladies." Only very recently had the introduction of a ladies' gallery made it possible for women even to hear debates (protected by a grille that kept them from being seen). How extraordinary it must have felt to walk on the floor of the House and sit on the bench occupied by cabinet ministers. On 11 June there was what the *Times* called a "Ladies' Parliament" of the Social Economy Department, where "gentlemen were in such a miserable minority that they were scarcely visible and . . . took good care not to make themselves heard."[72]

The room had also been jammed for Cobbe's paper the day before. Responding to the hearty applause when she finished, Henry Hart Milman, dean of St. Paul's and president of the Education Department, said that if the NAPSS had had the power of conferring degrees he would "be most happy to propose that Miss Cobbe receive from us the degree of M.A. . . . mistress of the art of discussing a subject with sound reason, with infinite

grace, and with perfect propriety."[73] Cobbe had declared that badly educated middle- and upper-class women were unfit even for philanthropic
work and demolished the argument about preserving gender differences:

> It is as absurd to try to keep a woman feminine in mind by making her learn
> French because a man learns Latin, as it would be to keep her so in person
> by making her eat mutton because a man eats beef! Endless are the absur-
> dities of this kind extant among us. Men ought to be well-informed: let
> women, then, know nothing. . . . Men ought to be strong and healthy: let
> a woman's cheek . . . display the charming *morbidezza* of partial disease.
> . . . Not, however, by narrowing and clipping every faculty, not by pinch-
> ing her in mental stays, shall we make a true woman. Such processes pro-
> duce Dolls, not Women.[74]

Cobbe's proposal grew from events earlier in 1862. Elizabeth Garrett had
applied to take the University of London matriculation (i.e., entrance)
examination to certify her intellectual preparation for medical study. After
Garrett's application was rejected, Emily Davies circulated a letter asking
the university senate to "give the widest interpretation to the words of their
Charter, and to 'hold forth to all classes and denominations' of her Majesty's
subjects . . . 'an encouragement for pursuing a regular and liberal course of
education.'"[75] (Established in 1836 so that Nonconformist and Jewish men,
who were barred from Oxford and Cambridge, could gain degrees by examination, London University had no requirement for collegiate residence and
was thus the most obvious place for women to enter an opening wedge.)

Although Emily Davies's letter carried the signatures of twenty-seven
persons of high status (including W. E. Gladstone, R. Monckton Milnes,
F. D. Maurice, and Matthew Davenport Hill, as well as Lady Goldsmid,
Harriet Martineau, Mary Howitt, and Frances Cobbe), it had very little
effect, whereas Cobbe's NAPSS paper attracted wide attention. The *Times*
led its 11 June report with an account that called her arguments "close and
well-sustained" and urged her to "take means to insure for her essay a more
general publicity," and the *Parthenon* said that she "deserved a doctorate on
the spot." The *Illustrated London News* praised her "rare combination of wit
and vigorous argument"; the *Daily Telegraph* used the same phrase, and its
summary of the paper was repeated almost verbatim by the *Morning Herald,* the *Morning Star,* and the *Morning Advertiser.* The *Daily News,* on the
other hand, produced a very clear, vigorous half-column analysis of the central argument. One suspects that the *Daily News* had received an advance
copy—or that Cobbe herself wrote the report.[76]

The Education Department held a special evening session at Burlington
House—for men only—at which William Shaen moved that the executive

American sculptor Harriet ("Hattie") Hosmer (1830–1908) as sketched by Cobbe at Newbridge in 1862. (Cobbe Papers, Alec Cobbe Collection)

council "represent to the Senate of the University of London the desire-ableness of their undertaking the duty of affording women an opportunity of testing their attainments in the more solid branches of learning." Almost all of the speakers said the issue was very important but, as so often happens in such meetings, raised legal and procedural questions; the discussion bogged down, and Shaen's motion did not come to a vote.[77]

Less favorable publicity set in once the essayists in weekly magazines had a chance to polish their phrases. The *Saturday Review* was scathing: "If Miss Cobbe means that sex is a mistake, why does she not say so?" In inimitable *Saturday Review* fashion, the writer also explained that he would be "read-ier to listen to the lecturers if they had not so many of them *Miss* before their names. . . . An unmarried woman is only half a woman, and therefore can only deliver half-truths." The *Spectator* appreciated the "vivacity and vigor" of Cobbe's paper but thought London's examination would put "half the young women in the country in brain fever or a lunatic asylum." Even Emily Davies, subsequently the founder of Girton College, thought Cobbe had demanded "too much too quickly" and made women "the butt for endless jokes."[78] Davies's own proposal was outlined at the Birmingham NAPSS meeting six years later. The separate institution she brought into being gave women the social as well as educational advantages of collegiate instruc-tion—if they could leave home and afford the fees. Cobbe's suggestion for degrees by examination was meant partly for young women like herself, who studied on their own with the help of family libraries; but, more importantly, it would have given working governesses, whatever their age or finances, a chance to certify their learning. Sixteen years later, when the University of London did finally amend its charter, Cobbe went with a delegation including Millicent Fawcett and the dowager Lady Stanley of Alderley to present the chancellor with a letter of thanks signed by nearly two thousand women. To Lord Granville's amusement, Cobbe also gave him a copy of her 1862 NAPSS paper and a collection of not only the favorable but also the hostile responses from the press.[79]

Cobbe spent much of the summer of 1862 in London visiting editors and arranging new projects; she found a publisher for the collected works of Theodore Parker and placed more essays in *Macmillan's, Fraser's,* and the *Spectator.* Since the NAPSS meeting almost coincided with the international exhibition opening at the rebuilt Crystal Palace in Sydenham, London was jammed with acquaintances from Rome as well as social-science friends. Harriet Hosmer's sculpture *Zenobia,* the heroic warrior queen captured and led in chains through Rome, attracted a great deal of attention from women moved both by the subject and by the sculptor's prowess. At the end of July Hosmer went with Cobbe for a holiday at Newbridge.

Maggie Elliot, meanwhile, was on her way home to Bristol. Benjamin Jowett's letter to her on 4 June was the last to be published. Rumor had it that he was "near the point of proposing" when someone else was elected to the only Balliol fellowship that then permitted its holder to be married. Maggie was ill during the autumn, and Cobbe blamed Jowett. "[I] fully expected that he would marry my friend—but I always feared that he wd cause her much pain," she wrote years later. "There was an ugly streak of moral *cruelty* in him, with all his goodness." A published article about Bishop Colenso contrasted the physically powerful "soldier of truth" with the "small retreating chin and delicate figure of the Oxford divine."[80]

In the midst of the busy and active autumn after the London NAPSS meeting, on 6 October 1862 Cobbe stepped off a train in Bath, twisted her foot on the platform, and sprained her ankle. She was not quite forty years old and "in splendid health and spirits." By the next week, she wrote, "I was a poor cripple on crutches, never to take a step without them for four long years, during which period I grew practically into an old woman, and (unhappily for me) into a very large and heavy one, for want of the exercise to which I had been accustomed." The lameness put an end to active social work and was an acceptable reason for changing her way of life. In "Social Science Congresses, and Women's Part in Them" she had suggested that "books like Mrs. Stowe's are each worth twenty lives of philanthropic labours." By the autumn of 1862 she was signing essays even for the *Journal of the Workhouse Visiting Society* with her full name instead of initials. Her work appeared regularly in *Fraser's,* although she complained to Froude in February 1863 about the pay. He blamed the publisher's penny-pinching and offered a quasi apology: "If you feel you cannot do any more for me I can only thank you for the *very good help* which you have given us so far."[81]

"What Shall We Do With Our Old Maids?"—in *Fraser's* for November 1862—replied to W. R. Greg's recent essay "Why are Women Redundant?" by poking holes in both Greg's solution and his euphemism and cheerfully claiming "old maid" status for the vigorous independent women earning fame as poets, novelists, artists, and especially sculptors. The passage on sculpture is the most intense; and although the name prominently mentioned is Hosmer's, Cobbe wrote the essay soon after meeting Lloyd. In December and January she was in London for medical advice and still hoped to recover quickly. Mary Somerville wrote to Harriet Hosmer, in Rome, on 5 February 1863, "Tell Mary Lloyd that I rejoice in the prospect of seeing her and my friend Miss Cobbe, and that I wish them much enjoyment in their journey to the Holy Land." They may even have considered going on to India. In the event, however, any such trip proved impossible; Cobbe remained in England for the time being. She had at least one long conversation with Emily Davies, who had taken over the editorship of *English Woman's Journal* and recognized the difference between the stolid earnestness of most social reformers and the wit and polish of an up-and-coming professional writer. Cobbe told Davies frankly "that to have a weak, poor, Journal, purporting to represent women, is decidedly worse than nothing." Davies realized that in order to have any real effect on public opinion, the *Journal* had to compete with more popular periodicals. Articles like "What Shall We Do With Our Old Maids?" would have been wonderfully helpful, but there was almost no money to pay contributors. "I don't find people *at all* willing to write for nothing," she explained to Barbara Bodichon. "Even writers like Miss Cobbe, who are interested in our object, require to be paid, & one does not see why they should be expected to work for nothing."[82]

While Cobbe was staying in London, J. A. Froude asked her to help him get Maggie Elliot to write, and polish, a story she had told him so that he could publish it in *Fraser's.*[83] And she had a very rewarding dinner with Mary Carpenter's younger brother William. He had been apprenticed to an apothecary at fifteen but was more interested in science and gradually stopped practicing medicine, although he remained an examiner in physiology and comparative anatomy. In 1856 he became the University of London's registrar—the man, that is, who had to inform Newson Garrett that his daughter Elizabeth could not take the matriculation exam—but whether or not they discussed women's education, William Carpenter was an active Unitarian of a more progressive bent than his sister, and at his dinner Cobbe met John William Colenso. Appointed bishop of Natal in 1853, Colenso first aroused controversy because he did not force polygamous converts to divorce their plural wives, which would have left the women and their children without protection. While examining the first books of the Old Testament to make clear explanations in Zulu, he had found them "impossibly deep in self-contradictions" and concluded that the narrative "cannot be regarded as historically true." At the end of October 1862 the first volume of Colenso's *The Pentateuch and the Book of Joshua Critically Examined* was published. Ten thousand copies were sold or ordered within six days.[84] The second volume came out in January, as did the geologist Charles Lyell's *Antiquity of Man* and T. H. Huxley's *Man's Place in Nature.* Cobbe owned all of these books. Colenso's work aroused a storm of controversy; he was not only ridiculed in Arnold's *Culture and Anarchy* (like Cobbe, but at much greater length) but also ousted from his bishopric, although he was later reinstated. In Colenso, Cobbe found an erudite ecclesiastic whose scholarship confirmed the rough chart of improbabilities she had so painfully worked out alone in her early twenties.

In February she was back in her lodgings at Durdham Down editing Theodore Parker's works. The fourteen volumes, which remained the only collected edition for half a century, were published at intervals from 1863 to 1871, although Cobbe's work was finished by November 1864. The "editing" consisted in assembling published versions, largely American, of Parker's books, essays, sermons, and speeches and sorting them by topic. Cobbe's only significant addition was a thirty-page preface to the first volume, *A Discourse of Matters Pertaining to Religion,* the book that had so comforted her in 1846. Praised in the *Inquirer* because Cobbe admired without worship— "She does not agree with all Mr. Parker's positions. . . . But she does justice to his eloquence, learning, genius, integrity, and piety"—the introduction was noticed by intellectual women on both sides of the Atlantic. George Eliot wrote to her friend Sara Sophia Hennel that it was "very honourable . . . a little too metaphorical here and there, but with real thought and good feeling in it." Lucretia Mott called it to the attention of her friends, while Lydia Maria Child wrote, "Miss Cobbe's introduction . . . I like extremely. It is a truly manly production; thus we are obliged to compliment the 'superior sex' when we seek to praise our own."[85]

In the spring of 1863 Cobbe became, like Mott, Child, and of course Parker, an active abolitionist. The *Times* had called Abraham Lincoln's Emancipation Proclamation a "wicked" policy and saw his plan to enroll Black regiments as an invitation for slaves to revolt. Recollecting the events of 1857 in India, the *Times* conjured up images of "horrible massacres of white women and children."[86] Most London newspapers followed suit; the *Spectator* and the *Daily News* were unusual in remaining sympathetic to the North. The January 1863 issue of the *Atlantic Monthly* carried a letter from Harriet Beecher Stowe to the women of England pleading for support. Mentia Taylor, who had once been denied membership in the London Anti-Slavery Society because of her sex, responded by forming the Ladies' London Emancipation Society. For its first effort, Cobbe wrote a "Rejoinder to Mrs. Stowe's Reply to the Address of the Women of England," which James Fields, who had often seen both Cobbe and Stowe in Florence in 1860, published in the April 1863 issue of the *Atlantic Monthly.* George Eliot wrote of "good Miss Cobbe's Rejoinder" that she was "glad to see how free the answer was from all tartness or conceit."[87] Cobbe had been energized by meeting Harriet Beecher Stowe in the emotional aftermath of Parker's death and by reading Parker's "Letter from Rome" on the slave's "natural right to kill everyone who seeks to prevent his enjoyment of liberty," but even her manuscript of "A Lady's Ride," written before the war began, was filled with distaste for southerners. "Slave-owners," she wrote, were "centuries behind the world in all matters of theology, literature, & science; & painfully overbearing & peremptory in their behavior to their inferiors."

Antislavery activism drew Cobbe into a London circle more widely radical than the Bristol social reformers or many of the feminists connected to the *English Women's Journal.* The executive committee of the Ladies' London Emancipation Society formally organized at Aubrey House, the home of P. A. and Mentia Taylor, on 20 March 1863 included Frances Power Cobbe, Sarah Remond (then living with Mentia Taylor and studying at Bedford College), Charlotte Manning (first mistress of the college at Hitchin, which later became Girton), and Elizabeth Malleson (founder of the Working Women's College opened in Bloomsbury in 1864 and secretary of the Ladies' National Association for Repeal of the Contagious Diseases Acts when it was formally organized in 1870). Moncure Conway, son of a slave-owning Virginia family who had become a Unitarian minister, was in England giving lectures in support of the Union. His autobiography described Cobbe as "the most distinguished" of the ladies who formed the society.[88]

The stated purpose of the Ladies' London Emancipation Society was to circulate documents exposing the evils of slavery; their goal was to convince British readers that the Union cause was a moral crusade and not a struggle for territory. The first pamphlet it issued was Cobbe's *Red Flag in John Bull's Eyes.* (The "Red Flag" was the threat of insurrection, which Confederate sympathizers continued using to enrage British public opinion.) Conway saw the manuscript and reported that she "had not only studied all the history of the negro in the West Indies," where, of course, her cousin Henry Clermont had been stationed for many years in command of African troops, "but carefully collected all the facts concerning the conduct of the slaves during our war; with power and accuracy her pamphlet tore the red flag to tatters."[89] Her final sentence, listing the cruelties of slave owners, includes, in italics, the phrase "crimes which we dare not name," a coded reference meant for women readers. Fanny Kemble's *Journal of a Residence on a Georgia Plantation,* which made the crime perfectly clear, was published in England the same month—May 1863—and was excerpted with her permission by Isa Craig for the second Ladies' London Emancipation Society tract.

Lameness continued to interfere with many of the things Cobbe wanted to do. She worked to find sources of additional income so she could travel. Nicholas Trübner, who was publishing Cobbe's edition of Theodore Parker's works and sympathized with women's causes, brought out the "Thanksgiving" chapter from Cobbe's *Religious Duty,* now with her name attached to it, as a separate volume. *Essays on the Pursuits of Women,* a collection of reprinted pieces, was published by Emily Faithfull and dedicated, without giving their names, to Mary Somerville, Mary Carpenter, and Harriet Hosmer. The *Spectator* printed a fairly respectful review, although much of its space was given to contrasting Cobbe's moderation with the polemics of Harriet Taylor and other writers, all unnamed, who "speak as though every woman were a slave," but the *English Churchman* warned readers that "even in literature of this practical and benevolent class, there may be unsound and dangerous doctrinal teaching." The *Athenaeum* first objected that "Miss Cobbe is under the impression that *men* are the especial opponents of what may be termed the 'woman's rights' cause" and then proceeded to dispute virtually every point she had made. In particular it worried about the undesirable consequences that would follow if "girls and boys" should "encounter each other in lecture-rooms" of colleges associated with London University.[90]

Thanks to her growing reputation, as well as her ability to stir up controversy, Cobbe no longer had to be a patient supplicant in her business dealings. Seeking a publisher to reprint the travel essays from *Fraser's Magazine,* she asked Froude for advice, while at the same time arguing with him about slavery (Froude was not an abolitionist, nor did he support the Union). She told Richard Bentley that his reader was "taking rather an unfair length of time" and said that if he was "hesitant about publishing a work so definitely heterodox . . . pray be very frank with me & tell me so." And despite her disappointment with Benjamin Jowett, she asked him for a letter to help her place a risky theological piece in the *National Review.*[91]

In mid-July 1863 Cobbe followed a course of medicinal baths at Aix-le-Bains, an Alpine resort known since Roman times for its hot sulfur springs.

By then she was accustomed to finding useful contacts everywhere. In Aix it was John Elliot Cairnes, an economist with Anglo-Irish origins (his father owned a brewery in Drogheda), who had made his reputation with *The Slave Power* (1862), a compelling defense of the Northern cause, and soon became an ardent supporter of women's suffrage. Cairnes and his bride were pleasant company, but the baths did nothing to help her ankle. She went on to the Grand Hotel des Diablerêts in Switzerland. Although she would write that she "lay all the bright summer long helpless and suffering,"[92] she accomplished enormous quantities of work. In August she wrote the preface to Parker's *Discourses of Slavery I,* chosen for publication in the crucial summer of 1863. A *Daily News* column dated 22 August and headed "The English In Switzerland" reports on crowded hotels, inflated prices, an unseasonable snowfall, and the "mountain climbing feats of Madame d'Augeville, who two weeks ago ascended the Oldenhorn (her age is just three months shy of 70)." Cobbe recycled much the same meditation on scenery, along with her poem "A Thunderstorm on the Diablerêts," as an essay published in the *Reader* for 3 October. By the end of September she had written her first major antivivisection piece, "The Rights of Man and the Claims of Brutes," and completed her book *Broken Lights.*

Throughout the autumn of 1863, from various cities in Italy, she continued to write anonymous journalism for the *Daily News* and essays for the *Reader.* (The latter did not usually print signatures, but about half the pieces in Cobbe's scrapbook have a published "F.P.C." at the end.) Although the *Reader* did not last long, it has been described as "one of the finest literary journals" of the century.[93] Its editor during this period was David Masson, who also edited *Macmillan's* and had accepted Cobbe's first commercial article. By 13 October Cobbe was in the Italian seaport of Spezzia (La Spezia) enjoying the company of Mary Somerville—who at eighty-three was at work on her last major scientific book, published in 1869 as *On Molecular and Microscopic Science*—and also, before the end of the month, completing the essay "Hades." Then Cobbe moved on to Florence, where she again stayed with Isa Blagden, now at Villa Giglioni in Bellosguardo; she provided a nice hostess gift by reviewing *The Cost of a Secret,* a three-volume novel by the author of "Agnes Tremorne"—that is, Isa Blagden—in the *Daily News.* Most of Cobbe's writing during the winter reveals her growing skill as a freelancer, making every experience pay for itself several times over. Her observations and research and interviews with public officials were used not only for the *Reader* and the *Daily News* but also to collect economic, demographic, and cultural information for a grand survey of Italy under independence, which she published in 1864.

In November 1863 the people in Isa Blagden's drawing room heard about "cruelties" practiced by Moritz Schiff, a physiologist at the Florence Museum of Natural History. On 18 and 21 December Cobbe wrote of "helpless dogs, and other creatures" kept alive for days "with their entrails out" or "other organs exposed." Schiff challenged the *Daily News* correspondent at Florence to come forward and prove the facts alleged in his letter. Cobbe replied, giving her name and address, but heard no more from Professor Schiff. Although this incident and the petition Cobbe then circulated in Florence are often described as the origin of the antivivisection movement, "The Rights of Man and the Claims of Brutes" had already been published in *Fraser's* for November. Inspired by *Times* reports about experimental operations on unanesthetized horses in France, to which even the *British Medical Journal* and the *Lancet* objected,[94] Cobbe analyzed "the duties of man as regards the welfare of the brutes." In 1863 she could justify scientific experimentation on animals if all possible means were used to avoid pain and the experiment was needed to discover a new truth, establish a questionable fact, or provide "general instruction" for students. Invoking the scientific prestige of Charles Darwin, she observed that humans were "allied in blood to all the beasts of the field."

Early in 1864 the travel pieces from *Fraser's* were republished as *Cities of the Past*. The *Saturday Review* on 16 January was, surprisingly, "delighted to meet with Miss Cobbe as a traveller, and to find that this stern champion of her sex is so pleasant, so intelligent, and so natural a companion."[95] *Broken Lights* also came out early in 1864. Identified in its subtitle as "an inquiry into the present condition and future prospects of religious faiths," the book poked holes in all contemporary brands of Christianity and supplied illustrative examples equally insulting to high church Anglicans, to evangelicals (whether Dissenters or in the low church party of the Church of England), and to broad church intellectuals, including Jowett; even English Unitarians were found wanting. She dismissed all faiths based on "inspired prophets" by references to Brother Prince of the Agapemone and condemned Thomas Carlyle for his worship of power without morality and his lack of fellow feeling for criminals, "Niggers" (Cobbe used quotation marks to emphasize that it was Carlyle's word, not hers), and poor people.[96] Even theism, she proposed, needed an infusion of warmth and emotion if it was to become "a Religion at all, and not a Philosophy."[97]

The first theological book published under her name from the outset, *Broken Lights* was widely and seriously reviewed on both sides of the Atlantic. The *New Englander and Yale Review* considered it jointly with John Henry Newman's *Apologia Pro Vita Sua*. "W.S." in Boston's *Monthly Religious Magazine* found *Broken Lights* "full of tenderness, reverence, and piety," while Susanna Winkworth, who worked among the poor in Bristol and had been

a Unitarian before returning to the Church of England in 1861, was respectful but uncomfortable. Frank Newman, virtually the only theologian she
had praised besides Parker, nevertheless mounted a strong argument against
her in *A Discourse Against Hero-Making in Religion*.[98] The *Theological Review*
was complimentary. The review appeared in the journal's second issue (May
1864) along with Cobbe's "Religion in Italy in 1864." Edited by Charles
Beard, the *Theological Review* intended to be a progressive Unitarian periodical with "the freest of discussion of controverted topics in theology."[99]
Cobbe became the only woman whose work appeared regularly in the periodical; it printed twenty-four of her essays in the period from May 1864 to
October 1877. In addition, the publicity generated by *Broken Lights* allowed
Trübner to bring out a new edition of *Religious Duty* under that title and
with Cobbe's name on the title page, which garnered far more attention than
its anonymous appearance in 1857 as part 2 of *An Essay on Intuitive Morals*.

The extent of controversy between people with quite similar ideas was
striking. Maggie Elliot wrote that the editor of the *North British Review* had
rejected an article by Cobbe "with a most civil note, admiring it much, saying he agrees with almost every part of it, etc., etc.; but that . . . it would be
represented as an attack on the 'Evangelical Church,' which would be very
damaging to the *Review*." By the end of the century it was hard for Cobbe
herself to remember how very iconoclastic her theism had once seemed.
Writing to George Bentley about her autobiography, she hoped that "the
days are past when Mudie tabooed me on account of my heresies! I have
heard (30 years ago) of more than one lady asking for my books at his counter
& being answered by the Assistant 'Do you know what sort of books they
are Madam' with dark hints which caused the enquirer to retreat horrified
under the impression that she had asked for something quite improper! How
long ago all that kind of thing seems!"[100]

Despite her complaints about mail service between Italy and London,
Cobbe continued to send new essays to British periodicals: "What Annexation Has Done For Italy" for the *National Review* and "A Day At Adelsberg" for *Victoria Magazine* in January 1864; "Hades" for *Fraser's* in March
and "The Nineteenth Century" for the same magazine in April. The latter
is an important analysis of the spirit of the age that has been much quoted
by twentieth-century scholars. The breadth and sweep of Cobbe's writing
improved during the Italian year, when she was away from her sources and
forced to depend on her own intelligence and on the general knowledge she
gained by entering varied circles of intellectual and social activists.

Her major work during the trip was *Italics: Brief Notes on Politics, People and Places in Italy, in 1864*. Most attention has been given to the chapter
"People One Meets in Italy," which is largely about English-speaking peo-

ple. Robert Browning, among others, disliked what he read; he wrote to Julia Wedgwood that he had "found a part in which I was concerned; well-meant, poor, inexact, painful and mistaken stuff. . . . I suspect Miss C. cannot understand, nor express herself, in Italian." William Dean Howells said the chapter on literature was absurd; instead of talking to people acquainted with Dante, he complains, Cobbe evidently had recorded the "indolent and flippant guesses" of foreigners. And the *Saturday Review* objected, typically, "Here we have Miss Frances Power Cobbe professing to write a book about Italian affairs, but really inveigling us into reading a series of homilies on the wrongs of her injured sex."[101]

But the literature and personalities were in fact a very minor part of *Italics*. Far more significant at the time were the political and economic information, the statistical summaries, the evaluations of railways and education and women's rights, the analysis of conflicts between Catholicism and modernization, the description of Italian newspapers and their politics. Some of the material was supplied by Count Guido Usedom, the Prussian ambassador. (The book is dedicated to Usedom's English wife.) Later, in London, the revolutionary leader Giuseppe Mazzini spent several hours "correcting" Cobbe's interpretation of Italian politics. Nevertheless, in contrast to the poets and authors who complained about personal details, the *Times* printed a very long review—four columns of summary and quotation describing it as "full of interesting facts and original reflections," praising the author's interest in economic reform, law courts, railways, normal schools, and a free press, saying how refreshing and how valuable it was to read of Italy something more than scenery, art galleries, and tourist attractions.[102] Cobbe's newspaper journalism gave her significant contacts; personal observation supplied the authority to repackage her research in a book that had wider interest than the theological and philanthropic writing she had previously published under her own name; and there was an eager market for *Italics* when it came out.

When she returned to England in 1864, Cobbe did not return to Bristol. After *Italics* she committed herself to writing professionally so that like the women she had known in Rome, she could become established in a metropolitan social and intellectual world. Mary Lloyd, who had been in England or Wales for much of the winter, wrote to her mentor John Gibson in February that she would return to Rome in April or May to pack up her things and sell her furniture. She then joined Cobbe in Genoa to begin a life together. On their way home they stopped in Fontainebleau, as a couple, to visit Rosa Bonheur and Nathalie Micas.

In less than six years, between December 1858 and the summer of 1864, Cobbe had tried and discarded a life of active personal social service, demonstrated that she was a dynamic public speaker, taken a leading part in emergent feminist causes, placed twenty essays in widely circulated journals, and published four substantial books, as well as making unpaid contributions to help friends who edited feminist magazines, bringing out pamphlets on social issues, contributing unsigned articles to weekly periodicals, doing journalism for the *Daily News,* and beginning a long-term connection with the *Theological Review* and the *Spectator.* Her name was known internationally; the books she published in 1864 were reviewed in the *New York Times* as well as the *Times* of London. "Cobbe" had also become a recognizable shorthand for "strong-minded female" and "man-hater" in journals such as the *Saturday Review.*

Cobbe had learned to craft logical arguments while constructing *Intuitive Morals,* had developed sharp observation and stylistic energy in the notes and journal written on her trip through the Middle East, and had demonstrated a capacity for social analysis in the earliest workhouse pieces. By the time she added the emotional energy Benjamin Jowett demanded and then, in "Social Science Congresses, and Women's Part in Them," allowed her own high spirits and pointed wit to reach the page, she had acquired a wonderfully appealing voice with a wide and flexible range of intellectual and stylistic tools. When she settled in London at age forty-two, she had abundant contacts among intellectuals, feminists, editors, and reformers: members of the NAPSS, advanced religious thinkers met through Bishop Colenso and Frank Newman, scientists introduced by William Carpenter, and women from the Ladies' London Emancipation Society, as well as the Langham Place circle and Emily Faithfull's Victoria Press. In addition, and not to be overlooked, some of her relatives and Anglo-Irish contacts were also valuable resources in the campaigns and the journalism of the next two decades.

# 7 Mary Lloyd

*～○ I thought ere this you would have had my better half with you. . . . Poor old darling, I am comforted by knowing she is happy & enjoying her little fling. Her life can never have too much of that to make up for the past—but I am very lonely & sad without her.*

FRANCES POWER COBBE TO MARY SOMERVILLE,
27 DECEMBER [1869]

Mary Lloyd's deep sense of privacy has made her very hard to picture or even imagine. Her name appears less than a dozen times in the 1894 edition of the *Life of Frances Power Cobbe:* "Of a friendship like this," Cobbe explains, "I shall not be expected to say more."[1] After Lloyd died Cobbe added a few paragraphs for the 1904 edition, but they do little more than create an idealized Mary Lloyd, not unlike the idealization of Cobbe's mother:

> It would be some poor comfort to me in my loneliness to write here some little account of Mary Charlotte Lloyd, and to describe her keen, highly-cultivated intellect, her quick sense of humour, her gifts as sculptor and painter (the pupil and friend of John Gibson and of Rosa Bonheur); her practical ability and strict justice in the administration of her estate; above all to speak of her character, "cast"—as one who knew her from childhood said,—"in an heroic mould," of fortitude and loftiness; her absolute unselfishness in all things large and small. But the reticence which belonged to the greatness of her nature made her always refuse to allow me to lead her into the more public life whereto my work necessarily brought me, and in her last sacred directions she forbids me to commemorate her by any written record.[2]

The few contemporary depictions use much darker colors. On 16 February 1867 Kate Amberley walked over to visit Cobbe at home and saw "the lady she lives with Miss Loyd [*sic*], an unamiable looking spinster, who said she hated philanthropists." Cobbe herself wrote that "'intense' was the only word in the language" to describe Lloyd's dog Nip, a comment that I suspect could be transferred to Nip's owner. Lady Battersea, a friend of Cobbe's since the time she had been young Constance de Rothschild, recorded the following account of Lloyd as an old woman: "severe & pessimistic as usual rather alarming at first; a stern moralist; a hater of cant, with no belief in humanity or I fear in God."[3]

Mary Lloyd was the eighth of seventeen children born to Edward Lloyd of Rhagatt and his wife, Frances Maddocks, in the years 1810–31. Seven died in infancy or childhood; ten lived to be adults. The middle group of children included six girls, whose births spanned little more than seven years: Mary in January 1819, Charlotte on 12 February 1820, Jane on 30 August 1822, Eliza on 6 January 1824, and Harriet on 25 July 1826; an earlier Harriet was born in 1821 and died four years later, when Mary would have been six.

Edward Lloyd, like Charles Cobbe, was a substantial squire with land in several counties. Rhagatt Hall, then in Merioneth (now in Denbighshire), is a Georgian stone house a mile and a half outside of Corwen, a market town with 1,980 inhabitants, "pleasantly situated," according to Samuel Lewis's 1833 *Topographical Dictionary,* "on the southern bank of the river Dee, on the great road from London to Holyhead and Dublin." Llangollen is ten miles to the east on the same road. Some of Edward Lloyd's land was archaeologically rich. In Llanbedr more than fifteen hundred Roman coins were unearthed in 1816, and Mary herself helped W. Boyd Dawkins excavate prehistoric human and animal bones on family property in 1869. Historically, Corwen was the home of Owain Glyndwr and the rendezvous for his army during the last significant Welsh rebellion against the English, early in the fifteenth century. The Lloyd family of Rhagatt were said to be descended from the Tudor conqueror who was made lord of the Marches of Wales.

I have discovered nothing about Mary's childhood or education. Since there is no drawing of her in an album of family portraits done by a governess when she was eight, she may have lived for a time with a maiden aunt, Margaret Lloyd of Berth. Born about 1780, Margaret Lloyd was a friend of the Ladies of Llangollen. Mary inherited several books inscribed "M. Lloyd. The gift of Lady Eleanor Butler and Miss Ponsonby" and also some letters written to her aunt Margaret by the poet Felicia Hemans, who until 1831 lived less than ten miles from Berth.[4]

Like Cobbe, Mary Lloyd had a wide range of intellectual interests. A commonplace book she began in 1849 opens with mottoes in Latin and Greek as well as English and a quotation from the New England Unitarian William Ellery Channing: "I call that mind free which protects itself against the usurpations of society." She culled sententious newspaper paragraphs on topics such as "a child's smile" and "beauty and ugliness," copied a great

Mary Charlotte Lloyd (1819–1896). Published by Cobbe in the *Abolitionist* on 15 December 1900, the photograph was probably taken by Mary's brother John Lloyd in 1864 or 1865. (From the collections of the Library of Congress)

many puns from the pages of *Punch,* included passages from *Pendennis* and the Canadian humorist "Sam Slick," quoted verse by Felicia Hemans and Eliza Cook. Most interestingly, she included a section of "Outrages by Husbands upon Wives" from the journal *Justice of the Peace.* It asserted that "the latter generally suffer when the former are punished," a proposition that, whether or not either of them remembered it at the time, lay behind the specific remedies proposed in Frances Power Cobbe's 1878 bill for the protection of wives.[5]

When she reached adulthood, Lloyd had younger sisters at home and some independent income from her aunt Margaret's will. By her early thirties, if not earlier, she was making clay models in the studio of the most celebrated nineteenth-century British sculptor. Born in North Wales, John Gibson had been in Rome since 1817. Elizabeth Eastlake's biography of him quotes a letter to "Miss Lloyd" in April 1832: "Your time has been well spent at Florence among the statues, but though I admire the genius and power of Michael Angelo very much, I am afraid your taste might be led astray by him."[6] The date seems rather unlikely since Mary would have been only thirteen at the time, although she could have been traveling with her aunt or with Margaret Sandbach, the granddaughter of Gibson's first patron. Margaret and Henry Sandbach were definitely in Rome during the winter of 1838–39, when Mary was turning twenty and had become their close friend. Whatever other experiences—or studies—intervened, by 1853 Lloyd and Hosmer were working in Gibson's studio.

When Cobbe and Lloyd met in the winter of 1861–62, both were mature single women (Cobbe was thirty-nine, Lloyd was forty-three) who had some private income, lived alone, and were fond of animals. Both had begun to establish a professional identity, Lloyd as a sculptor and Cobbe as a writer. In personality they could hardly have been more different. Contemporaries who wrote about Cobbe invariably described her "good-natured humour," her "wit, fun, sweetness," her "smile, at once so cheery & so infectious"; she was called a "full-hearted, jolly Irishwoman, full of good humor and good temper" who was "singularly genial, witty and merry, in conversation most amusing." Lloyd, in the words of Constance Battersea, was "devoted to Miss Cobbe & yet so unlike her. Pessimist, unsociable, gloomy."[7]

Their backgrounds, however, were strikingly similar. Both were children of relatively long-lived parents. In Wales and in Ireland their families were English-speaking gentry who had for generations exercised civil authority in Celtic countries without acquiring titles or knighthoods. Mary's grandfather, John Lloyd, born in 1746, was a well-known barrister who became chief justice of the Carmarthen circuit in 1779. Like Cobbe's great-great-grandfather, he did well in his profession and added land to the family holdings. Cobbe's father owned more than eleven thousand acres, while Lloyd's father had forty-three hundred, but their incomes were virtually the same; land in Wales brought in better rents.

Cobbe and her brothers spoke of their father as "The Master"; Lloyd's father was universally known as "The Old Squire." Both men were conscientious evangelical Anglicans who restored their property, built cottages, and supported schools and churches. In 1841 the parish that included Rhagatt had 41 inhabited houses and a population of 183; by 1851 there were 34 inhabited houses and a population of 137, of whom 23 were the Lloyd family and their servants. At Rhagatt, as at Newbridge, four or five sheep from the home farm were killed every month, although an additional three hundred to five hundred pounds of beef were purchased as "butcher meat." The crude numbers show more servants at Rhagatt; in 1830 there were seven men (ranging from a rat catcher who was paid £8 per year to a bailiff and agent who earned £100) and eleven women. At Newbridge, however, many workers lived elsewhere and were not counted as residents. The Rhagatt library contained more books on law and fewer of theology—reflecting the different ancestral vocations—but many of the same classical and mathematical texts, a good selection of travel accounts, and even a guidebook to Bath.[8] In both families the younger sons in succeeding generations went to the church, the bar, the military, and the empire. Both Cobbe and Lloyd had an uncle who was a naval officer during the Napoleonic Wars.

There were many other similarities. The eldest son in each family matriculated at Oxford in 1830, John Lloyd at Christ Church and Charles Cobbe at Exeter, and both became active landowners. John Lloyd was a magistrate in both Denbigh and Merioneth, served as high sheriff of Denbighshire in 1863, and was a deputy lieutenant of Merioneth. Upon inheriting, he almost at once got in touch with the architect George Gilbert Scott about building a church at Glenrafon, Llawr y Bettus (in the parish of Llanfawr), which was consecrated on 22 March 1864. And although both of the eldest brothers married, neither had children, and so the inheritance passed to or through a son of the second brother.

Howel William Lloyd and Henry Cobbe both went up to Oxford in 1835, and both entered the church. In 1842 both became curates, but in the same year that William Cobbe became a disciple of Henry James Prince, Howel Lloyd resigned his curacy in order to examine his faith. In 1846 he was received into the Roman Catholic Church. Charles Owen Lloyd, the youngest brother, arrived in Calcutta the same year that cousin Frank Cobbe went to Madras. On 12 September 1848, in an attack on the fortifications of Mooltan (Multan, now in Pakistan) during the second Sikh War, Ensign Charles Owen Lloyd of the 8th Native Infantry was, according to the *Annual Register*, "cut down while parleying with the enemy."[9] He was nineteen years old. Mary Lloyd's sister Eliza also spent time in India. She arrived in 1853 as the wife of Meredith Vibart of the Bengal Artillery. Vibart's uncle and aunt and their four children were massacred at Cawnpore "with such circumstances of fiendish atrocity as cannot be written, scarcely breathed," according to Eliza's letter of 2 September 1857. A column in the *Times* for 15 October 1857 headed "The Indian Mutinies. The following is from an officer at Almora," was, in fact, not by an officer but extracted from three letters written by Eliza Vibart. By 20 October she no longer called it a mutiny, but "the revolution which it may now be termed."[10] At almost the same time that Lloyd's sister was reporting from Almora, Cobbe's cousin Alick wrote a detailed letter on eight large sheets of thin paper about the siege of Delhi, including hand-drawn maps.[11]

There were also significant differences, of course. Lloyd may have acquired a glimmer of feminist consciousness from her mother. A touching homemade notebook marked on the cover "F. Lloyd—Rhagatt *Private*" contains a list of personal items that Mary's mother, Frances Lloyd, wanted her children to have, along with a sentence dated August 1841: "She believes that *legally,* a *Wife* possesses nothing of her own, but, she feels assured, that nothing will gratify her affectionate husband more, than to comply with the reasonable wishes of hers when no more, whom he tried his utmost to please in life."[12] And although Cobbe had girl cousins for friends, and spent more time with them than her *Life* would lead one to believe, Mary had many sisters very close to her age. The youngest, Harriet, born in 1826, never married and acted as "daughter at home" until the end of their parents' life.

When Cobbe and Lloyd first met, Mary's parents had quite recently died, her father on 14 October 1859 and her mother three months earlier. These deaths followed hard on the heels of two more. Her eldest sister, Frances, had died on 16 September 1858, and Frances's husband, Robert Williams Vaughan, on 29 April 1859. Mary had spent several months in Wales and London coping with legal business. Her father had insured his life to provide her with an income about twice as large as Cobbe's. She also had a one-third share in the Welsh estate of Hengwrt by way of her sister Frances and her husband. They died childless; Vaughan willed a life interest in Hengwrt to his wife's three unmarried sisters, Mary, Jane (later married to Henry Ffoulkes), and Harriet.[13] In addition to making Mary a "landed proprietor," a status she would usefully claim when signing petitions for women's suffrage, the inheritance gave the three sisters the right to appoint the vicar of Llanelltydd parish.

Of the siblings living in 1862, John and his wife Gertrude were at Rhagatt. Howel had briefly worked in the War Office during the Crimea and would later teach at the Catholic University College, which existed in London from 1874 to 1878, but his chief source of income was tutoring older boys who lived in his Kensington house along with his wife and son. Like Cobbe's brother Tom, Howel Lloyd was a serious amateur scholar. He investigated Welsh history, archaeology, and philology in the British Museum, wrote papers for antiquarian and archaeological journals, produced versions of the catechism and other Roman Catholic devotional works in Welsh, and translated ancient Welsh poems into English.

Charlotte, the sister closest to Mary in age, was married at nineteen to her first cousin Richard John Price of Rhiwlas, near Bala, some ten miles west of Corwen. He died at age thirty-eight, leaving her pregnant with a son, Richard John Lloyd Price, born on 17 April 1843, eight months after his father's death. Charlotte lived with her father-in-law at Rhiwlas; her son was at Christ Church, Oxford, when Cobbe and Lloyd settled in London. The next sister, Jane, married the clergyman Henry Powell Ffoulkes in 1861. Eliza's husband, Captain Meredith James Vibart, came from a family that had served the East India Company for several generations, but by 1862 the Vibarts and their two daughters were in England while Meredith looked for other ways to earn a living. Harriet probably joined the Clewer Community in 1862; she became a professed member as Sister Harriet Frances on 30 November 1864.[14] An Anglican sisterhood, officially the Community of St. John Baptist, the order was best known for its House of Mercy, an institution for rescuing prostitutes founded at Clewer in 1851.

In the year between Cobbe and Lloyd's first meeting and their decision to live together, Lloyd's second oldest brother—married only eight years and the father of three young children—died on 29 July 1863. According to the death certificate, he had "committed suicide by shotting [*sic*] himself whilst in a state of temporary insanity." No further information about the circumstances has been discovered. Suicide was still deeply feared, and it was concealed whenever possible. A coroner's jury almost always delivered a verdict of "temporary insanity" when the suicide was a person of any standing in the community; otherwise he would have been buried at night without Christian rites, and his goods and chattels would have been forfeited to the Crown.

By 1864, furthermore, Lloyd's oldest brother was seriously ill. The many recent tragedies might well explain the "fixed sadness" that became a theme in descriptions of Mary Lloyd, although her brother's suicide raises the possibility of a family vulnerable to depression. Oddly, however, her letters to John Gibson, even in the summer of 1864, are playful and teasing. Writing on Harriet Hosmer's stationery from North Wales on 25 August 1864, she scolded him for staying in the Italian heat during the summer: "But as the Imp [Hosmer] so justly remarks there is no knowing what follies men will commit when left to their own masculine devices without any feminine common sense to guide them in the ways of wisdom & prudence."[15] Perhaps this was the tone she had established with an elderly high-status men-

tor who served as a good father in the way that Cobbe considered Somerville
an approving mother, although it also suggests that the very private Mary
Lloyd may have been unlike the woman known even to Cobbe's close friends.

The Lloyd and Cobbe families thought of themselves as Welsh and Irish.
Cobbe used the words *Saxon* and *Celt* as racial designations but spoke of her
national identity as Irish rather than English or British. By the nineteenth
century gentry in Wales generally were not Welsh-speaking; in the 1891 census, Mary Lloyd listed her language as "English" rather than "both," although her father and brother must have known enough Welsh to carry out
their duties as magistrates. In 1877, in "The Celt of Wales and the Celt of
Ireland," Cobbe commented on the surprising differences between the two
peoples even though both were of the same "blood," lived under rainy skies,
were nourished by oatmeal, milk, and potatoes, and had been "for several
centuries . . . under the rule of the same conquerors." Yet both, she asserted,
were fervently religious, though the Welsh were Dissenters and the Irish were
Roman Catholic; and they were also similar in imagination and quick wits:
both had a strong sense of humor and playfulness. Perhaps in that sense too,
in private, Mary was as Welsh as Cobbe was Irish. Lloyd had wide-ranging
intellectual interests—ethnology, archaeology, ancient history, economics—
and the two women also shared an understanding of the unspoken secrets
that can shadow family history. When Cobbe and Lloyd settled in London
they had in common the experience of growing up as ruling-class outsiders
in their native lands; and they remained outsiders by birth and "nationality" in the metropolis. This combination of class empowerment and out-
sider status, I suspect, gave both of them a critical perspective and an ability to see—and ignore—some of the boundaries taken for granted by other
women.

## 8

# At Home in London
## 1865–1868

*For those men and women . . . who hold rather pronounced opinions of the sort not relished in country circles, who are heretics regarding the religious or political creed of their relatives and neighbours, London offers the real Broad Sanctuary, where they may rest in peace, and be no more looked upon as black sheep.*

FRANCES POWER COBBE, "THE TOWN MOUSE AND THE COUNTRY MOUSE"

When Cobbe and Lloyd got back to England in the summer of 1864, Cobbe stayed in London to put the finishing touches on *Italics* and write "The Philosophy of the Poor-Laws," which was published in *Fraser's* for September. A valuable overview both broad and specific, its theoretical analysis and some of its recommendations still provide useful ways of thinking about the welfare system. Then she joined Lloyd in Wales. They rented a small house in Corwen to be near John Lloyd, who was ill. (He would die the following May of cancer.) Mary helped her brother develop photographs and tried to ease the burden on his wife, Gertrude. A London friend, Jane Hampson, shared the house for a time. Although Cobbe could not yet walk easily, she was riding on a Welsh pony and enjoying it "immensely," as she wrote, underlining the word, to Mary Somerville.[1]

She continued to produce miscellaneous essays for the *Reader* and completed a two-part article on art for *Fraser's*. J. A. Froude, writing to her about it on 26 November 1864, again complained about anti-Confederate activists, including Cobbe. She also finished her editing for Parker's collected works. The eighth volume, published that autumn, included "On the Public Function of Woman." Although Cobbe's feminist ideas were not "derivative," rereading Parker's 1853 sermon may have supplied authority and shape for some of her work in the second half of the 1860s. Woman's domestic function, Parker argued, "does not exhaust her powers. . . . To make one-half of the human race consume all their energies in the functions of housekeeper, wife and mother, is a monstrous waste of the most precious material that God ever made." A woman "has the same natural rights as man." Although he believed that "man will always lead in affairs of intellect," woman "has the better heart, the truer intuition of the right, the lovely, the holy." And finally, Parker proclaimed, "By nature, woman has the same political rights that man has,—to vote, to hold office, to make and administer laws. These she has as a matter of right. The strong hand and the great head of man keep her down; nothing more."[2]

Early in 1865 Cobbe stayed with Jane Hampson in Brompton while she looked for a house to share with Lloyd. At first she hoped to find "a little detached cottage somewhere out in St. John's Wood—where we can have flowers & dogs." But despite the "*ugliness* of London—the fog—the noise—the small houses," she rejoiced at the presence of "so many people . . . interested in the subjects one cares for." In the end they settled on Kensington, not far from Jane Hampson. The lease to a three-story house on a pleasant square was transferred to Mary Lloyd on 15 March 1865. "I only hope in God's goodness," Cobbe wrote, "it may prove a source of happiness to dear Mary & that I may be the sort of friend she wants."[3] Lloyd put up fifteen hundred pounds from her inheritance to buy the lease; Cobbe paid her eighty pounds a year in rent, and they shared the other household expenses, including the wages for three women servants. The housekeeper, Ellen Parry Jones (who tended to grow only eight or nine years older at every decennial census), was a Welshwoman who may already have worked for Mary Lloyd; she remained with them for the rest of their lives.

Hereford Square was one of the new developments that changed Kensington from an agricultural to a suburban community between 1840 and 1860. Built on three sides of a long narrow "square" (the fourth side is Gloucester Road), the houses are not wholly identical but pleasingly uniform, in white stucco over solid brick, with drawing-room windows opening onto balconies that overlook the square. Number 26, which was a corner house, does not survive; it and two others were lost to a bomb in 1945. It had three full stories plus a typical Kensington basement opening onto an area that gave natural light to the kitchen. The garrets above the third story also had small but adequate windows. Number 26 had the advantage of "a uniquely large L-shaped back garden which extended behind some of the other gardens." The house was connected to piped water and gas as well as a sewer; it had a fireplace in almost every room. "Our little house is very nice & bright & I think we shall be very comfortable & happy by & bye," Cobbe wrote, "but poor Mary has had to undergo great worries with dilatory & cheating tradesmen." Indeed, Lloyd told Fanny Kemble that she "very nearly set fire to the house" before she discovered "all the gas pipes cut off."[4]

The new South Kensington Museum gave Lloyd access to Italian sculptures and contemporary decorative arts. Kensington and Chelsea attracted artists, intellectuals, and liberal social activists. Bishop Colenso and his wife were at 23 Sussex Place, near Gloucester Road, James Anthony Froude a short walk in the other direction, at 5 Onslow Gardens. Uncle George had been at 9 Sydney Place, just off Onslow Square, until his death on 8 February, but I rather doubt that Cobbe visited when she was hunting for a house; George had become difficult and troublesome during his final years. A little further north, just off Kensington High Street, a whole nest of activists lived on Phillimore Gardens: Charlotte Manning at number 44; Jessie Boucherett at number 9; William Shaen (who not only served as solicitor for an enormous number of radical organizations but also provided the "handsome head & face" for Millais's *Huguenot*),[5] and his intellectual wife, Emily, at number 15. Just north of them, Peter and Mentia Taylor had a substantial country house built in the 1690s for the first lord of Kensington manor. Among the immediate neighbors on Hereford Square, George Borrow (whose reputation was made by semifactual accounts of gypsy life) lived four houses up, at number 22. "My friend was amused by his quaint stories and his (real or sham) enthusiasm for Wales," Cobbe wrote. "I never liked him, thinking him more or less a hypocrite."[6] At the census of 1871 Cobbe gave her occupation as "writer," while Borrow described himself as a "literary man."

Not long before they moved in, Cobbe visited Maggie Elliot at 6 Grosvenor Crescent and met the younger John Russell, who had become Viscount Amberley when his father was raised to the peerage as Earl Russell, and his wife, Kate. Kate Amberley described Cobbe in her journal as "a very fat woman about 45, [she was in fact 42] walked with crutches fr. an accident to her leg—We were there about 1½ hours & had very pleasant talk on religion & various topics. I liked her very much—she is a very jovial merry woman and laughs rather loud & much—genial & seeming to enjoy life & take it all easy."[7] Here as in so many other comments it is clear that finishing school had miserably failed at turning Cobbe into an English lady and that her vigorous direct speech and hearty laugh, as well as her "manly" frame, gave her an impressive public presence that appealed to many women.

Cobbe and Lloyd had wanted their own house both for comfort and so they could entertain in a less Bohemian fashion than the studio parties in Rome; and they required servants to look after fires, lights, shopping, cooking, and cleaning so that both Cobbe and Lloyd would have time for their own work. Cobbe's inherited income did not cover all of her share, especially after they found that housekeeping brought expenses they had not anticipated. She reached an agreement with Trübner to publish, "very advantageously," another collection of essays and became thoroughly annoyed when Froude held the second part of "The Hierarchy of Art" until the March issue of *Fraser's,* since the delay made her late in getting the essay to Trüb-ner.[8] Her publication in *Macmillan's Magazine* for March, "Shadow of Death," was an odd little legend that may have been an attempt to discover how to work the more remunerative territory of fiction.

She may have felt a little bit guilty about wanting London for its social life. Mary Carpenter wrote on 22 January, in response to a letter from Cobbe, that she sometimes did "things quite contrary to my natural tastes & wishes," but since she had "never commenced any thing but from a distinct & clear conviction of its *necessity*" she always "plunged" onward. Then, seeming to recollect that Cobbe had not plunged onward with social work, Carpenter continued: "Your philosophic mind & literary talents combined with your good womanly & loving nature . . . enabled you to do an infinitely greater good to the country than by visiting." Yet Cobbe had not entirely withdrawn from voluntary social service, though she chose a mode more suited to her own talents: some time during the year she became an "occasional lecturer" at the College for Working Women established at 29 Queen Square, Blooms-bury, by Elizabeth Malleson, a coworker from the Ladies' London Emanci-pation Society.[9]

An important new network began forming when the Kensington Soci-ety issued its first set of questions on 25 March. Organized by Emily Davies, the group met at Charlotte Manning's house in Phillimore Gardens. Cobbe signed up even before she had a permanent London address. Others on the initial membership list of some thirty-three names included Jessie Bouche-rett, Dorothea Beale, and Elizabeth Garrett. (Garrett had finished her re-quired clinical work and would successfully take the Apothecaries' Hall licensing examination on 28 September.) Elizabeth Wolstenholme, from Manchester, was a corresponding member; forty years later, as Elizabeth Wolstenholme Elmy, she stood beside Sylvia Pankhurst at Women's Social and Political Union (WSPU) demonstrations, and she died six days after King George V signed the Representation of the People Act of 1918, which gave her the vote. Among other members added in the early months were Frances Mary Buss, Barbara Bodichon, and Anna Swanwick.[10] The com-mittee issued questions four times a year. Members could write anything from a sentence to an essay; their responses circulated in advance, so the meetings became not only a place to cement friendships but also a chance to grapple thoughtfully with issues that became central to the women's movement.

Cobbe's autobiographical chapters about social life in London tend, like many of the period's memoirs, to become lists of "great men I have known." Her overlapping but varied circles, however, were essential to her growing expertise and influence. Other important contacts came through James

Martineau's Sunday services at Little Portland Street Chapel, near Regent Street, just north of Oxford Street. "It was a long way from our home in South Kensington," she wrote, "and we had no carriage; yet I do not think we ever missed—rain or shine—a Sunday morning service when we were in London."[11]

Martineau had moved to London in 1857 to take up duties at Manchester New College, a nondenominational institution in Gordon Square. In February 1859 he also became minister of Little Portland Street Chapel, "a relic of the time when among dissenters there was a cult of ugliness,—fine architecture and stained glass being decorations of the 'Scarlet Woman.'" Cobbe and Lloyd never became Unitarians; one contemporary pointed out that "the Unitarian considers the Theist quite as far removed from orthodoxy as the ordinary Protestant does the Unitarian." Although Martineau's Unitarianism has been described as "a philosophical rather than a theological inspiration," his "free criticism of the Bible was united with an intense reverence for Jesus and a profound faith in God."[12] Both Theodore Parker and Frances Power Cobbe had moved much further away from the Bible, towards "a full recognition of the authority of reason and conscience." Cobbe also had difficulty with Martineau's optimism: she wrote that he "never really *felt* the agony of 'the riddle of the painful earth,' and only approached it from the intellectual side."[13]

The relationship between Martineau and Cobbe, however, was never one-sided, clergyman to parishioner. Moncure Conway believed that she "enlarged his theology," and letters show his almost humble dependence on her judgment. In 1865, for example, Martineau wrote to Cobbe, "Few things could so relieve my self-distrusts as such concurrence and approval as yours." And a few years later he wrote, "I am always deploring this diameter of London . . . which keeps Brompton and Bloomsbury in a state of such unnatural estrangement. I think of nothing worthy of much care without wishing I could know your thoughts upon it."[14] Their friendship would explain why Cobbe never met Harriet Martineau even though both wrote for the *Daily News* during the early 1860s: James Martineau and his sister were bitterly estranged after his scathing review of her *Letters on the Laws of Man's Nature and Development* (1851).

Since, as Cobbe once wrote, "a sermon of Mr. Martineau's always signified an 'Hour' . . . of very hard thinking indeed," his metaphysical and ethical arguments attracted a highly intellectual audience. Some of those who attended at one time or another were W. E. Gladstone, George Eliot, Charles Lyell, Charles Darwin ("a frequent visitor"), William Shaen, Anna Swanwick, Henry Crabb Robinson, and William Carpenter. Cobbe particularly valued her friendship with the geologist Charles Lyell and his family. His

Unitarian clergyman James
Martineau (1805–1900).
(I. Giberne Sieveking, *Mem-
oirs and Letters of Francis W.
Newman,* 1909)

John Locke (1805–1880), MP
for Southwark from 1857 until
his death and husband of
Cobbe's cousin Laura. The
lithograph, by J. Tissot, was
published in *Vanity Fair* on 12
August 1871.

house at 73 Harley Street, quite near Martineau's chapel, became "a recognised meeting-place of leading scientific, literary and political figures."[15]
Cobbe and Lloyd often went there on Sunday afternoon for a meal and good
conversation. Charles Lyell's wife and sister-in-law were daughters of another geologist; both women cared about scientific issues.

Yet another network was the small literary and artistic society called the
Pen and Pencil Club, which Mentia Taylor formed in 1864. After Arthur
Munby went to his first meeting, he noted in his diary: "Everyone has to
contribute something in prose or verse or in painting or sculpture. People
sat round the drawingroom & listened to the stories, and then looked at the
drawings &c afterwards. The subjects of the night were 'Suspense' and
'Witchcraft': there were two good eldritch stories, one by Miss Adelaide

Manning . . . & the other by a Miss Keary." The sisters Annie and Eliza Keary, both authors, were members, as were Edwin Arnold, Austin Dobson, Edmund Gosse, and William Allingham.[16]

With all these contacts, Cobbe, sometimes accompanied by Lloyd, went out to dinner two or three times a week, "without any kind of ulterior aim or object," she would say, since they had no "social ambition; not even daughters to bring out!" But of course dining was invaluable for making professional connections and for learning about, and promoting, social, political, and feminist issues. Only two weeks after moving to Hereford Square she dined with Walter Bagehot, then editor of the *National Review.* The guests included Richard Holt Hutton, the well-known critic and scholar who edited the *Spectator;* Arthur Arnold, soon to become editor of the *Echo;* as well as "other literary folk." She met barristers and MPs at 63 Eaton Place, the home of her cousin Laura and her husband, John Locke. With a very substantial house, an excellent cook, and a fine cellar, the Lockes entertained a circle rather different from the writers and reformers of South Kensington. Yet *Vanity Fair* called Locke "a sturdy Radical of the old style." As a member for Southwark, a borough of docks, tanneries, and decrepit working-class housing, he was "always to be found in the front of any struggle that may arise for the popular rights or privileges." And finally, *Vanity Fair* said, he had "a considerable reputation for dry humour . . . and he is the only man who is ever known to make Mr. Gladstone smile."[17]

Cobbe steadily looked for new markets, though not at the expense of her principles. John Douglas Cook had made the weekly *Saturday Review* interesting through its high Tory, Anglo-Catholic outlook—A. J. Beresford-Hope was one of the founders—and its biting criticism of contemporary life. (Its writers were protected by anonymity; none of the essays or reviews carried an author's name.) With a deliberate plan to "set woman against woman" in order to stir up controversy, the *Saturday Review,* in Cobbe's words, "squirted its venom every week like a toad by the roadside" on women's "new-born hopes of freedom and culture." Despite its insulting account of women's papers at the 1862 NAPSS meeting and its especially pointed attack on Cobbe, to say nothing of its review abusing *Italics,* the *Saturday Review* invited her to become a contributor. She told them, according to her 1 April letter to Mary Somerville, "I do not care what they said of *me* but I will only contribute on condition they do not attack women any more!"[18]

The annual exhibition of the Royal Academy of Arts always opened on the first Monday in May, which in 1865 was also the first day of May. "There is no public event," Margaret Oliphant wrote a few years later, "which creates more general interest. . . . From ten o'clock till six the rooms are

thronged with an interested, eager crowd." The 1865 exhibition—at the time
it still was held in the east wing of the National Gallery of Art, on Trafalgar
Square—featured Frederick Leighton's *David* ("seated in brooding thought
on a terrace which overlooks the hills of Judea," hills Cobbe had herself seen
only a few years earlier) and, among the sculptures, Mary Lloyd's marble
group *Horses at Play,* cataloged as exhibit number 1021.[19] Though I have
been unable to discover any contemporary comment on Lloyd's work as a
sculptor, to be accepted by the Royal Academy exhibition was a mark of
some distinction, a moment to bask in success and recognition. By the end
of the month, sadly, Lloyd's brother John, who had come to London for
medical treatment, had died. She wrote that "life was a misfortune in my
Brother's wretched state of suffering," and she "rejoiced when it was at last
over, sad as the parting was."[20] The nephew who would inherit the family
estate was only seven years old; John Lloyd's widow remained at Rhagatt
until he came of age.

At the end of May Cobbe attended the first Kensington Society meeting. Her paper—serious, well argued, and radical—is the only one summarized at length in the minutes. The question, proposed by Elizabeth Garrett,
was, "What is the true basis, and what are the limits of parental authority?"
(Cobbe's response, described in chapter 4, above, was later expanded for her
published essay "Self-Development and Self-Abnegation.") Notes of the discussion that evening in Charlotte Manning's drawing room reveal the difficulties encountered even by mature single women and how their ideas
expanded through conversation. The fifth commandment, they decided,
applied as absolute obligation only to children who had not reached the age
of moral reason. Elizabeth Garrett distinguished between a parent as parent
and a parent as the master of a household: "A father has no right to decide
what books a grown-up child may read, but he has a right to say that books
to which he objects should not be seen on his drawing room table." Before
the session ended, a much more significant issue was introduced: was a parent obliged to prepare his daughter for a profession? They concluded that
"if a parent cannot provide sufficiently for his daughter's maintenance, he
ought to enable her to support herself" and, more importantly, that even
"apart from pecuniary necessity," if she wanted to "enter upon some independent pursuit, he ought not to interpose obstacles."[21]

When the Kensington Society issued its topics for the November meeting, Helen Taylor proposed the question, "Is the extension of the Parliamentary suffrage to women desirable, and if so, under what conditions?"
Less than a month later Parliament dissolved and John Stuart Mill brought
women's suffrage into electoral politics as a part of his platform. Mill was
elected to represent Westminster; Henry Fawcett became a member for

Brighton; and when the new Parliament opened on 1 February 1866 there was reason to think it might become a real question, not merely a discussion-society topic.

In the meantime, however, there was a long parliamentary recess. Cobbe visited her brother Tom sometime in June. In November 1864 Tom and Jessie and their children had moved to a newly built house in the village of Liss, four miles from Petersfield and about fifty miles from London. On Saturday, 8 July, back in London, she gave a "jolly little party—not very little for there were nearly 40 people but our house held them all well." The guests included Charlotte Cushman, W. E. H. Lecky (a Dublin-born historian and writer on religion), the Colensos (just about to return to Natal), the Massons, John Cairnes and his wife, and the Bagehots. Mary Carpenter may also have been there; she wrote to her brother at the end of July that she had had "an hour's chat at Miss Cobbe's with the Bishop [Colenso]."[22]

Mary Lloyd was detained in London much of the summer by business. On 2 July she invited John Gibson to "stay with us in this quiet peace we have a spare room." By 4 August she was planning a get-together with Harriet Hosmer in Paris. Cobbe went to Ireland. Writing about the exhibition inaugurated that summer by the Prince of Wales, she described artwork including "a dog by Rosa Bonheur, and a portrait of a monk . . . by Henriette Browne," as well as sculpture by Emma Stebbins and Harriet Hosmer, whose *Faun* drew special praise: "We doubt if anyone could have thought of such an image of ease and joy, and pure, sensuous, delight-brimming *existence,* in our dull, orderly England. It needed to be born in a New World and to drink in Roman sunshine for a whole joyous youth to conceive this figure."[23]

"Ireland and Her Exhibition in 1865," however, had a political intent. Cobbe asked if the essay might appear anonymously; Froude replied on 8 August 1865, "You can do as you like about your *name.* You may perhaps be able to write more freely behind the veil."[24] Ultimately it was signed after all; perhaps she softened her criticism. On the Anglo-Irish side she pointed to "the unnatural insulation of such wealth and cultivation as exist in the midst of dreary wastes of poverty and neglect" with "great six-foot walls, which often go meandering for miles. . . . Within is a beautiful park. . . . Outside there is a miserable village, composed of a hundred mud-hovels." Yet though she casts blame on landowners' isolation (and the Newbridge demesne is surrounded by those six-foot walls), the most vivid writing depicts failings of the Celtic Irish. She then describes the famine and its consequences: the number of emigrants from 30 June 1841 to 31 July 1865 was 2,931,344. "Had the population, which twenty years ago almost touched eight millions, gone on increasing unchecked, it would by this time . . . have reached the sum of ten millions. Where there is now one mouth to feed there would have been two." But the famine had broken up the "vicious circle into which the evils of Ireland had run"; by 1865 "Famine and the Exodus ended the system of the peasant, and the Encumbered Estates Court the system of the landlord. Grievous remedies—cauteries for bleeding wounds; but they have done their work." The language is chilling, but Cobbe understood agricultural economics well enough to see the overwhelming difficulties in supporting an ever-increasing population on boggy land with a short growing season. The current population of the entire island is little more than half of what it was before the famine.

Cobbe published a great deal of miscellaneous journalism during 1865 to meet the expenses of London: the two-part series on art and the Ireland essay for *Fraser's*, one for *Macmillan's*, two for the *Theological Review*, and two new pieces for her collection *Studies New and Old*. All of these are substantial essays, typically twelve to fourteen pages of fairly small type in a journal. There were two pieces in the *Reader* in June, but with its subsequent troubles she lost one of her outlets. She placed two anonymous reviews in the *London Review*. She also introduced a volume of Parker's unpublished sermons selected by Rufus Leighton and wrote several pieces for less respectable magazines, including "The Spectral Rout" in the *Shilling Magazine* and "The Fenians of Ballybogmucky" for *Argosy*. "The Spectal Rout" may have been an attempt at fiction, though a legend or a tale (plot and moral without characterization) seems to be as close as she could get. The humorous Fenian piece may also have been a stab at finding a popular voice that would sell.

Frank Newman diligently tried to promote Cobbe's reputation as a serious writer. On 17 July 1865 he wrote an angry letter to John Chapman, editor of the *Westminster Review*, for not letting him discuss *Intuitive Morals*: "You assume I am likely to scandalize your readers by anything that I shall say about Miss Cobbe's philosophy." Chapman must have relented, since Newman's "Capacities of Women" appeared in the *Westminster Review* for October. Reviewing Bessie Parkes's *Essays on Women's Work* (1865), Anna Swanwick's *The Agamemnon, Choephori, and Eumenides of Æschylus* (1865), and seven of Cobbe's books, Newman declared his intention to "exhibit what, in their present cultivation, English women can achieve." His extended discussion of a large *oeuvre* identifies Cobbe as a major author, and although he criticizes some details, such as her errors in Greek, Newman lauds Cobbe as an important writer with great versatility and power.[25]

By October, when the essay appeared, Cobbe was back in London. In the middle of the month the prime minister, Henry John Temple, third viscount Palmerston, died; on 29 October Maggie Elliot's relative John Russell again briefly took office. And on 21 November the Kensington Society discussed women's suffrage. Helen Taylor, who proposed the question, was the daughter of Harriet Taylor, the longtime friend of John Stuart Mill who married him after her first husband's death. Harriet Taylor's anonymous article "The Enfranchisement of Women" in the *Westminster Review* for July 1851 was often attributed to Mill, although Charlotte Brontë, among other women, recognized its true authorship. After her mother died in 1858, Helen Taylor became Mill's "daughter at home," writing letters for his signature and looking after him in other ways. Because Mill spent half the year in Avignon, Taylor did not attend the November meeting but sent a paper. Barbara Bodichon also sent a paper, from Algiers, where she had spent her winters since her marriage in 1857.

The papers were followed by a heated discussion and an informal vote. Nearly all of the fifty women present expressed support for women's suffrage, and some wanted to begin a public agitation. Emily Davies "cautioned against forming a committee" because she was afraid that "such a radical demand would attract 'wild people'" and damage her efforts for women's education. But the genie was out of the bottle, and many Kensington Society women did not want it to be stuffed back in. Cobbe wrote Froude soon afterwards to propose a choice of topics for her next essay. In answer to his reply on 8 December that "ragged school life is an excellent subject. Pray deal with it in preference to any other," she produced "The Indigent Class: Their Schools and Dwellings" for the February 1866 issue of *Fraser's Magazine.* She may well have offered him a suffrage essay but, suspecting that he would refuse and because she did need the money, suggested other topics as well.[26]

Mary Lloyd left for Italy in late November. In the summer Cobbe had written to Somerville, "Mary swears she will go to Rome this winter . . . as if I were going to let my *wife* run about the world in that manner like an unprotected female & leave me behind!" But Cobbe needed to stay near her professional contacts. Meanwhile, Somerville's son from her first marriage had died suddenly, leaving confusion behind: his wife's marriage settlement restricted her inheritance to property specified in his will, and the fruitless search for a will turned up an adult child born to a maid who had worked for his mother when he was a young man. Whether or not this knowledge become public among women like Cobbe and Lloyd, who visited the widow several times and who cared for Somerville, Cobbe could not seriously forbid Lloyd to travel, although she wrote to Somerville on 18 December about her sadness "not to have [Mary] this winter."[27]

On 9 January 1866, while Lloyd was in Rome, John Gibson suffered a stroke. He was in his midseventies. Harriet Hosmer recorded that "good Miss Lloyd remained with him to the last, but I left a kiss on his forehead and came away. Oh! how cold and drear the stars looked that morning as I walked slowly home!"[28] And when Lloyd returned to London they found the pleasures of living in their own house diluted. In addition to unexpected repairs and the rising price of food, there were two robberies nearby in the space of two weeks. Country houses, Cobbe later pointed out in the *Echo,* were well defended with bolts and shutters, even though the country "affords but barren pasturage for burglarious art." Urban burglars observed their targets and made acquaintance with neighborhood servants and tradespeople. Living as they did, with no man in the house, even two independent women were anxious about their safety. Cobbe sold her mother's pearls so they could not be stolen—she also wanted to invest the proceeds—but she managed to turn their fears into a short humorous essay for *Once a Week:* "We bought a rattle; we bought a double-barrelled pistol; we bought a six-shot revolver . . . we hung bells on every door and window; we left brandy in the dining-room, in hopes the thieves would drink it and stop there; we . . . sold our trinkets, and put imitation ones in handsome boxes where the burglars could take them comfortably; we riddled our garden-door with bullets, and then drew chalk targets round the holes, to show how well we could shoot at a mark."[29]

On 1 February 1866 Parliament opened with Earl Russell as prime minister and William Gladstone as government leader in the House of Commons. Political friends returned to London. On 13 February Kate Amberley went "at ½ 9 to a party given by Mary Stanley & Maggie Elliot, an excellent party; made acquaintance with Froude—saw Miss Cobbe." Cobbe, she reported, was "interested in a bill just brought in to Parlt. by a Mr. Torrens to buy up the worst districts in London and build good dwellings for the poor." Cobbe was, in fact, actively lobbying. A few days later she managed to sit next to John Bright, generally a dependable supporter of reformist causes, at a dinner given by another MP. Her February essay for *Fraser's,* "The Indigent Class: Their Schools and Dwellings," described a housing problem caused not only by urban growth but also by the demolitions for railways and grand public buildings that were so changing mid-Victorian cities. She recommended compulsory purchase of property in "overcrowded and pestilential districts" and low-interest public financing to build houses. She was careful to emphasize arguments that appealed to the self-interest of middle-class readers and voters: slums bred epidemics, and improving poor people's health and education would "make the social fabric sound at the core" and diminish the expense for "workhouses, gaols, and hospitals." Thus, with this essay Cobbe stepped beyond the boundary of even very large philanthropic schemes into a first sketch of a welfare state. Her economist friend John Cairnes objected: "Would not this in practice amount to an undertaking by the State to provide comfortable lodgings for the population at large in any numbers that may apply?"[30] He was quite right; though her model may have been the conscientious paternalism of the Newbridge landlord who built cottages and paid for schools, she was, in fact, proposing public housing and free public education, and she continued to do so despite objections from even the most liberal policymakers about state competition with private enterprise.

The bill introduced by William Torrens gave local boards the power of compulsory purchase. Torrens was about the age of Cobbe's oldest brothers and came from a comfortable family of Anglo-Irish gentry in Glasnevin, then a mile and a half north of Dublin; his bill was cosponsored by John Locke and Arthur Kinnaird. Writing anonymously in the *London Review,* Cobbe argued that "we absolutely require the intervention of a new and higher power to act for the interests of the whole community. . . . This power—not the power of private capital, not the power of a handful of wealthy philanthropists, not the power of commercial companies—can only be the power of the State. The State alone can supply the enormous funds demanded to do the work effectually, and within the limits of a generation."[31]

Torrens's bill did not survive in its original form. The next year, when he introduced a new version, Cobbe turned up the rhetorical heat: "If we wait till private enterprise or private charity buy up all the slums of London alone, and build on their site fit dwellings for human health and decency, we may wait till generations have died in misery and squalor, and pestilence after pestilence has ravaged the land." Finally, much amended and further weakened, the bill became law in August 1868 as the Artizans & Labourers' Dwellings Act. "The prevailing philosophy," according to Anthony S. Wohl, "was that while it was a legitimate function of local government to demolish insanitary dwellings it was totally illegitimate for it to interfere in the free market to build houses."[32] Although the final version was far from the one Cobbe had wanted, contemporaries gave her some of the credit for its passage. Through this experience she learned a great deal about practical politics, the inevitability of compromise, and the strategies that might work when presenting unpopular ideas to the governing classes.

In mid-March of 1866 Cobbe inquired about publishing travel pieces in *Temple Bar.* She and Lloyd may once more have planned a long trip. Bishop Colenso (in Natal) heard that they were going to America.[33] But as it turned out, the spring was otherwise occupied. Although no plan of action had followed the Kensington Society's November vote in favor of women's suffrage, Cobbe placed an unsigned letter in the *Spectator* for 24 March 1866 that ran under the heading "Class Representation for Petticoats."

> Sir,—The right to the franchise of that great recently discovered creature, the working man, is presented to us under half-a-dozen different aspects.

. . . Labouring under the misfortune of not being a working man, I yet flatter myself with the fond belief that I may claim to be a "rational and moral being," and I know (alas! too well!) that I have reached double the age when the law fixes for such beings the era of political majority. I possess some little property. . . . This epistle will prove to you that I can write, and afford some presumption that I can also read. . . . if the injustices and sufferings to which unrepresented classes are liable be the proper reason for conferring representation on every class, I need only observe that the wrongs and disabilities of all kinds under which my particular class suffers are too notorious to require citation.

Perhaps the reader asks, What, then, is this class which is thus excluded from the franchise. . . . Possibly I may be an alien . . . or a criminal . . . or, at all events, a member of a class so small and inconsiderable that it has been overlooked by our legislators. None of these hypotheses will apply. . . . Am I very illogical in demanding one of two things, either that my class shall have provision made for its representation in the coming Reform, or that the friends of Reform should cease to distract us with the repetition of arguments at which they themselves shrug their shoulders with contempt for their unpracticalness, whenever they happen to be cited in behalf, not of bricklayers, but of women?

A Woman

Although the editor ruined Cobbe's rhetoric with the heading, which gave away her conclusion and also emphasized women's sexuality and frivolity by reference to their undergarments (R. H. Hutton never supported women's suffrage), the letter did two significant things: it identified women as a class, and it attached their cause to the reform bill then under discussion. The dimensions of reform were still indefinite. A month after Cobbe's letter, in the middle of a long speech not meant as a proposal, Benjamin Disraeli, then leader in the Commons for the Conservative opposition to the Liberal government, said that "if there is to be universal suffrage, women have as much right to vote as men. And more than that—a woman having property ought to have a vote in a country, in which she may hold manorial courts and sometimes elects churchwardens." The sentence was followed by laughter, according to the Times, but little more than a week later Barbara Bodichon wrote to Helen Taylor about "doing something immediately towards getting women votes." She did not want to act "without knowing what you and Mr J. S. Mill thought expedient." Taylor answered at once that if a "tolerably numerously signed petition can be got up"—the minimum later mentioned was one hundred names—Mill would present it to

Parliament. Taylor drafted a long petition, which Bodichon trimmed into a short statement calling for the "representation of all householders, without distinction of sex, who possess such property or rental qualifications as your honourable House may determine." Cobbe and other women with experience in the NAPSS went to work: Barbara Bodichon, Elizabeth Garrett, Emily Davies, Bessie Parkes, Jane Crowe, Jessie Boucherett, Florence Hill. Mentia Taylor was also enlisted. They not only asked friends but also got signatures from teachers, shopkeepers, dressmakers, that is, from working women who were heads of household and saw the practical advantages of voting. On 7 June, Davies and Garrett delivered the petition to Mill. That evening Arthur Munby went to "Notting Hill about 9, to a small party of women (Mr. Shaen & I the only men, for Mr. Taylor was at the House)." Louisa May Alcott was there; so was Cobbe, who "sat talking lively unpretending talk to a circle of admirers. The women's petition for the franchise, which she & Mme Bodichon & Mrs. Taylor have got up, was presented tonight by J. S. Mill. They say it has 1500 signatures."[34]

The next step was to get press coverage. As Cobbe had done for her workhouse papers, they prepared a pamphlet to send to editors, but it was not ready until 18 July. Cobbe managed to get a signed letter in the *Spectator* for 16 June. Responding to the *Spectator's* negative report on 9 June, she argued that "it would be the soundest of all possible policy, while a mass of uneducated *male* votes is being poured into the scales of the Constitution, to balance them by the admission of the votes of a class having much greater educational and moral advantages, namely, those of single women of property."[35] For twenty-first-century readers the argument about "moral advantages" may have unpleasant overtones, reminding Americans, in particular, of the racist arguments that infected the suffrage movement when the Fifteenth Amendment gave the vote to African American men. But the British franchise was still based on property, and rhetoric about moral and educational qualifications was already embedded in the debate. Placing any kind of notice favorable to women's suffrage proved difficult. Cobbe lamented that she did not have access to a good newspaper. "The Pall Mall," she reported to Davies, "put in my little paragraph on our Petition but the editor has said nothing to my proposal to write an article." She could not persuade Froude to take something for *Fraser's*. Davies was not sure an essay by Cobbe would do any good: "Miss Cobbe is thoroughly identified with the rights of women, so that anything she says comes with an *ex parte* air." Alexander Macmillan would not take Cobbe's article because he was already committed to Helen Taylor's "Women and Criticism," which was, as Taylor herself pointed out, "merely incidental to the subject" of suffrage. Davies suggested to Bodichon that "Froude might perhaps insert your article, with only your initials, & I think it would be to our advantage to have our subject brought forward by a new hand, rather than by Miss Cobbe."[36]

As these fragments of correspondence suggest, attempts to follow up on the first organized suffrage effort were sometimes at cross-purposes. Parliament also was in disarray. Russell's bill collapsed along with his government, a demonstration in favor of universal manhood suffrage turned into a riot, and Parliament rose with no decision in sight. After the triumph of obtaining 1,499 signatures in less than four weeks, underlying disagreements began to surface. Helen Taylor insisted that she be a member of any permanent suffrage committee even though she lived in Avignon for half of the year. Davies did not want to give too much time to suffrage because women's education was her first priority, and furthermore she thought Helen Taylor should stay in the background since newspapers were treating suffrage as "an individual crotchet of Mr. Mill's" with little support anywhere else.[37]

Davies, like Cobbe, understood how to use the press. Suffragists needed to get something into *Cornhill,* she wrote, to reach "commonplace people." Publishing in *Westminster* "would do us no credit" since it was allied in the public mind with John Stuart Mill and radical causes. "The Fortnightly is not so bad as the Westminster," Davies continued, "but Miss Boucherett says it is disapproved of by the sort of people she knows,"—that is, well-to-do people whose influence counted with politicians—"& I don't fancy it has much weight, in *itself,* with anybody."[38]

Even those at the center of the petition campaign disagreed about whether to explicitly exclude married women, though everyone knew that the property qualification excluded them in practical terms. Mill and Taylor thought the argument should be strictly equalitarian, with no reference to marriage. Davies favored pursuing the marginally possible. On 6 August she urged Helen Taylor that further petitions request the franchise only for single women and widows; if married women were included, the public would "insist on discussing wives and nothing else."[39] On suffrage questions Cobbe, like Davies, generally chose to favor pragmatic goals. Mill and Taylor would not compromise, the organization of a suffrage committee was delayed, and in the end Taylor refused to become a member.

The suffrage petition and the Torrens-Locke-Kinnaird housing bill did not exhaust Cobbe's political efforts during 1866. The Irish Republican ("Fenian") Brotherhood, organized to arouse Irish rebellion against English rule, had been founded in the United States in 1858. In 1865, when the end of the Civil War released large numbers of Irish-Americans from both armies, money, weapons, and soldiers became available for the cause. Cobbe had written "The Fenians of Ballybogmucky" amid rumors of a rising in Ireland planned for Christmas 1865. Its immediate republication in Boston's *Every Saturday* suggested the political as well as financial advantage of writing on such topics for American journals. "The Fenian 'Idea,'" in the May 1866 *Atlantic Monthly*, was a more temperate piece designed to discourage the *Atlantic*'s educated audience from making parallels between the American Revolution and the Fenian cause. At the end of May Cobbe wrote James Fields a tough but polite letter informing him that she had not yet received the ten pounds he had promised for the article.[40]

Another essay for an American journal is the first evidence of Cobbe's serious interest in psychological phenomena. "The Fallacies of Memory," published in *Galaxy* in May 1866, investigates the nature of failures in recollection, giving examples from commonplace experience, historical evidence, and courtroom testimony. In addition, Cobbe wrote often on American topics for the *London Review*. (She had become close friends with Louisa Lee Schuyler, of New York, who had done intensive Sanitary Commission work during the war and was later to form the State Charities Aid Association, which worked to improve prisons, poorhouses, public hospitals, and care for people who were mentally ill.) Other anonymous pieces in the *London Review* and signed letters to the *Pall Mall Gazette* developed her social thought. On the issue of healthcare for paupers, as on housing and education, she came closer to constructing a system of welfare entitlement as she began to recommend that serious illnesses should never be treated in the workhouse; she believed that the board of guardians ought to defray the cost of sending patients to a hospital.[41] She also continued to look for a voice she could sell to more popular journals, both for the income and perhaps for eventual political uses. "Alured," a strange "allegory" of love, death, and the uncanny, appeared in the shilling monthly *Temple Bar,* then edited by Edmund Yates, in August. She placed three narratives in Bradbury and Evans's inexpensive illustrated journal *Once a Week,* although she did not manage to become a regular contributor.

During the summer parliamentary season of this busy year, social events mixed pleasantly with politics. Cobbe had to decline an evening party given by Kate Amberley because she was dining with the Froudes, but she issued her own invitation to a "little gathering of *heterodox* friends for a 5 o'clock cup of tea under our lime tree." At more public events she learned, as did many busy women, to use her time well. "We seldom think out the subject of a new book or article, or elaborate a political or philanthropic scheme," she would write, "with so much precision and lucidity as when gazing with vacant respectfulness at a gentleman expatiating with elaborate stupidity on theology or science." And her well-known habit of unfashionable dress caught up with her when she put on something suitable for a large elegant party at the Amberleys' on 3 July. Geraldine Jewsbury wrote an embarrassed letter the next day:

> *Were* you last evening at 13 Deans Yard Westminster? There was a lady whom at the time I did not in the least associate with *you* on the contrary I took a fixed idea it was *somebody else*—a lady whom I have seen in a sort of way but to whom I have never been presented & she being a great lady, I did not even look at her much because I did not want to ask for recognition. . . . This morning on opening my eyes—it flashed on me that . . . it was *Miss Cobbe* who was in that jacket with those buttons last night! If *so* my stupidity had . . . brought its own punishment for I leave you to imagine how glad I wd have been to have got a word with you.[42]

In August Cobbe was out of town, perhaps to see her brothers. Sometime during 1866 Henry and his family—two daughters born in Switzerland as well as his wife, Sarah, and their eldest child, Mabel, who was eleven—returned to England. He became rector of Milton-Bryant in Bedfordshire, about forty miles from London but without an easy rail connection. It was a small parish with a proportionately meager income for its clergyman; *Crockford's Clerical Directory* for 1865 gives a population of 345 and an income of £252 in addition to a house.[43] Cobbe had tried to help either Henry or Tom get a book into print. On 7 March 1866 Froude wrote, "What can be done for your brother's book? . . . Could he not make semihumorous articles out of it? I can do nothing & know no one who can."[44] Whichever brother the letter refers to, this judgment from a noted historian must have been discouraging, and the project in question is undiscovered. Tom completed a historical manuscript some three and a half years later, but it is hard to imagine a work less possible to transform into "semihumorous articles." Henry may also have worked at history while living in Switzerland; a source note to the *Dictionary of National Biography* entry for John, Lord Wenlock, who died in 1471 at the Battle of Tewkesbury, acknowledges an unpublished manuscript by Henry Cobbe.

That autumn, when Cobbe and others were back in London, attempts to organize a suffrage committee began in earnest. The NAPSS had met in Manchester, and Barbara Bodichon's paper had stimulated Lydia Becker and other local women to develop a committee, which in turn prodded the London group into action. On 21 October 1866 nine women met and resolved to "form a Provisional Committee for obtaining the abolition of the legal disabilities which at present unqualifies women as such from voting for Members of Parliament." The nine were Barbara Bodichon, Jessie Boucherett, Frances Power Cobbe, Emily Davies, Elizabeth Garrett, Isa Craig Knox (the paid secretary of the NAPSS had married her cousin John Knox), Mary Lloyd, Bessie Parkes, and Mentia Taylor.[45]

Yet the conflicts in ideology and strategy had not been resolved. Helen Taylor refused to join but insisted on making her influence felt. Some members wanted men on the governing body to add political weight; others thought that if men were involved, they would get all the credit. Davies favored a small, informal committee; Helen Taylor believed there should be a larger, more structured society.[46] Mary Lloyd's presence was anomalous; she had not attended NAPSS meetings or demonstrated an interest in politics. However, Cobbe could count on her support in case of divisive questions, and as a single woman who was both a householder and a landowner she represented a class of women who would be enfranchised if the disqualification of gender were removed. It was also difficult to find anyone willing to take responsibility for leadership. At the first meeting, according to Bodichon, Davies "expressed her determination to withdraw altogether from the work finding the educational movement as much as she could do." Bodichon was in London only two months of the year. Davies worried about Mentia Taylor because she was "a woman with such well-known radical proclivities."[47] For the time, Isa Knox was named "honorary secretary," the usual title for the day-to-day head of voluntary associations during the period, with Mentia Taylor as secretary.

The group never did become organized formally enough to have stationery or even a name; Elizabeth Crawford calls it, for the sake of convenience, the "London Provisional Petition Committee." At the end of November the body was restructured as a society for "the Enfranchisement of Unmarried Women and Widows, Possessing the Due Property Qualification." By the end of the discussion Cobbe was no longer on its governing committee, a small but mixed group composed chiefly of high-status men and respectably married women. Louisa Smith, one of the Garrett sisters, who was married to James Smith and the mother of four children, was the honorary secretary, and Mentia Taylor, another married woman, with a husband in Parliament, served as treasurer. During the winter of 1866–67 the new society collected two sets of names. A women householder's petition was to be signed only by single or widowed women who would be eligible for the franchise, while a general petition would include signatures of others, both men and women. Although Cobbe was no longer on the executive, she made several "improvements"—the word is Helen Taylor's—in the petitions.[48]

Cobbe's essay in *Fraser's* for November attacked the "false conventional laws of society" that distinguish "between vice in high places and vice in low;

between vice in man and vice in women. . . . Let a man be very wealthy—
a powerful statesman—a brilliant writer. How does society condone his
debts and his dishonesties, his drunkenness, gambling, profligacy, domestic
cruelties?"[49] Far from questioning working-class moral judgment (as she
seemed to do in some arguments for women's suffrage), she struck much the
same note a few months later in "What Is Progress, and Are We Progressing?" Although statistics revealed a drop in crime since 1851, she argued, there
remained an "enormous class of delinquencies which only in extreme cases
finds it way into police reports": fraud, deception, manipulation of financial markets, adulteration of food, dishonesty in trade. Middle-class citizens
may believe that pickpockets and muggers are the chief representatives of
the "criminal classes," but "commercial corruption is the rottenness of the
bones," and national acts such as the "Burmese War of 1852 [and the] second Chinese War of 1856" were a source of disgrace and dishonor. Without
ever mentioning suffrage, both of these articles implicitly demonstrate wom-
en's qualification to vote intelligently on large public issues as well as on
"women's topics" such as charity and infant welfare.

One day in January 1867—an intensely cold month—Hajjin vanished
while walking with her mistress in Sloane Square. The police advised Cobbe
"to print handbills offering a reward" so the thief would return the dog.
"Had it been my watch which was stolen," she wrote, "the police would, of
course, have endeavoured to capture the thief. As it was only a dog, which
I valued ten times as much, nothing could be done but to aid me to bribe
the robber."[50] After a few days Hajjin turned up at the Lost Dog's Home in
Holloway. Cobbe at once wrote a short book to earn money and publicity
for the home. *The Confessions of a Lost Dog* was reviewed in the *Spectator* for
23 March 1867 with a lightly humorous critique of the "autobiographer's"
unwillingness to share her inner feelings. The book also began making
Cobbe's name known among the sentimental pet lovers who would become
ardent, if sometimes difficult, allies in the struggle against vivisection.

After the political establishment returned to town for the parliamentary season Cobbe invited the Amberleys to meet her cousin Elizabeth
Monck, whose husband was governor general of British America, along with
J. A. Froude and several scientific people, such as the Lyells and T. H. Huxley.[51] Parliament's chief business that session was still the question of reform.
When the bill introduced by the Liberals in 1866 was defeated, Russell's government resigned and the Conservatives formed a new administration with
the earl of Derby as prime minister and Benjamin Disraeli as party leader
in the House of Commons. Disraeli introduced a series of resolutions (not
yet a bill) on 11 February. Over the next few weeks a large number of proposals were in play. Most men in both parties wanted to add literate voters

from the lower middle class and the skilled working class without setting the qualification so low that the "responsible classes" would be overwhelmed by votes from "horny-handed laborers." But reducing the property qualification exacerbated women's disenfranchisement. Even if gender were removed, married women would not become voters; everything a woman owned passed into her husband's hands unless her family negotiated a marriage settlement, and marriage settlements, which were only provided by substantial families, generally took the form of investments or a charge on an estate rather than land or houses. But lowering the property qualification and removing gender would benefit a large number of widows and single women, especially among dressmakers, grocers, lodging-house keepers, and other tradeswomen, as well as among women farmers. In addition, both Lloyd (as a householder) and Cobbe (as a lodger paying £80 a year in rent) could become voters.

As soon as the parliamentary discussion began, women set to work along several lines. One was to renew agitation for a married women's property act. The issue had first come up in Parliament more than ten years earlier; a bill had even passed its second reading in July 1857, but it had gone no further because the divorce bill, then in the Lords, dealt with the most aggravated problems. Early in 1867 a committee headed by Josephine Butler, Jessie Boucherett, Elizabeth Wolstenholme, and Elizabeth Gloyn—both Butler and Gloyn were married; the other two were single—asked the NAPSS council to work toward "a full consideration in both Houses of Parliament." Meanwhile, suffragists continued collecting names for their two petitions. Cobbe asked Mary Somerville to sign—it was always useful to head the lists with the names of distinguished women—but Somerville refused. "I think the petition of the women to Parliament so ill timed that I cannot possibly sign it," she wrote. She believed that women would demean themselves "by joining the outcry of a disaffected mob whose real object is to overthrow the constitution."[52] But Somerville was in Italy, and events in England moved quickly ahead. Cobbe showed no sign of distancing herself because male laborers wanted to eliminate all property qualifications; indeed, she believed the fears aroused by working men's agitation would help women's cause.

Unfortunately, however, the Enfranchisement of Women Committee, established the previous November, had never jelled. On 4 March 1867 Mentia Taylor wrote to Helen Taylor: she believed that a new committee was needed, one on which she would "not feel myself as a Pariah," as well as an honorary secretary who could actually do the work. Louisa Smith had died of appendicitis early in February and had been replaced (on paper) by Barbara Bodichon, who was in Algeria. Emily Davies's tactics, or lack of them, were a major problem. Jessie Boucherett complained that "our affairs have been very ill managed" because "Miss Davies knows so little of what is going on." Mentia used strong language: "I cannot again work with a committee in which I meet with no support, no sympathy, in which I am regarded as a dangerous, go-a-head revolutionary person."[53]

On the next day, 5 March, Cobbe dined at Peter and Mentia Taylor's. Several MPs were there, including Henry Fawcett (who would marry Millicent Garrett in April). John Bright, a notable parliamentary orator, wrote in his diary: "Conversation on Women's Franchise, which I do not much favour. Miss Cobbe a very intelligent woman, with good sympathies." (Meeting him at another dinner a year earlier, she had asked, according to her note, "why he laboured so hard to get votes for working carpenters and bricklayers, and never stirred a finger to ask them for women, who possessed already the property qualification? He said: 'Much was to be said for women,' but then went on maundering about our proper sphere, and 'would they go into Parliament?'")[54]

On 28 March Henry Austin Bruce presented a general petition with 3,559 signatures to the House of Commons. Mill followed the next week with another 3,161 names. On the same day, a two-column letter to the editor headed "Female Franchise" and signed "Only a Woman" was printed in a new and very conservative newspaper, the *Day*. Its anonymous author was Frances Power Cobbe. Lydia Becker's "Female Suffrage" had come out in the March *Contemporary Review,* but the *Contemporary Review* was edited by Henry Alford, dean of Canterbury and a member of the London enfranchisement committee. Cobbe's success in placing a prosuffrage argument in an antisuffrage paper shows personal politics—and press politics—in action. The *Day,* billed as a "champion of enlightened Toryism," first appeared on 19 March 1867. Too conservative even for Disraeli, the paper survived only until 4 May, and its investors, including R. H. Hutton, who subscribed six thousand pounds, lost heavily.[55]

Cobbe was on the newspaper's staff—still remarkable for a woman in 1867, although not entirely without precedent—as a leader writer. Leaders, typically the longest items in each day's paper, took up serious political, social, or legal issues in the manner now found in signed editorial-page columns; they were expressions of opinion, with background and analysis, usually tied to current news. Since all such writing was anonymous—written as "we" in the voice of the paper and in Cobbe's case carefully without gender—discovery of Cobbe's work for the *Day* depends on her scrapbooks at the National Library of Wales. Her typical leaders were between twelve hundred and fourteen hundred words long. She wrote two or three leaders every week and earned three guineas for each one. The first of her leaders, on 1 April 1867, was about a trial of some Fenians arrested after a failed uprising in Dublin. It urged that even though the law permitted them to be whipped, some other penalty should be imposed: whipping would only "embitter hatred already deep enough." The second, on 3 April, argued for modifications and funding of the Artizans and Labourers' Dwellings Act.

Now the *Day,* as might be expected, very much opposed women's suffrage. Cobbe's "letter to the editor," however, is the same length as her leaders, and she was paid the usual three guineas. Although the editor would not admit it to the leader pages, where, unsigned, it would be taken as reflecting the newspaper's opinion, he was willing, after what sort of argument we can only imagine, to print it as correspondence with the signature "Only a Woman." Cobbe made some significant rhetorical concessions to conservative arguments about women's sphere, yet by adopting this tactic, and by her value as a journalist, she managed to promote women's suffrage in a high Tory newspaper. "Female Franchise" moved systematically through the arguments for and against granting political rights to "women otherwise qualified." On the question of women as an unrepresented class, she wrote, opponents tell us "as the *Times* did last week, that we are not a class at all . . . that we have no separate interests, or, if we have any, that they are well cared for by our male relations. Alas! alas! That . . . ideal family which Englishmen always refer to as woman's paradise, that region of earth or period of time when woman shall really have no separate interests from man, when her property, her life, and the children dearer to her than her life, shall be her own, never invaded or torn from her . . . That time, alas! is not in England to-day." And, nearing the letter's conclusion, if women's putative mental inferiority was an insurmountable barrier to their political rights, "then Mr. Carlyle is right, and all government except that of the strong is a delusion. . . . We have gone back to the *Droit du plus fort,* and all our civilisation is a mistake."[56]

While engaged with suffrage Cobbe discovered new aspects of the woman question. She looked for the first time at working women who were neither domestic servants nor middle class and began to question even the kind of volunteer labor she had done less than a decade earlier. In "The American Sanitary Commission and Its Lesson," which may reveal Louisa Schuyler's influence, Cobbe told ladies that to work in a hospital without pay was "*not* an heroic act of public charity, but a serious social mistake." If "ladies of independent means filled with religious zeal" refused to take a salary, they not only replaced women who "need to earn their own bread, and often the bread of their families" but also degraded the profession by making it seem as if the work had no monetary value.[57]

Suffrage activity intensified throughout the spring. Julia Ward Howe, the author of "Battle Hymn of the Republic" and a U.S. suffragist, came to tea.

By May Cobbe was talking with Helen Taylor and Mentia Taylor about a successor to the Enfranchisement of Women Committee. Meanwhile, the failure of reform in the previous year had combined with economic difficulties to revive interest in a much broader franchise for working men. There were massive demonstrations in Hyde Park despite the government's ban. "Intellectuals like Matthew Arnold and Thomas Carlyle," writes Theodore Hoppen, " . . . thought the world had come to an end. Arnold made the Hyde Park demonstrations a symbol of disorder in *Culture and Anarchy* (1869)," and Carlyle responded with the abusive spleen of "Shooting Niagara: And After?" in *Macmillan's Magazine* for August. Angered because men's physical force got attention, while law-abiding women were ignored, Cobbe composed a sly letter to the editor of *Day* suggesting how women could also stir up trouble:

> Sir,—I am a working woman, and I and millions of other women want our rights. We have settled to hold a grand meeting and demonstration on Monday in the Reading-room of the British Museum. It is a public place, paid for by the national taxes, and I am sure our tea costs us enough to give us a special right to use it. . . . What, sir! are not the rights of women to the franchise far more important than that a party of old fogies should sit poring over musty folios all day long, in that well-warmed and ventilated apartment for which *we* have paid? . . . Sir, I and my friends are resolved to try our rights, and let the base and cowardly curator and his myrmidons dread our parasols. If everybody's eye be poked out, on their heads be it!—Yours, not very obediently, Edmonia Bawles.[58]

As she wrote a year later, "Last summer the *Times* remarked that 'when working men desired to have votes *they* threw down the park palings, but that women have not shown their wish for the same privilege by any such proceedings.' . . . we should have supposed that the mob who attacked the police and spoiled the public park, and the women who stopped at home and signed Mr. Mill's petition, had respectively shown the one their *unfit-ness*, and the other their fitness for the franchise of a law-respecting nation."[59]

On 20 May 1867, while the Commons considered multiple changes in their effort to reach a formula for reform, John Stuart Mill moved to leave out "man" and substitute "person." Kate Amberley, Maggie Elliot, Millicent Fawcett, and other women were in the ladies' gallery to hear his speech. Although the amendment lost by 123 votes—196 MPs voted against it, 73 in favor—there was surprising encouragement to be found in the numbers. Even the *Saturday Review*, never a friend to women's causes, described it as a "respectable minority."[60] Nor did it become a party issue; about 10 of the

73 favorable votes came from Conservatives, one of whom, Russell Gurney, served as a teller. Some Liberals voted on purely ideological grounds, believing in equity for women, but one suspects that most of the Liberals and almost all of the Conservatives were more interested in adding women voters to balance the radicalism of working men. Disraeli, the Conservative leader in the Commons, did not vote on either side in the division over Mill's amendment. Gladstone voted against it, as did cousin Laura's husband, John Locke. Those voting in favor of women's suffrage at this earliest opportunity included Amberley, Henry Fawcett, F. H. Goldsmid, Duncan McLaren, James Stansfeld, and P. A. Taylor, all of whom were married to women active in the suffrage movement, as well as Thomas Hughes, Henry Labouchère, Lawrence Oliphant, and John Bright. (John Bright supported a great many radical causes, including universal male suffrage, during his long career but had already told Cobbe of his objection to enfranchising women. He voted in favor this one time, presumably out of respect for Mill, but not again, although his younger brother Jacob Bright became the suffragists' chief spokesman in Parliament.) Well more than half of the 658 men then in the House of Commons managed to avoid voting at all.[61]

Activists paused only briefly to take stock. On 26 May Cobbe invited the Amberleys to meet James Martineau. Kate Amberley reported in her diary: "Mr. Frank Newman was unexpectedly there it was the first I had met him and it gave me great pleasure. He was in his mg. [morning] clothes, thick warm ones, a woolen shirt and coarse comforter, iron grey hair, fine bright eyes and a good deal of colour in his face. His voice was soft and gentle. . . . We sat in an arbour of Miss Cobbe's in her back garden after dinner, where she writes, often. We left at 11—a delightful day."[62]

The London suffrage committee continued to struggle with internal difficulties. Jessie Boucherett had wanted to have all the women's suffrage petitions brought into the Commons on the same day. Emily Davies had told her that the committee "did not think there would be any advantage in so doing." Boucherett thought that was "extremely stupid on their part" because they had missed an opportunity to get press attention. Davies found it "clearly impossible to go on as we are. No secretary would, with her eyes open, undertake the task of keeping Mrs. Taylor in check." Boucherett suggested a large general committee with as many MPs as possible[63] and three small central committees, in London, Manchester, and Edinburgh. She hoped the London central committee would have Helen Taylor plus "Mrs. P. Taylor, Miss Cobbe, myself and half a dozen or a dozen more, active, zealous persons." Mentia Taylor spoke to Davies, and Davies agreed to retire. The version Davies recorded in her old age was that the committee had dis-

solved "by common consent" on 14 June 1867 because of "the incompati-
bility of its chief elements." Mentia Taylor, she continued, "belonged to the
extreme Left of the Liberal Party, & looked at matters from a different point
of view from other members."[64]

The next day Mentia wrote to Helen that she was "pleased to have had
the opportunity of introducing you and Miss Cobbe to each other—and
though she is somewhat conservative—and differs from us in many points—
she is so earnest in our present work—and so straightforward—that I feel
her cooperation will be of great value to us." The three of them—Helen Taylor, Mentia Taylor, and Frances Cobbe—were central in forming the new
organization. Davies wrote bitterly that the suffrage cause was for the moment "under the direction of the Radical section of the party."[65]

Cobbe, aware of her differences from advanced liberals on issues of party
politics—not, perhaps, in gender politics, but no one yet had the language
to conceptualize such a term—wanted a colleague who would be able to represent her when she could not attend meetings. She wrote to Helen Taylor
that she had spoken "to some of my friends in whose judgment I have much
confidence" and found "that three of them Miss Lloyd Miss Hampson &
probably Miss A Spottiswoode would in all probability" agree to work on
the committee "should it prove desirable." Two-way and three-way discussions, some recorded in letters and others only to be inferred, continued for
much of the summer. On 20 June, after consulting with Cobbe, Mentia
wrote to Helen that the organization's name would be London Woman
Suffrage Society. Two days later Cobbe reported to Mentia that Helen Taylor refused to be on the executive but said that she and Mill would join the
general committee. In early July Lydia Becker, from Manchester, wrote to
Helen Taylor on notepaper headed "Enfranchisement of Women" inquir-
ing about the proposed union among the organizations. She wanted to retain
enough independence so that each society would be "free to work in the
mode best adopted to the locality in which they are engaged." This letter
opened yet another set of questions that would come to haunt the infant
suffrage organizations in the months ahead.[66]

On 3 July, Mentia Taylor called a meeting for the fifth. When it was over,
Cobbe wrote to Helen Taylor that they had had "a fair preliminary meeting
& now consider ourselves constituted into the Exece Come of 'The London Society for obtaining political rights for Women.'"[67] (The name would
undergo several further changes.) Like the provisional committee of October 1866, the new executive was made up entirely of women. They included
Frances Power Cobbe and Mary Lloyd—both had been on the provisional
committee but not among the mixed governors of the Enfranchisement of

Women Committee—Millicent Garrett Fawcett, Jane Hampson, Katherine Hare, Margaret Bright Lucas, and Carolyn Stansfeld.[68] Mentia Taylor, the only direct holdover from the committee that had just dissolved in disarray, was head of the new executive under the title of honorary secretary.

Millicent Fawcett, the youngest of the activist Garrett sisters, was twenty years old and had been married in April to the Cambridge professor of political economy and liberal MP Henry Fawcett. Katherine Hare was a member of the Kensington discussion society; her father, the political reformer Thomas Hare, became honorary president of the suffrage organization after Mill's death. Margaret Bright Lucas, a sister of John and Jacob Bright, had worked in radical causes for more than twenty years. Carolyn Ashurst Stansfeld was a daughter of a freethinking solicitor who believed in the political and social equality of women and the wife of the radical MP James Stansfeld. Both Lucas and Stansfeld, along with Cobbe and Mentia Taylor, had been members of the Ladies' London Emancipation Society. Lloyd and Hampson were clearly out of place; it is probably unfortunate that Augusta Spottiswoode would not serve as Cobbe's ally. A longtime workhouse visitor, Spottiswoode had at least the potential for political activism; eventually, when it became possible for women to serve, she was elected to a post as a poor-law guardian.

As for the "radicalism" of Mentia Taylor, mentioned so often in accounts of the suffrage movement, it is hard to discover quite what form it took. Cobbe clearly was not frightened by it. Mentia and her husband were Unitarians whose efforts lay behind a great number of reformist organizations that had Cobbe's sympathy: the Friends of Italy, the Ladies' London Emancipation Society, the Ladies' Educational Association; Mentia was also a friend of George Eliot's and the initiator of the Pen and Pencil Club. Louisa May Alcott described her as "a far more interesting woman to me than Victoria . . . a model Englishwoman,—simple, sincere, and accomplished; full of good sense, intelligence, and energy." Daughter of a farmer, she was a governess before she married, and her parties at Aubrey House were "admirably free of class prejudice in persons and opinions" even though after Peter Taylor became a wealthy man through his partnership in the Courtauld silk-manufacturing firm their house in Notting Hill Gate had, according to Arthur Munby, a "drive and gardens in front and parklike grounds behind. . . . It was amusing to see how rooms and hall were made to express the owner's politics. Busts of Cromwell, portraits of Mazzini, memoirs of Abraham Lincoln, instead of Landseers & so on." Yet for all the descriptions of her hospitality and her radicalism, there seems to be no record of the specific actions or opinions that set women like Emily Davies on edge.[69]

On Sunday, 7 July, two days after the executive committee was formed, Cobbe and the Taylors dined with Mill and his stepdaughter at Blackheath. Among the topics of discussion was a name for the new society. Whatever proposals were made in the presence of Mill and Helen Taylor, by 11 July the executive committee had agreed on London National Society for Woman Suffrage. However, Helen Taylor, although unwilling to serve on the executive, insisted on using her power as their link with Mill to veto the committee's decision and demanded that the name be changed to London National Society for *Women's* Suffrage. On 15 July Mentia Taylor wrote to Helen explaining why the committee stood by its original choice; she "enclosed a blunt note from Frances Cobbe who said she preferred Woman to the genitive form and therefore was leaving it that way."[70] Helen Taylor refused to yield, and after several more exchanges Cobbe gave in rather than lose her support. The stationery already printed with the heading "London National Society for Woman Suffrage" was altered by hand to read "Women's." Both Peter Taylor and Moncure Conway were mystified by the dispute, according to Elizabeth Crawford, but apparently "Helen Taylor and Mill thought that 'Woman Suffrage' implied that of only unmarried women and widows."[71] The society's purpose, for the present, was to spread information by publishing and reprinting pamphlets (as the London Ladies' Emancipation Society had done). Cobbe and Helen Taylor at once began working to get newspaper publicity; Helen supplied data, and Cobbe wrote to editors. Before Parliament rose in August, however, the Representation of the People Act, generally called the Second Reform Bill, had passed. After a similar measure for Scotland in 1868 the electorate was doubled; in England, Wales, and Scotland one out of three adult males qualified to vote (in Ireland, one in six).

With the immediate cause for their activism suspended, the suffrage executive scattered for a summer holiday. Lloyd went to Wales; Cobbe visited her brother Charles. From Ireland she invited Mary Somerville to join the new society: "I am delighted you think we are all right about the women's franchise. It is indeed I think a conservative measure & one really needed in these very alarming times." After other news, she returned to her disappointment over the Reform Bill: "Many old Whigs who have always been liberal friends of the people are pretty frightened—for my own part I feel as if we were throwing heads you win, tails I lose & all for nothing." She blamed it on "wretched party spirit" that had "Tories & Whigs & radicals outbidding each other with that blessed Working Man—the origin of all evil." That last, disturbing phrase grew from her angry belief that the Commons had caved in to mob violence and her fear that representatives elected by workingmen with their own class causes would be even less likely to care about

Henry Fawcett (1833–1884) and Millicent Garrett Fawcett (1847–1929). Henry Fawcett was elected to Parliament in 1865. Millicent Fawcett was an active suffragist by the time she was twenty and lived just long enough to celebrate women's full political equality. The photograph was taken in 1868, not long after their marriage. (Mary Evans/The Women's Library)

John Stuart Mill (1806–1873) and his stepdaughter Helen Taylor (1831–1907). (Hulton/Archive by Getty Images)

women. But her general concern was very widely shared: even the earl of Derby, whose government had sponsored the bill, described it as "a leap in the dark."[72]

Harriet Hosmer was at 26 Hereford Square during the summer and went to Newbridge with Cobbe in August. She wrote that she was "in a delightful place and in the old home of a friend who is very dear to me. We are about ten miles from Dublin, and when I speak of a cool summer, I mean such weather as we have in the winter in Rome. . . . This seems the densest solitude in comparison with the rush and crush of London, though there is a gay party staying at the house, besides the family." A month later Cobbe and Hosmer were both in Wales. "We have been on a most delightful excursion nearly all day," wrote Hosmer. "Miss Lloyd is hospitality itself, Miss Cobbe jollity itself, and we three are as snug as possible. I received your last letter yesterday morning, just as we were booting and spurring ourselves for an expedition which turned out to be one of the most successful on record. I rather astonished Miss Lloyd, who is our tutelary deity, by my spring of leg and vigor of windpipe. The air is perfectly delicious, like champagne."[73]

Cobbe had hoped to winter in Rome, which was why she wanted Hampson on the committee, but nothing came of it. The reason may have been financial. On 29 October she wrote Charles a long letter about her income and her needs. Inflation in the decade since their father's death had reduced the value of her inheritance, which Charles paid quarterly as a charge on his income from the estate, so that "£200 a year now will only purchase as much as £140 would purchase ten years ago." She earned from £100 to £150 a year by writing:

> This is of course more than one woman in a thousand makes—& more than my father could have foreseen. Still it leaves me with an income on which I find it will be impossible for me to live here. For the first, & only time doubtless,—of my life I have the chance of a home—a real home with a friend whom I love & in the place where I am not only happiest but have the best chance of getting on in what I may call my profession as a writer. More than half the expense of our house & all the capital for it has been found by Mary Lloyd but my share—I see too clearly, will be beyond my means even with my best exertions. I shall have to relinquish it & resume my old solitary lodging house life without a servant—& without the great happiness of a friend. . . . The prices of food & coals &c have become so enormous that if I hold out this winter—(as I am inclined to do—in the hope of getting better employment) I must dip heavily into my capital. . . . I almost think I shd do best to break up at once—That I should do so with the bitterest regret there is no need to say.[74]

Charles generously provided the extra £100 a year she asked for. Whether or not she knew it, he had done much the same for two brothers: he had agreed to give Tom £200 a year on his second marriage, although the capital intended for Tom's inheritance was consumed in divorcing Azélie; and he had added £150 a year to Henry's income and also lent him money for moving to Milton-Bryant. Will, however, had written himself out of the family when he entered the Agapemone. In March 1866 Will sent Charles an angry and defensive letter demanding information about their father's will. Charles, himself stung into anger, reminded Will that he had not shown up for either parent's death. Their father, he wrote, had not made provision for his children "solely by their agreeing, or disagreeing with him in their religious views. . . . Your sister has views more remote from what were his than even yours." About the will, he concluded, "I would not hurt your feelings by sending the shilling left to you but as you now claim whatever may be coming to you, I send it in stamps, and you can give me an acknowledgment, as Executor."[75]

After her own letter to Charles, Cobbe briefly found regular work on the *Leader,* described in the *Newspaper Press Directory* for 1868 as a Saturday "political, literary, and social Review" that "combines the best qualities of journalism with the lighter attractions of a popular miscellany." (The "lighter attractions" included a serialized novel.) Cobbe wrote eighteen unsigned essays, primarily on social topics, between 5 October and 18 December 1867. On 26 October she insisted that education had "never gone far enough down in the social strata." It must be made universal, a task "which the State alone can perform." An American reviewer, J. W. Chadwick, writing a major essay on Cobbe in the U.S. *Christian Examiner* for November 1867, suggested that her "fondness for statistics" and "practical turn of mind" had led her toward a scientific approach to social problems.[76] Increasingly she demanded new legislation and public funding, the antithesis, perhaps, to mid-nineteenth-century laissez-faire liberalism but hardly a sign of the conservatism (at least as the term is now used) with which she is often charged.

Politics as well as money supplied a reason to stay in London. Cobbe, unlike some others, felt strongly that women alone should sign the next suffrage petition. With committees established in London, Manchester, and Edinburgh, Helen Taylor wanted to publish "*one list* of names—selecting the best of each committee." The London executive did not like Taylor's exclusionist tactic, high-profile though it might be, and agreed that any published list should include "*all* who pay their guinea to be on the General Committee."[77] Lydia Becker wanted to know what Manchester would gain by joining with the London society. Differences in the spirit and methods had become evident; Manchester hired a paid organizer to canvass for signatures rather than using London's more genteel letter writing. In addition, some Manchester members thought petitions were a waste of time unless there were a bill in Parliament; they wanted to bring a court case in the name of a woman otherwise qualified since most other laws used *man* generically to include both sexes.[78]

During these internal conflicts Cobbe resigned from the executive, although she continued to be a member of the general committee. She wrote to Helen Taylor that "the different ideas of radicals and conservatives as to what is admissible under a hundred circumstances are more various than I had ever imagined & I came to the conclusion that Miss Hampson & Miss Lloyd—& in many cases myself, would be mere obstructions to the action of the others." That was for public consumption. More pointedly, she resented Helen Taylor's continual interference; after all, Taylor had refused to lead or even serve on the executive. Cobbe was "rather vexed" that although she herself had yielded about the name after "that very difficult evening we spent at yr house," Taylor "continued to urge an amalgamation . . . to which I had shown such repugnance." Cobbe believed that they should not use Manchester's names "for our honour" unless they were "ready to stand by them in any action whose good taste might be questionable." She had no specific objection to anything the Manchester women had done, but— perhaps a sign of how unfamiliar women still were with organizing a mass movement—she very much disliked trusting people she did not know.[79]

Mary Somerville's reluctance to be involved with radicals might have influenced Cobbe, but it is worth noting that Helen Taylor herself resigned from the Manchester society in December 1868 "in protest against Lydia Becker's style and methods." Cobbe's difficulties in 1867 may not have been entirely unreasonable, although she and Becker later became friendly colleagues. Cobbe called her "a woman of singular political ability, for whom I had a sincere respect. . . . She gave me the impression of one of those ill-fated people whose outward persons do not represent their inward selves. . . . She was a most courageous and straightforward woman, with a single eye to the great political work which she had undertaken."[80]

Hampson and Lloyd, however, had never belonged on the executive. Without the experience of public work in the NAPSS, they were unfamiliar with the give-and-take of debate, unaccustomed to organizing, and far more bound by conventions of womanly privacy. Yet it must be remembered that even Emily Davies did not then want her name linked with the suffrage cause. Mary Lloyd continued to sign petitions, though she had no taste for activism. I suspect that Cobbe was disappointed by her friends' failure to understand the demands of political cooperation, but neither Hampson nor Lloyd had even attended Kensington Society meetings; they lacked the growing consciousness that prepared other committee members to work together.

Explaining her resignation to Helen Taylor, Cobbe wrote that "even this Woman's franchise question wherein all my definite politics centre is so far secondary to me to the religious ideas which I wd fain make my life's work to spread in the world." She worried especially about her reputation because "orthodox papers fasten on heretics any blot they can discover." And she was especially sensitive just then because the Agapemone had yet again grabbed public attention. Her acquaintance W. Boyd Dawkins wrote in the October 1867 *Macmillan's Magazine* about Henry Prince's "religious enthusiasm or mania" as a psychological aberration that explained the "foundation of a new creed." Despite its veneer of historical and philosophical investigation and its scholarly tone, the article emphasized the sect's luxury and women's wish to escape. Dawkins at least did not mention William Cobbe by name, but W. Hepworth Dixon did. *Spiritual Wives,* published in January 1868, was a sensational book on religious movements that illustrated man's "spiritual passions." Dixon, who then edited the *Athenaeum,* had written to Cobbe in September: "The Dean of Bristol tells me that you are likely to know the full name of Prince of the Agape. If so I want to write a letter to him." She supplied the address, he visited the Agapemone, and among the chief followers of Henry James Prince he named "William Cobbe, a brother of Miss Frances P. Cobbe, the writer on social subjects" as the member who had built their "handsome stone chapel."[81]

Cobbe wrote at once to complain. Dixon answered that he was "grieved to find that any words of mine have caused you pain." He would, as a personal favor, remove her name from the text. But he refused to admit any fault: "What I know of Mr. Cobbe I heard from yourself, and from his friend in the Abode of Love. You spoke to me without reserve in London, & the people at Spaxton spoke of you. . . . If you are annoyed, it must be with the facts, & not the historian. You are a public writer, I cannot think it a grievance to see your name in print."[82]

*Spiritual Wives* gives a picturesque account of the community and its setting. Dixon described rituals such as the "Two Anointed Ones, to whom has been given power to explain to men the mystery of the Seven Stars, to keep the Seven Golden Candlesticks, and to declare the Man whose name is the Branch." They also had "Seven Angels who sound the Seven Trumpets" and an elaborate catalog of apocalyptic symbols drawn from Revelation, a panoply of spiritual mumbo jumbo that must have disgusted a rationalist like Will Cobbe's sister. Prince believed that he had been, to use the current term, born again; he told Dixon that he had "died to the flesh, and was born a second time to the Spirit. He put off the old man, he discarded self, he ceased to commit sin, and even to be capable of sin." Although the Agapemonites' communal life was said to be purely spiritual—Dixon was told that "those who married in the world aforetime, live as though they had not. Men house apart from women, and know no craving after devil's love"—Prince, having declared that he was the Holy Spirit, took a virgin as his bride in order to save "the whole order of living men." He did so "by his own sovereign right; consulting no one, least of all the object of his choice." Dixon's account of this "Great Manifestation" is full of evasive language but implies that Prince consummated the relationship—or raped Miss Paterson, as the case may be—in full view of the congregation. He said that "under these bridals her nature was sublimed; her soul became free; her body was cleansed from taint." Not long thereafter, however, the bride "began to prove herself a mortal woman."[83] After the child was born, some members left the Agapemone, but others, including Cobbe's brother Will, remained among the faithful.

No wonder Cobbe was anxious about any unorthodox associations. After leaving the London National Society for Women's Suffrage executive committee she published an unusually large number of long articles on social, religious, political, and feminist topics in a wide range of magazines in the first months of 1868. "Household Service," in *Fraser's* for January, argued that women disliked domestic service because people no longer respected their servants. The *Theological Review* printed the third part of "The New Creed and the Old, in Their Secular Results," a long and serious analysis of religious belief and ethical behavior. Frances Colenso wrote from Natal to a friend that "the *Theological Review* is truly valuable. The last number we had, the January one, the most so. . . . I tried in vain to keep it for Sunday, but I had not strength of mind."[84] In February Cobbe published in *Fraser's* on Friedrich Max Müller's *Chips from a German Workshop* (a study of comparative religion), and also, in the much lighter *Temple Bar,* "French and English Epitaphs."

Yet a third essay for February, in another of the new popular monthlies, made a further entry into the debate on Irish questions. On 13 December 1867 Fenians blew up part of the Middlesex House of Detention, which was located in an overcrowded London neighborhood. They failed to rescue two Fenian prisoners, and the explosion killed 6 people and injured 120 more, most of them local residents. In this context Cobbe responded to an earlier *Tinsley's* article by "An American Fenian" who had complained that the British press "habitually deals with Irish questions exclusively from an English point of view." Yes, she answered in "Ireland For the Irish," that was true: the Celtic Irish, Fenian or not, had no outlet in the British press, but the Anglo-Irish were equally ignored. She admitted the "crimes of former English legislation for Ireland" but, and this was a point she would make again and again, "if the Fenians would go further, and claim that the confiscations of Irish lands should all be rescinded . . . we say such a scheme is hopeless and absurd. . . . Every inch of Irish land has been seized, granted, confiscated, bought and sold over and over again."

On 2 March Kate Amberley gave birth prematurely to a daughter, Rachel, and a twin who never breathed. Elizabeth Garrett attended the birth; Maggie Elliot was godmother. "If the tenth commandment had gone on to forbid coveting one's neighbour's *daughters,*" Cobbe wrote, "I am afraid my conscience as regards it would not be clear!" Kate Amberley would have noticed the pointed reference to scriptural sexism; by mid-April she was back at work on her own feminist projects. She invited Cobbe and Lloyd to meet Harriet Jacobs, the author of *Incidents in the Life of a Slave Girl,* who was in England raising money for a Savannah orphanage. They were otherwise engaged, but Cobbe put down her name to buy a copy of the book.[85]

Mary Lloyd had two paintings in the 1868 exhibition of the Society of Women Artists. Both were of dogs belonging to her nephew Richard Lloyd Price (who was by 1868 serving as high sheriff of Merioneth): number 336, *Mr. Price's 'King Dick', a bull dog,* and number 362, *Portrait of Mr Price's dogs with game.* On 1 April she and Cobbe dined with Frances and Hensleigh Wedgwood. Frances had helped gather signatures for the 1866 suffrage petition, Hensleigh was a mathematician and philologist who disagreed with many of Max Müller's ideas about the origin of language, and their daughter Julia Wedgwood, who was in her mid-thirties, would soon write the chapter on suffrage for Josephine Butler's *Woman's Work and Woman's Culture* (1869). Also at the dinner were Hensleigh Wedgwood's sister Emma and Emma's husband—Charles Darwin.[86]

During the winter and spring Cobbe finished the religious book published in October as *Dawning Lights.* She tried to place it with Richard Bentley, a publisher who was more mainstream than Nicholas Trübner and might have garnered more publicity and better sales. In May 1868 Geraldine Jewsbury, who read manuscripts for Bentley, wrote to him: "I am very sorry you have concluded *not* to publish for my friend Miss Cobbe. I think there wd have been a *credit* in it if even not great profit—but I stick like a good shoemaker to *my own* last! & only speak on novels!" It is unclear whether his refusal was on financial or on religious grounds; writing to his son, George, about her autobiography in the 1890s, Cobbe was afraid he might find it too heterodox. She put new effort into theological networks by getting in touch with Edward Enfield about the Free Christian Union he was organizing and later sending him information about people who might be interested. But Enfield had some difficulty with practical details. At one point she asked him to "tell me at what hour will begin the meeting of the F.C.U. next Friday & where *is* Freemason's Tavern?—We women principally know of it as a place where our company is *not* required!"[87]

A major step toward higher education for women took place on 28 March with a conference on establishing a college; the first name on the list of people attending is Frances Power Cobbe's. Names were also being gathered for the next petition to Parliament. Florence Hill started a suffrage society for Bristol and Clifton. The prospectus was written by Frank Newman, who had moved to Bristol after retiring from University College London, and issued in the name of Matthew Davenport Hill; it permitted "his daughter to invite so many as his drawing-room will hold to meet there on 24th January 1868, at 3 p.m."[88] On 14 April the Manchester society held a large public meeting at which, for the first time, women were among the speakers. (Was this the sort of thing Lloyd and Hampson were afraid of?) On 14 May John Stuart Mill brought to Parliament a petition containing 21,757 signatures. This time Mary Somerville's name was included; she and Florence Nightingale headed the list. Additional petitions were submitted on the same day by P. A. Taylor, Duncan McLaren (from Edinburgh), and H. F. Davie, a baronet with a career in the army behind him when he entered Parliament in 1847.

At the end of June Cobbe was in Bristol and had to decline an invitation from Kate Amberley to meet Henry Wadsworth Longfellow for tea. She and Maggie visited the workhouse, where they found "five survivors of our poor old friends."[89] After that she went to Ireland for three months; while there she produced the "Catalogue of Pictures" that documents the art collection at Newbridge and supplies some anecdotes about ancestors whose portraits were on the walls. Lloyd was in Wales. It was becoming more and more clear how much Lloyd disliked the city; yet although she spent more time each year in Wales, their commitment to building a life together evidently did not waver.

Cobbe's most important contribution to the women's cause during 1868—the year after she left the suffrage executive—took the form of a crucial article in support of the Married Women's Property Act. The new bill, prepared by the NAPSS, was introduced on 21 April; its sponsors were two Liberals, George Shaw Lefevre and John Stuart Mill, and one Conservative, Russell Gurney. Petitions circulated by the Married Women's Property Committee garnered 33,000 signatures. The result was a tied vote—123 aye, 123 no. (John Locke was among the ayes.) The bill thus failed to advance, but the women's committee redoubled their efforts for the next try.

In July Cobbe wrote to J. A. Froude proposing a topic about which he was unenthusiastic. He replied, on 6 August, "If you will promise to make your article entertaining I will make no objection. . . . I have not studied the subject. I only know it to be a difficult one. It is a horrible thing for a woman to be married to a brute who drinks away all her earnings but also a family goes on best with one head to it. There are other laws, the law of entail for instance . . . which I think far worse. . . . as I said, if you will season the dish to make it pleasant to the palate you can say your say." Froude's reply was typical of his editorial practice as well as his infuriating disinterest in women's issues. During the American Civil War, for example, he had printed a wide range of articles although he was himself pro-South, but he had made many suggestions about tone and rhetoric. Moncure Conway later explained: "Although my political articles were hard for Confederate sympathizers to bear, Froude never changed a sentence himself, and rarely induced me to alter them; and only in one case . . . did he print any disclaimer. . . . His usage, after I had selected a subject relating to the struggle, was to write me some thoughts, strongly put, meant to restrain my enthusiasm."[90]

As for the essay in question, however, Froude's demand that Cobbe "season the dish" did good service to the cause, for the article was "Criminals, Idiots, Women, and Minors," published in *Fraser's* for December 1868. Picking up a phrase that she said had been "complacently quoted by the *Times*" earlier in the year to designate the four categories of persons "excluded from many civil and all political rights in England," Cobbe gave it instant currency and lasting fame. As Froude requested, she gave her wit full play, opening with an attempt to explain to a visitor from another planet that the bridegroom's vow "With all my worldly goods I thee endow" was the reverse of truth. The visitor cannot understand why "the property of the woman who commits Murder, and the property of the woman who commits Matrimony, [are] dealt with alike by your law." Cobbe then acknowledged the legal, practical, and sentimental argument for the forfeiture—which, she pointed out, affected only middle-class and poor women, since the wealthy were protected by settlements—and demolished each in its turn. After well over a hundred years, the essay remains a persuasive and amusing example of finely tuned rhetoric, high quotability, and great clarity.[91]

In October Cobbe published "The Church of England, and Who Should Stop in It" in the *Theological Review* and the book *Dawning Lights: An Inquiry Concerning the Secular Results of the New Reformation*. Both analyzed the increasing disarray within England's Christian denominations as science and biblical criticism made headway. (Matthew Arnold's "Dover Beach" had been published in the previous year.) Cobbe described *Dawning Lights* to Kate Amberley as "a *wicked* little book. W. E. H. Lecky, who had anonymously published a volume of essays entitled *The Religious Tendencies of the Age* in 1860, wrote to Cobbe, "I am filled with admiration at your amazing courage—a courage I never mean to emulate—in nailing your colours so boldly to the mast—another proof of the alarming fact that men and women are rapidly changing attributes," and the naturalist John Edward Gray, who, unlike Lecky, was not a personal friend, wrote that since he knew how people who thought for themselves were treated, he felt impelled to write a letter of sympathy to "a kindred spirit." At this distance it is rather difficult to understand either the wickedness or the courage. The *Spectator* review suggests another problem: "While we fully understand," says the reviewer, "her negative views, her rejection of what is called 'authority' in religion, her disbelief in miracle . . . and her vigorous repudiation of the doctrine of everlasting punishment . . . when we come to ask what practically she looks to as the theological ideal of the future, we are as unable to sketch it as when we began her book." The reviewer seems especially baffled by the difference between "natural law" and "divine law," a difficulty arising, I suspect, because the great advance in scientific thinking (and scientific method) since the mid-1840s, when Cobbe had first formulated the essentials of her theology, made "natural law" a far more complex and less intuitive matter than she could explain.[92]

When Cobbe returned from Newbridge in October an election was looming—the first election under the broader electorate created by the 1867 Reform Bill. She found her name on the register for Chelsea, by mistake for "Francis," and asked Mill for advice; he recommended that she not go to the polls since there was "an actual mistake in the name," whereas ladies whose names were entered otherwise should try to vote. Parliament dissolved on 11 November; voting took place from 17 November to 7 December, and the new Parliament assembled on 10 December. The Conservatives were soundly defeated—there were 271 Conservative MPs and 387 Liberals—so the new government was formed by W. E. Gladstone. The Radical Charles Dilke was elected for the newly constituted borough of Chelsea, but Mill lost his seat to, as Munby put it, "Mr. W. H. Smith, universal newspaper-vendor, with money at command."[93] Amberley was also defeated, probably because of a remark in favor of birth control. Despite those losses, the increased number of MPs thought to favor suffrage seemed to bode well for the women's cause. And for Cobbe, the new political situation brought an exciting new opportunity.

## 9

Working Woman Scribbler
1869–1874

*Journalism enables me . . . both to live & to fight in every cause I care for & that is a great matter!*

FRANCES POWER COBBE TO SARAH WISTER, 17 MAY [1874]

The first respectable halfpenny newspaper, published "on the eve of the assembling of a Reformed Parliament" at a price within reach of new voters, the *Echo* gave Frances Power Cobbe a stunning opportunity as a regular staff writer responsible for three leaders a week. Its owners, the firm of Cassell, Petter and Galpin, had asked Moncure Conway to edit; when he refused, they had turned to Arthur Arnold. Trained as a surveyor, Arnold had been assistant commissioner of the public works that provided relief in Lancashire during the cotton famine; he also wrote two sensation novels and would later serve on the London County Council. Horace Voules, then only twenty-four years old, was business manager; T. H. S. Escott called him "the most universal utility man known to the press in his day," a man "equally able to write printer's copy and to set it up himself." Newsagents refused to handle the paper because its price allowed them hardly any profit, so Voules introduced a "brigade of boys" (and girls) to peddle it on the streets.[1]

The *Echo* said that its intention was not to compete with the morning dailies by printing "a folio edition of *Hansard*" but rather to find a place "after the labours of the day . . . in as many homes as we can reach with news which may be read without fatigue."[2] Its front page typically had two leaders. Often, though not always, the first was political, and the second more broadly social or sometimes just amusing. Cobbe's were usually second leaders. Inside were some columns of "Public Opinion" that cannibalized leaders from the morning papers, a "Summary of the News" in short paragraphs, a column of crime reports, letters to the editor, items from Reuters, notes from abroad, and some book reviews or a longer account of a public event. Finally, there were reports of sporting and financial news and a page or more of small ads. Except for a very brief court circular, it had no society news, no fashion notes, nothing in the nature of a "ladies' page."

According to the masthead, three editions were published—at 3:00, 5:00, and 6:30 P.M. The first edition went to press just after noon; it gave the 12:00 London temperature and a stock market report from 11:30. Arnold claimed that the *Echo* was the first paper "to publish tape-prices—our printers setting up from the tape . . . which for the first time placed the Stock Exchange in almost direct communication with the public." The late editions also had early racetrack results. These features made the *Echo* a paper for commuters, for city gents, clerks, civil servants, and artisans. Before very long its circulation topped 100,000—twenty times that of the *Daily News*. And though it was published after some men's workday ended, the *Echo* was out before Parliament went into session. Arnold had many friends in government and used them to good effect: "Very frequently when my first edition had gone to press I walked to the Foreign office and saw Lord Granville or Mr. Hammond, gathering hints or news enough . . . to make the success of a later edition. . . . Almost every day from noon to two o'clock I went out in search of news, and very often helped the fortunes of 'The Echo' by inferring events from the casual remarks of casual persons whom I saw in those mid-day hours."3

The *Echo*'s politics, as well as its success, grew from Arnold's ability to pick writers with ideological goals that made them willing to produce good copy for rather less money than was paid by the morning papers. (Cobbe got two guineas for an *Echo* leader, three for a piece the same length in the *Daily News*.)4 The staff included the clergyman H. R. Haweis, whose dramatic sermons made St. James, Marylebone, a tourist attraction; George Manville Fenn, whose boys' adventure stories gave lessons in geography and natural history; John Macdonnel, later master of the Supreme Court; George Shee, another barrister; William Black, a very successful novelist, now forgotten; and most surprisingly, Frances Power Cobbe, one of the very few women to have a regular staff position on a London paper. Arnold, recently married to Amelia Hyde, the daughter of an Anglo-Irish military man, knew Cobbe from NAPSS meetings and literary dinner parties and was attracted by her attention-getting essays in monthly magazines, her reporting for the *Daily News,* and her experience writing leaders for the short-lived *Day.* Her first leader appeared in the *Echo*'s third number, on 10 December 1868.

For almost seven years the *Echo* gave Cobbe an outlet for her political and social views. She was at the office by 10:00 A.M. three days a week—taking the underground from Gloucester Road station to the *Echo*'s premises on Catherine Street, just off the Strand opposite Somerset House—and she earned nearly three hundred pounds a year from a combination of leaders, reviews, and news reporting. Her distinctive style was sharpened by the need,

# The Echo.

No. 742.　　　　LONDON, THURSDAY, APRIL 27, 1871.　　　　ONE HALFPENNY.

THE REVISED BUDGET.

THE TEMPTATION OF MR. GLADSTONE.

THE AUSTRO-PRUSSIAN WAR.

MURDEROUS OUTRAGE AT ELTHAM.

A typical *Echo* front page (larger than a tabloid but somewhat smaller than a broadsheet) contained two "leading articles" of about twelve hundred words each. Cobbe generally wrote three every week.

in twelve hundred words, to marshal facts and create memorable phrases that would strike home with the city gent on his homeward commute. The deliberately nongendered voice, appearing in a paper that reached members of Parliament as well as men who only wanted racing news, gave her an unparalleled platform for feminist causes. The earliest version of her pamphlet *Why Women Desire the Franchise* was summarized in the *Echo* on 23 December 1868. She wrote columns on wife abuse, cruelty to children, girls' education, Girton College, and women candidates for the London School Board, she ran campaigns to gain clemency for women who attacked their abusers and wondered why, in infanticide cases, the guilty man who abandoned both woman and child was not also tracked down and tried. She could place letters to the editor written by friends such as Emily Faithfull, Maria Grey, Florence Hill, and Millicent Fawcett. Though she was officially anonymous—most readers had no idea that a regular front-page writer for the *Echo* was female—feminist women knew she was there. The paper's news notes supply information about women's meetings, publications, and accomplishments.

Like any writer who has to produce a twelve-hundred-word essay three times a week, Cobbe picked up material everywhere, from a neighborhood mugging to a friend's lost dog to information gleaned from relatives, including John Locke and her brother Charles. She wrote a surprising number of columns on military affairs; it is probably no coincidence that her cousin Alick, by then a lieutenant colonel, was stationed in the United Kingdom from November 1868 to January 1870. Alick's older brother Charles Augustus, who became inspector general of constabulary for the Midland counties in 1869, supplied inside information about crime and the justice system.

The Bow Street police court, just up the street from the *Echo* offices, and the central criminal court at Old Bailey were regular stops for *Echo* reporters. On 14 January 1869, when Susanna Palmer was indicted for wounding her husband in a scuffle, Cobbe at once understood the full extent of women's need for protection. As Russell Gurney said when he mentioned the case in Parliament, "It became clear to her that if she was to have a regard to her single daughter's honour, it was impossible for her to remain together with the daughter under the same roof with her husband." But it was Cobbe who made the case into a cause célèbre by following up the *Echo*'s brief news report of 15 January 1869. She visited Palmer in prison, wrote a leader using an argument she would pursue for the next decade—"Why is it . . . that the ruffians who throttle gentlemen on the highway receive (very properly) a flogging, while the far worse brutes who beat the woman whom they happen to have sworn to 'love and cherish' get off with, at most, a few weeks' hard labour?"—and put a letter, signed "F," in the *Echo*'s correspondence column asking for contributions to a fund for Palmer's relief.[5] It was not the only time she would parlay a news report into a leader, then a personal investigation, and then a public campaign or parliamentary action.

The importance of the *Echo* under Arthur Arnold's editorship lay in its reach as a halfpenny evening paper with racing results, political commentary, and business news; in its lack of identification with any specific faction; and in the freedom it supplied to an activist who created a lively, genderless voice that let her opinions speak for "the newspaper" rather than coming before the public as "a woman." At the same time, Cobbe learned through hard experience the physical and mental rigors of writing to order three days a week. "Few women," she advised aspiring journalists, "possess the steady health and equable brain-power which can enable them to perform the serious mental labour of original composition on a fresh subject every day (or, let us say, every alternate day), week in and week out, through the greater part of the year. . . . it is suicidal for a woman who cannot fairly rely on her own sustained powers to offer herself as a candidate for regular office work on a newspaper."[6]

She managed nevertheless to maintain some outside life. Rosa Bonheur visited in January 1869 and liked Mary Lloyd's plan for building herself a studio in the back garden. On 11 February Arthur Munby went "to a conversation-party in Blandford Square at Mme Bodichon's," where he found a "small & agreeable gathering of cultivated and accomplished women" including Cobbe. On 5 March Kate Amberley saw Cobbe, Froude, and Lecky at a "very pleasant & lively" party given by Maggie Elliot. Two days later she called at 26 Hereford Square and met "Rev. Mr. Channing a Boston man who lives in London & has a chapel, a Theist." Sometime during the spring Cobbe went to a dinner party at Peter and Mentia Taylor's, where she sat next to John Stuart Mill and very much enjoyed the "play and good humour" in his arguments.[7]

The next few years were crammed with busy complexity—popular journalism and intellectual essays, politics and social activism, friends and family and Mary Lloyd and their dogs, theology, science, and feminism. Cobbe was at the height of her powers, full of energy, enjoying life, a strong-minded woman confident in her own opinions and person but still open to friendly controversy. Yet even a woman of Cobbe's stature and reputation (and social contacts) could not share fully in London's intellectual life. The Metaphysical Society, formed on 21 April 1869, included such good friends as Froude, Carpenter, Martineau, and Hutton; they gathered to discuss mental and moral phenomena, questions about the existence of God and the nature of conscience, and the "logic of the sciences whether physical or social," topics in which Cobbe was crucially interested. "If it was once resolved to admit ladies," wrote one of its members, "I am sure that Miss Cobbe wd be elected by acclamation."[8]

Although no bill for women's parliamentary suffrage was yet in the offing, the House of Commons ratified a surprising measure for women's political rights in May 1869, when conditions for the municipal franchise were under debate. Jacob Bright proposed an amendment specifying that "wherever words occur which import the masculine gender, the same shall be held to include females." The amendment was agreed to, according to the *Englishwoman's Review,* "amid cheers," and thus "without discussion, and in the space of a few minutes, the disability of women ratepayers to vote for the election of Town Councilors and other municipal officers was abolished." The amendment was not, however, a complete surprise as Cobbe had promoted it beforehand in an *Echo* leader.[9]

John Stuart Mill's *On the Subjection of Women* was published on 24 May. A few days later Cobbe wrote him that she had already been "reading it over and over" with "intense satisfaction & exultation." She had advance sheets from the publisher so that she could write a review. "I should vainly try to tell you how grateful I feel to you," she wrote, "how I have longed to thank you as I read page after page—& said in my heart 'God bless you,' as I closed the whole magnificent argument." She signed the letter with "warmest gratitude & honour" and publicized the book with lengthy quotations in the *Echo* (7 and 8 July 1869) and a witty essay in the *Theological Review.* Yet much as she applauded his argument, Cobbe was not an equalitarian liberal; unlike Mill, she believed women were morally superior to men but not intellectual equals, or at least not until a woman could produce "one single really *great* work . . . in poetry, in history, in sculpture, in painting or in music."[10] In addition, she was always aware of the conditions specific to women—especially pregnancy and child care—that would affect their situations even if laws and opportunities were made entirely equal.[11]

Between political activism, some outside writing, and producing three columns a week, Cobbe was exhausted by the end of June. Mary Lloyd took a cottage in Wales for the summer; Cobbe joined her for two months. (She supplied several *Echo* columns for July, but many were on general topics and could have been written in advance. Even when she was in London there was some irregularity in her publication days, depending on other people's schedules as well as her own.) The first public suffrage meeting in London at which women spoke took place on 17 July 1869. Cobbe wrote with regrets that she would be out of town, but she was so thoroughly associated with the cause that the *Saturday Review* mentioned her name along with Fawcett's and Mentia Taylor's.

Back at her desk in August, she listed the "old bills" that had been "hung up to dry" during the year's parliamentary session. Proposals on married women's property, on marriage with a deceased wife's sister, even on removing the grating in front of the House of Commons ladies' gallery, had been blocked or postponed. "We are far from advocating the presence of women in Parliament," she wrote—the first time she had introduced the topic— but she insisted that as long as women remained unrepresented their interests would be ignored. Although Arthur Arnold personally supported women's suffrage, Cobbe made a request of Helen Taylor: "If Mr. Mill should see Mr. Arnold (the editor of the Echo) at any time, & would urge him to be a little less afraid of compromising his paper by speaking out, it would do much good." It is therefore not possible to know whether denials such as "we are far from advocating the presence of women in Parliament" express the *Echo*'s editorial policy or her own opinion at this date (as we shall see, she would later urge a woman to stand).[12]

Cobbe had spent her summer holiday happily riding, hiking, and enjoying outdoor life. The property in which Lloyd and her sisters had a life interest was named Hengwrt; the house stood just outside Dolgelley (Dolgellau), a market and assize town at the head of an estuary leading to the sea at Barmouth, ten miles away. Some of Lloyd's income came from renting the house, especially during the summer season, so in 1869 they had a cottage at Bontddu, about halfway between Dolgelley and Barmouth. Charles Darwin and his family were nearby in a house rented by his brother-in-law Hensleigh Wedgwood (who was sometimes Lloyd's tenant at Hengwrt). Encountering Darwin in the hills one day, Cobbe found him "greatly excited" about *On the Subjection of Women,* although he said that "Mill could learn some things from physical science; and that it is in the struggle for existence and (especially) for the possession of women that men acquire their vigour and courage." Reporting the incident in her *Life,* Cobbe highlights the absurdity of holding this conversation at the top of their lungs while they stood on paths sixty feet apart and shouted across the distance.[13] Did she also understand the serious conflict between Darwin's biological determinism and Mill's emphasis on the social conditions that shaped gendered human natures?

In the same summer, the geologist and paleontologist W. Boyd Dawkins explored caves ten miles east of Corwen on property belonging to the Lloyd family. Mary Lloyd was intensely interested in all such explorations of early human remains. Cobbe described driving "to the side of a small wood-covered hill rising abruptly out of the fields of yellowing corn. Into the heart of the hill run three or four deep and dark caverns, recently opened. . . . Overhead the trees hang in summer glory, and all around the sweet rich grass and endless wild flowers of Wales grow in luxuriance." Dawkins identified the remains of a dozen animals mixed with bones belonging to people of an "Iberian or Basque race in the Neolithic age."[14]

Writing from Wales to Mary Somerville, Cobbe mentioned a visit from Josephine Butler, who wanted to begin an international organization for changing laws about women. Both Somerville and Cobbe contributed essays to Butler's *Woman's Work and Woman's Culture,* which was in press when Mill's *On the Subjection of Women* came out. Cobbe's essay, "The Final Cause of Woman," opens by objecting to universalizing theories of "Woman (always to be written with a capital W)." Woman, she writes, is not "an Adjective," whose value lies in her relation to others, but rather "a Noun" and therefore "the first end of her being must be an end proper to herself." For the American *Putnam's Magazine* she wrote, more frankly than she had yet done in any English journal, of women's "Servile Vices, the propensities to cowardice, meanness, prevarication, and flattery, which are the natural products alike in male and female, black or white skins, of a condition of prolonged puerile or servile dependence."[15]

Although Cobbe went back to work in August, Lloyd stayed in Wales through the autumn. She missed "her ponys & her mountains" so badly that Cobbe began to "think we ought to go & live in the country." They tried to let the Hereford Square house but could not find a satisfactory tenant.[16] Cobbe's *Echo* income was becoming more important to them. Agricultural rents, the primary source of Lloyd's income, fell sharply as open farmland and steam transportation started bringing cheap food from North America and Australia; and Lloyd had also made a worrisome loan to the friend of a friend.

Late in September 1869 the NAPSS met in Bristol. For the first time there were separate sessions for ladies only. The council disliked the idea but agreed because Mary Carpenter hoped to hear from women unwilling to appear before a mixed audience. Writing for the *Echo* of 1 October, Cobbe masked her gender: "Reporters were not admitted, but a lady has communicated to the Press that Miss Carpenter took the chair, that a letter of sympathy and encouragement from Miss Nightingale was read, that Doctrix Elizabeth Blackwell, of New York, spoke upon the education of women for the medical profession," and so forth. The conference still let activist women see friends and make plans, but their sense of trespass had vanished, and the atmosphere was far different from that in Dublin only eight years earlier. Politics and public speaking no longer intimidated the regulars. Carpenter wanted the ladies' sessions to focus on women's traditional philanthropy, but on 2 October Kate Amberley and several others "revolted against Miss Carpenter for wishing to exclude all subjects whh were matters of legislation."[17] The *Echo* for 4 October discreetly avoided mentioning the conflict.

A more troublesome division among women emerged over the Contagious Diseases Acts, introduced in 1864 and extended in 1866, 1868, and
1869. Intended to reduce venereal disease among soldiers and sailors, the
acts called for compulsory vaginal examination of suspected prostitutes in
port and garrison towns. An 1867 recommendation to apply the acts universally throughout the country brought attention to their moral as well as
gender implications: inspecting women and placing those found to be dis-
eased in "lock hospitals" had the effect of policing women's bodies in order
to make nonmarital sex safe for men. At Bristol in 1869 Dr. Charles Bell
Taylor called a special session on the Contagious Diseases Acts and spoke so
forcefully that a motion opposing them passed by a vote of 2 to 1. (The only
woman allowed to attend was Elizabeth Blackwell.) Either before or after
that meeting, however, Elizabeth Wolstenholme spoke to Josephine Butler
about the effect of regulation, and Butler undertook a fact-finding journey
through the subjected districts.

Cobbe was very reluctant to enter a campaign over sexuality even though
it soon became a crusade to protect women's bodies against invasive examinations by prurient physicians. She told Kate Amberley that she was "*most*
anxious that none of us who are identified with the general cause of women
should get mixed up in this controversy which must do *us* harm & in which
I feel perfectly persuaded we can do no good." She could "conceive no way
so certain to injure our work in other directions as rushing into this most
difficult—& let us add—most disgusting business."[18] Aside from her fear
that suffragists would be linked with prostitutes, Cobbe thought none of
them were competent to deal with the medical issue. Florence Hill's brother
Matthew Berkeley Hill, a professor of clinical surgery at University College
London, strongly supported the acts as a measure important to public health.

At the NAPSS meeting in Bristol an organization of men only was formed
to work for repeal. By December 1869 a separate Ladies' National Association for Repeal of the Contagious Diseases Acts had written a manifesto
that was signed by 124 prominent women, including Harriet Martineau and
Florence Nightingale, and published in the *Daily News* for 31 December.
Josephine Butler became head of the organization; its supporters included
many of Cobbe's close friends. Many years later she wrote to Millicent Fawcett that "your sister—to whom I naturally appealed for guidance . . . put
me on the wrong track. . . . Only by degrees my own reflections made me
feel that Mrs Garrett Anderson had misdirected me. It was just the same sort
of misdirection as the men-doctors are giving to the laity all over the country every day on the subject of vivisection."[19]

In October 1869 a long-term project of Cobbe's brother Tom's reached
publication as *History of the Norman Kings of England. From a New Colla-*

*tion of the Contemporary Chronicles.* A conscientious and painstaking narrative of events during the reigns of William I, William II, Henry I, and Stephen, the book was drawn almost entirely from primary sources, with very little in the way of context or analysis. Tom's sister arranged for a long notice in the *Echo* on 28 October; whether or not she wrote it herself, the review carefully explained the author's aim in presenting contemporary sources without interpretation. *History of the Norman Kings* was enthusiastically reviewed by John Doran in the *Athenaeum* for 23 October. *Notes and Queries,* also on 23 October, was less laudatory but not overtly critical except for complaining about citations that did not include the edition or page. But the *Saturday Review* for 18 December printed what Cobbe called "a cruel and most unfair review" that "practically *killed*" the book. "This history of the Norman Kings," said the reviewer, "is a wonderful instance of what can be done by an ingenious writer when he once gets astride of a theory. There are a few passages in the preface which are quite sufficient to prove that, when Mr. Cobbe likes to write sensibly, he can write very sensibly indeed. It is from sheer choice and on a deliberate theory that he has chosen to write nonsense." Many years later Cobbe complained that the review by "Mr. Freeman (I have no doubt it was he)" had crushed "all the ambitions & hope of a life which had been most cruelly broken by a faithless wife & had just revived enough in advanced years to make that considerable literary effort."[20] And it is true that the subsequent reviews—often written by men under the influence of Edward Augustus Freeman, whose own three-volume *History of the Norman Conquest* came out in 1865–69—were never again as warm as the first notice in the *Athenaeum.*[21]

Socially, the autumn of 1869 was livelier than the spring; perhaps Cobbe was becoming accustomed to the routine of writing three times a week. At her parties, Julia Channing wrote, "one met representatives of the world of science and letters and art, and of the general advance of humanity towards something by somebody." Late in November Cobbe invited Geraldine Jewsbury along with the Huxleys. "If I had the choice of associating only with women, or only with men," she wrote, "I should have no hesitation in preferring women's society. But, as the children say, '*Both is best.*'"[22] Nevertheless, Cobbe's delight in mixing people from her various social and intellectual circles sometimes created embarrassments. Writing to H. R. Haweis after Froude's death, she recalled an incident from the days when she and Haweis had been colleagues at the *Echo:*

Do you remember asking me to invite Mr. Green to meet Mr. Froude? I did so, & they & you were in our drawing room in Hereford Sq. at one of my little afternoon parties . . . but, of course, [I] could not take the liberty of introducing a man to Mr. Froude without first asking his permission. . . . to my consternation Mr Froude said: "Let me see him first." I pointed him out amid the little crowd across the room, & Mr Froude looked at him & then put up his hands . . . "O No! No! Don't! *Saturday Review written all over his face.*" I was in despair, but there was nothing to be done, & when a few minutes later, you said to me "Now introduce them," I could only make an excuse to dive down to the tea room & *stay there* till Mr F. was gone![23]

There was pleasant amusement in another pretense at matchmaking for Maggie Elliot. The Dublin-born historian W. E. H. Lecky wrote to Cobbe soon after his *History of European Morals* was published (in 1869) that he was glad the "last chapter ['The Position of Women'] does not appear very scandalous to you. . . . I am so glad you think I understand the nature of women—a profound and conflicting subject." He liked to provoke praise from feminist acquaintances, for he also let Kate Amberley know of his relief that she was not planning to "crush" him "by an essay on Women . . . I am really substantially on your side & Miss Cobbe assured me that my conception of female nature was almost exactly hers." During August both Lecky and Maggie Elliot visited the Amberleys at their country house, and Kate Amberley hatched a romantic plan. Writing to her not long afterwards, Cobbe followed a reference to Maggie with a cryptic phrase: "Would that I *could* give that hint! But I am too proud for her to go a step in that direction."[24]

Hajjin died during the autumn and was buried in the garden at Hereford Square. In his memory, perhaps, Cobbe wrote "Instinct and Reason," a brief examination of dogs' creative intelligence in solving new problems, for the November 1869 issue of *Animal World.* Soon there was a new puppy, Yama, probably acquired not long after Cobbe reviewed Charlotte Manning's *Ancient and Medieval India,* which includes a quote from the *Mahabharata* in which the hero takes his dog Yama along with him to heaven. In her second half-year's work for the *Echo* Cobbe occupied the nonparliamentary season with a number of entertaining essays on general social topics, including the follies of fashion ("Artificial Woman-making," 28 August 1869), common sense versus superstition ("The Table-Twisting Faith," 19 August 1869), ostentatious weddings ("The Cost of Weddings," 4 September 1869), the vulgarity of elaborate funerals ("Mrs. Grundy at the Cemetery," 18 September 1869), railway accidents caused by overworked employees ("Tired to Death!" 13 October 1869), and hospitals so understaffed that patients were sent away immediately after surgery ("A Case of Hospital Charity," 16 November 1869"). On 9 November she mounted a campaign on behalf of Elizabeth Whelan, a homeless woman sentenced to prison when her baby died of exposure although a solicitor whose wife died of malnutrition was not even brought to court, nor was the father of Elizabeth Whelan's child.

At year's end Mary Lloyd went to Italy for several weeks. "Poor old darling," Cobbe wrote on 27 December, "I longed of course to accompany her & to see you dearest Mrs Somerville but I could not afford it. It must have made a final end of my work with the Echo by which I am earning about £300 a year." She asked for Somerville's opinion about the controversy among mathematicians over whether the solar system was "old enough to admit of the period needed for Darwin's hypothesis"; she also asked for her opinion about Lloyd's emotional health. "Tell me about my old woman when she comes to you pray,—how you think her in spirits & mind as well as looks. I do hope please God she is happier than she used to be."[25] During December and January the Echo printed a series of "Notes from Rome," which are mostly about art. Cobbe excerpted them from Lloyd's letters, kept a separate account of their length in column inches, and, one presumes, passed along the money thus earned.

By mid-January, when Lloyd was back home, Cobbe heard William Carpenter give "the first of a series of Sunday Lectures on Science (wonderful to tell!) in a large hall in Langham Place." The emphasis and the exclamation point are reminders of the widespread prohibition against any secular activities, even private reading, on Sundays during Cobbe's childhood. Subscribers to the Sunday Lecture Society paid a pound apiece for reserved seats to the entire series. The initial list contained about 270 names; perhaps one in twelve were women, including Cobbe (but not Lloyd), Helen Taylor, Mentia Taylor, and Maria Grey. Also attending were the Darwins, Lecky, Mill, Ruskin, Anthony Trollope, and Charles Voysey. Maurice Davies described the inaugural lecture on 16 January 1870 as "a new sensation, reminding one of that furtive visit to the theatre on a Sunday evening on one's first visit to Paris."[26]

In the Echo, Cobbe wrote more and more often about women's issues. A particularly vivid example, "The Right to Beat a Wife" (17 January 1870), described the case of a policeman disciplined for using his truncheon to subdue a man who was striking a woman, not because of any questions about excessive force but because, as it turned out, the woman was married to the man who hit her: "Can there be any doubt that all London constables will learn from it that women's claims to protection from violence in the streets are of the most doubtful kind. . . . Are single women . . . to set up flags in their bonnets, as the disengaged cabs ought to do, inscribed with the word 'Unmarried,' so that the police may know that nobody has a right to knock them down, and may safely go to their assistance if attacked?"

Once Parliament opened, Cobbe vigorously supported the Married Women's Property Bill, using approaches that would appeal to various kinds of readers. On 5 February it was "Money in Women's Hands," about a lawsuit over a wife's debts; the bill would protect both husbands, who now bore responsibility, and tradespeople, who suffered if they could not collect. On 26 March, when debate was postponed until mid-May, she recommended that anyone contemplating matrimony should wait to see the result. In April she called attention to Dinah Mulock Craik's *Brave Lady,* which deployed sentimental fiction to reveal how a good mother could be devastated by her inability to control her income.[27] As the bill made its way into the House of Lords, a long letter signed "A Weak-minded Female" opposed changing a system that had worked so well. "A Woman on Women" (11 June 1870) castigates her (or perhaps, Cobbe suggests, him) for ignoring women in less fortunate circumstances. "The Lords on Wives' Property" (23 June 1870) takes aim at the tone of debate: the bill's supporters provided facts, while the opponents made jokes. "Married Women in New York" (7 July 1870) outlines wives' extremely broad property rights under state law and asserts that its "practical working . . . has commended itself to the judgment of the people of New York."

Russell Gurney's 1870 bill, however, was so changed by amendments that, as the *Pall Mall Gazette* said on 12 July, "The House of Commons will find some little difficulty in recognizing their old acquaintance . . . on its return

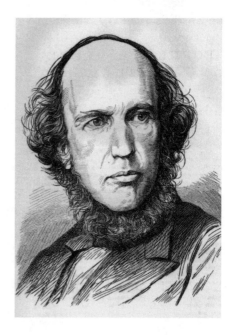

Physiologist, zoologist, and early psychologist William Benjamin Carpenter (1813–1885). Carpenter was a close friend of Cobbe's until she began her campaign against vivisection. (Hulton/Archive by Getty Images)

from its temporary absence in the House of Lords."[28] Nevertheless, the Commons passed it on 3 August without trying to restore it to its original form. As passed, the 1870 act gave working women some of the protection that marriage settlements provided for the wealthy: control of the wages they earned after marriage, of legacies under two hundred pounds, and of money deposited in savings banks (but not in investments women of substance might have). The Married Women's Property Committee knew at once that the amendments and limitations not only were troubling in themselves but also made further reform difficult, since many people would believe the problem had been solved. Cobbe continued to come up with new approaches. "What is Necessary?" (15 November 1870) took up a suit that hinged on whether the goods a wife had obtained on credit were necessities: "Had the original Married Women's Property Bill become law," Cobbe wrote, "these hateful cases of husbands disputing their wives' debts, and wives running into extravagance on their husbands' credit, would have been stopped for ever."

"Ancient and Medieval India," published in March 1870, was Cobbe's last essay for *Fraser's Magazine*. Although there is no clear evidence of any break with Froude—they continued to meet socially—a letter he dated 24 March begins, "I was very sorry to see from your manner yesterday that I had seriously offended you," and then explains that he was "deeply disappointed" in an article she had sent and had been "obliged to stop it" because of something about Christ. (Froude's handwriting, alas, always grows illegible when the subject is touchy.)[29] On the other hand, "Ancient and Medieval India" was little more than a summary of Charlotte Manning's book. Three columns a week for the *Echo* made it hard to find the time or the mental energy needed to write broad and thoughtful essays.

In the spring of 1870, with Jacob Bright's Women's Disabilities Removal Bill, women's suffrage came before the Commons for the first time as an independent cause. Using the words with which Bright had successfully amended the municipal franchise proposals in 1869, the new bill stipulated that in all acts describing the electoral franchise, "wherever words occur which import the masculine gender, the same shall be held to include females."[30] Cobbe went to a late-afternoon public meeting in support of the bill on 26 March. Arthur Munby noted that the "large room was full: the audience chiefly welldrest women, old & young. . . . Numbers of my acquaintance of the Aubrey House set were present; and in the chair was my friend Mrs [Mentia] Taylor herself. I had thought it would seem strange, but it seemed quite natural, to see that gentle earnest ladylike woman acting as chairman of a public meeting. . . . and the two best speeches I heard . . . were made by women: Miss Helen Taylor, who did the rhetoric ably, and Mrs Fawcett, who was logical and calm." Kate Amberley, as an insider, was free to be more critical: "Miss [Helen] Taylor made a long & much studied speech; it was good but too like acting. Mrs. Grote's was short but natural—Mrs. Fawcett's uninteresting & Mrs. Pet. Taylor (chairman) was inaudible fr sore throat." Nevertheless, she concluded, "it went off very well & was a great success."[31]

In addition to the usual arguments for suffrage, Cobbe consistently pointed out the economic advantages of having a vote. It was reason number five in her much-used pamphlet *Why Women Desire the Franchise*. She wrote for the *Englishwoman's Review* about a successful woman farmer who had been lucky enough to find a landlord (Cobbe's brother Charles) who would give her a lease even though she could not vote for his candidates. Jacob Bright's bill had its second reading on 3 May and passed by a vote of 124 to 91. The *Times* called it an accident: the "great majority of members" thought it was "one of those propositions which scarcely call for the trouble of refutation." On 12 May, when the next step had to be taken, Prime Minister W. E. Gladstone said he was "surprised and disappointed." He thought "it would be a very great mistake to proceed with this Bill." His opposition created a dilemma for Liberal MPs. Mentia Taylor counted 59 men who supported the bill on second reading but were absent from the following division.[32] Men like James Stansfeld, so dependable a supporter of women's causes that his biography is subtitled *A Victorian Champion of Sex Equality*, stayed away rather than choose between their principles and their party leader. Yet the total vote, even at 2:00 A.M., was much larger than the previous one. Anxious men in both parties, Conservative as well as Liberal, suddenly found a reason to show up for the division, and women's suffrage was rejected by more than two votes to one.

One of the chief items on Parliament's agenda for 1870 was W. E. Forster's Elementary Education Bill, which ensured that schools would be available in every part of England and Wales. Religious education had long been the chief stumbling block: what sort of scriptural and moral teaching should be provided, and how were the competing wishes of Nonconformists and the established church to be reconciled? Behind-the-scenes negotiation occupied much of the spring. On 16 June, when a compromise involving locally elected school boards had been reached, Forster was asked if the words *he* and *his* were "intended to exclude women [from] sitting on such boards." He answered that "words importing the masculine gender should be taken to include and mean the feminine gender unless the contrary was specifically declared" and that in the case of school boards he "looked forward to [women's] assistance in some cases being most valuable."[33] Thus, although the suffrage bill failed, women had for the second year in a row achieved a voice in local electoral politics.

While these interesting debates were going forward Cobbe became friends with Sarah Wister, of Philadelphia, born in 1835 to Fanny Kemble during her ill-fated marriage to the slave owner Frank Butler. Sarah, like her mother, became an active abolitionist. A dozen years younger than Cobbe, she was married to the Philadelphia physician Owen Jones Wister (their son, another Owen, wrote the archetypal "Western" novel, *The Virginian: A Horseman of the Plains,* published in 1902) and had been writing (anonymously) short critical notes for North American magazines. Wister left the United States for a European trip on 21 May and less than a month later was telling Cobbe about the "stormy debate" in Philadelphia "on women's rights, particularly on their right to study medicine." She gleefully described an incident in which the anonymous author of a prizewinning medical essay had turned out to be a woman; a local medical journal had published an editorial headed "Waterloo."[34]

Meanwhile, Kate Amberley had lectured on women at the Mechanics' Institute in Stroud. She thought the lecture had fallen "very flat," but it attracted attention—negative, of course—from the *Times.* She asked for advice about publication, and Cobbe recommended *Macmillan's,* the *Contemporary Review,* and the *Fortnightly Review* as the only magazines "in which

Sarah Butler Wister (1835–1908), Fanny Kemble's daughter and Frances Power Cobbe's longtime correspondent. (Germantown Historical Society, Philadelphia)

it would be fitting for you to appear in which entrance could be obtained for anything so strong" and offered letters of introduction.[35] Kate and her mother-in-law, Lady Russell, were still matchmaking. Cobbe wrote that "Mr. Lecky was *very empressé* the other day with a certain friend but did not avail himself of an opportunity I made for him of a tête a tête, & I have heard no more. I fear Lady Russell's communication was fatal to our little projects." Lady Russell, it turns out, had told Lecky how old Maggie was. "He was quite taken aback," she wrote to Kate Amberley, "hardly wd believe—returned to the subject next morning—'are you quite sure?' . . . Could you commit a pious fraud, tell him I was mistaken & that she's only 35?" (Margaret Elliot was born in 1828 and was therefore forty-two at the time; Lecky was thirty-two.) Later in the year, when Cobbe encountered Lecky in Dublin, she decided that "all our little schemes in a certain quarter are vain . . . I am so vexed—! I like him so much & I think both would make fine lives together & . . . poor ones apart."[36]

On 16 July 1870 France declared war on Prussia. Stimulated by conversation with her military cousins, Cobbe had written several columns about soldiers and their families during the year. Once war began, she produced both leaders on 13 August; ten days later she pointed out that a railway accident that killed a dozen people brought forth national mourning, whereas in a war between two nations of Europe, people barely notice headlines reading, "Fifty Thousand Killed and Wounded." On 4 September the Second Empire collapsed. Both leaders on 6 September were about the war, and both were Cobbe's. On 10 September she observed that the "Irish have made up their minds that this is a religious war—a sort of crusade on the part of Roman Catholic France against Protestant Germany."[37]

During the third week in September Cobbe went as a journalist and also as an interested observer to a meeting of the British Association for the Advancement of Science in Liverpool. The organization decided to consider guidelines for physiological experiments and appointed a committee of ten scientists to produce a report for the next year's meeting. After sitting through the proceedings at Liverpool Cobbe reported to Kate Amberley that she was "rather unhappy at the tone our friends Mr Huxley & Dr Tyndall were taking." She wrote a private letter to Huxley, who replied after a long delay. He was very annoyed by her criticism; the discoveries of his "honoured & valued friend B Séquard," he said, have "immediate and important practical application" in healing diseases of the nervous system. "I would sacrifice a hecatomb of dogs, tomorrow," he continued, "if I thought I could thereby cure a single epileptic or paralytic man."[38]

Barely a week later Cobbe told Somerville that "Huxley has taken to publishing defending vivisection so we are obliged to cut him." It is interesting to speculate that Cobbe herself, born a generation or two later, might have been drawn to scientific research. Her earliest writings on religion were based on what she then understood to be scientific method—making a hypothesis and testing it against available evidence—and she eagerly pursued conversations about current scientific issues with men such as William Carpenter and Charles Lyell. Before leaving for the Liverpool meeting she had contacted George Grove, then editor of *Macmillan's Magazine,* about writing an article for him; he published her "Unconscious Cerebration: A Psychological Study" in November. The term was Carpenter's; he and Cobbe had been corresponding about the topic since December 1867. Her even more interesting "Dreams As Illustrations of Unconscious Cerebration," published in April 1871, investigated the light shed by dreams on "the nature of brain-work, unregulated by the will."[39] Excerpts from both of these essays, as well as Cobbe's earlier "The Fallacies of Memory," are included in the section of Jenny Bourne Taylor and Sally Shuttleworth's 1998 anthology of Victorian psychological texts that examines developing theories of the unconscious mind.

The first London School Board was elected in November 1870. An *Echo* second leader, not by Cobbe, proclaimed its significance: "There probably has never yet been an election—not even when a Ministry has staked its reputation upon the verdict of the country . . . more important and interesting. . . . The work to be done, the regeneration of the great population of London, gives a dignity and gravity to the contest. . . . The candature [*sic*] of women side by side with men, of Peers with artisans, of a candidate such as Professor Huxley, in conjunction with Mr. Cremer, who urges amongst his qualifications his full knowledge of the due ignorance of his own class,—all this is new and strange."[40]

Cobbe worked hard to support Maria Grey in Chelsea and to publicize women candidates' meetings in the *Echo.* The campaign, she wrote to Mary Somerville, "has been a complete rehearsal of a parliamentary election for women & a great step in advance—All women ratepayers go to poll."[41] The school-board election used ballots (for the first time) and a system of cumulative voting: each elector had as many votes as there were open seats and could divide them in any way. In Marylebone, for example, there were twenty-two candidates for seven seats. A voter could choose seven different candidates; cast all seven votes for one of them; give four votes to one candidate and three to another; or use any other combination. This system helped ensure that some candidates from religious minorities would be elected, since supporters could "plump" the whole number of their votes for the candidate of their own faith.

A rather breathless anxiety surrounded all the new experiments. As a ratepayer, Mary Lloyd had a vote. Cobbe did not, but she visited London polling places and saw "ladies in their carriages, quiet and rather nervous middle-class maiden ladies in their cabs,—good honest washerwomen and needlewomen resolutely marching up on foot. Each and all passed in and out of the polling place without the slightest difficulty or annoyance." But later, when she went to the same polling places during a parliamentary election, "the air was foul with the smell of brandy and beer," and she heard "about a dozen curses and denunciations of 'bloody' people and things. This last was the superior constituency alone entrusted with the solemn charge of electing the legislature of the nation."[42]

On 1 December London woke up to the news that "Miss Garrett, M.D." had topped the poll for Marylebone by an astonishing plurality. She had received 47,858 votes; T. H. Huxley was in second place with 13,494. Newspapers agreed that it was an "extraordinary phenomenon in the history of electioneering" achieved by "thorough organization and indefatigable exertion." Elizabeth Garrett and her friends had "canvassed with an energy, an audacity, and a perseverance which no unpaid males could command."[43] Emily Davies, founder of the women's college at Hitchin, led the poll for Greenwich, though by a more conventional margin. But Maria Grey, in Chelsea, placed fifth among eleven candidates for four seats; with a total of 7,025 votes she trailed the successful fourth-place candidate by 108. Although crucially interested in middle-class girls' education, Grey had not been enthusiastic about campaigning. At first she had refused to run, but then, as she later wrote, she had heard a sermon by Stopford Brooke "which made me feel ashamed of my cowardice and see that it was my duty as a woman, free from absorbing home duties, with independent means, and some brains to do unpaid work for the people's education." The *Englishwoman's Review* blamed Grey's loss on a position Cobbe certainly supported and might even have proposed: she had rejected "special religious teaching" so that, in the words of the *Englishwoman's Review.* "all classes—even Jews and Roman Catholics—could receive the advantages of the Act."[44]

Actively campaigning could not help but educate or reeducate the women who took part. In Manchester, Lydia Becker, now editor of the *Women's Suffrage Journal,* was also elected. Cobbe immediately began using *Echo* leaders to advise the school board on policies. She may have emerged from the campaign with a better grasp of working-class realities. "The Witton Catastrophe" (13 December 1870), for example, described an explosion that had killed nearly one hundred women who worked loading gunpowder into cartridges, a trade that had not, she pointed out grimly, been found improper for the "timid sex." Her most scathing feminist piece for the end of 1870, however, was "The Modern Revolt" (3 December 1870), a response to Eliza

Lynn Linton's article in *Macmillan's* for December. Not willing even to dignify Linton by using her name, Cobbe rebuked her as a successful, well-paid woman who belittled other women's attempts to qualify for professions.

Amid all the politics and journalism Cobbe had not forgotten theology. By the end of October she was asking for contributions to a volume published as *Alone to the Alone: Prayers For Theists*. It contains seventy-one brief prayers or meditations supplied by fifteen people; she told friends that half were by women. In November she wrote an eyewitness account of Charles Voysey's appeal against his conviction for heresy. In 1864 Voysey, perpetual curate of Healaugh, a Yorkshire parish with a population of 260, had preached a sermon later published as "Is Every Statement in the Bible about our Heavenly Father Strictly True?" In 1868 he had "denied that Christ's sacrifice was necessary for man's salvation,"[45] for which he was found guilty of heresy. Cobbe's report of the appeal is full of interesting detail about the setting and process, but the substance of Voysey's argument is curiously muted: "But the subjects involved in this remarkable trial . . . are very unfit for newspaper discussion, and we must leave the matter for others to handle in its controversial bearings." It is difficult not to wonder whether the evasion is Cobbe's or the editor's and whether it grew from respect for readers' religious convictions or from the newspaper's susceptibility to legal action. When, on 11 February 1871, the Privy Council denied the appeal and revoked Voysey's position as a clergyman in the Church of England, Cobbe at once began writing to friends who might help him find a place in London.[46]

On the final day of 1870 Cobbe wrote the latter half of the *Echo's* annual summary of events. Only one person—Charles Dickens—had been buried in Westminster Abbey during the year. The Holborn viaduct and the Thames embankment had been completed, three new stations had been added to the Metropolitan Railway, and telegraph service was being transferred to the government. She concluded that few books of any real note had been published but that in a week or two "Mr. Darwin's long-anticipated treatise on 'The Descent of Man'" would appear.[47]

Almost as soon as the new year began, a romantic incident affirmed married women's right to sit on elected bodies. Maria Grey was a childless widow in her fifties when she ran for the school board; Elizabeth Garrett was single and two decades younger. On 7 December 1870 Arthur Munby had seen Garrett looking "youthful and charming—one of the belles of the room: 'tis amusing, to see this learned and distinguished M.D. moving about in rose-coloured silk and pointlace, with flowers in her hair, and receiving due homage, in both capacities, from the men."[48] On 6 January 1871 the *Times* reported that she was about to marry. The man, not yet named in the *Times,* was James George Skelton Anderson, treasurer of her campaign committee

Elizabeth Garrett (1836–1917), the first woman to qualify in England for a license
to practice medicine. The photograph was taken in 1866, before she became
Elizabeth Garrett Anderson. (Mary Evans/The Women's Library)

and a member of the managing board for the East London Hospital for Children, where she was an attending physician. The *Lancet* happily assumed
that "she forfeits by marriage her position on the School Board."[49]

Delighted with her friend's private happiness, although also believing
that it might end her public life, Cobbe produced a tidy parody of Longfellow's "Excelsior" with a "maid" in place of Longfellow's "youth." It began:

> The Woman's cause was rising fast
> When to the Surgeons' College past
> A maid who bore in fingers nice
> A banner with a new device
>
> > Excelsior![50]

The letter of thanks—"Your capital verses made us both shout with laughter"—signed "E. G. Anderson," said that no resignation was in prospect, not even, the language implies, in the case of pregnancy: "Seriously, dear Miss Cobbe, I am not going to give up anything. . . . Till I am convinced to the contrary I shall continue to hope that healthy women cd be in good working health thro most contingencies if they *resolve* to be so." And indeed, as the newspapers soon discovered, the Education Act had no explicit provision "forbidding a married lady from retaining her seat."[51]

Charles Darwin's "long-anticipated treatise" came out at the end of February. (The publisher begged Darwin not to let any notice by Cobbe, who had advance sheets, appear before the official publication day.) Her review, entitled "Darwinism in Morals," makes clear that she wholeheartedly accepted physical evolution but that applying the same principle to moral development raised difficulties (just as "sociobiology" and "evolutionary psychology" continue to trouble many intellectuals, especially feminists). Emma Darwin, who often handled correspondence for her husband, reported to Cobbe that "Mr. Darwin is reading the *Review* with the greatest interest and attention and feels so much the kind way you speak of him and the praise you give him, that it will make him bear your severity, when he reaches that part of the review." A further letter in Emma's handwriting passed along some of Darwin's questions, invited Cobbe and Lloyd to stop in for a visit, and then concluded, "Speaking in my private capacity I quite agree with *you*. I think the course of all modern thought is 'desolating' as removing God further off. . . . So you see I am a traitor in the camp."[52]

During 1871 Cobbe became a member of the Married Women's Property Committee executive. She had already published many essays in support of the bill, and aside from everything else, she knew that title to their own property was essential to married women's suffrage. Others then on the committee included friends such as Kate Amberley, Frances Wedgwood (Hensleigh Wedgwood's wife), and Lydia Becker as well as Jacob Bright, Charles Dilke, and Richard Pankhurst. Josephine Butler was also a member; although Cobbe may still have felt distaste for the campaign to repeal the Contagious Diseases Acts, she did not object to sitting on a responsible executive committee with its leader.

In the first half of 1871 Cobbe published seven anonymous pieces in the *Examiner,* a Sunday paper with a political focus. (The *Echo* came out only six days a week.) The work may have been done for the extra money—a scrap of paper in her brother Charles's handwriting accounts for her income during 1871, as if some difficulty had arisen—although she did manage to promote women's suffrage in two of the seven *Examiner* essays. On 13 February Jacob Bright again introduced his suffrage bill, and women once more organized to support it. Cobbe reported on the London public meeting of 25 March in an *Echo* leader that jocularly suggests a gentlemanly (rather than feminine) author: "The irrepressible woman is upon us again." Interestingly, two passages are altered in her scrapbook. The published conclusion read: "But if the truth be that to give us the solemn charge of moral freedom has been accounted an end so great that . . . there should be no more talk of women 'accepting with pride' a condition of universal dependence and inferiority—a condition which is, in fact, not accepted. It is as purely imaginary as the vision of ladies in Parliament, and ladies on the Bench of Bishops."[53] In the copy she saved, Cobbe crossed out the dash and the words that follow it, suggesting that they were added by an editor or subeditor who thereby (not coincidentally?) ruined her strong peroration and denied any prospect of women becoming bishops or members of Parliament.

A month later, as the vote approached, Cobbe dripped venomous irony on W. E. Gladstone: "The popular and urbane Minister—'the people's William' . . . will not see the persons who ask the privilege of an interview with him. . . . Who can they possibly be. . . . a party of Federal Communists. . . . a gang of pickpockets . . . the inmates of Bedlam or of Colney Hatch. . . . But it is unfortunately none of these people. . . . simply a few ladies. . . . What *can* Mr Gladstone be afraid of?" She publicized the same incident in the *Examiner,* concluding that Gladstone's refusal to meet with the suffragists was "the best argument which has yet been furnished to women for persisting in asserting their claims. No body of similar numerical or social importance which could command direct representation in Parliament would be liable to receive such a slight from the great *liberal* Premier."[54]

On 3 May Amberley wrote to his wife from the House of Commons: "Gladstone spoke in favour, said he would vote against & ran away finally, I believe—Disraeli voted with you." Although the *Times* reported that the bill had met "with the prompt negative it deserves"—the vote was 151 in favor and 220 opposed—Cobbe was enormously encouraged. "Our defeat last Wednesday," she wrote to Mary Somerville, "was in fact the earnest of now inevitable victory. We have now on our side *all* the men of real mark of *all* parties . . . in a year or two at most the franchise must be given to us." During the debate, A. J. Beresford-Hope had professed "great respect and no little fear" for "the strong minded phalanx." He "looked upon a woman's tongue, sharpened by debates and journalism, as a very formidable weapon, and one that was highly dangerous to encounter." Writing anonymously, though identifying herself as a woman, in the *Examiner* for 6 May, Cobbe went after the *Times,* which "outshone the M.P.'s," she said, "for the production out of its treasury of things new and old in the way of fallacies."

Never a week, and rarely a few days, elapse without the police reports recording some pitiful story of a wife beaten to death by her husband; or left to starve in poverty and disease . . . [yet] the *Times* sweetly tells women to be content without any political rights, because "as matters now stand, men undertake to provide for women a safe and sheltered sphere within which they may develop all the gentle powers of their nature!" *Do* they undertake it? Then, for god's sake, let the law compel them to fulfill their undertaking! Let us have one thing or the other. Let the State secure for every woman "a safe and sheltered sphere," and a freedom from all the burdens for which she has no corresponding privileges; or let her have equal rights with a man, and have done for ever with the cant of the "safe and sheltered sphere" which to thousands is only a mockery.[55]

Cobbe's next *Echo* leader, after defeat of the suffrage bill, was "The Eltham Tragedy" (6 May 1871): everyone knew when a dying mutilated girl was discovered at Eltham that it must be a tale of seduction and abandonment. "Is it not terrible that the appearance of a woman's mutilated corpse almost necessarily implies" that her former lover has killed her?

Cobbe's summer holiday was short but busy. She spent time with Lloyd in "her cottage which she has taken for 14 years & where she means to spend her summers near her own estate which always seems to want looking after." Lloyd was "helping to explore more caves & blackening her fingers with soot of the Stone-age." Sarah Wister paid a visit while they were both in Wales, but Cobbe did not stop in Bristol to see her old friend Matthew Davenport Hill. The ninety-nine-year-old Hill wrote in his teasing Regency style, "Falsest of woman-kind! You have cruelly jilted me. Florry wrote to say you were coming here as you ought to have done long ago." From Wales she went on to Newbridge. In her "dear old home" nearing her forty-ninth birthday, she paused to take stock. "Sometimes it comes over me there in the stately old rooms & beautiful parlours that I was born a gentlewoman & have rather had a downfall in becoming a hack scribbler to a halfpenny newspaper! But the scribbler is happier than ever the idle lady was (as if indeed I ever was idle) & my regrets always end in a laugh."[56]

Lloyd stayed in Wales through October; at the end of the month, Cobbe wrote to Mary Somerville that she would soon be coming "home to me like a truant husband." When she was in London, though, Lloyd (rather like Emma Darwin and other conscientious partners) helped attend to business. As Cobbe's public recognition grew, she was besieged with requests. People asked for advice about manuscripts and lectures; sought introductions to editors; sent books in hopes of a review ("as if I were likely to relish such rubbish," she complained on receiving *The Debatable Land Between This*

*World and the Next* from Robert Dale Owen). She visited the president of the Poor Law Board to help Florence Hill advocate boarding out for orphaned children. A surprising number of men, some of them quite well placed, asked her to "put in a word" with the home secretary or the India Office or the inspector of prisons when they were trying to find posts for a nephew or protégé. Naurozji Fardodunji hoped she would promote the National Indian Association; Keshub Chunder Sen depended on her introductions when he visited England; she was invited to speak at an International Conference on Prison Discipline. People with causes wanted publicity in the *Echo,* and they wanted her name. She let it be used on the council of the Cremation Society and then joked to Sarah Wister that she had never owned any land and, furthermore, never would "as I have joined the Cremation Society!!"[57]

Late in 1871 the women's suffrage movement finally established an effective national organization. Jacob Bright felt the need of "a body in London, representing all the various Associations" to arouse public support and lobby MPs. On 6 November the Central Committee of the National Society for Women's Suffrage came into being. The London National Society remained aloof; some of its leaders, including Millicent Fawcett, objected to being linked with women working to repeal the Contagious Diseases Acts.[58] But Cobbe immediately became a member of the executive committee. She no longer worried about the prominence of Manchester radicals and women campaigning against the Contagious Disease Acts within the organization, and in the four years since resigning from the executive committee of the London National Society she had lost her concern about the "personal publicity" of being on an executive with women of many different political stripes. She was also confident enough to do without the support of Lloyd and Hampson; indeed, the contrast between November 1867 and November 1871 reveals how very much Cobbe, as well as the women's movement itself, had changed in less than five years.

According to the *Annual Register,* 1872 would be remembered as "the most remarkable 'weather-year' of the century," with an earthquake, thunderstorms, snow, and hail in the first week; steady rains and cold far into the summer; and so much wind and rain in November that London had none of its usual "yellow fog." Mary Lloyd's dog Nip had died, probably during the autumn of 1871, when Cobbe wrote a letter to the *Spectator* making a playful argument in favor of the immortality of dogs. (If one granted that a "child of some six or eighteen months be certainly an immortal being," she wrote, then a dog, whose intelligence and moral knowledge "manifestly surpasses an average human infant," must also have a continued existence after death.) At about the same time Cobbe's new dog Yama, the Pomeranian who had replaced Hajjin, disappeared. She was recovered in January 1872 "so altered we had to hold quite a Tichborne trial about her identity! She . . . would not come to me when I called her. But then per contra, the old cat knew her & began to play at once, & the new cat spat at her. . . . the moment I held her to my cheek . . . she took hold of the lobe of my ear & gave me a gentle bite! After this her recognition was ecstatic on all sides & she has been ever since rushing over the house in a frenzy of self-congratulation."[59]

On 17 January the new central committee was "formally constituted" with a meeting at the Langham Hotel. Cobbe, once again officially at the movement's heart, reported the "loud unanimous cheer throughout the hall" when it was announced that Mary Somerville had subscribed to be a member. Before the next parliamentary vote, suffragists held 150 meetings around the country and collected at least 330,000 signatures for petitions.[60] When the Irish Society for Women's Suffrage met at Blackrock on 21 February, Cobbe's old neighbor Lord Talbot de Malahide was in the chair.

Writing in the *Echo* during the first part of the year, Cobbe often used her workhouse experience to argue for including women on official bodies. "The Hampstead Inquiry Report" (4 January 1872) described a typical pattern: well-intentioned gentlemen sat on the board of a public institution, scandal arose, an official inquiry was conducted, and a report exonerated everyone. But surely, she wrote, someone was to blame for "tainted food, lost and dead children, filthy linen, and patients troubled with lice and maggots." Two days later "Poor-Law Inspectors and Their Failures" pointed out that inspectors were appointed without any particular qualification and that women knew much more about nurseries, kitchens, childcare, and general housekeeping. On 26 April Cobbe attended Sophia Jex-Blake's lecture on women's medical education, and she joined a committee to start a women's hospital connected to Elizabeth Garrett Anderson's dispensary. Frances Morgan, who had earned her M.D. at Zurich in 1870 and would soon be Cobbe's friend and physician, also worked at the dispensary.

The women's suffrage bill was scheduled for debate on 1 May. A rally on 29 April in St. George's Hall drew such a large crowd that an overflow meeting was held in the Cavendish Rooms. Once again Amberley wrote to his wife from the House of Commons: "The Attorney Genl. for England spoke for the Ladies, the Attorney Genl for Ireland against—Three members jumped up in succession to announce their conversion from *support* of the Ladies to *opposition!* . . . Gladstone keeps away—I keep my letter open to you to inform you of the numbers: 143–222. a retrogression since last year!" The *Englishwoman's Review* discovered that opponents had circulated a message urging MPs to be in the house by four o'clock in order to prevent the bill's "accidental" passage.[61] Although the vote was disappointing, the non-party "whip" reveals that women were becoming a threat.

In the *Echo* Cobbe could do little more than regret that no "statesman of the first rank" had spoken against the bill. Beresford-Hope, she said, had indulged "*ad libitum* in his pendulum gestures" and given "selections from certain Irish songs and Irish stories." After filing her leader, she hurried off to speak at a meeting of suffragists from around the country who were planning their next move. In view of the defections among Liberal MPs, Cobbe wanted to emphasize the "Conservative principle" that "those who paid their taxes should have representation." At such meetings she began to call the Liberal prime minister "William the Woman-hater."[62]

With the coming of May and the London social season—and the post-

Cobbe's relative Alexander James Beresford-Hope (1820–1887), Conservative MP, publisher of the *Saturday Review,* supporter of Anglo-Catholic ritualism, and vocal opponent of women's suffrage. The caricature by "Ape" (Carlo Pellegrini) appeared in *Vanity Fair* on 10 September 1870.

vote lull in suffrage agitation—Fanny Kemble spent some time at 26 Hereford Square and read to Cobbe and Lloyd from the memoir she was beginning to assemble. The Amberleys' youngest child—mathematician, philosopher, social reformer, and Nobel Prize winner Bertrand Russell—was born in the middle of May. Activists from the United States came to London during the summer for a Women's Peace Congress at St. George's Hall. Julia Ward Howe spoke on 8 July, and Cobbe gave an afternoon reception for her, inviting J. A. Froude—would the old Confederate backer have wanted to meet the author of the most famous Union marching song?—as well as other "literary notabilities." The suffrage central committee met later in the month. Cobbe may have had a brief holiday in August, but the dreadful weather, or perhaps the money problem, changed Lloyd's usual plan: she rented out her cottage to James Martineau and his family.[63] On the way back to London, Martineau had at attack of vertigo, and on medical advice—he was already in his late sixties—stopped preaching, although he continued to teach at Manchester New College.

After Martineau left Little Portland Street, Cobbe attended Charles Voysey's services at St. George's Hall. Although Voysey had none of Martineau's intellectual depth, his ideas were drawn from very agreeable sources. Indeed, Charles Maurice Davies described a service at which, "instead of a Lesson from the Old Testament," Voysey read a passage on the rights of animals from F. W. Newman's "Theism"; the "Second Lesson was taken from the 'Heteropathy' of Miss Frances Power Cobbe"; and the service concluded with a "Hymn of Praise, taken from the Epilogue of F. W. Newman's 'Theism.'" Annie Besant, who was then a clergyman's wife but subsequently became notorious as a militant atheist who published a pamphlet on birth control, wrote that "a ray of light broke the darkness" of her religious dilemma when she heard Voysey preach. His theism "opened up . . . new views of religion. I read Theodore Parker's 'Discourse on Religion,' Francis Newman's works, those of Miss Frances Power Cobbe . . . the anguish of the tension relaxed; the nightmare of an Almighty Evil passed away." Before long Besant moved on—in the 1890s she would succeed Madame Blavatsky as leader of the Theosophical Society—but for her as for others in the 1870s, Parker, Newman, and Cobbe were guides to a new faith. Cobbe returned to serious theological work with the first part of "The Life After Death," published in the *Theological Review* for October. Although she had long since rejected "heaven" and "hell," she clung to the idea of immortality and sought ways to justify her belief. In the months after her mother's death, so far as she had known, she had been alone in her doubts, but now many intelligent people had adopted a position she could no longer share. "The great mass of the literary & scientific & even *reading* world has undergone a silent revolution of an enormous kind," she wrote; "I hardly know one man but a clergyman who believes in a life after death!"[64]

In the aftermath of Huxley's defense of vivisection at the 1870 meeting of the British Association for the Advancement of Science, Cobbe grew increasingly concerned that animal experimentation might spread to England. Interested for the present in arousing sympathy and fellow feeling for animals, she also concentrated on reaching the right audience with the right message. "The Consciousness of Dogs" was published in the October issue of *Quarterly Review.* With the largest circulation of any quarterly, the journal was generally conservative and drew readers from the educated upper and upper middle classes. For those readers, Cobbe carefully examined dogs' mental and emotional characteristics. Charles Darwin found it "the best analysis of the mind of an animal which I have ever read."[65] For the December *Cornhill* she created "Dogs Whom I Have Met," a collection of pleasant anecdotes suited for the holiday number of a popular magazine. Leaders in the *Echo* focused on class: boys' careless cruelty as opposed to eminent scientists' deliberate torture; the prosecution of men who kept a rat pit in Paddington in contrast to the social glitter of aristocrats shooting pigeons sprung from traps at Hurlingham.[66]

Mary Somerville died at Naples on 29 November 1872, a few weeks short of ninety-two. Cobbe wrote an obituary for the *Echo* "with such pain & tears as made me ill for a day after." She was so distraught that Lloyd sent their first condolence letter. Then they went to work trying to have Somerville's pension continued for her two daughters, who were both in their late fifties. Cobbe contacted scientists and asked Augusta Stanley, wife of the dean of Westminster, to speak to the queen. She hoped the daughters could also realize some money by publishing a memoir Somerville had worked on toward the end of her life. By late December Cobbe had a promise that she could review the book in the *Quarterly Review* when it came out, began to advise Martha Somerville about its editing, and urged her to write out everything she wanted Cobbe to say in the review.[67]

Even before the death of her "second mother" Cobbe had been thinking about family and about the mother who had died a quarter of a century earlier. A landmark birthday came near the end of 1872; Cobbe turned fifty on 4 December. When *Blackwood's Edinburgh Magazine* published an essay titled "La Bruyere" in November, she inquired about getting more information, since she thought the seventeenth-century French philosopher might have been an ancestor of Frances Conway's. John Blackwood passed Cobbe's letter along to the essay's anonymous author, but Anne Mozley would not write to Cobbe: "She is a very well known person, clever and amiable I hear in private life, but an advanced liberal." Besides, she was "clearly mistaken in supposing La Bruyere an ancestor" since "he died unmarried & without children."[68] During the 1870s Cobbe generally went to Ireland every two years or so. Cousins and in-laws and children evidently still filled Newbridge for summer visits. Azelie Thompson, a child of Uncle George's daughter Linda, married Matthew Poole, the eldest son of cousin Anne Conway. No trace of the other Conway relatives survives in Cobbe's correspondence, although Harriet, who spent so much time at Newbridge during their girl-hood, had returned from India after the death of her husband, Captain John Beville Layard, of the Madras Army. It is hard to believe that Cobbe was completely out of touch with her mother's side of the family, especially in a year when she had searched for Conway ancestors.

The cousins Cobbe saw most often were children of her uncle Thomas and the begum. The 1871 census recorded John Locke as living at 63 Eaton Place with his wife Laura (born in Calcutta), his son John Henry (age twenty-two, a law student), and his sister-in-law Azalia A. Talmadge (born in Delhi) along with six servants. "Azalia"—that is, Azélie, once the wife of Cobbe's brother Tom—is described as "married" rather than "widowed," so Talmadge was presumably still alive; since they generally lived in Paris, it would seem that she took refuge with her sister during the Franco-Prussian War. Charles Augustus often came to London. Eliza and Sophy lived to-gether in lodgings, sometimes in England and sometimes, during the off-season, at some Continental watering place.

Cobbe visited Tom and Jessie and their children at Liss, but, oddly, there is no evidence of visits to her brother Henry and his wife, Sarah, at Milton-Bryant. Perhaps, since it was less than fifty miles from London, the trips were short enough to escape mention; she did get information for Henry (probably for his daughter Mabel, who was seventeen) about the new wom-en's residence in Cambridge supervised by Anne Jemima Clough.[69] Brother Will remained unseen at the Agapemone, although he must still have been on her mind: references to "Mr. Prince" appeared not infrequently, and always pejoratively, in her *Echo* columns. Mary Lloyd's only surviving brother—Howell, who had converted to Catholicism—lived near them in Kensing-ton, but no evidence reveals whether they ever saw one another. Mary's nephew Edward, who would succeed to Rhagatt when he came of age, was at Eton; Cobbe and Lloyd sometimes took him to the theater as a weekend treat.

In 1873, with (unfulfilled) rumors that a new reform bill was in prospect, suffrage petitions were yet again sent to both Gladstone and Disraeli; the Married Women's Property Committee, of which Cobbe was still a mem-ber, worked closely with the jurisprudence section of the NAPSS; and Elizabeth Garrett Anderson was elected as the first, and for many years only, woman member of the British Medical Association. Two causes that Cobbe had often promoted—appointing women poor-law inspectors and putting orphans into foster care—came together early in January when her friend Jane Hughes Senior became an assistant inspector of workhouses. The first woman appointed to a significant government post, she had a salary of four hundred pounds a year and a special mandate "to look after the dwellings and general treatment of children who are boarded out."[70]

As she began her fifth year of regular work for the *Echo,* Cobbe looked for new instances and new language to offer up opinions on familiar themes: fraud, education, poverty, urban safety, police organization, the absurdity of women's fashions. Spiritualism and its believers were among her favorite targets; on 4 January 1873 she was astonished that a scientist as distinguished as Alfred Russel Wallace had asserted that some "manifestations" were "undoubtedly genuine." Some of her second leaders remain startlingly relevant, even after more than 130 years: "Eating Good Children's Tommy" (25 February 1873) disapproved of a proposal that would enable suicide but hoped the debate would make doctors pay more attention to relieving pain and providing a comfortable death; "Offence's Gilded Hand" (4 March 1873) pointed out that money and good lawyers kept rich men out of prison; "Book Stealing" (10 April 1873) describes bibliomaniacs, who steal not to sell but to possess, as the plague of all great libraries.

Her social life is glimpsed in the unpublished diary of Shirley Brooks, who became editor of *Punch* in 1870: "To Haweis, 16 Welbeck Street. Odd house, full of colour. Odd party, rather. The Alma-Tademas, Tom Taylors, Frances Cobbe, so fat & merry, but a strongminded woman. Arnold, the editor of the Echo." Hugh Reginald Haweis was Cobbe's coworker on the *Echo,* and the house "full of color" was no doubt the work of his wife, born Mary Joy, who had exhibited at the Royal Academy and wrote on fashion and domestic art. When he and Cobbe wrote the second leader on alternating days, she reported, he "willingly adopted the special tone in the treatment of social questions of which she had (from the starting of the paper), struck the key-note." On the other hand, as a clergyman he had a "vivid liking for an aesthetic form of worship,"[71] a liking that Cobbe certainly did not share.

In the spring of 1873 Cobbe and Lloyd tried a new plan to give Lloyd something more like country life and help with her financial difficulties. Declining an evening invitation from Helen Taylor, Cobbe wrote, "We have let our house for the season." April's letters were dated "Thayer's Park Farm, Beckenham, Kent." Although Beckenham is less than ten miles from central London, farm lodgings allowed Lloyd to enjoy horseback riding in the countryside in spring, while Cobbe had a convenient rail connection to London Bridge, Charing Cross, and the *Echo* office. In May she was at Sevenoaks, also in Kent, where Geraldine Jewsbury then lived, while Lloyd went to the Lake District.[72]

Cobbe spent much of the spring and summer coaxing and advising Martha Somerville. By 2 April the publisher had typeset Mary Somerville's manuscript autobiography and sent proofs to Cobbe. She wrote to Martha as diplomatically as possible: "Mary & I have read it up to the last two sheets, together with great care & I need hardly tell you with the deepest interest. . . . But now dear Martha I have to say what I fear will pain you. . . . I am sadly afraid about the impression the book will make on strangers." She saw no hope of commercial success and feared that the book would harm Somerville's reputation: people would "come to the conclusion she was a cold hearted person—or she could not so completely have omitted all reference to her feelings." Cobbe urged Martha to write an introduction and select parts of her mother's memoir, leaving "blanks with stars—& giving the whole somewhat the aspect of fragments," and to "call the book something like Memoirs of Mrs Somerville compiled from Recollections of her life edited by her daughter Martha Somerville or . . . something of the sort not claiming to be an Autobiography." She closed by offering to mark passages to omit and to help with the editing.[73]

Cobbe's work ultimately made her virtually a coauthor of the book: she told Martha what to write, revised it, suggested adding some of Somerville's letters, contacted scientific friends for advice, and removed a number of passages, sometimes quite deliberately to cast Somerville in a better light. "You should I think put in *all* she says about her studies . . . omitting however if you can conscientiously do so her attacks on Darwinism," Cobbe told Martha. "It wd do her great harm just now among the scientific indeed the whole thinking world." Or as she suggested in a subsequent letter, "paste & scissors are very useful in our trade!"[74]

Published in very much the form Cobbe suggested—whatever Somerville may have written about Darwin is glossed over with a brief reference to Cobbe's own "vigorous" but "kindly" critique in "Darwinism in Morals"— *Personal Recollections, from Early Life to Old Age, of Mary Somerville with Selections from her Correspondence,* "By Her Daughter, Martha Somerville," came out late in November. Continuing her literary midwifery, Cobbe not only reviewed the book in the *Quarterly Review* and the *Academy* but also, she told Martha Somerville, "got friends to review it at length in the Contemporary & more briefly in the Fortnightly." In hopes of correcting the rumor that Somerville's first husband had helped with her early mathematical work, Cobbe's review in the *Academy* emphasized her unhappiness during the three-year marriage to a "harsh, stern, and unsympathizing" man.[75] The longer essay in the *Quarterly Review* includes Cobbe's own recollections, quotes Somerville's letters to her, and emphasizes Somerville's support for women's university education and opposition to animal experimentation.[76]

To return to the late spring of 1873, a small domestic adventure featured the dog Yama. About to give birth, she was inspired to dig "a regular fox's hole" under the ground; the puppy was rescued just in time to keep it from being buried alive. "Such," wrote Cobbe in another sly dig at those who were beginning to equate "natural" with "good," "are the perils attendant on following hereditary instincts under altered conditions of society!" (Later in the summer she gave the puppy to Florence Clough, then fifteen, a daughter of Arthur Hugh Clough and his wife, Blanche.) John Stuart Mill's death on 8 May required Cobbe once more to struggle through tears to produce an obituary for the *Echo*.[77] Shortly afterwards, just before leaving to spend a few weeks in Wales, she said farewell to Sarah Wister, who was on her way home to Philadelphia. In August their correspondence began. Cobbe's first long letter suggestively describes Mary Lloyd's nature and hints at their tensions: "I have just come home leaving Mary in Wales & somehow the fixed sadness of that dear & noble heart next to mine in unbroken tête a tête for seven weeks has left me so saddened with the problems of life—human & animal—that I think it is a good thing you can't talk to me just now!"[78]

During these years when Cobbe was at the height of her intellectual reputation, she received a great many letters on literary, scientific, and philosophical matters. Maria Mitchell, the American astronomer and professor at Vassar, was in London during the summer and took a cab to Hereford Square:

> I was as much surprised as delighted when the girl said she was at home, for the house had painters in it, the carpets were up, and everything looked uninhabitable. The girl came back, after taking my card, and asked me if I would go into the studio, and so took me through a pretty garden into a small building of two rooms, the outer one filled with pictures and books. I had never heard that Miss Cobbe was an artist, and so I looked around, and was afraid that I had got the wrong Miss Cobbe. But as I glanced at the table I saw the 'Contemporary Review,' and I took up the first article and read it . . . . when a very white dog came bounding in upon me, and I dropped the book, knowing that the dog's mistress must be coming—and Miss Cobbe entered. She looked just as I expected, but even larger; but then her head is magnificent because so large.

In September William Carpenter sent proofs of his book in progress—*Principles of Mental Physiology*, published in 1874—and invited Cobbe to dinner so they could talk about her criticisms.[79]

London School Board terms expired in the autumn of 1873. Neither Emily Davies nor Elizabeth Garrett Anderson chose to stand again, and although two women were elected for Marylebone, Cobbe once more worked for a Chelsea candidate who did not succeed—Amelia Arnold, wife of the *Echo*'s editor. After attending her campaign events and seeing how men behaved even when supporting a woman candidate, Cobbe wrote a short, humorous essay for the *Women's Suffrage Journal.* "As George Eliot says," it begins, "'The masculine intellect—what there is of it—is always of a superior calibre;' but yet it seems to labour under one peculiar and unconquerable . . . congenital defect. It appears that no power of abstraction exists whereby a man can think of a woman except in her relation to himself." At one meeting "a venerable gentleman, with a white beard" introduced the woman candidate with a twenty-minute talk about the reason more attention should be paid to girls' education: "'Ill-trained girls,' he had observed, 'never did sew on their husband's buttons nor attend to the boiling of their eggs for breakfast.'"[80]

By that time even *Punch* had recognized the opening of Girton College in Cambridge by quoting, without comment, Cobbe's notice for the *Echo.* Cobbe publicized the new girls' secondary schools that Maria Grey was developing and spoke at a first-anniversary celebration for the Chelsea Girls' High School. Since Cobbe was not a ratepayer—the house she shared with Mary Lloyd was in Lloyd's name—she could not stand for public office even if she wanted to, but the variety of opportunities that grew from her personal networks and her work in journalism were perhaps more satisfying. "The truth is," she wrote not long after the 1873 election, "that one wants *to live*, not to vegetate . . . and this concentrated Life can be lived in London and nowhere else." Yet as a writer she could well have lived elsewhere, and she could not help sometimes feeling guilty about Lloyd's unhappiness. She told Wister in December 1873 that "Mary . . . growls over London but endures it. We have been to a play—& to a conjurer—& have given (for us) a big dinner party—& seen Holman Hunt's picture of a . . . wooden man sawing in the middle of a floor covered with exquisitely painted shavings—which is supposed to represent Jesus Christ & the Shadow of Death."[81]

From the beginning of 1874, Cobbe published in even more journals—"chopped up into little bits in the Echo Daily News & Examiner"—and took a larger role in activist organizations. Jacob Bright urged her to speak at a suffrage conference in Birmingham. "I mean to say," she wrote Wister, "that there is no use to go on using *logic* to prove our claims. If argument could gain them we should have had them long ago. . . . It is *sentiment* we have got to contend against not reason—& to conquer it we must show ourselves strong & calm & wise—& not pretty & silly & vociferous."[82] In its published version, *Our Policy: An Address to Women Concerning the Suffrage* was still being reprinted more than twenty years later.

For January 1874, aside from the two Somerville reviews and the schoolboard piece in the *Women's Suffrage Journal*, Cobbe had an essay in the *Theological Review.* "Heteropathy, Aversion, Sympathy" argued that sympathy was neither universal nor ahistorical but differed with the "stage of genuine civilization": animals attacked the weak, primitive peoples in unforgiving climates destroyed the elderly, "nations so far advanced in civilization as the ancient Greeks and the modern Chinese" practiced infanticide, and even gently nurtured children exhibited similar tendencies. Fox hunting and wife abuse, religious martyrdom and holy war, class prejudice and hypernationalism all grew from a lack of sympathy. The essay builds an argument to unify the causes that were most important for Cobbe: "Not only do our sympathies require to be more equally extended as regards nations, classes, sexes and ages; but there is sore need that they should spread outside the human race among the tribes of sentient creatures who lie beneath us and at our mercy." The *Examiner* for 17 January 1874 had a simplified version of the concluding argument, published over Cobbe's name. (The paper had been purchased in 1873 by her old radical friend P. A. Taylor.) "From the old

Lydia Becker (1829–1890), pioneer suffragist, elected member of the Manchester School Board, and editor of the *Women's Suffrage Journal.* The sketch was published in *The Graphic,* 10 January 1874. (Mary Evans Picture Library, London)

point of view," she wrote, "the brutes were separated from us by a clearly-defined and ineffaceable line of demarcation. . . . They were created to serve us, as the sun and moon were made to regulate our day and night." But in the new state of things, she asked, if the "theist philosopher" found it acceptable to torture animals with cruel experiments, where would he draw the line? At the idiot? the infant? the peasant? the Negro? the feeble woman? any man who was not a philosopher?

Meanwhile, the general election of early 1874 had an unexpected result: a Conservative majority with 350 seats to the Liberals' 302. Although most MPs who actively worked for suffrage were Liberals (and some lost their seats), Cobbe was delighted. To begin with, Benjamin Disraeli became prime minister, and three men in his cabinet had also voted for women's suffrage. Liberals would be freed from the danger of Gladstone's disapproval; Conservatives might show up to follow their leader's example. By the time Parliament opened on 5 March, however, the Married Women's Property Committee realized that eighty of their strongest supporters were missing and decided their bill could not pass. Lydia Becker urged the committee to suspend its efforts until suffrage was won, but Samuel Morley introduced, and Parliament passed, a narrow revision of the 1870 act that protected creditors but did nothing for women.[83] In the course of these disputes both Becker and Cobbe resigned from the committee's executive. In other words, Cobbe now aligned herself with the radical Miss Becker, whose presence had worried her in 1867.

Furthermore, Jacob Bright had lost his seat, so suffrage needed another parliamentary spokesman. William Forsyth, Conservative member for Marylebone, was willing to take up the cause, but his bill stipulated that only single women and widows could qualify as voters. Becker believed the change was "a fatal error," although eventually the *Women's Suffrage Journal* did support Forsyth's bill. Cobbe too was disillusioned. "Mr Forsyth tells me he has very fair hopes of getting us the suffrage in this session," she wrote, "but I do not build on it." She was quite correct. Another difficulty for suffragists grew from increasing government control of the time allowed for debate. The bill was deferred, then "unavoidably postponed" by the "pressure of Government business," and finally withdrawn because it was so late in the session. At the same time, a strong backlash against women's higher education had moved from the United States to England. In 1873 Dr. Edward H. Clarke, a professor of medicine at Harvard, had asserted in *Sex in Education* that rigorous mental work between the ages of twelve and twenty would damage women's capacity to produce healthy infants. On 21 March 1874 Cobbe complained to Sarah Wister that "President Elliot of Harvard has been in London & talking a great deal of what you justly call nonsense about

the physical difficulties in the way of women's education as announced by
. . . Dr. Clarke."[84]

In the course of these public and parliamentary setbacks Cobbe placed
a group of second leaders, most of them on women's issues, in the *Daily
News,* then edited by James Martineau's disciple Frank Harrison Hill. On
Tuesday, 14 April, for example, she responded to the education question in
an irony-laden essay:

> Some recent authorities seem to view the female of the human race as if she
> were an invalid by nature, a born patient, whose normal condition requires
> constant medical supervision. . . . It is true that, for ages, women of the
> working classes have performed physical tasks of agricultural and house-
> hold toil alarmingly at variance with the "invalid" theory of feminine exis-
> tence, and no medical warning has been raised. . . . Now, however, that a
> very serious effort is being made both by parents and by young women
> themselves to substitute for the old wretched shifty scramble for "accom-
> plishments" something which may be truly called Education, the voice of
> warning sounds from shore to shore across the Atlantic.

Yet despite the visit from Harvard's president and the medical opinions, on
13 May the University of London convocation did what Cobbe had asked
of it twelve years earlier. "Is it not splendid the Convocation of London University passing by large majority the resolution to give degrees to women!"
she wrote. "It will yet take a long time to go through the Senate—& to get
a new Charter, but the die is cast. We shall have women MA's & DD's too
I dare say some of these days!"[85]

A false start toward another of her goals took place in the House of
Commons on 18 May, when Colonel Egerton Leigh briefly introduced and
then withdrew a resolution about assaults on women. His speech was curiously light and patronizing, although he identified two key issues: that
women were reluctant to testify against an abuser and that the "sons of a
man who beat his wife treated it as a matter of course, and became women-
beaters when they grew up." Leigh proposed to give courts the "power to
order flogging" when necessary. *Punch* gallantly supported him with a verse
that began:

> There's preaching from platforms and fighting of fights
> By our sisters who shriek for "Woman's Rights,"
> But of *Punch's* sympathy more belongs
> To his sisters who suffer from "Woman's Wrongs."

The *Englishwoman's Review,* however, was suspicious, as Cobbe must have
been, when Disraeli asked Leigh to withdraw the resolution for additional

study. "We fear," it reported, that "Government is too deeply engaged with questions affecting the interests of constituents and voters to concern itself with those of a class which has no political influence."[86]

While Forsyth's bill was stalled in Parliament an article by Goldwin Smith stirred up new controversy. Smith, who had been regius professor of modern history at Oxford before accepting a chair at Cornell University, wrote that he had "once signed a petition for Female Household Suffrage got up by Mr. Mill" but had not then "seen the public life of women in the United States," which convinced him that the "very foundations of Society are touched when Party tampers with the relations of the sexes." In the *Daily News* for 3 June Cobbe had a fine time attacking Smith's logic as well as his arguments:

> As a political question interesting to Englishmen . . . we have, of course, nothing to do with Mr. Smith's references to Mrs. Victoria Woodhull, to Mr. Mill's mistakes about Mrs. Mill's capacity, to the Ohio Whisky War, to Queen Elizabeth's love for Leicester . . . to the immorality of Mrs Aphra Behn's novels . . .
>
> "The question," Mr. Goldwin Smith says, "whether female suffrage on an extended scale is good for the whole community [remains] . . . Is it good for us to have free institutions or not?" Glancing over this sentence, a hasty woman might assume that the writer was an ally of her sex, supposing that "us" naturally meant her half of the human race as well as the other.[87]

The suffrage central committee took a new office at 294 Regent Street during the summer. Cobbe often attended executive meetings. A younger woman remembered years later "the thrill of joy her entrance gave. It was as if a radiant sunbeam had lighted the office."[88] At the summer's general meeting, on a hot July day, Forsythe stubbornly argued that married women should be left out of the bill since they would not, in any case, be entitled to vote. Arthur Arnold, among others, insisted that the exclusion was "needless and offensive." As the meeting—in a "crowded, badly ventilated Hall"— grew ever longer and more exhausting, Cobbe managed to lighten the atmosphere with a humorous description of Goldwin Smith as the "Knight of the Rueful Countenance." Then, sadly, there was a tribute to Kate Amberley, dead on 28 June at age thirty-two of diphtheria caught while nursing her daughter Rachel, who also died.[89]

When she stayed in London through the early summer months, Cobbe liked to invite friends for tea in the garden or to sit out under the lime tree on long warm evenings. She appreciated women's company more and more, in contrast to the intense professional networking of her early days as a journalist:

Where men are present the women who are 1st pretty—2d flippant—3d subservient & flattering always keep the tone of conversation at their own level with the injurious assistance of the men. Where there are no men, such women either never care to come at all or put aside their nonsense & affectations & say what they think. . . . What men say is more entertaining & instructive on the whole than what women say—that is—perhaps three men in a party will say as many good things as four or five women. But then *per contra* I care to know what women think & feel, & I very rarely care a pin what a man thinks or feels or believe that he allows me to know his genuine thoughts or feelings (if he has any of the latter) but only what he chooses the world to suppose he has.[90]

Cobbe went as a journalist to the Royal Society for the Prevention of Cruelty to Animals (RSPCA) conference in celebration of its fiftieth anniversary and heard Arthur de Noé Walker deliver an address on vivisection that "showed how idly cruel" some of the experiments performed by London physicians were. No longer confined to Paris or Florence, medical callousness was coming much closer to home. Although Cobbe at this point still had no objection to experiments "made under the influence of some pain-destroying drug" provided that "care is taken to destroy the animal" before the anesthetic had worn off, the experiments Walker described disturbed her deeply.[91] Furthermore, he was the kind of man she trusted. Son of a naval captain who had served under Nelson, Walker had entered the 6th Madras Native Infantry in 1837, been wounded in the China expedition of 1842, studied medicine after leaving the East India Company, and volunteered as a surgeon in the Crimea, where he was present at the attack on the Redan in which Cobbe's cousin Henry Clermont died. Cobbe was a friend of his sister, Countess Baldelli, who had been trying to start a society to prevent animal cruelty in Florence.

Experiments on unanesthetized animals had appalled Cobbe since she wrote "The Rights of Man and the Claims of Brutes" in 1863. In the first half of the 1870s, however, the question began to coalesce with her mounting doubts about science in general, doctors in particular, and the male cruelty so vividly brought home by her newspaper work. The first British text for experimentation, the *Handbook for the Physiological Laboratory,* by Michael Foster, John Burdon Sanderson, Thomas Lauder Brunton, and Emmanuel Klein, was published in 1873. Cobbe tried unsuccessfully to "obtain a Queens Bench writ to prohibit the sale" of such works. In *Echo* leaders throughout 1873 and 1874 she pursued the topics of cruelty and medical indifference. She asked Sarah Wister to find out from her physician husband if it was true that "the diabolical practice of vivisection has been introduced

& is actually used as an *illustration of lectures* in physiological schools." Then in August 1874, at the British Medical Association meeting in Norwich, the French physiologist Eugene (Valentin) Magnan gave a lecture accompanied by a demonstration: he muzzled and spread-eagled two dogs and then injected one in the leg vein with alcohol and the other with absinthe. The first quickly died; the other "underwent a severe epileptic fit, which lasted for about an hour" and then recovered. "The Norwich Society for the Prevention of Cruelty to Animals," prodded the *Spectator,* has not "prosecuted the operator. Why not?"[92]

The prosecution would, in fact, take place later in the year. During the autumn, however, Cobbe's journalistic indignation was turned largely against ritualism, the Church of England, and William Gladstone. In "The High Church Mind," in the *Examiner* for 29 August, she condemned the patriarchal "High Church country parson," who busied himself "improving" every detail of his neighborhood and did "not like Jews, Roman Catholics, or heretics to buy or rent" property in the parish. She rang the changes with half a dozen leaders in the *Echo,* where she had long been fond of tweaking the "upholstery and millinery of religion." Although many people opposed ritualism primarily because the vestments and incense and candles came dangerously close to Roman Catholicism, Cobbe's objection was that emphasis on sacraments rather than individual conscience interfered with personal thought, restored dependence on priests, and significantly oppressed women. Ritualistic clergy, she wrote, established "another master beside the husband and father in every house."[93] Furthermore, they encouraged women to devote themselves to needlework and altar decoration rather than district visiting and social activism. She saw ritualism as yet another backlash movement, one designed to seduce women through art, beauty, and emotionality into becoming docile followers of male authority.

W. E. Gladstone's "Ritualism and Ritual," in the October *Contemporary Review,* took almost the same position as Cobbe, but she could not resist poking at him whenever she saw an opening. His criticism was too mild; she was surprised that he could not talk about religion without commenting on women's dress; even when the Pope called Gladstone "a viper," Cobbe was not certain that the former prime minister understood the limits of church and state. So fully had the suffrage battle transformed her opinion of Gladstone that she no longer fondly remembered the dinner party at which she had laughed at his imitations of distinguished preachers. "'But Mr. Gladstone,' said she, when he concluded, 'you have said nothing of *my* pastor.' 'And who is that?' 'The Rev. James Martineau.' Mr. Gladstone was silent for a moment, and then said deliberately. 'There is no doubt that Mr. Martineau is the greatest of living thinkers.'"[94]

Thank-you notes written during autumn 1874 reveal the continued variety of Cobbe's social life, although since letters from women were seldom preserved, it is not possible to discover what determined how she and Lloyd mixed and matched their guests. Yet as she became more and more exercised about both physiological experiments and women's causes, old intellectual relationships showed the strain. "There is something in the arrogance & overbearing ways of these men of science as bad as the old priestly misdeeds," she complained to Helen Taylor. The other night, she continued, Herbert Spencer had "attacked Mrs. William Grey & me about women's claims with a grinding voice & insulting manner such as I never experienced in a drawing room in my life. He literally defended wife beating and excused wife murder! the whole accompanied with expressions of contempt towards women which made every sentence an insult. We tried to change the subject (which we had not introduced) but in vain till at last, as dear Mrs Grey was ill & exhausted . . . he was stopped at last & sat looking at me with actual hatred for the rest of the evg!"[95]

Cobbe's *Hopes of the Human Race, Hereafter and Here: Essays on the Life after Death* was published in November 1874. Most of the essays were reprinted from the *Theological Review.* The one new piece was a sixty-page introduction responding to the posthumous publication of John Stuart Mill's *Essays on Religion* in which she vehemently criticized his assertion that faith in immortality required one to abandon rational inquiry. Before the book came out, Cobbe wrote to Helen Taylor that disputing Mill was "so inexpressibly painful to me that I feel as if I needed your assurance that you will forgive it. . . . It is a strange irony of fate that a man whose memory I honour so *profoundly*—to whom personally I owe such *great* kindness—& to whom I think every woman owes a debt of gratitude never to be discharged should have struck so terrible a blow at all which seems to me worth living for in life—& that I shd have the immeasurable presumption of striving to answer him." Taylor replied that if Cobbe had only let the book "lie bye" in her mind, she would have found it more palatable: "The temptation to lay down the law in a hurry is one thing that makes periodical writing very often as mischievous as it is useful." Despite the sharpness on both sides—Cobbe and Taylor were fairly well matched in argument—both letters are signed with unusually affectionate phrases that evidently served to maintain their politically useful relationship.[96]

Cobbe also sent copies of the book to both of the friends recently bereaved of young wives. In addition to Kate Amberley's death from diphtheria, Charles Dilke's first wife, also named Kate, had died in childbirth on 20 September, after only two years of marriage. Among the many patronizing post-Victorian comments about Cobbe that circulate in twentieth-century books is the following in Roy Jenkins's biography of Dilke: "He carried on a very strange correspondence about the existence of the human soul with a Miss Cobbe, the author of a little book entitled *Hopes of the Human Heart* [*sic*]." In the letter Dilke wrote on 23 December, however, he first praised *Hopes of the Human Race*—"I have read with much interest your new book & with especial delight the passages of singular beauty & great eloquence on which 'The Life After Death' is full"—and then proceeded to argue for about six pages against Cobbe's central premise. Amberley also responded with warm thanks, followed by ten pages of close argument.[97] If Cobbe did not convince two men with wives tragically lost, she at least gave them mental distraction.

Meanwhile, in mid-November the National Society for Women's Suffrage held its annual meeting in the Manchester Town Hall. A *Times* leader on the sixteenth conceded almost everything the suffragists argued about women's intellectual and moral fitness and about the justice of giving them the vote. Its central objection now was that women would exercise too much power, that women's questions would "always obtain an altogether disproportionate weight." Once they had the franchise, furthermore, "would it be possible to exclude them from the House of Commons?" It was, Cobbe pointed out, a "remarkable article . . . conceding everything except some small expediency."[98] On 9 December she spoke at a public meeting in London. Also on the platform were two relatively new friends with whom she would become very close, the young medical woman Frances Morgan, a fellow member of the central committee since 1872, and Morgan's new husband, another physician, George Hoggan.

Cobbe's *Daily News* column for the next day, which was unusually long, even for a leader, spoke confidently in a male constitutional and political voice, with no reference to the wrongs of women, crafting an argument to reassure conservatives and, more explicitly, to convince Benjamin Disraeli of the benefit to his party of enfranchising women. Women voters would be either "ladies who, having inherited independent means," had a fair education and the leisure to study public affairs or "a still more meritorious class—namely that of women who, in spite of all difficulties, have been enabled by their own industry, sobriety, and self-denial to support themselves and those dependent upon them." She concluded with a direct appeal to the prime minister: "No class of the community can be more deeply interested than women in the maintenance of order and the improvement of public morality." By taking the measure under government sponsorship, Disraeli would have "an opportunity for illustrating the paradox that your general Conservative alone is 'truly Liberal.'"[99]

At home, however, Cobbe and Lloyd were "overburdened with worry &

trouble about our tenure of this house & till it is settled whether we stop—
or go abroad for the winter—or find another house in town I have no brains
to spare." In addition to Lloyd's dislike of the city, they were "undergoing a
malicious suit" brought by "an artist who alleged that . . . Miss Lloyd's studio was a nuisance." The area around Gloucester Road station was becoming increasingly built up, with "new streets multiplying all around" and a
"red brick hotel . . . rising where what was last year a lane between privet
hedges."[100] They hoped, Cobbe wrote, to find a house "in Chelsea where
Miss Lloyd will have the relief to her artist eye of looking at the river." She
was also saddened by Jane Senior's letter reporting that poor health would
force her to resign her post as Poor Law inspector: "I need not tell *you* what
this has cost me.—To fail to keep the position so long hoped for, by so many
women. I feel such a traitor!" But Senior too was hoping soon to be free of
her large house and go to "a tiny house in Cheyne Walk Chelsea—so that I
may see the river."[101]

In the midst of her personal dislocations, and no doubt compounding
them, Cobbe was on the brink of public and organized antivivisection work.
The RSPCA's cruelty case against Magnan over the August demonstration
was dismissed on 9 December. Responding in the *Echo,* Cobbe urged the
RSPCA to "consider how legislative assistance can be obtained, not for the
suppression, but for the restriction, of Vivisection." By mid-December she
had written a petition asking the society to take action and sent copies to
her brother Charles and other dependable contacts, who agreed to collect
signatures. As she explained to Helen Taylor, she had made the petition
"studiedly moderate" so that humane scientists might be able to sign.[102]
Then she and Mary Lloyd went to work soliciting names.

Charles Darwin refused to sign; he had "long thought Physiology one
of the grandest of sciences, sure sooner or more probably later greatly to
benefit mankind." Darwin's wife, Emma, however, offered to get signatures
from other men she knew. Henry and Millicent Fawcett concluded that they
did "not know enough about the question" to justify using their names. But
Lewis Carroll (he signed that name rather than Charles Dodgson) felt "honoured and gratified at receiving so flattering a letter" from someone whose
latest book he greatly admired and was glad to enlist in the campaign, as
were a great many other notable men.[103] Cobbe was full of hope that the impressive roster of names would make members of the RSPCA executive pay
attention and that their own public and political weight would swiftly accomplish a necessary measure for the humane regulation of scientific research.

## 10

Parliamentary Politics
1875–1878

*Had I been a man, and had possessed my brother's facilities for entering
Parliament or any profession, I have sometimes dreamed I could have made my
mark and done some masculine service to my fellow-creatures.*
FRANCES POWER COBBE, *Life of Frances Power Cobbe*

Frances Power Cobbe mounted two major political efforts during the second half of the 1870s. For one she conducted a vigorous public-relations campaign, called in favors from men in Parliament, and won a major feminist victory. For the other she built an organization that consumed an enormous amount of time, ruined many of her friendships, sapped her energy, and ultimately damaged her reputation.

To begin with the latter—animal protection—the memorial Cobbe and Lloyd prepared asked the RSPCA to appoint a subcommittee on vivisection, prosecute cases that were illegal under existing laws, and discover whether a new law was needed. Cobbe had learned by experience to enlist lukewarm supporters by asking for an investigation instead of making immediate demands. She and Lloyd gathered signatures through family contacts, intellectual and artistic networks, and religious, military, and Anglo-Irish connections. They secured nearly a thousand supporters; and among the published names, all belonging to men with some prominence, were those of four archbishops (one Roman Catholic and three Anglican, including Cobbe's relative Marcus Beresford, the Primate of Ireland), ten bishops, more than five dozen peers, the lord chief justice of the court of common pleas, five admirals, a dozen generals, twenty-four members of Parliament (including A. J. Beresford-Hope—it would be interesting to know who contacted him), and some forty physicians, surgeons, anatomists, and other medical men. It was also signed by Alfred Tennyson, Robert Browning, Thomas Carlyle, John Ruskin, Benjamin Jowett, and James Martineau.[1]

For the meeting on 25 January 1875 Cobbe put together a deputation suited to the RSPCA executive: R. H. Hutton, editor of the *Spectator;* Sir Frederick Elliot, a permanent secretary at the Colonial Office; William Francis Cowper-Temple, a member of Parliament and nephew of a former prime

minister; the geologist William Pengelly; General Colin Mackenzie, a hero
of the first Afghan war; and Colonel Evelyn Wood, who, like Cobbe's cousin
Henry Clermont, had been wounded on 18 June 1855 but had survived to
win the Victoria Cross in India when he was barely twenty-one. Cousin
Laura's husband, MP John Locke, read the memorial, and several members
of the deputation, including Cobbe, made brief speeches.

The RSPCA appointed a subcommittee and invited Cobbe to its first
meeting, at which the chairman asked if she could get a bill restricting vivisection into Parliament. That was exactly what she did not want; the whole
point of the memorial was to have any bill come, not from a woman identified with minority causes, but from the RSPCA itself, backed by its influence and membership. The subcommittee then decided to send the RSPCA's
paid secretary to ask London physiologists about their own practices. Making appointments in advance to visit their laboratories ensured that he saw
nothing inhumane.[2]

Cobbe did what she could in the *Echo*. "The Restriction of Vivisection,"
on 26 January 1875, opened with a sentimental appeal ("How many aching
and embittered hearts have been soothed and consoled by the dumb faith-
fulness of a friend who is never weary of us"), moved to shocking descriptions from scientific literature, listed the most impressive names on her memorial, and then introduced an argument that would lose some feminist
friends: "Better forego those tempting promised fruits of the tree of knowledge," she wrote, than allow girls "to learn chemistry and physiology in their
boarding-schools with the help of animals poisoned and dissected alive for
their entertainment."

But even before Cobbe met with the RSPCA, T. H. Huxley was writing
to Darwin about ways of "taking the wind out of the enemy's sails" (either
he or the son who edited his letters politely removed her name): "My re-
liance as against —— and her fanatical following is not in the wisdom and
justice of the House of Commons, but in the large number of fox-hunters
therein. If physiological experimentation is put down by law, hunting, fishing and shooting, against which a much better case can be made out, will
soon follow."[3]

The powerful opposition made Cobbe irrational and sometimes careless. After the editor of the *British Medical Journal*, Ernest Hart, a strong
supporter of women's medical education, challenged some of the memorial's
assertions, Cobbe charged (privately) that he "had cheated his creditors
shamefully—& lies under heavy suspicion of having poisoned his wife *intentionally* as well as actually." At the same time her own sincere interest in the
developing science of psychology was again demonstrated in "Thoughts
about Thinking," a careful examination of conditions affecting the "perpet-

ual stream of thoughts" that passed through people's minds when they were awake.[4]

Also increasingly involved with working-class women, Cobbe gave the principal speech at a meeting to promote a union among dressmakers and milliners.[5] By 8 February both Lloyd and Cobbe were exhausted from overwork. Cobbe went to spend a few days with her brother Tom and his family in Hampshire. It was probably on this visit that she wrote the poem tipped into some copies of her privately printed volume of poetry, perhaps only the copies given to special friends:

To Mary C. Lloyd
Friend of my Life, when'er my eyes
Rest with sudden, glad surprise
On Nature's scenes of earth and air
Sublimely grand, or sweetly fair,
    I want you,— Mary.

When men and women gifted, free,
Speak their fresh thoughts ungrudgingly,
And springing forth each kindling mind
Streams like a meteor in the wind,
    I want you,— Mary.

When soft the summer evenings close,
And crimson in the sunset rose,
Our Cader glows, majestic, grand,
The crown of all your lovely land,
    I want you,— Mary.

When the dark winter nights come round
To our "ain fireside" cheerly bound,
With our dear Rembrandt girl, so brown,
Smiling serenely on us down,
    I want you,— Mary.

*Now,*—while the vigorous pulses leap
Still strong within my spirit's deep;
*Now,* while my yet unwearied brain
Weaves its thick web of thoughts amain,
    I want you,— Mary.

*Hereafter,* when slow ebbs the tide,
And age drains out my strength and pride,
And dim-grown eyes and palsied hand

No longer list my soul's command,
        I'll want you,— Mary.

In joy and grief, in good and ill,
Friend of my heart: I need you still,
My Guide, Companion, Playmate, Love,
To dwell with here, to clasp above,
        I want you,— Mary.

For O! if past the gates of Death
To me the Unseen openeth
Immortal joys, to angels given,
Upon the holy heights of Heaven,
        I'll want you,— Mary.[6]

Thoroughly happy in her personal life with Mary Lloyd, Cobbe also continued to attract ardent respect from younger woman. A new admirer in the
spring of 1875 was Constance de Rothschild. Her father was Anthony de
Rothschild, of the banking family; her mother had been born, as Louisa
Montefiore, into another prominent Jewish family, and her uncle Lionel had
in 1858 become the first practicing Jew seated in Parliament. The introduction was probably made by Anne Thackeray, William Makepeace Thackeray's daughter; an old friend of the de Rothschild sisters, Anne Thackeray
was then living nearby, in Onslow Square, with her sister and her brother-
in-law, Leslie Stephen. Constance de Rothschild remembered it as a "bright
and sunny afternoon" when she went to "a pleasant, cheerful house" where
the drawing room had "a comfortable and sociable aspect." She wrote in her
diary, "To me she is fascinating and interesting and I hope to see more of
her and to become better acquainted with her." Cobbe had "looked at me
curiously for a moment with her searching, piercing glance, and then asked
. . . 'Are you the lady who wrote the book on the Bible for Jewish children?'
I answered that I was, astonished that Miss Cobbe should have been aware
of so modest a venture in the field of literature; but, grasping my hand, she
said cordially, 'I have read the book, and am so very glad to make your
acquaintance.'"[7] De Rothschild continued to write breathless accounts of
her meetings with Cobbe: on 29 April she had "a long theological conversation with Miss Cobbe," and 2 May was "a glorious day" when Cobbe came
to lunch. Since de Rothschild was already past thirty, it is surprising how
young her diary entries make her sound, especially given that she was a woman
who often dined with Gladstone or Disraeli, went to house parties at which
the Prince of Wales was also a guest, and visited cousins in many European
capitals. Almost worshipful toward Cobbe and thrilled by her intellectual

authority, de Rothschild was clearly delighted to meet someone who took her own intelligence seriously.

After the beginning of 1875 Cobbe wrote for the *Echo* only once a week. An unusually large number of the columns were somewhat personal, another sign that she was no longer absorbed in the business of daily journalism. "A Plea for Speedy Burial" (14 January 1875) told an anecdote about her great-grandmother Frances Power of Coreny; "The Actual Condition of the Museum" (23 February 1875) complained about the "suffocating atmosphere" of the British Museum reading room and the annoyance of having to show one's ticket on every entrance, even when one had been "well known for twenty years." "What Remedy has Miss Wood?" refers to the 1849 case of Miss Nottidge and the Agapemone in which her brother Will had testified.

Published on 10 March 1875, "What Remedy has Miss Wood" is the last *Echo* leader in Cobbe's scrapbook. She and Arthur Arnold both left the paper when it was sold to Albert Grant, a Tory MP who had grown rich by selling shares in shaky enterprises to clergymen and widows hoping for a large return on their limited capital. Cobbe was already looking for other work. A separate, unlabeled scrapbook in the National Library of Wales contains about a dozen pieces from *The Bazaar, Exchange and Mart,* a weekly journal that existed primarily so that people could advertise articles for sale or exchange, on topics entirely unlike Cobbe's usual writing: "The Practical Rosery," "Colouring Photographs," "Wooden Houses for Dwellings," "The Radish, Its Characteristics and Culture." Nothing indicates why these articles were saved. Since Mary Lloyd was a gardener as well as an artist, they might have been her work, or hers and Cobbe's in collaboration. Richard Holt Hutton said that the *Spectator* would gladly publish antivivisection material but that he was "not a woman's suffrage man."[8] She reviewed a volume of Charles Beard's sermons in the *Theological Review* for April (Beard was the journal's editor) and published "The Moral Aspects of Vivisection" in the *New Quarterly Magazine* for the same month.

In the meantime, the *Morning Post* published a touching letter from George Hoggan about his experience working under "one of the greatest living experimental physiologists." The dogs brought into the laboratory would approach each person, using "eyes, ears, and tail" to make "a mute appeal for mercy." Although she had met Hoggan and knew his wife as Frances Morgan of the suffrage central committee, Cobbe did not know that he had worked for Claude Bernard. He followed up with an essay in the April *Fraser's* that pointed out a major flaw in Cobbe's memorial. Recognizing the difficulty in finding witnesses to testify about cruelty in laboratories, she had suggested making medical journals liable for prosecution. Hoggan knew that all scientists would fight hard to defeat anything that interfered with open review. Indeed, he thought that medical men who opposed unrestricted vivisection wanted "the fullest and most minute details of every cruel experiment" to be "published as clearly as possible" so that the experiments would never need to be repeated.[9] Hoggan's knowledge of science was therefore an extremely useful adjunct to her political and rhetorical skill.

Since the RSPCA had done nothing useful, Cobbe decided to go ahead on her own. She asked Frederick Elliot to draw up a bill. A younger brother of Gilbert Elliot, he was the uncle of two good friends from Bristol, Maggie Elliot and Nina, countess of Minto. When she went to talk over its provisions with William Cowper-Temple, who had been on the delegation to the RSPCA, his wife took her off to consult Lord Shaftesbury. Knowing of his "extreme Evangelicalism," Cobbe was afraid he would not "co-operate with such a heretic" as she was but was surprised to find him not only an extraordinary humanitarian but also much less bigoted than she had assumed. Continuing to use as much aristocratic prestige as she could command, Cobbe lunched one day with Lady Minto and Henrietta, countess of Ogilvie (a sister of Kate Amberley's) so that they could go over the bill clause by clause with the man who would introduce it in the House of Lords.[10]

While Cobbe was meeting with one set of politicians about vivisection, the women's suffrage bill came up for debate on 7 April. Forsyth had finally agreed to use Jacob Bright's wording (with no reference to marriage), but he was no more than four sentences into his speech when he repeated, "I say, emphatically, 'women not under the disability of coverture,' for I am strongly opposed to the claim of married women to vote at Parliamentary Elections, and there is nothing in the present Bill which will enable them to do so." He did at least manage to borrow language from Cobbe's "Criminals, Idiots, Women, and Minors," not only embroidering and refining the title phrase itself but also using her edged observation that "a man lost the control of his property only through the crime of felony [while] a woman lost the control of hers by marriage."[11]

In the debate Patrick Smollett was, as the *Englishwoman's Review* put it, "coarse without being humorous," and Beresford-Hope "became as usual facetious."[12] It was the first actual division under the Conservative government. Disraeli voted for the bill, Gladstone did not vote, and John Locke voted against it. The tally was 187 against and 152 in favor, a difference of only 35 votes, close enough to arouse real concern among opponents. "The woman's suffrage movement has entered upon a new phase," chortled the *Englishwoman's Review,* with the formation on 23 June of an Association to Defend the Constitution made up of "Peers, Members of Parliament, and other influential men" organized to oppose the claims of women. The chairman of the new committee was E. P. Bouverie, and its other members, in addition to Beresford-Hope, included Randolph Churchill, Henry Cecil Raikes, Samuel Whitbread, and Constance de Rothschild's cousin, Nathaniel Meyer de Rothschild.[13]

On 4 May Cobbe's bill for regulating the practice of vivisection was introduced in Parliament. It permitted experiments only on anesthetized animals and at registered locations, although special licenses good for six months might be granted by the home secretary for experimentation without anesthesia. Cobbe arranged with her friend William Hart Dyke, the Conservative whip—she probably knew him through her old Ardgillan neighbor Thomas Edward Taylor, Conservative MP for county Dublin since 1841, when Charles Cobbe and his family had helped in the campaign—to have the bill introduced with the government's sanction in the House of Lords by John Henniker-Major, an experienced parliamentarian who had been in the Commons before succeeding as fifth baron Henniker in 1870.

Eight days later an alternative version prepared by scientists under Darwin's coordination was introduced in the Commons by Dr. Lyon Playfair, a longtime suffragist and chair of chemistry at Edinburgh. The two bills were surprisingly similar. Playfair's made the license for unanesthetized vivisection good for a longer time but required that the animal be humanely killed immediately afterwards, and it prohibited demonstrations (as opposed to experiments) even under anesthesia. T. H. Huxley, who thought he had explained to Playfair what the bill should say, was "sorry to find that its present wording is such as to render it very unacceptable to all teachers of physiology."[14]

But though the Playfair bill seemed almost satisfactory, Cobbe preferred Henniker's and set about organizing petitions to support it. She managed to get more than twenty thousand signatures, including one from Darwin's daughter Henrietta Litchfield, and to arrange for other propaganda. On 7 May C. L. Dodgson (Lewis Carroll) asked Cobbe if she could place his article "Popular Fallacies about Vivisection." It had been turned down by the *Pall Mall Gazette* "on the ground of the fallacies being unheard of, though eight out of the thirteen came from a *Pall Mall* article!" Her response was impressive; less than two weeks later Dodgson wrote in his diary: "Heard from Mr. John Morley, editor of *The Fortnightly Review,* that he accepts my article."[15] It appeared in the issue for 1 June.

Faced with competing bills, Home Secretary R. A. Cross put a stop to parliamentary action by appointing a royal commission to make recommendations. The commission included activists from both sides—most notably T. H. Huxley and R. H. Hutton—as well as retired judges and others who presumably were neutral. Cobbe knew even before the members were announced on 22 June that Hutton was one of them and started trying to gather damning evidence. On 4 June, for example, she asked James Macaulay, the author of *Plea for Mercy for Animals* and soon to be editor of the *Boy's Own Paper,* if he knew a "servant or porter of one of the hospitals who would be willing to bear evidence of the number of animals procured & what is done with them."[16]

By then Cobbe was in Wales. She tried to see Dodgson on her way through Oxford in May, but the porter would not allow Yama—an experienced rail traveler who had learned to scoot quickly into an empty first-class compartment and hide under the seat—into Christ Church. "I much regret having missed the pleasure," Dodgson wrote. "The general law about dogs, to which you were an unfortunate victim, is beneficent in its general action (like so many laws of Nature 'So careful of the type she seems, So careless of the single life,') as you would allow if you could have seen the College as I knew it years ago, with *70* dogs on the premises, day & night! If only I had known of it, I would have convoyed you in, dog & all."[17]

In addition to the spring's exhausting political work, Cobbe and Lloyd continued to struggle about where to live, especially now that thrice-weekly trips to the *Echo* office were no longer essential. But with the loss of her newspaper desk the British Museum "ladies' tables" had become even more important to Cobbe. Aside from the library's other resources, all of the principal medical journals were on open shelves in the reading room.[18] In "The Town Mouse and the Country Mouse," published in July, the Town Mouse pleads for resources "to feel, to act, to *be* as much as possible in the few brief years of mortal existence," to which the Country Mouse responds: "If he live *faster* I live *longer;* and I have better health than he all the time. . . . I retain till the verge of old age much of the agility and vigour wherewith I walked the moors and climbed the mountains in my youth." The attempt to compromise in Hampstead, Richmond, or Wimbledon would be, Cobbe thought, not "the best of both worlds" but rather "the worst of the two," with days wasted "waiting at railway stations to go in or out of town."

Several friends were concerned. William Rathbone Greg, for example, wrote that "I shd have enjoyed your paper still more if I had not felt that it was suggested by your intention to quit London." Though Cobbe was working hard at miscellaneous essays, leaving the *Echo* had cut her dependable income in half. Fanny Kemble thought she was in such a "depressed tone of spirits" that she invited her to visit Philadelphia, but Cobbe answered that she could not "put the Atlantic between herself and M[ary] L[loyd]."[19]

Once more, however, she returned to London much sooner than Lloyd. Constance de Rothschild visited Hereford Square several times in August, thrilled with the encouragement she was getting. After one long visit she wrote that Cobbe "asked me to write an *article on Hebrew women* for The

New Quarterly"—Cobbe was sure enough of her ground to promise publication and name the journal—and a few days later de Rothschild "went to Miss Cobbe and read her my notes. She seemed pleased and made me hopeful and anxious to write. What a great piece of good fortune that I should know such a nice, distinguished woman." On 17 August she "spent the morning at home writing for my dear Cobbe feel embued with the spirit of my work," and two days later she "tried to continue writing a little." The twenty-second was recorded thus: "A glorious day. I wrote for an hour or two in bed, then ordered my phaeton & drove off to Miss Cobbe. She seemed very pleased with my performance, and gave me great encouragement." The following day she went to fetch her friend Alice Probyn, who lived with her sister at number 10 Hereford Square, and to her delight "had a sight of my dear Cobby."[20]

When the royal commission went to work during the autumn, Cobbe faced the difficulty of discovering people who would testify to incidents they had seen with their own eyes. Anna Kingsford, now studying medicine in Paris, provided information for two men who passed it on to Cobbe, but one of them appeared to have no way of gaining access to laboratories and the other would not allow Kingsford's name to be used. "We are too much tainted with our anonymous stories," Hutton wrote to Cobbe on 6 September 1875; even for publication in the *Spectator* he wanted to wait "till the student who authenticates these matters can give his name." By November the RSPCA had entirely withdrawn from the vivisection issue. Lacking the political support it could have supplied, Cobbe and Hoggan decided to form a new society that would have enough prestige to influence Parliament and the public. Cobbe knew from the suffrage battles about "the huge additional labour" of managing a society. In this cause she had "hitherto worked independently and freely, taking always the advice of the eminent men who were so good as to counsel me at every step. But I felt that . . . the authority of a formally constituted Society was needed to make headway against an evil which daily revealed itself as more formidable."[21]

George Hoggan was then thirty-eight, fifteen years younger than Cobbe. Trained as a naval engineer, he had served in the China war of 1860 (as had Cobbe's cousin Alick), but after failing to be appointed to accompany Livingston to Africa, he left the navy and studied medicine at the University of Edinburgh.[22] Both he and his wife were interested in scientific medicine; they published several joint papers on physiology, but they did their research with a microscope rather than a scalpel. Technically, Frances Hoggan was a doctor, and George was not; her degree, from Zurich, was an M.D., and his, from Edinburgh, was an M.B., or bachelor of medicine, the usual British degree at the time.

Cobbe and Hoggan sent out letters on 15 November and at once began collecting important names. The first two men to respond were Anthony Ashley Cooper, seventh earl of Shaftesbury, and William Thomson, archbishop of York. A lifelong evangelical with a strong sense of social duty, Shaftesbury was a prime mover in reforming lunacy laws, shortening the workday, regulating child labor, building model tenements, and establishing ragged schools. Tall and handsome even in old age (he was almost seventy-five in 1875), Shaftesbury had an aristocratic bearing and inherited sense of position that made him an enormously effective spokesman. In the matter of vivisection he preferred prohibition to restriction, but he agreed, as he wrote to Cobbe on 17 November, that at the time restriction was "as much as you will be able to attain."[23] Another early response came from Fitzroy Kelley, the chief baron (presiding judge) of the Court of Exchequer, which heard financial cases. By the time the as-yet-unnamed society held its first meeting, on 2 December at the Hoggans' house, Cobbe had also enlisted some of her dependably radical friends. James Stansfeld, a leader in the antislavery cause as well as a consistent women's advocate, was in the chair, and William Shaen, a member with Cobbe and Frances Hoggan of the women's suffrage central committee, also attended. Both of these men were then campaigning to abolish the Contagious Diseases Acts; it may well have been their antipathy to the medical profession that led them to oppose vivisection.

The Hoggans' house was somewhat more convenient, though smaller, than 26 Hereford Square, and Cobbe and Lloyd were just then in the process of moving. They had finally found a house on Cheyne Walk. Number 24 faced the river between Oakley and Manor Streets, just by Albert Bridge, across from the open green spaces of Battersea Park. The new Thames embankment shielded it from the noise of boatmen and scavengers. Dante Gabriel Rossetti was at number 16, a house twice as wide as the others and closer to Manor Street; the house Cobbe and Lloyd rented was near the corner of Oakley Street. Number 24 is rather odd, since a passage to the mews eats up nearly half its width at street level. The ground floor held two small rooms and a staircase, but the first floor had two good-sized rooms extending across the passageway and an elaborate cast-iron balcony overlooking the river. Two upper stories supplied bedrooms and servants' rooms, and there were the usual semibasement kitchens. Although it was smaller—and older—than 26 Hereford Square, the surroundings were far more pleasant. Vernon Lee wrote of dining with a friend who lived on the Chelsea embankment, "with a breezy, quiet view over reaches of the Thames & Battersea park, trees & distant hills; the only place in London where life seems otherwise than a grimy, empty scuffle."[24] Housekeeping was cheaper than in the bustling neighborhood near Gloucester Road station; they probably kept

two servants instead of three. Regular commuting would have been difficult, however, since the nearest underground station was nearly a mile away
at Sloane Square and cabs to central London were expensive. Without her
spacious studio, Lloyd could no longer work at sculpture, but she was already
beginning to be hampered by rheumatism, and the house did have a room
suitable for painting.

In January 1876 cousin Alick's daughter Gena (then age eight) was sent
home from India and received by John and Laura Locke, thus beginning
another cycle of home education for India-born children. Catherine Anne
Pelham died at an advanced age. A cousin of Cobbe's father, she was the last
remaining member of his generation. More shockingly, John Russell, viscount Amberley, died on 9 January at thirty-three, following his wife Kate
by less than eighteen months. Aside from the sadness of these two tragically
early deaths, Cobbe was deprived of two close friends who had been extremely well connected and dependable advocates for her causes.

A minor annoyance began in late 1875 or early 1876 when George Bentley started to receive letters and manuscripts signed "F. Power Cobbe,"
"F. P. Cobbe," or "Fanny Power Cobbe," a form Cobbe herself never used,
though close friends called her "Fanny." Since Bentley knew Cobbe's reputation, he asked the correspondent—who said she had "never . . . written
anything before"—to call. Eventually he did publish two of her pieces,
anonymously, in *Temple Bar*. A few other pieces, sometimes signed "Fanny
Power Cobbe," appeared in *Tinsley's Magazine* and *St. James's Magazine* during the late 1870s. Some of these letters and essays are mistakenly attributed
to Frances Power Cobbe, and the name led to an unsettling incident that
will be explained in chapter 11.[25]

Cobbe reviewed Octavia Hill's *Homes of the London Poor* in the 15 January 1876 issue of the *Spectator,* pointing out that although Hill had once
believed philanthropy could solve the housing problem, she now realized,
as Cobbe had done ten years earlier, that public funding was essential.
Cobbe's January publication in the *New Quarterly Magazine* was "Backward
Ho," a funny critique of the "Anti-Renaissance" in contemporary society,
"where we shout at once for 'Liberty, Equality, and the Feudal System.'"
Evidence of a return to the "Dead Sea of the Middle Ages" included church
ritualism, Gothic architecture, Pre-Raphaelite painting, "Pre-Miltonic poetry," carved oak furniture, and people's eager belief in spiritualism and
other superstitions. The essay aimed enough pointed barbs at its (generally
unnamed) targets to arouse a yelp from John Ruskin in *Fors Clavigera:*
"From the ductile and silent gold of ancient womanhood to the resonant
bronze, and tinkling—not cymbal, but shall we say—saucepan, of Miss
Frances Power Cobbe, there *is* an interval, with a vengeance." He followed

the published complaint with a letter to Katharine Bradley, later, if not already, a friend of Cobbe's: "I will . . . tell you more of Miss Cobbe. It is not the wrongness of her views, but her insolence in proclaiming them—contrary to St. Paul's order 'I suffer not a woman to teach'—which is deadly in her character and so harmful in its effects."[26]

The Royal Commission on Vivisection issued its report on 8 January 1876. The conclusion, endorsed by T. H. Huxley as well as the other members, recommended regulating but not prohibiting experiments. (The commission, like the antivivisection societies, used *vivisection* in its broad sense to include not only dissection or surgical experiments such as severing nerves but also injections, electrical shocks, oxygen deprivation, and all other painful or destructive work done to living mammals for the sake of scientific teaching, training, or research.) The next step was to make sure the report was not simply filed away as the results of so many other government investigations had been. On 18 February Cobbe and Hoggan's society met with Shaftesbury for the first time in the chair.

Someone, almost certainly Cobbe herself, sent one of her essays to W. E. Gladstone, still leader of the Liberal opposition; the reading listed in his diary for 29 February 1876 includes "Cobbe on Vivisection," probably "The Moral Aspects of Vivisection," from the *New Quarterly Magazine,* which had been reprinted as a pamphlet. The next day he thanked her for the article—"I seldom read a paper possessed with such a spirit of nobleness from first to last," he wrote—and invited her to one of his working breakfasts. Presumably he took the barrage of *Echo* leaders, if he had any idea who wrote them, as merely part of the general noise surrounding any politician, but Cobbe's opinion of him was only temporarily modified. At the breakfast they held some private conversation in his library, and she asked him to join their society; he "replied that he would rather not do so; but that if ever he returned to office he would help me to the best of his power."[27]

On 1 March the committee adopted a statement of purpose and took offices at 1 Victoria Street. Its official name, provided by George Hoggan, was The Society for Protection of Animals Liable to Vivisection. Although sometimes referred to as SPALV, common usage generally settled on the unofficial name Victoria Street Society, or VSS. Its officers were Shaftesbury as president; Cobbe and Hoggan as honorary secretaries (the equivalent of executive directors); and Archibald Prentice Childs, a fellow of the Royal College of Surgeons, as (paid) secretary. An executive committee, which was technically responsible for making policy and approving actions, met almost every week, but there were almost certainly no more than three or four insiders who attended regularly. In addition to Frederick Elliot, Colin Mackenzie, and Evelyn Wood—all of whom had been part of the delegation to the

RSPCA in January 1875—the executive committee members in 1876 were Mary Lloyd, Leslie Stephen, Frances Wedgwood, Frances Hoggan, William Shaen, Edith Best (whose husband was Baron Wynford of the Royal Horse Artillery), F. W. Chesson and Edward B. de Fonblanque (two men about whom I have discovered no further information), the Reverend Charles J. Vaughan (formerly headmaster of Harrow, then Master of the Temple), Julia Haldane-Duncan (widow of the second earl of Camperdown, whose obituary twenty-two years later would mention her "shrewd intelligence and good sense" and her "conspicuous sincerity," in addition to the usual womanly qualities),[28] and Eveline Alicia Wallop, countess of Portsmouth (president of the West of England Society for Women's Suffrage). Henry James would later describe a visit to Lady Portsmouth's home in Devon:

> The place and country are of course very beautiful and Lady P. "most kind"; but though there are several people in the house . . . the whole thing is dull. There is a large family, chiefly of infantine sons and daughters (there are 12!) who live in some mysterious part of the house and are never seen. Lord P. is simply a great hunting and racing magnate, who keeps the hounds in this part of the country and is absent all day with them. There is nothing in the house but pictures of horses—and awfully bad ones at that.[29]

The executive thus included a characteristic assembly of people with some weight—aristocrats, military men, doctors; representatives of the government, the church, and the law; intellectual Londoners; and members of good county families. The cavalrymen and fox hunters certified the group's manliness and helped deter accusations of soft-hearted sentimentality. A further cadre of vice presidents and honorary members collected over the next several years allowed a great many more important names to be listed in VSS publications.

The offices at 1 Victoria Street were near the Westminster Palace Hotel, close to the St. James's Park underground station, convenient for lobbying at the Houses of Parliament and the government offices along Whitehall and within easy reach of Dean Stanley at the Abbey. In addition to a committee room, a secretary's room, and space for clerks and volunteers, there was another room for Cobbe, where she put up bookshelves, pictures, curtains, "and various little feminine relaxations."[30] Although she did not need to go to the office every day or keep regular hours (the paid secretary did that), she considered the VSS to be her society and enjoyed having her own office where she could invite people to join her for tea.

Her immediate task was to arrange a delegation to urge the home secretary to sponsor a bill that would carry out the royal commission's recommendations. Although Cobbe did not herself attend—this was a deputation of important men calling on a cabinet minister—she organized the group. It included Shaftesbury, Cardinal Manning, Frederick Elliot and his great-nephew Gilbert Elliot, fourth earl of Minto (Nina's son, who subsequently became governor general of Canada and then viceroy of India), William Cowper-Temple, Colonel Evelyn Wood, Anthony John Mundella (another radical MP who consistently supported women's suffrage and fought against the Contagious Diseases Acts), Leslie Stephen, and James Anthony Froude. John Duke Coleridge, chief justice of the court of common pleas, said he would "certainly come" if he could but that he had to sit on that Monday; he would, however, "try to get away & join you at the Home Office." The day before the meeting, Cobbe had a letter from Froude: "Carlyle has determined that he cannot appear in a deputation along side the chief servant of Beelzebub as he regards the Cardinal. He is really sorry about it, and would have well liked to be present and to give Mr. Cross his opinion." But although she would have liked the weight of his presence, Cobbe herself saw Thomas Carlyle as the prophet of "a form of Demonolatry—the worship of Strength & Knowledge divorced from goodness."[31]

Since Cross had appointed the commission, he might already have decided to act on its recommendation, but he did invite the delegation to suggest a list of provisions. The VSS executive met on 30 March to compile their ideas. The bill was introduced by Henry Howard Molyneux, earl of Carnarvon, who had given his first public speech at age seven at a local RSPCA meeting. Cobbe worked hard to get petitions signed; Benjamin Jowett, for example, secured the names of the heads of "every College in Oxford."[32]

Cobbe did not neglect women's issues. "The Fitness of Women For the Ministry," in the *Theological Review* for April 1876, regretted the "loss out of our religion of all those ideas which may be ranked as the Doctrine of the Motherhood of God." Toward the end of the month the Women's Disabilities Removal Bill came up for debate. William Forsyth began with a reference to E. P. Bouverie's committee to "save the ark of the Constitution from the sacrilegious hands of audacious women." So far it had held no meetings, produced no petitions, and signed up fewer than thirty members, while the year's petitions supporting women's suffrage had more than 350,000 signatures. Forsyth was, however, a difficult champion. He believed "that public display and platform agitation" were "not the proper sphere of women" but that women were in a dilemma: if they did not speak out "it would instantly be said that they do not care for the suffrage. . . . and if they speak they are said to be unfeminine."[33]

The division produced 152 ayes and 239 nays, a loss by 87 votes; the same number of MPs voted for women's suffrage in 1876 as in 1875, but significantly more voted against it. Evidently the "defenders of the constitution," or someone, got more MPs into the house for the division. Disraeli dependably voted in favor of women's suffrage, though he did not speak. Gladstone, just as dependably, stayed away. On 13 May the central committee held an overcrowded public meeting at St. George's Hall, Langham Place. Russell Gurney took the chair, and a number of MPs—not including William Forsyth—were on the platform. Cobbe was not scheduled to speak, but she was furious with John Bright. Although never really in favor of women's suffrage, he had voted with Mill in 1867, but now, in opposition to his brother Jacob, he had not only voted against the bill but also spoken against it. Cobbe rose—to loud cheers—and proclaimed that "it calls upon every woman who has a heart and a tongue to say—'No; it is not true that women have no wrongs. No; their interests are not always considered and provided for by men. . . . and it is not true, in any sense whatever, that this demand for a voice in the legislation of the country ought to be regarded in the odious light of a war between the sexes.'" John Bright, she continued, "says that 'it is a scandalous and odious libel to say that women are a class,' or 'that they suffer the least from not having direct representation.' I am prepared to maintain, on the contrary, that they form the class of all others which needs the protection of direct representation, seeing that their special interests concern not only money or land, but things tenfold dearer—personal rights, and rights over children." Getting into the swing of her unplanned oratory, she distinguished between women as a political class and misleading ideas growing from social definitions of class.

> On one side I see women who are lapped in every luxury which the hands of loving fathers and husbands can give them. The wind of heaven never visits their cheeks too roughly; they never know any of the great realities of life. Life is from beginning to end one long sweet holiday. . . . and I am sorry to say that, though some of these are among the most excellent and unselfish of human beings . . . others are not so. They are spoiled by the indulgences which their vanity, their luxuriousness, their selfishness receive every hour of the day; they are heartless; they are silly; they are frivolous; their nobler faculties lie dormant; they live for stupid, silly fashion, and lead the lives of butterflies in a world of toil. . . . Well, these fine ladies meet with the members of Parliament . . . at their own splendid dinner-parties, and they sweetly assure them that everything is perfectly right as regards women; they want nothing. . . . and then members of Parliament come and tell us that all the "best" women they know say that they do not want the franchise. . . . I suppose there are from ten to twenty thousand—or let us be liberal, and say 40,000—of those very happy women. And then I see on the other side, not ten or twenty thousand, but several hundred thousand

women—perhaps there are a million or so—who are very poor, struggling sorrowfully, painfully, often failing under pressure of want of employment, of underpaid, unhealthful, unhopeful employment, or of grinding oppression and cruelty from those whose duty it is to protect them. . . . I say unhesitatingly that there is wrong, grievous wrong, somewhere.[34]

Cobbe's speech was interrupted with cheers and with laughter at her poignant jokes, which I suspect were sometimes told in dialect; she sat down to loud applause. The *Echo* years had given her an enormous wealth of experience in concise argument and sharp expression that made her a very popular public lecturer during the next decade. Lewis Morris remembered "being strongly impressed by her nimble changes from grave to gay, from exuberant humour to deep pathos. . . . And the figure, virile in its large proportions and careless garb, was a very remarkable one. But if there was a man's brain and form, there was always a noble woman's heart."[35]

The Cruelty to Animals Bill, introduced by Lord Carnarvon, had its second reading in the House of Lords on 22 May. It prohibited experiments of any kind on dogs and cats, required registration and licenses for all experiments, and forbade those that did not have definite practical aims. And Carnarvon was a powerful sponsor: in addition to his lifelong support for animal protection, he was then in the cabinet as colonial secretary, and Queen Victoria was the godmother of his eighteen-month-old daughter. Ten days later the VSS held its first public meeting. Although she tried unsuccessfully to get Gladstone to attend, Cobbe put together a notable roster of speakers, including herself. It was the first time, other than when she had presented papers at NAPSS conferences, that she had addressed an audience not composed primarily of suffragists; indeed, the *Times* found it noteworthy that a public political meeting had "several ladies in the room."[36] The VSS wanted to get the immunity for dogs and cats extended to horses, asses, and mules and, more significantly, to fight off crippling amendments. For the moment, the cause received favorable attention from many newspapers as well as steady support from the journals to which Cobbe had dependable access.

By month's end, however, the widespread support and the strength of Carnarvon's bill had led the medical profession to organize, advertise, petition, and send its own deputations to the Home Office. On 22 June the *Pall Mall Gazette* deplored "evils which are likely to accrue to the common-sense and scientific interest of the age, if legislation is to be interfered with by sentimental feminine agitators." *Punch,* another dependable opponent of women's rights, chimed in with "Dogs and Doctors," which criticized tenderhearted ladies for not also being vegetarians. Besides, according to Toby, the *Punch* dog, "No good dogs were ever vivisected," only curs. A crowd of several hundred medical men besieged the home secretary with a petition signed by thousands of doctors demanding complete withdrawal, not amendment, of the bill. While the opposition swelled, Carnarvon was away from London because of his mother's death and the family responsibilities that followed.[37]

Mary Lloyd took a much larger share of the work for animal protection than she had ever done for suffrage; she often worked in the office addressing envelopes, sorting handbills, and doing the dozens of other chores required to run an advocacy organization. One of the surviving letters about Carnarvon's bill is addressed to Lloyd, though it was written by Cobbe's longtime friend Charles Beard. Furthermore, she had become a member of the governing committee for the Home for Lost Dogs, which in the summer of 1876 was mired in financial problems arising from its move to Battersea. Lloyd borrowed two thousand pounds (with a mortgage on the Hereford Square house) to make a low-interest loan to the home.[38]

By mid-July both Cobbe and Lloyd were in Wales. On her way there Cobbe spent a week visiting Constance de Rothschild, no doubt lobbying as well, since the family's estate was only thirty-five miles from London and other visitors were there. Yet despite all Cobbe's efforts and high hopes, the bill was gradually mutilated, "clause by clause, under the sharp pressure of the Vivisectionists." It passed on 12 August. "We asked for an Act to protect animals from Vivisection," she wrote the next day. "The Home Secretary has given us an Act to protect Vivisectors from prosecution." Even twenty years later she would reflect that the world had "never seemed to me quite the same since that dreadful time. My hopes had been raised so high to be dashed so low as even to make me fear that I had done harm instead of good. . . . Justice and Mercy seemed to have gone from the earth."[39]

Many of the stubborn and sometimes irrational moves Cobbe made during the next quarter-century arose from her sense of guilt and responsibility for the 1876 act. She had set the whole train of events in motion by organizing a memorial to the RSPCA. In consequence the government had recognized vivisection as a mode of scientific research and thereby, she thought, promoted a great many more experiments. Scientists seemed wholly untrustworthy. T. H. Huxley had signed the commission report, which would have provided the basis for a satisfactory bill, and then connived to substitute a different measure. Doctors were even worse; though few of them actually did research, Ernest Hart had organized hundreds for an intimidating demonstration. With no act at all, it might, she imagined, have been possible to prosecute some of the vivisectors' worst abuses under existing animal-cruelty laws, but now, with licenses, the vivisectors, and not the animals, were protected.

With wholly uncharacteristic political indiscretion she sent "several letters of bitter reproach to the friends in Parliament." Shaftesbury reminded her that he had always said it was essential to have some sort of bill to "condemn the practice . . . and give us a foundation on which to build amendments hereafter." He added a blunt lecture on practical politics; if the House of Lords had rejected the amended bill, the home secretary would never again risk opposing the medical establishment, and no bill sponsored by a private member would have any chance whatever.[40] It was half-measures or none.

Throwing caution to the winds, Cobbe wrote to the *Home Chronicler,* a new animal-protection paper edited by former VSS secretary A. P. Childs, that "as we have been defeated in our efforts to make cruel Vivisection *illegal,* we must endeavour to make it *infamous.*" She did not mean just public relations and written appeals. She outlined a series of radical suggestions that included publishing the names and addresses of vivisectors; holding open-air meetings in Hyde Park, a working-class strategy that often led to riots; and "discourag[ing]" hospitals that allowed experimentation in their medical schools. Even some of "our friends," she soon realized, were shocked by the idea of boycotting hospitals and publicizing scientists' home addresses. Admitting that "we must now completely abandon the hope of putting an end to it by any immediate legislation," she more calmly proposed in mid-September "a Social, not a Political movement; an ethical and religious propagandism, rather than a Parliamentary agitation."[41]

Cobbe returned to London for October, while Lloyd stayed in Wales. The house at Cheyne Walk, as well as the one on Hereford Square, had been sublet; Cobbe's letters for October are dated from 1 Victoria Street, and she was back in Wales by early November. Her summer radicalism exposed serious divisions within the movement. Should the VSS work toward restrictions of the sort that had been in the bill before it was amended, or should they campaign to prohibit all experiments on living animals? Cobbe urged the society to "adopt the principle of total prohibition" and threatened to resign as honorary secretary. George Hoggan wanted to prohibit only experiments that caused pain but wrote that "the manner of opposition to the Bill has led me to acquiesce in Total Abolition, although I am not prepared, and possibly never shall be prepared, to take an active part in working for it." The VSS executive asked members to choose among five options: (1) dissolve the society, (2) carry on "with the object of watching the operations of the Act of last Session, and seeing that its provisions be enforced," (3) try to add agricultural animals to the act, (4) work toward prohibiting all painful experiments, or (5) reconstitute the society "upon the principle of total abolition of Vivisection."[42] At its meeting on 22 November the executive committee officially adopted the fourth option: to observe how the new act was enforced and work toward extending it to prohibit all painful experiments. Despite her threat of resignation, Cobbe agreed to the compromise; and Hoggan remained on the executive but ceased to act as joint honorary secretary.

In December Cobbe tried to reduce tension among the various anti-vivisection societies by writing from Wales that it was a waste of energy to "divide our camp because some of us ask for the total abolition of Vivisection, and others for the total suppression of painful experiments. . . . It is a mere question of which demand is most expedient to put forward while we strive to arouse the conscience of the nation." The expediency argument echoes the suffrage movement's struggle over the issue of married women; although Cobbe favored total abolition, she tried to focus on political realities and prepare for a long public-relations campaign. A. P. Childs and the *Home Chronicler,* however, blamed her for "surrendering a principle in order to get some apparent material or immediate advantage."[43]

During the VSS organizational turmoil Cobbe stayed active in other causes. She was among the forty thousand women who sent the queen a memorial about Turkish suppression of an uprising in Bulgaria. An exercise of political citizenship on a question of foreign policy—not one of the issues in women's special sphere—the memorial urging that in this war women were, "more even than in civilised wars, the chief sufferers" was promoted by a committee that included some antisuffragist women.[44] Although the memorial had no practical effect, the incident reveals how acceptable it had become for women to circulate petitions in the ten years since the Enfranchisement of Women Committee had organized its first memorial to John Stuart Mill.

In October 1876, after enabling legislation had been passed, the senate of Ireland's Queen's University resolved to admit female candidates to its medical examinations. (The resolution's supporters included Cobbe's old neighbor Lord Talbot de Malahide.) Frances Hoggan and Eliza Walker-Dunbar, who, like Hoggan, held a Zurich M.D., passed the examination early in 1877 and were licensed to practice in the United Kingdom—the first women to qualify by taking the same written papers and the identical "clinical and *viva voce*" examination "conducted at the same time and in the same room as the men students."[45]

When the triennial London School Board election came along in November, the Southwark Radical Association invited Helen Taylor to stand. Cobbe asked John Locke, who was still MP for Southwark, what help he could provide; he answered that since he was not a Southwark ratepayer (he and Laura lived across the river, near Belgrave Square), he could not vote for Taylor. One suspects that Locke, who consistently voted against women's suffrage, deliberately misunderstood the request for help and was not at all eager to have a radical woman school-board member in his constituency. Cobbe did not return to London to campaign, but she wrote that Taylor was "heartily welcome" to use her name: "I don't believe that I agree at all in your principles:—But my cry is 'Not Measures but *Women*'!"[46] Taylor was elected by a comfortable margin, as were three other women: Elizabeth Surr, Alice Westlake, and Florence Fenwick Miller. At age twenty-two Fenwick Miller had already studied midwifery and "ladies' medicine," written a popular book on physiology, and embarked on a successful career as a lecturer.

Cobbe pursued projects in two new voices during November and December 1876 while living at Tanllan, a house on the outskirts of Llanelltyd. Located across the river from Dolgelley, Llanelltyd was then "a scattering of some twenty cottages." Lloyd was, in effect, its resident squire; the church living was in the gift of Hengwrt, which also owned much of the farmland. On Christmas night in 1876 Cobbe and Lloyd were honored guests at a miniature Eisteddfod (competitive festival) of poets, essayists, and singers in a barn outside the village.[47]

By the start of 1877 Cobbe was back at Cheyne Walk working on another venture in anonymous journalism. An essay of hers appeared on 4 January in the first issue of *Truth*. A sixpenny magazine published every Wednesday, *Truth* featured, according to its advertisement in Mitchell's *Newspaper Press Directory*, "current topics" in Paris and London, which translated to society news, political commentary, investigative reports, witty reviews, and hard-edged opinions. Horace Voules was managing editor; he too had left the *Echo* when it changed hands.

*Truth* was owned by Henry Labouchère. Later to become notorious for extending the 1885 Criminal Law Amendment Act to cover "any act of gross indecency" between one "male person" and "another male person," Labouchère had ample family money and contacts in commerce, finance, the diplomatic corps (where he spent ten years), and politics. He had been a Liberal MP for Middlesex in 1867–68, had reported from Paris for the *Daily News* during the siege of 1870, and was married to an actress. *Society in London* described him as "a professed radical" who gave large Bohemian parties. During its first two years, Labouchère actively edited *Truth* and wrote many of its articles, operating as a political gadfly and working hard to expose "fraudulent enterprises of all sorts." Although he did not publish rumors of scandal in people's private lives, as other society journals did, no person was above his "candid observation." Cobbe's friend Kate Field, also a regular contributor, said *Truth* became a "paying property" in less than a year because it was "the cleverest weekly published." "When I want to be serious," she added, "I can write for *The Times*."[48]

Although Cobbe's autobiography is silent about her year-long connection with Labouchère and his journal, she must have gone regularly to the office on Bolt Court, just off Fleet Street. Her scrapbook contains not only a series of articles (generally of about fifteen hundred words, the length she perfected in the *Echo*) but also short paragraphs and fillers in the anonymous but personal voice typical of *Truth* (e.g., "I once met Miss Charlotte Williams Wynn, whose biography is the book of the month, in a country-house in Italy . . .").[49] Labouchère became a virulent antisuffragist when he returned to Parliament in the 1880s, but he had voted with Mill in 1867, and he was certainly willing to give free play to Cobbe's powerful feminist arguments. The journal's tone, her own growing radicalism, and the protection of anonymity gave her a sharper edge. For example, the first sentence of her series "Remunerative Employment for Women," on 25 January 1877, reads, "The only effectual solution of the Woman Question—we are sorry to arrive at the conclusion—is the introduction into Europe of the wholesome practice of female infanticide."

Cobbe had written a great deal while she was in Wales. In January 1877 a review of James Martineau's sermons appeared in the *Theological Review,* and she had an essay on Schopenhauer in the *New Quarterly Magazine.* More intriguing was the dystopian fiction that appeared as "*The Age of Science: A Newspaper of the Twentieth Century* by Merlin Nostradamus." In early December Cobbe offered it to John Blackwood and begged him to keep her name secret whether he published it or not.[50]

Brought out by Ward, Lock, and Tyler, successful publishers of cheap literature, *The Age of Science* had both an anonymous author and bright, illustrated paper covers to encourage impulse reading by people not interested in vivisection or in anything written by a strong-minded woman. Purporting to be a newspaper from 1 January 1977 delivered by the newly invented "Prospective Telegraph," the book projects a future when, in the words of the summary provided by the *Englishwoman's Review,* "scientific research and medical despotism will have taken the place of Christianity and moral and political freedom in governing society." In that future time Parliament, as a consequence of works such as Dr. Clarke's *Sex in Education,* will have forbidden women to read or write; all crime will have become medicalized, except such acts as treating one's own minor ailments (which will be a criminal offense); and any person might be committed to an asylum on the "certificate of any single Medical Graduate."[51] Primarily directed toward the professional arrogance of scientists and physicians, though it also aims shafts at imperialism, protective tariffs, and other national flaws, the book's satire of science and bureaucracy is still often pertinent.

As Cobbe was pushed into a defensive posture even within the antivivisection movement, her moral certainties grew increasingly rigid. On 19 January 1877 Louisa Carpenter, William Carpenter's wife, wrote a touching letter to thank Cobbe for frankly explaining why she and Mary Lloyd would no longer visit. Cobbe had delighted in the friendships she had made at the Carpenters' table, she had defended William against accusations that his science led to atheism, they had read each other's manuscripts and traded references, he had quoted her work, and she used his ideas about psychology. I have not discovered precisely what action or publication made Cobbe end "all personal intercourse," but she, as well as Louisa Carpenter, must have felt a "heavy heart" at the "painful interruption" of a "long and unbroken friendship."[52]

"Mr. Lowe and the Vivisection Act" came out in February in the *Contemporary Review,* the journal that became Cobbe's chief outlet for serious ethical and social essays. She may have decided to publish there because of the approaching failure of the *Theological Review* and because of Alexander Strahan's generally nonmaterialist side in theological disputes, and perhaps also because Strahan paid contributors unusually well, in part because he was an inept financial manager. Cobbe's essay was directed against Robert Lowe, a longtime Liberal MP and sometime cabinet minister who had helped draw up the 1875 antivivisection bill introduced for Cobbe by Lord Henniker but thereafter had opposed any legislation. Lowe had complained in the October *Contemporary Review* that doctors had been badly treated in the Cruelty to Animals Act of 1876; no government had previously exposed "any respectable trade, much less a highly-educated, liberal, and honourable profession," to such interference.[53] Cobbe's response, a virulent and often sarcastic attack on the medical profession for meddling with legislation, begins the obsessively picky argumentation that makes the disagreements between antivivisectionists and their opponents, as well as with each other, such tedious reading.

Beginning in February 1877, an enormous number of letters to Cobbe in the collection now at the Huntington Library are from Shaftesbury, most of them almost totally illegible, in spiky writing with a broad-nibbed pen on paper soft enough to blur the ink. The VSS executive seems to have met almost every Wednesday. During February they agreed to support a bill for total prohibition sponsored by James Holt. None of them believed the bill could succeed, but they thought that it might be used to raise public awareness. In March Cobbe went to give speeches in Clifton. On 8 March she addressed the Bristol and West of England Society for Women's Suffrage at the Victoria Rooms. Mary Carpenter sat on the platform. It was the only time she took part in a public suffrage event and the last time she and Cobbe were together; Carpenter died three months later. Cobbe brought along a niece—I do not know which one—to visit Carpenter at Red Lodge.[54] Henry's daughter Winifred and her younger sister were still at school—Winifred had entered Cheltenham Ladies' College in May 1876—but three other nieces were of an age to be appropriate traveling companions: Henry's eldest, Mabel, was twenty-two, and Tom's two daughters were twenty-one and twenty.

Then on 12 March there was an 8:00 P.M. antivivisection meeting in the same hall. It grew rowdy even before the meeting began; shortly after 8:00, hecklers started "shouting 'Time's up,' and stamping and whistling." People hissed when Gilbert Elliot, who was in the chair, read messages from Archdeacon Randall and from their own MP, Samuel Morley. Tormenters interrupted the opening speech by B. Douglas, who had replaced A. P. Childs as VSS secretary, called out rude answers to his rhetorical questions, and shouted silly jokes. They also heckled Cobbe: midway through her talk a stranger stood up and tried to make a speech of his own from the floor of the hall.[55] It was assumed that the hecklers were young medical students, but in any case, Cobbe discovered that speaking to a largely male audience at a public antivivisection meeting was very different from addressing enthusiastic supporters at women's suffrage events. Although she had better success at two smaller antivivisection lectures in nearby towns the next afternoon, it must have been a relief to get home.

Even there, however, Cobbe was under attack. At her suggestion the VSS had plastered the walls of London with "sensational illustrations of the alleged horrors of vivisection, and appeals to popular passion." Cobbe defended the posters against people who found them exaggerated and far too disturbing—most of them, she claimed, were enlarged reproductions taken directly from physiological handbooks—but even friends such as Fanny Kemble, who supported the cause, were disgusted by the "*pictorial* appeals to the national humanity—portraits of dogs and horses, etc., by famous masters, coarsely reproduced in common prints, with 'Is this the creature to torture?' printed above." By June Shaftesbury was sorry Cobbe had not consulted him more fully. "Public Opinion," he wrote, "is, with God, our only Hope." The vote on Holt's bill ended with the stark defeat they had expected: 83 in favor and 222 against. Even many antivivisectionists believed the bill went too far; R. H. Hutton's *Spectator* pointed out that it would have prohibited veterinarians from inoculating animals for their own protection.[56]

Her private life also suffered. Kemble said that Cobbe "saw comparatively few of her former pleasant intellectual associates." Discomfort with some longtime feminists was even more painful than the loss of male friends such as William Carpenter. Her relationship with Elizabeth Garrett Anderson, to whom she had sent the funny "Excelsior!" poem six years earlier, grew cool. Girton responded to a VSS accusation by insisting that "no vivisection whatever is practised at the College" but that students attending advanced lectures in physiology at the university laboratory could see demonstrations on dead animals or, very rarely, "on living animals, rendered insensible to pain by anæsthetics."[57] Cobbe's strong desire for women to enter the medical profession was thus almost inevitably coming into conflict with the training needed by advanced medical practitioners.

The annual debate on the Women's Disabilities Removal Bill was scheduled for 6 June 1877. In May, Stafford Northcote, chancellor of the exchequer in Disraeli's Conservative government, received a women's delegation and "fully admitted the claims of women ratepayers and householders to the vote." Although Northcote explained that no electoral reform would be encouraged at present, it was the first time any government had officially received suffragist women. The debate, however, was even more rowdy than usual; one MP saw the movement as "the vagary of 'those who had lost their wits, or who unfortunately never had any.'" A filibuster of last-minute questions and rebuttals used up the time and prevented a vote. Why, asked the *Englishwoman's Review,* do people claim that women would be "hysterical" politicians? Nothing could be "further removed from logical reasoning or sober debate than the conduct of our men-elected masculine Parliament."[58]

By this time the internal divisions among suffragists were fading. In 1872 the London National Society for Women's Suffrage had refused to join the Central Committee for Women's Suffrage because Millicent Fawcett and John Stuart Mill had objected to including Josephine Butler and others active in the fight against the Contagious Diseases Acts, but five years later it no longer seemed to matter. All of the societies were at last united as subscribers to the Central Committee of the National Society for Women's Suffrage; Cobbe remained on the executive committee. On 11 June Lady Anna Gore Langton, another staunch longtime suffragist, called a meeting at her London town house to plan the next year's work.

Cobbe, however, was not there; she and Mary Lloyd had already left for Wales. Her mood was not happy, to judge by a long grumpy letter published in a Welsh paper at the end of the summer criticizing spoiled scenery, cheaply built new hotels, omnipresent advertising posters, and tourists who pillaged the countryside for ferns and wildflowers. "I think Mary Lloyd really suffers from London; as Fanny would from living out of it," Kemble wrote. "They talk of going away, but there are impediments to their doing so."[59]

Cobbe's summer writing returned to theology. "The Peak in Darien: The Riddle of Death," published in the *New Quarterly Magazine* in July, presented anecdotes about the moment of death, when onlookers sometimes see "an expression of astonishment, sometimes developing instantly into joy." She made a more philosophical defense of human immortality in

"Magnanimous Atheism." The last of her essays published in the *Theological Review,* it was less a review than a meditation inspired by Harriet Martineau's posthumously published autobiography. Despite many similarities in their ideas and experience, the two women had never met. In later years Frances Wedgwood had hoped to introduce them, but Martineau had written, "I need not say how happy I should have been become [*sic*] acquainted with Miss Cobbe but the time is past; I am only fit to old friends who can excuse my shortcomings. I have lost ground so much of late that the case is clear—I must give up all hopes of so great a pleasure."[60]

Although still hunting for information to use in fighting vivisection—she asked an artist friend living in France to find out what happened to stray dogs in Paris—Cobbe was starting to focus on another crucial issue about men's cruelty. A short note signed "F.P.C." in the *Women's Suffrage Journal* for 1 August 1877 described Cadwallader Jones, "a sober and industrious young farmer, chapel-goer, and poet" who had hacked his former lover into sixteen pieces. Why, she asked, are "these peculiarly revolting murders always committed against women," and in particular against a woman with whom the murderer has had "intimate relations." She reported more about the case in *Truth* for 26 July and sent a photograph of the "pious scoundrel & murderer" to Francis Galton with a request for information about sexual crimes and mutilated corpses. A long letter to the *Spectator* for 6 October about a woman starved to death by her husband called for reforms of the Married Women's Property Act. Lydia Becker would have liked to print essays by Cobbe in the *Women's Suffrage Journal* but believed that women who wrote professionally should not be asked "for a part of life-blood" unless they could be paid. After publication of the items about murdered women, however, she asked Cobbe to send "little notes" whenever she could.[61] Subsequent issues of the *Women's Suffrage Journal* suggest that Cobbe often forwarded short news items or commentaries about men's maltreatment of women.

Cobbe was back in London by October, although Lloyd stayed in Wales with a sister who was seriously ill. Lloyd's nephew Edward had matriculated at Oxford in January 1877; Cobbe's nephew Leuric, her brother Tom's elder son, went up to Trinity in October. Once Cobbe was at home, Anne Thackeray wrote about calling to introduce her new husband, Richmond Ritchie.[62] Constance de Rothschild was married on 22 November to Cyril Flower.

On 1 November the VSS executive committee considered what to do next. Neither Cobbe nor Shaftesbury saw any hope of parliamentary action. They sent out a circular explaining to members that they would "utilize the coming year by redoubled efforts to awaken public feeling by Meetings, Lectures, Sermons, Placards, Advertisements in newspapers, and articles in periodicals." Adding to their difficulty was the "hydrophobia scare," which pro-

voked "prejudices of which physiologists will not fail to take advantage."
Cobbe pointed out in *Truth* that newspapers had avidly seized the story:
"Among human beings . . . children are smothered, men are poisoned, and
women are kicked to death, and the *Times* . . . takes only the smallest and
most dilatory notice. . . . But if some obscure little cur . . . presume to touch
with his teeth the sacred flesh of humanity, even in the person of a bullying
tramp . . . then instantly the telegraph wires are put into requisition." The
Metropolitan Police were ordered to destroy any dogs that might possibly
be rabid, but the *Home Chronicler* suspiciously wondered whether patholo-
gists had created the panic so they could get the Vivisection Act relaxed on
the grounds of investigating hydrophobia.[63]

When the fog season came, Cobbe had a spell of bronchitis, but she was
out and about by 12 November—she renewed her reader's ticket at the British Museum that day—and on the sixteenth she was in Bristol for a drawing-
room suffrage meeting. The strategy of drawing-room meetings, which had
been promoted by Priscilla McLaren at the contentious central committee
meeting in 1874, was designed to reach people who would not attend public events. The hostess invited almost 150 friends; Cobbe gently echoed popular stereotypes and pointed out the political need for women's superior
moral sense. Because drawing-room meetings were cast as social events and
included many husbands, polite dissent was not uncommon. A Dr. Stuart
remarked that "he was a great admirer of the other sex . . . but for that reason he was entirely averse to their mixing in the rough and rude world of
politics." And so on. Cobbe replied that "Dr. Stuart gave more weight to
the effect of sentiment in the world than it deserved. There was plenty of
sentiment for young, well-born, and beautiful women . . . but how about
those women who were not beautiful and not young, whose lives were hard
and lonely, and who had to go into the world and work for their bread?"
She concluded that she would gladly exchange "the uniform courtesy and
consideration which she had met all her life at the hands of men for simple
justice, if that justice were extended to all women in all ranks of life."[64]

On 12 December Cobbe took part in another effort to reach beyond the
core supporters of suffrage by speaking to an at-home at 64 Berners Street.
Like the Kensington Society meetings of the 1860s, these events encouraged
discussion of interesting topics. Cobbe presented a brief version of the essay
published in *Contemporary Review* for January 1878 as "The Little Health of
Ladies." A sensible and often amusing argument in favor of good food, adequate rest, comfortable clothing, outdoor exercise, and mental occupation,
Cobbe's talk also proposed that "much serious illness resulting from the neglect of early symptoms would be avoided if lady doctors could be more
readily consulted." In discussion, according to the *Times*, "one or two ladies

## COBBE TO THE RESCUE!

URELY not before it was wanted, Miss FRANCES POWER COBBE has been holding a Conference, preliminary to the publication of a paper, on the "Little Health of Women,"—a translation, no doubt, of the delicate French phrase "Petite santé," which means not so much positive illness as a general out-of-healthiness, something which justifies an interesting invalid in maintaining she is "not well," when at the same time she would hardly feel justified in proclaiming herself ill. It is a very dangerous crisis for affectionate and impressionable husbands, who often find feminine attacks made under cover of la petite santé peculiarly irresistible.

"Cobbe to the Rescue!" *Punch,* 22 December 1877.

blamed men for professing that admiration which tempted women" to submit to "the tyranny of fashion." The event generated a surprising amount of publicity on both sides of the Atlantic. Even *Punch* supplied a humorous but not inaccurate summary on 22 December, illustrated by a fine whimsical cartoon of a fashionable young lady with a whip and reins to control the equally stylish man who is drawing her three-wheeled invalid carriage.[65]

Writing in *Truth* soon after her fifty-fifth birthday, Cobbe thought about the transition to late middle age: "There comes a time, when we recognise, that, whatever our work has been, we shall not add to it any very considerable achievement; whatever knowledge we have gained, we shall not learn much more; whatever love and honour we have won, we have tasted the sweetest of them already. It is not that we have come to the end of work, or knowledge, or love. . . . Our work will be as good . . . but it will not be greater work than we have accomplished hitherto."[66]

And then she at once set out to make herself a liar. She may have been discouraged by wrangling within the antivivisection movement, by the growing virulence of antisuffragists, and even, as in the response to her recent lecture, by a press that provoked arguments about fashion but ignored what she said about working women's health. Experience had left her frustrated by endless meetings, the tedious labor of gathering signatures and gluing them to petitions, and the slow process of getting approval from an executive committee. Using everything she had learned about publicity and politics, Cobbe began a campaign that ended barely six months later with passage of a law that has been called "one of the most important, the most effective, and the least well known, nineteenth century statutes."[67] Using her own accomplished pen (and access to journals) and her contacts among influential men, she did without organizations, petitions, or committees to secure a law that was unquestionably feminist at its heart and especially valuable to poor and working women. Cobbe was not the only one to take up the cause of protection against domestic violence, but the 1878 law's most important provisions were hers, and its almost miraculously swift accomplishment was due to her well-orchestrated campaign.

The time was ripe partly because she had prepared the ground, despite the disclaimer in her dramatic narrative: "One day in 1878," she reports in her autobiography, "I was by chance reading a newspaper in which a whole series of frightful cases" of women "beaten, mangled, mutilated or trampled on by brutal husbands" appeared. "I got up out of my armchair, half dazed," she continues, "and said to myself: 'I will never rest till I have tried what I can do to stop this.'"[68] But Cobbe had been writing about women the law did not protect since the earliest days of her work with Mary Carpenter in Bristol; she had published a dozen or more *Echo* leaders on the subject and sent news accounts gleaned from the *Echo's* police-court reporters to Lydia Becker for the *Women's Suffrage Journal;* the Susanna Palmer campaign rested on evidence of a long history of abuse before Palmer stabbed her husband; and Cobbe's suffrage addresses had featured women's need for protection. As recently as the drawing-room meeting of 16 November she had asked why people believed that "women possessed such great influence" when it was impossible "to procure any protective legislation for those unfortunate wives whose husbands beat and kicked them to death."[69]

On 18 December 1877 the *Times* reported "three cases, occurring apparently simultaneously—of kicking in one woman's forehead, and another woman's eye, and throwing a burning paraffin lamp at a third." Cobbe wrote a signed letter to the *Spectator* headed "Protection for English Christians," a reference to the alleged massacres in the Turkish Empire that were then exciting outrage. It appeared, appropriately for the Christmas season, in the issue for 22 December. Her focus was still suffrage: "If we, the women of England, possessed constitutional rights, the very first exercise of our power of political pressure would undoubtedly be to compel the attention of our representatives in the Legislature to the prevention of these crimes of wife-beating and wife-murder. Can you, men of England, wholly acquit your consciences, while you tie *our* hands and never lift your own?"

The next week's *Spectator* had a wonderfully incendiary reply arguing that "to bring political passions into our homes and amongst our women is to strengthen conflict and aggravate their condition." True relations between men and women could only be established, the writer asserted, if women were withdrawn from the labor market, refused all political rights, and placed "where Nature intended." The letter was signed "F."—an initial Cobbe often used for her own newspaper correspondence—and it was so effective in fanning flames that I cannot help wondering whether she wrote it herself.[70]

John Stuart Mill and Harriet Taylor had written about domestic abuse thirty years earlier. In 1853 magistrates had gained the power to fine the abuser twenty pounds and sentence him to prison for up to six months, and further bills had been introduced but defeated during the late 1850s. With the Matrimonial Causes Act of 1857, physical cruelty became grounds for separation—if the wife had money to afford the divorce court. (Legal separation allowed a woman to choose her own domicile and handle her own property as a single woman, but neither she nor the man could remarry.) Demands to punish abusive men by flogging grew in the mid-1870s. As we have seen, Colonel Egerton Leigh briefly introduced a resolution on flogging in 1874. Although Disraeli was "disgusted with the accounts we frequently read of assaults committed upon women—upon the gentler—I will not say the feebler—sex," he asked for time to have a study conducted. Leigh withdrew his proposal, saying that "all he desired was fair play for the fairer sex." (Cobbe called it "one of the jokes which are so inexpressibly sickening in connection with this subject.")[71] The Home Office surveyed judges and magistrates, found that most of them considered flogging the best response, and in 1875 produced a blue book entitled "State of the Law relating to Brutal Assaults," which, like many such investigative reports, led nowhere. The NAPSS took up the subject at its 1876 conference, and still nothing happened.

It was against this background that the effort Cobbe opened with her letter (or perhaps letters) to the *Spectator* in December 1877 got off to a start. A series of responses in January 1878 suggested broad support for the call to protect women but also revealed that many sympathetic men, including the

*Spectator*'s editor, R. H. Hutton, did not understand the issues. Edward Strachey, on 12 January, asserted that brutality was "a large element in the character of most Englishmen." Cobbe's friend Maria Grey answered on the nineteenth that, on the contrary, most Englishman were compassionate to the helpless. Grey raised the flags of "national welfare" and "mothers of the race," arguments surely designed to elicit "compassion" and justice from men in Parliament so that the argument would not remain theoretical. Although I do not know whether Grey's letter was written at Cobbe's suggestion or was purely the act of another woman whose consciousness had been raised by the Kensington Society, other people's consciousness may well have been affected by the clergyman who proclaimed on 26 January that no stranger should ever come between a man and his wife, not even if he was beating her. He closed by quoting from Paul's Epistle to the Ephesians, as used in the Church of England marriage service: "As the Church is subject unto Christ, so let the wives be to their own husbands *in everything*."[72]

By that time Cobbe was already having a bill drafted by Matthew Davenport Hill's son Alfred Hill, a justice of the peace in Birmingham, with advice from John Duke Coleridge, lord chief justice of the court of common pleas. In addition, Cobbe herself owned a copy of Charles John Bunyon's *A Profitable Book Upon Domestic Law* (1875). She wrote to Kemble that on one Sunday she had had "a capital half hour with Lord Coleridge, and obtained his full approval of my Bill. . . . Then I went off to the M.P. who is getting up our deputation, and settled a great deal of business with him, and other business with his wife about amalgamating two women's suffrage societies; so, altogether, I broke the sabbath in a frightful manner." She hoped that Russell Gurney, recorder of London and a Conservative MP who had been a staunch friend of women's issues, would take charge of the bill, but by then his health was too fragile.[73]

Cobbe laid out the bill's key principles in an anonymous two-page article in *Truth* for 17 January 1878. Picking her rhetoric and examples carefully to arouse male chivalry, she argued that punishing brutal husbands would not protect abused wives. The essence of her proposal was succinctly stated:

> As our divorce laws recognize that a woman *(who can afford to pay for it)*, has a right to obtain a judicial separation (divorce *a mensa et thoro*, not *a vinculo*) from her husband, on the ground of cruelty, so the poorest women in the land, who are a hundredfold more exposed to such cruelty, should, in our opinion, have the same relief placed in their reach. The wife of a man convicted of an aggravated assault upon her (or of repeated brutal assaults), should be able to obtain from the magistrate who sentences her husband, a

Protection Order for life, which should have all the legal effects of a judicial separation. . . . [In addition] the children of the separated couple should be given into the exclusive custody of the wife, and the husband should be ordered to pay for their support such share of his weekly earnings as the magistrate may deem proper, as is done in the case of illegitimate children. This last proviso will be recognized by every one as absolutely just, in itself, and needful for the protection of the children . . . and it is also indispensable to the working of any law intended to set free the wife, since very few mothers would avail themselves of any such liberty unless they might take their children along with them, and out of the hands of their husbands.[74]

"Wife-Torture" was evidently the last piece she published in *Truth,* though as in the case of *Fraser's,* no explanation has come to light. Possibly she had offended Labouchère; or perhaps she was simply no longer interested once she had managed, in an anonymous and ungendered political essay, to place her argument in a magazine read by a great many members of Parliament. Aside from offering all women the same protection that was available to those rich enough to use divorce courts, Cobbe understood some of the practical reasons that women of any class stayed with abusive husbands. Most importantly, she perceived why the masculinist argument of men like Colonel Egerton Leigh—that the crime should be suppressed by imposing longer sentences, that the criminal should be humiliated by flogging—was the worst possible solution.

She never discussed the reasoning that led her to this conclusion. Was it pure practical thought? talking to Susanna Palmer and women like her? conversation with magistrates (such as her brother Charles) and police officials (like her cousin Charles Augustus)? Mary Lloyd's recollection of reading *Justice of the Peace* twenty-five years earlier? *Echo* leaders such as "More about Justices' Justice" (26 October 1871) had considered the difficulty of prison sentences: "When the wife and her children are dependent for support on the man who beats her," a term long enough to "exercise a reformatory influence on the husband's character" would lead them to starvation. But in 1871 she recommended punishment "by a week's imprisonment and the lash" since she thought fear of the lash, much more than fear of prison, would prevent men from beating their wives. By 1878 she realized that although the threat of flogging might sometimes be an effective deterrent, when faced with the actuality no sensible woman would testify. A mother might be able to support her children if their father were in prison, but a man who had been flogged would still have the right to live with his wife. It seemed almost inevitable that he would pay her back for the pain she had "caused."[75] The key parts of Cobbe's proposal—an immediate separation order, custody of her children, and payments to help support them—made it possible for a woman to give evidence against her abusive husband.

On 1 February the *Women's Suffrage Journal* summarized the article from *Truth*, "understood to be from the pen of Miss Frances Power Cobbe," and added its own plea. Coincidentally, a Matrimonial Causes Acts Amendment Bill was introduced on 14 February by Farrer Herschell, a barrister and member of the NAPSS council. Designed to remedy an anomaly in the support provisions of the 1857 divorce act, the bill was thoroughly uncontroversial and passed its second reading less than a week later. Meanwhile, Cobbe constructed the full-length essay "Wife-Torture in England" for April's *Contemporary Review* and arranged to get prepublication offprints for lobbying. And on 29 March, when Herschell's matrimonial-causes bill reached the House of Lords, Lord Penzance introduced an amendment about wife abuse. Made a peer in 1869 as Baron Penzance, James Plaisted Wilde had been only a lukewarm supporter of the Married Women's Property Act, but long experience as a divorce court judge had taught him about matrimonial horrors. Realizing the boon of getting a law through so quickly—her own bill had not even been introduced—Cobbe wrote at once to Penzance. He replied on 4 April, "I am much obliged by your letter and quite recognize the importance of the points to which you call my attention." His clause had been, he continued, "very hurriedly drawn," and he promised to propose alterations that would "give the fullest consideration to your very practical suggestions."[76]

"Wife-Torture in England" was thus being widely read while the bill was in Parliament and had been carefully constructed for that purpose. Beginning with a complimentary anecdote about "the better sort of Englishmen" and moving through a page or two of general reflections on violence, the essay quickly becomes an almost unreadable catalog of brutal assaults documented from NAPSS papers, judicial statistics, and chief constables' reports, and described in appalling detail. Cobbe blamed the violence not only on social circumstances but also on women's legal condition, especially the "notion that a man's wife is his PROPERTY." She insists that if women were "to obtain the franchise to-morrow, it is morally certain that a Bill for the Protection of Wives would pass through the legislature before a Session is over." Having thus thrown down the gauntlet, she explains the argument against flogging, clarifies the crucial points of her proposal, deals with possible objections, and closes by entreating "the gentlemen of England,—the bravest, humanest, and most generous in the world,—not to leave these helpless women to be trampled to death under their very eyes."

The article's pointed focus on the poor in contrast to the "gentlemen of

England" was quite deliberate. Cobbe was writing propaganda for a specific purpose: to persuade the "better sort" in Parliament to pass legislation needed by women who could not afford other protection. She knew perfectly well that "wife-beating exists in the upper and middle classes rather more . . . than is generally recognized."[77] As early as 1862 she had written about divorce-court revelations in "Celibacy v. Marriage": "Who could have imagined it possible, that well-born and well-educated men in honourable professions, should be guilty of the same brutality? Imagine a handsomely-furnished drawing-room, with its books, and flowers, and lights, and all the refinements of civilized life, for the scene of similar outrages. Imagine the offender a well-dressed gentleman, tall and powerful as English gentlemen are wont to be; the victim shrinking from his blows—a gentle high-bred English *lady!*"[78] In this campaign, however, her goal was to give poorer women equal access to separation orders, just as the 1870 Married Women's Property Act offered them the financial control that well-to-do women got through marriage settlements. (Appearing before a magistrate was not only cost-free but relatively simple; there were more than five hundred of them in London alone, and in the countryside most male landowners and many clergymen were magistrates.) And, of course, to convince members of Parliament to act, it was far easier to arouse benevolence toward poor victims than to demand an examination of their own behavior.

By 15 April the *Englishwoman's Review* was celebrating the "unlooked for progress" made during the past month: "There is a double gain in having this clause for the Protection of Wives added at this stage of its progress to another Bill which has already passed the House of Commons, because it has thus avoided all the dangerous trials of Second-reading, Committees, Report, &c." Two other journals where Cobbe's influence was strong, The *Women's Suffrage Journal* (1 May) and the *Spectator* (11 May), applauded the Penzance amendment. There were, however, significant differences between his proposal and the one constructed by Cobbe and Hill. The latter let the court issue a separation order at a woman's request, while Penzance proposed that the separation take place only if the magistrate found it necessary for her "future safety"; that is, the power was in the (male) magistrate's hands, not in the woman's. The Penzance amendment gave a wife custody of children under age ten; Cobbe would have awarded custody without any age limit, since she recognized both the danger of violence toward young children and the potential for sexual abuse when a pubescent daughter was put into the custody of a man who had been ordered to stay away from his wife. And as the *Englishwoman's Review* pointed out on 15 June 1878, neither version protected women who were not legally married to their abusers.

Even with these flaws, however, the rapid success of the key provisions was a matter to celebrate. On 17 May the amended Matrimonial Causes Act easily passed its third reading in the Lords; the Commons accepted the added clause without discussion, and with the queen's assent the bill became law on 27 May. All of the feminist journals gave the entire credit to Cobbe. The *Englishwoman's Review* drew a pointed moral: "This, and other improvements which have taken place in the condition of women within the last twenty years, originated in the efforts of women themselves, without which the old order would not change." American suffragists immediately sought out copies of "Wife-Torture in England" and managed to introduce comparable bills in various state legislatures.[79]

Of course Cobbe's success depended also on the growing climate of opinion and the preceding work by Mill, the home secretary, and the NAPSS. But Cobbe's autobiographical account of sudden conversion in 1878 entirely fails to describe the significant role she had played since the early 1860s in keeping brutality against women in the public eye. While essays in monthly and quarterly magazines were read by a few thousand people, and feminist journals counted their subscribers with three figures, the leaders Cobbe wrote for the *Echo* reached more than a hundred thousand readers. The law was, I think, fairly described in an obituary as Cobbe's "monument."[80]

Efforts to bring about this enormous success did not fill Cobbe's time, even at the beginning of 1878. In mid-January the VSS was on the verge of collapse. The executive committee's November decision to undertake no parliamentary action during the year had led to defections from both those who wanted to push for total prohibition and those who favored better regulation. Shaftesbury wrote that he "constantly" received "letters of a very sarcastic tone, charging me with destruction of a great cause, & imputing very bad motives." In November 1876 the VSS had more than six hundred members, but on 28 January 1878, when the marquis of Bute sent fifty pounds "for the present distress," he added that "for the future, we must surely have 300 members, or at least 150."[81]

As scientific experimentation grew in strength and prestige—Michael Foster founded the *Journal of Physiology* in 1878—Cobbe's uncompromising opposition began to demand her withdrawal from other causes. Though she could maintain friendly relationships with antisuffragists, including John Locke and R. H. Hutton, the defenders of vivisection became intolerable. She had enthusiastically supported the Albemarle Club, which admitted equal numbers of men and women and supplied a dining room, a drawing room, and (on the third floor) several dressing rooms and a meeting room reserved for ladies, but when a controversy arose over whether members could freely invite guests to join them for meals, she objected that "an unrestricted right of admission for guests would at once open the door to the possible entrance of very undesirable persons." After losing a vote over the issue, she resigned from the managing committee. Her vehemence became almost a joke among friends. James Martineau wrote a New Year's Day letter in 1878: "In the Theatre of the Royal Institution, on Friday evening [28 December], I looked round to see if you were present, to hear Huxley's lecture on Harvey. But as you did not jump up to contradict him, I am persuaded you were not there." She felt compelled to write to Henry Wentworth Acland, regius professor of medicine at Oxford, after her friend Felicia Skene "unguardedly betrayed" that Cobbe had written *Science in Excelsis*— a bitter dark comedy of the Last Judgment in which Azrael, the angel of death, prepares to vivisect a group of "eminent Physiologists" in a "celestial Laboratory"—to assure him that she did not believe that vivisectionists were "beyond the pale of God's mercy" but that she did believe cruelty, whatever its motive, was more heinous than any "sins of the flesh."[82]

Cobbe and Lloyd were both ill during the winter and spring of 1878. Fanny Kemble felt sorry for the "constant effort" of Cobbe's life, yet she wrote that "perpetual movement and interest" were "absolutely indispensable to Fanny Cobbe's existence; and I really do not think she could endure a life in Wales, or indeed anywhere but in the midst of all this excitement and occupation to which she is now accustomed." Yet there were difficulties with their hopeful compromise on Cheyne Walk; the next tenant found serious problems with the roof and uncomfortable drafts in the room over the passage to the mews. By mid-March they had arranged to move. "I am sure," wrote Kemble, "she will regret more and more leaving London. . . . She certainly is eminently social in her tastes and tendencies. In the midst of all the confusion and worry and disorder of her affairs, preparing to leave her house, etc., etc., she invites people to tea-parties, and luncheon-parties, and goes out to dinner parties."[83] The exact shape of their plans is unclear. For the moment, Lloyd went to Wales and Cobbe stayed in London, probably in lodgings or with a friend, since the Hereford Square house was still rented out.

In mid-May, when the new Matrimonial Causes Act was on the verge of passing, Cobbe's very first explicitly feminist appeal also came to victory. On 4 May, nearly sixteen years after Cobbe delivered "Female Education, and How it Would be Affected by University Examinations" at the London NAPSS meeting, the queen granted a new charter to the University of London. At a convocation on 15 May a delegation including Cobbe, the dowager Lady Stanley of Alderley (Kate Amberley's mother), Millicent Fawcett, and Emily Sherriff presented a letter signed by almost two thousand women expressing their "heartfelt gratitude for the noble part [the University of London] has taken in coming forward first among the Universities of Great

Britain to propose to open all its degrees to women."[84] Three days later, the Matrimonial Causes Act gained final approval in the House of Lords. It was an extraordinary congruence of achievements in one week.

Cobbe was in Wales by early June, though she briefly returned to London later in the summer for a VSS executive meeting. While not yet declaring itself a society devoted strictly to ending all experiments on animals, the committee carried a resolution, on Cobbe's motion, to "appeal henceforth to public opinion in favour of the total prohibition of Vivisection." George and Frances Hoggan abstained from voting and subsequently left the executive, although both continued to speak at VSS events. One or two other members resigned from the executive, but some who had left the previous autumn came back. Cobbe continued to write leaflets, and Shaftesbury started to edit them; he found her language too strong and sometimes inaccurate. "We must be exceedingly careful as to our evidence," he wrote on 17 September.[85]

She made a trip to Newbridge in August. Sometime in the past year the

Cobbe at age fifty-five. She called this photograph "the best which has been taken of me" even though it showed that "I am a formidable old woman."

begum Nuzzeer had died in Calcutta after more than forty years of widow-hood. Lloyd's nephew Edward Owen Vaughan Lloyd turned twenty-one during the summer and inherited the Rhagatt estate. His aunt Gertrude Lloyd, who as the widow of the previous landowner had occupied the house at Rhagatt since John Lloyd's death, moved to Hengwrt and stayed there for several years; having a steady tenant in the house made Mary Lloyd's fi-nances more secure. Despite her holiday, Cobbe's arm remained "unser-viceable" from too much writing. By 3 September she and Lloyd had made plans to go abroad.[86]

While Cobbe was in London during September, nevertheless, a whirl of fragmented activity kept her almost as busy as she had been during the spring. On 8 September she delivered a sermon, "The Kingdom of God," at the Free Unitarian Church of Reading. A few days later she asked in the *Spectator* why Isabel Grant had been sentenced to hang "for stabbing her husband in a sudden, tipsy quarrel, when homicides of like kind are almost uniformly punished as 'manslaughter' only?"[87] By 18 September she had written to the *Times* appealing for clemency and enlisted a fellow suffragist, Augusta Webster; a Hereford Square neighbor, Letitia Probyn; and John Verschoyle, an undergraduate at Cambridge from an Anglo-Irish clerical family with three generations of connections to the Cobbes, to organize petitions to the Home Office. A *Times* leader published the day following Cobbe's letter concluded that the case "comes so near the border line which divides murder from less capital offences that a remission of the extreme penalty would certainly be a welcome concession to public feeling." Three days before Grant's scheduled hanging the queen signed a reprieve.[88]

Cobbe applied for a passport on 11 October and left almost at once for an antivivisection meeting. Harriet Hosmer, then in London, wrote that she was "just home from a hunt for Miss Cobbe but she is as difficult to get hold of as an ignius fatuus (Mind I do not say Fat-uus)—how is it possible she is going away tomorrow just the day Miss Lloyd (so she wrote me) comes?" On 16 October, when Lloyd was indeed in London applying for her own passport, Cobbe spoke in Southampton. A *Punch* squib on 2 No-vember described her address: "Though womanly feeling was of course combined with masculine vigour, the former perhaps a little preponder-ated." *Punch* wondered why she did not find fox hunting (for sport) much more objectionable than vivisection (for science) and criticized her for con-tinuing to "devour [her] relations, the ox, the sheep, and the pig."[89]

Cobbe probably did not see *Punch* until later. When the meeting ended, she and Lloyd left almost at once for Fontainebleau (and Rosa Bonheur) on their way to Italy.[90] Twenty years after Cobbe's first joyous visit, many of her friends were gone. Isa Blagden had died in 1873; Cushman and her partner

Emma Stebbins had returned to the United States in 1870; and Theodosia Trollope, who had been at the center of so much English social life in Florence, had died in 1865. One of Mary Somerville's daughters was also dead, though Lloyd's good friend Martha was still living. Cobbe replanted the violets on Theodore Parker's grave in the English Cemetery but found it "far too humble & neglected." A few years later Theodore Stanton, Elizabeth Cady Stanton's son, raised a fund and put up a monument. Judging by photographs, he took Cobbe's suggestion for "a white marble headstone with a medallion & his head in intaglio-rilevato."[91]

Harriet Hosmer still maintained a Roman studio and might have arrived by winter, but it seems more likely that she remained in London working on her perpetual-motion machine.[92] Although Hosmer was no more than forty-eight, the bulk of her important work in sculpture was long since finished. One thing Cobbe did accomplish in Rome that winter was to have her picture taken. The photograph shows a confident woman of fifty-five. Although still heavy, she looks stronger and healthier than she had in pictures taken fifteen years earlier.

I have been unable to locate any other record of this trip; the only correspondence is a single postcard to turn down a speaking engagement. She did make one interesting new friendship, with a woman of twenty-two named Violet Paget, who was then living in Florence with her mother and had just started to publish essays on art, music, and poetry under the name Vernon Lee in *Fraser's,* the *New Quarterly Magazine,* the *Quarterly Review,* and *Cornhill.* Since Cobbe also wrote for those four periodicals during the 1870s, an editor may have suggested that she look up the new contributor. Paget's identity and gender were not yet public. She wrote to a friend on 18 December that the *Academy* had "found out (Heaven knows how) that Vernon Lee is not a real name and put it in inverted commas. I don't care that Vernon Lee should be known to be myself or any other young woman, as I am sure that no one reads a woman's writing on art, history or aesthetics with anything but unmitigated contempt."[93] A *Spectator* review of *Studies of the Eighteenth Century in Italy* on 26 June 1880 still referred to the author as "Mr. Lee," but Cobbe wished Paget would use her "own name for the honour of our sex. We cannot afford to have you numbered in the masculine ranks." Whatever else she may have done on her final trip to Italy, six months of public silence in the company of Mary Lloyd with Italian sunshine and freedom "glowing before us like one long bright holiday" was balm for the failures and a happy reward for the accomplishments of the past four years.[94]

*We must accept and seize every instrument of power, every vote, every influence which we can obtain to enable us to promote virtue and happiness.*
FRANCES POWER COBBE, *The Duties of Women*

Cobbe and Lloyd did not return from Italy until late in the spring of 1879. Lloyd went straight to Wales, and Cobbe probably stayed with friends, since she used the VSS office for her mailing address. On 18 June Cobbe spoke at a public meeting of the Society for Promoting the Employment of Women. Constance Flower, formerly Constance de Rothschild, "spent a long hour with that glorious woman Miss Cobbe" on 23 June. Soon afterwards Cobbe introduced her to Helen Taylor, another instance of her power to use networks for political ends. Taylor was still on the London School Board, and Constance's husband, Cyril Flower, was about to stand for Parliament, where he would take a strong interest in urban issues. Though Taylor sometimes offended suffragists with her high-handed ways, Flower found her "a quiet agreeable gentle, extremely clever woman."[1]

A flurry of antivivisection activity occupied July. While Cobbe was in Italy two members of the VSS committee enlisted Lord Truro to bring a bill for total abolition into the House of Lords. Cobbe asked Erasmus Darwin, who was a physician as well as a fellow member of the suffrage central committee, if he could persuade his brother Charles to support a clause limiting repeated experiments once results had been published. She met with Shaftesbury on 11 July to supply information for his speech and went to Westminster on the fifteenth to listen. But Shaftesbury had no hope of success and real doubts about the bill itself. His speech quoted a passage, supplied by Cobbe, from Claude Bernard, who had confessed that his thirty years of operations on living animals had achieved no results with therapeutic value: "Our hands, without doubt, are empty today, but our mouths full, it may be, of legitimate promises for the future."[2] But the result, as they expected, was overwhelming: 16 votes in favor of the bill, 97 opposed.

Using the tactic she had first employed almost thirty years earlier, Cobbe readied a pamphlet to publicize Shaftesbury's speech, but either because of

a careless paid secretary or because of Cobbe's own poor supervision, Shaftesbury received forty-eight copies of his 1876 speech instead of the new one.
George Hoggan, meanwhile, had been dismissed from his post as an attending physician at St. John's Hospital after writing to the press about mismanagement. The hospital's attorney, suing Hoggan for libel, described him
as a man "of an interfering or fussy nature."[3] And vivisection was beginning
to draw influential nonscientific support. The archbishop of York, one of
the first two people to join the VSS, voted against Lord Truro's bill; George
Eliot established a studentship in physiology to honor the memory of G.
H. Lewes, who had died in November 1878.

By early September Cobbe was doing business by post from Wales. Her
brother Charles, still fond of summer trips to the Continent, went as the
VSS delegate to an international congress of animal-protection societies at
Gotha, Germany, in August. Her brother Henry became the rector of Maulden in Bedfordshire. Although not far from his previous living, Maulden
was a bigger parish than Milton and provided him with a larger income.[4]
In addition, it was only forty-five miles from London and close to a rail station that had direct service, making it a better place to live with three daughters who were reaching young womanhood. During the summer of 1879
Oxford's first two women's colleges prepared to open. (Maggie Elliot declined an offer to become principal of Somerville.) Elizabeth Wordsworth,
principal of Lady Margaret Hall, wrote excitedly to a friend that "we . . .
'landed our first fish' when Mr. Cobbe (Maulden Rectory, Ampthill) defini-
tively put down his daughter Winifred's name." Whether or not Cobbe influenced that decision, she certainly spoke to Tom about the college named
for her dear friend. On 30 August, Mary Ward had a letter "from Miss
Frances Conway Cobbe, who desires to enter Somerville Hall in October"
but had a question about church attendance. Cobbe also wrote. Mary Ward
responded, "Clause necessary but will be liberally worded."[5] (Lady Margaret
Hall was associated with the Church of England, whereas Somerville was
carefully nonsectarian.) Seventeen years after Cobbe spoke to the NAPSS
about university degrees, the first twenty-one women students went into residence at Oxford. Two of them were her nieces.

Although she was writing occasional reviews for the *Spectator*, Cobbe's
last well-paid piece of journalism had been "Wife-Torture" in April 1878.
She needed more income to live in London. Public lectures, as Dickens and
Thackeray had discovered, put cash into a writer's pocket instead of the publisher's; and her friends Kate Field and Florence Fenwick Miller showed that
the occupation was not impossible for respectable women. On 4 October
1879 the *Spectator* advertised: "MISS FRANCES POWER COBBE proposes
to give (to Ladies only) next month in London, a Series of ADDRESSES

on the DUTIES OF WOMEN. Each address to be followed by a free Discussion. Tickets for the course, £2. For Prospectus and Tickets, apply to Miss GREEN, 80 Upper Gloster Place, N.W." The *Englishwoman's Review* for 15 October urged readers to get tickets at once, since "unless there is a sufficiently general response to the project it will be relinquished." Cobbe stirred up more interest by inviting women "who may feel inclined to debate anything which I may advance" to "speak freely on the subject at the close of each address."[6]

Cobbe's name and the urging of the feminist press drew a "very crowded attendance" to the lectures, delivered at the Westminster Palace Hotel at 3:00 P.M. on five Thursdays from 20 November through 18 December—a time and place convenient for middle-class women, even those who came alone. In the days before microphones, Cobbe's large frame was a distinct advantage, as was her experience. "It is vain," wrote one reporter, "to try in short space to give adequate impression of this noble address. The voice now of intense earnestness, now of deep pathos, now of sparkling humour, as Miss Cobbe lights up her subject with some incident or parable, is ringing in our ears as we write, reminding us that reproduction is impossible."[7]

By emphasizing duties instead of rights, Cobbe tapped into a familiar exhortatory tradition, but where Sarah Stickney Ellis wrote about women's duties as wives, mothers, daughters, and so forth, solely in relation to others, Cobbe covered those topics briskly in the opening lectures before moving on to women's duties as members of society and, finally, as citizens of the state. She knew well that even a woman such as Fanny Kemble, who gave up her daughters in order to divorce Pierce Butler, reflected social ideology when asked whether she shared Cobbe's opinions: "I know that I am quite willing that women should be allowed to do whatever they *can*—I mean, be politicians, members of Parliament, doctors, divines, lawyers, *soldiers, if they can,* and vote by all means, if they like. My own earnest ambition and desire for them is a better, more thorough education, and a higher estimate of their own great natural calling of wives and mothers, and a more intelligent apprehension of their duties in both capacities."[8]

Speaking of women as "Human Beings of the Mother Sex," Cobbe outlined a feminism of the sort Charlotte Perkins Gilman would promote in the United States a generation later: woman's special qualities required her to "share in the great housekeeping of the State." Like Gilman, she thought that any mercenary marriage, even if "solemnized by a bishop in the most fashionable churches of London," was as much a "sacrifice of true chastity" as the "painful subject" she would not name in front of listeners that included young unmarried women. In each lecture she saved the most radical passage for the climax. Her discussion of personal duty moved from the

conventionally feminine virtues of chastity and temperance to the somewhat more surprising veracity and courage—"We ought to take more pains
than men to steady our nerves . . . practise courage, I beseech you, at least
as diligently as you practise the piano"—and concluded with mention of "a
great Personal Duty of which some of you may never have thought, the duty
of MAINTAINING your own lawful FREEDOM, neither voluntarily ab-
dicating it nor suffering it to be wrested from you." She soon pointed out
the conflict between every person's duty of personal liberty and the "vow a
wife makes when married by the rites of the Church of England." While
Ruskin, in "Of Queen's Gardens," had said that women were to blame for
not hindering the world's suffering and injustice but would keep them
locked in their bowers, Cobbe demanded that women "strive to obtain *more
extended* powers." Only legislation, she reiterated, could touch "the *roots* of
great evils"; philanthropy merely eased the symptoms. Therefore it was a
"matter of *duty*" to demand "women's political emancipation."[9]

If Cobbe made any strategic error, it was in speaking to activists with an
approach that would prove very useful in acquiring new converts. Some
of the women at Westminster Palace Hotel objected to her old-fashioned
moralizing. The penultimate lecture, in particular, warned against adopting
"looser and more 'Bohemian' manners" and failing to censure "grave moral
transgressions." Two or three women, Cobbe said, "talked a great deal of
nonsense about receiving back offenders into Society or in short not exclud-
ing them at all." Supporters such as Anne Thackeray Ritchie thought "young
ladies like Miss Bewicke rushing in where angels &c might help their fellow
creatures rather in silence or in some way more suited to their years."[10]

But it was just because of the lectures' emphasis on duty and their morally
conservative tone that the published version, *The Duties of Women,* became
enormously useful to feminists on both sides of the Atlantic. Julia Ward
Howe reviewed it for the *Christian Register;* the *New York Times* wrote that
it would help convince men "that the spectre of the female politician who
abandons her family to neglect for the sake of passing bills in Parliament"
is an illusion. When Louisa May Alcott tried to get up a suffrage club, she
found that the women needed "so much coaxing" that she got copies of
*Duties of Women* for them to read. Frances Willard asked permission to bring
out an edition for Women's Christian Temperance Union (WCTU) reading groups; Mary Livermore wrote that introducing the book "into a neighborhood marks an epoch there. It sets women to thinking—opens long
sealed eyes—fructifies purpose."[11]

Some English reviewers took a darker view. Cobbe probably guessed that
the *Spectator*'s anonymous notice had been produced by R. H. Hutton. "It
does amuse us a little," he wrote, "to hear her speaking with such vast indig-

nation of the men who attack her sex generally, when there is a running fire of irony, and sometimes even subdued invective, against men, penetrating the whole substance of the book." Indeed, throughout the review he seems upset that a woman speaking to an audience of women had made so many mischievous comments about men. He was also still trying to prove that he had been right in objecting to Cobbe's 1862 proposal that women take University of London examinations, even though their admission was an accomplished fact when she gave her series of lectures.[12]

The 1879 London School Board election came along while Cobbe was midway through the series, indeed just before she reached the lecture on women's duties as citizens. Helen Taylor was reelected, as was Florence Fenwick Miller. Augusta Webster, a fellow member of the suffrage central committee who had moved into the house at 24 Cheyne Walk when Cobbe and Lloyd moved out, headed the poll for Chelsea. Another new member was Rosamond Davenport Hill, a good friend ever since she and Cobbe had taught together in Bristol; Cobbe introduced her to Helen Taylor so they could plan strategy together.[13] Henrietta Müller, an early Girton student, and the working women's advocate Edith Simcox also won. In all, nine women were elected, giving them almost one-fifth of the seats.

Even while Cobbe was preparing and delivering the lectures, she and Lloyd were moving to a different house. "The difficulties of a little Exodus," she wrote on 5 December, "have been greatly enhanced by the very coldest weather known in England for years."[14] Although she had written in "The Town Mouse and the Country Mouse" that commuting gave one the worst of both worlds, Mary Lloyd now took precedence. *The Duties of Women* defined "marriage" and "friendship" as equivalent: "I think that every one, at least some time or other in life, must have the chance offered to them of forming a true marriage with one of the opposite sex or else a true friendship with one of their own, and that we should look to such marriages and friendships as the supreme joy and glory of mortal life,—unions wherein we may steep our whole hearts." Women were "better suited for friendship than for marriage" if, like herself and Mary, they "do not need to *lean,* but to *clasp hands* along the journey of life."[15]

Their new residence was Albany House, in Byfleet, Surrey, a "quaint little house" just over twenty miles southwest of London. After the cramped quarters on Cheyne Walk it was an "unspeakable" comfort for Cobbe to possess "an atom of a study again." They had a "nice little trap and Mary's Welsh ponies and dogs." A direct train from Weybridge, two or three miles away, got to Waterloo station in fifty minutes.[16] Cobbe went into London at least once a week on VSS business; sometimes she stayed overnight, but her active life in town had diminished: there were no longer dinner parties two or three times a week, fewer suffrage committee meetings, a much smaller number of evening events. The new house did have enough room so that friends who came out for the afternoon or evening could spend the night and return to London the following day. Nevertheless, it was a different kind of life, and at first Cobbe was not sure that it was a life she entirely liked.

John Locke died in January 1880. Almost seventy-five years old, he was until his death an active MP and a dependable supporter of the antivivisection movement, though he had always voted against women's suffrage. Laura, who would soon be sixty, continued to live at 63 Eaton Place with their only child, then in his early thirties; also a barrister, he too was named John Locke (usually "Johnny," formally John Henry). Laura's orphaned niece Laura Ensor, her sister Florence's daughter, and like Florence a very witty woman, may have been with her for a time, although she had grown up primarily in France. Cobbe wrote letters to at least two of her school-board friends in February 1880 about Laura Ensor's interest in a post as inspector of needle-work.[17]

Another death notice in the *Times,* on 12 February, aroused sharp, if brief, anxiety among Cobbe's friends. "For a moment I sat *appalled,*" wrote Catherine Marsh, "& then, through thankful tears, I read an *additional* Christian name, which led me to believe that it was *not* the friend of every helpless & injured creature—Ld Shaftesburys friend,—& *my* friend,—who had left this Earth the poorer for her passing away." The Boston *Woman's Journal,* understandably less observant and less knowledgeable, published an obituary for Frances Power Cobbe on 6 March. It was picked up by other U.S. newspapers, and some dear friends across the Atlantic sent condolence letters to Mary Lloyd. "It is a curious experience that of learning what one's friend will feel when we have 'gone the way of all flesh'!" Cobbe wrote to Sarah Wister. "To me it has been infinitely comforting . . . to learn how much some dear ones would like yourself regret me & feel for Mary."[18]

Cobbe's explanation to the *Woman's Journal* was, however, somewhat disingenuous. "There is something half droll, half infinitely solemn, in thus seeing what will be said and felt of me some day," she wrote, but then added, "It was a poor lady—unknown to me personally—who took my name, and whose death was announced so as to mislead."[19] The *Times* notice read: "On the 6th inst. at South Kensington, FRANCES MARY POWER COBBE, youngest daughter of the late Lieut.-General Cobbe, R.A., in her 43rd year." It was the "Fanny Power Cobbe" who had written letters to George Bentley and published essays in *Temple Bar, Tinsley's Magazine,* and *St. James's Magazine* between 1876 and 1879. But if she was a daughter of Cobbe's uncle George and a near neighbor in South Kensington (her last address was less than two hundred yards from Hereford Square), why was she a "poor lady—

unknown to me personally" who "took" Cobbe's name? At age sixty-eight Uncle George had married Elizabeth Pulleyne (age forty-two and a spinster, according to the marriage certificate) in August 1852, only a few weeks after his first wife died. The two children who became known as Frances Mary Power Cobbe and George Power Cobbe were already teenagers. Although in the nineteenth century a subsequent marriage did not legitimate children born prior to the marriage, George Cobbe gave his name to two children of his (spinster) wife, Elizabeth Pulleyne. His will acknowledges that they were his children and thus Frances Power Cobbe's cousins.

So in strictest truth, Cobbe may not have "personally" known the "poor lady . . . who took my name," but she certainly knew of her, if only from the published essays and the curious questions asked by editors and acquaintances.[20] And she still lived at home in 1856 when one brother wrote to another that "the visit to Ireland of my uncle must have been a great annoyance to you all & those who wrote to him so decidedly must have felt anything but pleasure in meeting him."[21] In evaluating all of Cobbe's judgments about men and women and morality one must take into account that between 1847, when she was twenty-four, and the time she left home ten years later her cousin Azélie, who was married to her brother Tom, ran away with another man; her brother Henry and his bride had a baby less than three months after their marriage; her cousin Henry Clermont's illegitimate son got in touch with the family asking for financial help;[22] and it became evident that Uncle George had a second family while his first wife was still alive.

The aftermath of Frances Mary Power Cobbe's death perhaps made the spring of 1880 a good time to be away from London. Living in the country made Mary Lloyd very happy, and Cobbe grew more or less reconciled; by the end of March she would write that "Mary has been wonderfully well all this winter—owing I think chiefly to her beloved old Welsh pony" and that she herself liked the place "more & more" for its "splendid walks & drives," although "dissipations" such as dinner in town were "rare." Shaftesbury remembered Mary Lloyd by sending tickets for the opening of the Royal Academy show. They were also finding people to visit in the neighborhood, especially Matthew Arnold, who lived near Cobham and also took trains from Weybridge station. Although Arnold had criticized Cobbe's "religion of the future" in "The Function of Criticism at the Present Time" (1865), they were both fond of friendly arguments and were united by their love of dogs. Mary Lloyd "used all her skill" trying to "save poor dear Geist—who was a very ugly dog," and Arnold freely allowed Cobbe to reprint "Geist's Grave" in antivivisection publications.[23]

Cobbe had thought there was enough interest to make it worthwhile to repeat her lecture series in London, but she dropped the plan when Parliament dissolved in March so that she and Lloyd could work "tooth & nail at the Election—putting *the screw* on all the Candidates in our reach." Cobbe lined up influential men to speak with candidates about both women's suffrage and animal protection, and she also asked Helen Taylor to do what she could for Arthur Cohen, who was running to replace John Locke in Southwark. She was not alone; according to the *Englishwoman's Review,* the election of 1880 "differed from all former similar expressions of the national will in the important share that women have taken in it."[24] When the new Parliament opened on 29 April the government had changed hands. Gladstone was again prime minister, and the new Liberal MPs included Cobbe's old editor at the *Echo,* Arthur Arnold, and her friend Constance de Rothschild's husband, Cyril Flower. Henry Fawcett became postmaster general although, unusually, he was not a member of the cabinet. The common explanation is that his blindness would have proved awkward in that role, although one might wonder if the awkwardness lay in the fact that Millicent Fawcett generally served as his reader and would therefore have had direct access to a great deal of cabinet business.

Although she had not repeated her lectures in London, Cobbe gave a compressed series at the Bristol home of suffragist Agnes Montgomerie Beddoe. While in Bristol she also spoke at a suffrage meeting, at which she emphasized her work with Mary Carpenter; in her drawing-room talks she almost always praised a local woman philanthropist before pointing out that political power was essential for lasting social improvement. She lectured somewhere on vivisection as well, probably in London; Shaftesbury found it "admirable—we must be 'mealy mouthed' no longer"—even though he thought the "Duties of Women" lectures had been "a little too pugnacious."[25]

With a new prime minister in office, Cobbe created a fresh antivivisection memorial to be signed by "men of real eminence." Tennyson willingly added his name, and as Cobbe wrote to Violet Paget, "Ruskin gave his to Lord Mount-Temple little supposing they were my words he was endorsing!" John Morley was "anxious at present for various reasons to abstain from signing memorials"—he had just become editor of the *Pall Mall Gazette* and had parliamentary ambitions to boot—but did ask "if there was any chance of your being willing to write an occasional article for me in this paper, on any subject you please that is open to newspaper treatment." After Shaftesbury presented the memorial in July, Gladstone wrote yet another "very friendly letter" but again refused permission to make it public.[26]

Cobbe and Lloyd stayed in Byfleet for the summer. The Battersea Dog's Home had raised enough money to repay Lloyd's loan, so she could pay off her mortgage and put 26 Hereford Square on the market. Cobbe wrote that she liked the "nice little house" in Byfleet "tenfold better than London" and told another friend that "Miss Lloyd & I have settled ourselves down here in the country I hope (in all senses) for *good.*" Both nieces in Oxford earned certificates for the Oxford local examinations, which served to validate secondary education, and Winifred passed the women's preliminary examination in French, German, algebra, and arithmetic. (At this date, when neither Oxford nor Cambridge gave degrees to women, only Girton required women students to pass the men's preliminary examination, which demanded Latin and Greek.) Winifred's cousin Leuric (Cobbe's brother Tom's son) had matriculated at Trinity College, Oxford, in 1877 but left without taking a degree; in June 1880 he crossed the Atlantic to learn farming.[27] A year later he married an Iowa farmer's daughter, Emma Edith Corinne Brown.

Following up on the suggestion about the *Pall Mall Gazette,* Cobbe found that Morley wanted "middle articles of about a column or a column & a half in length," preferably on "the more general and semi-philosophic aspect of politics," but it was soon evident that her philosophy and his were not compatible. He asked for "an article or two on the question of co-operative trading from the shop-keepers point of view" done in "a genial & house-wifely spirit." She complied almost by return of post, but her essay was not to his liking. "I asked you to bless the tradesmen rather than otherwise," he wrote, "& lo! you have cursed them altogether. . . . Could we not have a talk about it when you are next in town?" They soon discovered insurmountable political differences, and by October she was asking him to return unpublished manuscripts. "But why does my very moderate Radicalism alarm you?" he wrote rather plaintively. "I always thought, ever since I met you at Mr. Mill's, that you were a radical. . . . If anything in the Pall Mall seems awry to you, why not write me a letter for publication?"[28]

By the end of June, however, she had found a home at the *Standard,* a penny morning paper that was second to the *Telegraph* in daily circulation. (The *Times* cost threepence, restricting it to quite prosperous readers.) With an average daily issue of more than two hundred thousand copies, the *Standard* was read throughout the middle and lower middle classes. In its advertisement in the *Newspaper Press Directory* for 1880 it claimed to maintain "Conservative principles" but to apply them "without regard to party politics." Edited by William Heseltine Mudford, who has been described as "one of the great editors of the nineteenth century," it emphasized news and was both prosperous and influential. Among other noteworthy *Standard* journalists of the period was the correspondent John Alexander Cameron, just back from reporting on the second Afghan war (1878–81), in which Cobbe's cousin Alick had served with distinction under General Roberts.[29]

Cobbe was paid four guineas for each of her columns—twice the amount she had earned at the *Echo*—and initially wrote two each week.[30] In sharp contrast to the voice she used in *Truth* and even, often, in the *Echo,* Cobbe's tone in the *Standard* was typically genial as well as genderless. She did, however, often use women as authorities; for example, she discussed Elizabeth Garrett Anderson's views on examination anxiety in children, and she recapitulated Mary Carpenter's arguments against sentencing young offenders to adult prisons. But if the *Pall Mall Gazette's* Morley was too radical for Cobbe, she had trouble being bland enough for Mudford and the *Standard.* In one leader Cobbe pointed out that artistic taste did not necessarily lead to "taste for high and pure living" (one of her prime examples was the Borgias). A half-paragraph praising Christian art was, according to a marginal note in her scrapbook, "Interpolated by Editor." Her own conclusion had read: "But this ever-renewed argument about the 'morality' of undraped statues and pictures will never be set at rest, till the advocates of Art learn that it is not their business to be moralists and pedagogues, but rather prophets of the Beautiful in itself, and for its own sake."[31]

Finally taking a vacation in October, after Cobbe had earned more than ninety pounds for three months' work at the *Standard,* she and Lloyd went to the Isle of Wight, perhaps at Lloyd's urging, to watch the excavation of a newly discovered Roman villa just outside Brading. A trip in that direction could easily have been combined with a visit to Cobbe's brother Tom at Liss. His daughter Frances, back at Somerville for her second year, evidently took after her aunt in some ways at least. An American student wrote home that Frances Conway Cobbe was the only person in college who was not "stiff" (underlined) and was "a strong character, independent, sharp, and, I guess, moody," while the next letter described a comic adventure with a horse in the rain. Yet by term's end the friend wrote sadly that "Oxford is a lovely, dear old place: and poor Miss Cobbe has got to leave it, to go home and take care of her father. We are all so sorry."[32] During the final years of their parents' lives, Frances was at Liss with her father, who suffered from heart trouble, and Helen was with her mother in the warm Mediterranean air of southern France. As dutiful daughters, they had ended their formal education or professional preparation by their mid-twenties.

On 21 January 1881 Cobbe appointed a new VSS secretary to keep the office open daily from ten until five and write for its publications. Then a widower in his late forties, Charles Warren Adams was the son of a judge but had not made much of his life. Initially placed in the army, he sold his commission after only a year, studied unsuccessfully for the bar, had a government appointment for six years but spent half of the time on sick leave, bought a publishing business that failed, among other misadventures.[33] The society's funding and membership had improved: Adams was hired with a salary of two hundred pounds per year, although two years earlier all salaries put together had come to only ninety pounds per half-year.

In another effort to increase visibility, Cobbe imported the suffrage tactic of drawing-room meetings for reaching out to animal lovers. On 24 February 1881 she spoke to guests invited by Catharine Louisa Pirkis.[34] A novelist—she is still sometimes recognized as the author in 1894 of *The Experiences of Loveday Brooke, Lady Detective*—Catharine Pirkis was soon providing tracts for the VSS, and her husband Frederick, a retired naval officer, joined its executive committee. In mid-March Cobbe visited Constance and Cyril Flower, gave an address on kindness to animals, and basked in admiration. The eighteenth was recorded in Constance's diary as "A glorious day. Cyril out hunting. Spent the afternoon at Hartwell with Miss Cobbe. We had one of our long intimate chats." When Cobbe left by an early train on the nineteenth, Constance Flower was "*saddened* to see her go."[35]

Cobbe and Lloyd had to give up their own experiment in country living early in the year when they failed to get a suitable offer for their London house. Some London friends were not displeased; James Martineau, for example, wrote that he would "take a brighter view of the world, now that you are less out of reach." Cobbe may well have silently agreed. Lloyd managed to keep her pony for riding and driving in London; the census taken on 3 April 1881 found them at 26 Hereford Square with a coachman in addition to their customary three women servants. The dinner parties resumed; one guest invited in April was Henry James. And the London poor-law election that month brought a result almost unimaginable back when Cobbe was on sufferance as a volunteer workhouse visitor: for the post of guardian of the poor in the St. Pancras district there were forty candidates for eighteen seats, and four of the five women, including Florence Davenport Hill, were elected.[36] Twenty years after they shared Cobbe's volunteer work in the Bristol ragged school and workhouse, both Florence and her sister had become elected public officials with real power to shape education and welfare in the world's largest city.

As for Cobbe's antivivisection efforts, Constance Flower wrote at the end of 1881: "What a grand thing it is to have a purpose in life and to live up to it, giving everything up to that one purpose practicing self denial, abnegation, sacrifice, giving up pleasures, happiness, peace, if necessary one's good name in the world all for one grand purpose."[37] Seen from another angle, it is clear that after the disappointment of 1876, when the act she initiated to protect animals was transformed into a "vivisector's charter," Cobbe became increasingly fanatical; her common sense and intelligence, as well as her relationships, were compromised. Physiology had not become a university subject in England until the 1870s. The immediate practical results of physiological experimentation were admittedly slender. When Cobbe's first bill was debated in 1875, very few people—even in Parliament—knew about scientific medicine. Cobbe and the VSS made them aware of the pain suffered by friendly animals when experiments were done without anesthetics or when the anesthesia wore off and the animal was revived. In the first rush of publicity, when people initially learned about animal experimentation, it was reasonable to believe that it could be heavily restricted. But with each passing year the task grew more difficult instead of easier. (In fact, the 1876 law would remain unchanged for more than a century.) Cobbe began her campaign against vivisection in Britain just when physiological experiments began to pay useful dividends. Closing her eyes to that evidence, she became more and more bitter about her failure.

Claude Bernard, the archfiend in Cobbe's pantheon, died before his research had led to any important therapeutic results, but he had discovered that some drugs acted only on localized receptors, and he had learned a great deal about the body's internal secretions. On 18 February 1878 Louis Pasteur argued before the French Academy of Medicine that specific microorganisms caused specific diseases; he did research on chicken cholera and on anthrax, and by 1881 he had achieved stunning results with vaccination. While the evidence from experimental science accumulated and the first medical advances came into sight, the opposition became stronger and, to many modern minds at least, more wrongheaded. For example, Peter Taylor's *Letter to Dr. W. B. Carpenter, C.B.* apologized for approving of vaccination ten years previously. "Vaccination," wrote Taylor in 1881, "does not protect against small-pox . . . the inevitable disturbance to health by introducing an artificial disease is uncompensated by any advantage." Surely one difficulty was that science became unintelligible to the general public as it advanced. Yet—this is so easy with the benefits of hindsight—vaccination against smallpox was just then yielding its results. After thirty years of increasingly rigorous efforts the epidemic of 1870–73 proved to be the last widespread outbreak in the United Kingdom.

The intensity of Cobbe's obsession does not seem to have any simple explanation. In her childhood dogs were often her only playmates and closest friends, but the same is true for many other children who feel misunderstood. Her idol, Mary Somerville, supported and perhaps even suggested her 1863 petition protesting the research of Moritz Schiff in Florence. In England, however, even the medical journals criticized the cruel operations on horses that Cobbe described in "The Rights of Man and the Claims of Brutes" (1863). Although it is often suggested that women antivivisectionists were inspired by their fear and hatred of the medical profession, Cobbe's various explanations for distrusting doctors—her mother's invalidism, the mistreatment of her sprained ankle, doctors' tendency to overdose women patients—were, first, criticisms of old-fashioned, unscientific medical practice and, second, written after her opposition to vivisection had hardened.

In 1876, when medical pressure on the home secretary gutted what Cobbe had thought was a perfectly reasonable bill to protect animals without crippling scientific medicine, physiologists who actually conducted experiments wanted licensing to prevent nuisance prosecutions under the Cruelty to Animals Act and to regulate experimental facilities so the results would be acceptable science. Doctors, however, objected to any control except the self-regulation of their own licensing bodies as interfering with their rights as professionals. With virtually the same breath Cobbe could vilify doctors and hold them up as admirable models. Misunderstanding, whether deliberately or not, the relation between medical research and the eventual use of its findings, she argued that "not one out of a dozen of the great vivisectors of Europe is a practical physician or surgeon." She framed the experimental method as an antagonist to other modes of medical study. Prohibiting vivisection would "not retard the progress of Science or of the Healing Art, but . . . drive investigation into the true and legitimate roads to discovery, namely, clinical observation and microscopical research."[38] That formulation reflected the interests of her medical supporters. Frances and George Hoggan did physiological research by microscope; Luther Holden was a longtime lecturer in descriptive anatomy as studied through dissecting cadavers; Charles Bell Taylor, who had an international reputation for cataract operations, opposed compulsory vaccination as well as vivisection; and Robert Lawson Tait, a pioneering gynecological surgeon, published a paper in 1882 on the uselessness of vivisecting animals.

In April 1881 Cobbe's strongest attack on physicians to appear in a general periodical rather than in an antivivisection forum was published in the *Modern Review.* At Cobbe's request, "The Medical Profession and Its Morality" was published anonymously, even though most *Modern Review* articles are signed and Cobbe had from the beginning of her career been particularly vigilant about insisting that her name appear. Despite a few disclaimers about hardworking country practitioners, she accused physicians in general of taking up medicine because the preparation was relatively cheap and the "pecuniary prizes" enormous. Doctors could buy poisons and commit [sexual] offenses "on narcotised victims." They were materialists and therefore agnostics, if not atheists. Returning again and again to the money question, she asserted that a doctor might perform unnecessary amputations "for the sake of either his skill or his fee." "Does the mad-doctor of the private asylum, who makes £200 or £300 a year by a wealthy patient," she asked, "really lay himself out, with all his skill, to heal the poor bewildered brain?" Doc-

tors exercised "tacit trades-unionism" in referrals; they made vast profits from
compulsory vaccination; and they had perverted science to discover that
"mental labour is peculiarly injurious to the weaker sex." Their efforts to exclude women from medical practice and their enforcement of the Contagious Diseases Acts made physicians "doubly treacherous to women." And
finally, their interference in acts of Parliament "holds out a serious threat to
the personal liberties of all the lay members of the community."[39]

The essay inevitably aroused a storm of controversy, especially because
of its assertions about grubby monetary motives in a profession only then
becoming acceptable for gentlemen. Shaftesbury wrote that it was bold,
clear, and "in many points incontrovertible," but he found some statements
too melodramatic. The July issue of the *Modern Review* carried a response
by William Carpenter, who had clearly identified the author. Trained in
medicine, although he no longer practiced, Carpenter scoffed at her denial
of the germ theory, pointed out the absurdity of expecting doctors to find
cures without experiment and trial, lambasted her ignorance of scientific
methodology, and reminded Cobbe that he had "advocated and promoted
the admission of women" to medical study, women, that is, "of *asexual* temperament—in whom the intellect (as in Men) dominates the judgment."[40]
Carpenter's attack on the intelligence of someone who had been an intellectual collaborator only a few years earlier was direct, brutal, and surely
wounding, and it demonstrates how far Cobbe had gone beyond the possibility of any civil or persuasive dialogue with the advocates of experimental
medicine.

The first issue of the VSS monthly magazine *Zoophilist* came out on 2
May 1881. It was funded by a gift of thirteen hundred pounds from Madame
Van Manen-Thesing, the wife of Dr. Juris Manen, of the Hague. Already
suffering from the cancer that killed her a year later, she wanted to pass the
money to the VSS while she could.[41] Cobbe made a quick trip to the Hague
in mid-May to receive the money from Madame Van Manen-Thesing. With
the new funds available and the extra work of editing the *Zoophilist,* Charles
Adams's salary was raised to £250 per year. Published monthly at a price of
sixpence, the paper generally ran to sixteen pages in roughly tabloid size. It
had essays on animal questions, book reviews, reports of VSS meetings and
speeches, reprints of letters to other periodicals, and advertisements for books
by Cobbe and other members. The constant circulation, recirculation,
reprinting, and publication of letters and articles from elsewhere in the *Zoophilist* and from the *Zoophilist* as pamphlets makes accurate dating and bib-
liographic control of antivivisection writing virtually impossible, but after
the exchange in the *Modern Review* it might fairly be said that positions were

generally fixed, and arguments on all sides were fatally infected by distrust, hyperbole, and melodramatic emotion.

On 26 May, barely a week after returning from the Hague, Cobbe spoke at a suffrage meeting attended by Millicent Fawcett, her sister Elizabeth Garrett Anderson, Lydia Becker from Manchester, and Florence, viscountess Harberton, who was president and cofounder of the new Rational Dress Society. (Soon afterwards Cobbe wrote a leader on rational dress for the *Standard*.) Since the meeting was "almost exclusively of friends," Cobbe suggested they consider how to win the support of women from the influential classes and offered a nineteenth-century version of "I'm not a feminist, but . . .": a lady friend, she said, "had not the slightest interest in the women's suffrage movement, in fact she disapproved of it altogether; 'only she wanted to be secured against' this, that, and the other injustice which she had learned . . . might befall her under the existing law."[42]

The American suffragist Mary Livermore made a "flying visit to England" in mid-June. Intentionally using Cobbe's phrase at Lydia Becker's request, she delivered a lecture "The Duties of Women in Regard to the Life of a Nation" at St. George's Hall, Langham Place. Cobbe followed with, in Livermore's words, "a speech of nearly half an hour, full of force and fire, and glittering with the satire which she knows how to use upon illogical opponents." On 25 June Livermore attended the VSS annual meeting, held this time at the house of Lord Chief Justice Coleridge. She was especially impressed that Cardinal Manning "deferred most respectfully to Miss Cobbe whenever she spoke, and in one or two instances when she uttered most pronounced opinions, he assented instantly and heartily, without waiting for the endorsement of others." Yet it was perhaps the accumulating frustration in both causes—suffrage and antivivisection—that made Cobbe recur to the dream that predated both. She told Mary Livermore "with tears in her eyes . . . how much she regretted that there was no pulpit open to her, from which she could utter her highest and holiest thoughts."[43]

Cobbe was so busy that Violet Paget, who came to England on 16 June, waited impatiently to see her. At last she was invited to an afternoon party on 4 July. She wrote to her mother: "Miss Cobbe, who is grown still more enormous, was extremely friendly, but as a good lot of people came in, I had no opportunity whatever for conversation with her. The company was of the rather heavy intellectual sort—eminent lawyers, parsons—that sort of thing; also one or two swells with powdered footmen. . . . Also the little odious Jew Haweis of *Music and Morals* whom I particularly declined knowing; and Lewis Morris—the 'Wrong Morris' as we call him. He is the most utterly repulsive huge brute I ever beheld." Cobbe and Lloyd gave the party so their guests could witness a performance by a "young man named Bishop," who, according to Violet Paget, was "quite a scientific curiosity as a sort of clairvoyant. He repudiates all ideas of spiritualism, and has been seriously taken up by many men of science, specially Dr. Carpenter. He is a strange, flabby, white degraded nerveless looking being, a gentleman & to all appearance no impostor."[44] The demonstration was "thought reading": someone would hide an object and keep his mind on where it was hidden, and Bishop, blindfolded, would find it.

Also in attendance were John Hoare, Bernard Coleridge, and Leslie Stephen. Since Cobbe so often observed the polite convention of not publishing women's names, it may seem that she entertained only political and literary men, yet surely the guests included other friends and neighbors, women such as Jane Hampson, Rose and Florence Davenport Hill, Maggie Elliot, Mary Joy Haweis (as well as her husband), Maria Grey, Alice Probyn, Anne Thackeray Ritchie, Frances Hoggan, Cobbe's cousins Sophy and Eliza (who now lived very near, in a small house just beyond the Gloucester Road underground station), and Caroline Stephen (Leslie's sister). The "swells with powdered footmen" may have been women such as Constance Flower, her mother, Louisa de Rothschild (who was very nearly the same age as Cobbe), or Florence Harberton. Matthew Arnold was invited; Robert Browning was sorry he could not come, since he thought "Mr. Bishop's performance must be instructive to those who need it, and amusing to everybody." Browning, of course, had not approved of his wife's engagement with spiritualism, and Cobbe's own skepticism is revealed in her comment that people were "unanimous in applauding his art, of whatever nature it may have been." John Hoare was very much impressed, but the *Standard*'s editor "detected trickery."[45]

Early in July, perhaps in the backwash of responses to "The Medical Profession and Its Morality," the *Standard* had a short column praising doctors' self-sacrifice and objecting to the antivivisectionist outcry. Cobbe pasted the column in her scrapbook with a note "July 8—resigned in consequence of this." Her memory, however, was inaccurate. After an exchange of letters with Mudford, who explained that he also detested "wanton cruelty" but thought slaughterhouses caused much more suffering than physiological laboratories,[46] she continued working for the *Standard* for another six months.

July of 1881 was as crowded as the previous two months had been. On the twelfth Cobbe spoke at a drawing-room meeting in Brompton Square. The next day, a Wednesday, she lunched with Constance Flower, who wrote in her diary about her "happy afternoon" with "Cobby." Violet Paget was still trying to schedule a private visit, but both were too busy to find a time.[47] On the eighteenth Arthur Penrhyn Stanley, dean of Westminster, died. A valued acquaintance for at least fifteen years, he had willingly accepted Cobbe's invitation to become a VSS vice president. The society's executive met on Wednesday the twentieth; on the twenty-first Cobbe went to spend a long weekend with one of her brothers. Finally, on 28 July she had lunch with Violet Paget. On 6 August she was in Edinburgh, giving a speech for the Scottish Society for the Total Suppression of Vivisection.[48] Then, after an extremely hectic seven months of moving, travel, politics, and projects old and new, she joined Mary Lloyd in Wales.

By November Cobbe was back at Hereford Square. People who lived in London, she had written, found that the "most agreeable Society is to be enjoyed in the brief dark days before Christmas. Then the more intimate gatherings, the informal dinners, take place. . . . There is a bountiful supply of new books, and even politics are a little less bitter and full of dregs than at the hot close of the Session."[49] Dining at the Stansfelds on Monday, 28 November, she made a bet with her host about which of them was oldest. She was then a week away from her fifty-ninth birthday. When she learned that he was already sixty-one, she promptly paid up with a pair of gray gloves so elegant that his wife, a fellow member of the Ladies' London Emancipation Society almost twenty years earlier, as well as a suffrage activist, joked that Cobbe must have a wide acquaintance "among the dandies of London to have known where to get such a pair."[50]

Trying to use the 1876 animal-protection act for some good purpose, the VSS had filed charges against David Ferrier over a demonstration of cerebral location in monkeys at an International Medical Congress held in London during August. Ferrier, a professor of forensic medicine at King's College, did not have a license for experimentation. The trial at the Bow Street police court turned into something of a farce. The *Times* reported that "several ladies, among whom [was] Miss Frances Cobbe," appeared in court, and "a large crowd of medical students" was kept outside by the police because of their "howling and cheering" in the streets. But the VSS had no eyewitness evidence; its case was based on published accounts. Eminent medical men who were present claimed that the experiments had been conducted by Gerald Yeo, who did hold a license, and that Ferrier had merely interpreted their significance on the basis of work he had done prior to 1876. The case collapsed amid howls of laughter from the professors of science and medicine who jammed the courtroom.[51]

The last months of 1881 were punctuated by constant letters from Shaftesbury about introducing another abolition bill, entering a coalition with other antivivisection societies, and further VSS business. They needed "men of real knowledge, forensic ability, and high reputation" to translate scientific evidence for judges and the public. "Unfortunately," he wrote, "it often happens that those who are wise cannot speak; & those who can speak are not wise." After the Ferrier fiasco, Shaftesbury was again checking the materials Cobbe produced. By the end of the year he was deeply discouraged. It was humbling "to look back on the past & see, after all, how little has been done!" he wrote. "The Scientific World is in an execrable state. The Political is one still more so. The Religious is the worst of all. God help us."[52]

Stormy conflicts carried over into 1882. Some physiologists used a tone as feverish as Cobbe's. Richard Owen's *Experimental Physiology: Its Benefits to Mankind* called Cobbe the "pen-woman of the 'Bestiarian Society'"; described her medical ignorance, while quoting a great deal of Latin; and pictured her at the seaside enjoying "fellow creatures" (such as shrimps and lobsters) that had been "boiled to death." Charles Adams answered with equally crude *ad hominem* arguments in *The Coward Science: Our Answer to Professor Owen*, which asked whether Dr. Owen knew "anything at all of the position Miss Cobbe holds in the world of Intellect and Thought." On 9 March 1882 the science periodical *Nature* summarized the "twelve or fourteen" arguments published during the past few months from its own perspective and found that "the advantage inclines largely to the side of the physiologists." Cobbe had squandered her intellectual credibility by claiming that nothing useful had been discovered through animal experimentation. The "*utility* of Vivisection," *Nature* proclaimed, was disputed only by women whose essays were "so extravagant and ill-advised that even an ignorant reader must feel their judgment upon this head to be valueless." *Nature* had some respect for men like Coleridge and Hutton, who recognized the benefits derived from animal research but nevertheless opposed it on purely moral grounds. But even in "Zoophily," a *Cornhill* essay about kindness to animals, Cobbe could not resist a footnote hurling accusations at William Carpenter.[53]

Far more amusing was a little attempt by Harry Hamilton Johnston, later an explorer and diplomat but at the time a very young man engaged in making sketches at the Zoological Gardens, to trivialize Cobbe through her gender. When she visited a "distinguished man of science," he wrote, she had "an ostrich feather in her bonnet; a bird of paradise in, on, or near her muff; and she carried an ivory-handled umbrella." Counting on roars of laughter from people who knew how badly she dressed, Cobbe had a fine opportunity to reply:

> Sir, these "facts" may possibly be *"accurate enough for scientific purposes"* . . . but they have given much merriment to those who happen to be acquainted with my real "outward presentments." Suffice it to say, that I . . .

never used an ivory-handled umbrella; never wore a bird of paradise, or any other bird, either in *or near* my muff, or any other portion of my attire; and, finally, having never possessed such an object in my whole life, am driven to think that the only Muff connected with the ridiculous story, must be the person who assures us he "knows" it to be true.[54]

But that was a small light moment in a difficult winter. Alfred Tennyson, a loyal supporter, found one of Cobbe's essays "too vehement to serve your purpose." Shaftesbury warned her that "we must be more than usually careful." In the *Standard* she began objecting not only to physiology but to all science teaching: "Among all the thousands of youths who are now learning chemistry in our new Schools of Science, can we venture to feel certain that there are none who will be stimulated either to concoct or to procure and employ the poisons of which they read?" Shaftesbury stopped her plan to have posters carried around near churches on Sundays, both because of the "censure" for Sabbath-breaking and because of the "terror and disgust" aroused by the illustrations.[55] Worried that she would involve the committee in serious difficulty, he urged her more than once to be careful with names and make sure that her facts were accurate.[56]

Shaftesbury's final letter in the previous year had mentioned a new friend of the cause, a "female M.D. of Paris!" Cobbe had known of Anna Kingsford for almost ten years. In 1872, before beginning to study medicine, Kingsford had briefly edited the *Lady's Own Paper* and appealed for correspondence on vivisection. Cobbe had sent her a piece by an American physician, along with a short letter that Kingsford had advertised as an article by "Miss F. P. Cobbe."[57] After returning to London, according to her friend and biographer Edward Maitland, Kingsford had "a strong desire to influence the leaders of her own sex" and asked Cobbe to nominate her for "the first woman's club, then recently founded, and called the S." Since Cobbe had "up to quite recently . . . corresponded with her in terms of unreserved affection and respect," Kingsford's "amazement was therefore as great as her distress was keen when she received for answer an abrupt refusal to act in any way as her sponsor in London."[58]

Anna Kingsford was at this point a married woman who lived, not with her husband and child, but "under the same roof" as her unmarried male friend. Even if her husband wholly approved, as she claimed, the Somerville club could not have accepted her membership. The first middle-class women's club in London had to avoid any appearance of impropriety; its qualifications were "two only: personal respectability, and interest in social and political questions." Kingsford thought that Cobbe needed her scientific knowledge and may have expected introductions to build a medical practice, but the far more experienced Frances Hoggan, a Zurich M.D. already licensed in Britain, was not only Cobbe's personal physician but also a published physiologist. Given the political realities and Cobbe's effort to cultivate people of high status, and the influence that went with it, for antivivisection work, it is hard to imagine anyone less suited than Anna Kingsford to enter leadership in London under Cobbe's sponsorship. Although she was married to a Church of England clergyman, by 1882 Kingsford was a Roman Catholic convert dedicated to spiritualism and dabbling in various occult arts. In 1883 she would become president of the Theosophical Society. Maitland, however, believed that Cobbe was "capable of indulging any amount of jealousy of one whose endowments bid fair to make her a formidable rival in the cause" and that she actively worked to discredit Kingsford.[59] Wherever the truth may lie—Maitland's overwrought advocate's biography does not inspire trust—the account must take its place in the bizarre sensitivity that infected many players on both sides of this cause.

A mismanaged public conflict in March again showed Cobbe's stubborn unwillingness to compromise. When the Battersea Home for Lost and Starving Dogs held its annual general meeting, Cobbe objected to the reelection of George Fleming as a member of the governing committee. An army veterinarian since the Crimea, Fleming was a leader in the profession. Less than four years earlier Cobbe had urged him to become superintendent of the Brown (veterinary) Institution in London so that no experimental physiologist would get the post.[60] Cobbe had asked him privately to withdraw from the governing committee of the dog's home. After the private effort failed, she delivered a long, vituperative public criticism during a meeting at which both Fleming and his wife were present.

Fleming rose to defend himself. It would seem, he said, "that you prefer to perpetuate the dreadful scourge of rabies to the performance of a few comparatively painless experiments made to prevent it." He did not approve of "vivisection in its proper sense," only of pathological investigations that did not involve "cutting operations" but rather "almost painless" procedures. "Ought we not all to be in favor," he asked "of reducing disease in those creatures which must remain defenceless against contagion if we do not protect them from it?" After several more impassioned speeches, a vote was taken by secret ballot. Cobbe was thoroughly defeated and promptly resigned from the board. So did Mary Lloyd, who had mortgaged her house to raise money for the home's new kennels. Perhaps in an effort to exercise some damage control, the *Zoophilist* reported only that several board members had resigned but did not provide details.[61]

On Saturday, 29 April 1882, Cobbe had an invitation from Louisa Egerton, whose husband, Francis, was a Liberal MP. "Mr. & Mrs. Gladstone," she wrote, were coming for Easter weekend "to get a little peace & quiet—but I happen to know that he wd like very much to meet you." (The word *meet* in nineteenth-century invitations meant "get together with" rather than "become acquainted for the first time.") Despite her caustic editorials in the *Echo* and her anger at the 1870 intervention overturning the Commons victory for women's suffrage, Cobbe still hoped that Gladstone would let the VSS publicize his dislike of vivisection. He promised help, she wrote after his death, "four times in conversation and once on one of his famous postcards," but in this as in many other causes, "when the moment for affording . . . practical & *promised* support came, he has invariably & utterly thrown them over" because of his "thirst for popularity."[62]

Soon afterwards, two deaths dramatically reshaped Cobbe's family. On 13 May her brother Tom, who was sixty-eight, suddenly "fell down dead off his chair while actually speaking cheerfully of some indifferent matter." His daughter Frances then joined her sister Helen in Biarritz, where "they had no friends and much cruel difficulty with landlords,"[63] while Jessie slowly died of tuberculosis. On 25 May Tom's first grandchild, Janet Corinne Cobbe, was born in the United States, where Leuric had remained with his American wife. And then on 2 June, barely three weeks after Tom's death, Louisa, Cobbe's brother Charles's wife, also died.

In the aftermath of Louisa's death it became evident that Charles had already, or at any rate much too soon, turned his attentions to Charlotte Moore, daughter of a clergyman and a much younger woman. Although they waited the honorable year, but only just barely, before being married on 7 June 1883, when Charles was seventy-one and she was thirty-four, Cobbe knew about their relationship by late summer of 1882. Writing in October to thank Sarah Wister for her "warm sympathy," Cobbe said she had "never wholly realized before now when it comes to one very near to us exhibiting unlooked-for defects the calamity seems not merely disappointing but *sickening*—like the heave of an earthquake. Besides Mary Lloyd—(that *rock,* thank God!) the one person on whom I relied most was my eldest brother—& now I find that what I thought was *he*—was a pale reflex of his poor wife—& that now he is the reflexion of a creature whom I will not trust myself to describe."[64]

With the death of Tom, the brother with whom she had been emotionally most engaged, and with Charles's second marriage, which ended all visits to Ireland, Cobbe seemed more alone in the world. Her brother Will's distance from the family shows in his belated response to the news that Charles had remarried: "Doubtless in so large a house & place as Newbridge to live *alone* you must have found it very loansome—I had heard nothing from anyone, but in my own mind I had thought whether Fanny would not have gone over to live with you to make you comfortable, but I suppose she was unwilling to give up her town life & her own personal friends to do so."[65] Although the 1851 census had counted sixty-five people living at the Agapemone, by 1881 there were half as many: three men in their sixties (including Will), fourteen women "members of the household," and fourteen servants.

Cobbe did become close to her nieces as they grew into womanhood. Henry's daughter Winifred left Lady Margaret Hall in 1882 after her three years in residence. Like her father, she failed the examination on her first try—the principal reported that Miss Cobbe had been "unfortunately rather out of health"—but succeeded in June 1883, with passes in French, German, and modern history.[66] Although modern languages were not yet examination subjects for men, her work was equivalent to what would, in time, become an Oxford degree. Meanwhile, her sister Amy had entered Lady Margaret Hall early in 1883.

On 8 June 1882 the final version of the Married Women's Property Act, the version with provisions activists had wanted from the beginning, had its second reading in the House of Commons. There was no real debate; it passed without division. When it came into force the following January, everything a woman owned, acquired, inherited, or earned before or during marriage became and remained her own separate property. The twenty-five-year legislative process—beginning with the 1857 bill that was pushed aside by divorce legislation, revived by a women's petition in 1867, publicized through Cobbe's "Criminals, Idiots, Women, and Minors" in 1868, passed in narrowly limited form in 1870, and revised after several further attempts into what Mary Lydon Shanley has called "arguably the single most important change in the legal status of women in the nineteenth century"[67]— might have seemed a reasonable long-term model for both suffrage and animal protection: once a small achievement brought a new principle into the legal universe, further publicity and gradual extension might lead to ultimate success. In addition, the 1882 act would make a substantial number of married women eligible to vote unless they were explicitly excluded in any bill that erased disqualification by gender. It was a significant advance, and it would create difficult new complications for suffragists.

On 21 June 1882 the VSS met at Shaftesbury's town house. Cobbe, as usual, was the only woman to speak. She was followed by Robert Lawson Tait, the pioneering gynecological surgeon. As recently as 1 December 1881 an unsigned editorial in the *Zoophilist* had fulminated against ovariotomy as useless and dangerous to women, yet Cobbe's relationship with Tait, an enormous bear of a man who had performed a great many of them, was friendly and even teasing. He seconded her motion with "fear and trembling concerning the dreadful threat uttered by Miss Cobbe" about suppressing his profession.[68] Another speaker was Edward Berdoe, an authority on Robert Browning as well as a physician with an East End practice and a writer of antivivisection fiction. Cobbe was also helping a much more significant novelist, Wilkie Collins, then at work on *Heart and Science*. He thanked her on 23 June for the letter and pamphlets that had given him "exactly what I most wanted for the purpose I have in view." He would have to "keep clear of terrifying and revolting the ordinary reader," so he would be careful to show the vivisector "as a man *not* infinitely wicked and cruel" but unable to "resist the inevitable hardening of the heart, the fatal stupefying of all the finer sensibilities" produced by the "merciless occupations of his life."[69]

Cobbe's own writing and speaking continued to be fueled by religion, politics, and social causes, as well as the antivivisection campaign. She had an article on the Salvation Army in the *Contemporary Review* in August and one entitled "Progressive Judaism" in November. The latter, she said, was received "with the utmost possible disfavour by the Jewish press." Her thoughts were inspired by conversations with Constance Flower and by "the proposed massive reformation & denationalization of the Jews" recently described by Claude Montefiore. Cobbe still believed, as she had in *Intuitive Morals,* that a universal nondoctrinal theism would emerge from progress in all religions, but she often read other people's work through the lens of her own preconceptions. Montefiore informed Cobbe that his dislike of intermarriage was not based on "race" or national pride. Rather, he wanted "to preserve Judaism": in an overwhelmingly Christian country the children of mixed marriages would be brought up as Christians, and "Judaism will surely diminish away."[70]

During the summer Cobbe presided at the annual meeting of the Women's Protective and Provident League.[71] Although she was never active in its work, she approved of the league's goals and willingly offered her name and speaking ability to draw attendance at its meeting. On 2 November she did the same for a very large event to support Florence Fenwick Miller's successful campaign for reelection to the London School Board.

By the next day, however, the VSS was embroiled in a public scandal with consequences for Cobbe personally as well as for the organization. It began when Charles Warren Adams asked to be paid for his writing in the *Zoophilist* and Cobbe refused. Although the budget included twelve guineas per month for "literary contributions" to the periodical, she insisted that his own work was covered by his salary, which had been raised to £250 per year when he began editing the journal. It is no longer possible to tell what else may have been involved; the origins of the conflict might have included per-

sonal disagreements, sloppy bookkeeping, escalating temperamental differences, and a general breakdown of civility, honesty, and, in Cobbe's opinion at any rate, moral probity. On 4 November Shaftesbury wrote that he
had "no respect for the man" but "much anxiety" for the "welfare of our
society." Cobbe was soon "*demented* with worry—Secretary & clerk both
going—& giving me quite incredible trouble by their wickedness." On 26
November a notice was sent out to members: "Mr. Adams has ceased to be
the Secretary of the Victoria Street Society. Till further notice, all communications should be addressed, and all cheques be made payable, to the Honorary Secretary, Miss Frances Power Cobbe."[72]

At this point one would have suspected merely a commonplace fuss over
payments, but the complex melodrama that ultimately came to light involved both the society's affairs and some of its most prominent members.
John Duke Coleridge, great-nephew of the poet and a fourth cousin of the
novelist Charlotte Mary Yonge, was one of the few dependable activists
among the largely honorary VSS vice presidents. After an outstanding career
at the bar and in Parliament, in 1880 he had become Lord Chief Justice of
England. An American observer described him as a "most agreeable companion at a dinner table," pious, thrifty, a reader of novels, and a "great
scholar." He was enormously skilled at getting information from witnesses.
Questioning with an air of "childlike wonder," he would treat the witness
"as a kind of superior being who has at his or her disposal just the information to extricate him from an appalling difficulty."[73] At the time he was a
widower; two of his grown sons and his daughter, Mildred, were also active
in the VSS.

In November 1882 Lord Coleridge became aware that something was
going on between Charles Adams and Mildred Coleridge. One version has
it that Mildred told her father that she "had been falsely accused at the committee of the Victoria-street Society, by Miss Cobbe, of undue familiarity
with Mr. Adams." Adams, on the other hand, said that Cobbe "unhappily
proposed to introduce to Miss Coleridge the editor of the *Malthusian Review*."[74] Notorious for promoting birth control, the *Malthusian Review* was
edited by Charles Drysdale. Although I have discovered no direct evidence
of a connection, he may have written for the *Echo* during the same period
as Cobbe. He served as medical mentor to Florence Fenwick Miller, whose
reelection Cobbe was just then promoting; and his domestic partner was
another of the very early registered medical women, Alice Vickery. Possibly
both versions are true: Cobbe may have said that Charles Adams and Mildred Coleridge were spending too much time in his private office with the
door closed, and Adams may have declared that Cobbe herself was more
likely to put Mildred in moral danger. It must be remembered, however,

John Duke Coleridge (1820–1894), who was made first baron Coleridge. The caricature by Alfred Thompson was published in *Vanity Fair* on 30 April 1870.

that Adams was a widower of forty-nine, and Mildred, although a single woman living in her widowed father's house, was thirty-five. At that age Cobbe had gone adventuring across Lebanon with only a hired muleteer for company.

Lord Coleridge told Mildred that he had full confidence in her behavior but that her intimacy with Adams "had better be broken off." Then he wrote several letters. Shaftesbury replied that he had not been at the committee meeting and had heard differing stories about what took place. "I had entertained a hope that, after some words of excitement from Mr. Adams & Miss Cobbe, the matter had ended in a decided, but friendly, separation," he wrote, but he thought the disagreement was entirely over money. No one had told Shaftesbury anything about Mildred or mentioned the *Malthusian Review*.[75]

When he heard more of the story, Shaftesbury informed Cobbe that he was distressed by the "astounding & novel statements by yourself about Miss Coleridge" and that he had not heard "*from any one*, the slightest hint of the actual, or possible, relations between Miss C. and our own Paid Secretary." His diary has a long entry about the contretemps; unfortunately, most of it is illegible. Both Cobbe and Adams had "kept from my knowledge things that I ought to have known." Cobbe had been insufficiently careful; Adams was "self-seeking, ambitious, deceptive"; and the outcome might well be the ruin of "this Society—God forbid—much to the joy of the Pandemoniums of Science."[76]

On the twenty-fourth Shaftesbury advised her to get rid of Adams "as cautiously as we can" and complained in his diary of "follies," "dishonesty," and "bad judgments." Both sides had "left me in the dark. If he—they— each of them pretend to give me light their light only makes 'darkness visible.'" On 29 November he warned Cobbe that she was "not 'out of the woods'" and told her to "*lose no time* in having all your accounts examined & put in order, by an efficient & professional Accountant." Two days later, Adams informed Shaftesbury that he intended to sue for his money, and Shaftesbury, now sure that the matter would go to court, promptly advised Cobbe not to commit herself to anything by making any complaints in correspondence to anyone.[77]

Cobbe, however, had already written to Lord Coleridge denying that she had made "any such accusation as was supposed" and asking to speak with him. Very anxious about damage not only to the VSS but to the public reputation of the Lord Chief Justice and his daughter, Shaftesbury suggested to Cobbe that Adams was reserving "the Young Lady" as "his Dynamite for explosion" and urged that they come to some compromise over the money. Coleridge asked for a meeting with the VSS executive committee. Cobbe resisted; indeed, she said that Coleridge was a vice president, not a member of the executive, and thus had no right to be present at their meeting. Shaftesbury was aghast that she would even consider bringing up a tiny legalistic point in order to deny a request from the Lord Chief Justice and appalled at the language she had used in letters that might become public. Yet by early 1883 even Shaftesbury did not believe it was all smoke without fire. He wrote to Cobbe that "this 'Mildred' business is simply disgusting" and asked what on earth she could see in Adams: "What misery she will bring on her poor Father, and the Family!"[78]

In mid-November, just as this turmoil reached the boiling point, the American suffrage leader Elizabeth Cady Stanton invited Cobbe to her daughter's wedding. Cobbe would almost certainly have liked to go, not only because of the suffrage connections but because the clergyman was to be her dear friend William Henry Channing. "Unfortunately," she wrote to Stanton, her whole day was "bespoken" for the antivivisection society. Although Cobbe invited Stanton for tea the following week,[79] the backwash of emotion from this turbulent period may have helped damage their relations, which grew distinctly cool during the next decade. Matters were still so frantic that Cobbe could not arrange a dinner with Sarah Wister, who was visiting her mother, Fanny Kemble, on 4 December, which was Cobbe's sixtieth birthday. "If you really knew the whole story," she wrote to Wister, "you wd think a whole troop of imps from the Pit had got up to possess the people with whom I have had most to do." Cobbe was overwhelmed with "endless telegrams & letters" but hoped "to be emerging into calmer seas & my dear blessed Mary who has laboured & borne everything with & for me is beginning to be hopeful." "When *she* 'hopes,'" continued Cobbe, "I ought to be quite confident—for Pandora's story is certainly reversed in her case. Every virtue was left in Mary's box *except* Hope!"[80]

Since 1883 began without a paid secretary, Cobbe took charge of the *Zoophilist*. Hoping to improve circulation, she reduced the price to threepence and tried to make it "more suitable for general reading" by keeping the "more painful features" in the background and adding anecdotes, poems, and fiction. She asked many friends, including Sarah Wister and Anne Thackeray Ritchie, to contribute, although only a few said yes. For two months Cobbe and Lloyd together "kept the office during all the regular hours" and between them "wrote, edited, folded, addressed and posted two issues of the *Zoophilist*."[81] By March the editorial duties belonged officially to Benjamin Bryan, a provincial journalist and former editor of the *Blackburn Standard*, who would remain the VSS secretary for a great many years, although Cobbe continued to supply much of the journal's contents.

With Parliament in session, Cobbe asked everyone she could think of to drum up support for the bill prohibiting all animal experiments, which had been introduced two years earlier. (Robert Browning's letter promising to write his MP is dated 3 March 1883.) The bill finally came to the House of Commons on 4 April, but after a very long debate—punctuated towards the end by "loud cries of 'Divide!'"—the hour for Wednesday's early rising arrived, and the bill expired without a vote.[82] Although Cobbe could not yet know it, no subsequent bill during her lifetime was even brought to debate.

On 7 March, however, a different proposal she had long backed was temporarily successful; the Cruelty to Animals Acts Amendments Bill, which covered pigeon shooting, passed its second reading by a large majority (195 in favor, 40 opposed). Shaftesbury had to explain that it would be futile for him to sponsor the bill in the House of Lords; it would have no chance unless it were managed by "a 'Sporting' Peer." It had been argued in the Commons that pigeon shooting in its recently popular form—in which pigeons were painfully mistreated so they would burst into the air when released to be fired at by waiting "sportsmen"—was as cruel as cockfighting; in other words, the pastimes of country laborers and the working classes had been outlawed, while rich men's sports were exempt. After the bill was crushed in the House of Lords, Shaftesbury warned another peer that the Commons vote reflected "the sentiments of a great bulk of the people, to mark their hatred of a sport considered as essentially 'Aristocratic.'"[83]

Success on another front, however, surprised even its advocates. On 20 April 1883 James Stansfeld's motion that "this House disapproves of the compulsory examination of women under the Contagious Diseases Acts" passed with a majority of seventy-two votes, and though it did not repeal the acts, it effectively suspended the most damaging clause.[84] Cobbe would have seen this success not only as a great victory for the poor and working-class women who had been victimized by doctors and the police but also as a defeat, at least on this one issue, for the medical establishment.

A French medical man who defended vivisection in the April 1883 issue of the *Contemporary Review* described its English opponents as "a few hypocritical humbugs and hysterical old maids." The stereotype of sexual repression and frenzied response remained current for generations; it was one reason why Cobbe tried mightily to discourage overheated emotionalism among supporters—"My life has been made a burden by 'screaming' partizans—of which not all are women!" she wrote at one point—though she was not always successful in controlling her own outbursts. Suffrage and antivivisection were sometimes uneasy partners. When Elizabeth Cady Stanton and her daughter visited the VSS office, Cobbe showed them a number of her more horrifying exhibits and asked, "Would you shake hands with a vivisectionist?" Harriot Stanton Blatch replied that she would gladly shake hands with the experimental physiologist who had not only admitted an American woman to his classes after other professors refused but also demanded that students treat her courteously. She asked if Cobbe would "refuse to shake hands with any of your statesmen, scientists, clergymen, lawyers, or physicians who treat women with constant indignities and insult?" In the version told by her mother in 1898, Cobbe said, "Oh, no!" and Harriot replied that she must then "estimate the physical sufferings of cats and dogs as of more consequence than the humiliation of human beings," although in another version Cobbe replied, after a hesitation, "Perhaps not" instead of "Oh, no!"[85]

Susan B. Anthony joined Stanton in England during the summer. On 25 June both of them spoke during an afternoon suffrage meeting at which Jacob Bright was in the chair. Three days later Ursula Bright gave a big reception, and on the thirtieth Cobbe entertained them at a more intimate event at Hereford Square. Violet Paget, who was not involved in suffrage activism, wrote to her mother from Kensington on the same day that she was "considerably disgusted with London. Even here, which is many degrees better than Bloomsbury, it is unendurable, hot & squalid, with a pervading smell of wet brown paper and fishmongers." Despite the horrid weather, more that two thousand people attended a rally at St. James's Hall, in Piccadilly, on the evening of Thursday, 5 July, in support of a resolution to be offered the next day in the Commons by Hugh Mason, the proprietor of Oxford Mills in Ashton-under-Lyme and a recently elected MP, for "extending the Parliamentary Franchise to Women who possess the qualifications which entitle men to Vote."[86] With the Married Women's Property Act, that had come into effect at the beginning of the year, "women who possess the qualifications" would include married women who independently owned land or other property, although under a system of "household franchise" they would not be eligible on the basis of a home shared with a husband. (Adult sons living in their father's house were still unable to vote unless they qualified through some other property or by a university franchise.)

The tactic of offering a resolution instead of a bill, perhaps inspired by Stansfeld's success with the Contagious Diseases Acts, was meant to shape legislation that had not yet been proposed. Sixteen years after the previous reform bill, the government again planned to extend voting rights to additional categories of men. Women, who had seen so many bills defeated in the 1870s, regathered their energies to press their case. Mason had already sent Gladstone a memorial signed by 108 Liberal MPs that held at least an implied threat not to support Gladstone's proposal unless it included women.[87]

The hot and badly ventilated ladies' gallery of the House of Commons was "densely crowded" on the night of 6 July, and many suffragists stayed until the bitter end at 1:30 A.M. And bitter it was: at the beginning of his introduction Mason carefully specified "women ratepayers who are spinsters and widows" as the objects of his motion. "I have not the slightest sympathy," he continued, "with those who advocate the conferring of this vote upon married women." (Jacob Bright spoke in support but told the Commons he regretted Mason's restriction.) The motion was rejected, although only by sixteen votes, and given the late hour, an impressive number of MPs remained for the division. When suffragists met the next day, even the "most timid," in the words of Susan B. Anthony, despised the way Mason had sold them down the river, though they could not help feeling a little optimistic about the narrow margin of difference.[88]

At midmonth Cobbe went back to Wales. Mary Lloyd, again interested

in prehistoric populations, corresponded with the anthropologist and physician John Beddoe, of Bristol, who was then at work on *The Races of Britain*
(1885). Lloyd was also studying economics. Both she and Cobbe admired
Henry Fawcett's article on state socialism in *Macmillan's* for July. Later
in the month Frank Newman came to visit. Now almost eighty, he still
worked for women's suffrage and temperance and against both vivisection
and vaccination.[89]

A few days before her essay "Agnostic Morality" came out in June's *Contemporary Review* Cobbe wrote to complain about the "outrageous mistakes"
she had found when reading proof. Anyone who has struggled with her
handwriting may well have a certain sympathy for the poor compositor, even
though he substituted (her list) "ariel" for "arid," "loving panorama" for
"long panorama," "nature" for "virtue," and "choir *miserable* (!!!)" for "choir
invisible."[90] "Agnostic Morality" responded to Vernon Lee's "Responsibilities of Unbelief" in the same periodical for May. "The 'Vernon Lee' whom
I have answered," wrote Cobbe to Sarah Wister, "is a *young* woman Violet
Paget, whom I have known for many years & who I expect will take rank
ere long as among the ablest of women. . . . Alas she has written to me in
acknowledgment of this article a letter full of that very 'blatant atheism' from
which I had exonerated her." Although Gladstone read Cobbe's article on
Sunday, 3 June, and a letter from Charles Barnes Upton shows that it was
taken quite seriously by philosophers of the Unitarian persuasion, Cobbe
was struggling with an intellectual world that had moved well beyond the
theism that was dangerously advanced when she published *Intuitive Morals*
almost thirty years earlier.[91]

To return to the melodrama that began in the VSS offices in 1882, although Mildred Coleridge had agreed not to see Charles Adams again and
not to correspond with him until Easter, it was no later than February when,
if Adams is to be believed, she took the initiative to start exchanging letters.
After Easter—it was 25 March that year—they began to meet, with the com-
plicity of her maternal aunt and two old family friends who were in London for the season. When Lord Coleridge found out, he asked Adams to see
him. Adams told Coleridge that Frances Power Cobbe was not only hysterical but also insanely jealous of his love for Mildred, and he spread the slander around. Coleridge wrote to Adams, in a letter that was subsequently read
in court, "You stated plainly that Miss Cobbe was actuated, among other
bad motives, by an unqualified passion for yourself." Further, Coleridge had
"heard the imputation from others, who, I think, must have heard it from
you."[92]

It is easy to imagine how furious and humiliated Cobbe must have been
if the rumors reached her in the summer of 1883. Coleridge told his daugh-

ter that "she had better drop her intercourse with Mr. Adams, or marry him at once." Adams had no means to support a wife, but he came up with a resourceful nod to social conventions. On 11 June he told Coleridge that he and Mildred were engaged but did not intend to marry; the nominal engagement, he proposed, would allow them to meet freely without interference.[93] Lord Coleridge's reply, written on 16 June 1883, was oddly evasive; perhaps he was trying to imagine some solution to the baffling hardheadedness of both Adams and his daughter. Adams refused to enter the Coleridge house again. According to Mildred, her father offered to ask Gladstone to find an appointment for Adams, but they declined; Mildred proposed to earn her own income by teaching. Aunts, cousins, and family friends stirred the troubled pot. On 17 July a Miss Blackford drew Lord Coleridge's sister— perhaps the sister who was married to the bishop of Oxford—into conversation about the situation and then went off and tattled to Mildred. (It is rather difficult to remember that the youngest person involved here was thirty-six and several of them were past sixty.) Lord Coleridge implored his sister "to abstain from any remarks whatever" about Adams to any one.[94]

In mid-August, Coleridge left for ten weeks in the United States on diplomatic business. Adams wrote a letter timed for reading on shipboard, when it was too late to respond. Even without parental permission, he wrote, "your daughter has 'engaged' herself to me." On 25 October Shaftesbury wrote to Cobbe asking, "Is this marriage between Miss C. and the jelly-fish gone off?" quite evidently expecting it to happen before her father came home. And meanwhile, just to add a further complication, Coleridge was, in Shaftesbury's words, "making a sad fool of himself."[95] While returning to England on the White Star Line's *Britannic,* the sixty-three-year-old widower had met and been charmed by a woman less than half his age, Amy Augusta Jackson Lawford, whose father was Henry Baring Lawford of the Bengal civil service.

In October Charles Adams gave notice that he intended to file suit against "Adlam, Cobbe, and Others" for the money they owed him. (Charles Adlam, founder of the International Association for Suppression of Vivisection, worked in close cooperation with the VSS, and his wife was on its committee.) William Henry Channing, then chair of the VSS executive, was in poor health but wrote on 30 October that if "our Society cannot now *honourably* settle this affair out of court," he would appear in the witness box. Channing thought Cobbe was the real target, not only because she had fired Adams but also because of her role in the Mildred Coleridge saga. "If when our late Secr learns, that he cannot compel you to become his 'victim' in a court crammed with your foes," Channing hoped, he might "decide to abandon his case."[96] Yet being named as a defendant in a court case, even a petty case over not very much money, could not help but be painful, regardless of the extent to which Cobbe had learned to ignore Victorian proprieties about coming before the public.

Meanwhile, the soap opera continued. No sooner was her father back home than Mildred asked to resume closer relations with Adams. Adams and Lord Coleridge met again on 12 November. The next day Coleridge offered to settle £300 a year on Mildred if—and it was a crucial if—after six months Adams had some means of support. Adams seems to have believed that Mildred's share of her father's estate should have produced a settlement of £17,000; at 5 percent interest the annual income would have come to £850. Mildred complained to the wives of her father's close friends and, even more audaciously, issued circulars offering to take pupils for instruction in music, thus implying that her father would no longer support her. On 20 November 1883 Lord Coleridge wrote once more to Adams: "I have had a long letter from Miss Cobbe and a long interview with Mr. Channing and with my daughter. . . . my daughter is my only daughter and she has no mother. I must see, therefore, that she is not unintentionally compromised by conduct even the most innocent. . . . Her intercourse with you has, I dare say quite inadvertently, assumed this character, and I must therefore request that for the present it shall cease. I write this with her knowledge and at her request."[97]

The case of *Adams v. Adlam, Cobbe, and Others* opened on 7 December. Adams claimed £158 11s. for *Zoophilist* articles; "literary contributions" were in the budget at a guinea per column, and his material, he said, filled 151 columns. It might have been possible to believe that Cobbe thought his extra £50 per year covered the additional writing, except that he produced a receipt for £32 for the work published between January and April of 1882. The case "came to an abrupt termination" without anyone from the VSS giving evidence. Their barrister conferred with Cobbe and the members of the executive who were in court and abandoned the claim that Adams's salary covered the *Zoophilist* articles, producing an inevitable verdict in favor of Adams. The judge commented: "How the committee failed to realize that the plaintiff was entitled to be paid for his literary work it is difficult to understand. . . . they must have overlooked the receipts . . . which have been put in evidence."[98]

After such a painful public rebuke, Cobbe wrote to Shaftesbury offering to pay the sum herself. To comfort her, Shaftesbury, who had not himself been in court, replied that the judge was probably a vivisectionist who "sought to do you an injury." The very next day, however, remembering Cobbe's tendencies, he hastily wrote again warning her not to publish any letters that would make accusations against the judge.[99] He was growing more and more concerned about her risky tactics. On 1 November the

*Zoophilist* started publishing *The Vivisectors' Directory*, a listing of names, addresses, and experiments, surely intended as a warning against using one of these physicians, if not an incitement to direct action. The next month it had a special halfpenny supplement headed, "Experiments on Hospital Patients by Licensed Vivisectors." Shaftesbury quickly vetoed Cobbe's proposal to "stand at the door of the Hospitals and thrust papers into the hands" of patients. His letter called the tactic "infra dig," in quotation marks, pointedly using public schoolboys' slang to emphasize gendered rules of social class that might be outside her ken.[100]

On Saturday 8 December, the same day that Adams won his lawsuit for £158 11s., Mildred Coleridge left her father's house. Her eldest brother, Bernard (who had represented the VSS in the Ferrier prosecution) wrote to warn her in strong terms, although largely in rhetorical questions, about "the character of the man to whom you are about to give yourself up."

> Do you know that he ran away with a girl who was under age? . . . Do you know of the life which he led that unhappy girl after she became his wife? . . . Do you know what sort of person his daughter is? . . . do you know that she has an irreconcilable temper, that she is boarded out of charity by her relatives to rescue her from her father? . . . Do you know that Mr. Adams has a violent temper?
>
> Can you disguise from yourself, in your vanity, that it is money and position, not you, which he is scheming to obtain? Are you ignorant that he has admitted that in his eyes you are devoid of personal attractions, that you would not make at all a good wife, and that you would be a "white Elephant" to him?[101]

There was a good deal more, and though it was a private letter from a man to his sister, one might have expected that a barrister of some years' standing would have enough sense not to send it. The following day, Mildred Coleridge answered with a demand that he retract everything or she would put the letter in Adams's hands. (She also pointed out that Bernard, as the eldest son, would profit if the money once promised to her remained in their father's estate.) He didn't, she did, and in the next year everyone had a chance to follow the entrancing court case involving a son and daughter of the Lord Chief Justice of England.

Early in 1884 Cobbe and Lloyd prepared to leave London. Though it is not certain when they decided to live year-round in Wales, they had vacated Hereford Square by 13 January. Cobbe stayed with Maggie Elliot in Onslow Gardens while Lloyd made repairs and alterations so her tenant would be happy, for she had rented the house to their old friend Fanny Kemble. Cobbe was still trying to get name contributors for the *Zoophilist*, but the cause grew more and more discouraging. Robert Louis Stevenson wrote that although he sympathized in many ways, he "would not willingly put sticks in the wheels of a man like Pasteur." On 5 February the University of Oxford convocation approved ten thousand pounds to build a physiological laboratory. Convinced that no new law could be passed until there had been a massive shift in public opinion, Cobbe worked on building local branches of the VSS. In mid-February she spoke in Torquay and Clifton. At Torquay she heard more gossip about Charles Adams and his first wife, who had been the daughter of a Devonshire clergyman, which she promptly spread, at least in private letters.[102]

In support of women's rights she wrote a letter for Susan B. Anthony to read at an American convention in early March. "Whether those who are as old as I am will live to enter the promised land," the letter concluded, "I cannot tell, nor do I very much care. The final and complete emancipation ere long is, I think, absolutely certain." But her introduction to Theodore Stanton's *The Woman Question in Europe* was realistically cynical about moral claims. "Noble and righteous as was the act by which the government of the United States extended the suffrage to the emancipated negroes," she pointed out, it would not have been done "had the lately freed slaves borne a much larger proportion to the whole white population of the Republic," and even the most radical Englishmen have not asked "for the admission of Hindoos to a share in the Legislative . . . government of India." She urged suffragists to recognize men's unspoken fear of being outnumbered and to concentrate on arguments emphasizing that "the enfranchisement of women will tend to the stability and prosperity of the State."[103]

In England the new Representation of the People Bill, now generally known to history as the 1885 Reform Act, moved very slowly through Parliament. A letter sent to all MPs urging that "the claim of duly qualified women for admission within the pale of the constitution is fully as pressing as that of the agricultural labourer" was signed by seventy women with well-known names, including Cobbe. Millicent Fawcett and several other women who were married to Liberal MPs asked Gladstone to meet with them. The ominous reply came from a secretary, who reported that Gladstone believed (the word actually used by the secretary was *fear*) that "any attempt to enlarge by material changes the provisions of the Franchise Bill, now before Parliament, might endanger the whole measure."[104]

Suffragists concentrated their efforts on women with influential husbands. An interesting account of a meeting on 1 April appeared in a syndicated "Lady's Letter" carried by provincial newspapers:

Mrs. Frank Morrison gave a highly-successful "At Home" the other day, at the South Kensington Hotel. . . . There was quite a brilliant company assembled. I noticed Lady Harberton and Lady Wilde amongst the guests. The meeting was held in a charming room, with cream-coloured panels picked out with a narrow line of pale pink and pale blue. . . . Miss Cobbe was the first speaker, and delighted the audience very much. She commenced by poking a little good-natured fun at Miss Lonsdale's recent article on "Platform Women," in the *Nineteenth Century*. She said she felt a certain awkwardness in speaking after the severe things Miss Lonsdale had said of platform women. Miss Lonsdale had said that public speaking "rubbed the bloom off" women. "What a dreadful thing," said Miss Cobbe, "to appear without one's bloom!" (Here she looked round at her audience in that pleasant unaffected way she has, with a humorous expression that was irresistible.) . . . Miss Cobbe then took a graver tone, and spoke of the duty of public spirit, and of all it comprehended, of the good work which was being done in the world by such women as Miss Octavia Hill, and of the desire which every woman ought to feel to throw her weight into the scale in the direction of righteousness and goodness. Miss Cobbe was very much applauded on the conclusion of her speech, which, whilst decidedly enthusiastic, was also temperate in tone.[105]

The signature on this breathless account is "Zingara," one of the pseudonyms used by Lucie Cobbe, whose father was Charles Henry Cobbe (Uncle George's son). Then in her early thirties, Lucie had studied music in Paris (where she lived in the same lodging house as Florence Fenwick Miller) but now earned her living as a journalist.

In April, after that meeting, Cobbe and Lloyd moved to Wales, although Cobbe was nowhere near ready to "retire" from active life and was back in London before the Reform Bill's final reading. The formula she used was no doubt partly accurate: "For twenty years [Mary] lived in London to please me and now I live in Wales to please her." But in addition to Lloyd's longstanding dislike of the city and Cobbe's frustration with the setbacks and humiliations of antivivisection work, there were probably growing financial problems. Cobbe was doing much less paying journalism; London grew ever more expensive. Their Kensington neighbor Maria Grey moved to a cheaper house because her rates and taxes had more than tripled over the past twenty years. And Fanny Kemble, it turned out, was not the easiest of tenants. Cobbe thanked Sarah Wister for writing to her mother about the house: "I really think it had a great effect in aiding her to see her own little difficulties in a ludicrous light. . . . I hope & believe she loves Mary Lloyd

& is happy in her relations with her as her 'landlord', as she always calls her—, & I *know* Mary loves and admires her with all her heart."[106]

Since Kemble intended to spend the summer in Switzerland, she offered Cobbe the use of the house at Hereford Square during the political high season. The Commons scheduled its debate over adding a women's suffrage clause for 10 June. The government had already made its opposition clear with "strenuous efforts" to have the clause withdrawn. A group of seventy-seven Liberal MPs, including Henry Fawcett, petitioned to leave the question open, but toward the end of the debate Gladstone said he had no opinion on women's suffrage; after almost twenty years, he still thought "nothing hasty should be done." As for the current bill, "the cargo which the vessel carries is, in our opinion, a cargo as large as she can carry safely." Therefore, said the prime minister, he offered the women's suffrage clause "the strongest opposition in my power."[107]

After Tuesday's session the house adjourned debate on the Reform Bill until Thursday. On the intervening day, 11 June, Cobbe presided at a special meeting of the National Society for Women's Suffrage. After briefly noting their "cruel disappointment," she moved swiftly to the real business: what could be done in the face of Gladstone's opposition? Lydia Becker offered a resolution expressing "astonishment that Her Majesty's Government refuse to allow this amendment to be discussed on its merits"; she believed it was "an infringement of the privileges of a free Parliament and an aggression on the rights of the people."

The MPs at the meeting warned that Gladstone's speech would do severe damage, something the women already knew; some of the MPs present felt that they were "not at liberty" to vote as they wished. Millicent Fawcett generously expressed her gratitude for their frankness and said that members of the suffrage organization "must not on that account suspect their attachment to the principles they have always professed." But Cobbe, like Becker, was in no mood for conciliation: "I think I understand Mr. Blennerhassett to say that he considered it would be inexpedient for us to go on at this moment; but it seems to me that the principle of the expediency of women allowing themselves to be put aside into the corner has been pushed a great deal too far." She hoped that a number of Tories would vote for the clause and said that she "could not have much respect for Liberals who decline to go into the division lobby with Tories on a great moral question like this." Even in an assembly dominated by women connected to the Liberal Party, Cobbe's rabble-rousing peroration was greeted with shouts and applause.[108]

The next day, when Parliament went back to work on the Reform Bill, Cobbe spoke at a drawing-room meeting sponsored by Mrs. Coleridge Kennard at 39 Upper Grosvenor Street. Kennard was a Conservative MP; the meeting, intended especially for "ladies who were not accustomed to take an active part in public affairs," was designed to look for support among people not swayed by the power of a Liberal prime minister. "Mr. Gladstone," said Cobbe, "was incurring a tremendous responsibility in thrusting the course he had suggested upon his supporters. . . . this idolatrous worship of Mr. Gladstone must soon cease." He had not "been the friend of women," so perhaps they, as Conservatives, should be glad rather than "sorry that the Prime Minister had thrust aside this important subject."[109]

As the debate continued that evening in Parliament, James Stansfeld, both a Liberal MP and an old and faithful supporter of the cause, spoke sadly: the women's suffrage clause was doomed once the prime minister spoke "almost in menacing terms" even though nothing in his speech had explained why the Reform Bill would be in danger if it included women householders. Therefore, men like himself must either vote for the amendment and be accused of risking "a great measure of enfranchisement" or else "be false to their principles and false to those numerous women—it was useless to laugh, he was impervious to laughter—to those numerous women who had sacrificed so much in the cause."[110]

The laughter when Stansfeld spoke of "numerous women" supporting suffrage was not a good omen. Gladstone had raised the stakes very high. Cobbe wrote to a friend that "those who stood by their guns had a hard time of it. One of them told me that Sir W. Harcourt when he saw him going with the 'Ayes,' actually called to him three times by name to come back!— as if he were a boy & the Home Secretary a schoolmaster! (This fact however must not be *published* please)." The clause lost by 136 votes, by far the largest defeat to date. It was the only time Conservatives outnumbered Liberals among the prosuffrage votes. Among the 271 "nays" were 104 "pledged supporters of suffrage";[111] the courageous Liberals voting aye included Jacob Bright, Arthur Arnold, Cyril Flower (Constance de Rothschild's husband), James Stansfeld, and Peter Alfred Taylor. (Taylor, who was sixty-five, retired from Parliament very soon afterwards.) But even such dependable suffragists as A. J. Mundella voted against the clause, and poor Henry Fawcett, who was a member of Gladstone's government, left the House early so he did not have to vote.

After the clause was defeated Cobbe made one more try. Unlike the wives of Liberal MPs, she was quite willing to sink the whole Reform Bill if women were left out. Contacting the few other members of the National Society for Women's Suffrage who identified themselves as Tories, she sent a letter to Conservative Party local associations urging them to reintroduce the clause since "prudence . . . requires that an important class of educated and philanthropic persons should not be left out, or their claims postponed, when a large addition is likely to be made to the less educated portion of the electorate."[112] The suffrage association had another major public meeting on 17 June. Although Cobbe did not speak, she continued to work independently on her last-ditch effort, writing to Coleridge Kennard's wife: "Mr Kennard will do us infinite service if he can induce the Lords to insert our clause. It wd be worth something to checkmate Mr Gladstone in this way; for if the Bill *including the clause,* goes down to the House of Commons, he will find himself in a cleft stick! The grounds of his objection to it 'that it wd hinder the Bill'—will be turned into the best reason for accepting it— 'that it will facilitate the passing of the Bill.'"[113]

The big annual meeting of the VSS was scheduled for Thursday, 26 June, so Cobbe had to temporarily disentangle herself from suffrage to make arrangements, write to speakers, and prepare materials. She also told members of the executive committee that she had decided to retire as honorary secretary (she and Lloyd remained on the executive committee). R. H. Hutton wrote a characteristic letter expressing gratitude that she had put him "on some of the best work I have done for the country." He then told her yet again that in the matter of suffrage she was "going all wrong in wishing to put women on to the scene of battle. If you give them the vote, you must admit them into parliament; if you admit them into parliament you must admit them, when they show themselves qualified, into governments. And if you do that, you make a grave & to my mind most disastrous alteration in the ideal of the feminine character."[114]

At the annual meeting Shaftesbury gave the expected speech praising a departing officer. Cobbe responded that she was "long past the age when officers of the British Army are now required, whether they will or no, to retire, so you must think of me as an officer . . . on the Reserve List." She hoped to "strike some good sound blows yet on the brazen skull-caps of the vivisectors." Despite his anxiety about some of her decisions, Shaftesbury's regret was sincere. Describing the meeting in his diary for 27 June, he added: "Miss Cobbe will leave office as Hon: Sec:—The loss is irreparable."[115]

Within less than two weeks, in June 1884, women's suffragists experienced the final defeat of any real hope for achieving their goal during the nineteenth century, and Cobbe withdrew from day-to-day involvement with the antivivisection cause. Of course she was not done with either of them— far from it—but the nature of her life changed. And she was certainly happy to flee the capital. Violet Paget saw her just after the middle of month: "I asked her to fix a day for me to call, but she wrote to me saying she was obliged to leave at once for Wales."[116]

*All these years of contest with cruelty & vile hypocrisy have told heavily on me. . . . the amount & the character of the evil in Nature is such that if we were rationally to hold our faith in God's goodness we must plainly refuse to accept the testimony of Nature.*

FRANCES POWER COBBE TO SARAH WISTER, 8 AUGUST [1888]

Physically and emotionally exhausted when she left London in the summer of 1884, Cobbe "fell into a state of somnolence which lasted nearly 3 weeks—sleeping 10 hours a night & once or twice every day in my chair." She told Wister that she had resigned because the "quantity of work" was "beyond my power to bear—*plus* all the worry those wretched people gave me," and she was so worn out that she also wrote, "I feel I have done my life's work."[1]

Dolgelley and Llanelltyd, where Cobbe and Lloyd would spend the rest of their lives, were much closer to London in 1884 than before (or after) the Great Western Railway flourished. "You leave Paddington at 10 with tickets for Dolgelley," wrote Cobbe to a visitor, "& if you change at all (which is not always), it is but once at Ruabon." The train got to Dolgelley about six. Summer tourists of a romantic bent were entranced by the scenery of North Wales. Constance de Rothschild had gone years before with her family: "We arrived . . . yesterday, after a most beautiful drive through the most lovely country. . . . Dolgelly is a queer little Welsh town with its sturdy grey houses, its church & chapels its drab streets and its background of mountains." By 1884 *The Gossiping Guide to Wales* mentioned two first-class hotels, the Royal Ship and the Golden Lion, and an easy connection to the seaside town of Barmouth, which was also very popular with English tourists. The guide-book advertised a circulating library "in connection with Mudie," and Cobbe's letters show that monthly and quarterly journals could be had from the railway bookstall. Hengwrt stood just outside Dolgelley, in "the angle of the Y formed by the meeting of [two] rivers, on a gradually rising wooded slope."[2] The name Hengwrt is known to literary scholars because one of the best *Canterbury Tales* manuscripts, in the collection of the Welsh anti-

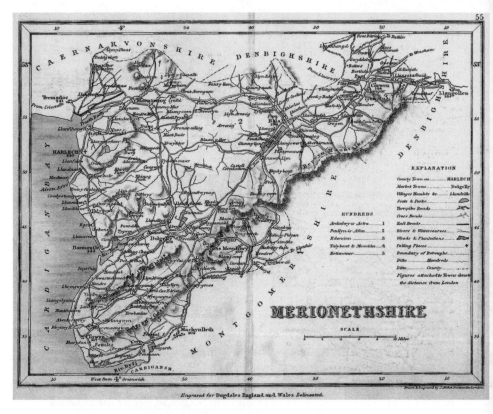

Engraved for Dugdales England and Wales Delineated.

Merionethshire in the nineteenth century. Following the road from Llangollen (at the right-hand edge of the map), one could pass through Corwen (home of Mary Lloyd's family), Bala (her nephew's estate, Rhiwlas, appears on the map), and then Dolgelly (near the head of the estuary stretching from the coast at Barmouth).

quarian Robert Vaughan, remained there until Mary Lloyd's brother-in-law Robert Williams Vaughan died in 1859.

Cobbe and Lloyd could not really afford to occupy the "grand old mansion," as Marianne Farningham called it, both because of the number of servants it required and because the life interest belonged jointly to Mary and two sisters, all of whom needed the income it provided. Harriet Lloyd had left the Clewer Community in 1873 but still lived as a "Sister of Mercy" in an East London refuge supported by its workers.[3] Jane's husband, the clergyman Henry Powell Ffoulkes, was almost seventy; she would be widowed within two years. Fortunately, tenants were easy to find during the summer and autumn. The house was conveniently located, perhaps half a mile from the railway station, with a view over open fields to Llanelltyd. Llanelltyd Bridge, at the foot of the hill, was said to be the best spot in North Wales for salmon fishing. In mid-August 1884 Hengwrt was rented for ten weeks at £210.[4] Cobbe and Lloyd went to Buxton, hoping the baths would help Lloyd's rheumatism. "The days when you saw her mounting that hill," Cobbe wrote, "& Dr Wister said he 'had heard of Welsh goats before but not of Welsh ladies'—those good days, are far behind us!"[5]

By that time Cobbe had recovered her energy and turned her mind to new schemes. She constructed two light essays for general magazines: "Girls' Schools in Past Times" (in *Time* for September 1884) was later incorporated in chapter 3 of her autobiography, and "A Glimpse of Wales a Hundred Years Ago" appeared in October's *Cornhill*. She wrote asking Stafford Northcote, then Conservative leader in the House of Commons, to raise the vivisection issue at party meetings. Because the House of Lords had rejected the Representation of the People Bill on 8 July, Parliament planned an unusual autumn session. Suffragists clung to a faint hope of still adding women. Northcote's reply about vivisection was not encouraging, but he accidentally provided an idea about suffrage that Cobbe picked up at once. He had said, in closing, "I wish Miss Muller had not made quite such a display. That is just the sort of thing which sets quiet conservatives against the movement."[6]

The incident he referred to was this: Henrietta Müller had announced that since she could not vote, she had refused to pay her taxes. On 28 June, when brokers seized furniture from her house, a "large party of friends" gathered outside. The strategy was not new with Müller—Charlotte Babb, an artist and member of the Central Committee for Women's Suffrage, had engaged in tax resistance since 1871—but Müller got enough publicity to disturb chivalric men. Seizing on Northcote's objection, Cobbe realized that an individual protest, which not many women could afford or risk, might be turned into a powerful political weapon. She proposed in the *Women's Suffrage Journal* that "we should next session promote a Bill for the *exemption from direct Taxation of the Property of Female Householders.*" As she wrote to Millicent Fawcett, "When we had got (as we easily could get) above a million women's signatures to this Petition—the alternative could be put pleasantly before Mr Gladstone!" And "when their Petitions for relief were rejected (as they wd be of course)," the injustice would be "brought home to tens of thousands of women . . . & we should have an immense influx of converts."[7]

Buxton turned out to be a "horrid place!"[8] The elegant Georgian crescent was overshadowed by new iron-and-glass promenades, Cobbe caught a cold that lingered for weeks, and the warm baths made Mary Lloyd weaker. "She walks a mile or two sometimes on the flat road," wrote Cobbe, "but always suffers for it." Her prickly independence, however, remained undiminished. "In writing to either of us," Cobbe begged, "do not say much of this. It pains her to talk of it." Lloyd especially hated not being able to do work outdoors. Cobbe dug and planted under her supervision to restore "a charming old Italian garden up far in the wood which must have been made many generations ago. . . . I have rebuilt the wall—, & cleared the dead trees & jungle, & planted a few more lovely shrubs & lots of violets & roses—& have made seats & walks & I am counting on a little paradise—out of which however I shall no doubt soon be thrown by seraphs (called tenants) with a flaming *purse.*"[9]

Both Cobbe and her brother Charles were rewriting their wills (as he would have had to do after his marriage). When he inquired about their mother's jewelry, she wrote a friendly but distant reply with an undertone of self-justification and closed without sending regards to Charlotte (Charles's new wife). This strikes me as distinctly rude, given the conventions of Victorian correspondence. Charles sold land to the Dublin waterworks for what became the Glenasmole reservoir and paid his sister four thousand pounds as the value of her patrimony, which freed his estate from the two-hundred-pound annual charge and also placed the capital under her own control. (He did continue to pay from his own income the additional one hundred pounds she had asked for fifteen years earlier.)[10]

For the next decade Cobbe's life was loosely structured by a few weeks in London in late spring, trips to Clifton, where her brother Tom's daughters were living, and visits to Dolgelley from old friends. Tom's widow Jessie, once the sister-in-law to whom Cobbe was closest, died in August 1884. Leuric had managed to bring Emma and their two very young children across the Atlantic just in time to see Jessie before she died. "I told you he had married in Iowa a farmer's daughter," wrote Cobbe, "and we were all rather in trepidation at meeting her but she proved so simple, so sensible—& warm hearted, that she has won us all. Nothing could ever make her a lady but she is a *fine human being* all the same!" Her attitude about class was not as simple as that sentence would suggest. Cobbe regretted the amount of time that American women such as Sarah Wister had to spend doing housework: "It seems to me that our form of civilization cannot survive a real democracy—There can be no Patrician life—with easy dignity—repose—& beautiful houses without a *Plebs* underneath it." Yet she realized that she lived "on the crumbling foundations of the old order—It is *possible* that there may be another civilization as fine or finer than ours erected in coming generations & on a broader platform."[11]

Mary Lloyd's nephew Richard John Lloyd Price and his wife Evelyn were less than twenty miles away, at Bala. The son of Charlotte Lloyd (the sister barely a year younger than Mary), R. J. Lloyd Price had inherited the Rhiwlas estate when his grandfather died in 1860. He was then seventeen years old. Educated at Eton and Christ Church, Lloyd Price owned sixty-four thousand acres and was not only an avid sportsman but also a savvy entrepreneur who developed subsidiary business ventures to provide income for himself and work for his tenants. He might have been an odd associate for his elderly aunt and her feminist companion had it not been for his enormous interest in dogs. In January 1876 he held forty-two dog licenses; he regularly sponsored sheepdog trials; the *Vanity Fair* cartoon of him (10 October 1885) is captioned "Pointers"; and his registered telegraph address was "Canis."[12]

Late in 1884 Cobbe saw a notice about the grave of an uncle she had never met, her mother's brother Thomas Conway, of the Madras Army, who had died of cholera in a remote Indian village nearly fifty years earlier. "Ever since," according to the *Times,* "his tomb has been carefully tended by the villagers," and General Roberts had recently expressed his thanks "for the respect shown to the last resting-place of a distinguished officer." Cobbe, in turn, thanked Roberts, then commander in chief in India, who replied that he was glad to have "afforded pleasure to a near relative of one whose name is a household word."[13] He was referring to Cobbe's cousin Alick, who had known Roberts since both were young captains and was just then on the point of retiring as General Alexander Hugh Cobbe, CB.

Meanwhile, the Adams-Coleridge saga got into the courtroom—and the newspapers. Although Charles Adams and Mildred Coleridge had agreed in October 1883 that they were really engaged, no marriage took place. There were rumors that Lord Coleridge had mistreated his daughter; in November 1884 Stephen Coleridge toured the United States and gave newspaper interviews in his father's defense. And then later in the month, Charles Adams sued Bernard Coleridge for libel on the basis of Bernard's letter implying that Adams had run away with his first wife when she was underage. As might be expected, a trial involving slander, sex, and two children of England's Lord Chief Justice turned into a media circus, with extra editions, leading articles, and plenty of malicious gossip. Adams, who was not a barrister, conducted his own case and kept trying to tell "his side" of the story, while the judge intervened again and again to make him keep to the points at issue. On 22 November the jury awarded damages of three thousand pounds to Adams, which was an enormous sum for a case of this sort, and the judge threw out their verdict. It had no legal ground, he ruled: a letter from a brother to his sister was privileged. Adams at once appealed; many critics thought the judge had acted out of deference to Bernard Coleridge's father; and the press feast continued as jurors and others tried, as the *Spectator* astutely remarked, to use public opinion as a court of appeal.[14]

But Adams had not yet finished: he had another letter in reserve. In October, before the trial began, Cecilia Bishop, a sister of Stafford North-cote and a very old friend of the Coleridge family, gave Adams a letter that Lord Coleridge had written to her almost two years earlier. Her motive, she said, was to save Mildred from being forced into an unsuitable marriage, though it is hard to fathom how the letter might help. Perhaps she imagined that Adams would make a gentlemanly withdrawal if he knew what his prospective father-in-law thought of him, or perhaps she was simply a meddler; Mildred Coleridge and Charles Adams had met in her rooms during the London season of 1882, when they were not supposed to be seeing each other. At any rate, with this additional letter in hand, Adams threatened to begin a new libel suit against the Lord Chief Justice himself if he did not get the three thousand pounds.

Even those who blamed Bernard Coleridge for his own accusations were appalled. "Lord Coleridge," argued the *Spectator,* "had absolutely done nothing except refuse to sanction, and therefore to assist, a marriage which he disapproved. If a father's right does not extend that far, what has become of it?" Elizabeth Eastlake wrote to Cobbe, "I can't write to you without thinking of Mildred Coleridge! Where is her *mind* to say nothing of heart, feeling & duty. . . . I hate the fashionable plea of insanity for crimes one can't comprehend, but a Coleridge mind thrown off its balance will account for much."[15] Lord Coleridge sought compromise, and the parties agreed on an arbitrator who would award "proper compensation" to Charles Adams.

Cobbe must have read each day's paper with high anxiety, wondering if her name would appear. Given her working relationship with Bernard Coleridge, who had served as VSS counsel, it has to be wondered if she supplied some of the rumors in his letter to Mildred. But Cobbe almost escaped; neither she nor the VSS was named in court, Adams having carefully testified that he and Mildred Coleridge were "thrown together on the committee of a charitable society" without mentioning its name, perhaps because any recollection that he had already sued the VSS on another issue might prejudice his case. Nevertheless, many people would have filled in the gaps and speculated about what actually happened in the committee rooms. Cobbe suffered something like a depression during the autumn. "I am getting old very rapidly," she wrote to Sarah Wister, and "feeling a sort of dumbness & cessation of the old desire to give expression to my thoughts & feelings."[16] She was saddened by the death of William Henry Channing; he had been both a living link to Theodore Parker and, more recently, a dependable VSS activist. And the women's movement as a whole suffered a loss when Henry Fawcett died on 6 November after a very short illness.

Cobbe's final essay in the first year of her "retirement" entered an ongoing debate about the consequence of atheism for public life. The topic was political as well as theological: the freethinker Charles Bradlaugh, elected to Parliament in 1880, had been denied his seat when he chose not to swear "so help me God." "You will have seen, perhaps, an article by Fitzjames Stephen . . . brother of Leslie & Carry on the *Unknowable & Unknown* in the *Nineteenth Century* for June last?" Cobbe wrote in October. "At the end of it he says that it will make little difference if people give up religion altogether—which indeed he obviously thinks science will soon compel them to do." She marked up her copy of Stephen's essay and set out to construct an answer, relieved to turn her thoughts "to such themes instead of the hideous one which has been my ten years nightmare."[17]

Cobbe's "A Faithless World" appeared in the issue of *Contemporary Review* dated December 1884. William Gladstone read it on Advent Sunday and found it "profoundly interesting." (R. H. Hutton knew that Cobbe would take a sly pleasure in hearing that Gladstone had spoken to him "in the warmest admiration of the essay.") But Annie Besant, who had found Cobbe's theism "a ray of light" in the darkness of her own religious dilemma, had, like many others over the past fifteen years, passed far beyond the ideas she had once found daringly advanced. (Besant was by now linked to Bradlaugh through not only their atheism but also their prosecution for publishing an "obscene" book that explained contraception.) Besant's book *A World Without God: A Reply to Miss Frances Power Cobbe* described "A Faithless World" as merely an attempt to "frighten people from Atheism."[18] Cobbe firmly declined to take part in Elizabeth Cady Stanton's projected demonstration that "the historical impact of Christian ideas . . . had been to degrade women." "The Bible is so rapidly ceasing to be, even among the most orthodox an armoury of text-bolts to be shot at opponents," she wrote, "that it is going needlessly backward to discuss at all (except as a matter of historical curiosity) what early Hebrews or early gentile Christians thought best to write about Women."[19]

Cobbe returned to vivisection in January 1885 with a long correspondence in the *Times* about surgery, in which most of the usual names said most of the same things. Mary Lloyd had been to London in December, staying with Fanny Kemble and attending an artistic event for which Shaftesbury had sent a card. When Sarah Wister invited both of them to visit Philadelphia, however, Cobbe wrote that they would have done it long ago were it not that Mary was "such a victim of sea sickness." Cobbe was intermittently ill for much of the year. Writing to Lydia Becker on 2 February, she regretfully turned down an invitation to speak at a mammoth suffrage rally at the Manchester Free Trade Hall. The VSS executive committee had raised funds for an annuity of one hundred pounds a year to reward her service and ease her retirement. They made the presentation in February 1885. Some of them must have been silently grateful that she was no longer quite so central to their work; R. H. Hutton's response to her thank-you note pointed out that published letters overstating the facts did harm to the cause. "Now & then," he wrote, "I wish you would not be so hot."[20]

Late in the previous year Cobbe had sent Violet Paget a letter filled with praise for Vernon Lee's novel *Miss Brown*. Her chief interest was in the novel's satire of aesthetes; once, when visiting a Rossetti exhibition, she wrote, she had been shaken by the "odious sensuality" and said to an acquaintance, "Do you understand this? I feel as if I had got into some horrible place. It might be a ward in the Consumptive hospital set apart for patients whose disease was complicated with erotic mania." Although Cobbe questioned some of the book's ethical conclusions, she found "whole chapters . . . as fine as subtle—as true as anything George Sand or George Eliot ever wrote"[21] and was not surprised to hear that Paget's venture into "dark places" had aroused critics "who take Miss Yonge for the model novelist of England." When Paget planned a trip to London in 1885, she asked for introductions "to any people who represent more practical interests than the aesthetes." As a novelist, she wanted "to see all kinds & conditions of men" and "especially would like to see something of the people who work among the poor." Cobbe tactfully discouraged an eager young writer who had spent very little time in England: "As to the active philanthropists I don't think they wd at all like to be *studied* by one who could not stop & work with them . . . & they are, so far as I know, almost to a man & woman fervently Evangelical or in some form, religious,—& wd regard yr philosophy with strong prejudice."[22]

The Adams-Coleridge saga should have ended on 21 June 1885, when the arbitrator sent out his decision awarding Adams five hundred pounds. Three days later Mildred Coleridge and Charles Warren Adams were married, and then two things happened to undo the resolution. First, Adams realized that Mildred's marriage settlement did not allow her to write a will in his favor if she should die first. And second, on 13 August 1885 Lord Coleridge was himself married, at age sixty-four, to Amy Lawford, who was thirty. Simple mathematics revealed that if Coleridge were to leave a life interest to his new bride, his estate was not likely to reach his children until well after Adams was dead. Almost at once he discovered grounds for yet another suit. When the arbitrator requested the letters involved in the lawsuit, Lord Coleridge's solicitor included some additional material, the arbitrator's clerk sent copies to Adams, and once again the pot began to simmer.

Cobbe was still linked to Coleridge family affairs through their multiple VSS connections. Bernard Coleridge served as honorary treasurer, Lord Coleridge remained a vice president, and Stephen Coleridge was becoming the most active member of the executive committee, although someone sent a warning to Cobbe: "I am fond of Stephen but could not trust him with money especially. I suppose you do not know all the *disgrace* he has been saved from by his father paying £15,000. Remember he is earnest about the Society and all that, but do not *lean* on him." The Coleridge presence became even more significant when Lord Shaftesbury died on 1 October at age eighty-four. "We knew the event would not be far off," wrote Cobbe, "but it was a great grief when it came—over & above the loss he is to me as kindest Friend & Helper, there is a curious sense that a great Personality has gone out of the world & out of my life & Mary's, are poorer & colder—I had grown to count on the sympathy of his great heart in everything."[23]

Although Parliamentary maneuvering during autumn 1884 had prevented any move to add women's suffrage to the Reform Bill, the earl of Carnarvon, a cabinet minister in every Conservative government since 1866, had said in the House of Lords that "the time was rapidly approaching when the claims of . . . duly-qualified women—must receive the attention of Parliament."[24] The political situation changed unexpectedly in June 1885, when the Liberals' budget failed to pass and Gladstone resigned. Ordinarily an election would have been called at once, but it seemed unwise to go to the polls before November, when the new qualifications for voters would take effect. The marquess of Salisbury formed a Conservative government that took office on 23 June, with Stafford Northcote, now earl of Iddesleigh, as first lord of the treasury and Carnarvon also in the cabinet. Suffragists spotted a small window of opportunity, since they believed a women's suffrage bill originating in the House of Lords would easily pass in the Commons. Cobbe was of course delighted. "Gladstone," she wrote to Lydia Becker, "has been the evil Genius of our sex—& of our country."[25]

Becker arranged at once to begin lobbying. Cobbe helped by getting in touch with the bishop of Winchester, who might influence the twenty-four bishops who voted in the House of Lords, but told Becker she could do no more at present. Still feeling old and ill, she had consulted a doctor, who had told her to avoid "excitement or agitation." But although she was no longer able to speak at meetings, she continued, "I may perhaps be of some use still with my pen now & then. I think I shall write for a last book a sketch of my life in which I shall make a point of shewing how I came to be converted to Women's Rights & why I uphold them. Do not however please mention this publicly—Perhaps I may not carry out the project."[26]

During the same summer it was rumored that Helen Taylor would become a parliamentary candidate in the November elections. Cobbe fired off an enthusiastic letter to Taylor, who replied, "Do you really think it would be such a gain to our cause for a woman to be elected to Parlt? I am not sure of it. Might it not frighten away many timid friends of the suffrage and so put off the day when we shall gain that—the real foundation of liberty? . . . For my own part I have never seriously thought of it except as a thing from the future, until your letter startled me by showing so different opinion from one so qualified to judge." When she wrote to Becker in August, Cobbe had "very little hope left to live to see our suffrage carried. Gladstone has been our ruin & I wish all the women of England would join the Primrose League to keep him & his party out of office forever."[27] By autumn the idea had taken root. Once more full of energy, she set about urging Primrose League women to campaign only for candidates who were committed to women's suffrage.

The Conservatives were the first political party to create a formal role for women. After the 1883 Corrupt Practices Act put a limit on paid workers, the party formed a Primrose Tory League of gentlemen volunteers. It soon enrolled "Dames" as well as "Knights" and dropped the word *Tory*. The Primrose League was not technically affiliated with the Conservative Party, although it always supported Tory candidates. In June 1885 a Ladies' Grand Council was formed. Cobbe seized the opportunity to contact women on the Ladies' Grand Council and other Dames whose names she could find. Writing as an individual rather than a member of the suffrage central committee, she did, however, ask for advice from Millicent Fawcett, who made some corrections to the proof. Given Cobbe's public radicalism, it is not surprising that one newspaper article began, "It will be news to most persons that Miss Cobbe is a Conservative of long standing." And if the circular provided no great help in the 1885 general election, it did at least yield a nice harvest of names preceded by *Baroness* or *Viscountess* for use in the next memorial.[28]

The Liberals continued to control Parliament—their majority was secure, however, only if Irish Nationalists voted with them—but several leading suffragists were defeated, including Arthur Arnold, Jacob Bright, and Coleridge Kennard. Helen Taylor was indeed put forward as a candidate by men from the Camberwell Radical Association, but the election authorities refused to accept her nomination.[29] As for the antivivisection cause, Bernard Coleridge was elected MP for the first time, while Ernest Hart, the *British Medical Journal* editor who had organized resistance to Lord Carnarvon's 1876 bill, ran "as radical candidate for Parliament in the supposedly radical Mile End district of Tower Hamlets" but was defeated, perhaps with the help of VSS propaganda.[30]

Cobbe's letter of regret to her friend Coleridge Kennard once the votes were counted urged him to have the Conservative Party make women's suffrage a pillar of its platform: "1st It would secure against the next election a large majority out of the 7 or 800,000 women to be enfranchised as supporters of the Conservative party," she wrote. "2d It will be a permanent, I venture to say an *historical* honour to the party. 3d—And it will be a tacit reproach to Mr Gladstone & his sham *Liberalism*." She told him that she believed, after looking at the returns, that a suffrage bill could be carried in the coming session; the question, then, would be, "Who is to have the credit of it?" Though nothing came of it, Kennard passed the suggestion at once to the Conservative Party leader, Lord Salisbury.[31]

Even after Gladstone formed a government Cobbe remained hopeful. "Public Opinion," she wrote to Theodore Stanton, "has ripened enormously during the recent elections & the part taken by the Primrose League has won over numbers of Tories & inspired the Dames themselves with the brilliant idea that they ought to have votes as well as their plough-boys!" On 18 February 1886 Leonard Courtney opened the debate, and A. J. Beresford-Hope promptly moved to adjourn. Even though it was past midnight, a motion made by Beresford-Hope was viewed as a transparent ruse, and when adjournment lost (by five votes), it seemed there might just possibly be a workable margin in favor of the bill. After a bizarre debate of extremely hurried speeches, it passed without division and went to committee. The *Times* leader complained that a surprise second reading "in the small hours of the night, in a thin house and practically without debate" was meaningless, but the prospect for passage must have seemed closer than the *Times* could bear. Its opposition no longer rested on any coherent argument but disclosed the real fear: "The fact remains that the women of England are more numerous than the men, and that to suffer them to enjoy the same political rights as the men would be almost a male-disfranchisement."[32]

Millicent Fawcett, again taking a public role now that her year of mourning had passed, counted among those MPs "who have declared themselves" three in support of women's suffrage for every one opposed. Cobbe went energetically to work revising the Primrose League circular, finding Conservative women to hold drawing-room meetings, and collecting signatures from "as many as possible of the titled Primrose Dames" for a petition to the House of Lords. But the central committee raised objections about sending out Cobbe's letter. Fawcett found that not only liberal but also "conservative members of the comee thought it was unwise in the interests of the W.S. question to issue a letter so decidedly 'party' in character" even after Cobbe revised it to make clear that she wrote as an individual and eliminated the society's name from the letterhead. Generously and carefully, Cobbe asked Fawcett to move that her proposal be withdrawn so the committee would not vote it down, thereby saving her "from the necessity of resignation to which I shd be very sorry to be driven."[33]

Gladstone's support of home rule for Ireland put the finishing touch on her disgust with the man and his politics. "The state of public affairs," she wrote to Wister, "is too terrible to talk of. Gladstone is the true Will(iam) of the Wisp—dancing from one quagmire to another morass—& leading thousands after him in a strange sort of infatuation." Another government proposal that aroused her ire was a coal mines regulation bill forbidding women to work at the pit brow. Women who did rough, outdoor aboveground labor in the coal fields were strongly against the proposal, which was backed by the all-male Miners' Federation since eliminating the competition would open more jobs for men. It was exactly the sort of thing Cobbe had feared two decades earlier when she intemperately, though privately, referred to political courtship of the "blessed Working Man" as "the origin of all evil." Writing to the *Times,* she urged Gladstone's supporters in Parliament not to demonstrate yet again "the lightsome readiness to play the game of follow-my-leader which distinguishes boy-minded people." It might be believed that they were seriously concerned about the moral effects of the "labour of well-conducted and exceptionally healthy women at the mouth of the coalpits," she continued, if they would first "prohibit immodest clothing and behavior on the stage" and in "fashionable ball-rooms" and close "all the airless and fetid workrooms" where seamstresses labored.[34]

The winter had been unusually cold and was only just relaxing at the end of March, when Cobbe and Lloyd planned to move permanently into a cottage just to the west of Llanelltyd. (Though Cobbe consistently calls it a cottage, Tyn-y-Celyn had been identified in one guidebook as a "boarding house," so it must have been reasonably substantial.) Early in the summer of 1886 Cobbe spent a few weeks in London while she did suffrage and antivivisection business and bought furniture for Tyn-y-Celyn. Though she always denied taking any pleasure in the "social season," she managed to attend a great many events. Going to hear James Martineau speak one evening, she found herself "obliged" to sit on the platform. The American physician and man of letters Oliver Wendell Holmes was "happy to meet Miss Frances Power Cobbe" when he went to lunch in late May with Juliana, Lady Camperdown, and he saw her again on 4 June "at the house of Mrs. Cyril Flower, one of the finest in London,—Surrey House, as it is called. Mr. Browning, who seems to go everywhere, and is one of the vital elements of London society, was of course there. Miss Cobbe, many of whose essays I have read with great satisfaction, though I cannot accept all her views, was a guest whom I was very glad to meet a second time."[35]

Cobbe had gone to London primarily to take the chair at the VSS annual meeting on 22 June, but political events were also compelling. The second reading of Gladstone's Irish home rule bill was scheduled for 7 June. In the wee hours of the morning it was voted down, and Parliament dissolved. In the midst of this turmoil Cobbe's brother Charles died at Newbridge on 5 July, a few weeks before his seventy-fifth birthday. Cobbe, who was still in London, almost certainly wrote the *Times* obituary that took care to exonerate him from any Irish nationalist grievances. Charles Cobbe, it said, was "like his father—of the same name—a representative of the very best class of Irish landlords. . . . As regards the management of his own estate—which was the largest in the county—there was not an acre of it rented above 40s., though the surrounding land, often of inferior quality, was made to pay 60s. and 70s. per acre."[36]

Since Charles had no children by either wife, his nephew Leuric, his brother Tom's son, expected to inherit the property; indeed, his farming experience in Iowa was better preparation than his unfinished Oxford degree for managing nearly ten thousand acres of Irish land. Charles's will, however, left a life interest in the house and estate to his widow, Charlotte, who was only ten years older than Leuric. Tom's children were bitterly disappointed; Cobbe wrote to Sarah Wister that Helen and Frances were "infamously ousted from the house they had been taught all their lives to look to as coming to them."[37] Unable to see past her own hard feelings, she failed to notice that Charlotte looked after house, church, and tenants, becoming an excellent "squire" in her own right.

The 1886 voting—the second general election in less than a year—took place in July. Despite a Conservative victory that defeated some of the "well known and faithful friends to the interests of women," suffragists believed they had, for the first time, an actual majority: they counted 344 votes in a House of Commons with 670 members. Lord Salisbury was again prime minister, the earl of Iddesleigh (Stafford Northcote, another known suffragist) headed the Foreign Office, and on the Liberal side, Cyril Flower, Constance de Rothschild's husband, served as whip. The Primrose League Ladies' Grand Council also elected new members, among them a Beresford connection whose help Cobbe had secured. In November the prime minister seemed to promise "modifications that will probably take place in the future" to give women more influence in politics.[38]

Just at this moment, when there was a real expectation of victory, the suffrage movement was crippled by internal splits. First there was a move to oust Lydia Becker as head of the Manchester National Society for Women's Suffrage. Cobbe wrote an impassioned letter in support of Becker intended for public use. Ousting Becker would be "nothing short of a calamity" for the movement, she wrote. "It would be in my judgment as unwise to put you aside at this juncture as for a man going into battle to put his right hand behind his back." And though the crisis passed and Becker was reelected, enough members withdrew to drain the committee's finances. The charges against Charles Dilke caused a separate disruption along moral lines. Constance Flower criticized her husband for seeming "to lose his proper judgment" in supporting Dilke; and the scandal also touched Maye Dilke, who was always known as Mrs. Ashton Dilke, the widow of Charles Dilke's younger brother and the author of *Women's Suffrage* (1885). Cobbe regretted that her "eloquent tongue" was "unavailable to us," though she did limit the statement to Primrose League lobbying ("at least with these Dames").[39]

And if the suffrage movement was in disarray just as it should have prepared for a major push, antivivisection also ran into a stumbling block. Louis Pasteur first succeeded with injections to prevent rabies from developing in people bitten by mad dogs during the summer of 1885. By 1 December the *Zoophilist* was arguing that since inoculations had to be given before symptoms developed, there was no way of knowing whether the person was actually infected. But logical arguments along those lines were difficult to pursue. Women who supported the cause for emotional reasons wrote letters such as those from Eleanor Vere Boyle, who said she "cannot, dare not, read what you enclose" because of the "fiendish details" but confusedly hoped or did not hope that "Pasteur will fall to the ground in time—One must not wish him to be carried off by his own Pasteurilean new disease!" while Cobbe's medical advisers were reluctant to oppose the new technique. "Mr Lawson Tait," she wrote, "professed to have no opinion at all—not having studied the subject. Dr. Hoggan, less cautious by far!—thinks I am sorry to say that Pasteur is on the right track."[40]

On 17 November the next installment of the Adams-Coleridge melodrama began in the High Court of Justice, Queen's Bench Division: Charles Adams sued his wife's brother and father for sending prejudicial letters to the arbitrator in the previous case. The courtroom was, as the *Times* reported with some restraint, "densely crowded in every part." In addition to the startling appearance of the Lord Chief Justice of England as a defendant, the witnesses included the foreign secretary (Lord Iddesleigh), the earl of Selborne, who had been lord chancellor in the previous government, and the bishop of Oxford (whose eldest daughter was married to her first cousin Bernard Coleridge). Henry James, the barrister MP who had been attorney general in the Liberal government of 1880–85, acted as the lead counsel for Lord Coleridge. Charles Adams once more conducted his own case, continually raising issues unrelated to the charge of libel. When he badgered the Lord Chief Justice in the witness box, the judge finally intervened: "This is not cross-examination," he said, "but persecution."[41]

Very early in the proceedings, as part of his self-justification, Adams testified (and the *Times* reported) that Miss Cobbe "unhappily proposed to introduce to Miss Coleridge the editor of the *Malthusian Review*." Adams said that he had warned Lord Coleridge and that when Cobbe learned about it, she "wrote to Lord Coleridge accusing him [Adams] of impropriety with his daughter." Cobbe's name came up again the next day in a statement prepared by Lord Coleridge's counsel. During November 1882 Coleridge's "daughter came to him in a considerable agitation and said that she had been falsely accused at the committee of the Victoria-street Society, by Miss Cobbe, of undue familiarity with Mr. Adams, and that after such a statement, made in the presence of other people, it was quite impossible she could continue to work with Miss Cobbe, or, indeed, to meet her at all." Coleridge had had a long meeting with Cobbe on 15 December, and it was "under the influence of this interview" that he had written the letter over which Adams sued. However, according to his attorney, "Lord Coleridge now believes that the inferences he drew from the communications made to him were erroneous."[42]

On the following day the *Times* published the letter in which Lord Coleridge reminded Adams that he too had made careless accusations: "To me you stated plainly that Miss Cobbe was actuated . . . by an unqualified passion for yourself." On 22 November Cobbe's name was mentioned again. Adams, moving into the fourth day of presenting his case, introduced a letter from Coleridge that began, "I have had a long letter from Miss Cobbe," and concluded, "I am not without hope that the society may be relieved from all connexion even of the most indirect kind with a publication like the 'Malthusian.'"[43]

Though the intervening passages drew no direct connection between Cobbe and "Malthusian," the letter was very short and, like the other published reports, must have been extremely painful for Cobbe to read. It was distasteful enough to find her name associated with sexual misbehavior in the VSS office and publications promoting birth control, which was almost always seen as a code for "free love," but her sense of rectitude was even more damaged by the implication that she had either lied or spoken so emotionally as to mislead the Lord Chief Justice. Under cross-examination by Adams on 23 November, Lord Coleridge elaborated on his understanding of the inappropriate behavior between Adams and Mildred Coleridge at the VSS office. In the news report that follows, the question opening each paragraph was asked by Adams, and the response was by Lord Coleridge:

Was it the first time you heard of the story of the "darkened room?"—
No; it is mentioned in the letter of 1882.

Did you at that time believe it?—I did at the time believe in it upon
authority I thought good, but subsequent events led me to think that her
impressions had been exaggerated.

It was Miss Cobbe?—It was. . . .

She told you the story of the darkened room?—She did. She told me a
great deal which unfavourably impressed my mind. I have since thought
that she was led away by warm feelings and may have exaggerated, and that
I ought not to have given implicit credence to her statements; and, more-
over, my subsequent acquaintance with you has led me to think I was unjust in making that particular charge against you, and I withdraw it.[44]

After seven days of argument, evidence, and cross-examination, the judge
carefully pointed out to the jury that the actual "publication" of the most
damaging statements had not taken place until Charles Adams read them
aloud in court. The jury took barely more than an hour to decide in favor
of the defendants, and the judge ordered Adams to pay the costs.[45] But
despite the vindication for Lord Coleridge and Bernard, damage had been
done not only to Cobbe's ego and her reputation but also to her relationship with the man whose eminence gave authority and dignity to the antivivisection cause. Nearly three years later, in the summer of 1889, Cardinal
Manning, according to Cobbe, "wrote & begged me to come & see him
which of course I did. . . . The object he had in view was—to reconcile me
to Lord Coleridge. . . . He took the proper priestly tone of telling me it wd
be a good action & good for my soul—& I laughed out at him & told him
I was too great a heretic to be guided. . . . I had to get off by telling him I
would 'think of it' but that I thought I had acted perfectly right—." "It is
obvious," she continued, seeing the incident only from her own viewpoint,
"that Lord C. must have begged his Eminence to patch up this business—
which is now three or four years old."[46]

Early in 1887 antivivisectionists worried that a proposed physiological
and pathological institute in London would become the "centre & sanction
of ever advancing vivisection." Cobbe wrote to the queen's private secretary
in fear, or perhaps in hope, that the institute would be a Jubilee proposal;
if it had been the latter, Ponsonby replied, it might have been a cause "in
which Her Majesty can directly interfere." Since the VSS held its 1887 annual meeting earlier than usual, probably to avoid conflict with the June
extravaganza, Cobbe and Lloyd went to London in March. Cobbe spoke at
the VSS meeting on the twenty-ninth—Cardinal Manning, rather than
Lord Coleridge, was in the chair—but found that Pasteur's apparent success

was taking a toll on members; Lewis Morris, for example, had written to her that "in the case of a specific disease like rabies which could be stamped out forever . . . I could not take the view of the Society."[47]

In addition, Cobbe's anxiety about teaching physiology led to difficulties with some of her oldest friends. Agitated over rumors of laboratory work at Girton, she wrote to Millicent Fawcett that she made "no protest against *killing* animals. . . . It is the *torturing* of them—turning their whole existence into a curse & misfortune—against which we lift our voices." Barbara Bodichon, now widowed and living near Hastings, tried to head off an open breach by asking their Kensington Society colleague Adelaide Manning, who had been one of the first Girton students and now sat on its executive committee, to see what she could do. "I called at Victa St. & saw Miss Cobbe & Miss Lloyd," reported Manning. "It is plain that they are going to make a tremendous point of this. . . . I told Miss Cobbe of our fear of exaggeration—she promised to be careful as to facts . . . I am afraid Miss Cobbe does feel it makes a *degree* of breach with her friends." Cobbe resigned from the committee governing the new University Club for Ladies on Bond Street,[48] but she did avoid public criticism of the women's colleges, at least for the time being.

"Faith Healing and Fear Killing," in the *Contemporary Review* for June 1887, analyzed the effect of mind on body and suggested that physicians "study Psychology a little more, and Physiology, possibly, a little less." In conclusion Cobbe argued that the enormous fear of rabies had been created by Pasteur's "success." If people realized "that many more men die every year from the kicks of horses than from the bites of dogs, Pasteur would have obtained no such apotheosis." In the summer of 1887 a House of Lords committee on rabies recommended conventional methods of control. Pasteur himself was puzzled by the interest in large-scale vaccination; he told Victor Horsley that since Britain was an island, if all dogs were muzzled the disease could be eradicated in a few years. Cobbe, however, also despised muzzling: combined with the fear of rabies it led to dreadful incidents when muzzled dogs, unable to drink or pant, suffered convulsions and were clubbed to death by frightened people.[49]

The order to muzzle dogs drew Mary Lloyd's nephew into the VSS. "People entirely forget that in muzzling the dog you deprive him absolutely of his only means of perspiration," he wrote; it would be far better for all dogs to wear a "regulation medal" certifying that they were free of disease.[50] In a spoof history produced in mock antique printing, R. J. Lloyd Price described himself, in the third person, as "chiefly remarkable for the swiftness and superiority of his pointer dogges . . . he did once refuse for one pointer bitche, named Belle, the large somme of five hundred guineas, she being champion of the Worlde."[51] He wrote articles for *The Field*, which called itself "the Country Gentleman's Newspaper," and books such as *Rabbits for Profit and Rabbits for Powder* (1888). Despite his intense enjoyment of shooting, and of the humane raising of rabbits and game birds so they would be healthy enough to provide good sport, Lloyd Price's books also reveal a sharp intelligence and a quirky wit that would have appealed to Cobbe.

During the summer of 1887 Cobbe negotiated with the publisher William Swan Sonnenschein over a piece of antivivisection fiction written by Edward Berdoe. *St. Bernard's; The Romance of a Medical Student,* by "Aesclaepius Scalpel," did not have much commercial appeal, but Sonnenschein was willing to publish it "subject to your generous proposal to subsidize the book to the amount of £50." Cobbe gave it additional support by using some of the antivivisection funds at her disposal to have free copies placed in public libraries. William Swan Sonnenschein, himself once intended for the medical profession, had just brought out the first English edition of Marx's *Capital* (1886) and published works by Edward Carpenter, George Moore, and George Bernard Shaw, as well as philosophical and feminist books, but since he had no list of bestselling fiction to support his scholarly interests, he was always looking for ways to share the cost of polemical work. For the next decade or more he found Cobbe a willing, if sometimes troublesome, partner in such projects.[52]

As her sixty-fifth birthday approached, Cobbe published a collection of her poems, *Rest In the Lord; And Other Small Pieces*. Printed "for private gift only" to "dear friends," it was meant to "serve perhaps, a little to draw closer those links of affection which, as the evening of life comes on, grow ever more precious." The poem to Mary Lloyd quoted in chapter 10 is tipped into a few copies; Cobbe knew that some people, but not others, would understand the emotional, intellectual, and physical desire it exposed.[53]

Late in September 1887 Cobbe visited her old NAPSS associate William Cowper, now Baron Mount-Temple, who had been president of the Workhouse Visiting Society when Cobbe gave papers on her projects in Bristol, and his wife Georgiana at Broadlands, their stunning eighteenth-century house near Southampton. After the visit she considered how the VSS could make use of three women with impressive titles and decided to invite them to become vice presidents: "Hitherto we have not had Lady V.Ps, but there is, of course, no reason why we should not. . . . This wd get over the very great objection of having names on the Executive of persons who never attend at all." Significant names were (then as now) especially important in unfamiliar or unpopular causes. On 3 December Amelia Edwards invited Cobbe to become a member of the Egypt Exploration Fund. "I assure you, it is not your money or your life that I want—but your *name*," wrote Ed-

Mary Lloyd's nephew Richard John Lloyd Price (1843-1923) as shown in the frontispiece of his *Dogs Ancient and Modern and Walks in Wales* (1893). (By permission
of the National Library of Wales)

wards. "I want eminent names quite as much as I want dollars & cents—& especially the names of eminent women." Cobbe proposed in exchange to make Edwards an honorary member of the VSS. Their correspondence was a delightful reminder of the Egyptian genealogies Cobbe had done just after leaving school. Having last seen Edwards "at that strange, ghostly awful house of D. G. Rossetti's" soon after his death in 1882, Cobbe now happily asked for information about female rulers. Edwards told her that "the whole scheme of Ancient Egyptian law as regards women was most extraordinary—& unlike that of any other nation." She had examined contracts, mortgages, deeds, and other legal papers and could demonstrate, she said, that the Egyptian woman's "independence—nay her *supremacy*—even in private life, was absolute."[54]

"We are getting on very quietly—as usual in our little cottage," wrote Cobbe in January 1888, even though gold had been discovered nearby and people were begging Mary Lloyd for permission to search her farms. In the wake of her sixty-fifth birthday, Cobbe could "only walk a mile or two instead of 8 or 10," but she had solved the problem of writer's cramp some two years earlier by learning to type. She told Sarah Wister that it was no harder than "picking out a tune with a finger on the piano."[55]

Cobbe's essay for January was "The Lord Was Not in the Earthquake," in the *Contemporary Review*. Emphasizing the evil in a nature "red in tooth and claw," she argued against those contemporaries who were starting to use instinct as a guide to ethics. In February, "The Education of the Emotions," in the *Fortnightly Review*, analyzed "contagiousness" of "emotions" such as fear, courage, admiration, and religious fanaticism before raising antivivisection and antimedical arguments. Questioning the "moral effects of our enormous Hospitals," Cobbe argued that it was dangerous to separate patients from their relatives "the moment that illness makes a claim for tenderness and care." Her antimedical passion made her forget what she had learned in Bristol about illness among uneducated and impoverished people. (Twenty years earlier, in the *Echo,* she had welcomed knowledge about the "infinitesimal germs with which the microscope alone can deal" and worried about people who were "senselessly careless about infection.")[56]

In London for political work during June, Cobbe met with Millicent Fawcett. Amid party fractures over the Irish question, Fawcett had left the Women's Liberal Federation and invited Cobbe to join her in forming another organization. "I am glad to hear of the new Liberal Unionist Association," Cobbe replied, "but do you not know that I have always been a Tory? I remember dear Mr Mill once saying in his sweet impressive way, when Mentia Taylor charged me at her dinner (between him & John Bright!)

with being 'a bitter Conservative'—, —'Miss Cobbe is a Conservative, I am sorry to say, but not a *bitter* one Mrs Taylor'—!"[57]

As part of her VSS business that summer, Cobbe pursued new names for the list of eminent vice presidents. On 14 June she had a letter of acceptance from the Chief Rabbi, Nathan Adler. Cobbe's own powers of persuasive charm, as well as the changing religious climate of the later nineteenth century, had done much to bridge the distance between men of widely different views. Lord Shaftesbury, a strict evangelical Protestant, said not long before his death that if the VSS had done nothing else but bring him together with (the Roman Catholic) Cardinal Manning to "sit and work at the same table for the same object, it would have been well worth while."[58]

A family delegation gathered to hear Cobbe's speech at the annual VSS meeting on 21 June: her brother Henry, her cousins Eliza and Sophy, her brother Tom's daughter Frances. Frances and her sister Helen had become a regular part of Cobbe's life since their mother died. They were, she reported to Sarah Wister, "as good as gold & very nice—even distinguished-looking—but not at all clever in any direction except in having plenty of that blessed thing,—good sense." While in London they tried to visit the Battersea Home for Lost and Starving Dogs in order to get information about its humane lethal chamber for sending to a similar institution in Italy (where they had spent the winter), but they were turned away. Someone must have intervened with the friends of their aunt who were still on the board, however, because an apology and invitation to visit were later forthcoming. In the summer of 1888 they took lodgings about a mile away from Cobbe and Lloyd. During a miserable summer, when fires were needed all day even during July and August, it was pleasant to have them nearby, though Cobbe later wrote to Wister, "I wish that their feeble health did not make them so silent & depressed."[59]

The gloomy weather was hard on everyone. Cobbe confessed that the "constant sole companionship of one whose eyes seem preternaturally open to pain & evil—& very dim sighted to happiness & good" had become a strain. The cloud over Mary Lloyd's nature, which had been noticed intermittently by Cobbe and outsiders ever since the 1860s, grew even darker as she became more restricted by pain. "Had I been *better*," Cobbe wrote sadly, "I might have borne her up, instead of being myself drawn to somewhat of her sad ways of looking at things."[60]

Yet by the end of the summer Cobbe was again full of energy and plans. Spending ten days in London at the height of the newspaper frenzy over "Jack the Ripper," she urged Scotland Yard to hire women detectives: "A clever woman of unobtrusive dress and appearance. . . . would pass unsuspected where a man would be instantly noticed; she could extract gossip from other women much more freely" and employ the "intuitive quickness and 'mother wit' with which her sex is commonly credited." Like many other antivivisectionists, she suspected that the "Whitechapel demon" was a physiologist gone over the edge and was glad to hear that the police were using bloodhounds: if they should be "the means of his capture, poetic justice will be complete."[61]

Late in November Cobbe was summoned to a special meeting of the Central Committee of the National Society for Women's Suffrage and hurried back to London to support her friends. The touchy question of political affiliation had been simmering since Cobbe was forbidden to use its letterhead when writing to the Primrose League in 1886. The central committee, it will be remembered, was an umbrella organization; its executive was composed of longtime activists such as Cobbe plus representatives from every suffrage organization in the United Kingdom. Its role was to provide literature, supply speakers, assemble petitions, and, especially, to maintain a London presence for lobbying and coordinating parliamentary efforts.

When the Primrose League was joined by the Women's Liberal Federation and then the Association of Liberal Unionists, a new question arose: could a local branch of, say, the Women's Liberal Federation—or, for that matter, the Primrose League—which adopted women's suffrage as part of its official policy be included in the central committee as a suffrage organization? Many older activists wanted to avoid party politics and retain the ability to work with MPs of all stripes. The other real difficulty, which Fawcett brought out in the open in her speech to the meeting, was that delegates representing the Women's Liberal Federation were likely to outnumber those from other organizations and turn the National Society for Women's Suffrage into a subsidiary of the Liberal Party,[62] the party headed still by William Gladstone, who had almost single-handedly prevented women's suffrage from getting fair consideration on the two occasions when success was really conceivable.

On 12 December members were admitted by ticket only so that no outsiders could attend. They were presented with a motion resolving that "in the opinion of this Meeting, the time has come for revising the rules of the Central Committee of the National Society for Women's Suffrage." Opponents promptly offered an amendment objecting to the new rules. After a reasonably polite debate the amendment was defeated by a vote of 94 to 63. Thomas Wallace Russell pointed out that anyone who "joined in discussing the [new] rules" would be pledged to accept them, and the dissidents, including Russell himself as well as Cobbe, "left the meeting in a body." The next day they met at Westminster Palace Hotel to "reconstruct the Central Committee under the old rules."[63] Fawcett was appointed leader, and Cobbe was on the executive committee, which included such old friends as Lydia Becker, Caroline Ashurst Biggs, Helen Blackburn, Jessie Boucherett, Florence Davenport Hill, Emily Davies, and Lady Goldsmid. The MPs on the executive represented all of the chief factions: Liberal Unionist T. W. Russell (who sat for county Dublin), Conservative Edward Thomas Cotton, Liberal Leonard Courtney, and nonaligned Unionist Justin Edwards-Heathcote. The breakaway organization retained the old name as well as the old rules. To avoid confusion, the old-rules group headed by Fawcett was generally identified as the Central Committee, Great College Street, and the new-rules faction was referred to as the Central National Committee, Parliament Street.

Revived in health and energy, Cobbe began several new projects during the winter. Though she had objected to politicizing the suffrage cause, the "new-rules" committee's welcome to organizations formed for other purposes may have suggested extending the tactic to antivivisection. She pursued her contact with Frances Willard to forge a link with the Women's Christian Temperance Union in North America. After Hannah Whitall Smith, a Philadelphia Quaker living in the United Kingdom, helped Cobbe identify a suitable leader in the United States, Willard quickly promised to "make Bands of Mercy a specialty in our work."[64] The alliance gave Cobbe access to almost two hundred thousand American women and to the children enrolled in the WCTU's various social-service programs.

She then turned her attention to British religious organizations. When the Society for Propagation of the Gospel published a sermon justifying animal experiments because God had given man "dominion" over brutes, she sent letters trying to get the Church of England to consider vivisection at its annual church congress. Most of the replies were discouraging, but the bishop of Winchester offered to "ask for a discussion on cruelty to animals: which might be utilized for antivivisection."[65] Her success with the Society of Friends was much more striking: she issued an appeal early in May, and by 23 May a Friends' Anti-Vivisection Association was being formed.

The VSS annual meeting in June 1889, which I believe was the last one Cobbe attended, was particularly depressing because the Prince of Wales and the Lord Mayor of London had just announced support for a Pasteur Institute in London. Antivivisection was increasingly viewed as a silly cause backed only by sentimental women. A month after Cobbe's death the *British Medical Journal* gleefully printed an old anecdote about Charles Darwin and T. H. Huxley: "Mr. R. H. Hutton, of the *Spectator,* had taken up the cudgels rather warmly against vivisection. 'Who is this Mr. Hutton?' said Darwin; 'he seems to be a kind of *female Miss Cobbe.*' Professor Huxley described it as the most beautiful double-barrelled 'score' he ever remembered." But in the summer of 1889 Cobbe too was "tortured by silly hysterical women who can do *nothing* & only make our movements appear foolish fads."[66]

On 9 July the Great College Street (old-rules) suffrage committee met at the Westminster Town Hall. Cobbe was reelected to the executive committee, and Mary Lloyd again became a subscriber. Trouble, or the wish to support old friends, had brought her back, though she had not paid dues since resigning from the 1867 committee. One focus of the July meeting was what the *Englishwoman's Review* called "The Battle of the Names."[67] The June issue of *Nineteenth Century* published "An Appeal against Female Suffrage," written by Mary Ward and signed by 103 others. Two, Mary Ward herself and the dowager Lady Stanley of Alderley, were prominent supporters of women's higher education, and a few more had some other public interests, but most were women whose names were familiar because of their husbands, such as Mrs. Leslie Stephen, Mrs. Huxley, Mrs. Frederic Harrison, Lady Randolph Churchill, Mrs. W. Bagehot, Mrs. Alma-Tadema, Mrs. Matthew Arnold, Mrs. Arnold Toynbee, and Mrs. Max Müller. Among professional women the exceptions included "Mrs. Lynn Linton" and two or three headmistresses of girls' schools.

The reply, organized by Fawcett's Great College Street central committee but supported by all factions of the suffrage movement, printed some six hundred names in the *Fortnightly Review* for July and produced a separate booklet with more than two thousand women classified by occupation to show their status. Included were dozens of founders and lecturers in women's colleges, the heads of forty high schools and page after page of teachers, thirty-three poor-law guardians, seventeen school-board members, twenty-three registered medical practitioners, and substantial numbers of aristocrats, clergymen's wives (among them the wives of the archbishop of Canterbury and the archbishop of York), artists, musicians, authors, social workers, and "women engaged in business," ranging from accountants, milliners, and type writers to housekeepers and lady's maids. The list of landowners included "Miss Lloyd, Dolgelly."[68]

The *Englishwoman's Review* for 15 July reported that "the leading reviews all deal this month with the question of Women's Suffrage in some form or another." In addition to the *Fortnightly Review*'s list of names, the *Nineteenth Century* had two responses to the antisuffrage essay it printed in June, one by Millicent Fawcett and one by Maye Dilke, by then a school-board member for Lambeth. The *National Review* published "one long wild shriek" from Eliza Lynn Linton entitled "The Threatened Abdication of Man." Julia Wedgwood's "calm, profound, scholarly paper" appeared in the *Contemporary Review*. By October the class-based voice of eugenics had made itself heard in Grant Allen's "Plain Words on the Woman Question," in the *Fortnightly Review,* which proposed that it was the moral duty of every (middle-class) woman to have "at least four children."[69]

All of this public attention makes the divisions and redivisions that diffused suffrage efforts even more regrettable. The Parliament Street committee, which opened itself to political organizations, struggled with the question of married women and finally decided to support all suffrage bills, both those restricted to single women and widows and those based on equal rights. (A householder franchise would be an equal-rights measure, although married women could not vote unless they occupied separate property in their own names, since an adult son living in his father's house would also be disenfranchised.) Politically, some Liberal MPs had objected to suffrage because they believed women were naturally conservative and would be unduly influenced by clergymen. Now many new voters were afraid that landowners would assign property to their wives, as—like Cobbe's father—they often did for sons when they came of age, and thereby double their own voting power, to the detriment of poorer men. The most radical members of the Parliament Street group, however, argued on ideological grounds to oppose any measure that explicitly excluded married women. Failing to win their point, they split yet again. The dissidents established the Women's Franchise League, which held its inaugural meeting on 25 July. Among the new league's early leaders were yet another group of Kensington Society members and old-line suffragists, including Elizabeth Wolstoneholme Elmy and Mentia Taylor, as well as Florence Fenwick Miller, Harriot Stanton Blatch, Alice Scatcherd, and Richard and Emmeline Pankhurst.

Once the Married Women's Property Act (1882) had come into force, the question about married women was no longer purely ideological, since even a property-based franchise could include some wives, especially women of the artisan class who occupied their own premises for a shop or workroom. Nevertheless, I am not sure that *conservative* and *radical* are the right terms to identify the two camps. Many of the single and widowed activists believed that most married women would vote with their husbands and ignore feminist causes. (Indeed, the signatures on the "Appeal against Female Suffrage" would seem to justify their suspicion.) Was it therefore "conservative" to believe that providing votes for such women would damage the reforming, or "radical," causes that activists such as Cobbe wanted to promote once they had influence over their parliamentary representatives? But whether the split was "conservative" versus "radical" or "pragmatists" versus "idealists," it squandered energy and goodwill that could have been put to other uses.

When Sarah Wister came to Wales for a visit in September, Cobbe experienced an emotional self-examination: "I think one's heart grows, if not cold, yet *dormant* to a great degree as one leaves the fifties & goes on far into the sixties, & the affections of the brighter years remain as beautiful & dear memories." Both she and Lloyd sometimes wished they "need not have always thought of *horrors* & might sometimes have reaped a little comfort & seen somebody the better or happier for our labours!" She hoped her book about dogs in literature might reach people's feelings and overcome the "effort on the part of the Biological *Gang* to make people dread & hate dogs."[70] With its references to Egypt, Persia, India, Judea, Greece, and Rome and its translations from both Middle Eastern and European works, as well as its English poetry, *The Friend of Man; and His Friends—the Poets* tried to accomplish for dogs what feminists during the period were learning to do for women: give them a history and scholarly worth. Cobbe recognized that her writing had lost its wit and charm (one reason that so much of the anti-vivisection material, unlike the feminist propaganda, is unpleasant and un-attractive reading). Ugly disputes, however, continued to erupt. By 1888 Charles Warren Adams had found the funds to edit and publish the *Veru-lam Review,* and he worked hard to claim the moral high ground. The *Zoo-philist,* he wrote, printed articles that were "unfit to be read, and impossible to be quoted, by any modest-minded woman." Though no names were mentioned, Adams clearly meant to imply that Cobbe was not "modest-minded," and he emphasized his own gentlemanliness (and masculinity) by closing with a long, untranslated quotation in Greek.[71]

At the end of the year, as so often happened now with the passage of time, Cobbe was on a committee to raise a memorial fund. In this case it was for Caroline Ashurst Biggs, a fellow member of the Ladies' London Emancipation Society and of the suffrage committee headed by Mentia Tay-lor in 1867. The following July it was for Lydia Becker, whose death Cobbe sincerely believed was an "*immeasurable*" loss to "the cause of women."[72]

Cobbe's holiday letter to Sarah Wister written on New Years' Day, 1890, was indignant about Robert Browning's funeral. He had been buried in the poet's corner of Westminster Abbey on the last day of 1889, and Frederick Leighton had been a pallbearer. She had once asked Leighton to sign a VSS memorial but received "a most contemptuous refusal." Made heedless by her anger, on the day after Browning's funeral Cobbe sent Leighton a quo-tation from Browning about "the people who wd not sign our Memorials," along with a copy of Browning's antivivisection poem "Arcades Ambo." "I think of all the people who rouse my indignation," she wrote to Wister, "the worst are the dilettantes, who live in a world of beauty & will not stoop to touch with their fingers the burden of a groaning world."[73]

She then went to Bristol for two weeks to see Helen and Frances and give an antivivisection speech. Mary Lloyd, no longer listed on the VSS exec-

utive committee, was having new problems with her health. Cobbe warned
Sarah Wister to write the word *private* across anything Lloyd should not read
since Lloyd hated any mention of her growing invalidism. But the real blow
of the new year came when Fanny Kemble left the house at Hereford Square.
The previous summer Cobbe had been "shocked" at the state of the conservatory but secretly arranged for repairs: "I shall be particularly anxious
that Mary shall not hear of anything I have done," she wrote to Wister, "so
you will please dear friend take care of this. She is such an unmanageable
old Welshwoman!" But the conservatory repairs were bungled, and fixing
the "downstairs WC" caused "an obstruction in the drains." Cobbe could
not suppress her annoyance even when writing to Kemble's daughter: "She
never expressed any pleasure in the things I had done—in the *garden* as well
as the house," and finally she had made demands that could not be met.
"We are very sorry for ourselves, for the loss of so good a tenant is very serious to Mary," wrote Cobbe. "But we are more mortified that all our hopes
& efforts to make yr Mother comfortable have failed. . . . Had *you* been in
England, dearest Sarah, I am quite sure this catastrophe wd never have
occurred."[74]

Cobbe was spending two or three hours every day on antivivisection.
The *Zoophilist* reprints dozens of her letters to newspapers; any occasion
would do to get some piece of the message into print. She produced several
clever series of tiny leaflets for handing out in public places, among them
*My Doctor Tells Me* (that Pasteur cures hydrophobia by means of vivisection,
that vivisection is not a cruel practice, etc.). At Swan Sonnenschein's suggestion she republished twenty-one articles and pamphlets in a hardbound
book, *The Modern Rack,* and had many copies placed in public libraries.[75]
She continued to order copies of the licensing reports, carefully read Home
Office returns of experiments, subscribed to the *Journal of Physiology* and
other scientific papers, and used a commercial agency in Southampton Row
for press cuttings to feed her work. And she began to write prefaces for children's stories promoting kindness to animals.[76]

Among reformers, and particularly among Americans, Cobbe's reputation continued to grow even after she had left London. A visitor in 1890
described her as the person who "now that George Eliot is dead, stands first
among the living women writers of England." Social activists wanted her
name—though not, any longer, her actual work—to support their causes.
She became a vice president of the new Association for the Advancement of
Boarding Out (i.e., foster care), was listed on a committee to oppose infant
marriage in India, and helped raise money to create a school for Hindu widows. She supported Mary Ward's appeal to raise funds for University Hall,
originally a residence for University of London students who were "in gen-

eral sympathy with . . . fearless investigation of the origins of Christianity, and the promotion of Religious, Social, and Educational work." Cobbe admired *Robert Elsmere,* Ward's very successful 1888 novel about a clergyman's crisis of faith, and approved of the University Hall project despite Ward's opposition to suffrage, though she was later annoyed to find her name listed on the governing committee since she had never been notified of any meetings or consulted about any decisions.[77]

Cobbe spent a July holiday at Grasmere with her cousins Sophy and Eliza. In August and September the Hengwrt tenants were R. J. Lloyd Price and his wife, Evelyn, who had rented their own house outside Bala for the shooting season at the astonishing price of sixteen hundred pounds. Though not herself living at Hengwrt, Mary Lloyd fiercely defended the property. That summer she found a doctor named Wolfenden making sketches and ordered him to leave. He refused and asked why. "Because you are a Vivisector & yr presence contaminates the ground," she answered, according to Cobbe's account. "He called her all sorts of names 'an old brute' being the kindest. She stood her ground & calling her steward made him 'make tracks'!"[78] Lloyd's copy of *Every Man's Own Lawyer; a Handy Book of the Principles of Law and Equity* is full of pencil marks and marginal notes in sections about trespass.

In November 1890 Cobbe delivered two public lectures in Birmingham. One, at a large VSS public meeting, was published as "The Bobliettes of Science." The other, entitled "Women's Duty to Women," was delivered at a conference of the National Union of Women Workers. Marianne Farningham recalled looking at "the great company of well-dressed women, chiefly young" and wondering "if they knew all that Miss Cobbe had done for our sex. But as soon as she entered the door the whole assembly with one accord rose in respectful greeting of this pioneer woman worker, who had shown so many of them the way. She was much touched by their evident admiration."[79]

And she could still give a fine, rousing speech. Describing "the great Masculine Myth,—that every girl and woman is amply and entirely provided for in mind, body, and estate from childhood to old age, by some individual man," she wondered why rich women have so often "followed in the ruts of the old masculine almsgivers." Thirty years earlier, while visiting workhouses and hospitals, she had found that "the *good* wards were given to the sick men, and the defective ones to the sick women!" But now, when rich women controlled their own charitable bequests, "how much worse it was when I went over Christ Church at Oxford, and compared that and all the other glorious old colleges where my own three brothers had been educated, to the humble little beginnings of Girton." She closed with a quotation from Terence, "I am a *Man*—nothing human is alien to me," and said, "I would have each of you add to this in an emphatic way. '*Mulier sum. Nihil muliebre a me alienum puto*,' 'I am a *woman*. Nothing concerning the interests of women is alien to me.'"[80]

And then almost at once she became embroiled in a dispute with Somerville College and published the whole set of letters on both sides in a pamphlet with the bitter title *Somerville Hall: A Misnomer*. At issue was the election to Somerville's governing council of Ghetal Burdon Sanderson, whose husband, an editor of the 1873 *Handbook for the Physiological Laboratory*, was a professor of physiology at Oxford. Knowing nothing about the woman herself, Cobbe nevertheless protested that having her name on the council would damage "not only Somerville Hall, but in a measure the whole movement for the advancement of female education." After a number of high-handed letters on both sides the vice president of Somerville tried to close the correspondence by firmly protesting "against any attempt to prejudice the Hall." Undeterred, Cobbe made the story public in letters to the *Spectator* and in the published pamphlet. On the whole it was one of those disputes in which no one looks good. The Somerville authorities were caught out in several errors; Cobbe's account of the facts grew more dramatic in each letter; and publishing the correspondence spread harm in all directions, quite aside from any question about the original issue of rejecting a woman with "great capacity for business [and] a strong interest in female education" because of her husband's name.[81]

Further damage was done, although perhaps unjustly, by Cobbe's next attempt to enlist religious opposition to vivisection. After her 1889 success with the Society of Friends she had directed attention to both Roman Catholics and the Church of England. Then in February 1891 she wrote to the *Jewish Chronicle* appealing to the "well-known humanity of English Jews" to protest against the fact that "throughout Germany and Austria the great majority of Vivisectors are Jews." Her letter aroused vehement objections. Claude Montefiore had already advised her that "a special *Jewish* appeal to *Jews* would be a mistake. Since the army is closed to Jews in Germany & Professorships in other sciences are very poor, they crowd into medicine. And as there is a greater proportion of Jewish Doctors, so there is a greater proportion of Jewish vivisectors." But Cobbe persisted. Her follow-up letter to the *Jewish Chronicle* pointed out that she had already published a great many British Christians' names in the *Vivisectors' Directory*. She also wrote to Jewish friends and to people such as Millicent Fawcett who had widespread contacts in the academic world asking for their help.[82]

The incident has left a taint of anti-Semitism around Cobbe's name, and it must be admitted that the English Jews she knew well were highly assimilated people such as Constance Flower, while her archenemy Ernest Hart, the leader of the physicians' protest in 1876, was indeed a man who had gone into medicine because of religious barriers at Cambridge when he was young. But I have not seen anywhere in Cobbe's writing the sort of brutally casual language used by many of her acquaintances. Walburga Paget, wife of the British ambassador in Vienna, wrote, for example, "The Jews are great cowards & I daresay that is what makes them dislike dogs." And Charles Adams, in the *Verulam Review,* consistently referred to the *British Medical Journal's* editor as "E. Abraham Hart" and spoke of "the blood of that pre-eminently pushing race" in his veins.[83]

Cobbe continued to fret about women students' becoming infected with the "passion for vivisection." She sent the pamphlet about Somerville to Millicent Fawcett in hopes of enlisting her influence and that of her daughter Philippa, a Newnham student who had in the previous June been stunningly placed "above the senior wrangler" in the mathematical tripos, to oppose vivisection at Cambridge. Fawcett made inquiries of Newnham's treasurer, Eleanor Sidgwick, who replied that women attended "two or three demonstrations" on anesthetized animals that were killed before the effect wore off. "These are the facts," she wrote, "but I hardly know whether you will think them worth communicating to Miss Cobbe. They might 'irritate' rather than 'soothe'!" It was, of course, inadequate; Cobbe still objected. But Cobbe wrote an unusually temperate letter to Fawcett that also gestured to their other alliance by enclosing a five-pound suffrage subscription.[84]

The census of 1891 found Cobbe and Lloyd living at Tyn-y-Celyn, Llanelltyd, with three servants. One of the servants was Ellen Parry Jones, who had been with them since the earliest years in London. All three servants were listed as bilingual, but Mary Lloyd spoke only English. Neither Lloyd nor Cobbe, therefore, could take part in the sort of neighborhood social work Cobbe had done as a girl in Ireland; their local contacts would have been limited largely to gentry and summer visitors. Lloyd's family made a significant contribution to their social life. In early June 1891 a two-day celebration at Rhiwlas marked the coming of age of Robert Kendrick Price, son of her nephew R. J. Lloyd Price. There were horse races, a tenants' dinner, a regatta on Bala Lake, sporting contests and food for the laborers, and entertainment for all with songs, dances, Punch and Judy, and so forth. Lloyd Price's wife, Evelyn, had become active in developing the local economy and especially in finding suitable employment for women. (The following year, Cobbe would write to the Society for Promoting the Employment of Women in London to locate skilled brushmakers for a factory Evelyn operated.)[85] Two very old American friends from London in the 1860s came to visit. Louisa Lee Schuyler had just secured passage of a New York State law that moved insane patients out of county poorhouses and into public hospitals. She lived with her sister Georgina, a competent musician, who tended the home fires while "Loo," as Cobbe called her, pursued her public life.

In early autumn Cobbe and Lloyd were again briefly living at Hengwrt, putting the garden in order and looking out the drawing-room window on "a panorama of splendid scenery . . . full of exquisite details of old stone bridge and ruined abbey, rivers, woods and rocks."[86] They expected to leave soon and probably for good, since Lloyd was about to come to terms with a man whose lease would last out her lifetime. Then an entirely unexpected inheritance changed everything. As Cobbe wrote in dramatic fashion to Sarah Wister:

> Some sixty years ago a country girl—very pretty & good & steady—went into service in Liverpool. Her first mistress told her she was too pretty to keep with her three sons & found her another place, as parlourmaid with a rich merchant, a Mr. Yates. . . . Her master's brother fell in love with her & at once sent her to be educated at Dr. Lant Carpenter's school in Bristol with Mary Carpenter for teacher & James Martineau for schoolmaster. At the end of a year Mr. Richard Vaughan Yates married her & soon after they went to Egypt on the famous journey with Harriet Martineau, commemorated in *"Eastern Life Past & Present."* Mr. Yates . . . died forty years ago, leaving his widow, as was believed, very moderately endowed. . . . while I was Hon. Sec. in Victoria St she several times came to the office & deposited £500 bank notes. . . . when she told me on one of the 4 or 5 occasions on which (in all) we ever met that she meant to make me her Residuary Legatee, I concluded it wd be a few hundred more at most.[87]

Anna Yates died on 1 October 1891. Her will, proved on 29 October, bequeathed houses to several women; legacies, annuities, and charitable bequests amounting to more than eight thousand pounds; and the residue, as she had promised, to Frances Power Cobbe. That residue, after taxes, amounted to about twenty-five thousand pounds. Cobbe found the lawyer's letter without warning in the morning mail.

> When Mary came down the stairs, she says she thought some dreadful news had come, I looked so floored. But wasn't it wonderful! In a couple of hours I had telegraphed to the would-be tenant: "Another offer per house accepted"—(the offer, of course, being our own)—& now we are, please God really housed in this dear house for the remainder of our joint lives— & Mary for all her life, whether I live or die as I have been able to secure in my will. It is a very great happiness to me, chiefly of course for her sake. . . . But also it is an immense pleasure to feel I can work for our Society *quite*

freely & largely so long as I live & leave it when I die probably some £15000 or more.[88]

She at once reassigned to the VSS the one-hundred-pound annuity that members had raised for her retirement, increased her contributions to many causes (including Mary Ward's University Hall and the *Women's Herald* free-circulation fund), bought herself a new pony, and for the first time hired a maid to be her own attendant, though since one of the woman's primary qualifications was the ability to use a typewriter, her duties were more those of a personal assistant than of a lady's maid.

On 6 November, in the wake of this stunning news, Cobbe traveled across England to deliver a speech entitled "Health and Holiness" at the Cambridge Ladies' Discussion Society. The invitation may well have been arranged by Eleanor Sidgwick or some other old friend as a gesture of reconciliation. Cobbe provided a nice, easy-to-follow spoken piece, expressing her distaste for doctors and fashions in reasonably temperate language. Happy to see "the young women of the new Colleges . . . taking to athletics and mountain climbing, short skirts and sensible shoes," she argued that for women "the worst of consulting medical advisers is; that we can scarcely help from taking from them the noxious idea (common to the profession) that our normal condition is to *be patients*."[89]

Happily settling in at Hengwrt and refurbishing it both inside and out, Cobbe and Lloyd could also delight in having far more friends to visit. Tourists came to Dolgelley not only to climb Cader Idris but for picturesque walks, the remains of Cymmer Abbey, and, in a field above Hengwrt, "traces of the ruins of Cymmer Castle." According to a guidebook written by Lloyd's ever-entrepreneurial nephew, the wood was "celebrated among entomologists as the haunt of many rare and wondrous moths." Maggie Elliot came for a month almost every autumn; the Schuylers made several more trips across the Atlantic. Cobbe's working room had a large, deep window with a view "of almost the whole valley of the Mawddach for nine or ten miles." A friend wrote that the "big open window of her drawing-room through which the beloved dogs came leaping and bounding; the spacious fields where the horses grazed . . . the fragrant room full of comfortable chairs and readable books were outward expressions of her own generous nature."[90]

Lloyd's own financial situation improved once she sold the lease to 26 Hereford Square and was no longer responsible for repairs or anxious about tenants. By March, although it had been a dreadful winter and was still snowing, Cobbe wrote happily to Sarah Wister: "I find my new strange wealth very pleasant! I have a perfect miracle of a former maid who type-writes—& translates & copies—& sews—& upholsters & walks all over the mountains & (I am informed) rows a boat & drives a trap & is the most good natured obliging creature in the world. We have redecorated the old drawing room entirely & a good deal else that was wanted about the house & shrubbery has been done & horses & carriages provided. So dearest Sarah when you come again to us it will be to be made comfortable!!"[91]

In addition, she continued, "I am (but this must be for friends' ears only) going to pay most of the election expenses of a young man who is to bring our AV Bill into Parliament as soon as possible." Although the VSS had an election fund—Cobbe had used some of the money earlier given to her by Anna Yates to set it up—this effort seems to have been entirely personal. And though I have not been able to discover a name for the (probably unsuccessful) candidate, the ability to fund a political campaign must have been almost a giddy experience for a woman who had spent more than thirty years chafing at her lack of a vote. Early in 1892, however, Cardinal Manning's death severed her last close personal connection to the men with major influence in the VSS. When the Parliamentary Franchise (Extension to Women) Bill came up for consideration in April, W. E. Gladstone was yet again an active opponent, and a suffragists' meeting was interrupted by supporters of the Women's Franchise League—some of whom, mostly men, stormed the stage—because the measure did not explicitly include married women.[92]

Cobbe was not in London at the time, though she made a trip in May for business connected with the Yates legacy. Meanwhile, she began another private effort that once more stirred up trouble. In February she sent a letter to the 261 local British societies for the protection of animals urging that the RSPCA hold a plebiscite on vivisection. "If a Temperance Society were to prohibit beer-drinking but permit its members to consume absinthe . . . what opinion should we form of that Association," she asked, making it once more a class issue: beer, like cockfighting or a poor cabdriver's overwork of his horse, was a working-class problem, and absinthe, like experimental medicine, was a vice of educated men. At the RSPCA annual meeting on 11 June Lord Aberdare criticized Cobbe by saying, among other things, that women were "absolutely without a sense of justice." This provided a fine opening for a double-pronged reply. "I am tempted to say that the man who made such a charge must be absolutely without sense of humor," she wrote. "*We* are pleading . . . for justice to men, that 6,000 carters and peasants should not be fined or imprisoned for misusing animals, while 150 gentlemen vivisectors are licensed and lauded for doing ten-fold worse." Furthermore, she asked, how could women have acquired that sense from their experience "of the dealings of his sex with ours." Although "neither a Criminal, nor an Idiot, nor a Pauper, nor (alas, for a long time back!) a Minor," she was still without "the franchise which is accorded to my groom. And, this being so, I am publicly taunted by a *man* with being one of a sex absolutely without sense of justice!"[93]

The incident gave Charles Adams an excuse to vent his enormous resentment of Cobbe. Although people generally believed of antivivisection that "Miss Cobbe *is* the movement; and the movement is Miss Cobbe," he wrote in the *Verulam Review,* that was in no way true. Cobbe, said Adams, had made herself important by the force of her personality and by her shamelessness. "For superabounding energy, for absolute self-conviction, for magnificent unscrupulousness of assertion, for entire imperviousness alike to reason and to ridicule, and for inextinguishable eloquence, especially in the direction of vituperation, she is, in these latter days, almost, if not quite, unsurpassed."[94]

For Cobbe's feelings and her reputation, however, there was far worse to come. In April she wrote the preface to an antivivisection book brought out through Swan Sonnenschein under the title *The Nine Circles of the Hell of the Innocent.* Now that she had money in hand, she managed the book as she would later do with her *Life,* undertaking all of the publisher's work except for advertising, distribution, and sale.[95] Like many of the earlier (and shorter) VSS productions, *Nine Circles* assembled extracts from medical and scientific reports under various headings—"Mangling," "Artificial Disease," "Poisoning," "Burning and Freezing," and so forth. In this instance, however, either because medical journals were not so freely available in Dolgelley or because she was busy with her autobiography, the excerpts were "Compiled by G. M. Rhodes." (Georgine Rhodes was probably the same "Mrs. Rhodes" who provided clerical help in the office during 1883.) Cobbe may have hurried the book into print because vivisection was finally on the agenda for the autumn's church congress at Folkestone. The session opened with one scientist and one clergyman arguing against vivisection and one of each defending the practice. The *Times* reported an attendance so large that "at one time the gangways near the platform were blocked" and the archbishop had to ask people to move "lest the County Council should withdraw its License." Rain pelting on the roof made speakers shout in order to be heard, but the debate remained almost civil until Victor Horsley spoke. Horsley was Pasteur's chief disciple in London, chairman of a society for preventing rabies, and in every way a notable opponent of Cobbe's agitations.

Horsley opened his offensive by asking if it was "too much to ask of a Church dignitary that, before speaking of the scientific work of honourable men as 'a moral offence,' 'cruelty,' and 'demoralization,' he should make some slight effort to learn the outlines of the subject on which he presumed to speak with dogmatic ignorance." Then he described *The Nine Circles* as "one of the rankest impostures that had for many years defaced English literature." Cobbe had "deliberately and fraudulently misrepresented the actual facts." The book mentioned twenty-six experiments in which English scientists had performed "cutting operations." In all of them, Horsley said, "chloroform, ether, or other anæsthetic agent was used. But of these 26 cases Miss Cobbe did not mention this fact at all in 20, and only stated it without qualification in two out of the remaining six." By the debate's end the clergymen were cowed by Horsley's authoritative analysis; in the closing moments the three bishops involved all made agreeable jokes to lighten the atmosphere and evade coming to any conclusion.[96]

Cobbe was not at Folkestone—sessions of the church congress were for Church of England communicants—but she read the *Times* report and promptly wrote a letter promising to investigate and to withdraw, with apologies, any accounts that were not accurate. But of course she also objected to Horsley's contention that vivisection meant only "cutting operations" and once more pointed out "the multitude of other experiments . . . baking to death, poisoning, starving, creating all manner of diseases." Horsley replied the next day that Cobbe was "adroitly seeking to throw dust in the eyes of the public." Facts, arguments, counterarguments, and accusations rushed forth in a flood of letters. Horsley's of 17 October alluded, without naming it, to the Adams-Coleridge trial in referring to her history of "false statements and insinuations." Other medical men and members of the public joined in, including a chivalric unnamed person who protested "against the tone of Mr. Horsley's letters. . . . 'You're a liar' is a favourite argument with ill-conditioned persons . . . but when the opponent is a lady it is an indication of cowardice as well as ill-breeding."[97]

Horsley, unabashed, defended himself: "I have documentary (printed) proof that she has chosen for 16 years or more to take an immoral course— namely, accusing medical men of murder, cruelty, falsehood, &c. . . . while supporting such charges by frauds of the kind I have now exposed." By 24 October a correspondent had recommended that Cobbe sue Horsley for slander, and T. H. Huxley volunteered to subscribe money for his defense. Horsley provided a list of passages from *The Nine Circles* in which anesthetics were explicitly mentioned in the original report but left out of the quotation; other scientists described errors made in reporting their own work; and "A Recovering Patient" expressed gratitude for skills physicians had gained in the laboratory. *Punch* had fun with both sides.[98]

Edward Berdoe, then the physician most active in the VSS, made the best case he could by explaining that Rhodes had failed to mention anesthesia only when "it could have had but the smallest possible effect on the sum-total of the animals' sufferings," and Georgine Rhodes added that

"Miss Cobbe had requested me to indicate the use of anæsthetics, and, not unnaturally, assumed that I had done so." Nevertheless, a great deal of damage had been done. At a VSS special meeting on 27 October Cobbe took full responsibility and promised to bring out a new edition that would be checked by Dr. Berdoe and Dr. Frances Hoggan. "I throw myself on your mercy," she said, "and I hope you will all consider me in the light of an old watchdog who has barked very conscientiously at the tramps for a long time, but once he has given a growl when there was no proper cause for it, and is much ashamed of it,—as every good dog would be." A speech of that sort was of course greeted with cheers, though the incident continued to sting. Damage had been done not only to her reputation and to antivivisection but also, to a degree, to the larger issue of women's political work. Years later Cobbe still harked back to "certain omissions by one of my assistants, for whose accuracy I had foolishly made myself responsible."[99]

Ernest Hart, who in addition to being a leading medical opponent had been defeated in his 1885 campaign for Parliament in the face of, if not because of, strong VSS opposition, gleefully wrote an article charging that Cobbe "takes refuge, when confronted with the facts, and when her falsities are exposed in a plain and convincing manner, behind 'The Privilege of Her Womanhood.'"

> Miss Cobbe appears on the platform, before a selected audience composed chiefly of women, and is introduced by a canon of the Church as "a white-souled and noble-hearted woman," and after joking and weeping by turns in true hysterical fashion, retires to her Welsh home "very happy and delighted." If these be claimed as the privileges of womanhood, it would be time that those who have any regard for the principles of morality in discussion, for the elementary laws of truth and fair dealing, should decline to have anything to do with women in public discussion.[100]

Cobbe's copy of the essay has a few large X marks in the margin, probably made when Basil Wilberforce (grandson of the evangelical abolitionist William Wilberforce and son of Samuel Wilberforce, the bishop of Oxford notorious for his debate with T. H. Huxley over Darwinism) asked her to "act as ghost" by providing some points for his reply. With her help, Wilberforce pointed out Hart's own errors and put a cheerful face on the diatribe as evidence of "the alarm in the camp of vivisectors." (He also, alas, carefully used Hart's full name, "Ernest Abraham Hart," and asked Cobbe hopefully whether it might be hyphenated as "Abraham-Hart.") But even the antivivisection *Spectator* wrote a dozen years later in its obituary of Cobbe that she had "contracted a wild distrust of the men of science, which once and again made both her action and her language exceedingly rash."[101] All in all, it was a painful "present" for her seventieth birthday (4 December 1892) and an unhappy close to a year that had begun with the erasure of all her financial worries. "I am hoping for *peace* more than anything," she wrote, "but failing powers, when peace is denied, are not very easy to bear cheerfully."[102]

13    The Oldest New Woman
      1893–1904

*How much this cheery old maid has done to make life brighter, richer, and deeper and more human for her fellow creatures. Whether we regard her as the grandmother of the New Woman or as the pioneer and prophet of the widest and most far-reaching manifestation of the divine thought in this our day and generation, Miss Cobbe has every claim to be regarded as one of the most notable among the notable of her sex.*

W. T. STEAD, "CHARACTER SKETCH"

During the winter after the Church of England's October 1892 congress, Cobbe soothed her soul with steady work, though she asked people not to mention that she was "trying to put down the story of my own rather interesting life before it comes to an end." Even a woman who lived in the public eye needed disclaimers; she freed herself for autobiography by deciding the book would not be published until after her death. A second piece of work also turned her mind to the past. Fanny Kemble died at eighty-three on 15 January 1893, leaving Cobbe to deal with the "mess of papers" Kemble had given her "from time to time for many years back." In 1872, when Kemble had begun writing her memoirs, she had stayed for several weeks at Hereford Square and asked permission to leave her letters and papers to Cobbe. Over the next dozen years Kemble had used much of the material in *Records of a Girlhood* (3 vols., 1878), *Records of a Later Life* (3 vols., 1882) and *Further Records* (2 vols., 1890) but continued giving Cobbe "large packets of all the letters she had received from interesting people, & also hers to some of her correspondents, returned to her after their deaths."[1]

After Kemble died, Cobbe opened up the boxes and returned the letters written by people who were still alive. Then, before letting any other papers out of her hands, she and Lloyd made sure nothing "could possibly hurt anybody."[2] (Kemble had made her promise that "not a word should ever be printed from her papers concerning Mr Butler in any way whatever.") Cobbe offered to sell George Bentley a series of letters to Kemble from Edward Fitzgerald but reserved the right to examine the proofs and exclude "anything which I might consider best kept private." There were also "two immense parcels" of letters written by Kemble. One seemed to be material already used in the three series of Kemble's *Records;* the other contained "a quantity of sheets & half sheets all piled with no order & in extreme confusion of dates (nearly illegible in many cases from crossings & faded ink). . . . Mary & I read one or two together most days & mark the passages which we think fit for publication . . . & then my (German) maid typewrites those passages & I correct them & again omit anything I think better omitted for any reason."[3] For a short time Cobbe considered putting together a further volume but dropped the project once she realized that Kemble had "used all the real material" and the rest would "only supply the *sweepings.*"[4] Ultimately she gave the remaining letters to Kemble's grandson Owen Wister.

This business kept both Cobbe and Lloyd occupied for much of the spring of 1893. Although Lloyd was still prickly about her independence, Cobbe was looking for an intelligent and faithful "attendant now she needs one sorely." Lloyd would sometimes go driving in Cobbe's "nice barouche" but preferred "her little old pony & chair for one." Cobbe herself remained hale and active, as revealed by an anecdote about her current dog, Colleen, who was lying asleep by the fire when Cobbe

> entered the room with my hat on and invited her to join me in a walk; but, after looking up at me for a moment, as canine politeness required, she dropped back among her cushions. . . . Thereupon I observed in a clear voice, "I am *not* going on the road" (a promenade disliked by the dogs because the walls on either side restrict the spirit of scientific research); "I am going up the mountain." Instantly my little friend jumped up, shook her ears, and, with a cheerful bark, announced herself as ready to join the party. . . . [She] has lived fewer years in the world than I have passed in Wales, but she knows just about as much English as I know Welsh, and has acquired it in just the same way.[5]

Public affairs remained deeply depressing. On 8 March the women's franchise bill was crowded out by extended debate on a noncontroversial measure that preceded it. Receiving a notice from Helen Blackburn about a suffrage committee meeting, Cobbe responded with angry discouragement: "It seems to me that after this last most insulting refusal to give a day to listen to our claims, the battle is utterly hopeless, & I for one have neither heart nor time in my old age to continue it any longer. Men are but playing with us."[6]

Since the death in 1891 of Sidney Williams, who had published much of Cobbe's social and theological work, she had arranged for Thomas Fisher Unwin to acquire the remaining unbound sheets and issue an Author's Edi-

tion with his imprint on the title page and "fresh little paper uniform taste-
ful covers."[7] (Unwin subscribed to the National Society for Women's Suffrage and in 1891 had published the first edition in nearly fifty years of Mary
Wollstonecraft's *Vindication of the Rights of Woman.*) Then, as her *Life* neared
completion, Cobbe changed her mind about waiting for posthumous publication and offered it to Unwin. By the end of the year she was beginning
to long for something more like her old public life. When Mary Haweis
organized a series of Sunday lunches in South Kensington at which distinguished people would discuss important topics, Cobbe wrote from Wales,
where she was eight hours from London, "It was almost *cruel* of you to send
me such a tantalizing series of invitations!"[8]

The work of assembling her autobiography did much to restore Cobbe's
emotional balance. An exercise in memory and imagination, the *Life of
Frances Power Cobbe as Told by Herself* let her revisit childhood, organize her
letters and papers, write to old friends for recollections to quote, and present a public self rather than a story of woman's domestic and emotional
life. "The world when I entered it was a very different place from the world
I must shortly quit," she wrote in the preface, "most markedly so as regards
the position in it of women and of persons like myself holding heterodox
opinions, and my experience practically bridges the gulf which divides the
English *ancien régime* from the new." In the tradition of exemplary lives, she
suggested that its value lay also in the evidence of "how pleasant and interesting" life could be for a woman who chose to remain single. Revisiting the
past revived some of her old interests. She began to read, and save, new essays
on biblical criticism and psychology; she also preserved "A Defense of the
'Wild Women'" by her acquaintance and fellow antivivisectionist Mona
Caird. Answering Frances Willard's plea that she write for the *Woman's Signal,* she replied to the antisuffragist Walter Besant by looking at her own accomplishments from the perspective gained through the year's work: "Every
woman of experience—be she even the happiest of us all, and blessed with
good relatives, health, vigour, and a competence, must yet feel how heavily
we are handicapped in the race of life."[9]

But as the *Life* neared completion Cobbe again grew anxious about the
arrogance of displaying her successful career. "I believe I shall only print the
book in England for private circulation during my life," she wrote to Sarah
Wister in the spring of 1894, "& let it be published after my death if desired.
But I believe I may safely let it be published in America if it wd create interest there—& secure my copyright under the new law." A month later she
changed her mind once more, referred to Unwin as "my publisher," and
reported on his own negotiations for U.S. rights. Meanwhile, although Wister could not interest Lippincott in Philadelphia, she contacted Houghton

Mifflin in Boston, who had responded by 27 May with a "most satisfactory" offer.[10] Cobbe had the printing done herself and got photographs copied for the illustrations since she thought engravings generally missed "all the finer points" and made faces look vulgar. Then in early June she learned that Unwin was also bringing out "the Autobiography of a woman I specially dread—& with whom it wd be too good fun for my enemies to bracket me in the reviews—namely Mrs Besant!"[11] Annie Besant was a freethinker and Fabian who had lost custody of her daughter for publishing a pamphlet on birth control; then, as if that were not enough, she had become a Theosophist. And Besant's *Autobiography* praises Cobbe's work for setting her free from conventional religion.

Early in the correspondence with George Bentley over Kemble's affairs, Cobbe had gently turned back his inquiry about publishing her autobiography. Although his firm was known especially for solid, middlebrow books of travel, history, and biography, as well as for novels by such bestselling writers as Ellen Price Wood and Rhoda Broughton, she told Bentley that "I think you & I are very much of the same opinions on politics, many social matters (if not all)—yet . . . you have never meddled with heterodox theology, & a very solid *core* of my book will concern my religious views & this you might not like." Now, with the pending crisis of joint reviews of her life and Annie Besant's, she asked Bentley if he would do "the immense service of publishing it for me when complete, on commission or in any other way." She anxiously sent proofs from the chapters on religion four days later; they might "very probably," she thought "cause you to feel you would not like to include it among your publications." By 20 June she had Bentley's acceptance in hand and began arranging a publication date. And she asked his advice as a publisher and "a man of the world" about the "propriety" of some of her unflattering references to Gladstone and other public figures.[12]

As the book neared exposure, Cobbe was filled with a combination of anxiety, excitement, and relief. Although she no longer went to London for VSS meetings, she still expected to be consulted on important issues. Lord Coleridge died on 14 June, Stephen Coleridge remained honorary treasurer, and Bernard, now "Lord Coleridge, QC," the first man to continue practice at the bar after succeeding to a peerage, was listed with the vice presidents. Nor did she go to the suffrage mass meeting at Queen's Hall on 9 June, a unified effort supported by the two central committees and also by the Women's Liberal Federation, the British Women's Temperance Association, and a number of women's trades unions; but despite having "withdrawn" from the cause a year earlier, she did send a letter, which was read aloud.[13]

And then in the middle of August, when she had invested a great deal of money in typesetting and printing, Cobbe had qualms yet again and urgently asked Bentley if it was "really desirable to *publish at all.*" Should she, after all, circulate the book privately? "The loss is nothing to me," she wrote, "compared to the peril of getting into hot water or being thought to have made a fool of myself!" Relieved by his prompt reassurance, she immediately wished she could talk with him about many other things "which it would not be fitting to put in a book." By 27 August she had sent a bound copy to Sarah Wister with careful instructions not to let it leave her hands before 22 September, which was the publication date required by Houghton Mifflin.[14]

For British circulation Cobbe had 1,000 copies printed but only 500 bound; she kept 50 for gifts and sent 450 to Bentley for "publication" on 22 September. By the twenty-seventh he had telegraphed to have the other 500 bound at once. In addition to gratifying sales and plentiful reviews on both sides of the Atlantic, she was soon basking in a wonderful harvest of letters from both friends and strangers. The most touching came from Margaret Froude: "My father wishes me to write at once to tell you what a pleasure reading your book has been to him. . . . We have been so glad to see him really interested & enjoying his reading," she began. "I think that when one is very ill as he is that recollections of old days are more pleasure & interest than anything new." James Anthony Froude would be dead within a month.[15]

As is generally the case with biographies and autobiographies, most reviewers summarized Cobbe's life and selected appealing passages to quote. Some, however, added their own affirmations. Walter Lewin wrote in the *Academy:* "Excepting John Stuart Mill, she has done more than anyone to give the dignity of principle to the woman's movement, which might otherwise have become a mere struggle for perquisites." Only *Punch* was vicious, describing it as "a slovenly-written, ill-digested mass of miscellaneous matter, including whole chapters devoted to digests of her published works"; coming from such an old enemy of her causes, the very venom was virtually a sign of her success. W. T. Stead named Cobbe "one of the most remarkable women of the Victorian era" and continued with his delightful phrase "the oldest New Woman now living on this planet." Coming at the height of the "New Woman" furor then occupying the press, as young, middle-class women demanded the right to go about unchaperoned, to have their own latchkey, to work for pay whether or not they had to be self-supporting, and to read and discuss whatever they chose without parental or masculine interference, Stead's description was a pointed reminder that some women had successfully led independent public lives for thirty years or more.[16]

A few reviewers and, later, some obituarists who were personal friends were distressed that vivisection had marred her later years. To that cause, wrote one, she had sacrificed "everything, her literary income . . . her work as a writer on religion, her friendship with distinguished scientific men, her leisure, and much of her great joy in life." But neither Cobbe's occasional gloominess nor our knowledge of the painful incidents left unrecorded in her autobiography should obscure the enormous fun people found with her, even late in life. She constantly sent gifts, especially of flowers picked from the garden at Hengwrt. Katharine Bradley, who together with her niece Edith Cooper published under the pen name Michael Field, for example, wrote, "Conceive my delight on coming home from a long day in town last evening to find awaiting me all that stretch of fairy country. . . . Edith is so paralysed by the beauty she does not feel she can begin. . . . If ever recovery from the paralysis takes place & the lovely little country vision is beholden you certainly shall see in M.S. the result."[17] Matilda Betham-Edwards "received an affectionate mid-winter invitation to [Cobbe's] Welsh retreat. . . . North Wales in the season of snowfalls! Not even the blazing logs and geniality of such a hostess could have warmed me there in December. But how happy we should have been together! With what quips, cranks, and wanton wiles should I have been beguiled!"[18]

With the book off her mind, Cobbe picked up social threads again. Constance, Lady Battersea (Cyril Flower had been made a peer as Baron Battersea in September 1892), came in August. "My dear old friend," she wrote of Cobbe, "is much aged but as dear & hearty & lovable as ever." On 2 August they spent "a nice long evening at the fireside, much talk"; the next day they drove through the splendid scenery to Barmouth. "Feel happy & contented here," Battersea continued. "Like that strange creature Miss Lloyd better than I thought." Cobbe still had a "bright mind & warm loving heart. . . . Time flies cruelly fast & I am very happy in this pretty mountain house. The two old ladies spoil & pet me with all their might and main—Cobby my own special one walks & drives with me & we talk by the hour. It is such a wholesome life with wh. I am in harmony."[19]

By 8 November Bentley's was sending "£300 on account," an action and a sum that made her breathless. "I never heard of such proceedings on the part of any publisher I have had to do with before!" she wrote to George Bentley. At year's end the British edition had sold 1,244 copies and brought her six hundred pounds. She had done only a little management about reviewers; a response from her old friend Peter Clayden, at the *Daily News*, promised that the book would not be assigned to "the writer you mention," who was, as a letter to Bentley makes clear, Andrew Lang. Gleeful responses to friends sowed favors as well as thanks: a letter of introduction to a leading Boston music critic for H. R. Haweis, who was setting off on a trip to

the United States, an assurance to Sarah Wister that she and Lloyd were sub-
scribing to *Harper's* on purpose to see the "spirited & original" work by Wister's son Owen, who was just beginning to publish stories about Wyoming
(where he, like his Harvard friend Theodore Roosevelt, had been sent for
his health). She even found a way to exercise her combination of hope and
wit over vivisection: "I could *not* bear it did I not believe in another life for
the poor harmless victims where their wrongs will be recompensed, & I may
add also in another life for their inhuman persecutors where they will all
repent in moral agony worse than the physical pain of their poor victims."[20]

Amid the praise heaped on her accomplishments, Cobbe was distressed
to learn that protection for abused wives was sliding into disrepair. Her
original bill, it may be recalled, required that a woman be granted a separation at her request, but the law as passed left the decision up to the magistrate. An essay in the *Westminster Review* by Mabel Crawford and follow-up
reports in women's newspapers demonstrated that magistrates sometimes
refused separation orders even when there was extreme cruelty. Cobbe
thought it was because of "High Church superstition about the sanctity of
marriage!" and told Helen Taylor that she was "earnestly seeking for some
M.P. who will take up the matter & try to strengthen the Act." As a first
step, she urged Walter McLaren to "ask for a Return of the cases in which
Separation Orders have been given & *refused* to wives whose husbands have
been convicted of aggravated assaults." McLaren, however, was suddenly
undermined as a feminist spokesman when his attempt to move that "no
person should be disqualified from exercising the Parliamentary franchise
on the grounds of sex" was blocked by an MP acting on the advice of Mary
Cozens, secretary of the so-called Parliamentary Committee for Woman
Suffrage, a committee unknown to Fawcett, Taylor, and other activists. "This
is certainly a justifiable case for blasphemy!" wrote Cobbe. "May Miss Cozens be scraped to death with oyster shells."[21]

It does not appear that any report about the refusal of separation orders
was ever prepared, although a new law in 1895 did allow a wife to leave a
cruel husband before she applied for separation. This was a significant
improvement—she would no longer be guilty of desertion if she took the
children and ran—but the key word was still *apply;* the power remained with
magistrates. The *Woman's Signal,* believing that Cobbe's focus on protecting
women had "done more towards checking wife-beating" than any other
action, argued that both laws were "made imperfect by the congenital incapacity of men to resist the masculine, deep-seated impression that the
woman is the property of the husband." Even the "good men" who brought
in the bill could not accept Cobbe's formulation: "When these enlightened
and good-hearted Members of Parliament cannot see that an assaulted

woman has a positive, inalienable and absolute right to be the person to say if she can 'give him another trial' it is not surprising" that unpaid magistrates should so often succumb to "their old ideals of the mastery of the husband" and order her back.[22]

The winter of 1895 was unusually harsh. "Between the deadly killing cold such as I never experienced before,—the blasted evergreens,—the dying & starving sheep & lambs & birds all over the country & the daily obituaries in the *Times* . . . the past months have been really *tragic*. Mary & I were both very ill with bronchitis & only pulled through with a new medicine called 'Codein' which magically stops paroxysms of coughing." Mary Lloyd's sister Charlotte Price of Corwen, mother of R. J. Lloyd Price, died on 8 February, and her sister-in-law Gertrude Lloyd (widow of her eldest brother, John) died on 31 March. Her brother Howell had died on 20 September 1893. And Mary herself, even after recovering from the winter's illness, grew "rather more still month after month."[23]

Putting real effort into antivivisection again for the first time since the church congress debacle, Cobbe found organized religion more and more an enemy to both animals and women. In October's *Contemporary Review* she responded to an article in the Jesuit periodical *The Month* for September. While reading the new English Revised Version of the Bible, she described to Millicent Fawcett a "masculine rule" that was as true for scriptures as for other histories: "If anything bad is done by women, make it quite clear that *women did it* & abuse the sex generally on the strength thereof. If anything *good* is done by women describe it in general terms applicable to both sexes, & draw no conclusions."[24]

With the new publicity of her *Life* and its reviews, feminists yet again found Cobbe's name excellent coin. The *Woman's Signal,* now edited by Florence Fenwick Miller, republished "Our Policy: An Address to Women Concerning the Suffrage," first printed in 1874. It also carried a sketch of Cobbe's second cousin, and Miller's good friend when they were students in Paris, "Mrs. Heaton Armstrong";[25] Lucie Cobbe was widowed six months after her 1885 marriage to J. C. Heaton Armstrong and continued to support herself through journalism. Best known for her etiquette columns in the *Ladies' Pictorial,* she also wrote on more professional topics, was active in the associations of women journalists, and became a vice president of the Women's National Liberal Association. As for her new friendships in Wales, Cobbe had been introduced to Blanche Atkinson sometime in the early 1890s. Two decades previously Atkinson had anxiously, and naively, pursued John Ruskin's approval as a young and enthusiastic "companion" of his Guild of St. George.[26] Now living in Barmouth with Frances Talbot, a wealthy widow and Ruskin patron, Atkinson had written children's stories and a few undis-

Llanelltyd church, engraving showing the view of mountains and estuary
described in Cobbe's 21 November 1896 letter to Sarah Wister. (From a drawing
by Henry Gastineau, published in 1830 or 1831)

tinguished novels about love, faith, and social service. Eagerly remaking herself into Cobbe's assistant and disciple, Atkinson came often to see her after
the middle of the decade.

The house was full of visitors in the summer of 1896. Maggie Elliot came
for her usual month; the Boston antivivisectionist Philip Peabody met Cobbe
for the first time; Loo and Georgiana Schuyler again spent several days. The
Schuylers may have told Sarah Wister how badly Mary Lloyd's health was
failing. Sarah, herself now widowed—Dr. Wister had died in February—
sent an unexpected and entrancing gift of fresh sun-ripened grapes from the
United States. Both Cobbe and Lloyd wrote thank-you notes on 4 October.
Cobbe's began, "We, 'The Ladies of Hengwrt' as undersigned—not to be
confounded with the Ladies of Llangollen" and said she was "so glad for
Mary to have them especially as she particularly enjoys grapes." Mary's concluded, "Frances is fairly well . . . that she walks less vigorously than hereto-
fore is I suppose only to be expected though it is a great annoyance to her
energetic temperament."[27]

Nine days later Mary Lloyd was dead at age seventy-seven. It was heart
disease that carried her off, though the death certificate mentions also "chronic

rheumatism 20 years." Responding to letters of condolence, Cobbe wrote that she had died "bravely resting on my arm & telling me we should not long be separated." She was buried as they had planned in the Llanelltyd churchyard, in a double plot that left room for Cobbe to rest beside her under the single headstone. "It is a most lovely spot with a great view of Cader—&˙ this place & woods—& the whole estuary down to the sea," Cobbe wrote, "& I have planted quantities of roses & other plants over it & over the high old wall behind under which I have placed a seat."[28]

But it was, she told Millicent Fawcett, "almost a mortal blow, & I have yet to learn how I am to live without the one who has shared all my thoughts & feelings so long." Cobbe described their relationship as "thirty four years of a friendship as nearly perfect as any earthly love may be—a friendship in which there never was a doubt or a break—or even a rough word—& which grew more tender as the evening closed." Florence Fenwick Miller paid tribute to all such friendships in the *Woman's Signal:* "Miss Frances Power Cobbe's many, loving admirers will regret for her the loss of her special woman friend, Miss Lloyd. . . . It is easy to understand how severe a blow this must be to the one who is left, and how dreary life alone must appear after so many years of sympathetic companionship." Rosa Bonheur's partner had also died not long since. Remembering Bonheur's role in the beginning of their relationship, Cobbe sent news of Mary Lloyd's death along with pictures of herself and Lloyd in the garden with their dog; Bonheur responded with a picture of herself with Nathalie Micas and their own dog, Gamine.[29]

By early 1897 Cobbe was seeing Barmouth friends, writing letters to the *Times,* and making generous contributions to the *Woman's Signal* free-circulation fund and a campaign against continued operation of the Contagious Diseases Acts in India. Her nieces came to visit, but though she was "glad to see them & thankful for their affection," she felt "perhaps even more alone than when alone." Writing to Sarah, Cobbe depicted her grief at second hand: Mary's "poor old pony died last week of old age—& the other pony still older which has shared its field & stable for many years goes about all day whinnying for her in the field under these windows till I go out & pet her as well as I can." But her public voice regained some of its old edge. She wrote to the *Times* that as a Jubilee tribute the queen should be officially titled Victoria the Great and that a column "such as that of Trajan or Antoninus" should be erected in London in her honor, a suggestion intended to contrast woman's rule to that of the kings who had preceded her. In a more formal Jubilee act, women active in public work sent their congratulations to the queen and asked for "a royal word of sympathy in the efforts . . . still further to enlarge the sphere of women's activity and usefulness." As with most such presentations, the signatures were arranged in order of rank, and Frances Power Cobbe's came first among the names of women without titles.[30]

On 3 February 1897 a women's suffrage bill introduced by Faithful Begg for "inhabitant occupier as owner or tenant," with no mention of marriage, passed its second reading in the House of Commons by a margin of seventy-one votes. It had a majority among members from every party. "We all met in the House of Commons where the excitement was great," wrote one woman who was there. "Women laughing and kissing and crying and some M.P.s running about like school boys." On 7 July, however, the time available for its third reading was absorbed by deliberately extended debate on other questions. Henry Labouchère, once a friend but now a raucous leader of opposition, made long speeches full of jokes, and others did the same. Even the *Spectator*—still an opponent of women's suffrage—wrote that "the spectacle of the House performing monkey tricks over the Verminous Persons' Bill, in order to dish the women, was not an agreeable one."[31] One consequence, however, was an effective reunion of the principal suffrage societies in the National Union of Women's Suffrage Societies under an executive committee ultimately headed by Millicent Garrett Fawcett. Although Cobbe was no longer formally a member of the executive, she continued to take an avid interest in suffrage activities.

Cobbe filled the house with visitors for much of the summer. Sarah Wister's sister Frances was among them. Her husband, James Leigh, then dean of Hereford, asked Cobbe to give copies of her theological books to the cathedral library. "How times are changed that ever such a request could be made to me," she wrote, "except with the view of burning them!" She was "glad to be able to give a healthful holiday" to many single women among her relatives: her nieces Frances and Helen, her cousins Sophy and Eliza, and probably some second cousins, such as Lucie Heaton Armstrong and Charles Augustus's daughters Estelle ("Stella") and Vanda.[32] The summer was unusually hot and fine. Cobbe's brother Henry brought his wife and daughters, all unmarried and now in their thirties and forties, for three weeks in August. The Schuyler sisters and Florence Davenport Hill came for ten days in September. But Cobbe was "no longer fit to sit at very long meals & join in long walks" and decided not to "repeat the experiment" the next summer. "Ones own relations are those who least of all understand how the loss of a *friend* leaves the world bare," she wrote to Sarah Wister. Even good friends, she wrote sadly, "are not like the one who is gone. I can hardly interest myself in their talk—nor I suppose they in mine."[33]

At the beginning of 1898 Stephen Coleridge completed his project to reshape the VSS in his own image rather than Cobbe's. At the annual meeting of 14 May 1896 Lord Coleridge, QC (i.e., Bernard), in the chair, had "urged the friends of animals to direct their efforts to the more important points, such as vivisection," and not to waste their time on smaller matters such as muzzling. Florence Fenwick Miller understood his intent; her address pointedly expressed gratitude to Cobbe for founding the society. In April 1897 Stephen Coleridge became honorary secretary, a title not used since Cobbe retired. The May annual meeting changed the organization's name to the National Anti-Vivisection Society. At a special meeting in July new regulations for governance were adopted; and a meeting at Stephen Coleridge's house on 6 October added new members to the executive committee. In January 1898 he issued a call for a special council meeting on 9 February to vote on a resolution that reads, in part: "While the demand for the total abolition of vivisection will ever remain the ultimate object of the National Anti-Vivisection Society, the Society is not thereby precluded from making efforts in Parliament for lesser measures, having for their object the saving of animals from scientific torture."[34]

Cobbe at once wrote a long, angry objection. If the resolution passed, she would sever her connection with the society and withhold the significant legacy she had intended. Coleridge argued that since a total abolition bill had "no chance whatever of becoming law within the lifetime of the youngest of us," it would be better to stop the torture of animals through securing open inspection "as opposed to the hopeless sterile policy of the last twenty years." All the members admired Miss Cobbe, he said, "for her stainless and beautiful life." (Was there a trace of sarcasm in his phrasing?) "But at this point of our path we believe that her judgment is astray." The meeting on 9 February was filled with wrangles about procedure and amendments; at one point Coleridge was annoyed at being called a "younger and newer member." The vote was 29–21 in favor of "lesser measures." Cobbe resigned the next day—someone must have sent her a telegram after the meeting—and was followed by a few vice presidents and executive committee members, almost all of them her very old friends and beyond active work. Julia Camperdown wrote literally from her deathbed to oppose the lesser-measures resolution.[35]

Some conflict of personalities was clearly involved, and Cobbe no doubt resented the arrogance of a young upstart who had seized control of "her" organization—Stephen Coleridge was then forty-four, and she was seventy-five—but the dispute rested on a complex mix of gender, tactics, and ideology as well as generation. Coleridge intended a return to lobbying in the corridors of power, while Cobbe was convinced that no legislation could succeed until public opinion led the way. The suffrage experience of the previous summer had confirmed her belief: not only had she learned in 1876 how thoroughly a bill could be gutted by powerful medical and scientific interests but she had just seen that any private member's bill, even one with a parliamentary majority, could be postponed into extinction by a few determined opponents. In the aftermath of that experience, the National Union of Women's Suffrage Societies drew back from the annual attempt to introduce a bill and concentrated on forming local societies in every constituency and building links with women's labor unions. And just at that moment Coleridge wanted to take up cozy masculine lobbying, while in Cobbe's opinion "the Whole hope of our cause rests on the success of our appeal to the heart and conscience of England."[36] Ideologically, because of her total distrust of scientific medicine Cobbe did not believe vivisection could ever be adequately policed; it had to be abolished. Coleridge, like those suffragists, including Cobbe, who were willing to exclude married women in order to get a foot in the door, hoped pragmatically to work toward abolition through increasingly restrictive steps. In the end it made no difference: no bill of any kind came to a vote until both of them were long dead.

Personally, however, leaving the society for which she and Mary Lloyd together had worked long hours on urgent tasks snapped Cobbe out of her inertia. By 27 April, when she wrote to congratulate Sarah Wister on Owen's marriage to Mary Channing Wister (a distant cousin, a great-granddaughter of William Ellery Channing, and a member of the Philadelphia School Board), she had decided to organize a new society, to be called the British Union for the Total Abolition of Vivisection, and her letter was full of excitement and energy. "I am going to hold a conference here next week for 3 days of 12 leading men & women workers in the cause (Half will have to sleep in Dolgelley!). . . . I must be President, & we shall have Branches all over the Kingdom immediately."[37]

Designed on the model of the suffrage central committee, the British Union was to be "a federation of Anti-Vivisection Societies acting independently in their own localities or special lines of work, but all joining in general plans for the anti-vivisection crusade throughout the kingdom." The Hengwrt conference of 3 and 4 May 1898 produced a constitution and set of rules under the guidance of an old Bristol friend, John Freeman Norris, formerly judge of the high court in Calcutta. The final clause, described in boldface as a "fundamental rule" never to be "modified or departed from," exposed Cobbe's fear of another gradualist takeover: it excluded any person from holding office who was a "member of, or a subscriber to, any Anti-Vivisection society advocating any measure short of Total Prohibition."[38]

The British Union was officially founded at a meeting in Bristol on 14 June. The Reverend Henry Cobbe became an "Honorary Correspondent." Her brother Tom's children Helen, Frances, and Hervic were all members, as were her cousins Eliza and Sophy. (With narrow incomes, they subscribed only 10s. 6d. apiece; Hervic gave £5, and Helen and Frances each pledged £2.) Other members came from among Cobbe's old friends—Maggie Elliot, Arthur Arnold, Jane Hampson, Felicia Skene, Lady de Rothschild, Mary Lloyd's sister Jane Ffoulkes, and R. J. Lloyd Price and his wife Evelyn. There were only ninety members in all, though some of the associated societies must have had their own membership lists.[39]

Physically and mentally full of energy, Cobbe acknowledged that depression had nearly overwhelmed her since Lloyd's death. She had "ceased to feel the object always in view of opposing her pessimism & finding arguments for hope & faith." Now she could laugh about "my old little joke about her which I used to make to her friends when she startled them by some expression of hopelessness—'Christian got to Heaven by having "Hopeful" for a companion—He would have gone the other way if he lived with Mary Lloyd'—How her sweet dear old laugh rings in my ears as I repeat her words now!"[40]

At the end of June Cobbe spoke at a meeting in Barmouth to establish a Welsh section of the British Union. The news report called it "a masterly presentation of the origin, history, and nature of vivisection" suited to an audience unfamiliar with the subject, and for the largely evangelical population of Wales she argued that God "could not possibly have so made His world as that man should be obliged to seek for the remedies of his diseases by tormenting His humbler creatures." In contrast, the speech of Evelyn Ashley, Shaftesbury's son, at the annual meeting of the National Anti-Vivisection Society (the former VSS) was full of manly jingoistic language designed to throw off antivivisection's "effeminate" associations. In one relatively short address Ashley managed to support the U.S. war in Cuba, praise field sports, laud battlefield surgeons in the Crimea, and quote from *Deeds That Won the Empire*.[41]

On 13 November Cobbe's brother Henry died after a short illness; an obituary described him as "till within a few weeks of his death, fully engaged with the activities of his parish and beaming with cheerfulness and good-nature, though in his 81st year." Cobbe wrote of him as "the last link to my old life & my dear good friend & comrade from our childhood," an accurate enough statement, perhaps, but it does emphasize how thoroughly her brother Will, who was still alive, had been erased from her consciousness.[42] It also meant that three more nieces, as well as their mother, were without a home—they had all been living at Maulden Rectory—and some concern about their finances. After her year of mourning, Winifred became the bursar at Lady Margaret Hall and then made a professional career supervising youth clubs and other social-welfare programs.

Frances Power Cobbe at work in the 1890s. (Cobbe Papers, Alec Cobbe Collection)

Cobbe was healthier than she had been a year or two earlier, though her eyes were failing: she could write only in the morning and spent the afternoon driving or "mooning about the place with my saw & scissors." She consulted her old friend Charles Bell Taylor, one of the physicians who had written tracts for the VSS and was internationally known for surgery on the eyes, but there was no sign of cataracts.[43] Among other work, she kept busy looking for people who could lend prestige to her new organization. "It is a very different thing combining with a few good hearted but unimportant men and women," she wrote, from working with "those dear friends— all now dead—who used to sit round our Council table in Victoria St." Lady Paget's daughter Alberta, wife of Baron Windsor, subsequently earl of Plymouth, became head of the branch in South Wales.[44] By mid-April 1899 Cobbe had several dependable acquaintances among her vice presidents, including Lady Battersea (Constance Flower); Lady Mount-Temple; the dowager Countess of Darnley, a distant connection through Cobbe's great-aunt Catherine Pelham; and Sir Charles Gordon, the former surgeon general.

Meanwhile Cobbe applied her feminist sensibility to the wreck of the *Stella*. A steamer that made regular journeys to Guernsey and Jersey, the *Stella* struck a rock at four o'clock in the afternoon of 30 March 1899 and sank eight minutes later. The ladies' cabin was full of women and children. The captain ordered them first into the lifeboats, and the stewardess, Mary Anne Rogers, kept them calm, got lifebelts onto the children, and went down with the ship. As the public began raising money for the widows of the officers and crew, Cobbe pointed out that one person had been mentioned only briefly and offered twenty-five pounds to begin a fund in her memory: "All honour is accorded, and justly so, to the captain of a ship who sinks with his vessel. This poor stewardess, pursuing her humbler duties, and courageously to the very last aiding the lady passengers . . . seems to me one of the most sublime figures in 'our island story.'"[45]

On 15 April 1899 the British Union brought out the first issue of its periodical *The Abolitionist*. Cobbe's "The Work Before Us," on the first three pages, set out her rationale and tried to reclaim the prestige of her first society: "The Abolitionist is founded to advocate the principles and policy of the Victoria Street Society such as they were under the Presidency of the late Lord Shaftesbury." Hoping to give the journal "literary & artistic distinction," she secured an experienced editor in her old disciple John Stuart Verschoyle, who had worked as an undergraduate on the campaign to reprieve Isabel Grant. During his ten years as a curate in London (1881–91) Verschoyle had spent as much time on journalism as on his clerical duties. Cobbe said that he had "for a long time edited the *Fortnightly Review*," though his name never appeared, and knew "everybody in the literary world."[46] Since 1893 he had been rector of a small parish near Taunton, Somerset.

In choosing *The Abolitionist* for the journal's name, Cobbe not only publicized its stand on vivisection but also claimed the emotional power of moral crusades against slavery and, more recently, against women's sexual slavery. She (or Verschoyle) did generate a few interesting features in the *Abolitionist*: medical contributions from William Gordon Stables, an immensely popular writer for the *Boy's Own Paper* who had served as an assis-

tant surgeon in the Royal Navy; a monthly insert with reasonably well produced drawings of old friends such as Mary Somerville and James Anthony
Froude; a contest offering five guineas for the best poem in English or Welsh
written to the tune of "March of the Men of Harlech." For the most part,
however, it was the same old collection of meeting notices, excerpted
speeches, and republished letters to newspapers. Virtually every issue had an
obituary for some old friend of Cobbe's.

Her brother Henry had spent many years working on a book that was
not yet published when he died. *Luton Church, Historical and Descriptive,*
brought out in 1899 by the firm of George Bell & Sons, which was headed
by Cobbe's friend Edward Bell, is a 650-page volume recording "as full an
account as practicable" of the church, which was in the market town closest to Henry's rectory at Maulden, along with biographies of people who
had been connected with it.[47] The account is indeed full, with quotations,
diagrams, lists of pastors, vicars, curates, and churchwardens, and long ap-
pendixes containing wills, Latin texts, indentures, and other material that
could not be worked into the central text. Cobbe wrote politic letters to a
few editors in an effort to secure favorable reviews, but the only one I have
been able to locate appeared in the *Athenaeum* for 13 January 1900.

"This is a sad winter in England," Cobbe wrote in January 1900, three
months after fighting began in South Africa, "owing to this abominable war
& the incapacity of our Ministers. . . . I used to call myself a Tory; but
assuredly will never do so again!" Her cousin Alick had died in September,
but all five of his sons were in military or imperial service, and the eldest was
in South Africa. After the disasters of "Black Week" in mid-December,
Redvers Buller was relieved as commander in chief. "I knew Buller a little,"
Cobbe reported, "and felt *sure* he wd be a bad General." She was happy to
know that he would be replaced by General Frederick Sligh Roberts, her
cousin Alick's old friend and commander.[48]

Spending the winter at Hengwrt alone, as she preferred, Cobbe quickly
produced two tributes when James Martineau died on 11 January. She was
yet again looking for someone to take over the remaining stock of her old
books. Unwin, she felt, had not promoted them adequately during the stir
of interest in her *Life,* perhaps because he was not pleased to lose the chance
of publishing it. Swan Sonnenschein agreed but then found that most were
"in an unsalable condition" from the years in storage. She also used Sonnenschein (or his clerks) as her agent in London, asking him to buy books
for her and, more interestingly, to forward copies of the *Zoophilist;* evidently
she did not want Stephen Coleridge to know she still subscribed. The effort
to sell her old publications was not pure vanity: she was spending heavily
on the British Union and on printing her own pamphlets for free distribu-

tion, and a troubled wartime stock market had diminished the value of her investments. She sold at least one valuable book to an American collector, a privately printed copy of *Shelley and Mary* which had been given to her by Jane Shelley, the widow of Percy Bysshe Shelley and Mary Shelley's son, Percy.[49]

In May she wrote to Moncure Conway that she was "very old and growing feebler, and losing sight and activity"; nevertheless, she managed to give a half-hour speech to the British Union branch in Barmouth on 22 August. According to a reporter, she "showed all the old characteristics, vigorous denunciation, pleasant satire, tender feeling and the true eloquence of an earnest-souled woman." She was especially incensed that W. E. H. Lecky, whom she did not name, had turned against suffrage: "An eminent living historian and member of Parliament, an old friend of mine in former years, has devoted several pages of one of his last books to showing that women ought not to be trusted with votes . . . because some of us are in the thick of the fight against vivisection!"[50] "It was good to feel," she wrote, "that I can still work & that I have not lost my voice." But intermittently she called herself "a poor lonely old woman" or "lonely beyond words" and quoted Tennyson, though, good theist that she still was, she substituted "O" in the first line for his "Ah, Christ":

O, that it were possible
For one short hour to see
The souls we loved, that they might tell us
What and where they be.[51]

In her loneliness, and free of Mary Lloyd's stern prohibitions, she began to mention Lloyd freely, and publicly, in a way she had not done in the *Life*. In "Recollections of James Martineau" she described her as "my own life-friend Mary Charlotte Lloyd," a "great-souled and . . . able" woman; and then the *Abolitionist* for 15 December 1900 carried a description of Lloyd and her work for the cause along with a photograph probably taken in the 1860s. Making additions to her *Life* for the one-volume edition Blanche Atkinson would bring out immediately after she died, she crafted a paragraph about Mary Lloyd and included the poem "To Mary C. Lloyd." "There is a price which every aged heart perforce must pay for the long enjoyment of one soul-satisfying affection," she wrote. "When that affection is lost, it must be evermore lonely."[52]

Early in January 1901 Cobbe lost another old friend, Maggie Elliot, whose "romances," including the one with W. E. H. Lecky, Cobbe and Kate Amberley had followed with such interest. When she reported this news to Sarah Wister a few days after Queen Victoria's death Cobbe indulged in a

fit of indignation at public events: "I have no hope of any good from King
Edward VII. He is—& has always been, a profligate,—& none but the bad
*fast* lot hail his reign. . . . These wars, yours in the Philippines & ours in
S. Africa—are miserable wicked things. I disapprove so utterly of all our
Government does that I shall call myself a Liberal in future." (A few sentences earlier, talking about the "fits of fury" she had as a child, Cobbe had
written that "it is now thirty years or so, since I have been really angry.")[53]

Cobbe had firmly listed herself as president of the British Union when
it was founded, but she did not attend its semiannual council meetings. In
Bristol there was a local paid secretary. Blanche Atkinson, who was honorary secretary of the North Wales branch, went often to Hengwrt to help
Cobbe with various antivivisection chores. Other active workers were Evelyn Lloyd Price and, in London, James Spencer, viscount Harberton, husband of Cobbe's suffragist friend Florence Harberton. The most important
new member she recruited was Walter Hadwen, a doctor who had moved
to Gloucester in 1896. A vegetarian, total abstainer, and opponent of vaccination, he had a reputation as a "firebrand" orator. After hiring a private in-
vestigator who learned that Hadwen was held in "high local esteem," Cobbe
selected him to succeed her as head of the British Union.[54]

Still possessed of a fine eye for publicity, Cobbe invented additional
schemes to spread the message among working- and lower-middle-class
people. One strategy was to briefly rent a vacant shop, display cute and appealing animal pictures in the window, and invite people inside to sign a
petition. A woman was hired at a salary of one hundred pounds a year to do
this in one town after another. "Working-men lecturers" were paid to speak
to suitable audiences. The Electoral Anti-Vivisection League, of which
Cobbe was still president, urged branches to concentrate on borough and
parish councils, school boards, poor-law guardians, and other local officers
who could have an immediate effect on healthcare and schools instead of
wasting time on parliamentary candidates.[55]

George Eyre Evans, a journalist and antiquary who served as unpaid
minister of the Unitarian chapel in Aberystwyth and admired Cobbe's
books, met her for the first time on 26 July 1901: "The hospitable door—
framed in pink & white everlasting peablossom stood open. . . . rising to
welcome me with outstretched hands was the venerable authoress. . . . there
is on [her face] a smile, at once so cheery & so infectious to which no portrait can do justice. . . . conversation like a stream of sparkling, living waters
flowed from her. . . . At tea we talked of Darwin, 'I fear he was at last really
an Atheist' . . . & then of Theodore Parker who had taught her with count-
less others to believe in the Absolute goodness of God."[56]

Other visitors came—James Martineau's daughter Gertrude and the

Schuyler sisters yet again (though Loo had been active in social service for more than forty years, she was still only in her mid-sixties)—but at the end of October Cobbe was exhausted and "shut up pretty well alone for the winter." Nevertheless, though she could provide only her name and her subscription, she formally joined the Women's Liberal Federation and followed public affairs at home and abroad. She wanted to know what Sarah Wister, the abolitionist daughter of a slave-owning man, felt about "[Theodore] Roosevelt's entertainment of [Booker T.] Washington" at the White House. "I think it very fine, & so do many of the better organs of opinion," she wrote, "but the *Spectator* 'regrets' it!" Cobbe had once exchanged letters with an Englishwoman living in Virginia but dropped the correspondence because of the "virulence & savagery of the things she wrote of the Negroes." She was startled, after years of silence, to have a letter "speaking with even additional horror of the Negroes . . . but not one word of reproach & shame for the Lynchings."[57]

During the winter of 1901–2 there were yet more annoying conflicts with Stephen Coleridge and the National Anti-Vivisection Society. Most amusing are the complaints in the *Zoophilist* about Cobbe's publication of "improper" material in the *Abolitionist*. "A Terrible Revelation: Vivisection and Sexual Psychopathy" reported that Dr. Krafft-Ebing, of the University of Vienna, had described "numerous cases" of men who *"make use of the sight of dying animals, or torture animals, to stimulate their lust."* The *Zoophilist* promptly condemned public airing of "subjects that are never mentioned by decent people even in private."[58] It is entertaining to find that middle-aged men in London were horrified by an old woman's knowledge; nevertheless, Cobbe repeated the information, if somewhat more discreetly, in her final antivivisection piece for a major journal. In the *Contemporary Review* for May 1902, she used the German term *Schadenfreude*, which suggested the new psychological terminology, to revise and update her observations about "heteropathy" by adding references to teachers' pleasure in using a birch and the "fierce joy" of men in close combat on the battlefield.[59]

In June 1902 Cobbe wrote a final letter to Coleridge. Beginning "Dear Stephen"—a form of address suitable either for a close friend or for an adult writing to a child—she returned his last letter unopened. She wrote that "I asked you six or more weeks ago, to allow our correspondence to fall into abeyance, "but she had nevertheless continued to get "more-or-less unpleasant letters." She concluded by assuring him that "though you have well nigh ruined the work of my life—& of a life dearer to me than my own, I am still yr old *friend*."[60] (Whether the last word was a final twist of the knife or had some other meaning I am at a loss to understand.)

Every few weeks in nice weather Cobbe had her coachman, David Evans, take her over to Barmouth to visit one or another of the elderly women who lived in the seaside town. Mrs. Talbot, whose house Blanche Atkinson shared, was still an active philanthropist; Marianne Hearn, who wrote under the name Marianne Farningham, had taught school in Bristol before becoming a novelist and editor of the *Sunday School Times*. On 16 July, after Cobbe got home, the Dolgelley police came to look at her horse; the Barmouth constable had sent a telegram reporting that it appeared unfit to drive. She and David Evans were charged with cruelty and ordered to trial at Barmouth Petty Sessions on 22 August. Experienced in the ways of the law and publicity, Cobbe at once got experienced counsel, sent for the Liverpool veterinarian who examined cases for the RSPCA, wrote to George Eyre Evans so a sympathetic newspaperman would be at the trial, and hired a stenographer to record the proceedings. She was in a state of high fury in the days just before the hearing, writing that "every one of the persons chiefly concerned (beginning with the Chief Constable) owe me a grudge."[61]

At the monthly magistrates' court (held in the Barmouth police station) on 22 August 1902, Cobbe's attorney called a parade of witnesses to testify that the horse—which was, admittedly, quite old—was always driven very slowly. Stafford Jackson, the veterinarian who served as her expert witness, was confident enough to make a small joke: "If I was asked whether he was a fit horse to be put into a carriage and driven . . . ten miles an hour I would say it would probably be an act of cruelty, but I have ridden in Miss Cobbe's carriage six times, and for a man who goes about the country pretty fast it is certainly a trying ordeal. We took an hour and twenty-nine minutes to come [the ten miles] from Dolgelly to-day."[62] The charges against both Cobbe and Evans were dismissed, and the *Cambrian News,* heading its report "An Absurd and Ridiculous Charge," described the case against a woman with "a world-wide reputation as the opponent of cruelty" as "a senseless practical joke." Nevertheless, the writer continued, "at four score, it is no small matter for a woman of great culture and refinement to be dragged into a police court to prove that she has not belied the professions of a lifetime by sanctioning cruelty to animals!"[63]

Relieved by the verdict, Cobbe nevertheless understood the risky nature of justice. "Had I not been able to procure clever Counsel to unmask their falsehoods, & a good Vet, of high distinction, to describe the state of my horse, I daresay a most unjust & mischievous sentence would have been passed against me." Whether it was lack of a common language, the local animal pastimes—cockfighting was "practically winked at" long after it became illegal in 1849—or simple class resentment, there were longstanding tensions between Cobbe and the Dolgelley Welsh. Constance Battersea had written during her 1894 visit: "This is beautiful country & a very pretty

place. But there seems to be no *entente* cordial between owner and tenants,
I should like to run into the village & see if they are as bad as they are
painted."[64] Even with the case settled in her favor, Cobbe remained "half
crazed with rage" at the men who had laid the charge and the papers that
had been "ringing with false reports & satirical remarks." She no longer felt
safe. "I have been afraid to take my usual drives which are indispensable to
my health now I am too feeble to walk—lest the mendacious police in their
anxiety to curry favour with their head should interpret any mishap (such
as dropping a shoe or picking up a stone) as 'torturing' a horse,—& make
me pay another lawyers bill of £97 for shewing up their falsehood."[65]

She had some relief in a visit from her friends the Buntings. Percy
Bunting edited the *Contemporary Review.* Cobbe thoroughly enjoyed "his
fine talk on all things to me most interesting—modern theological changes,
Higher Criticism, etc.—and her splendid philanthropy on the lines I once
followed." (Mary Bunting helped lead the Metropolitan Association for
Befriending Young Servants, which claimed as one of its ancestors the Sunday class run in Bristol by Cobbe and Maggie Elliot.) The visit, she said,
"made me go back years of life, and seem as if I were once more living in the
blessed Seventies."[66]

As autumn set in, however, she still felt uncomfortable in Dolgelley and
decided to spend the winter in Clifton, where Helen and Frances would be
nearby. She did not like the "eternal noise of a town"—the years at Hengwrt
had meant a return to the quiet of Newbridge—but at Clifton she was once
more in touch with social and political causes. She had "very large pretty
rooms" at 39 Royal York Crescent, a handsome curved street similar to the
more famous crescent at Bath where her mother had lived as a young woman.
A journalist interviewed her about changes in Bristol over the past forty
years; Helen came to tea every afternoon. On 7 November Cobbe presided
at the British Union semiannual managers' meeting. By the end of the month
she was writing to Lawrence Pearsall Jacks, a Unitarian clergyman who taught
at Manchester College, outlining a series of articles she would like to see in
his *Hibbert Journal,* which specialized in speculative philosophy and theology. The Unitarian clergyman Estlin Carpenter, a son of William Carpenter
and formerly a student of James Martineau's, was giving lectures on higher
criticism in the Victoria Rooms and came often to see her. In much better
spirits by the end of November, she joked that one person said charging her
with cruelty was "like charging Josephine Butler with [sexual] misconduct"
and another compared it to "saying that the Archbishop of Canterbury was
drunk!"[67]

Sarah Wister and other friends had been carefully quiet about the surprise they were preparing for Cobbe's eightieth birthday. On 4 December

1902 Mary Bunting and John Stuart Verschoyle brought a handsome album with an engrossed address of congratulations signed by 346 friends and admirers on both sides of the Atlantic. (As with the suffrage and other petitions, printed copies of the message had been sent to people, who returned their signatures; the signatures were cut out and glued into the album.) The address recognized Cobbe's pursuit of "equality of treatment" for women in university education and legal rights; her pioneering efforts in workhouse reform; the theological and ethical writing that had "contributed in no small degree to that broader and more humane view" in all creeds; and her leadership in extending "moral law" to animals. Signatures came from bishops, authors, politicians, professors, and well-known public figures such as Florence Nightingale, Josephine Butler, Henry James, W. T. Stead, Elizabeth Blackwell, and, from the United States, Grover Cleveland, Julia Ward Howe, Thomas Wentworth Higginson, W. D. Howells, and Mark Twain. In addition, there were separate congratulations and signatures from the National Union of Women Workers and the Ragged School Union.[68]

Another memorial was sent by the Central Committee for Women's Suffrage, "whose Councils you for so many years brightened by your presence," to recall "with deep gratitude how much you have contributed to inspire and uplift the hearts of toilers in the cause of the advancement of women, not only by your personal work or by your writings, but also by the cheering example of your whole life." Among the fifty signatures were those of a few survivors from the group that had signed the first petition to Parliament more than thirty-five years before, including Florence Davenport Hill and Jessie Boucherett. Cobbe replied—in the *Times*—with her old fighting spark: "Would that I could hope that the short span of life which alone can remain to me could see our sex enfranchised at last! Till we obtain the suffrage we are liable (and, I sometimes think, actually doomed) to have our other slowly-found rights taken from us again."[69]

Three reporters came "dodging in and out all day" to get the news, the story was published in the *Times* as well as in the local papers, and letters flooded in from others who had read the articles and written to add their best wishes. "Considering *all* my heresies," she wrote, the list of signers "is a curious testimony of the widening of sympathies & dropping of prejudices in the present day."[70] In Bristol, people "interested in theology and ethics and Egypt, and all things which interest me" made their way to visit her at Royal York Crescent. "You certainly succeeded in doing me a really great honour, and in *cheering* me," she wrote to Blanche Atkinson. "I confess I was very downhearted when I came here, but I am better now. I feel like the man who 'woke one morning and found himself famous.'"[71]

Filled with the energy of her friends' efforts and the stimulation of social contact, Cobbe agreed to give a lecture on suffrage. On 2 January 1903 she spoke for an hour to "something over a hundred ladies."[72] Published in the *Contemporary Review* for May under the title "Woman Suffrage"—in the title of this, her last significant publication, Cobbe returned to the form she was forced to abandon so many years before when Helen Taylor insisted on "Women's Suffrage"—the essay bears an italicized subtitle, "Justice for the Gander—Justice for the Goose," and explains, with her characteristic clarity and vivid examples, that in the twentieth century in England two principles of government "are almost universally accepted as just . . . That those who are called on to obey the laws should have a voice in making them; and That those who pay taxes should have a voice in their expenditure." At the end of the essay, summing up her own brand of difference feminism, she concluded that women's influence in public affairs would bring "greater humanity towards all the poor and suffering, to captives, to criminals, to children, to the aged, to animals," and, finally, to the cause of peace. "We are not a sex of saints and sages, though there have been some saints and sages here and there belonging to us; and also a great many sinners and fools. But on the whole we are less often criminals than are men; perhaps we are a little less selfish; and certainly more conscientious than ordinary men. In short, *in the lump,* women are better than men."

In early February, still in high spirits, she joked, "It is wonderful to be able to boast like an old gentleman known to Mrs. Ffoulkes—of being— an *Octogeranium!*" and got ready to spend two or three weeks in London. She longed "to see once more the place where I was so happy for so many blessed years" and had British Union business to do and friends to see. Among the callers at the rooms where she stayed in Thurloe Gardens, just opposite the Victoria and Albert Museum, were some from the Women's Liberal Federation.[73]

Back home in Wales, she sat in the garden when the cherry came into bloom and remembered sitting in the same place with Fanny Kemble. She wrote to Kemble's daughter:

> O! dear Sarah! what a *splendid human being* she was. The world seems very poor to me now. I wonder whether you, in America, have at all the experience which we old ones all seem to have here, that, with the Nineteenth Century—all the genius, the enthusiasm & the high principle went out of England? . . . To the *Duty Loving* old Queen has succeeded a *Pleasure-loving* King & the whole country seems to have deteriorated in the direction of Amusement-seeking in place of fidelity to Duty. . . . Perhaps all old folks are apt to think their times were best? But every body here does say how there are *no* politicians, *no* thinkers, *no* poets, *no* historians, *no* philan-

thropists, *no* artists, *no* novelists even, like those of 30 years ago—Is it the same in America?[74]

During the latter part of the year she was often exhausted and sometimes faint, and by early 1904 it was hard to give sustained attention to anything, though she still wrote "a leading article and a number of notes" for each issue of the *Abolitionist* and could laugh about reading in Richard Quain's *Dictionary of Medicine* that after seventy-five it was necessary "for old people 'to have *someone who loves them* to live with them!'—as if one could order 'some one who loves one' from the Chemist's Shop!" Yet the sadness was there. She had "nobody left who really loves me" and no one with whom she "could *endure* to live permanently."[75] George Eyre Evans, of Aberystwyth, visited her in early February: "The mountain peaks were lightly covered with snow, and nature was in a wild mood. . . . Some months had elapsed since I had last seen Miss Cobbe; today she was singularly bright, and her voice firm." They spoke of religious matters, of Estlin Carpenter's lectures in Aberystwyth, of recently published biographies of women and men she had known. She made a subscription in support of Evans's Unitarian congregation. "And then," he continued,

> we talked about her dear friend Miss Lloyd, and she led me to look at her portrait hanging on the wall beneath one of Miss Lloyd's water colour drawings. She told me of their first meeting in Rome, and of the "firm, true, & loving friendship," which had ever after remained between them. . . . In leaving, she came with me to the hall to shew me the group of horses modelled by Miss Lloyd, and of which Rosa Bonheur thought so highly. Then we parted with her injunction to "come & tell me all about Mr Carpenter's lectures when the course is over; And before you go, take a walk through the garden, & see the snowdrops." It was a memorable afternoon to me.[76]

On 4 April Cobbe drove out as usual, wrote letters, and had tea with a visiting neighbor. The next morning she was dead. Writing as a clergyman about a woman he had admired since he was young, John Verschoyle described what could be known and what could be hoped: "On the morning of her death she rose very early in the cold gray dawn, opened the shutters to let in the light, and as she walked across the room the gates of the unseen world opened to her with the merciful swiftness she had hoped and prayed for, and she passed the threshold, perhaps to find her loved ones waiting to receive her in the new life."[77]

Telegrams to notify her family and Dr. Hadwen were on the bedside table;[78] she must have been in the habit of getting them out every night and putting them away in the morning. On the day of her funeral, wrote Marianne Farningham, the wind was cold, "but it was not the tearing, raging wind which has lately swept up the valleys and attacked the hills of North Wales." Like her father almost fifty years earlier, she had requested a minimum of ceremony. George Eyre Evans's account was headed "A Simple Burying":

> No mourning, no hearse, no trappings of woe, no drawn blinds, marked the burying of all that was mortal of Frances Cobbe: a few old friends, groups of little children, faithful servants made up the company which gathered in Llanelltyd churchyard round the grave where but a few years ago Miss Cobbe had placed all that could die of a friend and companion Miss Mary Lloyd. The coffin of simplest make and without any name plate was borne from Hengwrt in the open "Victoria" which Miss Cobbe frequently used, driven by her own coachman. . . . In the churchyard prior to the lowering of the coffin into its unbricked grave, [J. Estlin] Carpenter delivered a short address dealing with the many phases of the active life of her, who had been at once the close friend of Darwin and Lord Shaftesbury, James Martineau, and Cardinal Manning, and a host of other leaders. It was a memorable service, and fittingly closed the earthly life of one who had worked with unselfish aim for more than 80 years to better her fellow-men and procure tenderness and mercy to animals.[79]

Years earlier Cobbe had marked the double grave where she and Lloyd would rest together with a single headstone bearing both their names and leaving a space for the date of her death. She chose a verse from Henry Wadsworth Longfellow to reflect the New England transcendentalism that had touched her long before at Newbridge when she first read the work of Theodore Parker:

> Take them, O Grave! and let them lie
> Folded upon thy narrow shelves,
> As garments by the soul laid by.
> And precious only to ourselves.

> Take them, O great Eternity
> Our little life is but a gust
> That bends the branches of thy tree
> And trails its blossoms in the dust.[80]

# Notes

## Abbreviations

| | |
|---|---|
| ALWL | Autograph Letter Collection. The Women's Library, London. |
| Bentley Archives | Richard Bentley & Son. Archives, 1829–1898. Published on microfilm by Chadwyck-Healey. |
| BUAV | British Union for the Abolition of Vivisection. Brynmor Jones Library, University of Hull. |
| CAC | Cobbe Autograph Collection. Bodleian Library, Oxford. |
| CC Diary | Charles Cobbe Diary. Cobbe Papers, Newbridge, Ireland. |
| CPAC | Cobbe Papers, Alec Cobbe Collection. |
| CPN | Cobbe Papers, Newbridge, Ireland. |
| *DNB* | *Dictionary of National Biography.* |
| ECS Papers | E. C. Stanton Papers. Theodore Stanton Collection. Special Collections and University Archives. Rutgers University Libraries, New Brunswick, New Jersey. |
| *EWR* | *Englishwoman's Review of Social and Industrial Questions.* |
| FPC | Frances Power Cobbe. |
| FPCP | Frances Power Cobbe Papers. The Huntington Library, San Marino, California. |
| *Hansard* | *Hansard Parliamentary Debates.* 3rd series. |
| MSFP | Mary Somerville Family Papers. Bodleian Library, Oxford. |
| M-T | Mill-Taylor Collection. Vol. 12. Archives Division. LSE Library, London School of Economics and Political Science. |
| NLW | National Library of Wales, Aberystwyth. |
| SSon | Swan Sonnenschein & Company. Archives, 1878–1911. Published on microfilm by Chadwyck-Healy. |
| *VL* | *Vernon Lee's Letters.* Preface by Irene Cooper Willis. London: privately printed, 1937. |
| VLC | Vernon Lee Collection. Special Collections. Colby College, Waterville, Maine. |
| VSS | Victoria Street Society. |
| WFP | Wister Family Papers. Historical Society of Pennsylvania, Philadelphia. |
| WSC | Women's Suffrage Collection. Manchester Archives and Local Studies, Manchester Central Library. |
| *WSJ* | *Women's Suffrage Journal.* |
| WSS | William Swan Sonnenschein. |

## Introduction

1. Paget, *In My Tower,* 1:187; Stanton, *Eighty Years and More,* 362; Cohen, *Lady De Rothschild,* 256; Verschoyle, "Frances Power Cobbe," 72.

2. Alcott, "Glimpses." Although Cobbe's *Essay on Intuitive Morals* had been published in 1855 without any author's name, she sent a copy to her Boston mentor, Theodore Parker. He was at that time also Louisa May Alcott's "beloved minister and friend" (see Alcott, *Journals,* 95). Alcott stayed with the Taylors for the first ten days of June in 1866. On 7 June John Stuart Mill presented to Parliament the women's suffrage petition circulated by Helen Taylor, Barbara Bodichon, Mentia Taylor, Emily Davies, Frances Power Cobbe, and others.

3. *Daily News,* 12 December 1893, quoted in *Zoophilist,* 1 January 1894, 179; Bosanquet, Review of *The Duties of Women;* W. E. H. Lecky to FPC, 7 November 1868, FPCP.

4. Willard, "Frances Power Cobbe," 597; Gross, *Man of Letters,* 67.

5. FPC to Millicent Garrett Fawcett, 24 February [1886], ALWL; James Anthony Froude to FPC, 19 March 1876, BUAV.

6. Cobbe's *Life of Frances Power Cobbe* was simultaneously published in two volumes by Richard Bentley & Son in London and Houghton Mifflin in Boston. A single-volume, posthumous edition with very few additions by Cobbe and a preface by Blanche Atkinson was published by Swan Sonnenschein in London in 1904.

7. [FPC], "The Writing of Biographies," *Echo,* 24 January 1874. Cobbe's *Echo* leaders and other anonymous journalism are identified on the basis of her scrapbooks, now located in NLW.

8. Corbett, *Representing Femininity,* 12.

9. FPC, *Life* (1894), 1:5. Quotations throughout are from the Bentley edition.

10. FPC to Sarah Wister, 1 February 1894, WFP.

11. FPC to Blanche Atkinson, December 1900, in Atkinson, Introduction, x.

12. Atkinson, Introduction, x–xi; FPC, "Recollections of Felicia Skene" (1902), 76; FPC, "Recollections of James Martineau" (1900), 175; FPC to Fawcett, 23 December [1889], ALWL (Cobbe's letters to Somerville are in the Bodleian Library, but her letters from Somerville have not been located); *Abolitionist,* 20 April 1904, 3.

13. [FPC], leader in the *Standard,* [December 1880]; Felicia Skene to FPC, 4 April 1894, in FPC, *Life* (1894), 1:27; Charles Cobbe to his brother Tom, 30 November 1846, CPN; [Stead], "Character Sketch," 329.

14. Caine, "Feminist Biography," 251.

15. FPC, *Life* (1894), 1:31.

16. FPC, *Our Policy* [1874], 4–5.

## 1 A Child Well Born

1. Verschoyle, "Frances Power Cobbe," 71.

2. Sanborn, "Frances Power Cobbe," 65.

3. Bates, *Donabate and Portrane,* 69; FPC, "Beresford and Cobbe" (1895), unpaged; Winifred Ada Cobbe, "Victorian in the Twentieth Century," 774; FPC, "Catalogue of Pictures" (1868). Another version of the story appears in FPC, *Life* (1894), 1:7–8.

4. William Laffan, "Through Ancestral Patterns Dance," in Laing, *Clerics and Connoisseurs,* 82.

5. FPC, "Beresford and Cobbe" (1895).

6. Alec Cobbe, "Portrait of Thomas Cobbe," in Laing, *Clerics and Connoisseurs,* 104; FPC, "Catalogue of Pictures" (1868).

7. FPC, "Beresford and Cobbe" (1895). Despite its small population, Swords returned two members. It has recently been called the "most notoriously corrupt borough in the Irish parliament" (Johnston-Liik, *Irish Parliament,* 438–39).

8. Many of the pictures in the family collection were exhibited at Kenwood House (London) in the autumn of 2001 and are reproduced in the exhibition catalog *Clerics and Connoisseurs,* edited by Alastair Laing.

9. Alec Cobbe, "Portrait of Charles Cobbe," in Laing, *Clerics and Connoisseurs,* 103; FPC, "Beresford and Cobbe" (1895).

10. FPC, *Life* (1894), 1:17.

11. Austen, *Persuasion* (1818), chap. 2.

12. FPC, *Life* (1894), 1:17; Peach, *Historic Houses in Bath,* 103.

13. FPC, *Life* (1894), 1:18.

14. Longford, *Wellington,* 80.

15. FPC *Life* (1894), 1:15. The passage, furthermore, reveals some confusion between her grandfather Charles Cobbe and her great-grandfather Thomas Cobbe.

16. Hardy, *New Picture of Dublin,* 89.

17. FPC, *Life* (1894), 1:20.

18. Haythornthwaite, *Colonial Wars,* 72; Cobbe, "Portrait of Charles Cobbe," 105. Unless otherwise noted, dates of commissions and promotions throughout are taken from annual volumes of the War Office's *Army List.*

19. Gardner, *East India Company,* 150.

20. Longford, *Wellington,* 80–93; Gardner, *East India Company,* 151; Weller, *Wellington in India,* 185; Hooper, *Wellington,* 76.

21. CC Diary, 23 September 1835, a date thirty-two rather than thirty years after the battle.

22. FPC, "Beresford and Cobbe" (1895); FPC, *Life* (1894), 1:23. *The Pleasures of Hope* was a volume of poetry by Thomas Campbell, first published in 1799.

23. Hodson's Index.

24. FPC, "Catalogue of Pictures" (1868); the account in *Life* is less specific. FPC gives Mrs. Champion's birth name as Frances Nind; V. C. P. Hodson's *List of Officers of the Bengal Army* gives the surname as Nynd.

25. See, e.g., the *DNB* entry for Thomas Leman. Further complications arise with the new genealogical research discussed in Susan Sloman, "Portrait of Mrs Elizabeth Nind," in Laing, *Clerics and Connoisseurs,* 145–46.

26. FPC, *Life* (1894), 1:208.

27. FPC, "Ireland and Her Exhibition in 1865" (1865), 407; CC Diary, 30 December 1826.

28. FPC, *Life* (1894), 1:25.

29. FPC, "Girls' Schools" (1884), 223 (the essay is repeated almost verbatim in *Life* [1894]).

30. It was not yet Kingstown nor, as it became after independence, Dun Laoghaire.

31. Office of Arms to Charles Cobbe, 18 August 1821, CPN.

32. Ledger, "Housekeeping 1810–1853," CPN.

33. CC Diary, 11 December 1825; FPC, "Evangelical Character" (1874), 454; FPC, *Life* (1894), 1:21.

34. Frances Conway Cobbe, Commonplace Book.

35. CC Diary, 13 March 1829.

36. CC Diary, 30 September 1824; Taylor, *Story of My Life,* 8.

37. Maxwell, *Mrs Gatty,* 58–59.

38. CC Diary, 20 December 1823.

39. CPAC.

40. As C. J. Hawes puts it in *Poor Relations,* 4, a very small proportion of the company's military or civilian servants between 1750 and 1800 were married, but a large number left property to Indian women or children in their wills.

41. Hyam, *Empire and Sexuality,* 116–17; James, *Raj,* 219. The sons are not mentioned in the *DNB* entry for Charles Theophilis Metcalfe.

42. [FPC], "Miss or Mrs.?" *Echo,* 2 November 1872.

43. CC Diary, 20 February 1824.

44. [Chadwick], "Philanthropic Autobiography," 328; FPC, "Catalogue of Pictures" (1868); FPC, *Life* (1894), 1:34.

45. FPC, "Girls' Schools" (1884), 223; Skene to FPC, 4 April 1894, in FPC, *Life* (1894), 1:26–27.

46. FPC, *Life* (1894), 1:4, 31.

47. CC Diary, 30 October 1824.


## 2  Childhood, Girlhood, School, 1827–1838

1. FPC, *Life* (1894), 1:32; FPC, "Swift and Stella" (1882), 569.

2. CC Diary, 10 August 1823; FPC, "Ireland and Her Exhibition in 1865" (1865), 410.

3. FPC to Nina Minto, 25 February [1874], Minto Papers; FPC, "Female Charity" (1862), 786; FPC, "Fitness of Women" (1876), 272.

4. Wakefield, *Mental Improvement,* 83–85.

5. FPC, "To Know" (1869), 777; CC Diary, 25 December 1824.

6. FPC, *Life* (1894), 1:33.

7. CC Diary, 7 March 1827, 12 October, 7 April 1829.

8. CC Diary, 20 November 1829. A few months later, probably at Anne Cobbe's suggestion, a certified translation of the contract of marriage between Thomas Cobbe and the begum Nuzzeer was sent from India, but since the wedding had been a Muslim ceremony, English law would not have recognized its validity.

9. FPC, "City of the Sun" (1861), 674; Edgeworth and Edgeworth, *Practical Education,* 1:24. The Edgeworths' book was still at Newbridge in 1852.

10. CC Diary, 27, 24 January 1831.

11. Low, "Distinguished Women and Their Dolls," 257; Anne Conway to Frances Cobbe, 26 November 1831, CPN; Will Cobbe to FPC, 30 September 1832, CPN.

12. FPC, *Life* (1894), 1:46, 173; Charles Power Cobbe to Charles Cobbe, 10 March [1851], CPN.

13. CC Diary, 30 October 1829.

14. CC Diary, 25 June 1827, 9 November 1830; Hall and Hall, *Hand-Books for Ireland,* 61.

15. CC Diary, 2 September 1825.

16. CC Diary, 12 October 1832. In Ireland, even with Catholic emancipation, the number of adult males eligible to vote was closer to 5 percent.

17. Stenton, *British Members of Parliament*, 131.

18. CC Diary, 28, 24 July 1832; Lecky, *Public Opinion in Ireland*, 2:135.

19. Miss Sawkins to Frances Cobbe, 13 November 1832, CPN; Harriet Conway to FPC, 6 August 1835, CPAC; FPC, "Fenians of Ballybogmucky" (1865), 88; FPC, "Defects of Women" (1869), 229; [FPC], "Bathers and Bathing," *Echo*, 15 July 1869.

20. Barmouth Library, *Frances Power Cobbe Bequest*.

21. Turner, "Crisis of Faith," 31. The incident is recounted in FPC, *Life* (1894), 1:86–87.

22. FPC, *Life* (1894), 1:39–40. Keith's book was published in Edinburgh in 1832.

23. CC Diary, 6 July 1833; Sawkins to Frances Cobbe, 30 August, 7 September 1833, CPN.

24. FPC, *Life* (1894), 1:65.

25. FPC, "Nineteenth Century" (1864), 485–86. Flora Long, whose family lived at Rood Ashton, had been engaged to Fan's uncle Henry, who died in 1823; she remained unmarried and was often included in Cobbe family gatherings.

26. FPC, *Life* (1894), 1:16; FPC, "Catalogue of Pictures" (1868); FPC, "Beresford and Cobbe" (1895). The gentleman was John Beresford, Lord Decies (1773–1863), a cousin of Fan's grandfather's.

27. Kidd and Richards, *Hadwen of Gloucester*, 146; FPC to Walter Hadwen, in Tebb, *Premature Burial*, 126. Cobbe alludes to this story in "A Plea for Speedy Burial," *Echo*, 14 January 1875.

28. FPC, "Nineteenth Century" (1864), 486; [FPC], "Family Reunions," *Echo*, 24 December 1872; CC Diary, 23 July 1836.

29. FPC, *Life* (1894), 1:18; CC Diary, 23 November 1834.

30. East India Company, *East-India Register*, xxiv.

31. FPC, *Life* (1894), 1:52. The name given there is "Mdlle. Montriou"; "Miss Montreau" appears in the account book recording her pay.

32. Hastings, *Private Journal*, 1:295. Hastings refers to his wife as Lady Loudoun; born Flora Muir, she was countess of Loudoun in her own right.

33. Mill and Wilson, *History of British India*, 3:426–27. Its name appears in nineteenth-century sources as Oodeypore, Udaypur, and several other variants.

34. Charles Cobbe to Elizabeth Tuite, 15 August 1836, CPN; CC Diary, 20 September 1823; Will of Thomas Alexander Cobbe, CPN.

35. Azélie Cobbe to Charles Cobbe, 29 August 1836, CPAC.

36. CC Diary, 21 October 1836.

37. FPC, "Girls' Schools" (1874), 222; FPC, *Female Education* (1862), 2.

38. FPC, "Girls' Schools" (1874), 224. The sum is derived from family account books. Travel expenses would bring the bill close to the £1,000 claimed in FPC, *Life* (1894), 1:60. Fan's two years at boarding school cost nearly twice as much as Will's four years at Sandhurst.

39. Prospectus for Miss Sawkins's school, CPN.

40. Lewes, *Three Sisters*, 12; FPC, "Girls' Schools" (1874), 225–28.

41. CC Diary, 9 April 1837.

42. CC Diary, 27 April, 24 August 1837.
43. CC Diary, 9 June 1837.
44. Will Cobbe to his father, 26 August 1837, CPN.
45. CC Diary, 20 September 1837.
46. CC Diary, 23 June 1838.
47. Haythornthwaite, *Colonial Wars,* 153–54, 271–72.
48. FPC, *Life* (1894), 1:196.
49. Azélie Cobbe to Charles Cobbe, 19 July 1838, CPAC; undated partial letter to his father in Tom Cobbe's handwriting, CPN.

## 3   Young Lady in Training, 1839–1845

1. Will Cobbe to his mother, 11 January 1839, CPN.
2. Hardy, *New Picture of Dublin,* 103; Pyle, *Kate Cullen,* 49, 53.
3. Will Cobbe to FPC, March 1839, CPN.
4. CC Diary, 27 June 1839.
5. FPC, *Life* (1894), 1:88.
6. Gatty, *Old Folks From Home,* 141, 135.
7. Nolan, "Society and Settlement," 189, 201; CC Diary, 8 November 1839. One of the paintings was Meindert Hobbema's *A Wooded Landscape* (1663), now held by the National Gallery of Art in Washington, D.C.
8. CPN. Further information, plans, and a photograph of one cottage still in use are in Arthur K. Wheelock Jr. and Alec Cobbe, "A Better Picture to the Christian Eye," in Laing, *Clerics and Connoisseurs,* 87–89.
9. FPC, *Life* (1894), 1:71; Will Cobbe to his father, 14 March 1840, CPN; [FPC], "Men at Women's Work," *Echo,* 18 April 1871; [FPC], "Poor-Law Inspectors and Their Failures," *Echo,* 6 January 1872.
10. Tom Cobbe to his father, 2 July 1840, CPN.
11. CC Diary, 10 November 1840; FPC, *Life* (1894), 1:170.
12. Marianne St. Leger Taylor Diaries, 29 August 1840.
13. Will Cobbe to his mother, 3 March 1841, CPN.
14. FPC, "Town Mouse and the Country Mouse" (1875), 505.
15. Charles Marriott to FPC, 27 August [ca. 1840], FPCP.
16. FPC, "All Sorts and Conditions" (1894), 103; FPC, *Life* (1894), 1:70–71; FPC to Constance Battersea, in Battersea, *Waifs and Strays,* 166–67.
17. CC Diary, 10, 14 July 1841.
18. CC Diary, 26, 27 January 1842.
19. FPC, *Life* (1894), 1:166.
20. FPC, "The Subjection of Women" (1869), 375; FPC, Note-Books, 1846–1863, vol. 2.
21. FPC, *Duties of Women* (1881), 10; FPC, "Little Health of Ladies" (1878), 289.
22. FPC to Martha Somerville, 13 [May 1873], MSFP.
23. FPC, "Nineteenth Century" (1864), 493.
24. FPC, "Woman's Work in the Church" (1865), 516.
25. Bates, *Donabate and Portrane,* 105.

26. See Kanner, *Women in English Social History,* 718. The book's author is evidently still unidentified.

27. Frank Cobbe to Charles Cobbe, 7 March 1843, CPN. In the end Frank too went into the military, as an officer in the Madras Artillery, though he spent much of his time in India supervising public works.

28. His name was variously spelled by family members as "Aleck" or "Alick"; I have chosen the form used by Fan. Sandhurst reports for both Alick and Charlie are in CPN.

29. Gross, "Unpublished Shakespeare Scholar," xxi. Most of Thomas Cobbe's Shakespeare manuscript is now at the University of Texas-Austin.

30. FPC, *Life* (1894), 1:89, 92.

31. FPC, "Recollections of James Martineau" (1900), 175; FPC to the *Bolton Free Christian Church Record,* April 1874, in Scrapbook, NLW.

32. FPC, "Morals of Literature" (1864), 128; FPC, "Evangelical Character" (1874), 457.

33. Gleadle, *Early Feminists,* 17.

34. Will Cobbe to his father, 23 March 1842, CPN.

35. Will Cobbe to his mother, 2 December 1839, CPN.

36. Schwieso, "Princes of Widcome," 31; Prince, *Charlinch Revival,* 9.

37. Prince, *Letters,* 20, 59–62.

38. Schwieso, "Founding of the Agapemone," 113–21. Schwieso's thesis, "Deluded Inmates, Frantic Ravers and Communists, a Sociological Study of the Agapemone, a Sect of Victorian Apocalyptic Millenarians" (Ph.D. diss., University of Reading, 1994), is the only nonsensational account of Henry James Prince and his sect.

39. Will Cobbe to his brother Tom, 4 October 1845, CPN.

40. Tom Conway to Charles Cobbe, undated, CPN. Will's withdrawal from the family explains why his letters home from school remain at Newbridge, although there are no similar letters from his brothers and sister. I assume that their mother had saved letters from all of her children and that, following the usual custom, Charles, Tom, Henry, and Fan took back their own letters after she died. Will's letters survive because he did not return home after his mother's death.

41. Prince, *Charlinch Revival,* 58.

42. *Hand Book to the Dublin & Drogheda Railway.* Passenger service began on 24 May 1844; trains started from each end at 6, 8, 11, 2, 5, 8; the journey time was slightly less than at present.

43. FPC, *Life* (1894), 1:69–70; FPC, "The Joy of Youth," in *Rest in the Lord* (1887), 28–29 (three stanzas are printed in *Life* [1894], 1:72); FPC, "Self-Development," in *Studies New and Old* (1887), 71–72.

44. The quotations are from FPC, "Recollections of Felicia Skene" (1902), 72–74.

45. FPC to Louisa Cobbe, [autumn 1845], CPAC.

46. Hall and Hall, *Hand-Books for Ireland,* 60.

47. CC Diary, November 1845.

## 4 The Family Heretic, 1845–1857

1. FPC, Note-Books, 1846–1863. Fan spells the village name "Balisk"; current maps have "Ballisk." Reporting the calculations in *Life* (1894), 1:140–41, she presents the same

numbers with a less shocking phraseology, saying that the man's "weekly wages scarcely covered bare food."

2. FPC, *Life* (1894), 1:70; Hardy, *New Picture of Dublin,* 224.

3. FPC, Note-Books, 1846–1863, vol. 1.

4. FPC, "Religious Demands" (1863), xvii–xviii. Theodore Parker was Louisa May Alcott's clergyman in Boston and appears as "Mr. Power" in Alcott's novel *Work* (1873).

5. Parker, *Discourse,* 44.

6. FPC, *Life* (1894), 1:43–44.

7. *Times,* 25 June 1849; Schwieso, "Religious Fanaticism," 173.

8. Mr. Allen to Tom Cobbe, 27 November 1846, CPN; Dixon, *Spiritual Wives,* 1:306; Charles Cobbe to his brother Tom, 30 November 1846, CPN.

9. FPC, "Ireland and Her Exhibition in 1865" (1865), 413; CC Diary, 8 October 1846; Charles Cobbe to his brother Tom, 30 November 1846, CPN.

10. Woodham-Smith, *Great Hunger,* 143; Accounts 1840–1845 and Accounts 1850–1855, CPN.

11. Charles Cobbe to his son Tom, 25 January 1847, and account book, 11 March 1847, CPN.

12. Thomas Conway to Charles Cobbe, [spring 1847], CPN.

13. "Cobbe's Divorce," *Times,* 24 April 1850.

14. FPC, "Grief," in *Rest in the Lord* (1887), 38; FPC, *Life* (1894), 1:99; FPC to Violet Paget, [26 March 1880], VLC; FPC, "Grief," in *Rest in the Lord* (1887), 37, 39.

15. Theodore Parker to FPC, 5 May 1848, in Weiss, *Theodore Parker,* 1:458; Parker, *Sermons of Theism,* 235. A paper-covered copy of the sermon, preached on 20 September 1846, inscribed "Miss Frances Power Cobbe with the best wishes of the author," is with Cobbe's boxes of offprints and pamphlets at NLW.

16. Touhill, *William Smith O'Brien,* 2.

17. "Caution," *Irish Felon,* 8 July 1848, 47.

18. CC Diary, 25 July 1848.

19. FPC, *Life* (1894), 1:100–101.

20. CC Diary, 18 January 1848.

21. FPC, "Life in Donegal" (1866), 436, 438.

22. [FPC], "The Homes of Unhappiness," *Echo,* 11 May 1869; [FPC], "Marriage—What Is It?" *Echo,* 3 November 1871; FPC, "Morals of Literature" (1864), 129.

23. *Times,* 25 June 1849.

24. "Nottidge v. Ripley," *Times,* 30 June 1849; Schwieso, "Religious Fanaticism," 167–70.

25. *Times,* 26 June 1849.

26. FPC, "Notes to An Essay on True Religion," in Note-Books, 1846–1863, vol. 1.

27. FPC, "Essay on True Religion" (1849).

28. FPC, "New Volume of Sermons" (1875), 300.

29. FPC, "What Is the True Basis" (1865).

30. FPC, *Life* (1894), 1:105; FPC, "What Is the True Basis" (1865); FPC, "Self-Development," in *Studies New and Old* (1887), 80.

31. CC Diary, 12 November 1850.

32. FPC to Alexander Hugh Cobbe, [August 1852], CPAC.

33. CPAC. Another version, by Fan's brother Tom, is in the possession of Hugh Cobbe.

34. "The Agapemone," *Illustrated London News,* 29 March 1851, 253.

35. FPC to her father, [April 1851], CPAC; Henry Cobbe to his father, 29 April 1851, CPN.

36. Mander, *Reverend Prince,* 104.

37. Adams, *Makers of British India,* 164.

38. FPC, Note-Books, 1846–1863, vol. 1.

39. FPC to Alexander Hugh Cobbe, [August 1852], CPAC.

40. Fan used John W. Semple's 1836 translation of part 2 of Kant's *Metaphysik der Sitten,* most recently available as *The Metaphysics of Morals,* trans. Mary Gregor (Cambridge: Cambridge University Press, 1996).

41. For extensive commentary on *Intuitive Morals* and an analysis of Cobbe's religious thought in the nineteenth-century intellectual context, see Peacock, *Theological and Ethical Writings.*

42. FPC, "Grief," in *Rest in the Lord* (1887), 40.

43. Jameson, *Commonplace Book,* 52, 86–88, 94.

44. CC Diary, 20 October 1855. Charles Cobbe's bark, however, was worse than his bite; a few months later Henry and Sarah, along with their baby, Mabel, were visiting Newbridge.

45. The marriage took place on 11 January 1855, according to the Register of Protestant Marriages, General Register Office, Dublin.

46. Parker to FPC, 5 June 1855, in Weiss, *Theodore Parker,* 1:459.

47. FPC, *Intuitive Morals, Part I* (1855), v, 2 (quotations from the 1859 edition by Crosby, Nichols and Company of Boston); [Buckingham], Review of *Intuitive Morals,* 370; FPC, *Intuitive Morals, Part I* (1855), 269.

48. Tyrrell, *War with Russia,* 166; Fortescue, *History of the British Army,* 201.

49. *Times,* 5 July 1855.

50. FPC, "Female Charity" (1862), 775.

51. H. C. Willet to Charles Cobbe, 7 January 1856, CPN. Willet's employer was listed in the P.O. London Directory for 1850 as George Schofield, haircutter, at 276 Regent St. The address, between Oxford Street and Great Castle Street, suggests a quite fashionable shop.

52. Charles Augustus Cobbe to Charles Cobbe, 12 February 1856, and H. C. Willet to Charles Cobbe, undated, CPN.

53. FPC, "Ireland and Her Exhibition in 1865" (1865), 421; FPC, *Life* (1894), 1:170.

54. F. W. Newman to James Martineau, 30 May 1857, in Sieveking, *Francis W. Newman,* 93.

55. [FPC], "Daughters," *Echo,* 29 June 1871.

56. Twining, *Recollections,* 132. See Jordan, "Woman's Work in the World," for the argument that a coherent feminist discourse emerged in 1857.

57. FPC to Harriet St. Leger, 14 November 1857, in FPC, *Life* (1894), 1:213.

58. FPC, *Anglo-Irish Landlord* (1890); Jessie Cobbe to George Finlay, 24 November 1857, Finlay Papers; Passport Register, 23 June 1857–8 January 1858.

## 5  Travel Alone, 1857–1858

1. "Englishwomen Abroad," *EWR,* 15 August 1882, 341–42.

2. Review of *The Cities of the Past;* FPC, *Life* (1894), 1:213; FPC to Eliza Cobbe, 9 April [1858], CPAC.

3. FPC, "City of Peace" (1863), 719.

4. FPC to Louisa Cobbe, 26 December 1857, CPN.

5. Hawthorne, *French and Italian Notebooks,* 158; FPC to Louisa Cobbe, 26 December 1857, CPN.

6. FPC to Louisa Cobbe, 26 December 1857, CPN; FPC to St. Leger, 21 January 1858, in FPC, *Life* (1894), 1:226.

7. FPC, "City of Victory" (1862), 317, 318.

8. FPC to Charles Cobbe, January [1858], CPN. In her letters she alternates between Symonds and Simmons as the name of the American couple. The wife had been a pupil of Elizabeth Sidgwick, who operated a well-known school in Lenox, Massachusetts, and who was a dear friend of Fanny Kemble's.

9. FPC, *Female Education* (1862), 14.

10. FPC, "City of Victory" (1862), 324; Nightingale, *Letters from Egypt,* 24; FPC, "Lady's Adventure" (1866), 409; Trollope, "Unprotected Female," 271.

11. FPC, "Lady's Adventure" (1866), 410–11; Martineau, *Eastern Life* (1848), 220.

12. FPC to Louisa Cobbe, 18–20 February [1858], CPN; FPC, "Hades" (1864), 309; FPC, "City of Victory" (1862), 328–29.

13. FPC to Louisa Cobbe, 18–20 February [1858], CPN; FPC, "City of Victory" (1862), 327.

14. FPC, "Lady's Adventure" (1866), 408; FPC, *Life* (1894), 1:234; FPC to Louisa Cobbe, 18–20 February [1858], CPN (in Egyptian mythology the bull was a symbol for the god Apis); FPC, "Lady's Adventure" (1866), 408.

15. FPC to Louisa Cobbe, 18–20 February [1858], CPN; FPC, "City of Victory" (1862), 326.

16. FPC to Louisa Cobbe, 18–20 February [1858], CPN.

17. Van Haaften and White, *Egypt and the Holy Land,* 60; FPC, "Lady's Ride Thro' Palestine" (1859) (evidently written in rough form as she went along, the manuscript was recopied in Bristol in 1859; its preface is dated Florence, 8 May 1858); FPC to Louisa Cobbe, 18–20 February [1858], CPN.

18. FPC, "Lady's Ride Thro' Palestine" (1859). Contemporary Ramla is in the Central Province of Israel, twelve miles southeast of Tel Aviv. Cobbe uses *Ramlek* and *Ramleh;* Anthony Trollope's "Ride Across Palestine" calls it *Ramlath* or *Ramath.* It is not the same city as Ramalla, in the West Bank, which is closer to Jerusalem.

19. FPC, "Lady's Ride Thro' Palestine" (1859).

20. FPC, "City of Peace" (1863), 722. Cobbe sketched the view from the roof of Hauser's hotel on 7 March 1858.

21. FPC to St. Leger, 6 March 1858, in FPC, *Life* (1894), 1:235; FPC to Eliza Cobbe, 8 March [1858], CPAC.

22. Trollope, *Bertrams,* 68; FPC, "City of Peace" (1863), 730.

23. FPC, "City of Peace" (1863), 733–34; FPC, "Lady's Ride Thro' Palestine" (1859); FPC to Eliza Cobbe, 8 March [1858], CPAC.

24. FPC, "Lady's Ride Thro' Palestine" (1859).

25. FPC, "Lady's Ride Thro' Palestine" (1859); FPC, "Fitness of Women" (1876), 251; FPC, "Day at the Dead Sea" (1863), 227.

26. FPC, "Day at the Dead Sea" (1863), 228–30.

27. FPC, "Lady's Ride Thro' Palestine" (1859) (pressed leaves in the manuscript are labeled "Dead Sea" and dated 13 March); FPC, "Day at the Dead Sea" (1863), 237.

28. FPC to Louisa Cobbe, 28 March [1858], CPN; FPC to Eliza Cobbe, 9–10 April [1858], CPAC.

29. FPC, "City of Peace" (1863), 734.

30. FPC, "Lady's Ride Thro' Palestine" (1859).

31. FPC, "City of the Sun" (1861), 674.

32. FPC, "Lady's Ride Thro' Palestine" (1859).

33. FPC, "Lady's Ride Thro' Palestine" (1859).

34. FPC, "Lady's Ride Thro' Palestine" (1859); FPC to Louisa Cobbe, 28 March [1858], CPN.

35. FPC to Louisa Cobbe, 28 March [1858], CPN.

36. FPC to Louisa Cobbe, 5 April [1858], CPN; FPC to St. Leger, 28 March 1858, in FPC, *Life* (1894), 1:252; FPC to Louisa Cobbe, 5 April [1858], CPN; "Positive Side of Modern Deism," 256.

37. FPC to Eliza Cobbe, 9–10 April [1858], CPAC.

38. FPC, *Life* (1894), 1:262.

39. FPC, "Day at Adelsberg" (1864), 202, 205. For Sappho's nineteenth-century reputation, see Prins, *Victorian Sappho.*

40. FPC, "Day at Adelsberg" (1864), 213, 211.

41. Obituary for Isa Blagden, *EWR,* April 1873, 157; Austen in Blagden, *Poems,* xi; additional information supplied by Sandra Donaldson, who kindly sent me a copy of her unpublished paper "'For Liberty of Friendship': Letters of Elizabeth Barrett Browning to Isa Blagden."

42. Ryals, *Robert Browning,* 102; James, *William Wetmore Story,* 2:95. My thanks to Herbert Tucker and Kathleen Peck for help on the issue of Blagden's ancestry.

43. FPC, *Life* (1894), 1:252.

44. FPC to Eliza Cobbe, 9–10 April [1858], CPAC. The Byron quotation is from canto 3 of *Don Juan.*

45. FPC, "Lady's Ride Thro' Palestine" (1859).

46. Eastlake, "Lady Travellers," 100; FPC to Louisa Cobbe, 28 March [1858], CPN.

## 6   From Winter into Summer, 1859–1864

1. FPC, "Mary Carpenter" (1880), 280; Elizabeth Barrett Browning to Isa Blagden, 2 October 1858, British Library Add. 42,231 (thanks to Lisa Merrill for supplying me with this reference); Theodore Parker to FPC, 9 November 1858, in Weiss, *Theodore Parker,* 2:254. Lady Byron, who had separated from the poet in 1816 after one year of marriage, lived for many years in East Sheen, where three of Cobbe's brothers went to prep school.

2. Carpenter, *Mary Carpenter,* 248 (Jo Manton finds it more likely that Carpenter's

brothers and sisters had urged her to "to take a 'nice friend' to live with her" [Manton, *Mary Carpenter*, 147]); FPC, *Life* (1894), 1:275–76.

3. FPC, "Mary Carpenter" (1880), 280; Carpenter to Miss Sanford, 5 July 1858, in Carpenter, *Mary Carpenter*, 249. See Manton, *Mary Carpenter*, 127–37, for the history of events in 1847–48.

4. Carpenter, *Mary Carpenter*, 252.

5. FPC to George Finlay, 8 November 1858, Finlay Papers.

6. There is a Thomas Cobbe of Swaraton in the Cobbe genealogy. The British Library and Bodleian catalogs tentatively attribute the book on unknown grounds to Thomas Grahame, possibly a relative of Jessie's, who might have made the arrangement with Smith and Elder.

7. FPC to St. Leger, [November 1868], [December 1868], in FPC, "Mary Carpenter" (1880), 282.

8. FPC, Note-Books, 1846–1863, vol. 3; F. W. Newman to FPC, 24 January 1859, FPCP.

9. FPC to St. Leger, [December 1868], in FPC, "Mary Carpenter" (1880), 282; FPC, "Mary Carpenter" (1880), 287.

10. Mary Carpenter to FPC, 17 March 1859, FPCP; FPC to an unidentified friend, 13 February 1859, in FPC, "Mary Carpenter" (1880), 292.

11. Simpson, *Many Memories*, 270; Crawford, *Women's Suffrage Movement*, 594; FPC, *Duties of Women* (1881), 6.

12. FPC, "Mary Carpenter" (1880), 281, 297, 283.

13. FPC, *Life* (1894), 1:279.

14. Parker to FPC, 5 July, 31 August 1859, in Weiss, *Theodore Parker*, 2:314, 348.

15. Mary Carpenter to FPC, 25 June, 12 August 1859, FPCP.

16. FPC, "Indigent Class" (1866), 146. The comment about Marian Erle, the lower-class woman rescued by the heroine of Elizabeth Barrett Browning's *Aurora Leigh* (1857), was published in 1866 and would not have endeared Cobbe to Barrett Browning's widower, but of course Barrett Browning had not liked Cobbe's absorption with practical charity or her lack of appreciation for Isa Blagden's "idle" life in Florence.

17. [FPC], "Ragged and Friendless," *Echo*, 14 November 1871; FPC, "Indigent Class" (1866), 151.

18. Strachey, *Cause*, 87.

19. Twining, *Recollections*, 170.

20. FPC, "Workhouse Sketches" (1861).

21. FPC, "Women's Duty to Women" (1890).

22. Minto, *Letters and Journals of Nina, Countess of Minto*, 236–37; Hinchliff, *Frederick Temple*, 86.

23. Elliot, *Workhouse Girls;* Obituary for Margaret Elliot, *EWR*, 15 April 1901, 142–43.

24. Mary Carpenter to FPC, 28 November, 1, 2 December 1859, FPCP.

25. FPC to St. Leger, undated, in FPC, "Mary Carpenter" (1880), 289.

26. FPC, "Eternal City" (1862), 572.

27. Henry James to Ellen Gosse, 14 April 1887, in James, *Traveling in Italy*, 219; FPC, *Life* (1894), 2:14. A sketch by Cobbe labeled "Drawing Room, Villa Brichieri, 1860" (CPAC) shows broad windows and several comfortable seating arrangements.

28. Kate Field to Cornelia Riddle Sanford, [March 1860], in Field, *Selected Letters,* 18; FPC to George Bentley, 11 September 1894, Bentley Archives, reel 25.

29. FPC, "Literature: *Personal Recollections of Mary Somerville*" (1874).

30. FPC, Note-Books, 1846–1863, vol. 3; FPC to F. W. Newman, in "Death of Theodore Parker," from an unidentified periodical, Scrapbook, NLW.

31. FPC, Note-Books, 1846–1863, vol. 3.

32. Elizabeth Barrett Browning to Sarianna Browning, [June 1860], in Browning, *Letters of Elizabeth Barrett Browning,* 398.

33. John Stuart Mill to Helen Taylor, 21 February 1860, in Mill, *Later Letters,* 683; Faber, *Jowett,* 301.

34. FPC to Mary Somerville, 18 August [1860], MSFP.

35. FPC, Note-Books, 1846–1863, vol. 3; Benjamin Jowett to Margaret Elliot, 22 January 1861, in FPC, *Life* (1894), 1:349.

36. FPC and Margaret Elliot, *Destitute Incurables* (1860).

37. FPC, "American Sanitary Commission" (1867), 411; FPC, *Life* (1894), 1:315.

38. FPC, Note-Books, 1846–1863, vol. 3; Carpenter, *Mary Carpenter,* 200. For the Hills, see Gorham, "Victorian Reform."

39. David Masson to FPC, 18 February 1861, in FPC, *Life* (1894), 1:314–15. In this case as in many others, the version in *Life* is slightly edited from the original, now in FPCP.

40. FPC, *Life* (1894), 1:315. Evidently, neither *Intuitive Morals* nor *Religious Duties* sold enough copies to pay the expense of publication.

41. Masson to FPC, 18 February 1861. This passage appears only in FPCP.

42. I am indebted to Andrea Broomfield for conversation about the value of name recognition to women journalists.

43. Trollope's "Unprotected Female At the Pyramids" appeared in *Cassell's Illustrated Family Paper* for 6 and 13 October 1860, and "Banks of the Jordan" (retitled "A Ride Across Palestine" when republished later) was serialized in the *London Review* for 5, 12, and 19 January 1861.

44. Froude to Cobbe, 28 March [1861], FPCP.

45. Morley, *Recollections,* 1:31.

46. [FPC], "Our Workhouse Poor," *Ecclesiastic and Theologian,* April 1861, 178–81; in Scrapbook, NLW.

47. Martel, "British Women," 85; Twining, *Recollections,* 182.

48. Cobbe's "Preventive Branch of the Bristol Female Mission" was published as the leading article in the *English Woman's Journal* for November 1861 and reprinted as *Friendless Girls and How to Help Them.* "The Sick in Workhouses," printed in the *Journal of the Workhouse Visiting Society* for September 1861, was also republished as a pamphlet.

49. Atkinson, "Social Science," 468.

50. Gatty, *Old Folks From Home,* 150–51, 167.

51. Masson to FPC, 6 November 1861, CAC.

52. Robert Browning to William Wetmore Story, 30 August 1861, in Hudson, *Browning,* 79; Jowett to Margaret Elliot, 10 October 1861, in FPC, *Life* (1894), 1:350.

53. All quotations from Scrapbook, NLW.

54. Bessie Parkes, undated fragmentary letter, Parkes Papers; Elizabeth Blackwell to Emily Blackwell, 20 November 1850, in Worzola, "Langham Place Circle," 58.

55. [FPC], *Daily News,* dated 3 January [1862], published 11 January.

56. Sherwood, *Harriet Hosmer,* 218; J. Beavington Atkinson to FPC, 28 February 1864, Hosmer Collection, Schlesinger Library, Radcliffe College, Cambridge, Massachusetts. I thank Martha Vicinus for showing me this letter.

57. [FPC], "The Fine Arts," *Daily News,* dated 15 April. (When publication dates are provided in Cobbe's scrapbook, they are generally 6–8 days subsequent to the dateline.) Hosmer's own version, "The Process of Sculpture," was printed in the *Atlantic Monthly* in December 1864.

58. The reports are dated 21, 25, and 27 February and 1 and 8 March.

59. FPC, "Women in Italy" (1862), 375. There is a similar half-veiled allusion in [FPC], "Why Romans Detest the Papacy," *Spectator,* 12 April 1862.

60. Elizabeth Barrett Browning to Arabel Barrett, [22 October 1852], in Browning, *Dearest Isa,* 26–27. The correct spelling is Matilda Hays, not Hayes as Browning has it.

61. Florence Hill to Barbara Leigh Smith, in Hirsch, *Barbara Leigh Smith Bodichon,* 102.

62. Ellet, *Women Artists,* 326; Barbara Leigh Smith to her father, undated, in Hirsch, *Barbara Leigh Smith Bodichon,* 103–4.

63. Album of sketches and photographs, CPAC.

64. FPC, *Italics* (1864), 398, 414; FPC, *Life* (1894), 2:30.

65. FPC, *Italics* (1864), 414; Stebbins, *Charlotte Cushman,* 106.

66. Harriet Hosmer to Cornelia Carr, 4 March 1858, in Hosmer, *Harriet Hosmer,* 122; FPC to George Finlay, 19 November [1859], Finlay Papers; FPC, "Nineteenth Century" (1864), 486.

67. FPC, *Rest in the Lord* (1887), 13.

68. FPC, *Life* (1894), 2:30–31.

69. Verschoyle, "Frances Power Cobbe," 79.

70. FPC, "Celibacy *v.* Marriage" (1862), 233; FPC, *Life* (1894), 2:32; *Woman's Signal,* 12 November 1896, where Bonheur's reply is quoted in the paper's message of condolence to Cobbe after Lloyd's death.

71. "The Ladies at Guildhall," *Saturday Review,* 14 June 1862.

72. "Social Science in Full Dress," *Spectator,* 14 June 1862; *Times,* 12 June 1862.

73. *Daily Telegraph,* 11 June 1862.

74. FPC, *Female Education* (1862), 10.

75. Emily Davies, "Family Chronicle," Emily Davies Papers.

76. All quotations from Scrapbook, NLW.

77. NAPSS, *Papers and Discussions on Education,* 109–12.

78. "The Ladies at Guildhall," *Saturday Review,* 14 June 1862; "Miss Cobbe on Degrees for Women," *Spectator,* 14 June 1862; Bennett, *Emily Davies,* 45.

79. *Times,* 16 May 1878; *EWR,* 15 December 1879, 529.

80. Adams, *Somerville for Women,* 15; FPC to Sarah Wister, 28 December [1897?], WFP; FPC, "Bishop Colenso" (1867), 13.

81. FPC, *Life* (1894), 1:341; FPC, "Social Science Congresses" (1861), 92; Froude to FPC, 16 February [1863], FPCP. *Fraser's* was then published by Parker, Son, and Bourn; Longman became publisher with the November 1863 issue.

82. Mary Somerville to Harriet Hosmer, 5 February 1863, in Hosmer, *Harriet Hos-*

*mer,* 189; Davies to Barbara Bodichon, 14 January 1863, 3 December 1862, Bodichon Papers; Davies to Anne Leigh Smith, 2 January 1863, Bodichon Papers.

83. Margaret Elliot's story appeared anonymously as "Jem Nash, the Dull Boy" in *Fraser's* 69 (March 1864): 336–46.

84. Schneewind, *Backgrounds,* 70; Colenso, *Letters from Natal,* 73.

85. *Inquirer,* 9 May 1863, 293; George Eliot to Sara Sophia Hennell, 9 March 1863, in Eliot, *Letters,* 4:78; Lucretia Mott to Martha C. Wright, 26 August 1863, in Hallowell, *James and Lucretia Mott,* 408–9; Lydia Maria Child to Eliza Scudder, 1864, in Child, *Letters,* 184.

86. Temperley, *British Antislavery,* 250; Dubrelle, "We Are Threatened," 609.

87. "Mrs. Peter Alfred Taylor," *EWR,* 15 July 1908, 147; George Eliot to Sara Sophia Hennell, 9 March 1863, in Eliot, *Letters,* 4:78. The rejoinder was published in England as a pamphlet, which Eliot could have seen before April.

88. Conway, *Autobiography,* 1:391.

89. Conway, *Autobiography,* 1:391. Cobbe's pamphlet is available online from the Victorian Women's Writing Project at the University of Indiana, <http://www.indiana .edu/~letrs/vwwp/>.

90. "Miss Cobbe on the Pursuits of Women," *Spectator,* 9 May 1863; *English Churchman,* 21 May 1863; *Athenaeum,* 15 August 1863, 199–200. The "Athenaeum Index: Author, Editor, Translator Record," which is available from City University (London) at <http:// oldspice.soi.city.ac.uk/project/athenaeum/reviews/home.html>, identifies the reviewer as John Cordy Jeaffreson.

91. Froude to FPC, 18 May [1863], FPCP; FPC to Richard Bentley, [5 June 1863], Bentley Archives, reel 25; FPC to C. H. Pearson, 5 May [1863], C. H. Pearson Correspondence.

92. FPC, "The Diablerêts," in *Hours of Work and Play* (1867), 167.

93. John F. Byrne, in Sullivan, *Victorian and Edwardian Age,* 346.

94. French, *Antivivisection and Medical Science,* 30.

95. Review of *The Cities of the Past.*

96. FPC, *Broken Lights* (1864), 235. Thomas Carlyle's "Occasional Discourse on the Negro Question," *Fraser's* 40 (December 1849): 670–79, was republished in 1853 as a pamphlet entitled *Occasional Discourse on the Nigger Question.*

97. Janet L. Larson's "Where Is the Woman in This Text?" provides a detailed, nuanced analysis of Cobbe's intellectual and rhetorical contributions to the "mid-Victorian Bible wars" (99) in *Broken Lights* (1864).

98. Review of *Broken Lights* and *Apologia pro Vita Sua;* Review of *Broken Lights,* 283; Winkworth, "Miss Cobbe's *Broken Lights.*" F. W. Newman's *Discourse* was originally delivered as a lecture on 24 April 1864 in South Place Chapel, Finsbury, where Moncure Conway had become pastor. Cobbe's papers at NLW include a printed copy inscribed "Frances Power Cobbe, from the writer."

99. Prospectus for *Theological Review,* [1863 or 1864], quoted in *Wellesley Index,* 3:507.

100. Minto, *Letters and Journals of Nina, Countess of Minto,* 237 (evidently writing about the article that appeared in the *Theological Review* in September 1864 as "Christian Ethics and the Ethics of Christ"); FPC to George Bentley, 5 October 1894, Bentley Archives, reel 25.

101. Robert Browning to Julia Wedgwood, 31 October 1864, in Curle, *Robert Browning and Julia Wedgwood*, 92–93; Howells, Review of *Italics*, 317; "Miss Cobbe's Italics," *Saturday Review*, 29 October 1864.

102. FPC, *Life* (1894), 2:5; "Old Italy and New Italy," *Times*, 16 May 1865.

## 7   Mary Lloyd

1. FPC, *Life* (1894), 2:31.

2. FPC, *Life* (1904), 708.

3. Russell and Russell, *Amberley Papers*, 2:18; FPC, "Dogs Whom I Have Met" (1872), 672; Battersea Papers, 2 August 1894.

4. See Rhagatt Papers; and Mrs. Hemans to Miss M. Lloyd, 7 April 1819, extracted in FPC, Note-Books, 1846–1863, vol. 3. Information about the inherited books was provided by Ceridwen Lloyd-Morgan, Assistant Archivist, NLW.

5. The commonplace book, apparently kept by Mary Lloyd from 1849 to the mid-1850s, is currently owned by Richard and Valerie Foulkes. I am grateful to them for showing it to Susan Hamilton, and to Susan Hamilton for sharing information with me. The Channing motto is from his "Spiritual Freedom" (1830).

6. Eastlake, *Life of John Gibson*, 89. The book's preface thanks Mary Lloyd for supplying materials and information.

7. The phrases, in sequence, are from Conway, *Autobiography*, 1:39; Frothingham, *William Henry Channing*, 339; Evans, "Cardiganshire Notes," vol. 2; [Stead], "Character Sketch," 329; Boucherett, "Frances Power Cobbe," 135; and Battersea Papers, 3 August 1894.

8. Rhagatt Papers.

9. *Annual Register*, 1848, 431. A longer, somewhat different account of Charles Owen Lloyd's death was in the *Times* for 2 November 1848.

10. Rhagad Collection (Additional). Eliza Vibart's letters of 21 July and 2 and 4 August 1857 are in an envelope with the cutting from the *Times* for 15 October 1857. Although I have no idea how the information reached the *Times*, it suggests that someone in the family had newspaper connections.

11. Alexander Hugh Cobbe to Charles Cobbe, 28 July 1857, CPN.

12. Rhagatt Papers.

13. FPC to her brother Charles, 29 October [1865 or 1867], CPAC; "Potted History of the Vaughan Estates." Robert Williams Vaughan's will passed the estate to offspring of distant relatives after all three sisters had died.

14. Information from the community's roll book was provided in a letter of 13 July 2001 from the Reverend Valerie Bonham, whose *A Place in Life* is a history of the Clewer sisterhood.

15. Mary Lloyd to John Gibson, 25 August 1864, Gibson Papers.

## 8   At Home in London, 1865–1868

1. FPC to Mary Somerville, 6 October [1864], MSFP. Jane Hampson's name crops up in various contexts, but facts have been hard to find. According to the 1881 census, she must have been born about 1827, she never married, and she was still alive to con-

tribute to a memorial fund after Cobbe died. Her father was a baronet, her brother George served in the Crimea, another brother was a clergyman, and she lived with a younger sister. I suspect that she was initially Mary Lloyd's friend rather than Cobbe's, but I have no evidence.

2. Froude to FPC, 26 November [1864], FPCP; Parker, "Public Function of Woman," 178, 192, 203–4, 197–98.

3. FPC to Mary Somerville, 8 January [1865], MSFP; Local Studies Department, Royal Borough of Kensington and Chelsea Central Library; FPC to Somerville, 1 April [1865], MSFP.

4. Hobhouse, *Southern Kensington*, 162; FPC to Mary Somerville, 1 April [1865], MSFP; Fanny Kemble to St. Leger, 27 March 1877, in Kemble, *Further Records*, 222.

5. FPC to Theodore Stanton, 11 May 1886, ECS Papers. *A Huguenot refusing to shield himself from danger by wearing the Roman Catholic badge*, by John Everett Millais (1829–96), was one of the most popular paintings of the Royal Academy exhibition of 1852.

6. FPC, *Life* (1894), 2:117.

7. Russell and Russell, *Amberley Papers*, 1:377.

8. FPC to Mary Somerville, 8 January [1865], MSFP; Froude to FPC, 19, 20 January [1865], FPCP.

9. Mary Carpenter to FPC, 22 January 1865, FPCP; Malleson, *Elizabeth Malleson*, 62.

10. Kensington Society file, Emily Davies Papers.

11. FPC, "Recollections of James Martineau" (1900), 175.

12. Conway, *Autobiography*, 2:48; Davies, *Unorthodox London*, 31; Davies, *Worship and Theology*, 268; Gow, *Unitarians*, 117. The outgrowth of a Dissenting academy founded in Manchester in 1786, Manchester New College moved to London in 1853 and presented its students for University of London degrees. Now in Oxford and chartered by the university as Harris Manchester College, it educates mature undergraduate and postgraduate students.

13. Gow, *Unitarians*, 151; FPC to Moncure Conway, 19 May 1900, in Conway, *Autobiography*, 2:441. "the riddle of the painful earth" is from Tennyson's "The Palace of Art" (1832).

14. Conway, *Autobiography*, 1:391; Carpenter, *James Martineau*, 413, 399.

15. FPC, "Hours of Thought" (1877), 29; Holt, *Unitarian Contribution*, 345; Colenso, *Letters from Natal*, 87.

16. Hudson, *Munby*, 217–18; *EWR*, 15 July 1908, 153–54.

17. FPC, *Life* (1894), 2:82; FPC to Mary Somerville, 1 April [1865], MSFP; *Vanity Fair*, 12 August 1871, 51.

18. Anderson, *Woman against Women*, 119; FPC, "Schadenfreude" (1902), 657; FPC to Mary Somerville, 1 April [1865], MSFP. A footnote to "Schadenfreude" reports a different, less clever response.

19. Oliphant, "Royal Academy," 753; "The Royal Academy," *Art-Journal*, 163; Graves, *Royal Academy of Arts*, 3:76. *Horses at Play* stood in the hall at Hengwrt during the 1890s and was left in Cobbe's will to the wife of Lloyd's nephew Richard Lloyd Price of Rhiwlas, near Bala. I have not been able to trace its subsequent location.

20. Mary Lloyd to John Gibson, 2 July 1865, Gibson Papers.

21. Kensington Society file, Emily Davies Papers.

22. FPC to Mary Somerville, 2 August [1865], MSFP; Carpenter, *Mary Carpenter,* 307.

23. Mary Lloyd to John Gibson, 2 July, 4 August 1865, Gibson Papers; FPC, "Ireland and Her Exhibition in 1865" (1865), 491–92.

24. Froude to FPC, 8 August [1865], FPCP.

25. F. W. Newman to John Chapman, 17 July 1865, Beinecke Library, Yale University, and *Wellesley Index* 3:368 (I thank Jeffrey M. Lipkes for providing the reference); Newman, "Capacities of Women," 166.

26. Worzola, "Langham Place Circle," 285; Holton, *Suffrage Days,* 19; Froude to FPC, 8 December [1865], FPCP.

27. FPC to Mary Somerville, 2 August [1865], MSFP; Jalland, *Death,* 227; FPC to Mary Somerville, 18 [December 1865], MSFP.

28. Eastlake, *Life of John Gibson,* 243. He died on 27 January. Gibson had added a codicil the day after his stroke leaving a bequest of two hundred pounds to Mary Lloyd, perhaps to compensate for the care she provided during the last weeks of his life.

29. [FPC], "Houses and Housebreakers," *Echo,* 24 September 1869; FPC to Charles Cobbe, 16 December [1884], CPAC (the pearls brought in £280, quite a significant sum); FPC, "Terrors of the Suburbs" (1866), 573.

30. Russell and Russell, *Amberley Papers,* 468, 471; FPC, *Life* (1894), 2:99–100; John Elliott Cairnes to FPC, 6 January 1866, FPCP.

31. [FPC], "The Homes of the Working Classes," *London Review,* 3 March 1866.

32. FPC, "American Sanitary Commission" (1867), 410; Wohl, *Endangered Lives,* 314.

33. Bishop Colenso to FPC, 4 May 1866, FPCP.

34. *Times,* 28 April 1866 (the wording is slightly different in *Hansard,* 27 April 1866, 99); Bodichon to Helen Taylor, and Helen Taylor to Bodichon, both 9 May 1866, in Hirsch, *Barbara Leigh Smith Bodichon,* 217; Crawford, *Women's Suffrage Movement,* 756; Hudson, *Munby,* 226.

35. *Spectator,* 16 June 1866.

36. FPC to Davies, [June 1866], MS 2340C, NLW; Davies to Helen Taylor, 7 July 1866, in Worzola, "Langham Place Circle," 287; FPC to Alexander MacMillan, 17 July [1866], Autograph Album, National Library of Scotland; Helen Taylor to Davies, 26 October 1866, in Robson and Robson, *Sexual Equality,* 103 ("Women and Criticism" was in *Macmillan's Magazine* for September 1866, signed "H.T."); Davies to Bodichon, 21 August [1866], Bodichon Papers.

37. Davies to Bodichon, 21 August [1866], Bodichon Papers.

38. Davies to Bodichon, 21 August [1866], Bodichon Papers.

39. Davies to Helen Taylor, 6 August 1866, in Worzola, "Langham Place Circle," 290.

40. FPC to James Fields, 27 May [1866], New England Hospital Records, Sophia Smith Collection. "The Fenians of Ballybogmucky," discussed in chapter 4, appeared in *Argosy* for December 1865 and in *Every Saturday* on 13 January 1866.

41. "Pauper Hospitals in the Country," signed "F.P.C.," *Pall Mall Gazette,* 26 October 1866.

42. FPC to Kate Amberley, [June 1866], Amberley Papers; FPC, "Thoughts about Thinking" (1875), 215; Geraldine Jewsbury to FPC, 4 July 1866, FPCP.

43. Even in 1898, *Kelly's Directory of Bedfordshire, Hunts and Northamptonshire* had only one listing for "gentry" besides the clergyman, a Miss Synnot, at Manor House; also listed were a pub, a Mrs. Mary Ann Dunkley (shopkeeper), a blacksmith, and five farmers.

44. Froude to FPC, 7 March [1866], FPCP.

45. Bodichon to Helen Taylor, 21 October [1866], M-T.

46. Helen Taylor to Bodichon, 8 June 1866, in Crawford, *Women's Suffrage Movement*, 354.

47. Bodichon to Helen Taylor, 21 October [1866], M-T; Worzola, "Langham Place Circle," 291.

48. Helen Taylor to Mentia Taylor, 2 November 1866, in Robson, "Founding," 15.

49. FPC, "Conventional Laws" (1866), 672.

50. FPC to *Pall Mall Gazette*, 8 March 1867.

51. FPC to Kate Amberley, [28 February or 28 March 1867], Amberley Papers.

52. Married Women's Property Committee, *Final Meeting*, 12; Mary Somerville to FPC, 8 February 1867, FPCP.

53. Mentia Taylor to Helen Taylor, 4 March 1867, in Rosen, "Emily Davies," 118; Boucherett to Helen Taylor, 9 April 1867, in Crawford, *Women's Suffrage Movement*, 207; Mentia Taylor to Helen Taylor, 4 March 1867, in Rosen, "Emily Davies," 118.

54. Walling, *Diaries of John Bright*, 298; FPC, *Life* (1894), 2:100.

55. Bourne, *English Newspapers*, 2:273; Koss, *Political Press*, 179–80.

56. [FPC], "Female Franchise," *Day*, 5 April 1867.

57. FPC, "American Sanitary Commission" (1867), 412–13.

58. Richards, Elliott, and Hall, *Julia Ward Howe*, 1:266; Crawford, *Women's Suffrage Movement*, 351; Hoppen, *Mid-Victorian Generation*, 252; *Day*, 3 May 1867. Edmond Beales was president of the Reform League, whose 23 July 1866 demonstration had as a consequence the pulling down of railings in Hyde Park. A second demonstration in Hyde Park, in defiance of government prohibition, was scheduled for 6 May 1867.

59. FPC, "Criminals, Idiots" (1868), 793.

60. "Female Suffrage," *Saturday Review*, 25 May 1867.

61. See the division list in *Hansard*, 30 May 1867, 843–45.

62. Russell and Russell, *Amberley Papers*, 2:39. That Newman had not changed from his everyday wear, or morning clothes, to go out in the evening was one more indication of his disregard for conventionality. I thank Paul Barlow and others on the VICTORIA Listserv for solving my mystification over "mg."

63. Boucherett to Helen Taylor, 9 April 1867, in Crawford, *Women's Suffrage Movement*, 207–8; Davies to Bodichon, 3 June 1867, in Worzola, "Langham Place Circle," 293; Boucherett to Helen Taylor, 9 April 1867, in Crawford, *Women's Suffrage Movement*, 207–8.

64. Boucherett to Helen Taylor, 7 June 1867, in Crawford, *Women's Suffrage Movement*, 208; Mentia Taylor to Helen Taylor, 8 June 1867, in Robson, "Founding," 17; Emily Davies, "Family Chronicle," Emily Davies Papers.

65. Mentia Taylor to Helen Taylor, 15 June 1867, in Crawford, *Women's Suffrage Movement*, 132–33; Emily Davies, "Family Chronicle," Emily Davies Papers.

66. FPC to Helen Taylor, [1867], M-T; Robson, "Founding," 17–18; Lydia Becker to Helen Taylor, 4 July 1867, in Crawford, *Women's Suffrage Movement,* 370.

67. FPC to Helen Taylor, 5 July [1867], M-T.

68. Katherine Hare's name is mentioned in some accounts and not in others. It does appear on the list published in *EWR,* October 1867, 13.

69. Alcott, *Aunt Jo's Scrap-Bag,* 206; Elizabeth Malleson, quoted in Crawford, *Women's Suffrage Movement,* 674; Hudson, *Munby,* 217.

70. Robson, "Founding," 19.

71. Mentia Taylor to Becker, 19 July 1867, WSC; Crawford, *Women's Suffrage Movement,* 351.

72. FPC to Mary Somerville, [August 1867], MSFP; *Hansard,* 6 August 1867, 952.

73. Hosmer to Wayman Crow, 10 August, 8 September 1867, in Hosmer, *Harriet Hosmer,* 230–31.

74. FPC to her brother Charles, 29 October [1865 or 1867?], CPAC.

75. William Cobbe to his brother Charles, 14 March 1866, and Charles Cobbe to William Cobbe (marked "copy"), 19 March 1866, CPN.

76. [FPC], "Education, Voluntary or Involuntary," *Leader,* 26 October 1867; Chadwick, "Frances Power Cobbe," 270.

77. Mentia Taylor to Becker, 8 August 1867, WSC.

78. Crawford, *Women's Suffrage Movement,* 371.

79. FPC to Helen Taylor, 4 December 1867, M-T. Hampson, said Cobbe, particularly disapproved of the "system of agency for obtaining signatures."

80. Crawford, *Women's Suffrage Movement,* 411; FPC, *Life* (1894), 2:212.

81. FPC to Helen Taylor, 4 December 1867, M-T; Dawkins, "Brother Prince," 464–65; Dixon, *Spiritual Wives,* 1:viii; Dixon to FPC, 3 September 1867, FPCP; Dixon, *Spiritual Wives,* 1:294–95, 298.

82. Dixon to FPC, 23 January 1868, CAC.

83. Dixon, *Spiritual Wives,* 1:232–33, 271–72, 249, 318, 320, 325.

84. Frances Colenso to Mary Elizabeth Lyell, 5 March 1868, in Colenso, *Letters from Natal,* 184. The January issue included Cobbe's "The New Creed and the Old, in Their Secular Results, III."

85. FPC to Kate Amberley, [March 1868], [April 1868], Amberley Papers.

86. Litchfield, *Emma Darwin,* 218.

87. Jewsbury to Richard Bentley, 8 May 1868, Bentley Archives, reel 47; FPC to Edward Enfield, undated, Free Christian Union Papers.

88. Blackburn, *Women's Suffrage,* 67.

89. FPC to Kate Amberley, [24 June 1868], Amberley Papers.

90. Froude to FPC, 6 August [1868], FPCP; Conway, "Working With Froude," 379.

91. See Hamilton, "Locating Victorian Feminism."

92. FPC to Kate Amberley, [24 June 1868], Amberley Papers; Lecky to FPC, 7 November 1868, FPCP; John Edward Gray to FPC, 5 December 1868, FPCP; "Miss Cobbe's Theology," *Spectator,* 9 January 1869.

93. Mill to Helen Taylor [November 1868], in Mill, *Later Letters,* 1475; Hudson, *Munby,* 264.

## 9   Working Woman Scribbler, 1869–1874

1. "The Story of *The Echo*," *Echo*, 1 March 1869; Nowell-Smith, *House of Cassell*, 118; Arnold, "Founding of 'The Echo.'" Terminology and attitudes had changed by the end of the century; Arnold called them all "boys" in his article for the paper's thirtieth anniversary issue, although on 1 March 1869 the paper was proud that "the sale of *The Echo* by hundreds of poor boys and girls and women in the streets of London has afforded the means of living to those who would otherwise have been chargeable as paupers, or possibly engaged in crime."

2. "The Story of *The Echo*," *Echo*, 1 March 1869.

3. Arnold, "Founding of 'The Echo.'"

4. The scrapbooks of Cobbe's anonymous newspaper work at the NLW often have dated notes of the amount she was paid; one purpose of her clipping file was no doubt to make sure that nothing was forgotten when payday came.

5. *Hansard*, 14 April 1869, 765. Cobbe's initial leader was "Even-Handed Justice," *Echo*, 19 January 1869; her letter was published on 6 February. She repeated the facts of the Susannah Palmer case in "The Rights of Married People," an *Echo* leader published on 23 February 1869, before Russell Gurney's motion for the first reading of the Married Women's Property Bill, and recurred to it yet again in "Wife-Torture in England" (1878).

6. FPC, "Journalism As a Profession For Women" (1888).

7. Rosa Bonheur to FPC, 20 January 1869, FPCP (although 26 Hereford Square no longer exists, the top-lit brick workspace constructed for Lloyd is now known as Number 1, Wetherby Studios); Hudson, *Munby*, 265–66; Russell and Russell, *Amberley Papers*, 2:261; FPC, *Life* (1894), 2:97. William Henry Channing, the principal editor of the 1852 *Memoirs of Margaret Fuller Ossoli*, became a clergyman to the Unitarian Society of Liverpool in 1854 and returned to live in England after serving as a chaplain during the American Civil War.

8. Brown, *Metaphysical Society*, 26; Thirlwall, *Letters to a Friend*, 266.

9. *EWR*, July 1869, 275–78; [FPC], "A Case for Consideration," *Echo*, 20 May 1869. Women ratepayers made up 17 percent of the electorate overall and as much as 25 percent in spa and cathedral towns where there was a concentration of widowed and single women with enough property to qualify as voters (Hollis, *Ladies Elect*, 31).

10. FPC to John Stuart Mill, 4 June [1869], John Stuart Mill Letters; FPC, "The Subjection of Women" (1869), 371.

11. See, e.g., [FPC], "Married Women's Property," *Echo*, 26 March 1870.

12. FPC to Helen Taylor, 17 June [1869], M-T; "The Female Franchise," *Saturday Review*, 24 July 1869; [FPC], "The Ladies' Bills," *Echo*, 7 August 1869; FPC to Helen Taylor, 17 June [1869], M-T.

13. FPC, *Life* (1894), 2:124–25.

14. [FPC], Review of *Cave Hunting*, by William Boyd Dawkins, *Daily News*, 29 October 1874; Dawkins, *Cave Hunting*, 152, 18.

15. FPC to Mary Somerville, [July 1869], MSFP; FPC, "Final Cause of Woman" (1869), 6, 21; FPC, "Defects of Women" (1869), 232.

16. FPC to Mary Somerville, 8 August [1869], MSFP; FPC to Jewsbury, 15 [November 1869], ALWL.

17. Russell and Russell, *Amberley Papers,* 2:291.

18. FPC to Kate Amberley, [autumn 1869], Amberley Papers.

19. FPC to Fawcett, 6 July [1897], ALWL.

20. FPC, *Life* (1894), 2:205; "Cobbe's Norman Kings," *Saturday Review,* 18 December 1869; FPC to H. R. Haweis, 15 November [1894], CPAC. Edward Augustus Freeman, who had won a university prize for his essay on the effects of the Norman conquest while he was an Oxford undergraduate, wrote for the *Saturday Review* from 1855 to 1877.

21. The review by Charles Henry Pearson in the *North British Review* in January 1870 praised the author's accuracy in drawing from chronicles but said that his style "is quaint even to affectation" and that the book's crucial defect was "the author's want of critical acquaintance with the institutions he describes. His contempt for philosophies of history seems to have led him deliberately to disregard, not only the knowledge that has been acquired since Kemble wrote, but all that a very ordinary man, with less than Mr. Cobbe's reading, might easily work out for himself" (530–31). Charles William Boase echoed the same charges in the *Academy* on 12 February 1870, and a year later, across the Atlantic, the *North American Review* for October 1870 complained about the author's "strange use of language": "Mr. Cobbe's style is indeed a very vicious one, abounding in participles and relatives, in unusual and obsolete words and in short, jerky sentences" (481).

22. Channing, *Blanche Mary Susan Ethelind Channing,* 27; FPC to Jewsbury, 15 [November 1869], ALWL; FPC, "Woman Suffrage" (1903), 658.

23. FPC to H. R. Haweis, 15 November [1894], CPAC. John Richard Green contributed essays on historical subjects to the *Saturday Review* from 1862 and later became extremely well known for his very popular *Short History of the English People* (1874). According to Herbert Paul's *Life of Froude,* 142–98, persistent attacks in the *Saturday Review* (written by Edward Augustus Freeman, not John Richard Green) damaged Froude's reputation as a historian in the mid-1860s.

24. Lecky to FPC, undated, CAC; Lecky to Kate Amberley, 16 September 1869, in Russell and Russell, *Amberley Papers,* 2:313; FPC to Kate Amberley, [autumn 1869], Amberley Papers.

25. FPC to Mary Somerville, 27 December [1869], MSFP.

26. FPC to Mary Somerville, 17 January [1870], MSFP; Sunday Lecture Society, [*Proceedings*]; Davies, *Unorthodox London,* 39–40. The lectures were held at 4:30 P.M. at St. George's Hall, Langham Place, which was also used for many suffrage meetings and, later, for Charles Voysey's Sunday services.

27. [FPC], "Married Women's Property," *Echo,* 26 March 1870; [FPC], Review of *A Brave Lady,* by Dinah Mulock Craik, *Echo,* 7 April 1870. She had also referred to the novel while it was running in serial parts in *Macmillan's* from May 1869 to April 1870 (see [FPC], "A Good Riddance," *Echo,* 9 December 1869).

28. *Pall Mall Gazette,* 12 July 1870, quoted in *EWR,* October 1870, 260. See Shanley, *Feminism, Marriage, and the Law,* 70–77, for details.

29. Froude to FPC, 24 March [1860s or 1870s], FPCP. Froude continued to edit *Fraser's* until 1874.

30. *EWR,* April 1871, 118.

31. Hudson, *Munby,* 281–82; Russell and Russell, *Amberley Papers,* 2:324–25.

32. "A Lady Farmer," signed "F.P.C.," *EWR,* April 1870, 58–59; *Times,* 4 May 1871 (discussing "last year's" vote); *Hansard,* 12 May 1870, 619–20; Mentia Taylor to *Pall Mall Gazette,* 14 May, reprinted in *EWR,* July 1870, 192.

33. *EWR,* July 1870, 225–26.

34. Wister, *That I May Tell You,* 79.

35. Crawford, *Women's Suffrage Movement,* 10; *Times,* 28 May 1870; FPC to Kate Amberley, 18 June 1870, Amberley Papers.

36. FPC to Kate Amberley, [July 1870], Amberley Papers; Lady Russell to Kate Amberley, 14 June 1870, in Russell and Russell, *Amberley Papers,* 2:355; FPC to Kate Amberley, [2] October [1870], Amberley Papers.

37. [FPC], "A Cracked 'Drum Ecclesiastic,'" *Echo,* 10 September 1870.

38. FPC to Kate Amberley, [2] October [1870], Amberley Papers; T. H. Huxley to FPC, 16 November 1870, FPCP. Charles Edward Brown Séquard was an experimental physiologist known for his research on the central nervous system.

39. FPC to Mary Somerville, 25 [November 1870], MSFP; George Grove to FPC, 2 September [1870], FPCP; FPC, "Dreams As Illustrations of Unconscious Cerebration" (1871), 512. That Cobbe might have been a frustrated scientist was initially suggested to me by Nina Auerbach.

40. "The Educational Election," *Echo,* 23 November 1870.

41. FPC to Mary Somerville, 25 [November 1870], MSFP.

42. FPC, "Municipal Woman Suffrage in England" (1879).

43. A selection of newspaper reports is quoted in *EWR,* January 1871, 12–18.

44. Maria Grey, *Memorials of Emily A. E. Shirreff,* 29; *EWR,* January 1871, 4.

45. Crowther, *Church Embattled,* 133.

46. [FPC], "A Modern Trial for Heresy," *Echo,* 11 November 1870; FPC to Kate Amberley [late March or early April 1871], Amberley Papers.

47. "The Year at Home," *Echo,* 31 December 1870.

48. Hudson, *Munby,* 293. In addition to her certification by the Society of Apothecaries, which provided the legal right to practice medicine in England, Garrett had qualified for the degree of M.D. at the University of Paris in the summer of 1870.

49. *Lancet,* quoted in the *Times,* 6 January 1871.

50. FPC, *Life* (1894), 2:105–6. Longfellow's poem was originally published in *Ballads and Other Poems* (1842).

51. Elizabeth Garrett Anderson to FPC, 25 February 1871, CAC; *Times,* 9 January 1871.

52. John Murray to Charles Darwin, 18 February [1871], in Burkhardt et al., *Calendar,* 328; Emma Darwin to FPC, undated, in FPC, *Life* (1894), 2:127; Emma Darwin to FPC, undated, FPCP.

53. [FPC], "Woman Suffrage," *Echo,* 28 March 1871.

54. [FPC], "The Temptation of Mr. Gladstone," *Echo,* 27 April 1871; [FPC], "The Female Franchise," *Examiner,* 29 April 1871.

55. Russell and Russell, *Amberley Papers,* 2:469 (Gladstone did not exactly speak in favor, though he admitted that women had many justified grievances [see *Hansard,* 3 May 1871, 91–94]); *Times,* 4 May 1871; FPC to Mary Somerville, 7 May [1871], MSFP; *Hansard,* 3 May 1871, 97–98; [FPC], "Women's Electoral Disabilities," *Examiner,* 6 May 1871. The *Times* quotation is from its leader of 4 May 1871.

56. FPC to Mary Somerville, 6 Sept [1871], MSFP; Matthew Davenport Hill to FPC, in FPC, *Life* (1894), 1:348; FPC to Somerville, 6 September [1871], MSFP.

57. FPC to Mary Somerville, 25 October [1871], 27 January [1872], MSFP; FPC to Sarah Wister, 17 May [1874], WFP. I am grateful to Stephen White for information about the Cremation Society. Its founders included Cobbe's friends H. R. Haweis and Charles Voysey; among the other council members were William Shaen, Francis Galton, and George DuMaurier.

58. Blackburn, *Women's Suffrage*, 119; National Society for Women's Suffrage, *First Report*; Malleson, *Elizabeth Malleson*, 118–19.

59. [FPC], "The Immortality of the Higher Animals" (signed "Philozooist"), *Spectator*, 18 November 1871; FPC to Mary Somerville, 27 January [1872], MSFP.

60. FPC to Mary Somerville, 27 January 1872, MSFP; Blackburn, *Women's Suffrage*, 119.

61. Russell and Russell, *Amberley Papers*, 2:481; *EWR*, July 1872, 204–5.

62. [FPC], "Women's Suffrage," *Echo*, 2 May 1872; *EWR*, July 1872, 210; Crawford, *Women's Suffrage Movement*, 133; Conway, *Autobiography*, 2:78.

63. "Women's Peace Congress," *Echo*, 9 July 1872; Howe, *Reminiscences*, 333; James Martineau to Mary Lloyd, 24 September 1872, FPCP.

64. FPC to Mary Somerville, 23 November [1872], MSFP; Davies, *Heterodox London*, 1:277, 280, 285; Besant, *Annie Besant*, 106–7; FPC to Martha Somerville, 13 [May 1873], MSFP.

65. Charles Darwin (in his wife's handwriting) to FPC, 28 November 1872, FPCP. As is often the case with the letters included in the *Life of Frances Power Cobbe*, the version published in 2:127–28 omits Darwin's "kind regards to Miss Lloyd" and some other names of living persons.

66. [FPC], "Cruelty to Animals," *Echo*, 13 June 1872; [FPC], "Nobody but Ladies and Gentlemen," *Echo*, 11 July 1872.

67. FPC to Martha Somerville, 6 December 1872, MSFP (the obituary was "Blessed Old Age," *Echo*, 3 December 1872); Mary Lloyd to Martha Somerville, 1 December 1872, MSFP; William Smith to FPC, 30 December 1872, CAC; FPC to Martha Somerville, [December 1872], MSFP.

68. FPC to John Blackwood, 8 November [1872], Blackwood Papers; Anne Mozley to John Blackwood, [November 1872], Blackwood Papers (I thank Ellen Jordan for sending me this passage).

69. Julia Wedgwood to FPC, 24 August 1871, CAC.

70. *EWR*, April 1873, 150. Jane Hughes Senior was the sister of the writer (and MP) Thomas Hughes, the widow of Nassau William Senior (whose report on poverty had led to the 1834 Poor Law), and a founder of the Metropolitan Association for Befriending Young Servants. Her initially temporary appointment was made permanent in February 1874.

71. Shirley Brooks, diary entry for 20 February 1873, supplied to me by Patrick Leary; FPC, Obituary for H. R. Haweis, *Abolitionist*, 15 February 1901; Hopkins, "Our Portrait Gallery," 398.

72. FPC to Helen Taylor, [24 March 1873], M-T; FPC to Martha Somerville, 10 May [1873], MSFP.

73. FPC to Martha Somerville, undated, MSFP.

74. FPC to Martha Somerville, 17 April [1873], 13 [May 1873], MSFP.

75. Somerville, *Personal Recollections,* 357–59; FPC to Martha Somerville, 1 , 6 December [1873], MSFP (the review in the *Fortnightly* was by Edith Simcox, in "New Books" for January 1874; but I have not located any notice in *Contemporary Review*). FPC's *Academy* review from 3 January 1874 was reprinted in *Every Saturday* (Boston) for 7 February 1874 and is quoted from that source.

76. FPC, "Mary Somerville" (1874).

77. FPC to *Animal World,* 1 October 1873, 156; FPC to Florence Clough, 9 August [1873], A. H. Clough Correspondence; [FPC], "A Philosopher's Grave," *Echo,* 13 May 1873.

78. FPC to Sarah Wister, 3 August [1873], WFP.

79. Maria Mitchell, diary entry for August 1873, in Kendall, *Maria Mitchell,* 216; William Carpenter to FPC, 4, 7 September 1873, FPCP.

80. FPC, "Deplorable Flaw" (1874). The Eliot quotation is truncated from Eliot's newly published *Middlemarch.*

81. *Punch,* 1 November 1873; *EWR,* January 1874, 69; FPC, "Town Mouse and the Country Mouse" (1875), 479; FPC to Sarah Wister, 10 December [1873], WFP.

82. FPC to Sarah Wister, 17 May [1874], 10 December [1873], WFP. Cobbe may have done less work for the *Echo* after January 1874, though it is hard to be certain; her scrapbook for this period is disordered, and she was paid for more leaders than she pasted on the pages that survive.

83. Shanley, *Feminism, Marriage, and the Law,* 107; *EWR,* October 1874, 277.

84. Becker to Edward Eastwick, 4 March 1874, in Blackburn, *Women's Suffrage,* 135; FPC to Sarah Wister, 17 May [1874], WFP; *EWR,* July 1874, 209; FPC to Sarah Wister, 21 March [1874], WFP.

85. FPC to Sarah Wister, 17 May [1874], WFP. Cobbe's suspicion about timing was right—the university senate reversed the decision by a vote of 17 to 10 on 1 July—but so, of course, was her conclusion.

86. *Hansard,* 18 May 1874, 398; "Women's Wrongs," *Punch,* 30 May 1874; *EWR,* October 1874, 206.

87. Smith, "Female Suffrage," 140, 139; *Daily News,* 3 June 1874. Although the leader was anonymous, *EWR* identified it as Cobbe's in October 1874, 262–63.

88. *EWR,* 15 January 1895, 59.

89. Details and quotations from *Women and Work,* 11 July 1874.

90. FPC to Sarah Wister, 17 May [1874], WFP.

91. [FPC], "Friends of the Lower Animals," *Echo,* 24 June 1874. She also reported on the conference in "The Jubilee of Brutes," signed "F.P.C.," *Examiner,* 28 June 1874.

92. FPC to Sarah Wister, 21 March [1874], WFP; [FPC], "Which is the Brute?" *Echo,* 3 March 1873; [FPC], "A Word With Our Surgeons," *Echo,* 9 August 1873; [FPC], "Ignorant and Scientific Cruelty," *Echo,* 23 December 1873; [FPC], "Mr. Cross on Cat-Killing," *Echo,* 1 April 1874; [FPC], "Fear of Hydrophobia," *Echo,* 27 May 1874; FPC to Sarah Wister, 10 December [1873], WFP; *Spectator,* 29 August 1874.

93. [FPC], "The Curse of St. Alban's," *Echo,* 14 March 1871; [FPC], "Priestcraft in the Church of England," *Leader,* 19 October 1867.

94. [FPC], "Mr. Gladstone Upon Ritualism," *Echo,* 28 September 1874; [FPC],

"Mr. Gladstone on Fashions," *Echo,* 29 September 1874; [FPC], "Mr. Gladstone and the Pope," *Echo,* 12 November 1874; Carpenter, *James Martineau,* 413.

95. FPC to Helen Taylor, 22 December [1874], M-T.

96. FPC to Helen Taylor, 20 October [1874], M-T; Helen Taylor to FPC, 22 October 1874, FPCP.

97. Jenkins, *Sir Charles Dilke,* 91; Charles Wentworth Dilke to FPC, 23 December [1874], FPCP; John Russell (Lord Amberley) to FPC, 25–26 November 1874, FPCP.

98. *Times,* 16 November 1874; FPC to Helen Taylor, 6 December [1874], M-T.

99. *Daily News,* 10 December 1874.

100. FPC to Mary Anne Estlin, undated, New England Hospital Records, Sophia Smith Collection; FPC to Helen Taylor, 6 December [1874], M-T; [FPC], "House Property in London," *Echo,* 22 December 1874.

101. FPC to Helen Taylor, 6 December [1874]; Jane Senior to FPC, 1 November 1874, FPCP.

102. [FPC], "The Vivisection Trial at Norwich," *Echo,* 12 December 1874, M-T; FPC to her brother Charles, [December 1874], CPAC; FPC to Helen Taylor, 22 December [1874], M-T.

103. A.V. Letters 1874–77, BUAV.

## 10 Parliamentary Politics, 1875–1878

1. *Animal World,* 1 March 1875, 38.

2. Hoggan, "Vivisection," 524.

3. T. H. Huxley to Charles Darwin, 22 January 1875, in Huxley, *Thomas Henry Huxley,* 1:470.

4. Ernest Hart to the *Times,* 28 January, 4 February 1875; FPC to Sarah Wister, 8 February [1875], WFP; FPC, "Thoughts about Thinking" (1875), 207.

5. *EWR,* 15 February 1875.

6. FPC, in some copies of *Rest in the Lord* (1887), 48–49. The poem is also published in FPC, *Life* (1904).

7. Battersea, *Waifs and Strays,* 163; Battersea Papers, 4 March 1875; Battersea, *Waifs and Strays,* 163–64.

8. Richard Holt Hutton to FPC, 15 March 1875, FPCP.

9. Printed in the *Morning Post* on 2 February, Hoggan's letter was republished in the *Spectator,* 6 February 1875; Hoggan, "Vivisection."

10. FPC, *Life* (1894), 2:187–88, 265.

11. *Hansard,* 7 April 1875, 418, 422.

12. *EWR,* April 1875, 164.

13. *EWR,* 15 July 1875, 311–12.

14. Huxley to Darwin, 19 May 1875, in Huxley, *Thomas Henry Huxley,* 1:471.

15. Desmond and Moore, *Darwin,* 615; C. L. Dodgson to FPC, 7 May 1875, FPCP (signed "C. L. Dodgson [alias 'Lewis Carroll']"); Carroll, *Diaries,* 339.

16. FPC to James Macaulay, 4 June [1875], Miscellaneous Papers, National Library of Scotland.

17. Dodgson to FPC, 21 May 1875, in Carroll, *Letters,* 226. The quoted passage is, of course, from the evolution section of Tennyson's *In Memoriam.*

18. Two tables, one on each side of the exit leading to the North Library—in the least public part of the reading room—were reserved for women readers, and the cloakroom had a female attendant to take their outdoor clothing (see Jones, Preface to *List of the Books of Reference*).

19. William Rathbone Greg to FPC, 6 August 1875, in FPC, *Life* (1894), 2:153; Kemble to St. Leger, 28 July, 14 September 1875, in Kemble, *Further Records*, 109, 119.

20. Cohen, *Lady De Rothschild*, 165; Battersea Papers, 23 August 1875.

21. Hutton to FPC, 6 September 1875, FPCP; FPC, *Life* (1894), 2:270.

22. Thomas, *Frances Elizabeth Hoggan*, 14–15.

23. Anthony Ashley Cooper, seventh earl of Shaftesbury, to FPC, 17 November 1875, in FPC, *Life* (1894), 1:271.

24. Violet Paget to her mother, 3 July 1894, in *VL*, 374.

25. Several letters in the Bentley Archives indexed as Frances Power Cobbe's clearly are not in her handwriting (see Mitchell, "Fanny Power Cobbe").

26. Ruskin, *Fors Clavigera*, letter 66 (June 1876); Field, *Works and Days*, 148–49. Thanks to Linda Hughes for supplying the latter reference.

27. Gladstone, *Diaries*, 9:108; William Ewart Gladstone to FPC, 1 March 1876, FPCP; FPC, *Life* (1904), 505.

28. *Times*, 8 February 1898.

29. Edel, *Henry James*, 235.

30. FPC, *Life* (1894), 2:276.

31. John Duke Coleridge to FPC, 17 March 1876, FPCP; Froude to FPC, 19 March 1876, BUAV; FPC to Sarah Wister, 21 March [1874], WFP.

32. FPC, *Life* (1894), 1:355.

33. FPC, "Fitness of Women" (1876), 272; *Hansard*, 26 April 1876, 1668–69.

34. *WSJ*, 1 June 1876, 88–89. The speech was published in *Victoria Magazine* for July and has been reprinted as "Speech At the Women's Suffrage Meeting, St. George's Hall, 13 May 1876" in *Before the Vote Was Won: Arguments For and Against Women's Suffrage,* edited by Jane Lewis (London: Routledge & Kegan Paul, 1987). And an American visitor had taken notes on the flyleaf of the 1874 Murray's *Handbook to London* I bought from a U.S. bookseller.

35. Morris, *New Rambler*, 303–4.

36. FPC to Gladstone, 21 April [1876], Gladstone Papers; "Vivisection," *Times*, 2 June 1876, 7.

37. *Pall Mall Gazette* for 22 June quoted in *EWR*, 15 July 1876, 329; "Dogs and Doctors," *Punch*, 29 July 1876; French, *Antivivisection and Medical Science*, 132. Henrietta Herbert, dowager Lady Carnarvon, died on 26 May 1876. Cobbe's *Life* says simply "Lady Carnarvon," and some accounts have assumed it was Carnarvon's wife, not his mother, who had died.

38. Charles Beard to Mary Lloyd, 19 August [1876], FPCP; Cottesloe, *Lost, Stolen, or Strayed*, 38–39; Local Studies Department, Royal Borough of Kensington and Chelsea Central Library.

39. FPC, "The Policy of the Future," *Home Chronicler*, 16 September 1876; FPC to *Home Chronicler*, 19 August 1876; FPC, *Life* (1894), 2:280.

40. FPC, *Life* (1894), 2:280; Shaftesbury to FPC, 16 August 1876, in FPC, *Life* (1894), 2:280–83.

41. *Home Chronicler,* 26 August, 16 September 1873.

42. FPC, *Life* (1894), 2:283; George Hoggan to *Home Chronicler,* 30 September 1876; Hutton to *Home Chronicler,* 28 October 1876.

43. FPC to *Home Chronicler,* 9 December 1876; *Home Chronicler,* 8 December 1877.

44. *EWR,* 14 October 1876, 452–55.

45. *EWR,* 15 March 1877, 130.

46. FPC to Helen Taylor, [8, 18 November 1876], M-T.

47. FPC, "Celt of Wales" (1877), 661.

48. Foreign Resident, *Society in London,* 278–80; R. A. Bennett in Thorold, *Henry Labouchère,* 448–50; Kate Field to Edward Clarence Stedman, 28 November 1877, in Field, *Selected Letters,* 138.

49. *Truth,* 8 November 1877.

50. FPC to John Blackwood, 4 December [1876], Blackwood Papers.

51. *EWR,* 15 February 1877, 95 (Cobbe no doubt told her friend Caroline Ashurst Biggs, who had become editor of the *Englishwoman's Review* in 1871, about the book's contents, or perhaps even supplied the "review" herself); FPC, *Age of Science* (1877), 44.

52. FPC, "Dr. Carpenter's Address," *Echo,* 6 September 1872; Louisa Carpenter to FPC, 19 January 1877, FPCP.

53. FPC, "Mr. Lowe" (1877), 335. Robert Lowe was also a consistent opponent of women's suffrage.

54. Carpenter, *Mary Carpenter,* 383.

55. "The Meeting at Clifton," *Home Chronicler,* 17 March 1877.

56. "Vivisection," *Saturday Review,* 5 May 1877; Kemble to St. Leger, 18 April 1877, in Kemble, *Further Records,* 226; Shaftesbury to Lady Portsmouth, 4 June 1877, FPCP; *Spectator,* 5 May 1877.

57. Kemble to St. Leger, 18 April 1877, in Kemble, *Further Records,* 226; *EWR,* 15 May 1877, 222–23.

58. *EWR,* 15 June 1877, 264–67.

59. [FPC], "Travelling in Wales," *Cambrian News,* October 1877; Kemble to St. Leger, 23 March 1877, in Kemble, *Further Records,* 221.

60. FPC, "Peak in Darien" (1877), 287; Frances Wedgwood to FPC, undated, FPCP.

61. Francis Galton to FPC, 27 August 1877, FPCP; [FPC], "A Lesson from the Penge Murder," *Spectator,* 6 October 1877, signed "F."; Becker to FPC, 6 October 1877, FPCP. The letter from Becker is very long with many familiar references to former conversations, suggesting that there must have been a good deal of additional (undiscovered) correspondence between Cobbe and Becker.

62. Anne Thackeray Ritchie to FPC, undated, CAC. The Ritchies had married on 2 August 1877.

63. *EWR,* 15 December 1877, 563–64; [FPC], "Mad Dogs," *Truth,* 11 January 1877; "The Vivisectionists and the Hydrophobia Cry," *Home Chronicler,* 8 December 1877.

64. "Drawing Room Meeting, Bristol," *WSJ,* 1 December 1877, 206.

65. *WSJ,* 1 January 1878, 10; "The Health of Women," *Times,* 14 December 1877; "Cobbe to the Rescue!" *Punch,* 22 December 1877.

66. [FPC], "The Halfway House," *Truth,* 20 December 1877.

67. Manchester, "Marital Violence," 131.

68. FPC, *Life* (1894), 2:218–19.

69. "Drawing Room Meeting, Bristol," *WSJ*, 1 December 1877, 205.

70. *Spectator*, 29 December 1877.

71. *Hansard*, 19 May 1874, 399; FPC, "Wife-Torture in England" (1878), 78.

72. F. W. Harper, "Wife-Beating," *Spectator*, 26 January 1878. Francis Whaley Harper, perpetual curate of the Abbey Church, Selby, Yorkshire, had written *The Incomes of the Clergy, What They Ought to Be and What They Are* (1856). Cobbe used his letter in a footnote to "Wife-Torture in England" (1878): "After thus bringing to our minds the beatings, and kickings, and blindings, and burnings, and 'cloggings,' which sicken us, he bids us remember that the true idea of marriage is 'the relation of Christ to his Church'!" (64).

73. Kemble to St. Leger, undated, in Kemble, *Further Records*, 245 (Cobbe's visit to Coleridge must have been made before his wife's death on 6 February 1878, and although I find no record of a deputation on this issue, Cobbe could well have spoken to Millicent Garrett Fawcett, wife of MP Henry Fawcett, about bringing the London National Society into the Central Committee); FPC to *Daily News*, 7 June 1878. Russell Gurney died on 31 May.

74. [FPC], "Wife-Torture," *Truth*, 17 January 1878.

75. In a letter to the *Women's Suffrage Journal* published on 1 July 1878, P. A. Taylor reported that when the home secretary had planned to introduce a flogging bill, he (Taylor) had been "instrumental in causing it to be withdrawn" because Cobbe "perceived the necessity of a sounder basis for such reform."

76. *Hansard*, 29 March 1878, 191; *EWR*, 14 December 1878, 533; Penzance to FPC, [4 April 1878], FPCP. Shanley, *Feminism, Marriage, and the Law*, 168–69, analyzes the difference between Cobbe's account in her *Life* and the bill's actual progress through Parliament.

77. FPC, "Wife-Torture in England" (1878), 58.

78. FPC, "Celibacy *v.* Marriage" (1862), 234.

79. "Protection to Wives," *EWR*, 15 June 1878, 250–52; Pleck, *Domestic Tyranny*, 104.

80. Boucherett, "Frances Power Cobbe," 133.

81. Shaftesbury to FPC, 23 January 1878, FPCP; Marquis of Bute to FPC, 28 January 1878, FPCP.

82. Mallet, "Albemarle Club," 38–40; James Martineau to FPC, 1 January 1878, in FPC, "Recollections of James Martineau" (1900), 185; FPC to Henry Wentworth Acland, [1878], Acland Papers. *Science in Excelsis*, originally published about 1875, is reprinted in FPC, *The Modern Rack* (1889).

83. Kemble to St. Leger, undated, in Kemble, *Further Records*, 245; Augusta Webster to FPC, 6 May 1878, FPCP; Kemble to St. Leger, 19 [February or March 1878], in Kemble, *Further Records*, 243 (ellipses in the original).

84. *Times*, 16 May 1878.

85. Shaftesbury to FPC, 17 September 1878, FPCP.

86. Augusta Webster to FPC, 9 August 1878, FPCP; Shaftesbury to FPC, 3 September 1878, FPCP.

87. FPC, "The Kingdom of God," *Inquirer*, 21 September 1878, 614–16; FPC, "Unequal Sentences," *Spectator*, 14 September 1878. The case of Isabel W. Thomason, also known as Isabel Grant, was reported in the *Times* on 6 September 1878.

88. Cobbe's letter was printed on 19 September; Webster's letter and the *Times*

leader were published on 20 September; news of the reprieve was published on 24 September.

89. Harriet Hosmer to Louisa Ashburton, Ashburton Papers, National Library of Scotland (supplied by Martha Vicinus); "Cannibalism *v.* Vivisection," *Punch,* 2 November 1878. Cobbe's speech is reported at length in "Meeting at Southampton," *Home Chronicler,* 26 October 1878.

90. FPC to Helen Taylor, 12 [October 1878], M-T.

91. FPC to Theodore Stanton, 3 January [1886], ECS Papers.

92. Martha Vicinus, e-mail message to author, 7 January 2002. Cobbe complained in *Life* (1894), 2:27, that Hosmer had been "lured away from sculpture by some invention of her own of a mechanical kind over which many years of her life have been lost."

93. Gunn, *Vernon Lee,* 66.

94. FPC to Violet Paget, 10 [September 1879], VLC; FPC, *Italics* (1864), 2.

## 11 Battles for the Unrepresented, 1879–1884

1. "Employment of Women," *EWR,* 15 July 1879, 320; Battersea Papers, 23 June, 3 July 1879.

2. Shaftesbury to FPC, 8 July 1879, FPCP; *Hansard,* 15 July 1879. Charles Robert Claude Wilde, second baron Truro (1816–91), was a barrister called from the Inner Temple in 1842; he must therefore have been at least an acquaintance of Cobbe's brother Tom, who also read law at the Inner Temple and was called to the bar in 1841.

3. Hoggan was dismissed in July 1879; the lawsuit against him was reported in the *Times* on 3 May 1881.

4. Directories of the period list five gentry families in Maulden, while Milton had only one in addition to the clergyman; Maulden had four pubs to Milton's one. The clergy income, according to *Crockford's Clerical Directory,* was £470 in Maulden compared with £252 in Milton.

5. Adams, *Somerville for Women,* 15–17; Wordsworth, *Glimpses,* 137; Mary Ward Diary, 30 August–5 September 1879. After much discussion, Somerville's constitution specified that "prayers will be read daily in the House" but remained silent about any requirement that students attend and inserted "as a rule" in the sentence mandating attendance at some place of worship on Sundays (Adams, *Somerville for Women,* 12).

6. "Lectures to Ladies," *EWR,* 15 October 1879, 464; *WSJ,* 1 November 1879, 190.

7. "Miss Cobbe's Lectures to Ladies," *WSJ,* 1 December 1879, 205.

8. Kemble to St. Leger, 10 January 1875, in Kemble, *Further Records,* 64.

9. Cobbe is quoted from the Boston edition of *The Duties of Women,* published by George H. Ellis in 1881. See the extended reading and commentary in Sears, "Politics and Gender of Duty."

10. FPC to Sarah Wister, 31 March [1880], WFP; Anne Thackeray Ritchie to FPC, 26 February [1880], FPCP. Alicia Bewicke had been a leading supporter of the British and Continental Federation for the Abolition of the State Regulation of Vice; later, as Alicia Bewick Little, she wrote on Tibet and China. Although Ritchie, who was in her early forties, called her a "young lady," Bewicke was then thirty-four. My thanks to Rachel Bright for the information about Bewicke.

11. Richards, Elliott, and Hall, *Julia Ward Howe,* 2:62; *New York Times,* 19 March

1881; Alcott, *Journals*, 231; FPC to Sarah Wister, 5 January [1888], WFP; Mary Livermore to FPC, 19 August 1882, FPCP.

12. *Spectator*, 15 January 1881. I identified Hutton's authorship through the *Spectator* contributors' book.

13. FPC to Rosamond Davenport Hill, [1879], M-T. Rosamond and her sister Florence began using the surname Davenport Hill instead of plain Hill when they settled in London in 1879 in order to avoid confusion with Octavia Hill, who was not a relative.

14. FPC to Miss Horner (probably a sister of Katherine Lyell's), 5 December [1879], CPAC.

15. FPC, *Duties of Women* (1881), 169–70.

16. FPC to Helen Taylor, [1880], M-T; FPC to Horatia Gatty, undated, NLW.

17. FPC to Helen Taylor [1880], M-T, which says that she was also writing to Augusta Webster.

18. Catherine Marsh to FPC, 14 February [1880], FPCP; Anne Thackeray Ritchie wrote of "such a horrible two minutes one evening over the paper" (26 February [1880], FPCP); FPC to Sarah Wister, 31 March [1880], WFP.

19. *Woman's Journal* (Boston), 3 April 1880.

20. On the other hand, the phrase "who took my name" may be accurate; George Cobbe's will refers to her as "Fanny Arabella Cobbe." I am grateful to D. W. Budworth for sending me his transcription of George Cobbe's will.

21. Cobbe's brother Charles to their brother Tom, 5 September 1856, CPN.

22. When he wrote to Charles Cobbe in 1856, Henry Willet had just finished his apprenticeship to a fashionable hairdresser. At the time of the 1881 census he, like Frances Mary Power Cobbe in the previous year, was living oddly close to 26 Hereford Square; he was at 74 Brompton Road, Kensington, with his wife Louisa, also a hairdresser, and his nephew Henry Perrin.

23. FPC to Sarah Wister, 31 March [1880], WFP; Shaftesbury to FPC, 20 April 1881, FPCP; FPC to Mary Joy Haweis, 22 October [1889], Haweis Family Papers; Matthew Arnold to FPC, 30 January [1883], FPCP.

24. FPC to Violet Paget, 26 March 1880 (Good Friday), VLC; Henry Taylor to FPC, 16 March 1880, FPCP; FPC to Helen Taylor, 11 [April 1880], M-T; *EWR*, 15 April 1880, 146.

25. "Bristol," *WSJ*, 1 June 1880, 117; Shaftesbury to FPC, 21, 14 May 1880, in FPC, *Life* (1894), 2:198, 197.

26. FPC to Violet Paget, 28 June [1880], VLC; John Morley to FPC, 31 May 1880, FPCP; Shaftesbury to FPC, 23 July 1880, in FPC, *Life* (1894), 2:198–99.

27. FPC to Sarah Wister, 28 June [1880], WFP; FPC to Arthur de Noé Walker, 29 [January 1880], CPAC; FPC to Sarah Wister, 28 June [1880], WFP.

28. John Morley to FPC, 2, 28, 30 June, 9 October 1880, FPCP.

29. Griffiths, "Early Management," 129. Brigadier General A. H. Cobbe commanded the Koorum Field Force during the invasion of Afghanistan. Wounded at the capture of Peiwar Kotal, he spent six months on sick leave and on 19 July 1879 was made a Companion of the Order of the Bath.

30. Cobbe's scrapbooks have fifty-five pieces from the *Standard* from the period 30 June 1880 to 14 January 1882, although many are not individually dated.

31. The clipping is not dated, but the context suggests October 1880.

32. Frances Sheldon, 17 October, 5 December 1880, Sheldon Letters.

33. *Times,* 24 November 1884. Since Adams sued everyone for everything, I would hate to suggest, even a century after his death, that the "ill health" which caused him to sell out in 1853 might have had anything to do with the prospect of being sent to the Crimea.

34. *EWR,* 15 March 1881, 136.

35. Battersea Papers, 17–19 March 1881.

36. James Martineau to FPC, 19 April 1881, in FPC, "Recollections of James Martineau" (1900), 186; Henry James to FPC, 28 August [1881], CAC; "Poor Law Guardian Election," *EWR,* 15 April 1881, 170–75.

37. Battersea Papers, 13 December 1881.

38. FPC, "The Higher Expediency" (1883) reprinted in FPC, *Modern Rack* (1889), 37; FPC, "Four Reasons for Total Prohibition of Vivisection," in FPC, *Modern Rack,* 224.

39. The editor included a note: "It is not without a grave sense of responsibility that we publish the above article from the pen of an esteemed contributor, who prefers to withhold his signature." The magazine's index, published at the end of the year, names Cobbe as author of the article. A further note following the article added one other point that Cobbe did not mention, although it is possible that she suggested it for the male editor to use: "Any one who will make a few casual inquiries will be amazed to discover the frequency with which medical men of high repute—men who are admitted to the friendship of good and unsuspecting women—offer counsel to young men and even to boys which strikes at the root of all morality."

40. Shaftesbury to FPC, 26 April 1881, FPCP; Carpenter, "Morality of the Medical Profession."

41. For information about Madame Van Manen-Thesing, see "Women's Share in the Anti-Vivisection Movement," *EWR,* 15 October 1884, 445–76; and FPC, *Life* (1894), 2:295–96. I do not know whether laws in the Netherlands at that time permitted married women to make bequests in their wills.

42. *WSJ,* 1 June 1881, 92.

43. *EWR,* 15 July 1881, 330–31; "Women and Politics," *WSJ,* 1 July 1881, 102–3; Livermore, *Story of My Life,* 565, 571, 565. The VSS meeting was also reported in the *Times,* 28 June 1881.

44. Violet Paget to her mother, 5 July 1881, in *VL,* 71. H. R. Haweis was a Church of England clergyman as well as a journalist. *Music and Morals* (1871) argued that music has a direct influence on the listener's moral character. Its enormous popularity helped bring music instruction into British elementary education. Lewis Morris was another friend from Cobbe's early days in London; they had met at Mentia Taylor's Pen and Pencil Club. He was a poet, a supporter of women's higher education, and an early advocate of the Aberystwyth college that became the University of Wales.

45. Arnold, *Letters,* 244; Robert Browning to FPC, 3 July 1881, in FPC, *Life* (1894), 2:17; Cobbe's comment, in FPC, *Life,* 2:17; John Hoare to FPC, 5 July [1881], FPCP; W. H. Mudford to FPC, 13 July 1881, FPCP.

46. Mudford to FPC, 12, 13 July 1881, FPCP.

47. *WSJ,* 1 August 1881, 123–24; Battersea Papers, 13 July 1881; *VL,* 79.

48. *VL*, 83. The Edinburgh speech was published by the VSS as "The Right of Tormenting" and reprinted in FPC, *Modern Rack* (1889).

49. The *Standard* leader quoted here was probably written during the summer; the note below it reads, "18th July 1881. The £63 above included this I believe."

50. James Stansfeld to FPC, 29 November 1881, with an annotation about the wager added in Cobbe's hand, FPCP.

51. *Times*, 4, 18 November 1881. A long transcript of the testimony appeared in the *British Medical Journal*, 19 November 1881, 836–42. Cobbe's account in *Life* (1894) 2:299–300 reports subsequent evidence showing that the experiments had been conducted jointly by Ferrier and Yeo, but the passage she quotes is, in my reading, still open to the interpretation that Yeo performed the surgery and Ferrier interpreted the results. Ferrier's experiments on electrical stimulation of the brain and his application of antiseptic procedures led ultimately to successful surgery for some types of brain tumors and brain injury.

52. Shaftesbury to FPC, 26 October, 30 November, 30 December 1881, FPCP.

53. Owen, *Experimental Physiology*, 129, 136; Adams, *Coward Science*, 10; "Vivisection," *Nature*, 9 March 1882, 429–33; FPC "Zoophily" (1882), 281.

54. Harry Hamilton Johnston to *Nature*, 16 March 1882; FPC to *Nature*, 23 March 1882. Johnston wrote a rather shame-faced apology that was published in *Nature* on 30 March.

55. Tennyson to FPC, 9 January 1882, in FPC, *Life* (1894), 2:180; Shaftesbury to FPC, 9 January 1882, FPCP; *Standard*, 14 January 1882; Shaftesbury to FPC, 21 January 1882, FPCP.

56. Shaftesbury Diaries, 21 January 1882; Shaftesbury to FPC, 4 January to 25 April 1882, FPCP.

57. Shaftesbury to FPC, 30 December 1881, FPCP; *Lady's Own Paper* wrapper, November 1872; FPC to Anna Kingsford, 12 October 1872. Although Edward Maitland's biography of Kingsford says that she edited the *Lady's Own Paper* for two years, the volumes in the British Library Newspaper Library at Colindale list other editors for all of the issues except the four numbers for October 1872, which have a new masthead, are identified as a new series, and have "Edited by Mrs. Algernon Kingsford" under the title.

58. Maitland, *Anna Kingsford*, 1:443.

59. Anna Kingsford to Lady Caithness, 5 April 1882, in Maitland, *Anna Kingsford*, 2:55–56; Anstruther, "Ladies' Clubs," 600; Maitland, *Anna Kingsford*, 1:444.

60. George Fleming to FPC, 21 August 1878, FPCP.

61. "Temporary Home for Lost and Starving Dogs," *Animal World*, 1 April 1882, 55; *Zoophilist*, 1 April 1882, 237.

62. Louisa Egerton to FPC, undated, FPCP (Gladstone's diaries show he was at the Egerton home on Saturday 29 April 1882 and the following day, which was Easter Sunday); FPC, *Life* (1904), 505; FPC to Bentley, 17 June 1894, Bentley Archives, reel 25.

63. FPC to Sarah Wister, 19 October [1889], WFP.

64. FPC to Sarah Wister, [October 1882], WFP.

65. William Cobbe to his brother Charles, 7 June 1884, CPN.

66. Principal's Reports, vol. 1, Lady Margaret Hall Archives; *EWR*, 15 September 1883, 413.

67. Shanley, *Feminism, Marriage, and the Law,* 103.

68. *Zoophilist,* 1 July 1882. A few months later Tait's stature increased exponentially when he for the first time performed an operation that saved the life of a woman who had suffered a ruptured tubal pregnancy. When Tait went to Philadelphia for a medical conference in 1884, Cobbe described him to Sarah Wister, whose husband was a physician, as "the queerest looking man I ever saw with an enormous head—but a fine one rather—& a very gentle voice," passed along the rumor that he was "the *(illegitimate)* son of the celebrated Edinburgh doctor Sir James Simpson," and suggested that the Wisters show him some attention (FPC to Sarah Wister, 4 August [1884], WFP).

69. Wilkie Collins to FPC, 23 June 1882, in FPC, *Life* (1894), 2:184–85.

70. FPC, *Scientific Spirit* (1888), 110; FPC, "Progressive Judaism" (1882), 752 (quoting from Claude Montefiore, "Is Judaism a Tribal Religion?" *Contemporary Review,* September 1882); Claude Montefiore to FPC, 4 December 1882, FPCP.

71. *EWR,* 15 July 1882, 320.

72. *Times,* 8 December 1883; Shaftesbury to FPC, 4 November 1882, FPCP; FPC to Sarah Wister, 22 November [1882], WFP; *Zoophilist,* 1 December 1882, 197.

73. Foreign Resident, *Society in London,* 132–34.

74. *Times,* 19, 18 November, 1886.

75. *Times,* 19 November 1886; Shaftesbury to John Duke Coleridge, 21 November 1882, FPCP.

76. Shaftesbury to FPC, 21 November 1882, FPCP; Shaftesbury Diaries, 21 November 1882.

77. Shaftesbury to FPC, 24 November 1882, FPCP; Shaftesbury Diaries, 25 November 1882; Shaftesbury to FPC, 29 November, 1 December (two letters) 1882, FPCP.

78. *Times,* 19 November 1886; Shaftesbury to FPC, 12, 13, 16 December 1882, FPCP; Shaftesbury to FPC, 16 January 1883, FPCP.

79. FPC to Elizabeth Cady Stanton, 14 November [1882], Elizabeth Cady Stanton Papers. Harriot Stanton married the English businessman William H. Blatch on 15 November 1882.

80. FPC to Sarah Wister, 13 [January 1883], WFP.

81. *Zoophilist,* 1 December 1882, 197; FPC to Sarah Wister, 13 [January 1883], WFP; Anne Thackeray Ritchie to FPC, 28 November [1882], FPCP; *Abolitionist,* 15 December 1900, 247.

82. Robert Browning to FPC, 3 March 1883, in Browning, *New Letters,* 283; *Hansard,* 4 April 1883, 1447–48.

83. Shaftesbury to Cobbe, 8 March 1883, FPCP; *Times,* 8 March 1883; Shaftesbury to Hugh Fortescue, third earl Fortescue, 20 August 1883, FPCP. Cobbe had written leaders on the topic since her first year with the *Echo;* "Peers and Pigeons" (17 July 1869) begins, "Is pigeon-shooting wicked, or stupid?"

84. See Jordan, *Josephine Butler,* 210–15.

85. *EWR,* 15 June 1883, 248, quoting Elie De Cyon, "The Anti-vivisectionist Agitation," *Contemporary Review* 43 (April 1883): 498–510; FPC to Dr. Owen Wister, 12 April [1885], Dr. Owen J. Wister Papers; Stanton, *Eighty Years and More,* 363; Stanton, *Bible and Church,* 2.

86. Violet Paget to her mother, 30 June 1883, in *VL;* Harper, *Susan B. Anthony,* 2:566.

87. "Preparations for the Reform Bill," *EWR,* 15 June 1883, 241–46.

88. I have drawn on *Hansard*, 6 July 1883, 664–724; *EWR*, 14 July 1883, 308–19; and Harper, *Susan B. Anthony*, 2:567.

89. John Beddoe to Mary Lloyd, 1 July 1883, FPCP; Sheldon Amos to FPC, 22 October 1883, FPCP; FPC to Millicent Fawcett, 15 July [1883], ALWL.

90. FPC to an unnamed person, 22 May [1883], Isbister Collection. The emphasis and exclamation marks are Cobbe's.

91. FPC to Sarah Wister, 17 [August 1883], WFP; Gladstone, *Diaries*, 10:257; Charles Barnes Upton to FPC, 13 June 1883, FPCP. Sandra Peacock argues persuasively that Cobbe's growing hatred for science was, by this time, changing the shape of her theology (Peacock, *Theological and Ethical Writings*, 249–55).

92. *Times*, 18, 19 November 1886; Coleridge to Adams, 17 July 1883, quoted in *Times*, 20 November 1886.

93. *Times*, 20, 25 November 1886.

94. *Times*, 20, 24 November 1884.

95. *Times*, 19 November 1886; Shaftesbury to FPC, 25, 29 October 1883, FPCP.

96. William Henry Channing to FPC, 30 October 1883, FPCP.

97. *Times*, 22 November 1886.

98. *Times*, 8, 10 December 1883.

99. Shaftesbury to FPC, 10, 11 December 1883, FPCP.

100. Shaftesbury to Cobbe, 20 November 1883, FPCP. (The Latin-based slang implies "not in accordance with one's position and character.")

101. *Times*, 22 November 1884.

102. Robert Louis Stevenson to FPC, 9 March 1884, FPCP; FPC to Sarah Wister, 26 February 1884, WFP.

103. FPC to Susan B. Anthony, 27 January 1884, in National Women's Suffrage Association, *Report*, 96–97; FPC, Introduction to *The Woman Question* (1884), xv–xvi. Cobbe had provided Elizabeth Cady Stanton's son Theodore with the names of people to write on several British topics, including Jessie Boucherett on employment, Maria Grey on education, and Frances Hoggan on medicine.

104. *EWR*, 15 May 1884, 223.

105. Reprinted in *WSJ*, 1 May 1884, 107.

106. Willard, "Frances Power Cobbe," 598; Grey, *Memorials of Emily A. E. Shirreff*, 55; FPC to Sarah Wister, 14 May 1884, WFP.

107. *EWR*, 16 June 1884, 260–61; *Hansard*, 10 June 1884, 1957–63.

108. *WSJ*, 1 July 1884, 179–81.

109. *WSJ*, 1 July 1884, 185–86.

110. *EWR*, 16 June 1884, 265.

111. FPC to Ellen (Mrs. Coleridge) Kennard, 17 June 1884, Kennard Papers; Fawcett, *Women's Suffrage*, 28.

112. *EWR*, 16 June 1884, 275–76. Others who signed were Louisa Boucherett, Jessie Boucherett, L. B. Courtenay, Emmeline Canning, and Clara S. I. Rayleigh.

113. FPC to Ellen Kennard, 17 June 1884, Kennard Papers.

114. Hutton to FPC, 24 June 1884, FPCP.

115. *Zoophilist*, 1 July 1884, 71–73; Shaftesbury Diaries, 27 June 1884.

116. Violet Paget to her mother, 23 July 1884, in *VL*, 158.

## 12 Tilting at Windmills, 1884–1892

1. FPC to Sarah Wister, 4 August [1884], WFP.

2. FPC to Sarah Wister, 30 April [1889], WFP; Battersea Papers, 26 August 1869; FPC, "Glimpse of Wales" (1884), 416.

3. Farningham, *Working Woman's Life*, 238. When Harriet Lloyd died in 1892, most of her estate was bequeathed to "Agnes Madeline Scott, sister of the Community of the Saving Name" for the use of the community. I have been unable to locate any information about the Community of the Saving Name, although it may have been located in Bromley, where Harriet was living at the time of the 1881 census.

4. Price, *Dogs*, 56; FPC to her brother Charles, 31 October [1884], CPAC.

5. FPC to Sarah Wister, 4 August, 14 May 1884, WFP.

6. FPC to Fawcett, 7 August [1884], ALWL; Stafford Henry Northcote to FPC, 5 August 1884, FPCP.

7. *EWR*, 15 July 1884, 329; *WSJ*, 1 September 1884, 213; FPC to Fawcett, 10 August [1884], ALWL.

8. FPC to her brother Charles, 31 October [1884], CPAC.

9. FPC to Sarah Wister, 31 October 1884, 15 March [1885], WFP.

10. FPC to her brother Charles, 16 December [1884], CPAC; Charles Cobbe, notes on financial affairs, December 1884, CPN. The annual interest on four thousand pounds at 5 percent would amount to the yearly two hundred pounds that their father's will had left her as a charge on the estate.

11. FPC to Sarah Wister, 31 October 1884, 6 January [1885], WFP.

12. Rhiwlas Estate Papers.

13. *Times*, 22 December 1884; Frederick Sleigh Roberts to FPC, 3 February 1885, FPCP.

14. *Times*, 25 November 1884; "Adams *versus* Coleridge," *Spectator*, 29 November 1884.

15. *Spectator*, 29 November 1884; Elizabeth Eastlake to FPC, 13 January 1885, FPCP.

16. *Times*, 22 November 1884; FPC to Sarah Wister, 31 October 1884, WFP.

17. FPC to Sarah Wister, 31 October 1884, WFP. Leslie Stephen's sister Caroline, who was active in both philanthropy and journalism, lived near Cobbe in Chelsea from 1875. Given her relationship with other members of the family, Cobbe probably knew that James Fitzjames Stephen was the anonymous author of a condescending dismissal of Theodore Parker's theology and of her introduction to Parker's *Collected Works* published in *Fraser's Magazine* in February 1864. As for the political issue, after further controversy and reelection Bradlaugh was seated in the House of Commons in 1886, thus essentially opening public office to men of any faith or none.

18. Gladstone, *Diaries*, 11:253; Hutton to FPC, 16 March 1885, FPCP; Besant, *Annie Besant*, 106–7; Besant, *World Without God*, 5.

19. DuBois, *Reader*, 228; FPC to Elizabeth Cady Stanton, 11 September [1888?], ECS Papers.

20. FPC to Sarah Wister, 6 January [1885], WFP; FPC to Becker, 2 February [1885], WSC; Hutton to FPC, 16 March 1885, FPCP.

21. FPC to Violet Paget, 9 December [1884], VLC.

22. FPC to Violet Paget, 1 May [1885], VLC; Violet Paget to FPC, 26 April 1885, FPCP; FPC to Violet Paget, 1 May [1885], VLC.

23. M. G. P. Martyn to FPC, [1885], BUAV; FPC to Sarah Wister, 13 November [1885], WFP.

24. *EWR*, 15 December 1884, 572.

25. FPC to Becker, undated, WSC.

26. FPC to Becker, 12 June [1885], WSC.

27. *EWR*, 15 June 1885, 249–50; Helen Taylor to FPC, 22 August [1885], FPCP (the date 1868 in Taylor's hand must certainly have been a slip of the pen); FPC to Becker, 5 August [1885], WSC.

28. Robb, *Primrose League,* 35–39, 50–53; FPC to Fawcett, 30 October [1885], ALWL; *Globe,* 11 November 1885, quoted in *WSJ,* 1 December 1885, 196; FPC to Becker, 26 November [1885], WSC.

29. *EWR*, 15 December 1885, 564.

30. French, *Antivivisection and Medical Science,* 166. French finds the VSS claim of credit "rather unlikely."

31. FPC to Coleridge Kennard, 19, 28 December [1885], Kennard Papers.

32. FPC to Theodore Stanton, 3 January [1886], ECS Papers; *Hansard,* 18 February 1886, 690–702; *Times,* 20 February 1886.

33. Millicent Garrett Fawcett to the *Times,* 22 February 1886; FPC to Fawcett, 24 February [1886], ALWL; Fawcett to FPC, 18 March 1886, FPCP; FPC to Fawcett, 16 March [1886], ALWL.

34. FPC to Sarah Wister, 26 March [1886], WFP; FPC to Mary Somerville, [August 1867], MSFP; FPC to the *Times,* 11 May 1886. See Feurer, "Meaning of 'Sisterhood,'" for a discussion of the Coal Mines Regulation Bill.

35. Roberts, *Gossiping Guide,* 107; FPC to Sarah Wister, 4 July [1886], WFP; Holmes, "Our Hundred Days," 534, 541.

36. The *Times* obituary, which appeared on 8 July 1886, is credited to "a correspondent."

37. FPC to Sarah Wister, 19 October [1889?], WFP.

38. *EWR*, 15 July 1886, 319, and 14 August 1886, 350; *Primrose League Gazette,* 15 December 1886.

39. FPC to Becker, 3, 18 December [1886], WSC (although Manchester Central Library's finding aid suggests a date of 1888, references to a new Conservative government and to Lord Iddesleigh, who died on 12 January 1887, require the earlier date); Israel, *Names and Stories,* 214; FPC to Fawcett, 24 February [1886], ALWL.

40. Eleanor Vere Boyle to FPC, 20, 24 January [mid-1880s], FPCP; FPC to Mr. White, 4 April [1886], NLW.

41. *Times,* 18, 24 November 1886.

42. *Times,* 18, 19 November 1886.

43. *Times* 20, 22 November 1886.

44. *Times,* 24 November 1886.

45. *Times,* 26 November 1886.

46. FPC to Sarah Wister, 13 July [1889], WFP.

47. Cardinal Manning to FPC, 27 January 1887, in FPC, *Life* (1894), 2:169–70;

Henry F. Ponsonby to FPC, 29 January 1887, FPCP; *Zoophilist,* 1 April 1887 (Cobbe misdates the meeting in *Life,* 2:173); Lewis Morris to FPC, 7 March [1887], FPCP.

48. FPC to Fawcett, 25 March [1887], ALWL; Adelaide Manning to Barbara Bodichon, 23 April 1887, Bodichon Papers; *EWR,* 15 March 1887, 110–12.

49. FPC, "Faith Healing and Fear Killing" (1887), 797, 808; Ritvo, *Animal Estate,* 194–95; FPC to the *Times,* 17 August 1886.

50. Price, *Dogs,* 13, 17.

51. Price, *History of Rulacc,* 28. The title page reads, "The History of Huracc, Or Rhiwlas"; the half-title reads "Rulacc, late Rhiwlas"; and the stiff paper cover on one of the two copies of the book in the NLW has yet another title, "Rulacc, Ruedok, and the Valley of the Welsh Dee," and "By an F.R.A."

52. WSS to FPC, 15 June 1887, 20, 22 December 1887, 2, 8 February 1888, SSon; Parry, "Swan Sonnenschein Limited," 291–95.

53. FPC, *Rest in the Lord* (1887), iv–v. The copy now in the Bodleian Library was given to "Miss Barham Smith" by "Miss Frances Conway Cobbe"; that is, the copy Cobbe gave to her niece Frances—all five of Cobbe's nieces remained single throughout their lives—did include "To Mary C. Lloyd," but the copy in the County Record Office at Dolgellau, which perhaps was given to Lloyd's nephew, did not.

54. Hannah Whitall Smith to FPC, 20 September 1887, FPCP; FPC to Georgiana Mount-Temple, 11 December [1887], CPAC; Amelia Edwards to FPC, 3 December [1887], FPCP (Edwards does write "dollars and cents," though another sentence includes the words "it is not the £.s.d. that I crave in asking you"); Edwards to FPC, 7 January 1888, FPCP.

55. FPC to Sarah Wister, 5 January [1888], 13 November [1885], WFP. Cobbe must have been among the earliest private users, for although typewriters were first produced in the late 1870s, they became widely available in Britain only in 1886.

56. FPC, "Education of the Emotions" (1888), 232; "From Pestilence!" *Echo,* 14 April 1870.

57. FPC to Fawcett, 28 June 1888, ALWL.

58. *Zoophilist,* 1 July 1888, 42 (dated with the Hebrew year as 14 June 5648); FPC, *Life* (1894), 2:176.

59. FPC to Sarah Wister, 5 January [1888], WFP; *Zoophilist,* 1 January 1889, 161; FPC to Sarah Wister, 8 August [1888], 19 October [1889?], WFP.

60. FPC to Sarah Wister, 8 August [1888], WFP.

61. FPC to the *Times,* 11 October 1888. The *Illustrated Police News* for 20 October summarized the letter and commented, "We are bound to assume that Miss Cobbe wrote her letter in sober earnest and after mature consideration. But the communicated certainly reads more like a grim joke than anything else. It is the female employment question carried to a ludicrous extreme."

62. *Women's Penny Paper,* 15 December 1888.

63. *EWR,* 15 December 1888, 557–60; *Women's Penny Paper,* 15 December 1888. In her autobiography Cobbe erroneously puts this schism after Lydia Becker's death, which took place on 18 July 1890, and assigns the blame to friction between Unionists and Home Rulers (*Life* [1894], 2:212).

64. Hannah Whitall Smith to FPC, 13 January 1889, FPCP; Frances Willard to FPC, 6 February 1889, FPCP.

65. FPC, "The Sanctification of Vivisection," *Zoophilist,* October 1888, 98–99; Edward Harold Browne to FPC, 8 February 1889, FPCP.

66. Monroe, "Frances Power Cobbe," 351; *British Medical Journal,* 28 May 1904, 1266; FPC to Sarah Wister, 13 July [1889], WFP.

67. National Society for Women's Suffrage Central Committee, *Report; EWR,* 15 July 1889, 289–91.

68. National Society for Women's Suffrage, *Declaration in Favour.*

69. *EWR,* 15 July 1889, 308–9, and 15 October 1889, 533–38.

70. FPC to Sarah Wister, 19 October [1889], 8 August [1888], WFP; FPC to William Blackwood, 11 April [1889], Blackwood Papers.

71. *Verulam Review* 1 (January–April 1888): 2–3.

72. FPC to Helen Blackburn, in Blackburn, *Women's Suffrage,* 187.

73. FPC to Sarah Wister, 1 January [1890], WFP.

74. FPC to Sarah Wister, 1 January [1890], 13 July [1889], 19 February 1890, WFP.

75. FPC, *The Modern Rack* (1889) contains twenty-one of Cobbe's antivivisection pieces, including speeches, essays reprinted from the *Fortnightly Review,* the *Contemporary Review,* and the *Zoophilist,* and pieces produced as pamphlets. Much of the work she did for the VSS was in ephemeral newsprint pamphlets and flyers for specific purposes, and those examples that do survive are difficult to locate. Thus *The Modern Rack,* published in hardcover and given to a large number of libraries, is, among other things, a convenient resource for contemporary scholars, though it contains only a fraction of Cobbe's often anonymous writing for the antivivisection movement.

76. Cobbe wrote prefaces for Helen Ekin Starrett's *Gypsy: The Story of a Dog* (1890) and Elizabeth Stuart Phelps's *Loveliness* (1900). These and other such titles sometimes misleadingly turn up in older library catalogs as books written by Cobbe.

77. Monroe, "Frances Power Cobbe," 350; Mary Ward to FPC, 28 May 1888, 15 August 1890, FPCP.

78. FPC to Sarah Wister, 30 July [1890], WFP.

79. Farningham, *Working Woman's Life,* 238. An account of the organization's history on the official website of the National Council of Women (its name was changed in 1918), <http://fp.ncwgb.f9.co.uk/htdocs/memblinks/history.htm>, says that the Union of Women Workers was formed in 1895 as a "platform for women who worked, mostly voluntarily, in the social sector" and that its first conference was held in Nottingham in 1895. However, the program for the 1890 conference is with Cobbe's papers in the NLW along with a typeset copy of her speech.

80. FPC, "Women's Duty to Women" (1890), is in a bound collection of Cobbe's proofs and/or offprints under the title "Themes of the Nineteenth Century," vol. 1, in the Department of Manuscripts and Archives, NLW.

81. FPC, *Somerville Hall: A Misnomer* (1891). I quote from a copy in the Somerville College Archives, Oxford, which is inscribed "With Miss Cobbe's Comp'ts" in her hand.

82. FPC to *Jewish Chronicle,* 13 February 1891, in *Zoophilist,* March 1891, 211–12; Claude G. Montefiore to FPC, 27 March [1890], FPCP; FPC to Fawcett, 14 February [1891], ALWL; FPC to Mrs. Michell, 21 March 1891, CPAC.

83. Walburga Paget to FPC, 22 November 1889, NLW; French, *Antivivisection and Medical Science,* 347.

84. FPC to Fawcett, 16 January [1891], ALWL; Eleanor Sidgwick to Fawcett, 25 February 1891, ALWL; FPC to Fawcett, 28 February [1891], ALWL.

85. Rhiwlas Estate Papers; Society for Promoting the Employment of Women, Management Committee Minute Books, 15 July 1892, Girton College Archives. I thank Ellen Jordan for supplying this information.

86. FPC, *Life* (1894), 2:331.

87. FPC to Sarah Wister, 3 December 1891, WFP.

88. FPC to Sarah Wister, 3 December 1891, WFP.

89. FPC, *Health and Holiness* (1891), 8, 7.

90. Roberts, *Gossiping Guide,* 101; Price, *Dogs,* 59; Evans, "Cardiganshire Notes," vol. 2; Battersea, *Waifs and Strays,* 168. The house was destroyed by fire some time after World War II, but the three outbuildings, much remodeled, remain, and the site still has a clear view of the church at Llanelltyd, where Cobbe and Lloyd are buried.

91. FPC to Sarah Wister, 14 March [1892], WFP.

92. FPC to Sarah Wister, 14 March [1892], WFP; *EWR,* 15 July 1892, 163–64; *Times,* 27 April 1892; Holton, "To Educate Women," 1133–34. Even Harriot Stanton Blatch thought the league's perspective was unrealistic and resigned from its leadership.

93. *Zoophilist,* 1 March, 1 July 1892. The *New York Times* reported on Aberdare's speech and quoted Cobbe's response on 17 July 1892.

94. Adams, "The Antivivisection Movement and Miss Cobbe," 199, 201.

95. In this case she contracted with Pewtress and Co., 28 Little Queen Street, to do the printing, including the Swan Sonnenschein's imprint on the title page, and delivered bound copies ready for sale (WSS to FPC, 18 March 1892, SSon).

96. *Times,* 7 October 1892.

97. *Times,* 11–18 October 1892.

98. *Times,* 20–25 October 1892; "Polite Learning," *Punch,* 29 October 1892.

99. "Miss Cobbe and 'The Nine Circles,'" *Spectator,* 5, 12 November 1892; *Zoophilist,* 1 November 1892, 194; FPC, "Recollections of James Martineau" (1900), 180.

100. Hart, "Women, Clergymen, and Doctors," 711.

101. Basil Wilberforce to FPC, 3 December 1892, FPCP; Wilberforce, "'Women, Clergymen, and Doctors': A Reply," 95; Wilberforce to FPC, undated, FPCP; *Spectator,* 16 April 1904. Horsley and Hart were scarcely better. A year or two later Horsley provided information for a pamphlet that accused the antivivisection movement of an "attempt to introduce Anti-Semitism into England" (*Zoophilist,* 2 December 1895, 275), and Hart spread slanders about Lawson Tait's immoral behavior with a nurse, which caused a writer in the *Boston Medical and Surgical Journal* to cast doubt also on the accuracy of the data in some of Tait's gynecological writing (Shepherd, *Lawson Tait,* 174–79).

102. FPC to Mr. King, 17 November [1892], Historical Society of Pennsylvania, Foreign Hymn Writers Collection.

## 13 The Oldest New Woman, 1893–1904

1. FPC to George Bentley, 31, 20 January, 16 February 1893, Bentley Archives, reel 25.

2. FPC to Sarah Wister, 4 March [1893], WFP. She returned letters written to Kemble by Henry James, Hamilton Aide, Frederick Leighton, Anne Thackeray Ritchie, and Rhoda Broughton.

3. FPC to George Bentley, 16 February 1893, Bentley Archives, reel 25 (Bentley ultimately published Fitzgerald's letters in *Temple Bar* and then as a book); FPC to Sarah Wister, 4 March [1893], WFP.

4. FPC to Sarah Wister, 25 March [1893], WFP.

5. FPC to Sarah Wister, 24 May, 25 March [1893], WFP; *Abolitionist*, 15 December 1905, 69.

6. FPC to Helen Blackburn, 6 April [1893?], ALWL.

7. FPC to George Bentley, 23 November 1894, Bentley Archives, reel 25. The Author's Edition titles are *A Faithless World, Alone to the Alone, Dawning Lights, The Duties of Women, The Hopes of the Human Race, The Peak in Darien,* and *Religious Duty.* Most are dated 1894, though they were issued late in 1893, and they are unchanged from the original texts.

8. FPC to Mary Joy Haweis, 1 December [1893], Haweis Family Papers.

9. FPC, *Life* (1894), 1:v, 5; FPC, "All Sorts and Conditions" (1894), 103.

10. FPC to Sarah Wister, undated, 25 May and 27 May 1894, WFP.

11. FPC to George Bentley, 3 January [1893], Bentley Archives, reel 25; FPC to Sarah Wister, 7 June 1894, WFP.

12. FPC to George Bentley, 28 February, 7, 11, 20 June, 3 July 1894, Bentley Archives, reel 25.

13. "Suffrage Mass Meeting in London," *Woman's Tribune* (Washington, D.C.), 30 June 1894, 118.

14. FPC to George Bentley, 12 and 16 August 1894, Bentley Archives, reel 25; FPC to Sarah Wister, 27 August 1894, WFP. Houghton Mifflin reset the type and provided an index, making it a very convenient edition to use, though the pagination differs from the Bentley volumes.

15. Margaret Froude to FPC [October 1894], FPCP. James Anthony Froude died on 20 October.

16. Lewin, Review of *Life of Frances Power Cobbe,* 321; "Our Booking Office," *Punch,* 13 October 1894; [Stead], "Character Sketch," 329.

17. Verschoyle, "Frances Power Cobbe," 75–76; Katharine Bradley to FPC, December [1892], FPCP. Enclosed was a manuscript poem in Edith Cooper's handwriting beginning, "The iris was yellow, the moon was pale," published in *Underneath the Bough* (1893) and composed, according to *The Michael Field Catalogue* (1998), in December 1892. My thanks to Dorothy Mermin for providing this information.

18. Betham-Edwards, *Mid-Victorian Memories,* 149.

19. Battersea Papers, 2–5 August 1894.

20. FPC to George Bentley, 8 November 1894, Bentley Archives, reel 25; Peter Clayden to FPC, 10 September 1894, FPCP; FPC to George Bentley, 11 September 1894, Bentley Archives, reel 25; FPC to Mary Joy Haweis, 23 November [1894], Haweis Family Papers; FPC to Sarah Wister, 20 November 1894, WFP; FPC to Walburga Paget, British Library Add. 51,239A, fol. 78.

21. FPC to Helen Taylor, 6 February [1895], M-T; FPC to Fawcett, 25 February [1895], ALWL; Walter McLaren to the *Times,* 23 February 1895; *EWR,* 15 April 1895, 97; FPC to Fawcett, 5 March [1895], ALWL.

22. "Whose is the Guilt?" *Woman's Signal,* 14 November 1895, 312–13.

23. FPC to Sarah Wister, 24 March, 7 October 1895, WFP.

24. FPC to Fawcett, 7 December [1895], ALWL.

25. FPC, "Our Policy," *Woman's Signal*, 6 February 1896; "Mrs. Heaton Armstrong," *Woman's Signal*, 11 June 1896.

26. See Spence, "Ruskin's Correspondence."

27. FPC to Sarah Wister, and Mary Lloyd to Sarah Wister, both 4 October [1896], WFP.

28. FPC to Fawcett, 11 November 1896, ALWL; FPC to Sarah Wister, 14 March [1897], WFP.

29. FPC to Fawcett, 11 November 1896, ALWL; FPC to Sarah Wister, 21 November 1896, WFP; *Woman's Signal*, 12 November 1896; Rosa Bonheur to FPC, 31 March 1898, FPCP.

30. FPC to Sarah Wister, 14 March [1897], WFP; FPC to the *Times*, 15 February 1897; "Women's Address to the Queen," *Woman's Signal*, 15 April 1897.

31. *EWR*, 15 April 1897, 99–101; Mary Joy Haweis to her son Lionel, 31 March 1897, in Howe, *Arbiter of Elegance*, 262; *Spectator* response quoted from *EWR*, 15 July 1897, 158.

32. FPC to Sarah Wister, 1 December [1898], WFP. Cobbe's will left legacies of £2,000 apiece to her five nieces; an annuity of £115 a year to Sophy and Eliza; and a bequest of £200 to Lucie Heaton Armstrong, as well as money to Frances Hoggan and to her servants. Stella and Vanda sent flowers to Cobbe's funeral.

33. FPC to Sarah Wister, 15 August [1897], WFP; FPC to her brother Henry, 1 August [1897], CPAC; FPC to an unidentified friend, 22 July [1897?], CPAC.

34. "Victoria Street Society," *Woman's Signal*, 21 May 1896; *Journal of Zoöphily*, December 1897, 133–34; *Zoophilist*, 1 February 1898, 171.

35. *Zoophilist*, 1 February 1898, 171–72, and 1 March 1898, 209; *Journal of Zoöphily*, May 1898.

36. *Woman's Signal*, 17 February 1898.

37. FPC to Sarah Wister, 27 April 1898, WFP.

38. "New Anti-Vivisection Union," *Woman's Signal*, 12 May 1898; Executive Committee Minutes, 1898–1904, BUAV.

39. Executive Committee Minutes, 1898–1904, BUAV.

40. FPC to Sarah Wister, 29 May 1898, WFP.

41. *Journal of Zoöphily*, August 1898, 85, 93–94.

42. *Zoophilist*, 1 December 1898; FPC to Sarah Wister, 1 December [1898], WFP.

43. FPC to Sarah Wister, 1 December [1898], WFP. Bell Taylor, a bachelor vegetarian and abstainer, was also one of the few physicians who had campaigned vigorously for repeal of the Contagious Diseases Acts. At his death in 1909 his estate of £160,000 was willed to various reformist organizations, including the British Union for the Abolition of Vivisection.

44. FPC to Sarah Wister, 29 May 1898, WFP; FPC to Lady Windsor, 24 March [1899], British Library Add. 51,239A, fol. 200.

45. FPC to the *Times*, 13 April 1899. A memorial fountain to Rogers was unveiled at Southampton on 27 July 1901.

46. FPC, "The Work Before Us," *Abolitionist*, 15 April 1899; FPC to Sarah Wister, 16 April [1899], WFP.

47. Henry Cobbe, *Luton Church*, viii.

48. FPC to Sarah Wister, 10 January [1900], WFP.

49. WSS to FPC, 20 March 1900–7 July 1902, SSon; FPC to Frederick Halsey, 11 May [1900], in *Huntington Library Quarterly* 28 (May 1965): 283–85. The Huntington purchased Halsey's entire collection, including *Shelley and Mary*, in 1915. Only twelve copies of the book had been printed. In a letter of 26 March [1886] to Sarah Wister, Cobbe described the "private journals & letters of Shelley & Mary which Lady Shelley has printed a very few copies . . . & endowed me with one."

50. FPC to Moncure Conway, 19 May 1900, in Conway, *Autobiography*, 2:441–42; "Miss Cobbe Speaks Again," *Woman's Tribune* (Washington, D.C.), 3 November 1900; *Journal of Zoöphily*, December 1900, 137. The book by Lecky was *Democracy and Liberty* (1896); Lecky's depiction of the danger in women's "wild gusts of unreasoning, uncalculating, hysterical emotion" is in the last few pages of the second volume.

51. FPC to Sarah Wister, 27 August [1900], 5 February [1901], WFP; FPC, undated meditation, CPAC. The lines are from "Maud," pt. 2, sec. 4, st. 3; Tennyson wrote the passage originally as a separate lyric soon after Arthur Hallam's death in 1833.

52. FPC, "Recollections of James Martineau" (1900), 186; FPC, *Life* (1904), 711.

53. FPC to Sarah Wister, 5 February [1901], WFP.

54. Kidd and Richards, *Hadwen of Gloucester*, 140–41; Hopley, *Campaigning*, 7.

55. *Abolitionist*, 15 August 1900; Executive Committee Minutes, 1898–1904, BUAV; *Abolitionist*, 15 March 1901.

56. Evans, "Cardiganshire Notes," vol. 2.

57. FPC to Sarah Wister, 27 October [1901], 5 January 1903, WFP. It is interesting that Cobbe had begun to capitalize *Negroes;* she had used a small *n* in the 1860s and 1870s.

58. *Abolitionist*, 15 February 1901; *Zoophilist's* condemnation reported in *Abolitionist*, 15 March 1901.

59. FPC, "Schadenfreude" (1902), 660.

60. FPC to Stephen Coleridge, 22 June [1902], BUAV.

61. "Miss Cobbe and her Persecutors," *Nature Notes* 13 (1902): 205; FPC to George Eyre Evans, 17 August [1902], in Evans, "Treasured Letters."

62. "The Charge of Cruelty to a Horse against Miss Frances Power Cobbe and Her Coachman, David Evans," in album of newspaper cuttings, owner unidentified, NLW. Cobbe also had the report by Stafford Jackson printed and sent a copy to Sarah Wister with her letter of 3 August [1902], WFP.

63. *Cambrian News*, 29 August 1902.

64. FPC to George Eyre Evans, 23 August [1902], in Evans, "Treasured Letters"; Owen, *Echoes of Old Merioneth*, 65; Battersea Papers, 4 August 1894.

65. FPC to Sarah Wister, 26 August [1902], WFP; FPC to George Evans, 2 October [1902], in Evans, "Cardiganshire Notes," vol. 4.

66. FPC to Blanche Atkinson, 6 September 1902, in Atkinson, Introduction, xiii–xiv.

67. FPC to Blanche Atkinson, 16 November 1902, in Atkinson, Introduction, xv; FPC to Lawrence Pearsall Jacks, 31 October [1902], Jacks Papers; FPC to Sarah Wister, 23 November [1902], WFP.

68. "Addresses to Miss Cobbe." Copies are in NLW and ALWL, and the album itself is in CPAC.

69. *EWR,* 15 April 1903, 90–91; FPC to the *Times,* 9 December 1902.

70. FPC to Blanche Atkinson, 5 December 1902, in Atkinson, Introduction, xvii; "Presentation to Miss Frances Power Cobbe," *Times,* 6 December 1902; FPC to Mrs. Edwards, Christmas [1902], ALWL.

71. FPC to Blanche Atkinson, 8, 24 December 1902, in Atkinson, Introduction, xvii.

72. FPC to Sarah Wister, 5 January [1903], WFP.

73. FPC to Sarah Wister, 6 February [1903], WFP; FPC to unidentified woman, 16 February [1903], CPAC.

74. FPC to Sarah Wister, 9 May [1903], WFP.

75. *Abolitionist,* 15 April 1904, 6; FPC to Sarah Wister, 4 January [1904], WFP. An 1894 copy of the *Dictionary of Medicine* was in Cobbe's library.

76. Evans, "Cardiganshire Notes," vol. 4.

77. Verschoyle, "Frances Power Cobbe," 79–80.

78. Kidd and Richards, *Hadwen of Gloucester,* 146. Afraid (like many other Victorians) of premature burial, Cobbe requested that Hadwen sever the arteries in her neck before her body was interred.

79. Marianne Farningham, "A Unique Funeral," and George Eyre Evans, "A Simple Burying," both in Evans, "Cardiganshire Notes," vol. 5.

80. These are the second and last stanzas of the three-stanza "Suspiria," by Henry Wadsworth Longfellow, first published in his collection *The Seaside and the Fireside* (1849).

# Bibliography

Works by Frances Power Cobbe

MANUSCRIPT AND ARCHIVAL SOURCES

Note-Books, 1846–1863. 3 vols. Department of Archives. National Library of Wales, Aberystwyth.
"Essay on True Religion." 2 vols. 1849. Department of Archives. National Library of Wales, Aberystwyth.
"Catalogue of Books in Library at Newbridge." 1852. Cobbe Papers, Alec Cobbe Collection.
"A Lady's Ride Thro' Palestine." 1859. Cobbe Papers, Newbridge, Ireland.
"What Is the True Basis, and What Are the Limits of Parental Authority?" 1865. Kensington Society file. Emily Davies Papers. Girton College Archives, Cambridge.
"Catalogue of Pictures in the Possession of Charles Cobbe at Newbridge House." 1868. Cobbe Papers, Newbridge, Ireland.
"Women's Duty to Women." Paper read at a meeting of the Conference of Women Workers, Birmingham, 1890. In "Themes of the Nineteenth Century," vol. 1. Department of Manuscripts and Archives. National Library of Wales, Aberystwyth.

*Manuscript and Archival Sources Not Listed Individually*

Miscellaneous papers, including pamphlets, offprints, leaflets, and periodical essays (largely by other people). Department of Printed Books. National Library of Wales, Aberystwyth.
Scrapbooks of published journalism from the *Daily News,* the *Echo,* the *Examiner,* the *Inquirer,* the *Spectator,* the *Standard, Truth,* and other newspapers and periodicals. Department of Printed Books. National Library of Wales, Aberystwyth.
Sketchbooks, album of sketches and photographs, illuminated family genealogy, and other mementos. Cobbe Papers, Alec Cobbe Collection.

PUBLISHED WORKS, IN CHRONOLOGICAL ORDER

*An Essay on Intuitive Morals. Part I, Theory of Morals.* London: Longman's, 1855; Boston: Crosby, Nichols, 1859. Initially anonymous; republished as *Theory of Morals* by Trübner in 1864 with Cobbe's name on the title page.
*An Essay on Intuitive Morals. Part II, Practice of Morals. Book I, Religious Duty.* London: Chapman, 1857. Initially anonymous; republished as *Religious Duty* by Trübner in 1864 with Cobbe's name on the title page.
With Margaret Elliot. *Destitute Incurables in Workhouses.* London: James Nisbet, 1860.

Also published in *Journal of the Workhouse Visiting Society,* no. 11 (January 1861): 329–38.

"Workhouse Sketches." *Macmillan's Magazine* 3 (April 1861): 448–61.

"The City of the Sun." *Fraser's Magazine* 63 (June 1861): 670–84.

"The Sick in Workhouses." *Journal of the Workhouse Visiting Society,* no. 15 (September 1861): 480–89. Reprinted as *The Sick in Workhouses: Who They Are and How They Should Be Treated.* London: James Nisbet, 1861.

"The Preventive Branch of the Bristol Female Mission." *English Woman's Journal* 8 (November 1861): 145–51. Reprinted as *Friendless Girls, and How to Help Them: Being an Account of the Preventive Mission At Bristol.* London: Emily Faithfull, [1861].

With Margaret Elliot. "Hints to Workhouse Visitors." *Journal of the Workhouse Visiting Society,* no. 16 (November 1861): 509–10.

*The Workhouse as an Hospital.* London: Emily Faithfull, 1861.

"Social Science Congresses, and Women's Part in Them." *Macmillan's Magazine* 5 (December 1861): 81–94.

"Celibacy *v.* Marriage." *Fraser's Magazine* 65 (February 1862): 228–35.

"The City of Victory." *Fraser's Magazine* 65 (March 1862): 317–31.

"The Eternal City (in a temporary phase)." *Fraser's Magazine* 65 (May 1862): 565–79.

"Women in Italy in 1862." *Macmillan's Magazine* 6 (September 1862): 363–75.

*Female Education, and How it Would be Affected by University Examinations.* London: Emily Faithfull, 1862.

"Home For Incurable and Infirm Women." *Journal of the Workhouse Visiting Society,* no. 22 (November 1862): 713–18.

"What Shall We Do With Our Old Maids?" *Fraser's Magazine* 66 (November 1862): 594–610.

"Female Charity: Lay and Monastic." *Fraser's Magazine* 66 (December 1862): 774–88.

"Remarks on Victor Hugo's *Les Misérables.*" *English Woman's Journal* 10 (December 1862): 217–24.

*Essays on the Pursuits of Women. Also a Paper on Female Education.* London: Emily Faithfull, 1863. Contains "Social Science Congresses, and Women's Part in Them," "Celibacy *v.* Marriage," "What Shall We Do With Our Old Maids?" "Female Charity: Lay and Monastic," "Women in Italy in 1862," "Workhouse Sketches," and "The Education of Women, and How it Would be Affected by University Examinations."

*Thanksgiving: A Chapter of Religious Duty.* London: Trübner, 1863.

"The Religious Demands of the Age." Preface to *The Collected Works of Theodore Parker.* Vol. 1. London: Trübner, 1863. The fourteen volumes of Cobbe's edition were published in 1863–71.

"A Day at the Dead Sea." *Fraser's Magazine* 67 (February 1863): 226–38.

*Rejoinder to Mrs. Stowe's Reply to the Address of the Women of England.* London: Emily Faithfull, 1863. Also published in *Atlantic Monthly* 11 (April 1863): 525–28.

"A Day at Athens." *Fraser's Magazine* 67 (May 1863): 601–12.

*The Red Flag in John Bull's Eyes.* Ladies' London Emancipation Society, tract 1. London: Emily Faithfull, 1863.

"The City of Peace." *Fraser's Magazine* 67 (June 1863): 719–38.

"The Humour of Various Nations." *Victoria Magazine* 1 (July 1863): 193–206.

"The Rights of Man and the Claims of Brutes." *Fraser's Magazine* 68 (November 1863): 586–602.

*The Cities of the Past.* London: Trübner, 1864. Contains "The City of the Sun," "The City of Victory," "The Eternal City (in a temporary phase)," "A Day at the Dead Sea," "A Day at Athens," and "The City of Peace," all reprinted from *Fraser's Magazine.*

"A Day at Adelsberg." *Victoria Magazine* 2 (January 1864): 202–13.

"What Annexation Has Done For Italy." *National Review* 18 (January 1864): 19–51.

"Hades." *Fraser's Magazine* 69 (March 1864): 293–311.

"The Nineteenth Century." *Fraser's Magazine* 69 (April 1864): 481–94.

*Broken Lights: An Inquiry Into the Present Condition and Future Prospects of Religious Faith.* London: Trübner, 1864.

"Religion in Italy in 1864." *Theological Review* 1 (May 1864): 198–214.

"The State Vault of Christ Church." *Macmillan's Magazine* 10 (May 1864): 70–72.

"The Morals of Literature." *Fraser's Magazine* 70 (July 1864): 124–33.

"Christian Ethics and the Ethics of Christ." *Theological Review* 1 (September 1864): 396–423.

"The Philosophy of the Poor-Laws." *Fraser's Magazine* 70 (September 1864): 373–94.

*Italics: Brief Notes on Politics, People and Places in Italy, in 1864.* London: Trübner, 1864.

"The Hierarchy of Art." Part 1. *Fraser's Magazine* 71 (January 1865): 97–108.

"The Hierarchy of Art." Part 2. *Fraser's Magazine* 71 (March 1865): 334–46.

"Shadow of Death." *Macmillan's Magazine* 11 (March 1865): 373–74.

"The Writings of Félix Pécaut." *Theological Review* 2 (May 1865): 262–76.

*Studies New and Old of Ethical and Social Subjects.* London: Trübner, 1865. Contains two new essays, "Self-Development and Self-Abnegation" and "The Sacred Books of the Zoroastrians"; reprints "Christian Ethics and the Ethics of Christ," "The Philosophy of the Poor-Laws," "The Morals of Literature," "The Heirarchy of Art," "Decemnovarianism" (originally "The Nineteenth Century"), and "Hades."

Editor. *Lessons from the World of Matter and the World of Man, Selected by Rufus Leighton from Notes of Unpublished Sermons of Theodore Parker.* London: Trübner, 1865.

"Woman's Work in the Church." *Theological Review* 2 (September 1865): 505–21.

"Ireland and Her Exhibition in 1865." *Fraser's Magazine* 72 (October 1865): 403–22.

"The Fenians of Ballybogmucky." *Argosy* 1 (December 1865): 80–91.

"The Spectral Rout." *Shilling Magazine* 2 (December 1865): 461–79.

"The Fallacies of Memory." *Galaxy,* 15 May 1866, 149–62.

"The Fenian 'Idea.'" *Atlantic Monthly* 17 (May 1866): 572–77.

"Robertson's *Life and Letters.*" *Theological Review* 3 (January 1866): 21–49.

"The Indigent Class: Their Schools and Dwellings." *Fraser's Magazine* 73 (February 1866): 143–60.

"A Lady's Adventure in the Great Pyramid." *Once a Week,* 14 April 1866, 408–11.

"The Religion of Childhood." *Theological Review* 3 (July 1866): 317–41.

"Alured: An Allegory." *Temple Bar* 18 (August 1866): 35–43.

"The Brahmo Samaj." *Fraser's Magazine* 74 (August 1866): 199–211.

"Life in Donegal." *Once a Week,* 20 October 1866, 436–38.

"The Conventional Laws of Society." *Fraser's Magazine* 74 (November 1866): 667–73.

"The Terrors of the Suburbs." *Once a Week,* 24 November 1866, 573–54.

"The New Creed and the Old, in Their Secular Results." Part 1. *Theological Review* 4 (January 1867): 1–21.

*Hours of Work and Play.* London: Trübner, 1867. Contains two new essays, "Public Morality and its Teachers" and "The Diablerêts"; reprints "The Indigent Class," "The Brahmo Samaj," "The Fallacies of Memory," "The Fenian 'Idea,'" "A Day at Adelsberg," "A Lady's Adventure in the Great Pyramid," "The State Vault of Christ Church," "The Shadow of Death," "Alured: An Allegory," "The Spectral Rout," "The Humour of Various Nations," and "The Fenians of Ballybogmucky."

"Critical Notice: Hugh Bryan, *The Autobiography of an Irish Rebel.*" *Fortnightly Review* 7 (February 1867): 258–59.

"The American Sanitary Commission and Its Lesson." *Fraser's Magazine* 75 (March 1867): 401–14.

"What Is Progress, and Are We Progressing?" *Fortnightly Review* 7 (March 1867): 357–70.

"The New Creed and the Old, in Their Secular Results." Part 2. *Theological Review* 4 (April 1867): 241–58.

*The Confessions of a Lost Dog.* London: Griffith & Farran, 1867.

"Bishop Colenso." *Christian Examiner* (New York) 83 (July 1867): 1–15.

"The Organization of Charity." *Theological Review* 4 (October 1867): 553–72.

"Household Service." *Fraser's Magazine* 77 (January 1868): 121–34.

"The New Creed and the Old, in Their Secular Results." Part 3. *Theological Review* 5 (January 1868): 26–51.

"French and English Epitaphs." *Temple Bar* 22 (February 1868): 349–57.

"Ireland For the Irish." *Tinsley's Magazine* 2 (February 1868): 39–49.

"Max Müller's *Chips.*" *Fraser's Magazine* 77 (February 1868): 187–204.

"Bunsen's Life and Last Book." *Fraser's Magazine* 77 (June 1868): 783–800.

"The Church of England, and Who Should Stop in It." *Theological Review* 5 (October 1868): 482–508.

*Dawning Lights: An Inquiry Concerning the Secular Results of the New Reformation.* London: E. T. Whitfield, 1868. Portions of some chapters reprinted from *Theological Review.*

"Criminals, Idiots, Women, and Minors." *Fraser's Magazine* 78 (December 1868): 777–94.

*Why Women Desire the Franchise.* London: National Society for Women's Suffrage, [1869]. Frequently updated and reissued to the end of the century.

"Fergusson's *Tree and Serpent Worship.*" *Fraser's Magazine* 79 (April 1869): 417–30.

"Milman's *Annals of St. Paul's.*" *Theological Review* 6 (April 1869): 131–48.

"The Subjection of Women." *Theological Review* 6 (July 1869): 355–75.

"The Defects of Women, and How to Remedy Them." *Putnam's Magazine,* n.s., 4 (August 1869): 226–33.

"The Final Cause of Woman." In *Woman's Work and Woman's Culture,* edited by Josephine E. Butler, 1–26. London: Macmillan, 1869.

"Instinct and Reason." *Animal World,* 1 November 1869, 40–41.

"To Know, or Not to Know." *Fraser's Magazine* 80 (December 1869): 776–87.

"Ladies' Amusements." *Every Saturday,* 12 February 1870, 101–102.

"Ancient and Medieval India." *Fraser's Magazine* 81 (March 1870): 343–61.

"Hereditary Piety." *Theological Review* 7 (April 1870): 211–34.

"Unconscious Cerebration: A Psychological Study." *Macmillan's Magazine* 23 (November 1870): 24–37.

Editor. *Alone to the Alone: Prayers For Theists.* London: Williams & Norgate, 1871.

"Darwinism in Morals." *Theological Review* 8 (April 1871): 167–92.

"Dreams As Illustrations of Unconscious Cerebration." *Macmillan's Magazine* 23 (April 1871): 512–23.

"The Devil." *Fortnightly Review* 16 (August 1871): 180–91.

"Auricular Confession in the Church of England." *Theological Review* 9 (January 1872): 17–38.

"The Evolution of Morals and Religion." *Manchester Friend,* 15 January 1872.

*Darwinism in Morals, and Other Essays.* London: Williams & Norgate, 1872. Reprints "Darwinism in Morals," "Hereditary Piety," "The Religion of Childhood," "An English Broad Churchman" (originally "Robertson's *Life and Letters*"), "A French Theist" (originally "The Writings of Félix Pécaut"), "The Devil," "A Pre-Historic Religion" (originally "Fergusson's *Tree and Serpent Worship*"), "The Religions of the World" (originally "Bunsen's Life and Last Book"), "The Religions of the East" (originally "Max Müller's *Chips*"), "The Religion and Literature of India" (originally "Ancient and Medieval India"), "Unconscious Cerebration: A Psychological Study," "Dreams, as Illustrations of Involuntary [*sic*] Cerebration," "Auricular Confession in the Church of England," and "The Evolution of Morals and Religion."

"The Consciousness of Dogs." *Quarterly Review* 133 (October 1872): 419–51.

"The Life after Death." Part 1. *Theological Review* 9 (October 1872): 506–35.

"Dogs Whom I Have Met." *Cornhill* 26 (December 1872): 662–78.

"The Life after Death." Part 2. *Theological Review* 10 (July 1873): 438–66.

*Doomed to be Saved: A Discourse.* London: Williams & Norgate, 1874.

"Deplorable Flaw in the Great Masculine Mind." *Women's Suffrage Journal* 5 (January 1874): 13.

"Heteropathy, Aversion, Sympathy." *Theological Review* 11 (January 1874): 1–35.

"Literature: *Personal Recollections . . . Of Mary Somerville.*" *Academy,* 3 January 1874, 1–2.

"Mary Somerville." *Quarterly Review* 136 (January 1874): 74–103.

*Our Policy: An Address to Women Concerning the Suffrage.* London: London National Society for Women's Suffrage [1874]. Frequently reprinted to the end of the century.

"Animals in Fable and Art." *New Quarterly Magazine* 2 (April 1874): 563–94.

"Modern Sorcery." *Cornhill* 30 (July 1874): 36–43.

"Evangelical Character." *Theological Review* 11 (October 1874): 447–69.

"The Fauna of Fancy." *New Quarterly Magazine* 3 (October 1874): 26–49.

*The Hopes of the Human Race, Hereafter and Here: Essays on the Life after Death.* London: Williams & Norgate, 1874. Contains "Introduction (Having Special Reference to Mr. Mill's Essay on Religion)" and reprints "The Life after Death," "The Evolution of Social Sentiment" (originally "Heteropathy, Aversion, Sympathy"), and "Doomed to be Saved."

"Thoughts about Thinking." *Cornhill* 31 (February 1875): 207–19.

"The Moral Aspects of Vivisection." *New Quarterly Magazine* 4 (April 1875): 222–37.

"A New Volume of Sermons." *Theological Review* 12 (April 1875): 292–300.

"The Town Mouse and the Country Mouse." *New Quarterly Magazine* 4 (July 1875): 475–510.

"Sacrificial Medicine." *Cornhill* 32 (October 1875): 427–38.

*Science in Excelsis: A New Vision of Judgment.* London: Victoria Street Society, [1875].

*False Beasts and True, Essays on Natural (and Unnatural) History.* Country House Library, no. 2. London: Ward, Lock, [1876]. Contains "Animals in Fable and Art," "The Fauna of Fancy," "The Consciousness of Dogs," and "Dogs Whom I Have Met."

"Backward Ho!" *New Quarterly Magazine* 5 (January 1876): 231–62.

*Re-Echoes.* London: Williams & Norgate, 1876. Fifty-two leaders from the *Echo.*

"The Fitness of Women For the Ministry." *Theological Review* 13 (April 1876): 239–73.

Nostradamus, Merlin [pseud.]. *The Age of Science: A Newspaper of the Twentieth Century.* London: Ward, Lock & Tyler, 1877.

"Hours of Thought on Sacred Things." *Theological Review* 14 (January 1877): 29–35.

"Pessimism, and One of Its Professors." *New Quarterly Magazine* 7 (January 1877): 283–301.

"Mr. Lowe and the Vivisection Act." *Contemporary Review* 29 (February 1877): 335–47.

"The Peak in Darien: The Riddle of Death." *New Quarterly Magazine* 8 (July 1877): 283–93.

"Magnanimous Atheism." *Theological Review* 14 (October 1877): 447–89.

"The Celt of Wales and the Celt of Ireland." *Cornhill* 36 (December 1877): 661–78.

"The Little Health of Ladies." *Contemporary Review* 31 (January 1878): 276–96.

"Wife-Torture in England." *Contemporary Review* 32 (April 1878): 55–87.

"Municipal Woman Suffrage in England." *Woman's Journal* (Boston), 15 March 1879.

Editor. *Bernard's Martyrs, a Comment on Leçons De Physiologie Opératoire.* Westminster: National Anti-Vivisection Society, 1879.

"The Tides of the Inner Life." *Modern Review* 1 (January 1880): 183–90.

"Personal Recollections of Mary Carpenter." *Modern Review* 1 (April 1880): 279–300.

*The Duties of Women, a Course of Lectures.* London: Williams & Norgate; Boston: George H. Ellis, 1881.

"The Roman Villa At Brading." *Magazine of Art* 4 (1881): 154–57.

"The Medical Profession and Its Morality." *Modern Review* 2 (April 1881): 296–326.

Review of James Martineau's *Loss and Gain in Recent Theology. Modern Review* 2 (July 1881): 855–57.

"M. Laborde At the Trocadero." *Ashley Grove Annual,* 1882, 13–16.

"Vivisection: Four Replies." *Fortnightly Review* 37 (January 1882): 88–104.

"Zoophily." *Cornhill* 45 (March 1882): 279–88.

"Vivisection and Its Two-Faced Advocates." *Contemporary Review* 41 (April 1882): 610–26.

"The Salvation Army, No. II." *Contemporary Review* 42 (August 1882): 182–89.

*The Peak in Darien, with Some Other Inquiries Touching Concerns of the Soul and the Body.* London: Williams & Norgate, 1882. Contains two new essays, "Hygieolatry" and "The House on the Shore of Eternity: An Allegory"; reprints "Magnanimous Atheism," "Pessimism, and One of Its Professors," "Zoophily," "Sacrificial Medicine," "The Fitness of Women for the Ministry of Religion," and "The Peak in Darien: The Riddle of Death."

"Progressive Judaism." *Contemporary Review* 42 (November 1882): 747–63.

"A Relic of Swift and Stella." *Temple Bar* 66 (December 1882): 568–72.

"The Higher Expediency." In *The Vivisection Controversy; A Selection of Speeches and Articles.* London: Victoria Street Society, 1883.

*Light in Dark Places.* London: Victoria Street Society, [1883].

"Agnostic Morality." *Contemporary Review* 43 (June 1883): 783–94.

Introduction to *The Woman Question in Europe,* edited by Theodore Stanton. New York: G. P. Putnam's Sons, 1884.

Preface to *The Vivisector's Directory,* edited by Benjamin Bryan. [London: Victoria Street Society], 1884.

"Girls' Schools in Past Times: A Personal Reminiscence." *Time* 11 (September 1884): 222–29.

"A Glimpse of Wales a Hundred Years Ago." *Cornhill* 50 (October 1884): 410–24.

"A Faithless World." *Contemporary Review* 46 (December 1884): 795–810. Reprinted with additions as *A Faithless World.* London: Norgate, 1885.

*Rest in the Lord; And Other Small Pieces.* London: privately printed, 1887.

"Faith Healing and Fear Killing." *Contemporary Review* 51 (June 1887): 784–813.

Editor. *Illustrations of Vivisection; Or, Experiments on Living Animals, From the Works of Physiologists.* Philadelphia: American Antivivisection Society, 1888.

"The Lord Was Not in the Earthquake." *Contemporary Review* 53 (January 1888): 70–83.

"The Education of the Emotions." *Fortnightly Review* 49 (February 1888): 223–36.

"The Scientific Spirit of the Age." *Contemporary Review* 54 (July 1888): 126–39.

*The Scientific Spirit of the Age, and Other Pleas and Discussions.* London: Smith & Elder, 1888. Contains "The Scientific Spirit of the Age," "The Education of the Emotions," "Progressive Judaism," "Thoughts about Thinking," "To Know, or Not to Know," and "The Town Mouse and the Country Mouse."

"Journalism As a Profession For Women." *Women's Penny Paper,* 3 November 1888.

*A Controversy in a Nutshell.* London: Victoria Street Society, 1889.

*The Modern Rack, Papers on Vivisection.* London: Swan Sonnenschein, 1889.

*The Friend of Man; And His Friends—the Poets.* London: G. Bell & Sons, 1889.

"The Love of Notoriety." *Forum* 8 (October 1889): 170–79.

With Benjamin Bryan. *Vivisection in America.* London: Swan, Sonnenschein, 1889.

"Secular Changes in Human Nature." *Forum* 9 (April 1890): 169–86.

*An Anglo-Irish Landlord.* London: privately printed, October 1890.

"Pity, Genuine and Spurious." *Forum* 10 (December 1890): 423–32.

"The Two Religions." *Contemporary Review* 58 (December 1890): 839–48.

*Somerville Hall: A Misnomer.* London: Victoria Street Society, 1891.

*Health and Holiness.* London: G. Bell & Sons, 1891.

*Public Money. An Enquiry Concerning an Item of Its Expenditure.* London: Society for the Protection of Animals from Vivisection, 1892.

Preface to *The Nine Circles of the Hell of the Innocent,* by G. M. Rhodes. London: Swan Sonnenschein, 1892.

"'All Sorts and Conditions of'—Women: Replies to Mr. Besant." *Woman's Signal,* 15 February 1894, 102–3.

*Life of Frances Power Cobbe.* 2 vols. London: Richard Bentley & Son; Boston: Houghton, Mifflin, 1894.

"Beresford and Cobbe." In *Beresford of Beresford: Eight Centuries of a Gentle Family. Preliminary Sketch. Part III,* edited by William Beresford. Leek: W. H. Eaton, 1895.

*The Divine Law of Love in Application to the Relations of Man to the Lower Animals.* Dol-
    gelley, Wales: n.p., 1895.
"The Ethics of Zoophily: A Reply." *Contemporary Review* 68 (October 1895): 497–508.
"Three Reasons for Humanity to Animals." *Woman's Signal*, 11 and 18 June 1896.
Preface to *Loveliness*, by Elizabeth Stuart Phelps. London: James Clarke, 1900.
"Dr. Martineau's Sermons." *Inquirer*, 20 January 1900, 11.
"Recollections of James Martineau, the Sage of the Nineteenth Century." *Contempo-
    rary Review* 77 (February 1900): 174–86.
"Recollections of Felicia Skene." In *Felicia Skene of Oxford: A Memoir*, edited by
    E. C. Rickards, 71–77. London: John Murray, 1902.
"Schadenfreude." *Contemporary Review* 81 (May 1902): 655–66.
"A False Philosophy—the Cause of the Evil." In *Public Morals*, edited by James Mar-
    chant, 251–52. London: Morgan & Scott, 1903.
Introduction to *Consecrated Womanhood*, edited by Frederic Rowland Marvin. New
    York: J. O. Wright, 1903.
"Woman Suffrage." *Contemporary Review* 83 (May 1903): 653–60.
"Keshub Chunder Sen." *East and West* 2 (June 1903): 1008–24.
"Youth and Age: An Unpublished Essay By the Late Miss Cobbe." *Spectator*, 14 May
    1904, 771.
*Life of Frances Power Cobbe as Told by Herself.* Edited by Blanche Atkinson. London:
    Swan Sonnenschein, 1904.

*Publications Not Listed Individually*

Unsigned essays in the *Echo*, *Truth*, the *Spectator*, the *Inquirer*, the *Day*, the *Standard*,
    the *Daily News*, and other daily and weekly journals.
Signed and unsigned essays in the *Zoophilist* (1881–97) and the *Abolitionist* (1899–1904);
    signed and anonymous antivivisection leaflets.
Essays reprinted in U.S. periodicals (often in the form of retitled selections); most U.S.
    editions of books; translations of Cobbe's books.

Works Consulted

### MANUSCRIPT AND ARCHIVAL SOURCES

Acland, Henry Wentworth. Papers. Bodleian Library, Oxford.
Amberley Papers. The William Ready Division of Archives and Research Collections.
    McMaster University Library, Hamilton, Ontario.
American Antivivisection Society. Archives. Jenkintown, Pennsylvania.
Autograph Album. National Library of Scotland, Edinburgh.
Autograph Letter Collection. The Women's Library, London.
Battersea Papers. Diaries of Constance de Rothschild Flower, Lady Battersea. Depart-
    ment of Manuscripts. British Library. Add. 47,913–47,947.
Bentley, Richard, & Son. Archives, 1829–1898. Documents held by University of Illi-
    nois at Urbana-Champaign and published on microfilm by Chadwyck-Healey.
Blackwood, William, and Sons. Papers. National Library of Scotland, Edinburgh.
Bodichon, Barbara. Papers. Girton College Archives, Cambridge.

Briggs Collection. Department of Manuscripts and Special Collections. Hallward Library, University of Nottingham.

British Census and National Index for 1881. Family History Resource File on CD-ROM from Church of Jesus Christ of Latter-Day Saints, Salt Lake City, Utah.

British Museum Reading Room Papers. Department of Manuscripts. British Library.

British Union for the Abolition of Vivisection. Letters, Minute Books, Annual Reports, and Miscellaneous Files. Brynmor Jones Library, University of Hull.

Clough, A. H. Correspondence. Bodleian Library, Oxford.

Cobbe, Charles. Diary. 9 vols. Cobbe Papers, Newbridge, Ireland.

Cobbe, Frances Conway. Commonplace Book. Department of Archives. National Library of Wales, Aberystwyth.

Cobbe, Frances Power. Papers. Letters addressed to Frances Power Cobbe. The Huntington Library, San Marino, California.

Cobbe, Thomas. A Memoir of the Cobbe Family, Genealogic and Heraldic. Cobbe Papers, Newbridge, Ireland.

Cobbe Autograph Collection. Letters and autographs, mainly addressed to Henry Cobbe or to Frances Power Cobbe. Bodleian Library, Oxford.

Cobbe Papers, Alec Cobbe Collection. Papers, letters, drawings, and photographs.

Cobbe Papers, Newbridge, Ireland. Papers, letters, account books, and other materials.

Davies, Emily. Papers. Girton College Archives, Cambridge.

Davis, Paulina. Papers. Special Collections. Vassar College Library, Northampton, Massachusetts.

Dilke Papers. Department of Manuscripts. British Library.

Elliot, Margaret. Correspondence. Department of Manuscripts. British Library.

Evans, George Eyre. "Cardiganshire Notes." 5 vols. Department of Archives. National Library of Wales, Aberystwyth.

———. "Treasured Letters from Many Correspondents." G.E.E. Department of Archives. National Library of Wales, Aberystwyth.

Family Records Centre, London. Census records, records of births, marriages, and deaths.

Free Christian Union Papers. Dr. Williams's Library, London.

Finlay Papers. British School at Athens.

Gerritsen Collection: Women's History Online. Chadwyck-Healey.

Gibson Papers. Royal Academy of Arts, London.

Gladstone Papers. Department of Manuscripts. British Library.

Goddard, May. Papers. Schlesinger Library, Radcliffe College, Cambridge, Massachusetts.

Haweis Family Papers. University Archives. University of British Columbia Library, Vancouver.

Hodson's Index. National Army Museum, London.

Isbister Collection. Manuscripts Division. Department of Rare Books and Special Collections. Princeton University Library.

Jacks, Lawrence Pearsall. Papers. Harris Manchester College, Oxford.

Kennard Papers. Special Collections. University of Adelaide.

Lady Margaret Hall. Archives. Registers, Principal's Reports, Photograph Album. Oxford.

Lloyd, Mary. Commonplace Book, 1849–ca. 1855. In private hands.

Local Studies Department. Royal Borough of Kensington and Chelsea Central Library, London.

Mill, John Stuart. Letters. Milton Eisenhower Library, The Johns Hopkins University, Baltimore.

Mill-Taylor Collection. Archives Division. LSE Library, London School of Economics and Political Science.

Minto Papers. National Library of Scotland, Edinburgh.

Miscellaneous Papers. National Library of Scotland, Edinburgh. MS 966.

Paget Papers. Department of Manuscripts. British Library. Add. 51,239A.

Parkes, Bessie Rayner. Papers. Girton College Archives, Cambridge.

Parrish Collection. Princeton University Library.

Passport Registers. Public Records Office, Kew.

Pearson, C. H. Correspondence. Bodleian Library, Oxford.

"Potted History of the Vaughan Estates." Gwynedd Archives, Dolgellau, Wales.

Principal Registry of the Family Division, London. Wills.

Register of Protestant Marriages. General Register Office, Dublin.

Rhagad Collection (Additional). Gwynedd Archives, Dolgellau, Wales.

Rhagatt Papers. Gwynedd Archives, Dolgellau, Wales.

Rhiwlas Estate Papers (1949 deposit). National Library of Wales, Aberystwyth.

Rhiwlas Papers. Gwynedd Archives, Dolgellau, Wales.

Shaftesbury, Anthony Ashley Cooper, seventh earl. Diaries. Broadlands Papers. Division of Special Collections. Hartley Library, University of Southampton. Quoted by permission of the Trustees of the Broadlands Archives.

Sheldon, Frances Elizabeth. Letters (transcribed by Frances I. Davis). Somerville College Archives, Oxford.

Somerville, Mary. Family Papers. Bodleian Library. Quoted by permission of the Principal and Fellows of Somerville College, Oxford.

Sophia Smith Collection. Smith College, Northampton, Massachusetts.

*Spectator* Contributors' Book. *Spectator* offices, London.

Swan Sonnenschein & Company. Archives, 1878–1911. Published on microfilm by Chadwyck-Healey.

Taylor, Marianne St. Leger. Diaries. Manuscript Department. National Library of Ireland, Dublin.

Stanton, E. C. Papers. Theodore Stanton Collection. Special Collections and University Archives. Rutgers University Libraries, New Brunswick, New Jersey.

Stanton, Elizabeth Cady. Papers. Library of Congress.

Vernon Lee Collection. Special Collections. Colby College, Waterville, Maine.

Ward, Mary. Diary, 1879. Somerville College Archives, Oxford.

Wister, Dr. Owen J. Papers. Historical Society of Pennsylvania, Philadelphia.

Wister Family Papers. Historical Society of Pennsylvania, Philadelphia.

Women's Suffrage Collection. Manchester Archives and Local Studies, Manchester Central Library. Microfilm collection by Adam Matthew Publications.

SECONDARY SOURCES

Abbott, Evelyn, and Lewis Campbell. *The Life and Letters of Benjamin Jowett.* 2 vols. London: John Murray, 1897.

Adams, Charles. "The Anti-Vivisection Movement and Miss Cobbe." *Verulam Review* 3 (October 1892): 197–209.

———. *The Coward Science: Our Answer to Professor Owen.* London: Hatchards, 1882.

Adams, Pauline. *Somerville for Women: An Oxford College, 1879–1993.* Oxford: Oxford University Press, 1996.

Adams, William H. Davenport. *The Makers of British India.* London: John Hogg, [1888].

"Agapemone." *Illustrated London News,* 29 March 1851, 253–54.

Alcott, Louisa May. *Aunt Jo's Scrap-Bag: Shawl-Straps.* 1872. Reprint, Boston: Little, Brown, 1927.

———. "Glimpses of Eminent Persons." *Independent* (New York), 1 November 1866.

———. *The Journals of Louisa May Alcott.* Edited by Joel Myerson, Daniel Shealy, and Madeleine B. Stern. Boston: Little, Brown, 1989.

Anderson, Nancy Fix. *Woman against Women in Victorian England: A Life of Eliza Lynn Linton.* Bloomington: Indiana University Press, 1987.

Anstruther, Eva. "Ladies' Clubs." *Nineteenth Century* 45 (April 1899): 598–611.

Archer, Mildred, and Gervase Jackson-Stops. "Mr Cobbe's Cabinet of Curiosities." *Country Life,* 10 March 1988, 130–33.

Arnold, Arthur. "The Founding of 'The Echo.'" *Echo,* 8 December, 1898.

Arnold, Matthew. *The Letters of Matthew Arnold.* Edited by Cecil Y. Lang. Vol. 4, *1871–78.* Charlottesville: University Press of Virginia, 1996.

Arrowsmith, R. L., comp. *Charterhouse Register, 1769–1872.* London: Phillimore, 1974.

Atkinson, Blanche. Introduction to *Life of Frances Power Cobbe as Told by Herself.* Edited by Blanche Atkinson. London: Swan Sonnenschein, 1904.

Atkinson, J. Beavington. "Social Science." *Blackwood's Edinburgh Magazine* 90 (October 1861): 468–78.

Austen, Jane. *Persuasion.* 1818. Vol. 5 of *The Novels of Jane Austen,* edited by R. W. Chapman. 3rd ed. London: Oxford University Press, 1933.

Baile de Laperriere, Charles, and Joanna Soden. *The Society of Women Artists Exhibitors, 1855–1996.* 4 vols. Calne, Wiltshire: Hilmarton Manor, 1996.

Barmouth Library. *The Frances Power Cobbe Bequest: Catalogue of Books.* Barmouth: Barmouth Press, 1904.

Bates, Peadar. *Donabate and Portrane—A History.* N.p.: privately printed, 1988.

Battersea, Constance. *Waifs and Strays.* London: Arthur L. Humphreys, 1921.

Bauer, Carol. "The Role of Religion in the Creation of a Philosophy of Feminism: The Case of Frances Power Cobbe." *Anima* 10 (1983): 59–70.

Bauer, Carol, and Lawrence Ritt. "Wife-Abuse, Late Victorian English Feminists, and the Legacy of Frances Power Cobbe." *International Journal of Women's Studies* 6 (1983): 195–207.

Beales, Derek. *England and Italy, 1859–60.* London: T. Nelson & Sons, [1961].

Bence-Jones, Mark. *A Guide to Irish Country Houses.* Rev. ed. London: Constable, 1988.

Benn, J. Miriam. *The Predicaments of Love.* London: Pluto, 1992.

Bennett, Daphne. *Emily Davies and the Liberation of Women, 1830–1921.* London: Deutsch, 1990.

Besant, Annie. *Annie Besant: An Autobiography.* 3rd impression with new preface. London: T. Fisher Unwin, 1908.

———. *A World Without God: A Reply to Miss Frances Power Cobbe.* London: Freethought Publishing, 1885.

Betham-Edwards, Matilda. *Mid-Victorian Memories.* London: John Murray, 1919.

Biggs, Caroline Ashurst. "Great Britain." In *History of Woman Suffrage,* edited by Elizabeth Cady Stanton, Susan B. Anthony, and Matilda Joslyn Gage, vol. 3. Rochester N.Y.: Susan B. Anthony, 1887.

Blackburn, Helen. *Women's Suffrage.* 1902. Reprint, New York: Kraus Reprint, 1971.

Blagden, Isa. *Poems.* Edited with a memoir by Alfred Austin. Edinburgh: William Blackwood & Sons, 1873.

Boase, Charles Williams. Review of *History of the Norman Kings of England,* by Thomas Cobbe. *Academy,* 12 February 1870, 134–35.

Bonham, Valerie. *A Place in Life: The Clewer House of Mercy, 1849–83.* Windsor, England: Valerie Bonham, 1992.

Bosanquet, Helen. Review of *The Duties of Women,* by Frances Power Cobbe. *Ethics* 16 (April 1906): 398.

Boucherett, Jessie. "Frances Power Cobbe." *Englishwoman's Review of Social and Industrial Questions,* 15 April 1904, 133–35.

Bourne, H. R. Fox. *English Newspapers.* 2 vols. 1887. Reprint, New York: Russell & Russell, 1966.

Brown, Alan Willard. *The Metaphysical Society: Victorian Minds in Crisis, 1869–1880.* New York: Columbia University Press, 1947.

Browning, Elizabeth Barrett. *Elizabeth Barrett Browning: Letters to Her Sister, 1846–59.* Edited by Leonard Huxley. London: John Murray, 1929.

———. *The Letters of Elizabeth Barrett Browning.* Edited by Frederick G. Kenyon. Vol. 2. New York: Macmillan, 1897.

Browning, Robert. *Dearest Isa: Robert Browning's Letters to Isabella Blagdon.* Edited by Edward C. McAleer. Austin: University of Texas Press, 1951.

———. *New Letters.* Edited by William Clyde DeVane and Kenneth Leslie Knickerbocker. New Haven: Yale University Press, 1950.

[Buckingham, Rev.]. Review of *Intuitive Morals,* by Frances Power Cobbe. *Christian Examiner* 63 (November 1857): 370–84.

Bunyon, John [Perkins, junior, pseud.]. *A Profitable Book Upon Domestic Law—Essays For English Women and Law Students.* London: Longmans & Green, 1875.

Burkhardt, Frederick, et al. *A Calendar of the Correspondence of Charles Darwin, 1821–1882.* Rev. ed. Cambridge: Cambridge University Press, 1994.

Caine, Barbara. "Feminist Biography and Feminist History." *Women's History Review* 3 (1994): 247–61.

———. *Victorian Feminists.* Oxford: Oxford University Press, 1992.

Carney, Karen M. "The Publisher's Reader as Feminist: The Career of Geraldine Endsor Jewsbury." *Victorian Periodicals Review* 29 (1996): 146–58.

Carpenter, J. Estlin. *James Martineau, Theologian and Teacher.* London: Philip Green, 1905.

———. *The Life and Work of Mary Carpenter.* London: Macmillan, 1879.

Carpenter, William B. "The Morality of the Medical Profession: A Reply." *Modern Review* 2 (July 1881): 489–532.

Carroll, Lewis. *The Diaries of Lewis Carroll.* Edited by Roger Lancelyn Green. Vol. 2. New York: Oxford University Press, 1954.

———. *The Letters of Lewis Carroll.* Edited by Morton N. Cohen and Roger Lancelyn Green. New York: Oxford University Press, 1979.

Chadwick, John White. "Frances Power Cobbe." *Christian Examiner* 83 (November 1867): 265–86.

———. "Frances Power Cobbe." *New World* (Boston) 4 (June 1894): 207–25.

[Chadwick, John White]. "A Philanthropic Autobiography." Review of *Life of Frances Power Cobbe,* by Frances Power Cobbe. *Nation,* 1 November 1894, 328–29.

Channing, Francis Allston. *Blanche Mary Susan Ethelind Channing.* Edinburgh: privately printed, 1905.

Chappell, Jennie. *Women of Worth.* London: S. W. Partridge, [1908].

Child, Lydia Maria. *Letters of Lydia Maria Child.* Boston: Houghton Mifflin, 1883.

Cobbe, Henry. *Luton Church: Historical and Descriptive.* London: George Bell & Sons, 1899.

Cobbe, Thomas. *History of the Norman Kings of England. From a New Collation of the Contemporary Chronicles.* London: Longmans, Green, 1869.

Cobbe, Thomas [Thomas of Swarraton, Armiger, pseud.]. *The Noble Traytour: A Chronicle.* 3 vols. London: Smith & Elder, 1857.

Cobbe, Winifred Ada. "A Victorian in the Twentieth Century." *English Review* 39 (December 1924): 773–76.

Cochrane, Jeanie Douglas. "Frances Power Cobbe." In *Peerless Women: A Book for Girls,* 200–220. London: Collins' Clear-Type, [1904].

Cohen, Lucy. *Lady De Rothschild and Her Daughters, 1821–1931.* London: John Murray, 1935.

Colenso, Frances. *Colenso Letters from Natal.* Edited by Wyn Rees. Pietermaritzburg: Shuter & Shooter, 1958.

Coleridge, Ernest Hartley. *The Life and Correspondence of John Duke Coleridge, Lord Chief Justice of England.* 2 vols. New York: Appleton, 1904.

Collins, Wilkie. *Heart and Science.* 1883. Edited by Steve Farmer. Peterborough, Ontario: Broadview, 1996.

Commager, Henry Steele. *Theodore Parker.* Boston: Little, Brown, 1936.

Conway, Moncure. *Autobiography: Memories and Experiences.* 2 vols. Boston: Hougton, Mifflin, 1904.

———. "Working With Froude on *Fraser's Magazine.*" *Nation,* 22 and 29 November 1894, 378–79 and 401–2.

Corbett, Mary Jean. *Representing Femininity: Middle-Class Subjectivity in Victorian and Edwardian Women's Autobiographies.* New York: Oxford University Press, 1992.

Cottesloe, Gloria. *Lost, Stolen, or Strayed: The Story of the Battersea Dogs' Home.* London: Arthur Baker, [1971].

Cox, George W. *The Life of John William Colenso.* London: W. Ridgway, 1888.

Crawford, Elizabeth. *The Women's Suffrage Movement: A Reference Guide, 1866–1928.* London: UCL, 1999.

Crawford, Mabel Sharman. "Maltreatment of Wives." *Westminster Review* 139 (March 1893): 292–303.

*Crockford's Clerical Directory for 1865.* 3rd issue. 1865. Reprint, Edinburgh: Peter Bell, 1995.

Crowther, Margaret Anne. *Church Embattled: Religious Controversy in Mid-Victorian Britain.* Newton Abbot: David & Charles, 1970.

Cunliffe, Barry. *The City of Bath.* 1986. Reprint, New Haven: Yale University Press, 1987.

Curle, Richard, ed. *Robert Browning and Julia Wedgwood: A Broken Friendship as Revealed by Their Letters.* New York: Frederick A. Stokes, 1937.

Dale, Antony. *Fashionable Brighton, 1820–1860.* [1947]. Reprint, London: Oriel, 1987.

Davies, Charles Maurice. *Heterodox London: Or, Phases of Free Thought in the Metropolis.* 1874. Reprint (2 vols. in 1), New York: Augustus M. Kelley, 1969.

———. *Unorthodox London: Or, Phases of Religious Life in the Metropolis.* 3rd ed. 1875. Reprint, New York: Augustus M. Kelley, 1969.

Davies, Emily. *Thoughts on Some Questions Relating to Women, 1860–1908.* 1910. Reprint, New York: Kraus Reprint, 1971.

[Davies, Emily]. "The Influence of University Degrees on the Education of Women." *Victoria Magazine* 1 (July 1863): 260–71.

Davies, Horton. *Worship and Theology in England.* Vol. 4, *From Newman to Martineau, 1850–1900.* Princeton: Princeton University Press, 1962.

Dawkins, William Boyd. "Brother Prince." *Macmillan's Magazine* 16 (October 1867): 464–73.

———. *Cave Hunting: Researches on the Evidence of Caves Regarding the Early Inhabitants of Europe.* London: Macmillan, 1874.

Desmond, Adrian, and James Moore. *Darwin.* London: Michael Joseph, 1991.

Diamond, Marion. *Emigration and Empire: The Life of Maria S. Rye.* New York: Garland, 1999.

Dicey, Edward. "Journalism New and Old." *Fortnightly Review* 83 (May 1905): 904–18.

Dixon, William Hepworth. *Spiritual Wives.* 2nd ed. 2 vols. London: Hurst & Blackett, 1868.

[Dixon, William Hepworth]. Review of *Italics,* by Frances Power Cobbe. *Athenaeum,* 22 October 1864, 524–25.

Doggett, Maeve E. *Marriage, Wife-Beating, and the Law in Victorian England.* Columbia: University of South Carolina Press, 1993.

Donaldson, Sandra. "'For Liberty of Friendship': Letters of Elizabeth Barrett Browning to Isa Blagden." Paper presented at the British Institute of Florence, Florence, 8 October 1985.

Driver, Leota S. *Fanny Kemble.* 1933. Reprint, New York: Negro Universities Press, [1969].

DuBois, Ellen, ed. *The Elizabeth Cady Stanton–Susan B. Anthony Reader.* Rev. ed. Boston: Northeastern University Press, 1992.

Dubrelle, Hugh. "'We Are Threatened with . . . Anarchy and Ruin': Fear of Americanization and the Emergence of an Anglo-Saxon Confederacy in England during the American Civil War." *Albion* 33 (winter 2002): 583–613.

Dunn, Waldo Hilary. *James Anthony Froude: A Biography.* 2 vols. Oxford: Clarendon, 1961–63.

East India Company. *East-India Register and Directory for 1842.* London: William H. Allen, 1842.

Eastlake, Elizabeth. *Journals and Correspondence of Lady Eastlake.* Edited by Charles Eastlake Smith. Vol. 2. London: John Murray, 1895.

———. "Lady Travellers." *Quarterly Review* 76 (June 1845): 98–136.

———, ed. *Life of John Gibson, R.A., Sculptor.* London: Longmans, Green, 1870.

Edel, Leon. *Henry James: A Life.* New York: Harper & Row, 1985.

Edgeworth, Maria, and R. L. Edgeworth. *Practical Education.* 2nd ed. 3 vols. London: J. Johnson, 1801.

Eliot, George. *The George Eliot Letters.* Edited by Gordon S. Haight. 9 vols. New Haven: Yale University Press, 1954–78.

Ellet, Elizabeth F. *Women Artists in All Ages and Countries.* London: Richard Bentley, 1859.

Elliot, Margaret. *Workhouse Girls: Notes of an Attempt to Help Them.* London: James Nisbett, 1875.

Ellis, Thomas Peter. *The Story of Two Parishes, Dolgelley and Llanelltyd.* Newtown: Welsh Outlook, 1928.

Escott, T. H. S. *Masters of English Journalism.* 1911. Reprint, Westport, Conn.: Greenwood, 1970.

Faber, Geoffrey. *Jowett: A Portrait with Background.* Cambridge: Harvard University Press, 1958.

Farningham, Marianne. *A Working Woman's Life: An Autobiography.* London: James Clarke, 1907.

Fawcett, Millicent Garrett. *What I Remember.* New York: Putnam, 1925.

———. *Women's Suffrage: A Short History of a Great Movement.* London: T. C. & E. C. Jack, [1912].

Feurer, Rosemary. "The Meaning of 'Sisterhood': The British Women's Movement and Protective Labor Legislation, 1870–1900." *Victorian Studies* 31 (winter 1988): 233–60.

Field, Kate. *Kate Field: Selected Letters.* Edited by Carolyn J. Moss. Carbondale: Southern Illinois University Press, 1996.

Field, Michael. *Works and Days: From the Journal of Michael Field.* Edited by Thomas Sturge Moore and D. C. Sturge Moore. London: John Murray, 1933.

Finlayson, Geoffrey B. A. M. *The Seventh Earl of Shaftesbury, 1801–1885.* London: Eyre Methuen, 1981.

Fison, Margaret. *Handbook of the National Association For the Promotion of Social Science.* London: Longman, Green, Longman & Roberts, 1859.

Foreign Resident. *Society in London.* 3rd ed. London: Chatto & Windus, 1885.

Fortescue, J. W. *A History of the British Army.* Vol. 13. New York: Macmillan, 1930.

French, Richard D. *Antivivisection and Medical Science in Victorian Society.* Princeton: Princeton University Press, 1975.

Frothingham, Octavius Brooks. *Memoir of William Henry Channing.* Boston: Houghton, Mifflin, 1886.

Gardner, Brian. *The East India Company: A History.* New York: McCall, 1972.

Gates, Barbara T. *Victorian Suicide: Mad Crimes and Sad Histories.* Princeton: Princeton University Press, 1988.

Gatty, Margaret. *The Old Folks From Home; Or A Holiday in Ireland in 1861.* London: Bell & Daldy, 1862.

Gilbert, John T. *A History of the City of Dublin.* 3 vols. 1854–59. Reprint, Shannon: Irish University Press, 1972.

Gladstone, William Ewart. *The Gladstone Diaries.* Edited by M. R. D. Foot and H. C. G. Matthew. 14 vols. Oxford: Clarendon, 1968–94.

Gleadle, Kathryn. *The Early Feminists, Radical Unitarians, and the Emergence of the Women's Rights Movements, 1831–51.* New York: St. Martin's, 1995.

Goldman, Lawrence. *Science, Reform, and Politics in Victorian Britain: The Social Science Association, 1857–1886.* Cambridge: Cambridge University Press, 2002.

Gorham, Deborah. "Victorian Reform as a Family Business: The Hill Family." In *The Victorian Family,* edited by Anthony Wohl. New York: St. Martin's, 1978.

Gow, Henry. *The Unitarians.* New York: Doubleday, Doran, 1928.

Graves, Algernon. *The Royal Academy of Arts: A Complete Dictionary of Contributors . . . 1769–1904.* 8 vols. London: George Bell & Sons, 1905–6.

Graves, Charles L. *The Life and Letters of Sir George Grove.* London: Macmillan, 1903.

Grey, Maria. *Memorials of Emily A. E. Shirreff, with a Sketch of Her Life.* N.p.: privately printed, 1897.

———. *The School Board of London: Three Addresses of Mrs William Grey.* London: W. Ridgway, 1871.

Griffiths, Dennis. "The Early Management of the *Standard.*" In *Investigating Victorian Journalism,* edited by Aled Jones, Laurel Brake, and Lionel Madden. New York: St. Martin's, 1990.

Grodzins, Dean. *American Heretic: Theodore Parker and Transcendentalism.* Chapel Hill: University of North Carolina Press, 2002.

Gross, John. *The Rise and Fall of the Man of Letters.* 1969. London: Penguin Books, 1991.

Gross, Mary Jean Holland. "An Unpublished Shakespeare Scholar: Selections from Thomas Cobbe's Nineteenth-Century Edition of the Plays." Ph.D. diss., University of Texas at Austin, 1979.

Gunn, Peter. *Vernon Lee: Violet Paget, 1856–1935.* London: Oxford University Press, 1964.

Hall, Samuel Carter, and Anna Maria Hall. *Hand-Books for Ireland: Dublin and Wicklow.* London: Virtue, Hall & Virtue, 1853.

Hallowell, Anna Davis. *James and Lucretia Mott: Life and Letters.* Boston: Houghton, Mifflin, 1884.

Hamilton, Susan. "Locating Victorian Feminism: Frances Power Cobbe, Feminist Writing, and the Periodical Press." *Nineteenth-Century Feminisms,* no. 2 (spring–summer 2000): 48–66.

———. "Making History with Frances Power Cobbe: Victorian Feminism, Domestic Violence, and the Language of Imperialism." *Victorian Studies* 43 (spring 2001): 437–61.

Hammerton, A. James. *Cruelty and Companionship: Conflict in Nineteenth-Century Married Life.* 1992. Reprint, London: Routledge, 1995.

Hammond, J. L., and Barbara Hammond. *James Stansfield: A Victorian Champion of Sex Equality.* London: Longmans, 1932.

*The Hand Book to the Dublin & Drogheda Railway.* Dublin: N. Walsh, [1844].

Hardy, Philip Dixon. *The New Picture of Dublin; or, Stranger's Guide through the Irish Metropolis.* Dublin: William Curry, 1831.

Harper, Ida Husted. *Life and Work of Susan B. Anthony.* 3 vols. [1898–1908]. Reprint, New York: Arno, 1969.

Harris, Mary Corbett. "Frances Power Cobbe (1822–1904) of Hengwrt." *Journal of the Merioneth Historical and Record Society* 7 (1976): 416–23.

Harrison, J. F. C. *The Second Coming: Popular Millenarianism, 1780–1850.* New Brunswick, N.J.: Rutgers University Press, 1979.

Hart, Ernest. "Women, Clergymen, and Doctors." *New Review* 7 (December 1892): 708–18.

Hart, H. G. *The New Annual Army List for 1849.* London: John Murray, 1849.

Hastings, Francis Rawdon. *The Private Journal of the Marquess of Hastings.* Edited by Sophia Hastings. 2 vols. London: Saunders & Otley, 1858.

Hawes, C. J. *Poor Relations: The Making of a Eurasian Community in British India, 1733–1833.* Richmond, England: Curzon, 1996.

Hawthorne, Nathaniel. *The French and Italian Notebooks.* Edited by Thomas Woodson. Vol. 14 of *The Centenary Edition of the Works of Nathaniel Hawthorne.* Columbus: Ohio State University Press, 1980.

Haythornthwaite, Philip J. *The Colonial Wars Source Book.* 1995. Reprint, London: Arms & Armour, 1997.

Herstein, Sheila R. *A Mid-Victorian Feminist, Barbara Leigh Smith Bodichon.* New Haven: Yale University Press, 1985.

Hinchliff, Peter. *Frederick Temple, Archbishop of Canterbury: A Life.* Oxford: Clarendon, 1998.

Hirsch, Pam. *Barbara Leigh Smith Bodichon: Feminist, Artist, and Rebel.* London: Pimlico, 1999.

Hobhouse, Hermione, ed. *Southern Kensington: Kensington Square to Earl's Court.* Greater London Council, Survey of London, no. 42. London: Athlone, 1986.

Hodson, V. C. P. *List of the Officers of the Bengal Army, 1758–1834.* London: Constable, 1927.

Hoggan, George. "Vivisection." *Fraser's Magazine* 91 (April 1875): 521–28.

Holcombe, Lee. *Wives and Property: Reform of the Married Women's Property Law in Nineteenth-Century England.* Toronto: University of Toronto Press, 1983.

Hollis, Patricia. *Ladies Elect: Women in English Local Government, 1865–1914.* Oxford: Clarendon, 1987.

Holmes, Oliver Wendell. "Our Hundred Days in Europe." Part 2. *Atlantic Monthly* 59 (April 1887): 533–45.

Holt, Raymond V. *The Unitarian Contribution to Social Progress in England.* London: George Allen & Unwin, 1938.

Holton, Sandra Stanley. *Suffrage Days: Stories from the Women's Suffrage Movement.* London: Routledge, 1996.

———. "'To Educate Women into Rebellion': Elizabeth Cady Stanton and the Creation of a Transatlantic Network of Radical Suffragists." *American Historical Review* 99 (1994): 1112–36.

Hooper, George. *Wellington.* London: Macmillan, 1889.

Hopkins, Tighe. "Our Portrait Gallery: The Rev. Hugh Reginald Haweis, M.A." *Dublin University Magazine* 90 (October 1877): 396–414.

Hopley, Emma. *Campaigning against Cruelty: The Hundred Year History of the British Union for the Abolition of Vivisection.* London: BUAV, 1998.

Hoppen, K. Theodore. *The Mid-Victorian Generation, 1846–1886.* Oxford: Oxford University Press, 1998.

Hosmer, Harriet. *Harriet Hosmer: Letters and Memories.* Edited by Cornelia Carr. New York: Moffat, Yard, 1912.

———. "The Process of Sculpture." *Atlantic Monthly* 14 (December 1864): 734–38.

Howe, Bea. *Arbiter of Elegance.* London: Harvill, 1967.

Howe, Julia Ward. *Reminiscences, 1819–1899.* Boston: Houghton, Mifflin, 1899.

Howells, William Dean. Review of *Italics,* by Frances Power Cobbe. *North American Review* 103 (October 1866): 313–45.

Hudson, Derek. *Munby, Man of Two Worlds: The Life and Diaries of Arthur J. Munby, 1828–1910.* Boston: Gambit, 1972.

Hudson, Gertrude Rose, ed. *Browning to His American Friends: Letters between the Brownings, the Storys, and James Russell Lowell.* New York: Barnes & Noble, 1965.

Hussey, J. M., comp. *The Finlay Papers: A Catalogue.* N.p.: Thames & Hudson, 1973.

[Hutton, R. H.]. Review of *The Duties of Women,* by Frances Power Cobbe. *Spectator,* 15 January 1881, 87–88.

Huxley, Leonard, ed. *Life and Letters of Thomas Henry Huxley.* 2 vols. New York: Appleton, 1900.

Hyam, Ronald. *Empire and Sexuality: The British Experience.* Manchester: Manchester University Press, 1990.

Israel, Kali. *Names and Stories: Emilia Dilke and Victorian Culture.* New York: Oxford University Press, 1999.

Jackson, A. W. *James Martineau: A Biography and Study.* Boston: Little, Brown, 1901.

Jalland, Pat. *Death in the Victorian Family.* Oxford: Oxford University Press, 1996.

James, Henry. *Letters.* Edited by Leon Edel. Vol. 3, *1875–1883.* Cambridge: Belknap, 1975.

———. *Traveling in Italy with Henry James: Essays.* Edited by Fred Kaplan. New York: William Morrow, 1994.

———. *William Wetmore Story and His Friends.* 2 vols. Boston: Houghton, Mifflin, 1903.

James, Lawrence. *Raj: The Making and Unmaking of British India.* 1997. Reprint, New York: St. Martin's, 1998.

Jameson, Anna. *A Commonplace Book of Thoughts, Memories and Fancies.* London: Longman, Brown, Green and Longmans, 1854.

[Jeaffreson, John Cordy.] Review of *The Collected Works of Theodore Parker,* by Frances Power Cobbe. *Athenaeum,* 20 August 1864, 234–36.

———. Review of *Essays on the Pursuits of Women,* by Frances Power Cobbe. *Athenaeum,* 15 August 1863, 199–200.

———. Review of *Hours of Work and Play*, by Frances Power Cobbe. *Athenaeum*, 2 February 1867, 149–50.

Jenkins, Roy. *Sir Charles Dilke: A Victorian Tragedy.* London: Collins, 1958.

Johnson, Maurice L. "Frances Power Cobbe." *Primitive Methodist Quarterly Review* 38 (April 1896): 223–35.

———. "A Priestess of Humanity." *Westminster Review* 156 (June 1904): 653–56.

Johnston-Liik, Edith Mary. *History of the Irish Parliament, 1692–1800.* Vol. 3. Belfast: Ulster Historical Foundation, 2002.

Jones, E. Rosalie. *A History of Barmouth and Its Vicinity.* Barmouth: John Evans & Nephew, 1909.

Jones, J. Winter. Preface to *A List of the Books of Reference in the Reading Room of the British Museum.* 2nd ed. rev. London: Trustees of the British Museum, 1871.

Jordan, Ellen. *The Women's Movement and Women's Employment in Nineteenth Century Britain.* London: Routledge, 1999.

———. "'Women's Work in the World': The Birth of a Discourse, London, 1857." *Nineteenth Century Feminisms*, no. 1 (fall–winter 1999): 12–38.

Jordan, Jane. *Josephine Butler.* London: John Murray, 2001.

Jowett, Benjamin. *Letters of Benjamin Jowett.* Edited by Evelyn Abbott and Lewis Campbell. London: John Murray, 1899.

Kanner, Barbara. *Women in English Social History, 1800–1914: A Guide to Research.* Vol. 1. New York: Garland, 1990.

Keane, Rory, Anne Hughes, and Ronan Swan, eds. *Ardgillan Castle and the Taylor Family.* Balbriggan, Ireland: Ardgillan Castle, 1995.

Kelly, Audrey. *Lydia Becker and the Cause.* Lancaster: University of Lancaster, Centre for North-West Regional Studies, 1992.

Kemble, Frances Anne. *Further Records, 1848–1883: A Series of Letters.* 1890. Reprint, New York: Henry Holt, 1891.

Kendall, Phebe Mitchell, comp. *Maria Mitchell: Life, Letters, and Journals.* Boston: Lee & Shepard, 1896.

Kennedy, Liam, Paul S. Ell, E. M. Crawford, and L. A. Clarkson. *Mapping the Great Irish Famine: A Survey of the Famine Decades.* Dublin: Four Courts, 1999.

Kidd, Beatrice E., and M. Edith Richards. *Hadwen of Gloucester, Man, Medico, Martyr.* London: John Murray, 1933.

Klumpke, Anna. *Rosa Bonheur: The Artist's (Auto)Biography.* Translated by Gretchen van Slyke. Ann Arbor: University of Michigan Press, 1997.

Koss, Stephen. *The Rise and Fall of the Political Press in Britain.* Vol. 1, *The Nineteenth Century.* London: Hamish Hamilton, 1981.

Laing, Alastair, ed. *Clerics and Connoisseurs: The Rev. Matthew Pilkington, the Cobbe Family, and the Fortunes of an Irish Art Collection through Three Centuries.* Exh. cat. London: English Heritage, 2001.

Larson, Janet L. "Where Is the Woman in This Text? Frances Power Cobbe's Voices in *Broken Lights.*" *Victorian Literature and Culture* 31 (2003): 99–129.

Lecky, W. E. H. *Leaders of Public Opinion in Ireland.* 1861. 2 vols. Reprint, London: Longmans, Green, 1912.

Lee, Vernon. *Vernon Lee's Letters.* Preface by Irene Cooper Willis. London: privately printed, 1937.

Lewes, G. H. *Three Sisters and Three Fortunes; Or, Rose, Blanche, and Violet.* 3 vols. 1848. Reprint (3 vols. in 1), New York: Harper & Brothers, 1864.

Lewin, Walter. Review of *Life of Frances Power Cobbe,* by Frances Power Cobbe. *Academy,* 27 October 1894, 321–22.

Lewis, Samuel. *A Topographical Dictionary of Ireland.* 2 vols. 1839. Reprint, Baltimore: Genealogical Publishing, 1995.

———. *A Topographical Dictionary of Wales.* 2 vols. London: S. Lewis, 1833.

Linton, Eliza Lynn. "The Modern Revolt." *Macmillan's Magazine* 23 (December 1870): 142–49.

*A List of the Royal Military College at Sandhurst.* London: T. Egerton, 1835.

Litchfield, Henrietta Emma, ed. *Emma Darwin, Wife of Charles Darwin: A Century of Family Letters.* Vol. 2. Cambridge: privately printed at the University Press, 1904.

Livermore, Mary. *The Story of My Life.* Hartford, Conn.: A. D. Worthington, 1897.

Longford, Elizabeth. *Wellington: The Years of the Sword.* New York: Harper & Row, 1969.

Low, Frances H. "Distinguished Women and Their Dolls." *Strand* 8 (September 1894): 250–57.

Low, Sidney, and Lloyd C. Sanders. *The History of England during the Reign of Victoria.* 1907. Reprint, New York: Haskell House, 1969.

Lowndes, William. *They Came to Bath.* Bristol: Redcliffe, 1982.

Maitland, Edward. *Anna Kingsford: Her Life, Letters, Diary, and Work.* 2 vols. London: George Redway, 1896.

Malleson, Elizabeth. *Elizabeth Malleson, 1828–1916: Autobiographical Notes and Letters.* Edited by Hope Malleson. London: privately printed, 1926.

Mallett, Mrs. Charles. "The Albemarle Club." *Womanhood* 2 (June 1899): 38–40.

Manchester, A. H. "Marital Violence and the Act of 1878." In *Droit Sans Frontieres: Essays in Honour of L. Neville Brown,* edited by Geoffrey Hand and Jeremy McBride. Birmingham, England: Holdsworth Club, 1991.

Mander, Charles. *The Reverend Prince and His Abode of Love.* Wakefield, Yorkshire: EP Publishing, 1976.

Manton, Jo. *Mary Carpenter and the Children of the Streets.* London: Heinemann, 1976.

Married Women's Property Committee. *Report Presented At the Final Meeting of Their Friends and Subscribers, 18 November 1882.* Manchester: A. Ireland, 1882.

Martel, Carol Freeborough. "British Women in the National Association for the Promotion of Social Science, 1857–1886." Ph.D. diss., Arizona State University, 1986.

Martineau, Harriet. *British Rule in India: A Historical Sketch.* London: Smith, Elder, 1857.

———. *Eastern Life Present and Past.* Philadelphia: Lea & Blanchard, 1848.

*The Mary Anne Rogers Memorial.* Southampton: John Adams, 1901.

Maxwell, Christabel. *Mrs Gatty and Mrs Ewing.* London: Constable, 1949.

Merrill, Lisa. *When Romeo Was a Woman: Charlotte Cushman and Her Circle of Female Spectators.* Ann Arbor: University of Michigan Press, 1999.

Metcalfe, Ethel E. *Memoir of Rosamond Davenport Hill.* London: Longmans, 1904.

Midgley, Clare. *Women against Slavery: The British Campaigns, 1780–1870.* 1992. Reprint, London: Routledge, 1995.

Mill, James, and Horace Hayman Wilson. *The History of British India from 1805 to 1835.* 3 vols. London: James Madden, 1845–48.

Mill, John Stuart. *The Later Letters of John Stuart Mill, 1849–1873.* Edited by Francis E. Mineka and Dwight N. Lindley. Toronto: University of Toronto Press, 1972.

Minto, Nina, Countess of. *Letters and Journals of Nina, Countess of Minto.* Edited by Arthur D. Elliot. N.p.: privately printed, 1920.

Mitchell, Sally. "'Fanny Power Cobbe'—a Case of Slightly Borrowed Identity and Two Misattributions in the *Wellesley Index.*" *Victorian Periodicals Review* 34 (winter 2001): 383–87.

Monroe, Mrs. H. E. "Frances Power Cobbe and Her Work." *Education* (Boston) 10 (February 1890): 350–55.

Morley, John. *Recollections.* 2 vols. New York: Macmillan, 1917.

Morris, Lewis. *The New Rambler: From Desk to Platform.* London: Longmans, 1905.

*Murray's Handbook of Rome and its Environs.* 11th ed. London: John Murray, 1873.

*Murray's Modern London: A Handbook to London as It Is.* New ed. London: John Murray, 1874.

National Anti-Vivisection Society. *The Vivisection Controversy: A Selection of Speeches and Articles.* London: Victoria Street Society, 1883.

———. *The Vivisection Controversy: A Selection of Speeches and Articles.* New ed. London: Victoria Street Society, 1890.

National Association for the Promotion of Social Science (NAPSS). *Papers and Discussions on Education.* London: Emily Faithfull, 1862.

National Society for Women's Suffrage. *Declaration in Favour of Women's Suffrage.* London, 1 August 1889.

———. *First Report of the Executive Committee.* London, 1872.

National Society for Women's Suffrage Central Committee. *Report of the Executive Committee.* London: National Society for Women's Suffrage, 1889.

National Women's Suffrage Association (U.S.). *Report of the Sixteenth Annual Washington Convention.* Rochester, N.Y.: Charles Mann, 1884.

Newman, Francis W. "Capacities of Women." *Westminster Review* (New York) 84 (October 1865): 167–78.

———. *A Discourse Against Hero-Making in Religion.* London: Trübner, 1864.

Nightingale, E. Constance. "Frances Power Cobbe, 1861–1961." *Women in Council,* n.s., no. 9 (winter 1962): 24–25.

Nightingale, Florence. *Cassandra and Other Selections from Suggestions For Thought.* Edited by Mary Poovey. New York: New York University Press, 1993.

———. *Letters from Egypt: A Journey on the Nile, 1849–1850.* Edited by Anthony Sattin. New York: Weidenfeld & Nicholson, 1987.

Nolan, William. "Society and Settlement in the Valley of Glenasmole, c. 1750–c. 1900." In *Dublin City and County: From Prehistory to Present,* edited by F. H. A. Aalen and Kevin Whelan. Dublin: Geography Publications, 1992.

Nowell-Smith, Simon. *The House of Cassell, 1848–1958.* London: Cassell, 1958.

O'Brien, Jacqueline, and Desmond Guiness. *Great Irish Houses and Castles.* New York: Harry N. Abrams, 1992.

Oliphant, Margaret. "The Royal Academy." *Blackwood's Edinburgh Magazine* 119 (June 1876): 753–69.

Onslow, Barbara. *Women of the Press in Nineteenth-Century Britain.* London: Macmillan, 2000.

Owen, Hugh J. *Echoes of Old Merioneth.* Dolgelley, Wales: Hughes Brothers, 1946.

Owen, Richard. *Experimental Physiology: Its Benefits to Mankind.* London: Longmans, 1882.

Paget, Walpurga [Walburga]. *In My Tower.* 2 vols. New York: George H. Doran, 1924.

Parker, Theodore. *A Discourse of Matters Pertaining to Religion.* 3rd ed. Boston: Little & Brown, 1847.

———. "The Public Function of Woman. A Sermon, Preached At the Music Hall, March 27, 1853." In *Sins and Safeguards of Society.* Vol. 9 of *The Centenary Edition of Theodore Parker's Works,* edited by Samuel B. Stewart. Boston: American Unitarian Association, 1907.

———. *Sermons of Theism, Atheism, and Popular Theology.* 4th ed. Boston: Horace B. Fuller, 1870.

Parry, Ann. "Swan Sonnenschein Limited." In *British Literary Publishing Houses, 1820–1880,* edited by Patricia J. Anderson and Jonathan Rose. Vol. 106 of *Dictionary of Literary Biography.* Detroit: Gale, 1991.

Paul, Herbert. *Life of Froude.* New York: Charles Scribner's Sons, 1905.

Peabody, Francis Greenwood. "Louisa and Georgina Schuyler." In *Reminiscences of Present-Day Saints.* Boston: Houghton, Mifflin, 1927.

Peach, Robert Edward. *Historic Houses in Bath and their Associations.* London: Simpkin, Marshall, 1883.

Peacock, Sandra J. *The Theological and Ethical Writings of Frances Power Cobbe, 1822–1904.* Lewiston: Edwin Mellen, 2002.

Pearson, C. H. Review of *The History of the Norman Kings of England,* by Thomas Cobbe. *North British Review* 51 (January 1870): 530–32.

Pleck, Elizabeth. *Domestic Tyranny: The Making of Social Policy against Family Violence from Colonial Times to the Present.* New York: Oxford University Press, 1987.

Porter, Roy. *The Greatest Benefit to Mankind: A Medical History of Humanity.* New York: W. W. Norton, 1997.

"The Positive Side of Modern Deism." Review of *Intuitive Morals* (both volumes), by Frances Power Cobbe, and *Theism,* by F. W. Newman. *Eclectic Review,* 6th ser., 3 (March 1858): 253–65.

Pratt, Edwin A. *A Woman's Work For Women.* London: G. Newnes, 1898.

Price, Richard John Lloyd. *Dogs Ancient and Modern, and Walks in Wales.* London: Eglington, 1893.

———. *The History of Rulacc, Or Rhiwlas.* London: Pewtress, 1899.

Prince, Henry James. *The Charlinch Revival.* London: James Nisbet, 1842.

———. *Letters Addressed by the Rev. Henry James Prince, to his Christian Brethren at St. David's College, Lampeter.* 2nd ed. Landovery, Wales: William Rees, 1841.

Prins, Yopie. *Victorian Sappho.* Princeton: Princeton University Press, 1999.

Prinsep, Henry T. *A Narrative of the Political and Military Transactions of British India Under the Administration of the Marquess of Hastings, 1813 to 1818.* London: John Murray, 1820.

Pugh, Martin. *The March of the Women: A Revisionist Analysis of the Campaign for Women's Suffrage, 1866–1914.* Oxford: Oxford University Press, 2000.

Pyle, Hilary. *The Sligo-Leitrim World of Kate Cullen, 1832–1913.* Dublin: Woodfield, 1997.

Raftery, Deirdre. "Frances Power Cobbe." In *Women, Power, and Consciousness in Nineteenth Century Ireland,* edited by Mary Cullen and Maria Luddy. Dublin: Attic, 1995.

Ragette, Friedrich. *Baalbek.* Park Ridge, N.J.: Noyes, 1980.

Rees, T. Mardy. *Welsh Painters, Engravers, Sculptors, 1527–1911.* Caernarfon: Welsh Publishing, [1913].

Review of *Broken Lights,* by Frances Power Cobbe. *Monthly Religious Magazine* (Boston) 32 (November 1864): 283–92.

Review of *Broken Lights,* by Frances Power Cobbe, and *Apologia pro Vita Sua,* by John Henry Newman. *New Englander and Yale Review* 24 (January 1865): 190–94.

Review of *The Cities of the Past,* by Frances Power Cobbe. *Saturday Review,* 16 January 1864, 79–80.

Review of *History of the Norman Kings of England,* by Thomas Cobbe. *North American Review* 112 (October 1870): 480–83.

Review of *Religious Duty,* by Frances Power Cobbe. *Theological Review* 1 (November 1864): 598.

Réville, Albert. Review of *Hopes of the Human Race Hereafter and Here,* by Frances Power Cobbe. *Academy,* 17 July 1875, 56–57.

Richards, Laura E., Maud Howe Elliott, and Florence Howe Hall. *Julia Ward Howe, 1819–1910.* 2 vols. Boston: Houghton Mifflin, 1916.

Rickards, E. C. *Felicia Skene of Oxford: A Memoir.* London: John Murray, 1902.

Ritvo, Harriet. *The Animal Estate: The English and Other Creatures in the Victorian Age.* Cambridge: Harvard University Press, 1987.

Robb, Janet Henderson. *The Primrose League: 1883–1906.* Studies in History, Economics, and Public Law, no. 492. New York: Columbia University Press, 1942.

Roberts, Askew. *The Gossiping Guide to Wales.* London: Hodder & Stoughton, 1884.

Robson, Ann P. "The Founding of the National Society for Women's Suffrage, 1866–1867." *Canadian Journal of History* 8 (1973): 1–22.

Robson, Ann P., and John M. Robson, eds. *Sexual Equality: Writings by John Stuart Mill, Harriet Taylor Mill, and Helen Taylor.* Toronto: University of Toronto Press, 1994.

Rosen, Andrew. "Emily Davies and the Women's Movement, 1862–67." *Journal of British Studies* 19 (1979): 101–21.

Rossetti, William Michael. "The Royal Academy Exhibition." *Fraser's Magazine* 71 (June 1865): 736–53.

Rover, Constance. *Women's Suffrage and Party Politics in Britain, 1866–1914.* London: Routledge & Kegan Paul, 1967.

"The Royal Academy." *Art-Journal,* 1 June 1865, 161–72.

Rubinstein, David. *A Different World for Women: The Life of Millicent Garrett Fawcett.* Columbus: Ohio State University Press, 1991.

Rupke, Nicolaas A., ed. *Vivisection in Historical Perspective.* London: Croom Helm, 1987.

Ruskin, John. *Fors Clavigera Letters 37–72.* Vol. 28 of *The Works of Ruskin,* edited by E. T. Cook and Alexander Wedderburn. London: George Allen, 1907.

Russell, Bertrand, and Patricia Russell. *The Amberley Papers: The Letters and Diaries of Lord and Lady Amberley.* 2 vols. London: Hogarth, 1937.

Ryals, Clyde. *The Life of Robert Browning: A Critical Biography.* Oxford: Blackwell, 1993.

Sanborn, F. B. "Frances Power Cobbe: A Life Devoted to the Promotion of Social Science." *Journal of Social Science,* no. 42 (September 1904): 63–68.

Schneewind, J. B. *Backgrounds of English Victorian Literature.* New York: Random House, 1970.

Schwieso, Joshua J. "The Founding of the Agapemone at Spaxton, 1845–6." *Somerset Archaeology and Natural History* 135 (1991): 113–21.

———. "The Princes of Widcome—A Most Unusual Family." *Notes and Queries for Somerset and Dorset* 34 (March 1996): 27–31.

———. "'Religious Fanaticism' and Wrongful Confinement in Victorian England: The Affair of Louisa Nottidge." *Social History of Medicine* 9 (1996): 159–74.

Sears, Albert C. "The Politics and Gender of Duty in Frances Power Cobbe's *The Duties of Women.*" *Nineteenth-Century Feminisms,* no. 2 (spring–summer 2000): 67–78.

Shanley, Mary Lyndon. *Feminism, Marriage, and the Law in Victorian England, 1850–1895.* London: I. B. Tauris, 1989.

Shepherd, J. A. *Lawson Tait: The Rebellious Surgeon.* Lawrence, Kans.: Coronado, 1980.

Sheppard, F. H. W., ed. *Southern Kensington: Brompton.* Greater London Council, Survey of London, no. 41. London: Athlone, 1983.

Sherwood, Dolly. *Harriet Hosmer, American Sculptor, 1830–1908.* Columbia: University of Missouri Press, 1991.

Sieveking, I. Giberne. *Memoir and Letters of Francis W. Newman.* London: Kegan Paul, Trench, Trübner, 1909.

Simpson, M. C. M. *Many Memories of Many People.* London: Arnold, 1898.

Smith, Goldwin. "Female Suffrage." *Macmillan's Magazine* 30 (June 1874): 139–50.

Somerville, Martha. *Personal Recollections, from Early Life to Old Age, of Mary Somerville.* Boston: Roberts Brothers, 1874.

Somerville-Large, Peter. *The Irish Country House: A Social History.* London: Sinclair-Stevenson, 1995.

Spence, Margaret E. "Ruskin's Correspondence with Miss Blanche Atkinson." *John Rylands Library Bulletin* 42 (1959): 194–219.

Srebrnik, Patricia Thomas. *Alexander Strahan, Victorian Publisher.* Ann Arbor: University of Michigan Press, 1986.

Stanton, Elizabeth Cady. *Bible and Church Degrade Women.* 3rd ed. Chicago: H. L. Green, 1899.

———. *Eighty Years and More.* New York: European Publishing, 1898.

Stanton, Theodore, ed. *The Woman Question in Europe.* 1884. Reprint, New York: Source Book, 1970.

[Stead, W. T.]. "Character Sketch: Frances Power Cobbe." *Review of Reviews* 10 (October 1894): 329–38. Published as "Autobiography of Frances Power Cobbe" in New York edition, 12 (November 1894): 562–69.

Stebbins, Emma, ed. *Charlotte Cushman: Her Letters and Memories of Her Life.* Boston: Houghton, Osgood, 1879.

Stenton, Michael, ed. *Who's Who of British Members of Parliament.* Vol. 1, *1832–1885.* Sussex: Harvester, 1976.

[Stephen, James Fitzjames]. "Life and Writings of Theodore Parker." *Fraser's Magazine* 69 (February 1864): 229–45.

Strachey, Ray. *The Cause: A Short History of the Women's Movement in Great Britain.* 1928. Reprint, London: Virago, 1978.

———. *Millicent Garrett Fawcett.* London: John Murray, 1931.

Sullivan, Alan, ed. *The Victorian and Edwardian Age, 1837–1913.* Vol. 3, *British Literary Magazines.* Westport, Conn.: Greenwood, 1984.

Sunday Lecture Society. [*Proceedings.*] London, 1869–90.

Taylor, Jenny Bourne. "Fallacies of Memory in Nineteenth-Century Psychology: Henry Holland, William Carpenter, and Frances Power Cobbe." *Victorian Review* 26 (2000): 98–118.

Taylor, Jenny Bourne, and Sally Shuttleworth, eds. *Embodied Selves: An Anthology of Psychological Texts, 1830–1890.* Oxford: Clarendon, 1998.

Taylor, Philip Meadows. *The Story of My Life.* Edited by Alice Meadows Taylor. 1877. New ed. Edited by Henry Bruce. London: Oxford University Press, 1920.

Tebb, William. *Premature Burial and How It May Be Prevented.* 2nd ed. Edited by Walter R. Hadwen. London: Swan Sonnenschein, 1905.

Temperley, Howard. *British Antislavery, 1833–1870.* London: Longman, 1972.

Thayer, William M. "Frances Power Cobbe—Self-Made Scholar." In *Women Who Win; Or, Making Things Happen.* London: T. Nelson & Sons, 1897.

Thirlwall, Connop. *Letters to a Friend.* Edited by A. P. Stanley. London: Bentley & Son, 1881.

Thomas, Onfel. *Frances Elizabeth Hoggan, 1843–1927.* Newport, Wales: R. H. Johns, [1971].

Thomson, David, and Moyra McGusty, eds. *The Irish Journals of Elizabeth Smith, 1840–1850.* Oxford: Clarendon, 1980.

Thorold, Algar Labouchere. *The Life of Henry Labouchere.* London: Constable, 1913.

Touhill, Blanche M. *William Smith O'Brien and His Irish Revolutionary Companions in Penal Exile.* Columbia: University of Missouri Press, 1981.

Trollope, Anthony. *The Bertrams.* 1859. Edited by Geoffrey Harvey. Oxford: Oxford University Press, 1991.

———. "A Ride Across Palestine." In *Tales of All Countries, Second Series.* 1863. London: Penguin, 1993.

———. "An Unprotected Female At the Pyramids." In *Tales of All Countries, First Series.* 1861. London: Penguin, 1993.

Turner, Frank M. "The Crisis of Faith and the Faith That Was Lost." In *Victorian Faith in Crisis,* edited by Richard J. Helmstadter and Bernard Lightman. Stanford: Stanford University Press, 1990.

Turner, James. *Reckoning with the Beast: Animals, Pain, and Humanity in the Victorian Mind.* Baltimore: Johns Hopkins University Press, 1980.

Twining, Louisa. *Recollections of Life and Work.* London: E. Arnold, 1893.

Tyrrell, Henry. *The History of the War with Russia.* Vol. 3. London: London Printing & Publishing, [1858].

Van Arsdel, Rosemary T. *Florence Fenwick Miller: Victorian Feminist, Journalist, and Educator.* Aldershot: Ashgate, 2001.

Van Haaften, Julia, and Jon E. Manchip White. *Egypt and the Holy Land in Historic Photographs: Seventy-seven Views by Francis Frith.* New York: Dover, 1980.

Verschoyle, John. "Frances Power Cobbe." *Living Age* 242 (July 1904): 70–80. First published in *Contemporary Review* 85 (June 1904): 829–40.

———. "The Funeral of Frances Power Cobbe." *Abolitionist* 5 (20 April 1904): 1–2.

Voelz, Peter M. *Slave and Soldier: The Military Impact of Blacks in the Colonial Americas.* New York: Garland, 1993.

Vyvyan, John. *In Pity and in Anger: A Study of the Use of Animals in Science.* London: Michael Joseph, 1969.

Wakefield, Priscilla. *Mental Improvement; or, the Beauties and Wonders of Nature and Art in a Series of Instructive Conversations.* Dublin: P. Wogan, 1799.

Walker, Arthur De Noé. *Address on Vivisection Read At the International Congress For the Prevention of Cruelty to Animals, Held in London, 1874.* London: Bailliere, Tindall & Cox, 1875.

Walling, R. A. J., ed. *The Diaries of John Bright.* New York: William Morrow, 1931.

Weber, Gary. "Henry Labouchere, *Truth,* and the New Journalism of Late Victorian Britain." *Victorian Periodicals Review* 26 (1993): 36–43.

Weiss, John. *Life and Correspondence of Theodore Parker.* 2 vols. New York: Appleton, 1864.

Weller, Jac. *Wellington in India.* 1972. Reprint, London: Greenhill, 2000.

*Wellesley Index to Victorian Periodicals.* Edited by Walter Houghton. 5 vols. Toronto: University of Toronto Press, 1966–90.

Westacott, Evalyn. *A Century of Vivisection and Anti-Vivisection.* Rochford, England: C. W. Daniel, 1949.

Wheatley, Vera. *The Life and Work of Harriet Martineau.* Fair Lawn, N.J.: Essential Books, 1957.

Wilberforce, Basil. "'Women, Clergymen, and Doctors': A Reply." *New Review* 8 (January 1893): 85–95.

Willard, Frances E. "Frances Power Cobbe." *Chautauquan* 7 (1897): 597–99.

———. Introduction to *The Duties of Women,* by Frances Power Cobbe. 8th American ed. 1881. Reprint, London: Williams & Norgate, 1888.

Williamson, Lori Lynn. "Viceregent of God: The Public Crusades of Frances Power Cobbe, 1822–1904." Ph.D. diss., University of Toronto, 1994.

Winkworth, Susanna. "Miss Cobbe's *Broken Lights.*" *Victoria Magazine* 3 (July 1864): 193–208.

Wister, Fanny Kemble, ed. *That I May Tell You: Journals and Letters of the Owen Wister Family.* Wayne, Pa.: Haverford House, 1979.

Wohl, Anthony S. *Endangered Lives: Public Health in Victorian Britain.* London: J. M. Dent, 1983.

Woodham-Smith, Cecil. *The Great Hunger.* 1962. Reprint, New York: Old Town Books, 1989.

Wordsworth, Elizabeth. *Glimpses of the Past.* Oxford: A. R. Mowbray, 1912.

Worzola, Diana. "The Langham Place Circle: The Beginnings of the Organized Women's Movement in England, 1854–1870." Ph.D. diss., University of Wisconsin–Madison, 1982.

SERIAL PUBLICATIONS

*Abolitionist*
*Animal World*
*Annual Register*
*Army List*
*Athenaeum*
*Echo*
*Englishwoman's Review of Social and Industrial Questions*
*Hansard Parliamentary Debates,* 3rd series
*Home Chronicler*
*Illustrated London News*
*Irish Felon*
*Journal of Zoöphily* (Philadelphia)
*Newspaper Press Directory*
*Punch*
*Saturday Review*
*Spectator*
*Times*
*Transactions of the National Association for the Promotion of Social Science*
*Truth*
*Vanity Fair*
*Verulam Review*
*Victoria Magazine*
*Woman's Journal* (Boston)
*Woman's Signal*
*Women and Work*
*Women's Penny Paper*
*Women's Suffrage Journal*
*Zoophilist*

# Index

*Italicized page numbers refer to illustrations*